# ARAMAIC CATHOLICISM:
# MARONITE HISTORY AND IDENTITY

A Journey from the Ancient Middle East
to the Modern West

# Aramaic Catholicism:
# Maronite History and Identity

**Peter J. El Khouri**

## A Journey from the Ancient Middle East to the Modern West

**Connor Court Publishing**

Connor Court Publishing Pty Ltd

Copyright © Peter J. El Khouri 2017

Nihil Obstat: +Bishop Antoine-Charbel Tarabay

Maronite Bishop of Australia, Eparchy of St Maroun

Date: 10 August 2017

The *Nihil obstat* comprises a declaration that a book or pamphlet is considered to be free from doctrinal and moral error. It is not implied that those who have granted the *Nihil obstat* agree with the contents, opinions or statements expressed.

Note to the Reader:

PO Box 7257

Redlands Bay, Qld 4165

sales@connorcourt.com

www.connorcourt.com

ISBN: 9781925501667 (pbk.)

Cover design by Maria Giordano. The cover illustration is the earliest illuminated motif of a Christian cross in existence today – from the Rabbula Gospels, 586 AD (from negatives of Fr. A. Badwi).

Printed in Australia

# TABLE OF CONTENTS

# Chapter 3

## St Maroun, St Abraham, and St Simon the Stylite 49

# Chapter 4

## Syria, Phoenicia, Lebanon, Palestine: The Christian Interlink 71

# Chapter 5

## The Formation of Aramaic Catholicism and 'Orthodoxy' 95

## Chapter 8

# Chapter 9

## The Legend of Maronite Monothelitism

# Chapter 10

## Aramaic Catholic Culture in the Medieval Period

## Chapter 11
## The Impact Of The Crusades          397

## Chapter 12
## The Maronites Under Mamlouk and Ottoman Rule          431

# Chapter 13
# Modern Maronite Identity     467

# ABOUT THE AUTHOR

Peter holds degrees from the University of Sydney in Economics (1982) and Law (1984). He has practised as a lawyer, director, and consultant in Sydney since 1986 and is the co-author of a legal textbook. He spent twelve years in the early part of his legal career engaged in various major crime cases as a defence lawyer. Peter has published on the Cronulla Riots, and ancestry and ethnic descriptors in Australia.

From 2015, Peter served two years on the NSW Government Advisory Board of Multicultural NSW. He has advised the Australasian-Middle East Christian Apostolic Churches Conference of Bishops and Clergy representatives (AMEC).

For close to thirty years, Peter has been a member of various Maronite Catholic parish and Eparchy committees and boards and has also assisted on Roman Catholic parish and school committees. He has authored works and given lectures on early Christian and Maronite history for nearly twenty years. Peter was the curator of Maronite History in the Middle East at the Maronite Heritage Centre in Sydney. He co-convened a World Youth Day 2008 international forum in Sydney hosted by IACE Australian Catholic University.

# ACKNOWLEDGEMENTS

I met Joseph Azize at Law School in the early 1980s. As friends, we co-founded with others the think tank Australian Middle East Christian Council. He assisted me in editing its confidential investigative report Cronulla Riots & Ethnic Descriptors presented to NSW police in 2006. I did not expect to have been invited by Joseph in 2007 to join him in lecturing law at university and co-authoring a legal textbook Pleading Precedents (2009). The now Father Yuhanna Azize encouraged me to lecture on Maronite history at the Catholic Adult Education Centre in Sydney in 2013-2014, where he was also lecturing in the Maronite faith. This further advanced my previous lecture notes, draft manuscripts, and research, prompting this publication. Today, I have the great honour to be involved with him for the fifth project together, this book, as a companion to his An Introduction to the Maronite Faith. Father Yuhanna has been a tremendous support and mentor to me over the decades.

There are many monks, nuns, priests, and bishops that have also been long-time friends and a source of spiritual guidance to me. Amongst so many, I must acknowledge His Excellency Bishop Antoine-Charbel Tarabay, Maronite Bishop of Australia and Associate Professor Father Abdo Badwi, Dean of the Department of Syriac and Antiochian Sciences (Faculty of Religious and Oriental Studies) at the University of the Holy Spirit at Kaslik in Lebanon.

A special thanks to Professor Carole Cusack from The University of Sydney, a most important and sincere contributor to the world's study of religion, who unselfishly spent much time in reading my manuscript and writing the foreword. Thanks also to Dr Venetia Robertson for her editing work.

Thanks go to all of my family, and particularly my wife and my children. To my late parents, Karam and Mary, who devoted much of their time to assisting new migrants from Lebanon to Australia from the 1950s, this book is dedicated in their memory.

# FOREWORD

Christianity is the largest religion in the world; slightly less than one-third of the 7.5 billion people living on planet Earth are Christians. The two thousand years of Christian history has seen many changes in the tradition; we are presently in the era when the 'Global South' (in particular the continents of Africa and South America) is the site of the greatest growth in Christianity, as numbers retreat in the 'Global North' (Europe and North America). From its origin, Christianity has been a missionary faith: in Matthew's Gospel the risen Jesus Christ says to his apostles: "All authority in heaven and on earth has been given to me. Therefore go and make disciples of all nations, baptizing them in the name of the Father and of the Son and of the Holy Spirit, and teaching them to obey everything I have commanded you" (Matthew 28:18-20). What began as a movement within Judaism had spread throughout the Greco-Roman world by the end of the first century, and has since become truly global. There are even seven churches that have been constructed on the largely uninhabited continent of Antarctica – these recall the seven churches listed in the Book of Revelation; Ephesus, Smyrna, Pergamum, Thiyatira, Sardis, Philadelphia, and Laodicea (Revelation 2-3).

Modern scholarship on Christianity encompasses archaeological investigation, textual reconstruction, historical ecclesiology and theology, and a range of cross-disciplinary efforts that draw together an increasingly large and unwieldy body of information in an ever-expanding number of languages. The other Abrahamic religions, Judaism and Islam, retain their scriptures in the original languages of Hebrew and Arabic, but Christianity embraced the translation of the Bible, and in October 2016 Wycliffe Bible Translators confirmed that the entire Bible has been rendered into 636 languages, while the New Testament has been published in 1,442 languages, and the total number of languages in which some parts of the scriptures exist is a remarkable 3,223. For those seeking to know more about the historical Jesus of Nazareth and the early Christian church, Aramaic, the language that Jesus spoke and which is recorded on occasion in the Greek New Testament, exercises a special fascination. Peter El Khouri, lawyer and co-founder (with Joseph Azize, now Father Yuhanna Azize) of the think tank Australian Middle Eastern Christian Council, has traced both the linguistic and Catholic identity of the Maronite Christian community in his book, Aramaic Catholicism: Maronite History and Identity.

The Middle East was the heartland of Christianity until the rise of Islam in the seventh century. El Khouri has examined the earliest inhabitants of modern Lebanon and adjoining countries, drawing on ancient and medieval sources, to establish that even after the schism of 451 AD, when the five patriarchates (Rome, Alexandria, Antioch, Constantinople, and Jerusalem) met at the Council of Chalcedon, a division arose between those Christians who remained loyal to Rome and the affirmation of the two natures of Christ, and those who were 'Monophysite' (one nature) including the Egyptian Coptic church, the Syriac churches, and the Armenian Orthodox church. The Chalcedonian Aramaic-speaking church was led by the monastic community of Beit Maroun ('House of Maroun'), a confederation that acknowledged St Maroun as its patron. El Khouri has shown that while the sources for Maronite history between the seventh and the twelfth centuries are limited, there is no reason to doubt that this church was in communion with the Holy See of Rome. The Crusades (late eleventh to late twelfth centuries AD) reconnected these Eastern Catholics with Roman Catholics in the West. The deep connections of Maronite Catholics with the Melkite, Antiochian Orthodox, and the Syriac churches are another valuable aspect of El Khouri's detailed history.

Aramaic Catholicism: Maronite History and Identity is a significant contribution to the history of an ancient and important early Christian church. It is of especial value to me that the context in which Peter El Khouri has produced this detailed and painstaking history is that of contemporary Australia. I have researched and taught the religious history of my country for nearly two decades, and during that time have come to appreciate that the Christian tradition of Australia often neglects or excludes the vibrant migrant churches in favour of an Anglo-Saxon, Church of England emphasis. In the twenty-first century the faith and fervour of migrant churches in Australia, which includes the Maronites as well as the full array of Orthodox communions, the Assyrian Church of the East, the Coptic and Armenian Orthodox churches and many others, is a vibrant and important aspect of contemporary Australian Christianity in particular, and religion in general. This book is a revisionist history of the Maronites, and merits a wide readership; members of the Australian and the worldwide Maronite community undoubtedly will welcome it, but it has significance and power for Christians around the world. Peter El Khouri deserves commendation for his patient and careful analysis of a far more diverse Christianity than most Australians in the twenty-first century have ever heard of. I am delighted to warmly recommend this book.

**Carole M. Cusack**
**University of Sydney**

# LIST OF MAPS, PICTURES AND DIAGRAMS

## *Chapter 10 (pp. 355-362)* continued

**Pictures:**

- Islamic Minaret likely influenced by St Simon Stylite pillar.
- Aramaic Maronite Madonna – Rabulla Gospel 586AD.
- Our Lady of Ilige Maronite Madonna – 10th century.
- Maronite nun.
- Iranian female Muslim tourist (headdress), Lebanon.
- Equal armed Aramaic cross, 5th century AD, Maarat Namaan, Syria.
- Equal armed Aramaic cross, Rabbula Gospels, 586 AD.
- Emblems most likely replicating ancient Aramaic equal armed cross motifs: Lebanese Maronite Order, Crusaders' Knights of St John, western ambulances, International Red Cross.
- Kadisha Valley, North Lebanon.
- Typical flat roofed Maronite village church with bell tower.
- Typical house, ancient Sejilla, Northern Syria, 4th-5th century AD.
- Ancient Sejilla town, Northern Syria, 4th-5th century AD.
- Rabbula Gospel illumination, 586 AD.
- Rabbula Gospel, 586 AD, scene of crucifixion and resurrection.

# INTRODUCTION

This book began as an endeavour into Maronite history. During its progress, it became apparent that this required tracing back to the first Christian century to follow the history of Catholics from the indigenous Aramaic-speaking Christian populations, the 'Aramaic Catholics'. This appears to be a lacuna in the published English writing on Maronite history, and furthermore, in sifting through the written sources available, it became clear that history has overlooked, misconstrued, or misrepresented this Catholic demographic. There are numerous considerations the present work intends to bring to the fore to address this dearth of discussion and shed further light on the culture and identity of the Maronite people and the origins of their Church.

Greco-Roman focused history often passes by the significant cultural attributes of the Middle East. The history of this area tends to hone in on the worlds of Antioch and Alexandria cities as capitals of the very broad regions of the patriarchates under their names. The large territory between these cities has been extensively overlooked. A void in history therefore appears in a lack of reference to Palestine, Lebanon, Phoenicia, and areas of Western Syria (away from Antioch and far Northern Syria). This is but one of many voids or incorrect general perceptions perpetuated in historical discourses.

In the first century AD, Jesus Christ was born in Bethlehem at the time of King Herod when the town was part of the administration of Judaea in the Roman province of Syria Palaestina. The Romans allocated the name 'Syria' to their three large provinces to encompass all its imperial land in the Middle East.[1] This broad Roman region came to be known as the 'Syrian Orient'. Aramaic, probably Jesus' primary native tongue, was the regional language of the ancient Middle East.

---

[1] Reference to the ancient Middle East here does not include Asia Minor (such as modern day Turkey) and North African countries such as Egypt.

1

The first and majority of early Christians were Aramaic-speaking Jews.[2] The populations residing closer to the Mediterranean and Jerusalem spoke a 'Western Aramaic dialect'. Those further to the East, such as in modern day Iraq spoke an 'Eastern Aramaic dialect', which was centred on the city of Edessa (modern Şanlıurfa in South-Eastern Turkey).

The Syriac alphabet developed from the Aramaic alphabet. From about the second or third century AD it was used as a literary and liturgical language of the Eastern Aramaic-speaking Christians. By the sixth century it began to be more widely embraced, particularly in Northern Syria. Eventually the term Aramaic ('Aramaya') became known as Syriac ('Suryaya', today pronounced 'Suryani'). For many centuries it is possible that we can refer to Aramaic, Syriac and Aramaic-Syriac interchangeably and written Syriac had little, if any, impact on the spoken Western Aramaic dialects until after the sixth century. Likely by the ninth century, Arabic also became a common spoken language in the region.

In the early Christian centuries we read of Greeks, Syrians and Egyptians in the East, yet there is a virtual silence concerning the five Roman provinces of Phoenicia, Phoenicia-Lebanon, and Palestine I, II, III, all established in the year 395 AD after a reshuffling of the regional boundaries by the ancient Romans. These five provinces became the bulk of the land belonging to the Roman Empire's portion of the Levant; the two other provinces, Syria I and II, formed the balance.

The word 'Syria' was no longer represented in five of the seven Roman Middle Eastern provinces. Nonetheless, both ancient and modern historians have continued to embrace the antiquated references to the former 'Syrian Orient' or 'Syria'. This was an accustomed use from the first four Christian centuries when the Roman Middle East was known by provinces connected to the principal term Syria (such as Syria Palaestina and Syria Phoenicia).

---

[2] It is generally accepted Aramaic, as the regional language, was the primary native tongue of the Jews at the time of Jesus Christ, and Hebrew was their second native tongue. Many Jews and likely Jesus Christ, also spoke the international language of Greek.

After 395, the outdated term 'Syria' for the Middle East continued to be primarily used during the fifth to the early seventh centuries. For Christianity in this region these centuries were the most significant in terms of its world population and comprehensive civil and religious development. Four of the five Christian patriarchates of the world would form in the East: Antioch, Alexandria, Constantinople, and Jerusalem, Rome being the only patriarchate of the West.

Alexandria in Egypt and Antioch in Syria were commonly regarded as having Greek-speaking populations. Whilst Greek was the international language of these two cities, there is scant reference to, or study of, their indigenous populations. They were naturally substantial in number and cultural contribution. Native Egyptians who spoke Coptic no doubt resided in Alexandria. Native Syrians, speaking Aramaic must have resided in Antioch. Their languages and cultures significantly influenced the diversity of these Christian capital cities, as did other less populous cultures and languages. The societies were multicultural and multilingual. Their ethnic diversity was generally harmonious, immersed in cross-cultural coexistence. Accordingly, another historical void appears related to the indigenous population of Antioch.

From 313 AD under the Emperor Constantine, Christians were free to practise their religion. In 380, theirs was the official religion of the Roman Byzantine Empire. The economy of the Middle East had been flourishing. Land was fertile, water was abundant, and many valleys in Phoenicia and Syria provided a large part of the food bowl in the East for the Roman Empire. There was a burgeoning program of construction of churches, monasteries, and hostels for pilgrims. Up until 451, the Christian faithful were almost entirely Catholic, whether residing in the East or the West. Each region retained its language and special customs in the liturgy of the Mass.

Given the passionate commitment to their belief and the predominance of Catholics in this region, the great theological debates of this time emanated from the East. The emperors, as Christians, often intervened in debates and occasionally exhibited partisanship. Unfortunately, misunderstandings led to schisms. The Council of Chalcedon, convened by the Emperor Marcian in 451 to solidify a canonical understanding of the two natures of Christ as divine and human, and a rejection of Monophysitism – the notion that Christ has only a singular nature – resulted in a schism. Some Eastern churches were no longer in communion with the Catholic Church, and were deemed heretical. These were principally the 'Monophysite' Egyptian Coptic, 'Monophysite' Syriac Church, and the Armenian Church.

After the schism of 451, we have been incorrectly led to assume that almost all, if not all, indigenous peoples from the large expanse of the Middle East had become principally Monophysite in their belief and therefore 'heretics' in the eyes of the Catholic Church. In other words, there were very few, if any Aramaic Catholics. The continual references to 'ancient Syria' and the 'Syrian Orient' have retained this generalisation, despite the diversity of the provinces and populations within them. Historians have therefore inadvertently not been fully alert to the Catholic presence in the region, which has thus gone largely unmonitored. As for the ancient Phoenicians, and much later the Phoenician-Lebanese in Roman times, studies of the early Christian period of history tend to provide little reference to Aramaic Catholics.

The split following Chalcedon is often marked as a precedent to the long history of Christian division in the East. However, in terms of proportional population size, it was far less significant than the Protestant Reformation, which led to the Western schism of the Catholic Church in the sixteenth century. In terms of the numbers of churches, the schism of 451 finds us today with only a handful of non-Catholic churches in the modern Middle East, whilst the sixteenth century Western schism has resulted in the hundreds of individual Protestant churches found in the West in the current age.

Contrary to popular perception, there was only one schismatic church in the Middle East created by the Council of Chalcedon decree, the church of the Syriac Monophysites established in 518 by an ethnic Greek former patriarch of Antioch named Severus. As for the indigenous peoples of Egypt, the Syriac Monophysites also believed in the one nature of Christ, divine. This Syriac church today is known as the Syriac Orthodox Church.

The fifth century schism between the Catholic Church and some Christians of the East was followed by Islamic rule from the mid-seventh century. This seems to have brought a perception there were little or no Middle East (Aramaic) indigenous Catholics remaining. The great Byzantine/East and Latin/West schism of the Catholic Church in the eleventh century created yet another void or misperception, that the only Catholics in the world were Latin or Roman Catholics. This remains the general perception today.

In the modern era most believe any Catholicism besides the Roman rite cannot exist, but if it does, it could not be pure and is thus treated with trepidation; hence the myopic idea that there is only one true form of Catholicism, and that is Roman Catholicism. Certainly, the modern Middle East is typically regarded as synonymous with Islam, thus any Christians in that region are considered a fractional minority only, and certainly not as true, that is Roman, Catholics.

Whilst tracing the history and identity of Aramaic Catholics from early Christianity, this book aims to pinpoint whether this Christian denomination survives in the modern Middle East of today and if so, if it has successively retained Aramaic in their liturgy and remained Catholic throughout the ages. Despite the many historical lacunae, challenges, and misconceptions, every path the research for this project took converged on the Maronite Church, that exists predominately in today's Middle East in the country of Lebanon.

The Maronite Church appeared unintentionally as a church in the late seventh century, decades after the arrival of Islam, and likely during a schism between the churches of Rome and Constantinople at the time. Upon independence of Lebanon in 1943, it was accepted that the Maronites were the largest religious denomination in the country, Christian or Muslim. As a result, the President of Lebanon remains Maronite by Constitution and is the only Christian head of state in the modern Middle East, and the only Christian leader that retains a seat on the Arab League of Nations.

Lebanon's demographics have certainly changed since the last census in 1932. Although the Lebanese democracy has its own nuances by Western standards, the country remains a message for the modern Middle East and the rest of the world. Following the bloody 'civil war' from 1975 to 1990,[3] the Lebanese have returned to their traditional life of peaceful and harmonious coexistence that was, for the most part, previously entrenched for hundreds of years.

The Taif Agreement of 1989 brought the Lebanese civil war to a close and enshrined the principle of mutual coexistence between different sects and their proper political representation in a new post-civil war parliament. This agreement transferred much of the powers of the Lebanese president to the prime minister (a Sunni Muslim) as part of the attempts to realign to a fairer democratic parliamentary system. Nonetheless, the president keeps an important role and its symbolic position nationally and regionally representing a Christian president should not be underestimated, particularly in the world's current religious and political environment.

The customs of mutual respect between religious faiths in Lebanon are today a shining light for the modern Middle East and the world. They are also a striking example for Western nations to follow given the new dynamic, for the first time in history, of very recent mass migration of Muslims to Western shores. The Lebanese and others from the Middle East, of all faiths, and their descendants throughout the world, are now well placed to partake in the skilled diplomacy required in this challenging arena.

Who the Maronites are and how their primacy in Lebanon came about is a worthwhile question considering their existence in an almost exclusively Islamic and Arab domain. The answer requires systematic overview of history starting from ancient Biblical times. To undertake this mammoth task, the reader must be immersed in Middle Eastern culture, religion, politics, and economics of many centuries. In providing such an overview, this study proposes to explore, in some

---

[3] Which appeared to be at first a localised Christian verses Muslim religious conflict, but many regard was in fact more a regional and international conflict.

6

instances for the first time, a multitude of fascinating and relatively unknown discoveries.

Prior to the sixteenth century and unlike most other Eastern churches, the Maronites have almost no written religious history available and no church historians. An exception is the Maronite history written in Arabic by the author Qays al-Maruni in the early tenth century but which is no longer extant. Like many church customs or rites, those of the Maronite Church were founded on oral traditions and not manuscripts. Reliance is placed on the tens and hundreds of generations who have passed down these traditions orally, by word of mouth, and through continual practice.

Starting from the mid or late seventh century under Muslim rule, Christians in Arab nations faced persecution. Their maltreatment was dependent on factors such as the personality of the rulers and governors, tolerance levels between faiths, Christian resistance, and the occasional waves of Islamic fanaticism both localized and generalized. At certain stages, additional matters influenced the struggles of the Maronite Church.

Upon the arrival of the Muslim conquerors in the Middle East the Maronites, as Melkites loyal to the Byzantine emperor, appeared as a dominant Christian sect in the Western region of the patriarchate of Antioch. As royalists, they were also firmly established as the Middle East's beacon of indigenous Aramaic Christian orthodoxy for the Byzantine Emperor and for the Catholic Church, including the Pope in Rome and Patriarch of Constantinople. For nearly six hundred years after the Crusades it was the only Christian church in the entire East in perpetual communion with the Catholic Church. Nonetheless, these aspects of the Maronite Church have been often misconstrued and overlooked.

Muslim rulers were suspicious of the Maronites for their links to the West, particularly to the Vatican, Italy, and France, who led the Catholic world. Numerous relocations of the Maronite Patriarchate were endured, as was martyrdom, and the destruction of monasteries, convents, and churches. Valuable historical records and literature were destroyed, misplaced, lost, or left behind in the melee. Upon the exit of the Crusaders, the Maronite's isolation as the only Catholics in the region drew attention not just from Muslims, but from the other Christian denominations of the Middle East. Both Muslim and Christian historians have spilled much ink over the millennia concerning the Maronites, and some of these works have unfavourably questioned aspects of Maronite history and identity. Accordingly, Maronites are often left to defend their own heritage.

The predominant focus in historical studies on Greek/East and Latin/West Christianity and culture has left a great volume of important Christian manuscripts and writings in Syriac virtually unexamined. This has been exacerbated in the Middle East by Muslim rule from the seventh to the early twentieth century, excepting the Crusade interlude of the twelfth and thirteenth century. Only in recent decades have we witnessed a flurry of interest in Syriac studies. Subsequently, there are many scholarly Aramaic-Syriac works in languages other than English, including Arabic, French, and German.

This book goes some way in addressing the voids of history regarding the development of Aramaic Catholicism and rise of the Maronite Church. Two periods of history, the fifth to seventh centuries and the crusades era of late eleventh to thirteenth century, will be of especial focus. For these two periods, and it seems for the first time in English, this book sets out the relevant full texts of important ancient historical sources concerning Aramaic Catholicism for the reader to consider. Drawing on the opinion of scholars, both Maronite and non-Maronite, and these original manuscripts, some conclusions can be drawn. The work validates the importance of a great deal more research required in the field, only modestly represented in the present work.

For the chapters of this book up to the fourth Christian century and after the end of the Crusades, a general background and overview is provided for the reader. For the period in between, the book adopts a more academic approach and focus. Despite the scarcity, the limited historical references provide insight into the unintentional formation of the Maronite Church during the fifth to seventh Christian centuries.

A number of relatively unknown parallels between Judaism, Aramaic Christianity, and Islam are proposed in the process. The influence on Islamic female headwear, architecture, and the minaret is discussed and the rapid rise of Islam is explored.

During the formative years of the fifth to seventh centuries, the weight of evidence allows the firm conclusion the bulk of Aramaic-speaking Catholics were located nearer to the Mediterranean. Two principal Christian opposition parties had established themselves in the patriarchate of Antioch after 451 AD: the Aramaic-Syriac Monophysites or 'non-Chalcedonian party' led by their monks on the one hand, and the 'Chalcedonian party' as Catholics on the other. The monastic confederations of St Maroun (or Maron) under the Beit Maroun monastery came to dominate the leadership of the Chalcedonian party, and were the strongest opposition to the non-Chalcedonian party.

The St Maroun monastic confederation was named after the eponymous St Maroun (d. 410-423), revered in the Middle East as the first open-air monk hermit. The monastic network was known as 'Beit Maroun' or House of Maroun. On the occasion of the Acacian schism in 471-518 between Rome and Constantinople, Beit Maroun appeared at the forefront of the Aramaic-speaking Christians who kept their Catholic orthodoxy and allegiance to Rome. Eventually this Chalcedonian party became known as Maronites – the 'followers of Maron' – before the Maronite Church was formed. For close to four hundred years, it seems Maronite communication was severed from the Catholic Church in the West shortly following the introduction of Islamic rule. There are virtually no ancient sources that assist us in tracking what exactly happened to the Aramaic Christians during this period who were adherent to the Chalcedon doctrine. Thereafter on the arrival of the Crusaders, the extraction of English translations of original sources relevant to the Maronites from Crusader chroniclers is set out for the period twelfth to thirteenth centuries. Shortly after the arrival of the Crusades until today, documents undisputedly confirm the Maronite Church in communion with the Catholic Church.

Since the great schism of the eleventh century between Constantinople and Rome, the Maronites remain today the only Eastern Catholics who can claim to be perpetual Aramaic Catholics from the first century. During the Crusades of the eleventh to thirteenth centuries, the Maronites as the only non-Roman Catholics and only Aramaic-speaking Catholics, reinvigorated Rome's ecumenism and today the churches of the Middle East, like the churches around the world, are in unprecedented close ecumenical dialogue. This movement officially began in earnest by the Catholic Church in the sixteenth century and has developed extensively during the latter half of the twentieth century to all Christian denominations. Following the end of the Crusades, the church history of Maronites is less controversial. The original sources are far more voluminous, particularly in Arabic. Accordingly, this study provides only a general overview of this period.

Although a great many of the Aramaic Catholics spoke the Western dialect, the Aramaic of today in the Maronite liturgy is in the form of the Eastern Aramaic dialect. This Eastern dialect became the written Syriac liturgical language of the Middle East Christians in the very early Christian centuries. However, the Western Aramaic dialect likely survives today in many forms of the day to day language of principally the Lebanese, Syrians, Palestinians, and Jordanians including many of their place names and Christian names. An important note is necessary regarding names of people and places. Historians have adopted a Greek or Latin name for the Aramaic names of people and places. For example, the Aramaic 'Sarkis' is known as Sergius, 'Yuhanna' is John, and the city 'Afamiyah' is Apamea. For consistency with historical recordings, this book keeps the Greek or Latin translations or phraseology.

Dateline summaries and milestones are provided throughout the book, allowing for event reminders amongst the complexity of ancient history. The study suggests, for the first time, the likely influence of Aramaic Christian symbolism on the Crusaders and into modern times in many ubiquitous Western emblems. In 2011, UNESCO declared the ancient villages and sites of Northern Syria, abandoned around the time of the Arab Muslim conquest of the seventh century, as world heritage listed. These most likely belonged substantially to Aramaic Catholic populations and accordingly the Maronites and details are provided in this book. Not previously undertaken is an interesting overview of Maronite history in Italy, including Roman streets named after the Maronites and election of 'Maronite' popes following a mass emigration of Aramaic Catholics.

Multiculturalism in the Christian church began at its birth. When Christianity was declared the official religion of the Byzantine Empire in 380, there was no mention of liturgical languages or customs. At no time through history has Rome, the Pope, the Vatican, the Church of Constantinople or the Byzantine emperor decreed an official liturgical language or cultural practice of the Catholic Church. This equally applies to the Byzantine Church after the eleventh century Roman-Byzantine schism. Although Aramaic was likely Jesus Christ's first native tongue and the language in which he preached to the Jews as the first Christian converts, Aramaic has never been imposed as the official liturgical or religious language for Christians. The Judeo-Aramaic religious practices of Christ and the first Messianic Jews have never been decreed as the official liturgical practices of Christians. This phenomenon perhaps provides a distinction with other religions such as Islam.

The beauty, richness, and diversity of every culture and its language have been cherished and allowed to flourish in Christianity from inception. The liturgies and languages of all Christian churches are significant in their own right. They include the Roman, Byzantine, Syriac (Aramaic), Coptic, Armenian, Ethiopian, and others. The Catholic Church is the largest organisation or institution in the world today. National, regional, and global multicultural policy and administration has been led by the Catholic Church for over 2000 years. In contrast, Western governments are still developing their multicultural policies with significant segments of their societies still resisting the concept.

The Second Vatican Council in the early 1960s declared the Eastern Catholic churches as duty-bound to retain their own rite and declared them of equal dignity, so that none of them is superior to the others as regards rite and they enjoy the same rights and are under the same obligations, also in respect of preaching the Gospel to the whole world (cf. Mark 16, 15) under the guidance of the Roman Pontiff.[4]

While the Roman liturgy today presides over many countries cultures and languages throughout all continents of the world, it matters not that today the faithful of the Roman rite dominate the numbers in the Catholic Church as indeed at one stage in history it was the Aramaic liturgy and thereafter the Byzantine liturgy that were in common use.

All liturgies must be retained in their glory. Some congregations of Christians in ancient times had shared liturgies and languages. They included for example a mix of Greek and Latin both in Rome and in Constantinople, and a mix of Greek and Aramaic in the Middle East. Eastern Catholics live two Christian cultures, their own indigenous rite and that of the Roman rite. They would have no difficulty attending mass at the Vatican, or if living in the West, at the local Roman Catholic parish.

In the reverse, the same does not apply to Roman Catholics. Perhaps we may see a change in the future with so many Eastern Catholic churches on Western shores in modern times. The penultimate chapter of this thesis gives one such example and discusses mass emigration of Maronites since the mid 1800s accompanied by the expansion to the West of the rich liturgical beauty and splendour of Aramaic Catholicism. It is timely as the last words of this study were being typed in May 2017, that His Eminence Cardinal Leonardo Sandri from Rome had just arrived to Australia. He is the first Vatican Prefect of the Congregation for the Oriental Churches to visit Australia. It symbolises the growing importance and new dynamic the Vatican is now placing on the Eastern Churches, not just in the East but now in the West.

This study confirms Maronites are the largest Christian denomina-

---

[4] "Decree on The Catholic Churches of the Eastern Rite," *Orientalium Ecclesiarum*, 21 November 1964, available at: http://www.vatican.va/archive/hist_councils/ii_vatican_council/documents/vatii_decree_19641121_Orientalium-ecclesiarum_en.html.

tion in the world today originating from the Middle East who retain in their liturgy the closest form of Jesus Christ's native tongue, Aramaic, the Jewish customs of the first Christians, and the melodies chanted by the first Christians indigenous to the Middle East. No recording of history is perfect, especially without a complete immersion for a narrowly defined period and topic. However, the aim of this research is to demonstrate significant voids, defects and misrepresentations in present accounts of Maronite and Aramaic Catholic history. Many new aspects of Maronite history are set out in this study, or the generally accepted history re-written. This book also seeks to open, for the first time, a new academic discussion on 'Aramaic Catholicism'. Considering the evidence and traditions with the history as a whole, it is argued here that the Maronite Church is the only Eastern Church that can claim a perpetual communion with the Catholic Church and perpetual succession to its Aramaic-speaking Catholic arm.

# CHAPTER 1

# THE ANCIENT MIDDLE EAST

## Timeline of Key Dates

**BC**

3000   Canaanites present in 'Syria', including Lebanon and Palestine.

1200   Egyptian Pharaoh Snefru brings back forty shiploads of cedar logs from Lebanon. Reports of shipbuilding from cedar wood. Canaanites become known as 'Phoenicians'. Phoenician city coastal states flourish and the Phoenicians begin to colonise the Mediterranean and beyond.

954   King Solomon starts construction of the first temple in Jerusalem. Cedar trees of Mount Lebanon used.

800   Phoenicians settle in Malta and Sardinia.

750   Phoenicians found Carthage (near modern Tunis) as their imperial capital.

332   Persian Empire conquest of geographical Syria and end of Phoenician independence.

332   Alexander the Great, born in Macedonia, seizes Palestine from the Persians. The start of the Greek Empire. One of his Macedonian generals, Seleucus I, rules Persia, Babylon and Syria. Capital of the Hellenistic Seleucid kingdom in Syria was Antioch.

63   Roman Empire under Pompey seizes Jerusalem. Syria (including modern-day Lebanon) becomes a Roman province.

**AD**

270   St Anthony the Great enters the ascetic life in the desert outside Alexandria, Egypt.

313   Roman Emperor Constantine (born in modern Serbia) declares freedom of religion.

330   Constantine renames Byzantium (modern Istanbul) Constantinople and makes it the new capital of the Roman Empire.

356   Death of St Anthony the Great.

360   Life of Anthony written in Greek about St Anthony by Athanasius of Alexandria, the first written reference to a hermit monk.

373   Death of St Ephrem the Syrian.

380   Emperor Theodosius declares Christianity the official religion of the Roman Empire.

PHOENICIA

SYRIA

Arwad

MEDITERRANEAN
SEA

Tripolis

LEBANON

Byblos

Beirut

Baalbek

TIMBER

Sidon

Sarepta

PURPLE DYE

WOOL

Tyre

WINE

Akko

POTTERY
OLIVE OIL

SYRIA

Atlit

Dor

ISRAEL

WINE

Jaffa

JORDAN

Jerusalem

Ashkelon

Dead Sea

GAZA
STRIP

Former
extent of
cedars

0 mi                    50

PERFUME

0 km        50

Map 1: Ancient Phoenicia. (Source: National Geographic Society, 2004).

15

Map 2: Eastern Oriental Dioceses of the Roman Empire (administrative), c 400 AD. The map relies on original Roman administrative maps Notitia Dignitatum and the Synecdemus. Source: E. Honigmann (Le Synekdèmos d'Hiéroklès et l'opuscule géographique de Georges de Chypre; Brussels, 1939).

16

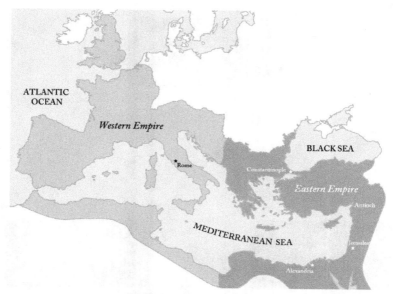

Map 3: Map, c. 395 AD, of the Western Roman Empire (capital Rome) and Eastern Roman Empire (capital Constantinople). This formed the basis for the modern day distinction between 'Western nations' and 'Eastern nations'. Source the author.

Typical mountain cedar forest overlooking the Mediterranean continually rejuvenating from ancient times. Location, Niha, North Lebanon, 1400m altitude above sea level.

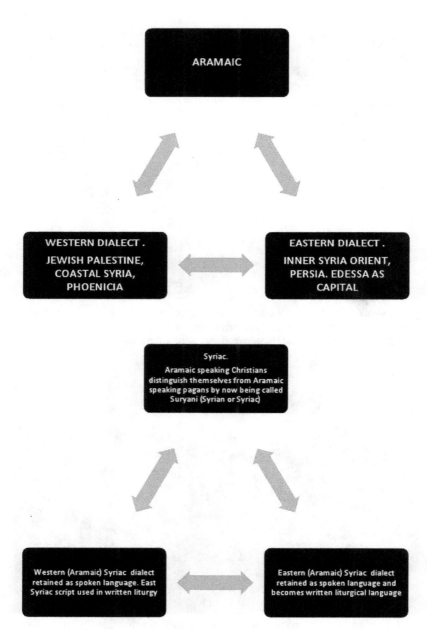

Diagrammatic explanation of Aramaic – Syriac language

## 1.1 Peoples and Places of the Ancient Middle East

### 1.1.1 The Semites and Canaanites

The Book of Genesis is the first book of the Jewish Torah and the Christian Old Testament Bible. It sets out the genealogy of tribes commencing from Noah and provides a useful insight into Biblical explanation of ethnic origins and terms relevant to our study of early Middle Eastern Christianity, principally in its western region. Shem, the son of Noah, was the ancestor of all the Hebrews. He had a son, Aram, who was the ancestor of the Aramaeans of ancient Syria (Genesis 9:18, 10:21). Another of Noah's sons, Ham, had a son Canaan who was the ancestor of the Canaanites (Genesis 9:18, 10:6).

The Canaanites were spread principally through what was to become known in the early Christian period as Phoenicia, Lebanon, Palestine, and western Syria. The Hebrews were also known as the Israelites or Twelve Tribes of Israel, named after the Israelite Kingdom of Judah, part of the land of the Canaanites. The ancient land of the Aramaeans and of the Canaanites will be the principal geographic region for our study of the early Church.

The scholar Philip K. Hitti holds the view that a Semite is a member of a speech family (not ethnic origin) comprising the Hebrews, Arabs, Aramaeans, Canaanites, Assyro Babylonians.[5] *The Macquarie Dictionary* describes a 'Semite' as: "1. A member of a speech family comprising the Hebrews, Arabs, Assyrians, etc., supposedly descended from Shem, the eldest son of Noah. 2. A Jew."[6] The coastal region of ancient Syria (Syria, Palestine, Phoenicia including Mount Lebanon) was Canaanite.

Many people in the region of ancient Syria, even to the fourth century AD, remained believers in the ancient Canaanite polytheistic folk religion. Pagan temples were built in prominent places such as Baalbek (up to 330 AD) and on many mountaintops devoting idol worship to a triad of deities, El, Adon, and Astarte. There is an extensive list

---

[5] Philip K. Hitti, *The Near East in History: A 5000 Year Story*, D. Van Nostrand Company, 1966, p. 33.

[6] *The Macquarie Dictionary*, Second Edition, The Macquarie Library Pty Ltd, 1996.

of towns and villages in Lebanon containing these temples, which are still standing today.

## 1.1.2 The Aramaeans and Aramaic

In the fourteenth and thirteenth centuries BC the Semitic tribe, the Aramaeans, took over a large part of Mesopotamia and north and central Syria. Damascus became the capital of the Aramaean state. The Aramaeans maintained their original dialect. The language became the medium of international commercial communication as far as India. Aramaic became for a time the language of diplomacy and was so used by the Persians who adopted Aramaic as their official language around the fifth century BC.

Once the size of the Persian Empire had increased, the use of Aramaic became widely spread. 'Aram' became synonymous with what the Greeks later called 'Syria'. By the eighth century BC, Aramaic had displaced Canaanite as the language of ancient Syria. There it remained entrenched until the Muslim conquest of the seventh Christian century, after which its Arabic cousin replaced it as the official language.

Aramaic, not Hebrew, was the language in which Christ communicated his message, however the message survived only in its Greek translation, often with the context lost in the translation. Most modern translations of the Old Testament were made from the Jewish scriptures. The majority of Jewish scripture is written in Hebrew, but there are also some sections that are written in Aramaic. Some of the Dead Sea Scrolls are written in Aramaic manuscript as well as Hebrew.

The Christian Bible was written as a result of three languages. Hebrew was the language of the Old Testament. Aramaic was the common spoken language of the Middle East for many centuries before and after Christ. Greek is primarily the New Testament language and was the international language at the time of Christ, much like English is today in the world.

Aramaic was the regional language of the Middle East, and Greek the international language. Aramaic was divided into two dialects: western Aramaic was used in the western region of ancient Syria and also the lower Mesopotamia. It was the dialect of the Jews around the time of Jesus Christ. Eastern Aramaic was used in Babylonia and upper Mesopotamia. Although today the Syrians, Lebanese, Jordanians, and Palestinians have for many centuries now spoken Arabic as their day-to-day language, they have done so in a dialect that has retained many western Aramaic peculiarities. The Aramaic language is a fundamental component of their history and the dialect spoken there today is most likely Arabic influenced by Aramaic.

Aramaic is sometimes called 'Syriac', from the Hebrew word Aram, meaning northern Syria. The Syriac alphabet developed from the Aramaic alphabet. It was used to write the dialect of the Aramaic-speaking Christians from about the second or third century AD. Eventually it became their liturgical language. Hitti provides an interesting insight into the transition of the term 'Aramaic' to 'Syriac', noting the influence of the Maronites:

> Christ's sermons, delivered in Aramaic, and His biography written in that language have not survived. Translated into barbarous Greek in the early Roman Imperial period, however, they have had a more enduring and wholesome influence on the progress of humanity than perhaps the entire Greco- Latin output. With the Christianisation of the area Syriac, a branch of Aramaic, became with local variations the language of the churches of Syria, Lebanon and Mesopotamia. From the third century on, its use for literary purposes became widespread, not so much because of a fresh invigoration of national feeling as because of the need felt for the propagation of the Christian faith. Syriac literature started with a translation of the Gospels and centred in Edessa (al-Ruha, Urfa). As Aramaic Christians adopted the Edessan dialect and made it the language of the church, of literature and of cultivated society, they all became known as Syrians (Suryan). Their early name, having by that time acquired in their minds a heathen connotation, became distasteful to them. Last did the original semantic name, Aramaic, come to be generally avoided and was replaced by the Greek 'Syrian' for the people and 'Syriac' for the language. Syriac did not

assume its central position in Lebanese literature until after the advent of the Maronites.[7]

The valley of Qadisha in the mountains of northern Lebanon refers to the Aramaic 'sainted' or 'sacred'. There are many hermitages and monasteries spread throughout the holy valley including the monastery of St Anthony of Kozhaya. The word 'Kozhaya' is of Aramaic origin and means 'treasure of life'. The famous area on the sea in Beirut, Lebanon called 'Rausheh' is the Aramaic name for *ras* in Arabic or 'headland' in English. Hitti provides us with an insight into Aramaic's influence on names in modern day Lebanon:

> A large number of plants in this conquered area (Lebanon), both wild and domestic, have preserved their pre-Arab Semitic names. Technical terms used in farming and agriculture are mostly Syriac and Aramaic, as are terms relating to theology and ritual (such as 'imad', baptism; 'karz', preaching; 'qissis', monk; 'mazmur', psalm). The overwhelming majority of Lebanese villages still bear Aramaic or Phoenician names, not Arabic. In al-Mashriq there is a list of 530 such villages all called Syriac. In all, Lebanon comprises some 1500 villages and towns. Those compound with 'bayt' (house of) or its attenuated form 'ba' ('Bayt al Din' or 'Bataddin', house of judgment; 'Batarram', house of the high; 'Basalim', house of the idol) were mostly nucleated around an ancient Semitic temple. Others compound with 'ayn' (spring) or 'mayy' (water), such as Ayn Turah (spring of the mountain), Rishmayya (source of water), owed their origins to springs of water. Other villages developed around forts: Majdalayya (tower place), Majdalun (small tower). A large number of place names are introduced by the Syriac 'kafa' (village): Kafar Faqud (village of the officer), Kafar Maya (field of water), Kafar Shima (village of silver). Even the coastal towns betray no Arabic influence in their nomenclature.[8]

The complexity of linguistic diversion is evident when the Semitic

---

[7] Philip K. Hitti, *Lebanon in History: From the Earliest Times to the Present*, Macmillan Company, 1957, p. 204.

[8] Hitti, *Lebanon in History*, pp. 244-255.

origin of a term is translated into Greek, and then Latin, and then English. For example, in Aramaic Syriac, Jesus Christ is referred to as the Messiah (modern day vulgar *Mesih*) taking its true Semitic meaning. The word Christ in English comes from the Greek word *Christos* meaning Messiah. So rather than say in English 'Jesus the Messiah' we say 'Jesus Christ'. However, the term 'Messiah' may for some provide a deeper meaning and historical context.

The same can be said of other translations from the spoken indigenous Aramaic language and culture of Jesus the Messiah and His fellow indigenous followers. The full and broadest contextual meanings of terms are retained in their original language in the environment of their indigenous culture. A translation of the Lord's Prayer, the 'Our Father', direct from Aramaic to English, rather than from Aramaic to Greek to Latin to English, provides another example of the possibility of contextual meaning lost in translation.

### 1.1.3  The Phoenicians and Written Language

The land of Phoenicia included coastal states of the eastern Mediterranean, today Lebanon and parts of surrounding nations, from Latakia (modern Syria) to Acre (Akko in modern Israel). The Phoenicians begin to colonise the Mediterranean and beyond, for example, Gadis (today Cadiz in south-western Spain on the Atlantic). The Canaanites who traded with the Greeks were given the name 'Phoenicians' in the beginning of the twelfth century BC, from the Greek word *phoinix* for purple-red, after the luxurious colour of the cloth that they sold or bartered and for which they became famous. Tyre and Sidon were the principal centres of the industry and trade. Mostly only the wealthy could afford the product. Cleopatra of Egypt, Jewish high priests, and Roman emperors all took pride in wearing their purple garments. Oriental church patriarchs and Roman Catholic cardinals later perpetuated the tradition.[9]

A key centre of trade in the ancient world, Lebanon was also known for its cedar timber. The pharaoh Snerfu, circa 2650 BC, re-

---

[9] Philip K. Hitti, *A Short History of the Near East*, Van Nostrand, 1966, p. 48.

cords a voyage by sea to Lebanon bringing back forty ship loads of cedar logs and also reporting shipbuilding from cedar wood,[10] and the Old Testament has numerous references to the cedar tree of Lebanon.[11] In 954 BC the construction of King Solomon's temple in Jerusalem was commenced and cedar trees from Lebanon were used. There were 153,600 foreigners, 70,000 for transporting materials, 3600 overseers, and 80,000 to cut stone in the mountains.

The Bible tells us that Solomon sent a message to King Hiram of Tyre requesting his skilled cutters to send him cedar, cypress, and juniper logs from Lebanon in exchange for wheat, barley, wine, and olive oil. Hiram replied he would cut down all the cedars Solomon needed from the mountains of Lebanon, tie them together in rafts and float them by sea to as far as Joppa so that from there they could be taken to Jerusalem (Chronicles 2:2). The cedar provided the Phoenicians with the finest timber for constructing their seafaring ships.

With a large labour intensive economy powered by cedar logging and trade, many from afar would have migrated to Phoenician land, as they did for the construction of Solomon's temple. Once settled, its attractive geography, climate, abundant water, fertile land, and papyrus trade would have inspired them to remain. This was the beginning of a wider cross-cultural mix that would make up the Phoenician population. This too can be said of a broad area of ancient Syria that, by historical accounts, was fecund and a strategic location for trade routes.

While the oldest records of the written language come from Mesopotamia around 3000 BC, the Phoenicians were integral to the invention of writing as we know it today. The first inscriptions of language were Sumerian and pre-Semitic in a script called cuneiform, meaning 'wedge shaped' because of the arrow headed characters produced by a stylus pressed on a soft clay tablet. Egyptian hieroglyphics came shortly after, and the invention of papyrus and a sort of ink. Both scripts indicate a beginning in picture drawing or pictographs and then

---

[10] Hitti, *Lebanon in History*, p. 67.
[11] For example see Psalms 104:16, 29:5; Jeremiah 22:14; 2 Kings 14:9, 19:23; Zechariah 11:1-2; Isaiah 14:14-15, 2:13, 35:2, 60:13; Ezekiel 17:22.

ideographs, symbols and images that portray an idea. For example, a representation of a human body with uplifted arms conveyed the idea of prayer; a hand at the mouth indicated the concept of eating.

Around the fifteenth century BC, the Phoenicians developed the pictographs into syllables and were the first to invent a true alphabet with easy to write symbols called letters.[12] As Hitti aptly summarises: "Phoenician traders passed the magic signs westward to the Greeks (c. 800 BC) and eastward to the Aramaeans. The Greeks in turn transmitted them through Latin to other Europeans. The Aramaeans transmitted them to the Hebrews and the Arabs."[13] The Phoenician script continued to be used in the Phoenician colonies in North Africa, the most famous of which was Carthage, until the early third century AD. In addition to the formal script, there was a cursive script employed for writing business and administrative documents. This script is described as Punic.[14]

## 1.1.4 The Greeks and Hellenism

The commercial, economic prosperity, and cultural aspects of the ancient Greeks influenced its colonies including those in the eastern Mediterranean. Greek influence or Hellenism was primarily an urban feature. Aspirants for government positions or scholarly and literary careers received education in Greek and were in varying measures Hellenised. Latin dominated in the army and the law, Greek was the language of political power and became the international language, but Aramaic was the regional language of the Middle East. Country folk, however, isolated and uninterested in higher education, remained relatively unaffected, persisting in their ancestral way of life and in the use of their vernacular. In the towns and cities, most in the Middle East would have been bilingual in Aramaic and Greek.[15]

---

[12] Hitti, *The Near East in History*, pp. 29-31, *Lebanon in History*, p. 6.

[13] Hitti, *A Short History of the Near East*, p. 53.

[14] Sebastian P. Brock (ed.), *The Hidden Pearl: The Syrian Orthodox Church and its Ancient Aramaic Heritage*, Vol. 1, Gorgias Press, 2001, p. 31.

[15] Sebastian P. Brock, *Ephrem to Romanos: Interactions between Syriac and Greek in Late Antiquity*, Routledge, 1999, pp. 149-150.

There were a large number of Greek settlements in Syria such as Antioch (modern Antakiyah in Turkey) and Apamea on the Orontes (Afamiyah, now Qalat al-Madiq in Syria). Phoenician cities began to take the form of their Greek counterparts comprising theatres, baths, gymnasiums and other institutions through which the individuals expressed themselves as members of society. Several cities joined in celebrating Greek festivals. The Phoenicians and Greeks, after a long record of commercial relations must have felt at home with each other. The cultural interchange was by no means one-way, for example, the Greeks assimilated Phoenician deities into their own pantheons. Baal became Zeus. Melkarth was rebirthed as Herakles, and the mysteries of Tamuz and Ashtarte began to be associated with Adonis and Aphrodite.

However, the Phoenicians of Lebanon and the Aramaeans of Syria did not lose their Semitic character. Aramaic remained the vernacular. A slightly different dialect of Aramaic, the 'western Aramaic' dialect, likely developed from the Canaanite vernacular used in areas closer to the Mediterranean coast. Theodoret of Cyrus, a theologian from the School of Antioch and bishop, noted differences between the Aramaic dialects of Syria, Palestine, Phoenicia, Euphrates and Osrhoene.[16] The question of who spoke which language, Greek or Aramaic, and where, is a complex one, and the evidence is scattered and often elusive. Even after the Romans took over the East from the Greeks, the language of political power was still predominantly Greek.

In the urban centres, the educated natives must have been bilingual, using the colloquial mother tongue at home and for daily purposes, and Greek for learned and official purposes. Aramaic was clearly the language for the native lower classes. Greek was the political language and Syriac was the literary and cultural language. Wealthy families who had ambitions for their child's career would need to ensure that they received a good education in the language of power. Theodoret was born (393 AD) to rich parents and wrote in Greek but likely normally spoke in Aramaic-Syriac (he could therefore converse

---

[16] Brock, *Ephrem to Romanos*, p. 149.

with the monks of Syria, most of whom knew no Greek and nine of which he met and wrote about).

Christianity provided Syriac with the necessary prestige to enable it to compete as a literary language with the Greek language of contemporary political power. Many monasteries used both Greek and Syriac languages. The use of two or even three (including Latin) languages side-by-side in the liturgy seems to have been common. This is reflected in a number of earlier surviving liturgical manuscripts from the early seventh century, where both Greek and Syriac feature. In this instance, the Greek is written in Syriac characters, indicating that by this time it was the subordinate language, soon to be displaced altogether by Syriac and then in turn by Arabic in the course of the Middle Ages.[17]

Therefore, the commonly held view that equates Antioch with an ethnic Greek city simply as result it was a Greek-speaking city must be reviewed. Greek was extensively used due to its political influence. However, at least by the mid-seventh century, there is evidence the population may well have been principally ethnic Aramaic. It cannot be ruled out for an earlier period and further investigation is warranted.

## 1.2  The Syrian Orient

In 63 BC, the Greek Empire fell to the expanding interests of what was then the Roman Republic. The general Pompey introduced a province in the Syrian Orient known as 'Syrian Palestine' (Syria Palaestina) leaving the remainder of the Syrian Orient as 'Syria Proper.' By 194 AD, Syria Proper was divided into two provinces making a total of three Roman provinces for Syria: Syria Palaestina, Syria Magna (or Syria Coela), and Syria Phoenicia. In 395 AD, the three Syrian provinces were divided into seven provinces:

- Syria Prima (which included Antioch for the purposes of our study)

---

[17] Ibid., pp. 149-160.

- Syria Secunda (which included Apamaea for the purposes of our study)
- Euphratia (which included Cyr for the purposes of our study)
- Phoenicia (which included Tyre, Sidon, Berytus [Beirut], Byblos, Tripoli, Akko [Acre in   northern modern Israel])
- Lebanese Phoenicia (which included Homs, Heliopolis [Baalbek], Damascus, Palmyra)
- Palaestina Prima (which included Aelia Capitolina [Jerusulem])
- Palaestina Secunda (which included Tiberius on the shores of the Sea of Galilee)

### 1.2.1  Antioch: A Multicultural City

Antiochia was a city founded on the Orontes River in the fourth century BC by one of Alexander the Great's generals, the Macedonian Seleucus I Nicator. During the first century BC (the late period of the Greek or Hellenistic Empire and the beginnings of the Roman Empire), the population swelled to perhaps hundreds of thousands of people and it became the third most populous city in the world after Rome and Alexandria. In that period it was a centre of Hellenistic Judaism and was the most Hellenised city in Roman Syria. It was also the capital of Roman Syrian Palestine (Syria Palaestina) when Syria was founded as a Roman province in 64 BC.

Julius Caesar visited Antioch in 47 BC and the Romans tried to make it an Eastern Rome. It had a stadium, theatre, amphitheatre, a forum, and baths. The Roman emperors favoured the city over Alexandria as the chief city of the eastern part of the Empire. Antioch had a spice trade, and the major trade routes the Silk Road and the Persian Royal Road. Antioch was the Southern capital (Sebastes in Cappadocia the Northern) of the Roman Empire's great road network, commercial communication routes, and defence lines between the Mediterranean, the Middle East, and Asia.

Under Roman rule, four Syrian cities achieved high distinction:

28

Antioch, Heliopolis (Baalbek), Beirut, and Jerusalem. In fame, splendour, and luxury, the capital city Antioch yielded only to the imperial one. With its suburb and consecrated park Daphne, it attracted pilgrims and pleasure seekers from near and far. The theatre built by Julius Caesar was the site of the Daphnian festival comprising games, dances, dramatic performances, chariot racing, gladiatorial contests, and sexual indulgences. Of the city historian Edward Gibbon wrote:

> Fashion was the only law, pleasure the only pursuit, and the splendour of dress and furniture was the only distinction of the citizens of Antioch. The arts of luxury were honoured, the serious and manly virtues were the subject of ridicule, and the contempt for female modesty and reverent age pronounced the universal corruption of the capital of the East.[18]

The Jewish people had their own autonomous quarter in Antioch, which attracted the earliest Christian missionaries (Acts 11:19). Antioch is where Saint Peter established the first Patriarchate before establishing one in Rome as the office of the Roman Patriarch. It is the location where the disciples of Jesus Christ were first called Christians sometime in the second half of the first century (Acts 11:23-26). With such a large and confined population, the number of its Jewish population may have exceeded elsewhere. The ancient city lies near the modern city of Antakya in Turkey, not far from the northern border of Syria, and is known as the cradle of the Church.

Antioch's population and language was originally of Aramaean origin. With the advent of conquests this changed. In northern Syria, Antioch together with the cities of Apamaea, Seleucia and Laodicea were the most Hellenised parts of Syria. In the first six centuries after Christ, Antioch could easily claim it was the most cosmopolitan and multicultural city in the world. St John Chrysostom mentions Antioch's population of about 200,000 by the fourth century (not including slaves). There were many other locations called Antioch and so this city was sometimes known as 'Antioch the Great', especially in Greek.

---

[18] Edward Gibbon, *The Decline and Fall of the Roman*, Folio Society, 1985, p. 800.

In addition to the indigenous Aramaeans who would have maintained many of their cultures, it had Jews, Greeks, Romans, Armenians, Arabs, and Persians. Outside of the city there is no doubt that the Syrian Aramaeans were the predominant demographic. The large influx of migrants, and the multiculturalism in cities and countries is not just the talk of today. The Christian Bible New Testament book of Acts, when relating to the event of Pentecost in Jerusalem, informs us:

> We are from Parthia, Media, and Elam; from Mesopotamia, Judea, and Cappadocia; from Pontus and Asia, from Phyrgia and Pamphylia, from Egypt and the regions of Libya near Cyrene. Some of us are from Rome, both Jews and Gentiles converted to Judaism, and some of us are from Crete and Arabia (Acts 2:9-11).

Greek remained the language used in government, with Latin used in the army and judiciary. Even so, people still spoke fluent Aramaic in the city and the native Aramaic-speaking population would not have considered themselves an inferior race. There is evidence many Greeks of the city were fluent in Aramaic, for example the well-known Bishop of Cyr, Theodoret wrote his *Religious History* (here *A History of the Monks of Syria*) in Syriac in about 444. Antioch was pronounced in Aramaic-Syriac: *Anṭiokia*; Hebrew: *antiyokhya*; and Latin: *Antiochia ad Orontem*.

## 1.2.2  Apamaea: The Aramaic Capital

Apamaea was on the right bank of the Orontes River. It was a base for thousands of horse studs for the Seleucid (Macedonian) kings. The site today is known as Qalaat al-Madiq, found about 55 km to the north-west of Hama, Syria. It was located at a strategic commercial crossroads. The city may have swelled to a population of hundreds of thousands. It became the most prominent Aramaic-speaking city. The city had one of the largest theatres in the Roman world, and a monumental colonnade. It was standing as ruins until recently today, to a fate unknown since the Syrian War from 2011.

## 1.2.3  Phoenicia: Lebanon's Ancient Past

In the early history of the Christian church the Phoenicians would have been amongst the first non-Jewish converts. Christ himself preached near upper Galilee in the cities of Tyre and Sidon (Matthew 15:21; Mark 7:31) and the people travelled from these cities to other places, including the shores of the Galilee, to hear Jesus preach (Luke 6:17; Mark 3:8). In the countryside near to Tyre and Sidon, Jesus healed the daughter of a Canaanite woman (Matthew 15:21-28; Mark 7:24-30). Christ's first miracle turning water into wine at the wedding of Cana (John 2:1-11) is arguably in the town of Cana in (modern) Southern Lebanon (although other towns in modern Israel make the same claim).

St Paul had friends in Sidon (Acts 27:3) surely Christian in faith, and he stayed at Tyre for many days where there were numerous disciples (Acts 21: 5-6). The church in Phoenicia flourished in the first two Christian centuries before significant persecution by the emperors Diocletian and Maxentius. Tradition holds that St Peter founded a church in Byblos and appointed John Mark as Bishop. The bulk of these early converts were Jews, however, many Phoenicians remained pagan and their temples were dotted all over the landscape, forming a multi-ethic and multi-faith society of Christians, Jews, pagans, and others. The most famous and revered temple was high in the mountains at Afqa, dedicated to Adonis. Worshippers came from all over the world. The location has been acclaimed as one of the most beautiful in the world.

Tyre, a city close to Galilee, likely had the first and largest cathedral of Christianity when its construction commenced in 314. This was before the construction of the Church of Nativity in Bethlehem and before construction of the Church of the Holy Sepulchre in Jerusalem. There is evidence the Cathedral had an iconostasis, a wall of icons and religious paintings, separating the nave from the sanctuary in a church in the Byzantine style. Bishop and church historian Eusebius (c. 264-340) published its inaugural speech which included comments the ceiling was made from the cedars of Lebanon. The authority

31

of the archbishop of Tyre extended over thirteen dioceses included all the cities of the Phoenician-Lebanese coast. The archdiocese's patriarch was in Antioch, not Alexandria.

## 1.3   The Byzantine Church and East-West Geographical Divisions

In 290 AD, the emperor Diocletian divided the Roman Empire into two major administrative units, which gradually became the empire of the West and the empire of the East. Diocletian's line of demarcation ran north and south along the twentieth degree longitude. Today that line would run roughly from Belgrade in Yugoslavia to Bengasi in Libya. In 330 AD, Constantine renamed the old Greek colony Byzantium as Constantinople (today Istanbul in Turkey) and made it the new capital of the Roman Empire. The two parts of the Empire were subsequently known as the Western Roman Empire and the Eastern or Byzantine Roman Empire.

Constantinople was Greek in language and Christian in religion. With Rome's eventual decline in the West as a city of influence, Constantinople as the residence of the emperor and his court grew in prestige and in 381 officially became the fourth patriarchal See after Alexandria, Antioch, and Rome. Jerusalem was promoted in 451 to the patriarchal rank out of respect for the place of origin of Christianity making a total five patriarchates. This ancient division of East and West remains the basis today for the definition of the Western world and the East.

# CHAPTER 2

# ARAMAIC CHRISTIANITY IN THE FIRST CENTURIES

## 2.1 Introduction to the Period

Jesus Christ was born in Bethlehem in the first century AD, when the town was part of the administration of Judaea under King Herod in the Roman province of Syria Palaestina. The Romans allocated the name 'Syria' to their three large provinces to encompass all its imperial land in the Middle East.[19] This broad Roman region came to be known as the 'Syrian Orient'. Aramaic, probably Jesus' primary native tongue, was the regional language of the ancient Middle East. The first and majority of early Christians were Aramaic-speaking Jews.[20] The populations residing closer to the Mediterranean and Jerusalem spoke a 'Western Aramaic dialect'. Those further to the East, such as in modern day Iraq spoke an 'Eastern Aramaic dialect', which was centred on the city of Edessa (modern Şanlıurfa in South-Eastern Turkey).

The Syriac alphabet developed from the Aramaic alphabet. From about the second or third century AD it was used as a literary and liturgical language of the Eastern Aramaic-speaking Christians. By the sixth century it began to be more widely embraced, particularly in Northern Syria. Eventually the term Aramaic ('Aramaya') became known as Syriac ('Suryaya', today pronounced 'Suryani'). For many centuries it is possible that we can refer to Aramaic, Syriac and

---

[19] Reference to the ancient Middle East here does not include Asia Minor (such as modern day Turkey) and North African countries such as Egypt.

[20] It is generally accepted Aramaic, as the regional language, was the primary native tongue of the Jews at the time of Jesus Christ, and Hebrew was their second native tongue. Many Jews, and likely Jesus Christ, also spoke the international language of Greek.

Aramaic-Syriac interchangeably and written Syriac had little, if any, impact on the spoken Western Aramaic dialects until after the sixth century. Likely by the ninth century, Arabic also became a common spoken language in the region.

Alexandria in Egypt and Antioch in Syria are commonly regarded as having Greek-speaking populations. Whilst Greek was the international language of these two cities, there is scant reference to, or study of, their indigenous populations. They were naturally substantial in number and cultural contribution. Native Egyptians who spoke Coptic no doubt resided in Alexandria. Native Syrians, speaking Aramaic, must have resided in Antioch. Their languages and cultures significantly influenced the diversity of these Christian capital cities.

These societies were multicultural and multilingual, and they lived in general harmony, immersed in their cross-cultural coexistence. Yet a void exists in the historical coverage of the indigenous population of Antioch. This chapter will outline some of what we do know about the Christian Aramaic-Syriac speaking peoples of the Middle East in the first centuries after the birth of Jesus Christ, and discuss their links to neighbouring faith, linguistic, and cultural groups. Special attention will be paid to both lay and monastic communities of the Syrian Orient in this study.

## 2.2 Links between Aramaic Christianity and Jewish Traditions

The natural influence of Judaism on Christianity is evident in Aramaic Christianity. The concept of prayer, for example, comes from the Jewish tradition, especially as it became widespread for the Jews as a replacement for the Temple sacrifices after the destruction of the Second Temple in 70 AD. At the time of Jesus Christ, the scriptures of the Jewish Temple in Jerusalem were no longer understood in Hebrew, but were adopted according to the Aramaic version of the sacred books. These books were the ancient Targumim. They were rephrased and transliterated into the Aramaic language in the western Aramaic dialect, as used in Jordan, Phoenicia, Lebanon, and northern Syria.

Phraseology in the Aramaic-Syriac Christian Peshitta (short summarised versions of the Old and New Testaments) is often that of the Jewish Targumim (Targum) or has its origins in it. Many examples of the inclusion of specific Jewish traditions have been found in the Syriac Peshitta. Targum traditions, as paraphrases of Jewish scripture used for preaching, are found in considerable number in the literary writings of the Aramaic Christians including the famous Aphrahat and Ephrem. The Syriac Peshitta was of the Aramaic spoken language as was the Jewish Palestinian Targum. When using the Targum, there was no Greek influence or need for translation. It is highly probable the Gospel of Matthew was written in Aramaic and not Greek, and accordingly no loss of meaning in translation from one language to another. It is thought Hebrew and Aramaic shared about sixty percent of the same words.

Although Greek was the international language at the time, Aramaic was the indigenous language of the Middle East. Jesus Christ, born a Jew in Bethlehem, would likely have spoken Aramaic as his native tongue, and may have spoken Hebrew and Greek as well. Jesus Christ's first followers, Jewish Aramaic-speaking converts, were from the Galilee and Jerusalem regions. The Jews were spread out across the Middle East particularly after 70 AD. Aramaic was likely their first native tongue, as it was for the non-Jews or Gentiles.

As Jews who believed in the coming of the Messiah, they may have initially shared the Temple with other Jews, and were not subject to expulsion. Jewish customs would certainly have continued for these Messianic Jews. The indigenous gentile and pagan population who converted as Christians may have joined the Messianic Jews in the Temple but this is not certain. As Chorbishop Seely Beggiani states, Aramaic Christianity reflects its origins in the first century converts to Christianity.[21]

By the fourth century, there is clear evidence of monastic life in the Middle East beginning to flourish, particularly in a Jewish Biblical

---

[21] Chorbishop Seely Beggiani, *Introduction to Eastern Christian Spirituality: The Syriac Tradition*, University of Scanton, 1991, p. 11.

context. This appears to have significantly influenced the development of Christian religious practice in the Middle East. R.M. Price, in his introduction to *The History of the Monks of Syria by Theodoret*, provides us with a trite account to the uniqueness of early Aramaic asceticism[22] imitating great Biblical figures:

> Asceticism in Syrian Christianity may be traced back to the presumed Syrian origin of the Gospel according to Matthew, with its emphasis on the theme of discipleship, on a following of Christ involving celibacy (19:11-12), poverty (19:21) and homelessness (19:29) in the service of announcing the kingdom, in a proclamation to be accompanied by miraculous signs of exorcism and healing (10:7 ff) ... Their central theme remains that full access to God can be enjoyed only by those who follow Christ in strict chastity and poverty ... Celibates are described as following in the footsteps of the great virgins of the Bible- Elijah, Elisha, Mary, John Baptist, the beloved disciple, St Paul ... Now it is surely this tradition, native to Syria, from which stem the ascetics of Theodoret. In them we find the same asceticism-celibacy, fasting, vigils, the same charismatic powers of healing and exorcism, and the same scenes of asceticism as an imitation of the great Biblical saints and a sharing in the life of the angels.[23]

The ancient reference to Jewish priests sounding the trumpet, calling to gather in the Temple God's army of warriors in their fight against the enemy devil, is thought to have been practised by Christian Aramaic-speaking priests.

In the geographical context of our study, there is evidence the descendants of the first Christians were likely to have retained many ancient Jewish customs and Temple rites. Several hundred years on,

---

[22] Generally, references to an anchorite, ascetic, or eremite means a religious person living in a solitary or secluded place – that is a hermit or recluse. A cenobite is one of a religious order living in a community such as a convent or monastery. A 'hypethrite' is an ascetic living in the open air.

[23] R.M. Price, "Introduction," in *A History of the Monks of Syria by Theodoret of Cyrrhus*, Cistercian Press, 1987.

some may have been extinguished, yet others retained. For example, at Antioch, and in several neighbouring provinces, Easter was tradition-ally celebrated in immediate proximity to the Jewish Passover, a prac-tice that was condemned in 325 at the Council of Nicaea.[24] In contrast, one important ritual likely to have been passed on to today is choral singing. In his chapter on James of Cyrrhus (written around 445), The-odoret informs us on the arrival to Cyrrhus of John the Baptist's relics from Palestine and Phoenicia, they were enthusiastically "welcomed with Davidic choral singing" by "the shepherd and the people, towns folk and countrymen."[25]

Who are the descendants of the first Aramaic-speaking Christians that witnessed Jesus Christ walking through the streets, heard him preach, saw his miracles, touched him, talked to him and attended the Temple with him? Could it be that the Aramaic-speaking churches originating from the Middle East are the direct heirs or representatives to the first Christian liturgical language and rituals? If there is any an-swer, it must point to the Aramaic-speaking churches today originat-ing from the Middle East. They may be the only Christians who can claim retention in their liturgy to the closest form of Jesus Christ's na-tive tongue – Aramaic – and melodies chanted by the early Christians indigenous to the Middle East.

## 2.3   Early Syrian Monasticism

Sozomen (c. 380-450 AD) was a historian of the early Christian Church period from 324 to 425 AD. He was born in Palestine and became a Christian lawyer in Constantinople. Although he had limited theologi-cal knowledge, his history included many sources and is regarded as a reliable account. He states that the Christians of the city of Antioch did not convert those in the countryside around Antioch. Antioch was a Greek-speaking administration capital. The region outside of Antioch was Aramaic-speaking. Sozomen recounts that the Christian city folk

---

[24] Theodoret, *A History of the Monks of Syria by Theodoret of Cyrrhus*, trans. by R.M. Price, Cistercian Press, 1987, p. 171.
[25] Ibid., Chapter 3 on Marcian.

did not influence the pagan countryside. Christian conversion was left to the hermit monks.[26]

Price provides us with a suitable introduction to this era of the uniqueness and influence of early Aramaic monasticism and its distinction from the monasticism of Egypt:

> [T]he ideal and practice of 'monasticism', that is the single life of the monachos (Greek) or ihidaya (Syriac), goes back in Syrian Christianity through the celibates of the second and third centuries ... but we know enough to be able to assert that the standard textbook treatment of monasticism, that starts with Antony of Egypt of the late third century and proceeds to Syrian monasticism as if it were a subsequent and dependent development, is seriously misleading.[27]

Anthony the Great (c. 251–356), also known as Saint Anthony, is reportedly the first hermit monk to live in the wilderness. He became a hermit in the desert just outside Alexandria Egypt in about 270-271. He is the most well known 'Desert Father' and is also regarded as both the father and founder of desert monasticism. Importantly for the history of early Aramaic monasticism, St Anthony and the Egyptian desert fathers did not live in the open air but in caves.

Athanasius of Alexandria wrote the *Life of Anthony* in Greek around 360.[28] Athanasius stated that around the time of Anthony's death in 356, "the desert had become a city" with thousands of Christian monks and nuns living there following Anthony's example. Although it is often said that these communities, which were originally informal gatherings of hermit monks, became the model for Christian monasticism, we know today this did not apply to the Aramaic monks of the Syrian Orient.

Price distinguishes the social and economic hardship of Egypt in the fourth century from the Aramaic position. The region of Theodo-

---

[26] Sozomen, *A History of the Church in Nine Books, from A.D.324 to A.D.440*, trans. by E. Walford, S. Bagster, 1846.

[27] Price, "Introduction," *A History of the Monks*, pp. xx-xxii.

[28] Athanasius, *Life of St. Anthony of Egypt*, trans. by David Brakke, Garland, 2000.

ret's holy men and women, that of northern Syria, experienced economic development in the fourth and fifth century whereby huge rural areas, under-exploited, enjoyed an unprecedented agricultural expansion accompanied by the breakdown of many large estates into a massive number of modest farms.

Price dismisses various explanations for the notable expansion in the fourth and fifth centuries, both in the number of ascetics in Syria, and in the attention and respect they received from other members of the church.[29] He rules out the theory of any link between monastic expansion and the end of the Roman persecution of Christians, and states many Aramaic monks, especially the leading ones, were not oppressed peasants at all, but came from the prosperous classes of society. He believes it is more so the fact that the primitive Christians had a strong sense of themselves as holy people, existing in the flesh but not in accordance with the flesh, living on earth but exhibiting a heavenly citizenship.

For the first time asceticism was widely pursued as the only way to obtain salvation. Through the strictest self-denial, the Aramaic hermits had won the access to God. For the ordinary Christian layperson not seeking the ascetic life, there was a spiritual anxiety; a sense of their own spiritual inadequacy where they no longer had the confidence their own prayers were acceptable to God. The ordinary folk sought intercession from the ascetics in their traditional role as mediators. Hermits, therefore, were not left alone. This brought a flood of 'clients' to the hermits in quest of the assurance afforded by their prayers and blessings. This, according to Price, provides the essential explanation of the growth both in the number of Christians who chose the ascetic path to salvation, and in the attention and respect these ascetics received from those who remained in the world.

Simon Stylite (as we will study in the next chapter) ascended a pillar not to achieve a positive effect on his soul or those of others, but simply to manifest the ascent of the whole person to God. In this way Aramaic ascetics, while mortifying the flesh, esteemed the body. The

---

[29] Price, "Introduction," *A History of the Monks*, pp. xxiii, ff.

holy Aramaic monks and nuns Theodoret mentioned offered to the beholder a spiritual life that was visible and a direct object of veneration, quite apart from conjecture on the state of the soul.

Arthur Vööbus, in his introduction to *History of Asceticism in the Syrian Orient*, comments that the grotesque and bizarre manners of Aramaic monasticism fascinated the Syrians.[30] Their personal habits and dress were distinct from the monks of Egypt:

> For the monastic philosophy there was no question about sleep. Only wakefulness and vigils were consistent with the spiritual life. Sleep on the contrary furthered laziness, laxity and the rise of all low instincts. Ephrem says bluntly that he who lives in fear of God, sleeps little, but he who falls away from the fear of God sleeps much ...
>
> The appearance of the dress, too, was framed in conformity with ascetic mentality. It was forbidden to use dress ostentatious in appearance. Black was regarded as the only proper colour. Not only was it an indication of simplicity, but the generally understood symbol of sorrow and mourning as well. Therefore, the black garments suited the ascetic mentality, giving an external testimony to the inward attitude. The monastic garb is spoken of as a sign of mourning. The white garments used by the monks in Egypt and by the Manichaean monks were avoided by the Syrians ... Those who decided to leave the world to enter the monastery knew what the outward sign of inward grief and sadness was-the selecting of a worn mantle or a miserable dress.[31]

The religious and moral life of the masses slipped into their hands. The Byzantine rulers joined the adoring masses rather than risk conflict with these powerful men and to a far lesser extent in number, women. The monks secured an entrance into ecclesiastical affairs. The monks then became significant in their missionary activities in trans-

---

[30] Arthur Vööbus, *A History of Asceticism in the Syrian Orient*, Vols 1-3, Louvain, 1960.

[31] Vööbus, *A History of Asceticism*, Vol. 1, pp. 264-9.

forming the semi-pagan and pagan communities in the orbit of the Syrian Orient and beyond to Mesopotamia and Persia.

The geographical landscape of the monks of Egypt differed somewhat from those in northern Syria Theodoret wrote about. St Anthony's ascetics practised a milder discipline due to the harsh climate of the deserts. Severe heat, very cold nights, and a lack of rainfall restricted these monks to their cells. Egyptian ascetics lived in cells in complete solitude. Later, through the formation of the cenobitic communities in monasteries, these ascetics lived communally but apart from society.

The Aramaic ascetics, on the other hand, lived in a more conducive climate and so their discipline focused on a greater rigourous discipline of the body. There were no true deserts. The terrain was mountainous and provided relief from the heat of summer. Occasional snow and a more consistent rainfall during non-summer months ensured water was always available. The ascetics could roam the wilderness and mountains, and were not confined to cells. As opposed to the Egyptian counterpart, self-inflicted suffering was therefore more a constant practice as part of fasting, praying and meditating.

The Egyptian monks spoke either or both Greek and Coptic (the ancient Egyptian language). The monks of the Syrian Orient spoke Aramaic-Syriac. Monasticism of the Aramaic speakers was not monolithic, and unlike Greek monasticism did not have one single founder. The ascetic monks of both Egypt and Aramaic world were venerated by the faithful as the 'new martyrs' because of their 'superhuman' practices.

After the early fourth century, this was an age without the persecution and without the Christian martyrdom of the previous centuries. There was a spiritual rather than a physical martyrdom, but both forms were of suffering and dying in Jesus Christ's name. These were the 'new athletes' to be admired and venerated, rather than the olympians.

Naturally, upon their death, the physical remains of the ascetics were highly sought after as a reminder of their sacrifice, devotion, and miracles. Battles would ensue between neighbouring towns and villages over the relics, which may have included clothing, hair, and personal belongings. In one case of James, as mentioned by Theodoret and discussed in the following chapters, the battle began even before the death of the holy man, whilst he was close to and presumed dead.

Once communities of monks developed as a less informal gathering for the ascetics, the Egyptian monasteries remained contemplative, reflective, and inwardly focused. Aramaic monasteries became active, missionary, and outwardly focused but at the same time retaining hermitages for those monks seeking the ascetic life. The Aramaic hermitages, although linked to the monastery and subject to the orders of the superior, may have been a sizeable distance away. Unlike the spread of Manichaeism throughout Syria and eastern provinces in the previous centuries, the monks of the Aramaic Christian monasteries did not rely on the support of the lay faithful.

The Aramaic monasteries promoted an image of self-sufficiency and many were centres of learning, craft, and art and had a direct influence on culture. Schools became attached to the monasteries, as did the cultivation of calligraphy, book production, and artistic declaration of manuscripts in the form of miniatures, such as the Rabbula Gospels. Most of the Syriac literature and manuscripts were produced by monastics. The first Christian university was founded by the Aramaic monk Narsai in Nisibis on the banks of the Tigris River.[32] As missionaries, Aramaic monks and their monasticism spread to Arabia, Ethiopia, Central Asia, India, Persia, and China.

There was a distinctive martial motif in the monasticism of the Middle East, with the practice of Christian hermits traditionally identified as that of soldiers with prayer as their weapon. Their holy war was against the sworn enemy, the devil. They were persons who fought with the physical comfort and pleasures of the world. Possessions, marriage, and any links with society were sacrificed. In ancient

---

[32] Arthur Vööbus, "The Contribution of Ancient Syrian Christianity to West European Culture," *Journal of the Syrian Academic Studies* 2 (1988): pp. 8-14.

Aramaic linguistic terms, the holy war of the thousands of Aramaic-speaking Christian hermits was reflected in the military terminology they employed: the struggle, fight, battle, and war. These were warriors of God, the fighters in the army of God. Theodoret also refers to them as part of wrestling schools,[33] and in about 375 AD, Ephrem wrote of "how great an army lies on the mountain."

This ethos, clearly understood in terms of warfare, may well have come from a Jewish tradition inherited by the Middle Eastern Christians and which continued for many centuries after Christ. There is ancient reference to the Jewish priests sounding the trumpet calling for the warriors to gather in the temple. This Jewish tradition continues today with the sounding of the trumpet at the Jewish Wailing Wall in Jerusalem. It is reported the Christian Aramaic-speaking priests in the Middle East would blow their trumpets signaling the engagement in battle with the enemy, the devil, as brave fighters in God's army.[34]

In January 387, through the bishop and historian Theodoret, we hear of thousands of anchorites living in the mountains and in the vicinity around Antioch coming into the marketplace within the supposedly Greek-speaking city of Antioch to support the population in its dispute with Emperor Theodosius and that these monks spoke Aramaic-Syriac and needed the help of an interpreter to speak with the royal emissaries. By the end of the fourth century, Constantinople in the Syrian Orient was regarded as the place of the monks of fame. Monasticism in the Syrian Orient was flourishing just as much as it was in Egypt, but entirely independent of each other.

In the countryside monks would be able to change their locations to follow rainfall and more fertile grounds, likewise for the mountainous regions, which became too cold during the winter. Still, the mountains were popular among the Aramaic speakers in the Orient offering natural protection and shelter in caves, clefts and hollows. The

---

[33] Theodoret, *A History of the Monks*, p. 56.
[34] See also 'holy war' in the Christian Old Testament book of Deuteronomy 20 and the story of Gideon.

growing number of monks in the mountains and deserts escaping from the world united them all. They would have lived in close proximity to one another being so many. Accordingly, they began to assist each other but retain the basic convictions for anchoritism. This propagated a communal spirit and fellowship and many would have desired to live in close proximity to an experienced 'fighter' wanting voluntarily to follow his or her instructions. The wild form of asceticism, hostile to civilisation, was gradually tempered and softened.

The Church was involved in taming the independence of these hermits and tying the monks and nuns to the Church. The Church began to appoint great monastic figures as bishops. We are told many of these men did not change their ascetic practices but combined them with their new duties as bishops. Other monks felt their place was in the Church and cooperation with the Church was the proper and natural course allowing the other groups, who kept alive the traditions of the original and somewhat archaic monastic origins to retain their independence. Eventually the ascetic life had been retained within the monastic communities and one could enter the ascetic life under the direction of these monastic communities.

We understand from Theodoret that there were possibly hundreds if not thousands of monasteries in the Orient including in Palestine, Egypt, Asia, and Pontus. Magnificent monasteries were built with gardens, orchards, plantations, fields and herds necessary for their maintenance. By the fifth century in the communal monasteries, it was not unusual to find in one monastery hundreds of monks and in some cases over a thousand. These monasteries then transformed the previous individual independent practice, and became the centres for launching the athletes and heroes: the hermits. Theodoret records monasteries with both Greek-speaking and Aramaic-Syriac-speaking monks each with their own superiors:

> (they) assembled (in the monastery church) at the beginning
> and close of the day in order to offer the evening and morn-
> ing hymnody to God; this they were divided into two and

each using their own language, while sending up their song in return.[35]

The ancient Semitic people regarded the mountains as holy and venerated places. It led to a significant amount of sites for monasteries resting in the mountains with the additional practical consideration of the security of the region. The mountain regions were the most attractive sites for monastic founding. They were inaccessible, pathways were narrow and ladders were used inside caves that could be lowered from above and drawn up when not in use. Criticism began to spread about the loss of tranquil spaces by the growth of community monasticism in a new grandiose style that left the primitive and austere behind.

Naturally, some of the monks of the monastery were required to undertake business transactions on behalf of their community. The monasteries developed management and housekeeping techniques, including the necessary supply of provisions. This was seen as abandoning the ancient principle of poverty. However, it was required so that this large community could be independent of help from others. Being so large, they could not remain dependent on the surrounding population. A compromise was achieved by appointing leaders to the monasteries.

Emperor Theodosius in 392 removed all obstacles to monasteries being established in towns and villages. Over time, many monasteries were established closer to communities of villages and towns to more readily serve in their missionary work. Monastic buildings began to appear in urban centres. People willingly and freely donated, as they do today, money or materials or manpower to help build churches and monasteries and many ancient buildings or parts of buildings still bear the names of the donors acknowledging the generosity of those who had made the gifts and donations to the monastery. Others volunteered their assistance to the monks in their pastoral and charitable work. Monasteries were now dotted throughout cities, towns, villages, and the countryside.

---

[35] Theodoret, *A History of the Monks*, p. 60.

## 2.4 Sons and Daughters of the Covenant

The *Bnai* and *Bnat Qyama* or *bnay qyama* (Sons and Daughters of the Covenant), was a form of Aramaic-Syriac monasticism originating in the third century and which became widespread throughout the Syrian Orient by the fourth century. It was a special order, an intermediate level between the laity and the ordained clergy. We best know it from the Sixth Demonstration of Aphrahat the Persian, written in 337.

St Aphrahat (c. 270-345) was an Aramaic-Syriac Christian author born in Persia. He wrote twenty-three homilies on Christian doctrine and practice, collectively known as the *Demonstrations.*[36] He was an ascetic and celibate, and was almost definitely a 'son of the covenant'. He may have been a bishop, and later Syriac tradition places him at the head of Mar Matti monastery near Mosul, now in modern day northern Iraq. He lived within the sphere of the Persian Empire, in a region beyond the eastern boundaries of the Roman Empire.

These sons and daughters of the Covenant were committed to life-long celibacy; however, they were not monks and nuns and could possess property. The *bnay qyama* practised a mild form of austerity. It was characterised by vows of celibacy, voluntary poverty, and service to the local priest or bishop. Its members were to live separately with others of the same office or with their families. It involved an intense commitment to ascetical life as a celibate, but not in separating from the Christian community by fleeing to the wilderness. They were to remain disciples, living and working normally in the community.

The members of the Covenant included married people who later decided to practise this form of abstinence. They were not required to live in monasteries as cenobites. They assisted at public celebrations, in the Divine Office, and abstained from meat and wine. There were virgins *or bthule* (meaning for both sexes) who renounced marriage and the 'holy ones' or *qaddishe* who were married but decided to live a life of celibacy thereafter. They were modest in dress and

---

[36] Aphrahat, *The Demonstrations of Aphrahat, the Persian Sage*, trans. by Adam Lehto, Gorgias Press, 2010.

avoided feasting, and strove to have no enemies and to refrain from using harmful words.[37]

The Daughters of the Covenant were responsible under the Rabbula Canon laws of the Aramaic-Syriac church for the singing of psalms and hymns in civic liturgical celebrations (civic mass or mass for the people).[38] It is likely that female choirs also included younger unmarried girls, 'virgins', who were not necessarily dedicated to life-long celibacy. The Aramaic-Syriac poet Jacob of Serugh (d. 521) tells us that St Ephrem had founded these choirs of consecrated virgins, training them through melody set to Aramaic-Syriac folk tunes in the forum of Edessa to directly instruct the congregations in right doctrine.

It is likely that St Ephrem was part of the *Bnai* and *Bnat Qyama*. He is a Doctor of the Church in Roman Catholicism and is venerated by the Greek Orthodox and of course the Aramaic-Syriac Churches. St Ephrem the Syrian (c. 306-373) is known as the great father of the Aramaic-Syriac-speaking Church traditions. He was an Aramaic-Syriac deacon and teacher and founder of the School of Nisibis and continued teaching in the School of Edessa.

Over four hundred hymns composed by Ephrem still exist as well as many sermons in verse and poems. His most important works are the poetic-lyric teaching hymns or *mādršê*. Ephrem used models of early Rabbinic Judaism, Greek science and philosophy, and the Mesopotamian/ Persian tradition of mystery symbolism in his writings. He used his *Hymns Against Heresies* as practical teaching to Christians not to succumb to the many heresies that were attempting to divide the early Church at that time. He advised other ascetics and taught that spiritual vocation was not just for the celibate but the married as well, espousing a far more moderate and common sense view to monasticism than the extremes.

[37] Vööbus, *A History of Asceticism* and Beggiani *Introduction to Eastern Christian Spirituality.*
[38] Susan A. Harvey, "Revisiting the Daughters of the Covenant: Women's Choirs and Sacred Song in Ancient Syriac Christianity," *Hugoye: Journal of Syriac Studies* 8, pp. 125-149.

Separate to the Daughters of the Covenant were the deaconesses. Their ministry was for women only – to visit and instruct them, attend on them if they were ill, assist in their baptism, and keep order in the women's sections of the churches during mass. It interesting that in the Western churches, without any knowledge of these Aramaic-Syriac traditions, the roles of women are coming in to play for the first time in 1700 years after it began in the Middle East.

It appears the practice of the *Bnay qyama* was widespread throughout Aramaic-Syriac-speaking villages, towns and cities of late antiquity. It is significant that the Aramaic-speaking Christians for almost five hundred years did not use the Greek equivalent of *monachos* for the name of a monk. Instead, they used the Aramaic term *ihidaya* meaning 'solitary, hermit' and single minded to Christ. This Aramaic term is used to refer to Christ and is also found in the Jewish Palestinian Targum (i.e. the Aramaic version of the Hebrew Old Testament paraphrased), referring to Adam as a single in the world prior to his fall when he is tempted by Eve.

# CHAPTER 3

# ST MAROUN, ST ABRAHAM, AND ST SIMON THE STYLITE

## Timeline of Key Dates

**Fourth Century**

313   Roman Emperor Constantine (born in Serbia) declares freedom of religion.

330   Constantine renames Byzantium (today Istanbul) Constantinople and makes it the new capital of the Roman Empire. The Roman Empire is subsequently known as the Western Roman Empire and the Byzantine Empire.

350   St Maroun is born.

356   Death of St Anthony the Great (he entered the ascetic life in the desert outside Alexandria, Egypt in 270 AD).

360   Life of Anthony written in Greek (about St Anthony) by Athanasius of Alexandria, the first written reference to a hermit monk.

373   Death of St Ephrem the Syrian.

380   Emperor Theodosius declares Christianity official religion of the Roman Empire.

380   St Maroun is the first hermit/monk to practise living in the open air in northern Syria. Famous for his miracles he attracted followers and visitors.

**Fifth Century**

410   Death of St Maroun (d. 410-423) near Antioch in northern Syria. A war over his remains arose between neighbouring villages. A great shrine was built honouring the 'victor' with public festivals.

422   Death of St Abraham, a hermit monk from Cyrrhus, the same region as St Maroun. He converted a town in Lebanon to Christianity and established a monastic community.

444   Theodoret, Bishop of Cyrrhus writes Religious History about Syrian monasticism.

451   Council of Chalcedon condemns the Monophysites as heretics. The communion is broken between the Universal Catholic Church and various churches including Coptic, Gregorian Armenians, Syrians (later known as the Jacobites), and Ethiopians.

452   Founding of Beit Maroun monastery honouring St Maroun as patron saint at Apamaea in northern Syria, built with the support of Byzantine Emperor Marcian.

459   A network of monasteries and followers flourish under the leadership of Beit Maroun monastery and follow the Antiochean Syro-Aramaic traditions. After the Council of Chalcedon they remain the only Catholics indigenous to the Middle East within the Patriarchate of Antioch.

460   Death of St Simon the Stylite.

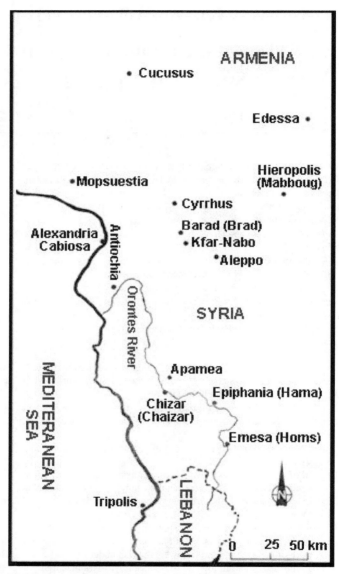

Map 4: Ancient geographical sites associated with Saint Maroun and the Maronites. Source: Guita G, "Saint Maron's Relic, 'Ornament of the Divine Choir of Saints'", The Journal of Maronite Studies (JMS), The Maronite Research Institute, http://maronite-institute.org Vol 1 , No 1, 1997 MARI website.

Fifth century St Simon Stylite's Church centred on St Simon's pillar, 30km from Aleppo, Northern Syria. UNESCO reported the Church was heavily damaged in an air strike in May 2016 during the Syrian Civil War (http://whc.unesco.org/en/news/1499/). Photos taken in 2005 by the author.

Remnants in the middle of St Simon Stylite's 18m high pillar around which the Church was built after his death. The top of the pillar was protected by a canopy of palm trees which was removed by St Simon in the last three years of his life. Earthenware pipe extended from the top platform to a pit at the bottom ground for the lavatory.

## 3.1 Syria and Phoenicia in the Fourth and Fifth Centuries

In the third and fourth centuries, the Roman Empire had allocated three Syrian provinces: Syria Palaestina, Syria Magna (or Syria-Coela) and Syria Phoenicia. At the Council of Nicaea in 325, seventeen bishops were represented from northern Syria (Syria-Coela), including Antioch and Cyrrhus (the latter, a region adjoining Antioch). By that time, there were a large number of Christians living in the countryside around Antioch, as well as the city of Antioch itself. The cenobitic monastery of Teleda in the country region of Antioch referred to by Theodoret was by 367 the greatest monastery of the region.

During these early centuries Christians faced strong persecution. Conversion to the faith was gradual. In 313 AD, the Roman Byzantine Empire granted freedom to its denizens to practise their religious rites. From then, the Christian faith expanded at a greater pace, as did its monasticism. In 380 AD, Christianity was proclaimed the official religion of the Roman Empire. The Emperor began to openly support the Church, including financially.

In general terms, if we place a world map in front of us during the early Christian centuries, we would see the Latin church in the West, the Greek church in the middle, the Aramaic-Syriac church to the East and the Coptics in Egypt. Each of these traditions would spread the gospel in those areas. The Latins moved through western Europe, the Greeks northwards through eastern Europe, the Aramaic-Syriacs through the Middle East and Asia, and the Coptics through Egypt and North Africa. For many of the early centuries after Christ, the Middle East region must have comprised an overwhelming majority of Christians throughout the world. By the early to mid-fifth century, its region was predominantly Christian.

After Christianity was declared the official religion of the Empire in 380, the Church actively sought to convert any pagans that remained in the Middle East, particularly near to the Holy Land and extending to Constantinople. In this present chapter, the focus is on the pagans left in north Syria and Phoenician region, remembering much of Europe remained pagan at this time. The translations of the relevant ancient sources are set out at the end of the chapter.

Eleven bishops represented Phoenicia at the Church Council of Nicaea in 325 from Tyre, Ptolemais, Damascus, Sidon, Tripolis (Tripoli), Paneas (Caesarea Philippi or Banias today in Golan Heights), Berytus (Beirut), Palmyra, Alassus, Emesa (today, Homs in Syria), and Antardus (today, Tartus in Syria). Whilst it is abundantly clear the coastal and inland cities of Phoenicia represented at Nicaea had significant Christian populations, there is no historical information to indicate the borders of the jurisdiction of each bishop, but it would have included all of the various countryside areas.

Accordingly, scholars have assumed the inland countryside of Phoenicia remained pagan for the most part whilst accepting the countryside of northern Syria had a more substantial Christian population. It is possible Christians were present alongside pagans in the countryside and mountains of Phoenicia and Lebanon at the time of the Council of Nicaea, but no direct records assist us on the issue. It is accepted that pagans lived alongside Christians and other faiths in the cities. The same would have applied in the countryside, except the conversion rate may have been slower than the city.

The only principal written sources known today that mention Christian conversion in Mount Lebanon relate to the life of anchorites in northern Syria in the late fourth and up to mid-fifth centuries. Contrary to the generally accepted view, these records suggest some or many villages, but not all, in this region of Lebanon remained believers in ancient (Phoenician) religion. Some scholars suggest the construction of pagan temples built in prominent places such as Baalbek and on many mountaintops devoting idol worship to the triad, El, Adon, and Astarte, continued up until the time of the mid-fourth century.

With particular reference to Mount Lebanon, two northern Syrian anchorites who practised open-air asceticism – St Abraham and St Simon the Stylite – help us understand how pagan villages converted to Christianity. The area St Abraham was from, Cyrrhus in northern Syria, became famous as the heartbeat of Theodoret's world of early Aramaic-Syriac monasticism. Several decades later saw great crowds visit St Simon Stylite in his neighbourhood of the Antioch countryside near to Cyrrhus. Tourists and pilgrims alike came from afar to witness this new unique athleticism. These anchorite monks were from the same region in which St Maroun was a pioneer in practicing this form of Christian religious secluded life.

## 3.2  St Maroun of Cyrrhus

Around the later half of the fourth century, scholars accept that St Maroun (in Aramaic-Syriac thought to mean 'small Lord'; written as Maron in the USA and France; also written as Maro, Marun, Maroon, Moron, Moro, Mroy), likely lived in the northern Syrian region of Cyrrhus. He resided in the open air near a pagan temple that he had converted into a church. The principal primary source about him is from *Religious History*, written in Greek by Theodoret. The region of Cyrrhus is now Huru Pegamber in south-eastern Turkey, bordering modern northern Syria.

In Theodoret's work on the lives of thirty notable holy men and women, he says Maroun's life was one of penance and prayer. He took refuge at rare times under a tent made of skins, in order to avoid bad weather. Crowds invaded his place of solitude. Men and women went to seek his prayers or partake in his discipline. He gave in abundance the gift of miracle healing to the sick, this "his fame circulated every-where, [and] attracted everyone from every side." Theodoret did not specifically mention how far Maroun's fame travelled. It is plausible from the words he used that it was an extensive area including outside of his 'Syria'.

Theodoret writes that on Maroun's death (d. 410-423 AD):

A bitter war over his body arose between his neighbours.
One of the adjacent villages that was well populated came

out in mass, drove off the others and seized this thrice desired treasure; building a great shrine, they reap benefits therefrom even to this day, honouring this victor with a public festival. We ourselves reap his blessing even at a distance; for sufficient for us instead of his tomb is his memory.

It is likely this is the same Maroun that St John Chrysostom in his 36th Epistle addressed his short letter in 405 AD "To Maroun, the monk priest." This description is consistent with Theodoret's reference to Maroun as not only a monk hermit, but implying he was a priest for he consecrated a place of worship of God and blessed the sick. There does not appear to be any evidence of another anchorite by the name of Maroun that John Chrysostom would have written to.

It appears Maroun was important in his time for being, to quote Theodoret, "he who planted for God the garden that now flourishes in the region of Cyrrhus." That is, he was likely the first, and if not one of the first, influential hermits in northern Syria to practise living in the open air rather than the monastic way of life in cells or caves founded by St Anthony the Great. It is not clear whether Maroun's hermitage was tied to or governed by a monastery but Theodoret directly mentions three of the thirty holy men and women as immediate disciples of St Maroun – James (Yacoub) of Cyrrhestica, Limnaeus, and a female, Domnina. It is possible other monks Theodoret wrote about were also Maroun's disciples but were not mentioned as such.[39] Theodoret mentions James as one of Maroun's disciples and his intention to mention more – "and also all the others whom, with God's help, I shall recall individually" – Price suggests at least John as one of those.[40]

It is significant that from the thirty monks in Theodoret's book, it

---

[39] Youhanna Sader, *Crosses and Symbols in Ancient Christian Art of Lebanon*, Dar Sader, 2006, p. 249, refers to Theodoret visiting the anchorite Thalelaios (Chapter 28) in 'Jbail' (Byblos) in Phoenicia. Price refers to the same visit to be at 'Gabala' in northern Syria. Sader's translation has not been relied upon in this thesis. Should he be correct, this would be a significant fact supporting Maronite traditions.

[40] The chapter on John is immediately after the chapters on James and Limnaeus.

appears only Maroun had such an extensive list of disciples directly or indirectly mentioned. When speaking of James as a 'product' of Maroun's 'planting', Theodoret mentions James as "to whom one could reasonably apply the prophetic utterance, *the righteous man will flower as the palm tree, and be multiplied like the cedar of Lebanon.*" It seems Theodoret inferred a connection between Maroun and/or James and a multiplication of the Christian faith in Lebanon. It is said St Maroun set the scene for contemporary monks such as St Abraham and St Simon the Stylite. According to documentary evidence, as detailed later in this chapter, these monks converted pagan villages in Mount Lebanon to Christianity.

Price states Syrian asceticism was prevalent and widespread in the Antioch region as early as 340 AD. He notes that Christianisation of the largely pagan countryside in the territory of Antioch took place roughly between 336 and 368 based on inscriptions in that period recorded in the works by Georges Tchalenko and John Hugo Wolfgang Liebeschuetz. Price believes Theodoret's list of Syrian monks and monasteries is uncomprehensive. However, he acknowledges Theodoret states in Chapter 30 "to recount everything is impossible not only for me but all writers."

Theodoret's knowledge of the past history of Syrian monasticism was 'patchy' according to Price.[41] We can provide an example of Price's last comment. In the chapter on Maroun, Theodoret as bishop would have known the name of the likely three towns that fought over St Maroun's relics. No doubt he was also aware of the town name housing the shrine of St Maroun and holding the (annual) public festival. However, he makes no mention of the names.

We can say that Theodoret was no thorough historian nor did he intend to be. On his journeys and daily life as a bishop, the extent of diary notes, recordings and memories would have varied depending on the time, circumstances and energy available. One may set out to write a comprehensive history but, as Theodoret warns, this is a daunt-

---

[41] Price, "Introduction," *A History of the Monks*, pp. xvii, xviii.

ing and near-impossible task. Compared to most of the other monks Theodoret wrote about, his chapter on Maroun was brief. Price suggests that the chapter is exceedingly thin and slight as "Maroun's disciples had been more concerned to imitate him than to transmit a detailed tradition of his life and labours."[42] Including Maroun, twenty-one of the thirty monks were deceased when Theodoret wrote his book. It is possible at least one other author or historian had already extensively written about St Maroun, but no evidence can confirm that.

It likely follows then that the fame of St Maroun, the towns that fought over his relics, and the town that housed his shrine with the public festivals, would have been so well known that Theodoret need only provide summary and passing detail. His objective was to elaborate on others. As we will see in Chapter 6, Theodoret's memory of honouring St Maroun was vivid to the extent it likely influenced the emperor to found a monastery in Maroun's name only a short number of decades after his death. Theodoret informs us that the open-air life of Domnina, a female disciple of Maroun, was imitated by other women and that there were convents averaging two hundred and fifty nuns.

Theodoret's Maroun was certainly no ordinary monk. It is believed a monastery was built after him at Apamaea in Syria, known as Beit Maroun or St Maroun's monastery. It accommodated at least three hundred monks. There is correspondence in 517/518 AD between the monks of a monastery in this name and Pope Hormisdas in Rome which indicates it was the leading monastery in a network of monasteries in Syria. Nearly all scholars accept that this St Maroun (and the monastic network which honoured him) formed the basis of what was much later to be unintentionally known as the Maronite Church. In the Maronite Catholic rite, the feast day of St Maroun is celebrated on February 9.

---

[42] Ibid., p. xviii.

### 3.3 St Abraham of Cyrrhus

Theodoret wrote about St Abraham (c. 350-422) a monk who was born in Cyrrhus, the cenobitic region sowed by St Maroun, and where Abraham gathered there "the wealth of ascetic virtue." After living as a hermit, he and his companions left to the mountains of Lebanon[43] after hearing that a large village "was engulfed in the darkness of impiety." He successfully converted the village to Christianity after almost being killed by its citizens in his attempts, such as when the citizens heard the singing of psalms and the Divine Liturgy.

He served as a priest there for three years and then had another of his companions appointed in his place and returned to ascetic life for a period of time. Based on legend, many have suggested this village may possibly be Afka near the top of the river Adonis. Tradition has it that the Adonis River, which is named after a Phoenician god, was changed to Abraham (or Ibrahim) River for the saint after the region was Christianised by Abraham and his companions.

We do not know how many companions were with Abraham but it is possible that with them was established a monastic community in Mount Lebanon in this village or at least a monastic mission in the form of at least one or more monks linked to the monks from their former hermitage or domicile or monastery in northern Syria. It is likely Christians were already living in Mount Lebanon prior to St Abraham visiting the area. Theodoret only mentions one village that was engulfed in impiety rather than a number of villages.

Abraham was later made bishop of the largely pagan city of Carrhae in Mesopotamia. A tale tells of the Emperor Theodosius (408-450) summoning Abraham because of his fame. When Abraham arrived, the Emperor "embraced him, and considered his rustic goats hair cloak more honourable than his own purple robe. The choir of the

---

[43] Theodoret refers to "the Lebanon" and not the mountains of Lebanon. The Lebanon was usually a reference to the mountains rather than the broader Roman province of Phoenicia Lebanon that extended as far East as Palmyra. Theodoret elsewhere in his book refers to 'Phoenicia' adding weight to his general distinction.

empresses[44] clasped his hands and knees; and they made supplication to a man who did not even understand Greek." It is possible, if not likely, Abraham would have mentioned Maroun to his imperial hosts. The Maronite Catholic Church celebrates the feast day of St Abraham on February 14.

## 3.4   St Simon Stylite of Syria

St Simon (Symeon) the Stylite (c. 389-459), another monk featured in Theodoret's book, was a contemporary to St Maroun and St Abraham. He lived for almost forty years in the open air on a stone pillar at a hilltop in the countryside region of Antioch in northern Syria, not far from modern day Aleppo. The pillar eventually reached eighteen metres high. The fame of his sanctity and miracles brought pilgrims to visit from all over Asia, Europe, Britain and the Middle East. He is often referred to as St Simon the Stylite the Elder, and his epithet is derived from the Greek 'stylos', meaning pillar. An enormous church was built around the famous pillar and completed in 490 AD. At that time it was the largest church in the world. Prior to the commencement of the Syrian War in 2011, it remained relatively intact. However, UNESCO website news reported the church was severely damaged, possibly as a result of an air strike in May 2016.

Syriac manuscript MS 160, c. 473 AD, gives an account of the conversion of "a great crowd" who had visited Simon from the mountains of Lebanon.[45] The pilgrims promised to convert to Christianity if Simon's advice proved correct, namely that the placement of crosses around their villages would protect them against wild beasts that were eating people and children even from inside their homes. His recommendation worked and the village converted. The manuscript was translated from Syriac into Latin in 1719 by the Maronite scholar Simon Assemani who lived in Rome and was in charge of the Vatican

---

[44] The empresses were the Emperor's sister Pulcheria and the Emperor's wife Eudocia. See Price, *A History of the Monks*, footnote 6, p. 125.
[45] The account is by Cosmos, a disciple of St Simon the Stylite.

library and collection of ancient manuscripts from the Middle East. In his book *Bibliotheca Orientalis*, also written in Latin, Assemani recalls during his time that the Maronites of Jibbet in north Lebanon were still spreading the news of this miracle and pointed him to the rocks where the crosses were carved in the towns of Hasroun, Bsharri, Ehden, and Aitou. Today, several churches exist in the mountain towns of north Lebanon in honour of St Simon Stylite. In the Maronite Catholic rite, the feast day of St Simon the Stylite is celebrated on September 1.

## 3.5  Key Historical Sources

### 3.5.1  St John Chrysostom's Letter to Maroun, c. 405

The first source discussed here is a letter to "Maron, the monk priest" in Greek by St John Chrysostom from c. 405. St John was known as 'John the Golden Mouth' for his sermons in the Cathedral of Antioch or Golden Church. He was Patriarch of Constantinople from 397 to 403. It is possible John dedicated his sixth epistle to Saint Maroun while exiled in Caucasus (Cucussus) Armenia, around the year 405. Born to 'Greco-Syrian' parents, his sixth epistle reads as follows:

> To Maron, the Monk Priest:
>
> We are bound to you by love and interior disposition, and see you here before us as if you were actually present. For such are the eyes of love; their vision is neither interrupted by distance nor dimmed by time. We wished to write more frequently to your reverence, but since this is not easy on account of the difficulty of the road and the problems to which travellers are subject, whenever opportunity allows we address ourselves to your honour and assure you that we hold you constantly in our mind and carry you about in our soul wherever we may be. And take care yourself that you write to us as often as you can, telling us how you are, so that although separated physically we might be cheered by learning constantly about your health and receive much consolation as

we sit in solitude. For it brings us no small joy to hear about your health. And above all please pray for us.[46]

Both scholars Pierre Dib and R.M. Price state this is, or is likely to be, the same Maroun as Theodoret's Maroun.[47] Maronite tradition as recorded by Patriarch Doueihi (1630-1704) believes St John Chrysostom was a friend of St Maroun even before the letter, claiming they were students together in Antioch. Abbott and historian Paul Naaman states that although far from conclusive, indications are not lacking in support of the idea that they knew each other in Syria before 398, which draws on the detailed summaries of Syrian monasticism Chrysostom provided in his biographies.[48]

## 3.5.2 Theodoret of Cyr, *Religious History*, c. 440-445

Theodoret, as Bishop of Cyrrhus (a region today in northern Syria and eastern Turkey), wrote in Greek a prologue and then thirty chapters entitled *Religious History*. He likely began writing from the year 423 and completed it around 440-445 AD. R.M. Price translated it into English in 1987 in a book entitled *A History of the Monks of Syria by Theodoret of Cyrrhus*. Each chapter is devoted to a religious person; twenty of who were already dead at the time Theodoret commenced writing his book. Most of the other hermits he visited and knew personally. Fourteen chapters were devoted to ascetics. He wrote about two deceased monks who passed away as early as 337/8.

We can learn much about the life of Aramaic anchorites and, for the first time, in eyewitness testimonial detail from Theodoret's work. It includes their practices and reputation for miracles. It does not infer

---

[46] Quoted by Guita G. Hourani, *Saint Maron's Relic*, which cited the epistle in Shafiq AbouZayd, *Ihidayutha: A Study of the Life of Singleness in the Syrian Orient: From Ignatius of Antioch to Chalcedon 451 A.D.*, Aram Society for Syro-Mesopotamian Studies, 1993, p. 363.

[47] Pierre Dib, *History of the Maronite Church*, Maronite Exarchate, 1962, pp. 3-4; Price, *A History of the Monks of Syria*, p. 119.

[48] Paul Naaman, *The Maronites. The Origins of an Antiochene Church. A Historical and Geographical Study of the Fifth to Seventh Centuries*, Cisterian Publications, 2009, p. 57.

there were no other ascetics, as Theodoret mentions in his prologue that he only spoke about those "whose rays have reached the boundaries of the universe." Most of the monks were hermits from Theodoret's region as bishop of Cyrrhus. This included small parts of the country-side regions of Antioch, Gabala, and Beroea (now Aleppo). The list of monks is mostly in chronological and geographical order.

Chapter 16 of Theodoret's book relates to Maroun quoted here in its entirety:

> After him I shall recall Maron, for he too adorned the godly choir of the saints. Embracing the open-air life, he repaired to a hilltop formally honoured by the impious. Consecrating to God the precinct of demons on it, he lived there pitching a small tent which he seldom used. He practised not only the usual labours, but devised others as well, heaping up the wealth of philosophy.
>
> 2. The Umpire measured out grace according to his labours: so the magnificent one gave in abundance the gift of healing, with the result that his fame circulated everywhere, attracted everyone from every side and taught by experience the truth of the report. One could see fevers quenched by the dew of his blessing, shivering quieted, demons put to flight, and varied diseases of every kind cured by a single remedy; the progeny of physicians apply to each disease the appropriate remedy, but the prayer of the saint is a common antiodote for every distress.
>
> 3. He cured not only infirmities of the body, but applied suitable treatment to souls as well, healing this man's greed and that man's anger, to this man supplying teaching in self-control and to that providing lessons in justice, correcting this man's intemperance and shaking up another man's sloth. Applying this mode of cultivation, he produced many plants of philosophy and it was he who planted for God the garden that now flourishes in the region of Cyrrhus. A product of his planting was the great James, to whom one could reasonably apply the prophetic utterance, 'the righteous man will flower

as the palm tree, and be multiplied like the cedar of Lebanon', and also all the others whom, with God's help, I shall recall individually.

4. Attending in this way to the divine cultivation and treating souls and bodies alike, he himself underwent a short illness, so that we might learn the weakness of nature and the manliness of resolution, and departed from life. A bitter war over his body arose between his neighbours. One of the adjacent villages that was well populated came out in mass, drove off the others and seized this thrice desired treasure; building a great shrine, they reap benefit therefrom even to this day, honouring this victor with a public festival. We ourselves reap his blessing even at a distance; for sufficient for us instead of his tomb is his memory.[49]

Importantly, Price states in his footnote 1:

Maron, while professing himself the disciple of Zebinas (Chapter XXIV) emerges from the *Religious History* as the first influential hermit of the region of Cyrrhus. His pattern of life in the open air, exposed to the extremes of the climate, was imitated by many-James (Chapter 21), Limnaeus (Chapter 22), and others (Chapter 23) – and gave the asceticism of Cyrrhestica a distinctive character, for elsewhere hermits normally lived in cells or caves. Since his disciple James entered on his labours in 402, Maron must still have been alive then but he must have died before Theodoret came to Cyrrhus in 423, since it appears that they never met. It is surprising, in view of Maron's importance, that this chapter is so brief and sketchy. A partial explanation is provided by the fact that Maron's fame was eclipsed by that of his disciple James (Chapter 21). Maron is also mentioned at Chapters 6, 22, 24, 30. He may be the 'Maron priest and monk' who received a letter from John Chrysostom between 404 and 407, but he is not to be identified with Maron of Apamea.

---

[49] The spelling 'Maroun' is used in this book rather than Price's 'Maron'.

Chapter 6 relates to St Symeon the Elder (not St Simon the Stylite), which mentions Maroun relating to an incident where Jews had witnessed a miracle from a Christian:

> Let no one think this story a myth, for I have as witnesses to its truth the common enemies of the truth-for it is those who benefited from this good deed who persisted in celebrating it. This was recounted to me by the great James, who said he had been present when they recounted the miracle to the inspired Maron.

Chapter 21 is a lengthy chapter relating to James (Yacoub) of Cyrrhus (who became a hermit in 405 AD)[50] and includes a short reference to Maroun:

> A companion of the great Maroun and a recipient of his divine teaching, he has eclipsed his teacher by greater labours. For Maroun had a precinct of the ancient imposture as enclosure, pitched a tent of hairy skins, and used this to ward off the assaults of rain and snow. But this man, bidding farewell to all these things, tent and heart and enclosure, has the sky for roof, and lets in all the contrasting assaults of the air, as he is now inundated by torrential rain, now frozen by frost and snow, and other times burnt and consumed by the rays of the sun, and exercises endurance over everything ...
>
> Living in this place he is observed by all comers, since he has, as I said, no cave or tent or hut or enclosure or obstructing wall; but he is to be seen praying or resting, standing or sitting, in health or in the grip of some infirmity, so that it is unceasingly under the eyes of spectators that he strives in combat and repels the necessities of nature.

Chapter 22 relates to Limnaeus also a disciple of Maroun and who visited him at the same time as James. It includes a short reference to Maroun:

> When he had received sufficiently the teaching of the godly

---

[50] Price, "Introduction," *A History of the Monks of Syria*, p. xiv.

old man and made himself an impress of his virtue, he came to the great Maroun, whom we recalled above – he came at the same time as the godly James. After reaping much benefit from there again, and keenly embracing the open-air life, he repaired to another hilltop, lying above a village called Targalla. Here he has continued until today, without a cell or tent or heart, but fenced round by a bare wall built of stones and not joined with day ...

Chapter 24 relates to Zebinas and mentions Maroun:

He was also exceedingly admired by the great Maroun, who would tell all who visited him to hasten and reap the old man's blessing, naming him father and teacher and calling him the model of every virtue. He even asked to share his grave: but this was disallowed by those who seized his sacred body and carried it off to the place mentioned above ...

Chapter 30 relates to Domnina and mentions Maroun:

Emulating the life of the inspired Maroun, whom we recalled above, the wonderful Domnina set up a small hut in the garden of her mother's house; her hut is made of millet stalks. Passing the whole day there, she wets with incessant tears not only her cheeks but also her garments of hair, for such is the clothing with which she covers her body. Going at cockcrow to the divine shrine nearby, she offers hymnody to the Master of the universe, together with the rest, both men and women. This she does not only at the beginning of the day but also at its close, thinking the place consecrated to God to be more venerable than every other spot and teaching others so. Judging it, for this reason, worthy of every attention, she has persuaded her mother and brothers to spend their fortune on it ...

But how long can I expatiate in my eagerness to recall all her virtue, when I ought to bring into the open the life of the other women who have imitated both her and those we recalled above? For there are many others, of whom some have embraced the solitary life and others have preferred life with many companions – in such a way that communities of two hundred and fifty, or more, or less, share the same life, putting up with the same food, choosing to sleep on rushmats alone, assigning their hands to card wool, and consecrating their tongues with hymns ...

Chapter 17 relates to Abraham the most important extracts of which are as follows:

This man too was a fruit of the region of Cyrrhus, for it was born and reared there that he gathered the wealth of ascetic virtue. Those who were with him say that he tamed his body with such vigils, standing, and fasting that for a long time he remained without movement, quite unable to walk. Freed of this weakness by divine providence, he resolved to run the risks of piety as the price of divine favour, and repaired to the Lebanon, where, he had heard, a large village was engulfed in the darkness of impiety. Hiding his monastic character under the mask of a trader, he with his companions brought along sacks as if coming to buy nuts-for this was the main produce of the village. Renting a house, for which he paid the owners a small sum in advance, he kept quiet for three or four days. Then, little by little he began in a soft voice to perform the divine liturgy. When they heard the singing of Psalms, the public crier called out to summon everyone together. Men, children and women assembled; they walled up the doors from outside, and heaping up a great pile of earth poured it down from the roof above. But when they saw them being suffocated and buried, and willing to do or say nothing apart from addressing prayer to God, they ceased from their frenzy, at the suggestion of their elders. Then opening the doors and pulling them out from the mass of earth they told them to depart immediately ...

When he promised his consent if they undertook to build a church, they begged him to start operations at once ... After three years with them ... he got another of his companions appointed in his place and went back to his monastic dwelling ...

Not to make the narrating long by narrating all he did after gaining fame among them, he received the see of Carrhae, a city which was steeped in the sottishness of impiety and had given itself up to the frenzy of the demons ...

Even the emperor desired to see him ... He summoned him and when he arrived embraced him, and considered his rustic goat's hair cloak more honourable than his own purple cloak. The choir of the empresses clasped his hands and knees; and they made supplication to a man who did not even speak Greek.

Chapter 26 of Theodoret's book relates to Simon (Stylite) some extracts of which are as follows:

As his fame circulated everywhere, everyone hastened to him, not only the people of the neighbourhood but also people many days journey distant, some bringing the paralysed in body, others requesting health for the sick, others asking to become fathers; and they begged to receive from him what they could not receive from nature. On receiving it and obtaining their requests, they returned with joy: and by proclaiming the benefits they had gained, they sent out many times more, asking for the same things. So with everyone arriving from every side and every road resembling a river, one can behold a sea of men standing together in that place, receiving rivers from every side. Not only do the inhabitants of our part of the world flock together, but also Ishmaelites, Persians, Armenians subject to them, Iberians, Homerites ... and men even more distant than these; and there came many inhabitants of the extreme West, Spaniards, Britons, and the Gauls who live between them. Of Italy it is superfluous to speak. It is said that the man became so celebrated in the great city of Rome that at the entrance of all the workshops men have set up small representations of him, to provide thereby some protection and safety for themselves.

Since the visitors were beyond counting and they all tried to touch him and reap some blessing from his garments of skins … he devised standing on a pillar, ordering the cutting of a pillar first of six cubes, then of twelve, afterwards of twenty two and now of thirty six.[51]

### 3.5.3   Syriac Manuscript, MS160, c. 473

Syriac Manuscript MS160, c. 473 AD, is held in the Vatican. It details the life of St Simon the Stylite. In 1992 it was translated into English as *The Lives of Simeon Stylites*.[52] The most important extract for this study relates to the passage referring to conversion of visitors from Lebanon:

> 62. After this a great crowd came to the saint from Lebanon. They told him about evil animals who roamed over all the mountain of Lebanon ravaging and attacking and devouring men. Wailing and mourning were raised throughout the whole region, for there was not one village of the whole mountainous region in which two or three people were not being devoured every day at least.

> 63. As they told it, sometimes (the creatures) looked like women with shorn hair, wandering and lamenting; sometimes like wild beasts. They would even enter into houses and seize people and snatch children from their nursing mothers' arms and eat them right in front of their eyes and (the mothers) could not lift a finger to help their little ones, so that there was mourning and lamentation. No one could go out into the open country alone but only in groups armed with swords and clubs. Even then the animals did not turn aside out of peoples way except for a little distance-then (the animals) would fol-

---

[51] Footnote by Price in the Chapter on Maroun: "When Simon Stylite died, Antioch sent a whole convoy of notables and soldiers to seize his body from the local inhabitants and bring it into the city."

[52] Robert Doran (trans.), *The Lives of Simeon Stylites*, Cistercian Press, 1992.

low in their footsteps. When the saint heard these things from them he said, 'God has repaid you according to your deeds. For you forsook the one who in his benevolence made you and provides for you and nourishes you in his mercy, and you fled for help to dumb, useless idols who can neither help nor harm you. Because of this God handed you over to wicked beasts who wreaked vengeance on you as your deeds deserved. Go now and call on these idols whom you worship...'

With heartfelt sorrow they all answered as if with one voice and said, 'if you pray for us and this rod of wrath passes from us, we will make a covenant in writing before your holiness that we will become Christians and receive baptism, that we will renounce idols, uproot their shrines and break their images. Only let this affliction pass from us'.

When the saint saw them promise to turn to God, he said to them, 'In the name of our Lord Jesus Christ take some of this *hnana*. Go and set up for stones on all the borders of the villages. If any priests are there, summon them, and make on the stone three crosses. Keep a vigil for three days, and you will see what God works there. For I have hope in my Lord Jesus Christ that from that day on they will not destroy the image of humans there'. This is indeed what God worked ... For from all that region came a great crowd without number – men, women, youths and children. They received baptism and became Christians, they turned to God from their worthless error as they had promised. Before all the people they related, 'we went and set up those stones and made crosses on them as your holiness commanded, and kept for vigil for three days. After that we saw those animals going to and fro marching around where the crosses had been made and howling so loud it carried over the mountain. Some of them fell down and burst open on the spot beside those stones, some went away howling. At night they sounded like women lamenting and crying out' ... After the people of that region had received baptism and became Christians, had renounced idols and graven images and believed in our Lord Jesus Christ, they remained at the saint's enclosure about a week. Then they returned home rejoicing and giving thanks and praising God who had worked this double kindness among them. From that time on they did not cease to visit the saint frequently. Those who had not received baptism did so, as did their children. This was for their advantage and salvation.

# CHAPTER 4

# SYRIA, PHOENICIA, LEBANON, PALESTINE: THE CHRISTIAN INTERLINK

## 4.1 Jews, Christians, and Pagans: A Multi-Faith Society

Theodoret mentions that St Abraham (c. 350-422) "repaired to the Lebanon, where, he had heard, a large village was engulfed in the darkness of impiety." We can deduce only certain pockets of the mountains of Lebanon or Phoenicia remained pagan. It could not have been *all* the mountain region otherwise Theodoret would not have hesitated to state so. This is consistent with the account of Cosmos, a disciple of St Simon the Stylite, relating to St Simon's conversion of the Lebanese from the mountains.

It is likely Christians were already living in Mount Lebanon at St Simon's time. St Simon, in addressing the Lebanese, says: "Go and set up four stones on all borders of the villages. If any priests are there, summon them, and make on the stone three crosses." The reference to priests implies that St Simon had knowledge of the presence of Christians and/or priests nearby, or priests visiting the village. For example, we know the Monastery of St Anthony in the Qadisha Valley of Mount Lebanon has its origins dating to the fourth century.

The proportion of Christians to pagans at the time cannot be determined, nor can any specific date or regional area of conversion. No doubt it was gradual in time and area from the first century up to the mid-fifth century. Historians throughout the ages have painted the image that pagans were not able to effectively communicate, interact, and trade with Jews and Christians, and vice versa. They have overlooked the fact the Middle East and its Syrian Orient, including the

71

Phoenician and Lebanese mountain range, has from inception been a multi-cultural, multi-ethnic, multi-lingual, and multi-faith society. Numerous passages in Jewish scriptures and the Bible refer to varied ethnicities as well as Jews, gentiles, pagans, Christians, and persons of other faiths living together, and considerable social cohesiveness was necessary for these civilisations to operate.

Authors have taken a narrow view of the extent of paganism in Mount Lebanon, and elsewhere, in the early Christian centuries. Throughout history up to today, one author after another has accepted that the entire Lebanon mountain range remained exclusively pagan for these early Christian centuries. However, this cannot be correct. The Lebanon mountain range is quite extensive in area. Its rugged terrain and deep gorges make for limited accessibility between the hills, peaks, and valleys. Often, to travel to a nearby town at a similar altitude one has to journey a considerable distance down from their own mountain range on a narrow path to the bottom of the ravine below and then up to the other side of the mountain also on a narrow path, even when the gorge or valley between the two towns is only a few hundred metres across. The dense forests in those times would have added to the isolation and inaccessibility.

While dialects, faiths, and ethnicities may have varied, certainly the Aramaic-Syriac language and inter-town trade was shared throughout the area. We know today that from one Syrian, Palestinian, or Lebanese mountain village, town, or city to the next you can find a slight difference in dialect, culture, and faith. This may have been more pronounced in those times. A foreign labour force involved in timber cutting, transportation, and stone building was likely to be present as it was in the region for the construction of King Solomon's Temple. No doubt they had their own language, faith, and culture living alongside the local population. It cannot confidently be asserted that one town was exclusively pagan, Jewish, or Christian.

Today, many villages and towns throughout Lebanon and its mountains are a mix of Christian and Muslim peoples. Lebanese and Jewish culture through the ages has been one of co-existence due to the continually varied foreign occupying forces, migrants, and faiths. Jewish populations could be expected in the early Christian period to be dotted through the Lebanese mountain range as they were on the coastal fringes. Some or many of these settlements may have become Jewish Christians in the first or subsequent centuries. For those that did not, they would have continued to co-exist with local Christian or pagan settlements.

No firm conclusion can be reached about the extent of Christian conversion in Mount Lebanon prior to the fourth or early fifth century. Bishops from nearby coastal and inland cities were present at the Council of Nicaea in 325. The towns and villages within their jurisdiction are not documented. Accordingly, around the early fifth century, before the conversions by St Abraham and St Simon Stylite, we can conclude there were Christians, in addition to pagans, in Mount Lebanon, though the extent of their population size and specific locales remain unknown.

## 4.2 North Syria, Lebanon, Phoenicia, and North Palestine: Shared Identity in the Geo-Political and Ecclesiastical Context

In the geo-political context of the Roman provinces of Syria up to 395 AD, a reference to Syrians and their monks would have included a reference to those from Phoenicia-Lebanon and Palestine. In reverse, a reference to Phoenicia would have included parts of modern day northern Syria and northern Galilee. The Roman Empire's boundaries were established for administrative and political purposes. Certain populations, including those in Lebanon, may have remained without a sense of nationalism.

After 395, the adaptation to the Empire's new political boundaries and terms around Phoenicia and Syria would likely have been gradual rather than instant. In the ecclesiastical context, we can conveniently summarise three major engagements of the Church from the period 313 to 452 in this region. Considered as a group, they are not recorded by historians or the Church. They have been outlined here as an overview for the reader. The first major engagement was from 313 AD. It was the period following the Emperor's announcement of freedom to practise religion. This was to have profound consequences on the Syrian Orient region as it did throughout the entire world of the Empire. The second major engagement followed the declaration in 380 that Christianity was the official religion of the Empire. By this time there was little evidence of pagans in northern Syria. The focus became on the pagan settlements remaining in Phoenicia.

The third major engagement was after the Council of Chalcedonian in 451 ensuring the doctrine of Christ's dual divine and physical nature was to be upheld throughout the Empire. The Church was aware this would create the first significant schism and would be met with strong opposition from the new Monophysite churches who denied that Christ had both a divine and human nature – that is, he was physically God and man – and said Christ only had one nature and that was divine. By this time, the practice of paganism was virtually insignificant in all locations of the Empire's Middle East. The Monophysite controversy and schism was the new focus. This is discussed in more detail in later chapters.

### 4.2.1  St Maroun and the Cyrrhus Hermits

St Maroun's fame was no doubt circulated by the Cyrrhus town folk, hermits, and the disciples of Maroun. Three well populated villages from the Cyrrhus region in northern Syria fought over St Maroun's relics. One of them built a great shrine, and Theodoret, who would have spoken publically about St Maroun and not just written about him, notes there was a public festival that was almost certainly annual. There is no reference to Maroun leaving for Lebanon or elsewhere. However, it cannot be ruled out that Maroun's visitors during his lifetime, and after to his shrine, may not only have been Syrians but perhaps Lebanese, Phoenicians, and others. At the least, many of the initial visitors were likely from the region of Cyrrhus, and to a lesser degree, the adjoining regions of Antioch and Edessa.

Around the lifetime of St Maroun or shortly thereafter, it is difficult to refute the proposition that St Abraham from Cyrrhus and his companions became interlocutors and direct links between the large Christian converted village in Mount Lebanon and the region of Cyrrhus and Antioch in northern Syria. Abraham (and expectedly his companions) were from Cyrrhus and provided the physical connection. It is possible the fame of Maroun, and the 'garden' of anchorites he planted that Theodoret tells us flourished in the region of Cyrrhus, would have been preached to or at least mentioned by these intermediaries. The news of St Maroun would have also spread by the monks and locals to their neighbouring villagers and town folk.

This could be the reason behind Theodoret mentioning that the righteous "multiplied like the cedar of Lebanon." The veneration of saints' relics was one of the most popular and well recorded Middle Eastern Christian traditions of the early centuries. As chronicled by Theodoret, this was especially so for the relics of the saintly anchorites of northern Syria. Any relic, even an infinitesimal fragment of cloth or hair of Maroun and other saintly anchorites were highly sought after as personal possessions or for safe custody in the shrine at one's parish, church, monastery, or home. The guardians, lobbyists, and transporters of saints' relics were primarily monks.

The unprecedented enthusiasm of this ancient period for the parish lay faithful may have also meant a personal journey and pilgrimage to the countryside regions of Cyrrhus and Antioch. Often this would have been a delegation of persons and sometimes a large delegation to include many residents of the town. This is demonstrated by the recount of the large number of Lebanese visiting St Simon Stylite. Although we do not have any evidence available, we cannot rule out similar practices of anchorites rapidly developing in the balance of the western regions of the patriarchate of Antioch. The mere fact of silence cannot support the proposition that it did not happen or that it was not recorded. In fact, it is more likely than not that the practice spread across the region.

Abraham and his companions were contemporaries of Maroun

75

and from the same region of Cyrrhus. Abraham probably followed the open-air practice of Maroun. It is expected these contemporaries would have introduced relics to the Lebanese village. This meant erecting a shrine to the saint, and celebrating their annual feast day. This religious practice is confirmed in Theodoret. At this period of time, St Maroun's relics must have been foremost amongst those sought from northern Syria as the first influential saint of this heroic open-air religious practice.

As they do today, neighbouring villages and towns join the annual celebrations and also become visitors to the shrine throughout the year. The neighbouring town folk then lobby for a relic of the saint in order to erect a shrine in their town. Decades later, monks like St Maroun's disciple James and St Simon Stylite may have become more popular, but the veneration and fame of St Maroun has not diminished, particularly in the locations where he was already venerated.

Theodoret only mentions one village that was engulfed in the "darkness of impiety" that Abraham and his companions attended to. There is little doubt any other pagan villages they found nearby or along the way would have been placed on the radar, not only for them but for their fellow monks in Cyrrhus. These monks would have visited adjoining villages, and those along the journey for Abraham, that were already Christian. The locals received first-hand the many stories of the holy anchorites from northern Syria. This is a plausible explanation for the very first beginnings of the veneration of St Maroun in Lebanon.

Theodoret mentions that Maroun's fame was widely circulated and it is possible that this included the regions of Phoenicia and Lebanon even before Abraham visited Lebanon. In the unlikely event Abraham and his companions did not preach about the fame of St Maroun, the Lebanese from the newly converted mountain village, enthused by their new faith and trust in God and inspired by Abraham and his companions, would have been eager to witness the hotbed of faith and athletic monasticism in the Cyrrhus and Antioch countryside regions. St Maroun's shrine and public festival was at their doorstep. The patriarch's residence was nearby to Cyrrhus in the city of Antioch. Many other Lebanese-Phoenicians would likely have also spoken about these holy athletes or perhaps their visit or intended visit to them.

The record of the visits to St Simon Stylite from the Lebanese mountain folk demonstrate the willingness and manoeuvrability of mass crowds, even of those without Christian faith, to travel long distances seeking to witness first-hand the 'new athletes' and 'new martyrs'. If some of the contents of Cosmos' story were legend or exaggeration, as at least one academic has proposed,[53] news was sure to have spread to any other pagan or Christian towns and villages of the intercession of this great new 'protector'.

Four of the eleven anchorites from the countryside region of Antioch that Theodoret wrote about appeared to be not from his jurisdiction as Bishop of Cyrrhus. Simon Stylite, whom Theodoret visited and wrote about, lived in a hermitage that fell just outside Theodoret's area of influence. The Church would have seen the anchorites without jurisdictional distinction in an interconnecting area between the bordering countryside of Antioch and Cyrrhus. Theodoret must have felt a special affiliation to Simon as virtually one of his own.

It is well accepted that crowds came from all over the world to visit St Simon Stylite, and no doubt that would have included visits to many of the hundreds, if not thousands, of anchorites around him, the overwhelming majority of which it seems were in the jurisdiction of Cyrrhus. This was a monastic movement unprecedented in history, including up to modern times. Christians and pagans alike visited.

Pilgrims from nearby and afar came to the regions of Antioch and Cyrrhus. Cyrrhus was between the cities of Antioch and Edessa. Naturally, there would have been much travel between Antioch (the patriarchal capital) and Edessa (the great Syriac Christian centre of literature, knowledge and learning). Cyrrhus (or Cyr) was the capital of the large district of Cyrrhestica. It was a Roman administrative, military, and

---

[53] See Matti Moosa, *The Maronites in History*, Syracuse University Press, 1986, whose ideas are discussed at length in Chapter 7 of this book.

commercial centre on the trade route between Antioch and the Euphrates River crossing at Zeugma, leading to Edessa.

The primary sources quoted and set out in detail in the previous chapter allow us to state St Abraham (from Cyrrhus) and St Simon the Stylite (from the countryside region of Antioch near to Cyrrhus) directly brought Christian conversion to many in Mount Lebanon around the late fourth century and up to the mid fifth century. As for St Maroun (whose hermitage was in Cyrrhus), we can say that it was he who, not exclusively or intentionally, helped plant the seeds in the region of northern Syria for the 'garden of monks' that were to follow in his time. Abraham and Simon Stylite may have carried the memory of St Maroun. At best we can only say they were likely monks from Maroun's 'garden', but we cannot be sure they passed on the memory of Maroun. It was certainly more likely for Abraham than Simon.

However, given the account of Theodoret about Maroun's fame and the saint being the first great monastic athlete and hero of the region, and given what we know a short while later about the prevalence of the monastery of Maroun, it is quite possible both Abraham and Simon spoke of Maroun. These monks were humble and were not seeking credit for themselves. The life and fame of saints before them would have been on the tip of their tongue. St Maroun was first ranked not only as the founder of open-air asceticism, but in time.

The region of Cyrrhus has always been a vital focus of study for Maronites in their attempt to find the location of the shrine of St Maroun. For the Lebanese Christian faithful in the time of the fifth to perhaps seventh centuries, Cyrrhus and the countryside of Antioch provided commonality and cause for visitation by pilgrims as a result of the following list of connections: the magnificent basilica of Cyrrhus holding the relics of Saints Cosmos and Damien who died as martyrs in 287; the fame of the hermitage and later shrine of St Maroun as likely one of the foremost shrines of Cyrrhus; the hermitage and later likely shrine of St Abraham who converted the Lebanese; the hermitage and shrine of St Simon Stylite who converted the Lebanese; the relics of John the Baptist; the hermitage and later likely shrine of

James (as a disciple of Maroun) and where the relics of St John the Baptist visited; the hermitage and later likely shrine of Limnaeus (as a disciple of Maroun); the hermitage and later likely shrine of Domnina (as a disciple of St Maroun); patriarch of Antioch nearby; and the location of Cyrrhus between Antioch and Edessa.

This commonality provides the basis for links between St Maroun, Syria, Phoenicia, and Lebanon (and even Palestine up to 451). In combination, these links seem to have never been thoroughly explored by scholars, yet they give plausible weight to the traditions that speak of the connection between St Maroun and Lebanon. But alone this is not sufficient to allow us to make final conclusions; it can only add another light to all of the traditions and documentation that must be considered as a whole. It does, however, provide further background information for scholars when considering evidence from any new manuscripts that may come to light.

### 4.2.2 James of Cyrrhestica

We know from Theodoret that James, Limnaeus, Domnina and others (likely not just the monks Theodoret wrote about), were disciples of Maroun. Theodoret could have inferred a link to Lebanon for Maroun's disciples. In the chapter regarding Maroun, he states:

> A product of his planting was the great James, to whom one could reasonably apply the prophetic utterance, 'the righteous man will flower as the palm tree, and be multiplied like the cedar of Lebanon', and also all the others whom, with God's help, I shall recall individually.

There is no reference to James leaving Syria for Lebanon or elsewhere. It is to be expected James, as for other disciples of Maroun, did spread the word about Maroun to visitors. Some of these visitors may have been from Lebanon and Mount Lebanon, but again there is no direct evidence to support this conclusion, only that it was possible. One can suggest it was likely in the context of the unprecedented times and circumstances.

Theodoret's reference to James (in the chapter on Maroun) being "multiplied like the cedar of Lebanon" notes in the same sentence that he was to "recall" others. This could have implied Abraham, who was the only one of Theodoret's thirty monks mentioned as travelling to Lebanon. Although Abraham and James were anchorites at the same time, James also lived a number of decades after Abraham. Abraham, either during James' lifetime or shortly after, had formed a connection between Lebanon and Cyrrhus. This connection is irrefutable. There is also the likelihood of a connection between James and Abraham providing another link between Lebanon and St Maroun.

Theodoret spent time with James and said he "eclipsed his teacher [Maroun] by greater labours." It would be expected of James, as a disciple of Maroun, to have at least publicly acknowledged the fact Maroun was the first open-air ascetic and James' teacher. The locals in Cyrrhus, as honoured hosts and to promote the fame of their region, would have spoken about Maroun in the same way to visitors passing through, as well as to the great majority who would have made overnight stays in the region in the numerous hostels that would have been built to cater for the massive pilgrimage trade. As a normal course, visitors to Cyrrhus may have also added to their journey a visit to St Maroun's shrine, which was within close reach. Perhaps it is no coincidence that Theodoret mentions the arrival from Phoenicia (and Palestine) of John the Baptist's relics in the chapter on James, and mentions Lebanon in the chapter on Maroun that James as a "righteous man will flower as the palm tree, and be multiplied like the cedar of Lebanon."

### 4.2.3 The Relics of St John the Baptist

Theodoret records a conversation with James relating to when Theodoret, as Bishop of Cyrrhus, was present to accept the arrival of the relics of John the Baptist from Phoenicia and Palestine. A permanent shrine in Cyrrhus waited for one of the most valued relics in Christian history. Theodoret details how he brought these "city guardians" (relics) to James. It is here we can propose there were visitors to Cyrrhus in Syria from Phoenicia-Lebanon and Palestine who brought the relics of John the Baptist with them. Though Theodoret gives no detail on the journey of these relics, no doubt there would have been significant welcoming, interest and of course veneration in many of the cities, towns and villages of Phoenicia and Palestine through which the relics travelled and remained overnight.

It is probable that news spread quickly back home in Phoenicia (and Palestine) of the journey and the relocation of the new shrine of the Prophet. Pilgrims naturally flowed in from afar to Cyrrhus. This mid-fifth century relocation of one of the most important Church relics from the Holy Land suggests the significance the Church, or at least the patriarch and bishops within the patriarchate of Antioch, placed on the monks and monasteries of the area of Cyrrhus. We recall Cyrrhus was about one hundred kilometres north east of Antioch and approximately mid-distance between Antioch and the great Syriac Christian city of Edessa.

Once again, as for St Maroun, Theodoret makes only a passing mention of the relocation of the relics of the great Prophet despite such a significant moment in history, particularly for his region of Cyrrhus. To the same extent, he did not mention such as simple a detail as the name of the town in Cyrrhus region where the shrine of the Prophet was located. Perhaps the fame of the Prophet's relics, the relocation journey and its new location was so widespread Theodoret saw no need for its detail. It is consistent with his pattern of limited detail for St Maroun. It raises the possibility that the reputation of Cyrrhus, via the relics of St John the Baptist and of St Maroun, was so renowned it did not warrant elaboration.

Theodoret had temporarily taken the Prophet's relics away from their permanent shrine in order to visit James. This would have added to the recognition of James, a personal visit and blessing virtually beyond precedent in the history of the Church. In addition to visiting the permanent shrine of the relics of the 'Prophet' (likely not far away), many may also have stopped by at the hermitage of the holy anchorite James, not just for his monastic athleticism but now as an added blessing as the site of a former visitation of the Prophet's relics.

### 4.2.4 The Patriarch in Antioch

As they do today, the Aramaic-Syriac church faithful, including Maronites, remain unshakably loyal to their patriarch. Given his importance in the church, frequent and sometimes daily matters need be addressed in person to the patriarch by the bishops, religious and faithful. Tradition also provides for visits to the patriarch in large delegations to join in celebration and commemoration on important feast days and events in the church's calendar. No doubt the various cross roads to visit the patriarch in Antioch were well worn. The great monks and monasteries in the countryside of northern Syria were not far from the path of travel to the capital. Cyrrhus, with its great fame, was also not far away.

Though this does not diminish the importance at the time of pilgrimage to Jerusalem and other holy Christian sites throughout Palestine, up to 451 AD, (before the patriarchate of Jerusalem was established), many of the religious and faithful would have also travelled to Antioch to visit the patriarch. This included pilgrims from as far as Palestine. In reverse, the patriarch of Antioch would have travelled throughout his jurisdiction or regularly sent delegations of bishops and priests. As a largely oral culture there is no documentary evidence for this tradition, nonetheless, the voluntary visitation to the patriarch by the faithful continues today.

After 451, Phoenicia remained under the patriarchate of Antioch. Palestine, though to what extent it is not clear, was now under the patriarchate of Jerusalem. The Palestinian devotees no longer needed to travel to Antioch to attend on their patriarch. The patriarchate of Antioch was now smaller in size. At the same time, the establishment of Beit Maroun, St Maroun's monastery in Apamaea on the accessible route from Phoenicia to Antioch, was the focus of the Emperor (as we will see in the forthcoming chapter).

### 4.2.5 St John Chrysostom

It is possible St John Chrysostom, Patriarch of Constantinople from 397 to 403, dedicated his 36th epistle or letter to St Maroun. With both

Greek and Syrian origins, St John Chrysostom was enthusiastic about Aramaic monasticism in Syria and Phoenicia. We have letters written from him to Constantinus, Nicholas, Gerontius, and Rufinus pleading for assistance to convert pagans in Phoenicia.[54]

Veneration of relics by the faithful was important to the Church. St John Chrysostom ends his letter to Rufinus, who was in Phoenicia, as follows:

> I have sent the venerable priest Terentius to my most pious lord Otreius, bishop of Arabissa, who has many well authenticated relics, and in a few days I shall send them to you in Phoenicia. Make haste to finish the churches which have no roofs before winter.[55]

Youhanna Sader suggests that the arrival of relics in Phoenicia as part of the conversion of the pagans is why the ancient churches of Phoenicia are dedicated to saints whose relics came from as far as Constantinople and other areas of the Empire.[56] Certainly, given the edict of the Emperor to retain the architectural value of pagan temples, almost all temples would have been utilised to form the basis of new church constructions.

It is worthy of a reminder that St John Chrysostom's jurisdiction, as patriarch of Constantinople, did not include Phoenicia and Syria. These regions were the domain of the patriarch of Antioch. Accordingly, this provides support for the focus of the Church, in the late fourth and early fifth centuries, on Phoenicia and the conversion of any remaining pagan villages and towns. This could quite easily have been achieved by spreading the glorious news of the north Syrian open-air anchorites through the foundation of St Maroun. It is important to note that some hundred years after the death of St Maroun in the early sixth

---

[54] Extracts of the letters are set out in Youhanna Sader, *Crosses and Symbols in Ancient Christian Art of Lebanon*, Dar Sader, 2006, pp. 237-242.

[55] The full letter is set out in Sader, *Crosses and Symbols*, pp. 241-242. Sader translates from M. Jeanin's 1887, version, which is apparently the complete works of St John Chrysostom's letters translated into French.

[56] Sader, *Crosses and Symbols*, p. 248.

century there appears little or no reference to paganism in Phoenicia or the Church's concern regarding the issue.

Maronite Patriarch Stephen Doueihi (1630-1704) believes St John Chrysostom was a friend of St Maroun even before the time of the letter, claiming they were students together in Antioch. Chrysostom was therefore well-placed in the Church to connect the remaining pagan towns of Phoenicia with the anchorite world of Cyrrhus and Antioch. When one considers all of the above circumstances, it is unlikely to be a coincidence that St John Chrysostom was a contemporary of Theodoret's Maroun and of Abraham, who converted a pagan village in Phoenicia.

The pointing to Lebanon and Phoenicia by St John Chrysostom and Theodoret (in his chapters on Maroun, James of Cyrrhestica as a disciple of Maroun, 'others' and Abraham), appears not to be a coincidence. Many church customs are founded on tradition and not texts. The Maronite Church is no exception. There are extensive lists of 'coincidences' in the study of Maroun for the Maronites that have been entirely dismissed by some who oppose traditional rendition of Maronite history. However, when multiplied as a sum total these 'coincidences', documented throughout this book, appear interlinked, causal, and considerable, and add weight to the church's oral traditions.

### 4.2.6 Beit Maroun Monastery and Apamaea in Syria

We know that by the middle of the fifth century huge crowds were coming to visit St Simon Stylite from the Lebanese mountains. As visitors came from all around the world, no doubt they also came from other parts of Lebanon including the coastal cities. Not far from Simon's open-air abode was the adjoining district of Cyrrhus. Prior to St Simon Stylite's fame, northern Syria's region of Cyrrhus near the border of the Antioch region would have been the predominant area for witnessing the life and shrines of the holy anchorites.

In this formative period, St Maroun would have been no exception and likely one of the most, if not the most famous, as the first to practise this form of asceticism in the open-air. As we will study in

Chapter 6, tradition honoured St Maroun by establishing a monastery in his name, Beit Maroun in Apamaea, Syria, approximately thirty to forty years after his death. It was about one hundred kilometres further south from Cyrrhus, not far from Roman Lebanon province and Mount Lebanon.

It appears a similar, but perhaps not as extensive, anchorite movement was flourishing in the countryside around Apamaea. We know from Theodoret of two cenobitic monasteries that were established there between 350 to 400 by Agapetus and Simon of Cyrrhus, following the moderate rules of their teacher Marcian. One of the monasteries had four hundred monks. It is reasonable to assume that some of the monks from these monasteries set out as missionaries, including to nearby Lebanon. At least one of these monasteries would have likely become pre-eminent amongst all monasteries in Syria Secunda until the founding of the monastery of Maroun in 452 by the emperor Marcian. Documentary evidence from the sixth century informs us that the monastery of Agapetus in Syria Secunda was ranked second to St Maroun's monastery.

Theodoret chose to live and study in one of these Apamaea monasteries (most likely Agapetus) when he was attracted to the monastic life and before he was, almost against his will, called away to become Bishop of Cyrrhus in 423. In the discussion in Chapter 6 of this book, it is demonstrated that Theodoret likely had an influence on the Emperor Marcian in establishing a new Apamaea monastery named after St Maroun. Syria Secunda hosted over time a religious confederation of monasteries that Theodoret said was "almost beyond counting" and subject to the same rules. Paul Naaman says a confederation of monasteries between the Syria Secunda/Apamaea area and the region of Cyrrhus was likely to have been established in part by Theodoret himself. As Naaman suggests "it would otherwise be a remarkable coincidence that Theodoret would be the only historian of these two monastic movements from Northern Syria."[57]

It is at this juncture we can propose a link, not only between the

---

[57] Naaman, *The Maronites*, p. 64.

anchorites and monasteries of Cyrrhus and Apamaea, but between them the memory of St Maroun. Theodoret must have witnessed first-hand the memory of St Maroun preserved by monks of both regions. One or more of Abraham, Simon Stylite, James, Limnaeus, Domnina, the three towns who fought over St Maroun's relics, the town which housed St Maroun's shrine and an (annual) public festival, or Theodoret and his fellow religious (priests, monks and nuns), must have passed down the memory of St Maroun through Syria and to the Lebanese and Phoenicians. If they hadn't, then by only several decades later and over the next century or two the monks of Beit Maroun monastery would have and likely to as far as Palestine as well.

The next chapters detail how immediately following the Council of Chalcedon, Beit Maroun was established in 452 with one of its primary roles being to uphold the doctrine of the two natures of Christ. Intentionally, through its network of monasteries, it became the beacon and leading monastery of Catholic Church orthodoxy for the Aramaic-speaking Christians throughout the Syrian Orient including in Syria, Phoenicia-Lebanon, and likely Palestine.

There is evidence to suggest the 'Syrian' monks (generally those from within the land of the Persian empire) conducted missionary work in Arabia and as far as India and China. As we have discussed, letters from St John Chrysostom (d. 407), Patriarch of Constantinople, to Constantinus, Nicholas, Gerontius, and Rufinus plead for assistance to convert the pagans in Phoenicia.[58] There is little doubt that slightly more than half a century later missionary monks from Beit Maroun and its network of monasteries were active not just in Syria but in Lebanon a short distance to the south. How many Lebanese imitated the lives of the anchorites is unknown. Whether they went to the same extent of open-air asceticism is also unknown. What is more certain is that the monks from Apamaea would have ensured not only the doctrine of Chalcedon was in place but so too that ascetic life was properly regulated through the environment of cenobitic monasteries.

As we have recounted in the previous chapter, Theodoret informs

---

[58] Extracts of the letters are set out in Sader, *Crosses and Symbols*, pp. 237-242.

us the Emperor Theodosius (408-450) summoned to see Abraham of Cyrrhus because of his fame. When Abraham arrived, the Emperor

> embraced him, and considered his rustic goat's hair cloak more honourable than his own purple robe. The choir of the empresses (the Emperor's sister Pulcheria and the Emperor's wife Eudocia)[59] clasped his hands and knees; and they made supplication to a man who did not even understand Greek.

Here we have another fascinating but plausible reason to link Abraham's Lebanon and Theodoret with St Maroun. Emperor Theodosius' sister Pulcheria married Marcian, the latter succeeding his wife's brother as Emperor. Marcian, and it is thought Pulcheria, were responsible for the decree to establish Beit Maroun. Abraham was previously in Lebanon converting the pagans. This would have been known to both emperors, their wives, and their families.

In addition to Theodoret, it is reasonable to suggest Abraham mentioned to the emperor and his sister Pulcheria the memory of St Maroun continuing in Cyrrhus, Apamaea, and Lebanon. If so, surely Pulcheria's husband Marcian was influenced by the news. Perhaps Abraham's lack of Greek encouraged the emperor to promote the study of Greek language amongst the indigenous Aramaic-speaking monks and clergy outside of the city of Antioch as another reason for establishing Beit Maroun.

As will be seen in later chapters, it cannot be denied that there was a well-bonded inter-connection of monasteries, churches, the religious (including anchorites) and faithful throughout the patriarchate of Antioch, from at least the latter half of the fifth century. Authors, particularly Moosa, opposed to Maronite tradition are somehow in denial of this critical historical fact. They imply there were no Christians in the Lebanon Mountains until later. If there were Christians, they intimate they were cut off and devoid of what was taking place in the rest of the region around them, amongst their brethren, and amongst their religious leaders and patriarch.

---

[59] Price, *A History of the Monks of Syria*, footnote 6, p. 125.

Another misconception must be dispelled. Many have penned St Maroun was the founder of the Maronite Church. However, the evidence is clear that Theodoret's Maroun never founded a church, nor was it his intention. As will be discussed in the following chapters, it was later and due to the circumstances of history that the Maronite Church was established through the steadfastness of the monastery St Maroun, its networked monasteries, and the faithfulness of the religious and people loyal to it and to the Catholic Church.

## 4.3  The Continuously Inhabited Settlements of Mount Lebanon

It is widely accepted that the traditions of the Aramaic Syriac monastic life (which continue today) developed as Christian village and town communities were built up around or networked with the nearby local monastery. The monastery's church served as the local parish church. If the monastery was not close enough in distance, missionary monks might have served as visiting parish priests.

At some point, though it is not clear when, Lebanese mountain folk were likely to have venerated St Maroun for his miracles and for his particular type of monastic living and teaching. They may have visited him, or his shrine, or heard about him through his disciples, other hermits, and via the general population of Cyrrhus. His life might have been communicated to them either during their conversion via St Abraham and St Simon the Stylite, or as a result of the missionaries from Beit Maroun at some stage after its construction. They may have become part of the Chalcedonian party whose leadership was eventually dominated by the Beit Maroun network.

The indigenous Lebanese would have remained well entrenched in their village traditions and the honouring of patron saints such as St Abraham and St Simon Stylite. To have accepted Theodoret's St Maroun or some other St Maroun as patron saint centuries later appears too far remote in time. If the accounts are correct that a significant number of Syrian Christians (with or without the first Maronite patriarch John [or Yuhanna] Maroun and his faithful in the late seventh century) migrated to Lebanon fleeing persecution, it is unlikely they would have converted the indigenous Lebanese if they were still largely pagans. However, there is no evidence to suggest that the Lebanese mountain folk at that time would have been pagans. If the locals were principally Christian (and already set in their Christian ways), it is improbable they would have convinced them to honour St Maroun as the patron saint and father of their church.

In considering all of the evidence we have relating to the formation of the Maronite Church and its community, it is more reasonable to propose that the Lebanese who were later to be known as Maronites embraced St Maroun from the fifth century. The memory of St Maroun would only be as a patron saint and a father of the church, but not its founder. As the following chapters will confirm, the first documented reference to the term 'Maronites' we are able to find is in the late sixth century, more than one hundred years before the Syriac monk Yuhanna Maroun became the first Maronite Patriarch and nearly two hundred years after the death of Theodoret's Maroun. There was no founder, as such, of the Maronite Church. In time, Mount Lebanon became for the Maronite majority their homeland, stronghold and refuge from persecution. It is not to say the faithful of Lebanon, if they did, stopped honouring St Abraham and St Simon Stylite. It is clear Lebanese Maronite villages and towns and the Maronites generally still retain the memory of these saints and of course at the same time honour St Maroun as the patron saint and a father (but it stressed again not founder) of their Church.

Mount Lebanon's geography and relative proximity to Beit Maroun brought together the mountain native Maronites with non-native Maronites such as those from Syria, all of whom today maintain the common tradition of honouring the memory of St Maroun. To deny this proposition presents an inconceivable coincidence for the traditional Maronite dominance of the Christian population in Lebanon. It also dismisses the value modern society places today on the importance of oral traditions of any ethnic, ancestral, religious or indigenous population.

A relic of *a* St Maroun, his skull, was gifted to the Crusaders in Lebanon almost one thousand years ago from the monastery of St Maroun's 'Skull' in Kafarhai, Lebanon. When considering all of the documentary sources together in their geographical and historical context and Maronite traditions, it is difficult to accept this was not Theodoret's St Maroun. It is important to present this analysis and evidence as the prelude to demonstrating how scholars such as Kamal Salibi have erred and should review their opposition to the traditions of Maronite history. This book demonstrates the need for scholars to more extensively examine what has been omitted and missed and engage with the more recent documentary evidence that has come to light.

Salibi is considered one of the foremost contemporary historians on Lebanon. His 1988 book in English, *A House of Many Mansions, The History of Lebanon Reconsidered*, remains today the pre-eminent contemporary authority for the history of Lebanon. He suggests the Maronites were originally Arabian Christian tribes and migrated from Arabia to Syria and Lebanon. He states:

> It is very possible that the Maronites, as a community of Arabian origin, were among the last Arabian Christian tribes to arrive in Syria before Islam. The area of their settlement, generally described as the valley of the Orontes, actually comprised the hill country on either side, including the northern reaches of Mount Lebanon to the west; those of the ante-Lebanon to the east; and the line of hills extending from this point towards the north, all the way to Aleppo. They were still found in considerable numbers, in all these regions, in the tenth century, at the time of al-Masudi. Thus, contrary to the assertion of Patriarch Duwayhi, their alleged flight from the Orontes valley to Mount Lebanon could not have occurred in 685. Ibn al Qilai ... was more correct in estimating that Mount Lebanon became the principal homeland of the Maronites in about 900. Considering that al-Masudi found the community still inhabiting the Orontes valley in the middle

decades of the tenth century, the date of their final eviction to Mount Lebanon must have been closer to the year 1000 ...[60]

Certainly since the twelfth century, from which time their history is better known, the Maronites have behaved as a tribe or confederation of tribes, often more than as a sect. As certainly, since the ninth century, their language has been Arabic, which indicates that they must have originated as an Arab tribal community, even if they had not actually arrived in Syria from Arabia. The fact that Syriac remains the language of the liturgy, in this respect, is irrelevant. Syriac, which is the Christian literary form of Aramaic, was originally the liturgical language of all the Arab and Arameo-Arab Christian sects, in Arabia as well as in Syria and Iraq ...[61]

The Maronites, as a Christian community in historical Syria, are roughly as old as Islam. According to Eastern as well as Western Christian sources, the Church was founded as a Syrian Monothelite communion in 680, which was the year in which the Monothelite doctrine of the Two Natures but only One Will and Energy in Christ was condemned as heresy by the Sixth Ecumenical Council. Patriarch Duwayhi also maintained that the Maronite Church was founded in that year, although he argued that it was established, from the very beginning, as a staunchly Orthodox eastern Christian communion recognising the supremacy of Rome ...

The earliest known references to the Maronites, however, are to be found in the works of two Moslem scholars of the tenth century, the historian al-Masudi and the theologian Abd al-Jabbar, both of whom describe the Maronites as monothelite Christians, explaining exactly what that meant. In their time, the Maronites still had their main settlements in the valley of the Orontes, in the Syrian interior – a fact which al-Masudi notes in some detail.[62]

[60] Kamal Salibi, *A House of Many Mansions, The History of Lebanon Reconsidered*, J.B. Tauris, 1988, p. 89.
[61] Salibi, *A House of Many Mansions*, p. 90.
[62] Salibi, *A House of Many Mansions*, p. 87.

These propositions, very much at odds with the sources and commentary discussed in this and following chapters, have now filtered through to modern day travel guide-books on Lebanon and the Middle East. Contrary to Salibi's opinion, the early documented Syrian and Lebanese Christian conversions that took place provide a basis for the tradition of the conversion to Christianity of Syrians and Lebanese who would likely have had a link to St Maroun.

The geographical area of the study relating to our primary sources both in the context of Syria and Lebanon, and the study of Beit Maroun in the following chapters, lands us substantially within native Syria, Phoenicia, Mount Lebanon and their fringe. It cannot be denied that some members of Arab Christian tribes who *may* have migrated before or around the time of Islam to Syria and Lebanon *may* have later become Maronites. However, it cannot be proposed that they were other than a minority. It is peculiar that a whole caravan of thousands in the form of an Arab Christian tribe (highly probable Monophysite) having Arabian city roots would spend weeks on a journey including over desert lands and suddenly end up in Syria and Lebanon amongst the land of their traditional Chalcedonian opposition.

No plausible explanation is given by Salibi for the documented link between Beit Maroun and the term 'Maronite' used in ancient correspondence before the alleged flight of Arab Christian tribes to Syria. Salibi implies that there was a great vacuum in Mount Lebanon, void of any population, Christian or otherwise, until the year 900. Yet, it is well known that by the time of the arrival of the Crusaders the Maronites overwhelmingly dominated the Christian population of Mount Lebanon. Salibi's claims reject the physical evidence of ancient churches, monasteries, and hermitages scattered throughout Mount Lebanon hundreds of years before the tenth century, as well as the written accounts of conversion of the Lebanese mountain folk by St Abraham and St Simon Stylite.

Salibi does not consider, and provides no explanation of, what was to come of the permanent continuously occupied settlements of Phoenician pagans dotted throughout the Lebanese mountain range. The trade in cedar was enormous, well before the birth of Jesus and even up to the Ottoman period of the second millennia. Towns and villages lived off the cedar trade in the heart or fringe of the cedar forests.

The locations of the mountain settlements were strategic, ensuring an abundant supply of spring water from close to its naturally gushing source from various points on the mountain ranges. This made the town agriculturally self-sufficient and would have also allowed trade in agricultural surplus. Ancient Phoenician and Roman ruins throughout the Lebanon mountain range are testament to these settlements. There can be little doubt, with the large population and migrant labour force that lived off the cedar (and likely agricultural) trade that these mountain towns and villages have remained in permanent settlement for thousands of years.

Given their strategic worth, the settlements would not have been temporarily or permanently vacated at any time, as remains the status quo today even with mass migration to the West. It is difficult to accept that any of Salibi's "Arab Christian tribes" or for that matter any other migrant Christian 'tribe', would be able to take over these permanent settlements, pagan or Christian, without force or conquest. Indeed, no historian or scholar has suggested such. Establishing a new town or village, without water supply from permanency of springs and natural wells, could not be sustained.

In his assessment Salibi tells us nothing of the descendants of the Lebanese pagans in the mountains who were converted by St Abraham and his companions, St Simon the Stylite and others. Did they vanish or were they, as one Christian sect, exterminated to make way for another Christian sect? Surely not. What Eastern church and patriarch did these Lebanese mountain folk belong to? Who are they today? They are the Maronites, heirs to the indigenous of the area and, importantly, the *only* Christian denomination that make such a claim to such large areas of the mountains.

Maronites see many of their ancestors as indigenous to Phoenicia and Lebanon before the birth of Jesus Christ. But they are also often unaware of the Syrian links to Phoenicia. Relying on oral tradition,

Maronites (with other Aramaic-Syriac churches) pride themselves as descendants of indigenous Aramaic speakers who today retain the native tongue of Jesus Christ in their liturgy. This is not to deny that a percentage of Maronites cannot trace their ancestry to Phoenicia due to immigration and cultural cross-fertilisation. Nonetheless, modern Maronites continue to show pride in Phoenician and Aramaic-Syriac history and heritage.

Maronites do not claim their populations completely left Syria. They admit some of their populations remained in Syria. The population of the Maronites in Syria immediately before the 2011 Syrian Civil War was significant both in Damascus and Aleppo with three Maronite bishops presiding over the faithful. Importantly, there is no evidence of Maronite migration *to* Syria. Most indigenous communities around the world are respected for their oral traditions. In contrast to many of those communities, the Maronites have a variety of documentary sources that support their oral history. Regrettably however, throughout history and today, some in the Arab and western world and in Lebanon, both Muslim and those from other Christian denominations, have sought to refute Maronite oral tradition and its historical links to Phoenicia and beyond.

The two main scholarly antagonists appear to be Salibi and Moosa whose works have gained recent prominence. Salibi's comments in his book about the Maronites were merely of a passing nature, ancillary to a more political history of Lebanon, but his brief comments lack an academic basis. His description of the Maronites as Monothelites will be dealt with in Chapter 9 of this book. On the other hand, the author Moosa dedicates a whole book to Maronite history – *The Maronites in History* (1986), which appears to be a scholarly work but as demonstrated in Chapter 7 of this book is to be dismissed as a work of poor scholarship whose claims are unsubstantiated and misleading.

# CHAPTER 5

# THE FORMATION OF ARAMAIC CATHOLICISM AND 'ORTHODOXY'

## 5.1 The Antioch Region and Early Aramaic Catholic Identity

Before the addition of Constantinople as a patriarchate in 381, Antioch was only one of three patriarchates, Rome and Alexandria being the other two. Constantinople and then Jerusalem in the fifth century were added to make a total of five patriarchates. Excepting Rome, four of the five Patriarchates were in the East. This was the Christian belt of the world, the heart of Christianity and its teachings, its mindset, its debates, its Councils, its arguments.

From about 395 to 535, Antioch was the capital of the Roman Byzantine Empire's province of *Dioecesis Orientis* or Diocese of the East. This encompassed fifteen provinces extending to the eastern border with the Persian Empire. It included Cyprus, Mesopotamia, Arabia, the two provinces of Syria, two provinces of Phoenicia and three provinces of Palestine.

Following the establishment of the patriarchate of Constantinople in 381, the patriarchate of Antioch must have lost most of its native Greek areas to the north and north-east. Only the city of Antioch, the island of Cyprus, and perhaps Apamaea retained substantial Greek ethnic populations. Aramaic-Syriac-speaking Christians came to dominate the population of the patriarchate of Antioch.

Out of several cities on the mainland, the main Greek-speaking city of the patriarchate was the city of Antioch. Although containing a large ethnic Greek population, many would have been bilingual in Greek and Aramaic-Syriac. In reverse, the indigenous of the city would have been also bilingual. Cyprus was principally ethnic Greek, and Greek-speaking. The rest of the patriarchate was in the main Aramaic-Syriac-speaking. Most of its religious were native Aramaic speakers but would have known Greek. The administrative city centres throughout the patriarchate would have comprised ethnic Greeks employed in the main as part of Byzantine bureaucracy.

Antioch is the western part of a massive limestone plateau extending to the east at Aleppo, to the north at Cyr, and to the south at Apamaea. The flat terrain between these cities naturally connected them as part of the Roman Empire's important road network and communication routes. The plateau is about 150 kilometres in a north-south direction and about 30 kilometres wide in a west-east direction. It is surrounded by the Orontes River and fertile plains. Theodoret wrote about some of the most famous hermits living in this region and no doubt they were all following the Antiochian religious principles. Naaman states "this formed the cradle of those who were later called *the monks of Beit Maron,* or simply the Maronites."[63]

As will be seen in later chapters, after Chalcedon, these monks were a united block to defend the Chalcedon doctrine of the Antiochians and its most prominent father, Theodoret. In the eyes of the pope of Rome, the emperor and the Catholic Church generally, these monks were the champions, leaders, and centre of indigenous orthodoxy in the Diocese of the East, the Syrian orient, with Antioch as its capital.

The great Roman route of the Orontes was the Antioch-Apamaea-Heliopolis (Baalbek) route. Much of it travelled along the Orontes River. It placed Antioch in direct communication with Emesa (Homs) and the Bekaa Valley between the mountain ranges of Lebanon and ante-Lebanon. This is a large plateau and easily accessible from the flat inland route, running parallel to the Mediterranean coast. It contains the most fertile plains of the region. In terms of geographical study in the context of the early formation of the Maronite Church, Naaman summarises its importance: "This road would be taken later by a group of Syrians, the Maronites, going to settle in north Lebanon,

[63] Naaman, *The Maronites*, pp. 22, 126.

following the economic decline of the limestone massif, and motivated by other political and religious reasons."[64]

Heliopolis (that is, Baalbek, not to be confused with Hieropolis north east of Aleppo), and its surrounding valley (Bekaa) was undoubtedly the biggest food bowl of any single area in the eastern part of the Byzantine Empire and the eastern Mediterranean. Uniquely it can be classified as an alpine plateau, or flat valley, between the almost all year round snow-capped Lebanon Mountain and adjacent ante-Lebanon mountain range, providing the permanent reliability of water. Its climate at an altitude of 1000 metres is comfortable both in terms of temperature and humidity as an average across all seasons. It gives easier access to the heights of the Lebanon mountain range than from sea level on the Mediterranean coast.

We must understand the intertwining of geography, politics, economics, religion, and the history of the ancient period before we can understand Maronite origins. For example, the American archaeological expeditions to Syria in 1899-1900 resulted in H.C. Butler finding evidence from the fourth and fifth century of advanced sanitary plumbing with pipes connected to sewers or reservoirs. He also found bathrooms in houses with brackets on walls for water jars and wash hand basins corbelled out of walls. He states that the degree of advancement in sanitation and personal cleanliness is an index of the progress in civilisation of Syria in the fourth and fifth century, considerably in advance of large parts of Europe in the early twentieth century.[65]

## 5.2 Lebanon and the Orontes River

The source of the Orontes River that extends through Syria to Antioch is the snow-capped Mount Lebanon. Its western slopes fall towards the Mediterranean Sea. Its eastern slopes provide the source of the

---

[64] Naaman, *The Maronites*, pp. 27-28.
[65] Howard Crosby Butler, *Early Churches in Syria Fourth to Seventh Centuries*, Princeton University Press, 1921, p. 233.

Orontes River (Nahr el Assi today) below Mount Lebanon's highest peaks of around 3,000 metres above sea level in the vicinity above the Qadisha valley. The highest peak is at an altitude of 3,088 metres.

The water torrent at the source of the Orontes River is ferocious. This is as a result of the dramatic steep decline from the peak of Mount Lebanon at over 3000 metres to a rapid decline to about 900 metres below. This steep terrain is unable to provide settlements the way the seaside western slopes of the Lebanese mountain range provide. The Orontes River eventually feeds the great lake outside the city of Homs (ancient Emesa) in southern Syria, then through the city of Hama (ancient Ephiphania), extending to northern Syria at Antioch (now in Turkey), and then reaching its mouth at the Mediterranean in modern Turkey. The River supplied water to the ancient city of Palmyra in Syria. It is the chief river of the Levant.

The Orontes River was and still is a vital supply of water for so many villages, towns and cities spread through the Bekka valley of Lebanon, northern Syria and today part of Turkey. It runs for almost 500 kilometres providing rich fertile plains and valleys along the way. Its waters in more modern times have turned the famous water wheels in northern Syria as around the clock turbines providing water for townships on its course. Water was a vital resource in the past, as it is today. The communities the River feeds in Syria and Turkey would be well aware of its source – in this case Lebanon.

In ancient days, some would have travelled, intrigued, to reach the source of the Orontes waters, others wanting the water in its purest form. The people living at or above its source, those in the mountains of Lebanon, would not have been aware of its importance to so many below. This would not doubt still be the case today. It is the Orontes that has always sustained the food supply in this large fertile rural and city belt. Naaman states it is the Orontes that gave its origins to and nurtured the great bulk of what was later to be identified as Maronite colonies that formed in the Syrian Orient.

The hermitage of St Maroun at Hermel in the north of the Bekka valley near to the border with Syria, was apparently abandoned during the early days of Islamic conquest. It is situated about 90 metres above the spring, Ain Zarqa, which is one of the sources to the Orontes. Perhaps the hermitage's location is no coincidence.

Before the Syrian War that commenced in 2011, Maronite colonies remained in the cities further along the Orontes in northern Syria. Due to the devastation and destruction caused by the present Syrian War, the fate of these Maronites, their bishops, parishes, and churches is unknown. A small Maronite colony still resides in Antakya (Antioch) Turkey.

## 5.3   Theodoret and the Aramaic Language

Theodoret was born in 393 to a generational Christian upper class family of Antioch who owned many properties. His mother married at the age of seventeen. Theodoret wrote that his mother was cured of ophthalmia or inflammation of the eye by the intercession of Peter of Chalcis, a saintly ascetic outside of Antioch, after numerous and lengthy visits. She then became pious.[66]

After many years of childless marriage, his father visited the hermits just outside Antioch asking for their intercession for the blessing of a child. Another hermit, Macedonius, advised Theodoret's mother to consecrate her child to God if conceived. After thirteen years of marriage she fell pregnant and was close to death, but was cured by the intercession of the prayers of Peter of Chalcis. Theodoret was an only child. His mother took him frequently to be blessed by the anchorite Macedonius, by Aphraates, and every week by Saint Peter of Chalcis. He studied theology and wrote that Diodore of Tarsus and Theodore of Mopsuestia were his 'masters'.[67] Naaman wrote:

> Thus, for his religious education, Theodoret had powerful models in his parents and especially the monks around Antioch ... Destined by his parents, even before his birth, to

---

[66] Naaman, *The Maronites*, p. 68. See also Theodoret, *Therapeutique* and *Religious History*.

[67] Naaman, *The Maronites*, pp. 68-69.

the monastic life, Theodoret very likely remained in Antioch until the time of their death. He was then twenty-three years old, and a church lector. Being the sole heir, he distributed his riches to the poor, and retreated to one of the two monasteries in Nikertai; as we have seen, this was three miles away from Apamaea, seventy-five miles from Antioch, and one hundred and twenty miles from Cyr.[68]

It was likely during his seven years at this monastery following Marcian's rule and before he was called to be Bishop of Cyr in 423, that he wrote his first literary work, *Therapeutique*.[69] His bishopric included a large population and extended region in northern Syria and included the city of Cyr to the north and the city of Beroea (Aleppo today) to the east.

Theodoret faced intense hostility from the proponents of the Unitarian doctrine. At the Second Council of Ephesus in 449, the Unitarians or Monophysites, led by the Syrian monk Barsauma, arranged for one thousand monks to converge on the assembly wielding sticks and swords.[70] Barsauma branded the heretics 'Nestorians' as those who did not follow the Unitarian doctrine of Eutychius, who had much influence on the Emperor and arranged for many who opposed his views to be expelled. Nestorius was a well-known Dualistic Christology father, and was declared a heretic at the First Council of Ephesus in 431. The Council opposed his view that Mary was the mother of Jesus Christ rather than the Mother of God. Theodoret, the leading dualistic partisan, was confusingly also called a Nestorian by the Unitarians and was declared a heretic and exiled by the Council in 449.[71]

When in exile, Theodoret returned to the monasteries in Nikertai, approximately twenty-five years after his first residency there. It is

---

[68] Ibid., p. 69.

[69] Ibid., p. 71.

[70] Evagrius, *The Ecclesiastical History of Evagrius Scholarasticus*, translated by Michael Whitby, Liverpool University Press, 2000, p. 121. Evagrius was an ancient Greek writer at the end of the sixth century.

[71] Confusingly again, even from the correspondence in 592 between the Jacobites and Maronites, the Unitarians also called themselves 'orthodox'.

clear that he was then heavily influenced by the lives of the saintly hermits and monastic life as an imitation of the life lived in heaven. His preference in these influences was the Aramaic-Syriac spirituality, language and environment, rather than the Greek. His dominant thinking was certainly not in the context of St Anthony of Alexandria's monasticism, or Alexandrine doctrine, or the Hellenistic spirituality. Nor was it the Greek influences that were part of life in the city of Antioch where he was born.

The dwelling of Theodoret in the monastery at Nikertai on two different occasions is significant for the understanding of the location of the establishment of Beit Maroun, as will be seen later in Chapter 6. It is likely Theodoret was the stimulus for Emperor Marcian to build the monastery of Maroun near Apamaea, the capital of Syria Secunda, where Aramaic culture prevailed over Hellenistic culture.[72] However, Theodoret's glory often remains in the context as a 'pure Greek'. It appears his native tongue was Aramaic as he only spoke in this language when meeting with many of the hermit monks he wrote about noting they did not speak Greek.[73] Brock suggests although Theodoret wrote exclusively in Greek, he normally spoke Syriac (Aramaic) by reference to where he tells of a demon speaking to him in that language urging him not to persecute the Marcionites.[74] As Naaman writes:

> this is just one of the distortions caused by Hellenocentric misconceptions. "Theodoret must be given back to Syria," states Peeters. Theodoret was Syrian Antiochian not only by origin, birth, and language but above all by feeling and thought.[75]

---

[72] Naaman, *The Maronites*, p. 129.
[73] For example, the monks Abraham, Macedonius, and Aphrahat in Theodoret's *Religious History.*
[74] Brock, *From Ephrem to Romanus*, p. 154, citing Theodoret's *Religious History*, Chapter 21.15.
[75] Naaman, *The Maronites*, p. 78. Again, the same 'giving back to Syria' could apply to the well known sixth century Christian Greek historian, Evagrius Scholasticus, who was born in the city of Epiphania on the Orontes River (present-day Hama in Syria), not far from Apamaea.

The same would apply to Theodore, bishop of Mopsuestia[76] from 392-428, who was born in Antioch. He was a leading religious writer in his time from the school of Antioch. Like Theodoret he was from a wealthy family and wrote exclusively in Greek following his Greek education, but Aramaic seemed his native tongue. Other prominent Greek writers were likely native Aramaic including the notable Christian writer Eusbeius of Emesa and the poet Romanus from Emesa.[77]

Several of St John Chrysostom's letters were addressed to Theodore's cousin, Paeanius, who was a senior government official. Theodore's brother, Polychronius, became archbishop of Apamaea. Theodore was a companion and friend of Chrysostom having met in Antioch as students. When Chrysostom was appointed Archbishop of Constantinople in 397 without his knowledge, apparently he had to secretly leave Antioch for fear his departure, as a most popular figure, would cause a virtual riot.

The background of Theodoret, Theodore, and others mentioned here points to a Greek-speaking and writing city of Antioch but with a substantial well-to-do indigenous Aramaic population. The prominence of the Greek language in the city does not necessarily equate to an overarching and dominant ethnic Greek population. Brock gives an analogy of Lebanon during the French mandate after the First World War. French was the language of power but Arabic and French flourished side by side in language and culture with French the choice of written language for many Lebanese writers (even today).[78]

We know by the seventh century the written Syriac prevailed over the written Greek in Antioch. It may prove elusive to determine the extent of the ethnicities in Antioch city prior to this time. However, there is evidence of a potential ethnic Aramaic domination of the city in the early sixth century with an Aramaic patriarch and 'anti-Greek/ pro-Rome' riots.

---

[76] Mopsuestia was 20 kilometres east of Antioch city.

[77] Brock, *From Ephrem to Romanus*, p. 154.

[78] Ibid., p. 158.

## 5.3.1 The Absence of Writings from a 'Theodoret of Lebanon'

As previously detailed, St John Chrysostom, the Patriarch of Constantinople (397-407), requested missionaries to Phoenicia as he was particularly concerned about the practice of paganism. He sent letters to monks and clergy rallying the mission. It seems monks had a special lead role to play in the mission of conversion. In his letter to Rufinus, Chrysostom talks of:

> some great misfortunes have occurred in Phoenicia. The fury of the pagans has grown to deplorable excess and of the monks engaged in their conversion, several have been wounded and others killed. Thus I insist again, and more strongly than ever, that you hasten to battle without further delay. I am sure that if you make an appearance there, your prayers, your goodness, your grief, patience, strength of soul and even your very presence, will suffice to put the enemy to flight, to restrain the infidel, to give courage to our own ...

> As for the relics of the martyrs, do not concern yourself. I have sent the venerable priest Terentius to my most pious lord Otreius, bishop of Arabissa, who has many well authenticated relics, and in a few days I shall send them to you in Phoenicia. Make haste to finish the churches which have no roofs before winter.[79]

This passage provides evidence of missionary monks directly involved in conversion of pagans around 400 AD. These monks were either from Phoenicia or if from elsewhere, more likely from northern Syria. Nonetheless, it is a written record, perhaps one of the earliest, of monastic missionary movements in Phoenicia. It corresponds with the time of Theodoret's Abraham and fellow monks converting the Lebanese town folk.

It has been suggested that many historians inappropriately attri-

---

[79] Sader, *Crosses and Symbols*, pp. 237-242. Whilst Sader's works warrant careful examination, he may be incorrect on occasion. For example, his reference to Gabala in Theodoret's Chapter 28 on Thalelaeus is likely to be mistakenly located as Jbail/Byblos in Lebanon rather than Jabala in northern Syria.

bute Christian conversion of Phoenicia to St John Chrysostom.[80] Sader informs us in his investigation of St John Chrysostom's missions to Phoenicia that he "found no trace of the missions, not even an oratory, a hermitage or a monastery dedicated to St John Chrysostom."[81] Outside of any bias or mistake on this subject, we must also consider information from Theodoret about Abraham in Lebanon and also the Syriac Manuscript MS 160 of the conversion of a large number of people from the Lebanon. It does appear Helleno-centric thinking may have created a myth and skewed historical truths. The date of the letters from St John Chrysostom concerning Phoenicia were relatively contemporary to the visit to Phoenicia (recorded by Theodoret) of the monk St Abraham and the visit of the Lebanese to Simon Stylite only a short number of decades later.

On the other hand, one can discover in Syria and Lebanon still today many churches named after St Simon the Stylite.[82] For the Maronites, the conversion of the Phoenicians by St Simon Stylite is not apocryphal (of doubtful authenticity) as stated by the author Moosa.[83] Moosa suggests there is no evidence any Maronite community existed in Lebanon in the fifth century.[84] That is correct, as we know through historical circumstances it was not until the late sixth century there is a first reference in documents to 'Maronites' whether in Syria or Lebanon. However, there is no explanation for Cosmos, as a disciple of St Simon, to randomly fabricate a story about a mass crowd from Lebanon visiting St Simon Stylite and converting to Christianity, even if the narrative about the wild beasts in the village was exaggerated or a legend.

It seems probable that after 451 the Chalcedonian monasteries, as principal intermediaries for the Churches of Antioch, Constantinople, and Rome, would have sent their monks to nearby Phoenicia, Syria

---

[80] Sader, *Crosses and Symbols*, p. 243.

[81] Ibid., p. 244.

[82] See also Sader, *Crosses and Symbols*, p. 245.

[83] Sader, *Crosses and Symbols*, pp. 245-246, agrees.

[84] Moosa, *The Maronites in History*, p. 20.

and likely Palestine to uphold the doctrine of the Council and ensure any remaining pagan villagers were preached the good news. Its head monastery, Beit Maroun, lay just north of the Lebanon coast and mountain range. One of its purposes was to uphold the doctrine. They were also competing with the Syrian monks who were now declared Monophysite. The whole region was at stake.

This network of monasteries must have supplied the great bulk of missionaries that spread out to those parts of Aramaic-speaking Syria and Lebanon which were not Christian or not Catholic as Christian Chalcedonian adherents. If any pagans remained, the monks would likely find a vacant pagan sanctuary, as they were numerous, and lived inside or constructed wooden dwellings nearby. The Christian emperors forbade the destruction of the temples due to their architectural and aesthetic value. The new Christians were encouraged to transform these splendid stone temple buildings into a church. Many churches and monasteries today are built on and from these temples and include remnants of the large temple columns and structures.

For those who were Christian, the monk missionaries would have ensured they upheld the doctrine of the Council. It must follow the Beit Maroun network expanded. The monks also brought relics of the saints including from Constantinople, Antioch, and other locations of the Empire. As detailed in Butler's notes on the Princeton University expeditions of the late nineteenth century, crosses and Christian symbols would have began to be engraved on stone work, on church walls and above windows and doors of residences.[85]

Some monasteries were likely to have been deliberately constructed close to the location of some of the most famous hermitages. In any event, a culture eventually developed whereby all monasteries of the Antiochian Syriac world were built for the communal monks (cenobites) and geared for any hermitage. The faithful gradually formed communities and work around the monastery. The monks and any hermit were viewed as soldiers living in the presence of God. The locals

---

[85] Butler, *Early Churches in Syria*, p. 233.

believed they were protected by these holy men and would receive blessings of God (through the monks) to them, their families, and their work.

There can be little doubt the anchorite and cenobitic monastic expansion in northern Syria that has been the focus of Syriac studies, did in fact take place in Lebanon just to its south at some stage at least by the latter half of the fifth century, after Theodoret's *Religious History*. Many archaeological monastic and hermitage sites in the mountains of Lebanon are testament, as are ancient monasteries and churches still in use today. No doubt there were priests, who are not monks, also active in missionary work. However, it is suggested that for the period primarily focussed on in this book, the fifth to seventh centuries, the theological leadership and missionary work of the monks dominated the ecclesiastical environment of the Aramaic-speaking world.

Lebanon, Phoenicia, and Palestine's history is relatively absent in Aramaic-Syriac studies because we have not found a 'Theodoret of Lebanon' writing about it at the time. Since we have not found an ancient source does not mean that a similar monastic movement to that recorded by Theodoret was not taking place outside of Syria. Perhaps there was a contemporary writer(s) but the source has since been destroyed. Perhaps and more likely in Theodoret's time, it was less prevalent outside of northern Syria. Nonetheless, the various independent sources, only when amassed, assist in painting the picture. The history, significance, and size of the population of Antioch, Cyrrhus, and its immediate surrounds deserved the attention. Equally would Antioch's importance as the capital of the patriarchate and so too the great city and monasteries of Apamaea and its surrounds.

## 5.4  Hermit Monks and Public Visits

As mentioned in previous chapters, Aramaic monasticism was a different type of cenobitic monasticism than the Greek and Egyptian practice that followed St Anthony. The Aramaic version would be likely to have been one in which a monk could choose between a contemplative life as inward away from the world, or an active mission-ary life outward in full communion with the community around it or the community that would likely establish itself around it. As will be revealed in Chapter 6, by the fourth century at the latest, there is evi-dence of anchorites attached to cenobitic monasteries and as part of a network of monasteries. One example was the practice of Agapetus and Simon in memory of Theodoret's anchorite Marcian around the late fourth century.

For the typical traits of the Aramaic anchorite Theodoret wrote about, Naaman writes:

> Such were the monks of Cyr who lived in the open air, sim-ple, humble, of a rudimentary culture, who often spoke only Syriac and who were filled with the love of Christ. They were virtuous to the point of heroism ... above all remarkable for their love of contemplation, sometimes excessive penances, and complete submission to the hierarchy.[86]

They would chant the Psalms and the hymns, pray, and read the Holy Scripture. They possessed a deep sense of their misery and wept continuously day and night seeking God's forgiveness. They practised chastity and poverty and many included females such as Marana, Cyra, and Domnina who Theodoret wrote about in his *Religious History.*

The chapter on Domnina, is the final chapter for Theodoret's thirty monks. In his concluding comments of that chapter, he gives us an insight into the reasons for his accounts of the life of the anchorite monks:

> But to recount everything is impossible not only for me but for all writers. Even if it were possible, I consider it superflu-ous and an ambition without gain; for those who wish to cull some profit, what has been said is sufficient to provide what they desire. We have recalled different lives, and added ac-counts of women to those of men, for this reason: that men of old and young, and women too, may have models of philoso-

---

[86] Naaman, *The Maronites,* p. 60.

phy, and that each person, as he receives the impress of his favourite life, may have as a rule and regulator of his own life the one presented in our account.[87]

In the concluding chapter of *Epilogue on Divine Love*,[88] Theodoret gives the principal reason for the life of these thirty anchorites. It is based in the Jewish tradition, the example of great Biblical figures such as Moses, Abraham, Isaac, Jacob, and Joseph, and the belief that "Divine love despises all earthly things." Theodoret's monks were exposed to the elements, the fierce sun, heat and cold. They ate and drank little and their diets were vegetarian principally of grass, beans, lentils and peas. Hunger on account of love was more delightful than any luxury. Their fatigue at night was greater than the day. They deliberately struggled against sleep and continued all night chanting hymns to God. It was only through their heavenly desires that they achieved these great heroic feats of athleticism. Theirs was not a life of pleasure.

The anchorites received visitors. This was regardless of whether they were not linked to a monastery – as in the early period of Aramaic monasticism – or linked – as in the later period when the hermitage was under the authority of the monk superior of a nearby monastery. The public visits were the result of insistence, persistence, and sometimes the force of mass crowds. Privately to themselves, the anchorites may have wished not to receive visitors. The peculiar contradiction prevailed, and although the anchorites were living a contemplative life not wanting of human contact they were in fact in regular contact with the outside community. These frequent and lengthy visits came from locals seeking the anchorite's blessings and spiritual advice. This was discomforting and often very annoying to the anchorite as James of Cyrrhus told Theodoret "it was not for their sakes I came to this mountain. It was for mine."[89] The exception to the annoyance was

---

[87] Theodoret, *A History of the Monks of Syria*, p. 187.

[88] Ibid., pp. 190-205.

[89] Naaman makes no reference to the name James of Cyrrhus from Theodoret. Instead he uses the name Jacob in English for the same monk Price translates to the name James. Whilst Naaman's translation may be correct, given this study relies on Price's

when their hierarchy would visit, including their Bishop Theodoret, as they would show absolute obedience to him. Perhaps Theodoret's Limnaeus, a disciple of St Maroun and in the same way as his master, was not part of a cenobitic monastery but still faithful to the Church as it was recorded he never opened the door for visitors except to Bishop Theodoret.

### 5.4.1 A Modern Example: Father Dario the Maronite Hermit Monk

The practice of visitation of anchorites continues in the Maronite Church today. With the permission of Father Superior of the monastery of St Anthony of Khozhaya, an interview by the present author of hermit Father Dario Escobar in 2005 in his hermitage in Lebanon reveals the persistence of visitors and the preference to be left alone, much the same as the monks in the first centuries.

Father Dario was a Roman Catholic priest from Colombia in South America. He had no Middle Eastern or Lebanese heritage. Whilst serving in a parish in Miami, he became interested in living life as an anchorite, after hearing about the life of hermit St Charbel from the Lebanese Maronite Order (LMO). Upon deciding to emulate St Charbel's life, Father Dario sought permission from Pope John Paul II to join the LMO. Although the Maronites are Catholic and in communion with the Latin Church of Rome, the Maronite Church was Eastern Catholic and Father Dario required consent being from the Latin Catholic Church.

After several years, the permission was granted and he joined the LMO, initially as a novitiate, and studied with them for a number of years before becoming a hermit. During that time he learnt Syriac and Arabic. In the summer of 2005, Father Superior of the monastery honoured the author of this book with the blessings of his consent to interview Father Dario. Father Dario was not warned as he lived the traditional way without technology. He was in an ancient hermitage known

---

translation, Price's name translation for James is retained for use in this study.

as Our Lady of Hawqa, thought to have its origins in the period fifth to seventh century. It was in the Qadisha Valley several kilometres away from the monastery, accessible only by foot.

Information provided by the Superior indicated the easier path by foot was the one that started from the village of Hawqa many kilometres away by road, and at an altitude of 1200 metres. The rugged, narrow, and sharply winding dirt and natural rock path from Hawqa to the ancient hermitage clung tenuously to the side of the mountain with no safety support. The drop of the vertical cliff face immediately below was up to 700 metres. After approximately a forty-minute hike, the hermitage appeared inside a natural grotto halfway down the spectacular gorge. The natural recessed cavern housed an entry gate leading upstairs to the chapel, small monastery and a natural stone terrace. There was also a bell tower and small agricultural terraces below.

Upon arrival, a family of three had just left visiting him. A man with a camera had been sitting on the terrace overlooking the breathtaking views of the valley. After enquiry from the author, it was established he was a reporter from the *LA Times* and had been 'hanging around' photographing Father Dario for the past five days. When asked about the whereabouts of Father Dario, the reporter replied: "there is a girl from the village in confession inside the chapel with him." There were other Maronite hermits living in the mountains of Lebanon at the time. They were attached to ancient monasteries elsewhere. Similarly, those hermits also received many visitors virtually on a daily basis. Occasionally, there might be a queue to see these hermits, such as on the weekend.

On interviewing Father Dario, his English was broken but adequate. He had been at the monastery for several years. Visitors sought out Father Dario in his traditional role of intercessor, that is, they believe that through strict self-denial he had won access to God and can act as a mediator through prayers and blessings. Father said he did not like the visitations but had never refused anyone. He respected the ancient traditions of Maronite monasticism.

110

Cliff edge mountain path leading to ancient hermitage of Our Lady of Hawa, North Lebanon. (Photos taken in 2005 by author).

Entry to ancient hermitage of Our Lady of Hawa, North Lebanon currently occupied by Father Dario Escobar.

Entry to the hermitage of Our Lady of Hawa. The bifurcated cross on the left of the arch also appears in many Aramaic sixth century church buildings in Lebanon.

Colombian born Father Dario Escobar, formerly a Roman Catholic priest, joined the Lebanese Maronite Order of monks to become a hermit.

## 5.5 Fifth Century Divisions in the Eastern Churches and the Formation of the 'Orthodox'

These years saw a complex and lengthy series of historical events and theological debates. The most detailed account as it relates to this period can be found in Naaman's 2009 publication. In 431, the Catholic Church held its Third Ecumenical Council in the Asia Minor Greek city of Ephesus (now Selcuk in Izmir province Turkey). The Council condemned the teaching of Nestorius, Patriarch of Constantinople. He was accused of preaching that though Mary was the mother of Christ, she was not the Mother of God. Facing persecution from the Byzantine emperor, the 'Nestorians' fled to land under Persian rule on the other side of the Euphrates River, particularly south Mesopotamia.

In 451, the Fourth Ecumenical Council was held at Chalcedon. This was a former Greek maritime city, now Kadıköy in Istanbul, Turkey. The Council declared the Monophysite teaching as a heresy. The Monophysites believed Christ the Son of God had only one nature being divine and not two natures of physical and divine. The Catholic Church lost a great many faithful. This was the start of the schismatic Monophysite churches of the Egyptian Copts, Aramaic-Syriacs, Armenians, and Ethiopians.

The Unitarian theology was promoted by the fathers of Alexandria: Clement, Origen, Athanasius, and Cyril. Its starting point is Heaven as in words of the Gospel of John, "the Word made flesh," emphasize divinity over humanity. Theodoret noticed monks in general were inclined towards the Alexandrine theology as it favoured mystical contemplation and rapture. Because of St Anthony, Alexandria was placed as the cradle of monastic life and holy place.[90]

The dualistic theology of the Dyophysites starts at Earth from the "man assumed" who is the son of Mary and is based on the Synoptic Gospels (Matthew, Mark, and Luke) explaining the humanity and divinity of Christ as one. As Naaman explains, "Dualistic Christology developed only where Christianity was deeply marked by Semit-

---

[90] Naaman, *The Maronites*, p. 125.

ic thought, Hebrew and Aramaic."[91] The Church of Antioch and its 'fathers' including Diodore of Tarsus, Theodore of Mopsuestia, John Chrysostom, and Theodoret of Cyr, promoted this concept of Christ.

From the time Constantinople was declared the New Rome in 381, the theological disagreements between the cities of Alexandria and Antioch intensified. As Constantinople chose its bishops from the monks of Antioch, the Alexandrians were outraged. At the first Council of Ephesus in 431 the Alexandrians were represented by their Bishop Cyril, and the Antiochians by Bishop Theodoret of Cyr. They were the two most brilliant theologians of their time.[92]

Cyril, Bishop/Patriarch of Alexandria, died in 444. In the same year, Patriarch Domnus of Antioch made Theodoret his counsellor and built him a house in Antioch. Theodoret wrote his *Religious History* at this time (440-445) seizing the period of calm to bring unity amongst his monks and for them to regain confidence in their vocation and local traditions, and reduce any attraction to Cyril's theology imported from Egypt.[93]

In 448, Eutychius arrived on the scene. He was the superior of the monks of Constantinople and supported the pro-Unitarian theology. He was an important figure in the empirical capital having much influence on the emperor Theodosius II. He was also a friend of Cyril until he died and was supported by Bishop Dioscorus of Alexandria, Cyril's successor. Patriarch Flavian of Constantinople and Patriarch Domnus of Antioch opposed them and engaged Theodoret who wrote a three-part book entitled *Eranistes* refuting Eutychius. In 448, Flavian called a meeting of forty bishops in Constantinople and deposed Eutychius.

Emperor Theodosius II, wanting to support Eutychius and Dioscorus called the second Council of Ephesus in 449 and Theodoret, Flavian, and Domnus were excommunicated (anathematized). Pope Leo in Rome refused to attend and refused to accept the decision. He nullified the excommunication accepting Theodoret's doctrines. The

[91] Ibid., p. 123.
[92] Ibid., p. 125.
[93] Ibid., p. 126.

Emperor issued a second order exiling Bishop Theodoret, the latter with approval from the Emperor deciding to return to the monastery in Nikertai. Theodoret sent letters around the world during this twenty-six-month period but only thirty-five have been located.[94]

In 451, Marcian became emperor and was a dualistic thinker, that is, Catholic 'orthodox'. He immediately banished Eutychius and brought Theodoret and his followers back from exile and called the Council of Chalcedon. The doctrines of the Ephesus Council of 449 were overturned. The Council was heated. When Theodoret entered to take his seat, the Monophysite bishops of Alexandria, Palestine and others yelled "mercy, the faith is lost. Get out of here master of Nestorius." The opposing bishops cried: "get out of here Dioscorus, it is the assassins of Flavian who should be expelled... Theodoret is worthy of attending this assembly."[95] At the conclusion of the assembly, Dioscorus was deposed and Theodoret was declared a "master of orthodoxy." The Roman legates favoured Theodoret's view.

To comprehend these developments it is helpful to be familiar with the last canon, Canon 28, of the Chalcedon Council: "that the city [Constantinople] which was honoured with the sovereignty and the Senate, and which enjoyed equal privileges with the elder royal Rome, should also be magnified, like her, in ecclesiastical matters, and be second after her." The sixth canon of Nicaea (325), which insisted on "the preservation of the rights and privileges of the bishops of Alexandria, Antioch, and other provinces," was abrogated in favour of Constantinople. Accordingly the leadership of the See of Alexandria, being the most important in the whole of the East from the prestige of ancient Egypt and Hellenistic Alexandria, was lost. Thus, the Alexandrines would not be governed by the Council.

The Egyptians and Aramaic-speaking Monophysites felt let down by the Council of Chalcedon. The Monophysites had little or no chance of political independence under the Empire and the theologi-

---

[94] Ibid., p. 87.
[95] Ibid., p. 91.

cal disagreement over the nature of Christ had bred bitter resentment towards the Chalcedonian bishops and the faithful. Nonetheless, the doctrine of Chalcedon became the religion of the empire. The emperor enforced the decrees of 451, and those who dissented suffered heavy penalties.

Native Egypt was united behind the Patriarch of Alexandria and the subsequent stirring of nationalism sparked the development of the Church of Egypt, the Coptic Church.[96] Monophysitism became a national patriotic symbol for the Egyptian Coptics. They were different ethnically and linguistically to the Byzantines as were the Aramaic speakers. Importantly, the Aramaic-speaking Monophysites did not immediately form a schismatic church like the Coptics. It is proposed this was a result of the many Aramaic-speaking pro-Chalcedons (within the lands of the Roman empire) who remained Catholic.

The Aramaic-speaking Monophysites did not officially form their own 'Syriac Orthodox Church' until the year 518, almost seventy years after the Council of Chalcedon.[97] At that time, they officially refused to acknowledge the pro-Chalcedon patriarch of Antioch. Significantly this was not, and could not be, a national church or identity. Rather, there were too many pro-Chalcedon Aramaic-speaking Catholics not just in the two Roman Syrian provinces but also in the provinces of Phoenicia, Phoenicia Lebanon, and the three Palestinian provinces.

Compared to the indigenous Coptics and Aramaic-speaking Monophysites, the ethnic Greeks were only small in number in the patriarchates of Alexandria and Antioch. They principally lived in the patriarchal capital cities and like the rest of the Greek-speaking world, remained pro-Chalcedon and Catholic. The Greeks retained the positions in government as officials. As minorities, their loyalty was to the empire, which was chiefly centred on Constantinople.

---

[96] Aziz Atiya, *A History of Eastern Christianity*, Methuen, 1968, pp. 57-58.
[97] See Chapter 7 for further detail.

## 5.6 Early Use of the Identity Terms
## 'Catholic', 'Chalcedonian', 'Orthodox', and 'Melkite'

The word 'Catholic' is derived from the Greek word *katholikos* meaning the whole or universal. The combination 'the Catholic Church' (*he katholike ekklesia*) is found for the first time in the letter of St. Ignatius to the Smyrnaeans, written about the year 110.[98] St Cyril of Jerusalem's definition is often quoted by Catholics:

> The Church is called Catholic because she is diffused throughout the whole world [i.e. the habitable world, *oikoumenes*] from one end of the earth to the other, and because she teaches universally and without curtailment all the truths of faith which ought to be known to men whether they concern visible or invisible things, heavenly things or the things of earth; further because she brings under the yoke of God's true service all races of men, the mighty and the lowly, the learned and the simple; and finally because she tends and heals every kind of sin committed by body or soul and because there is no form of virtue, whether in word or deed or in spiritual gifts of any kind whatever, which she does not possess as her own.[99]

The ecclesiastical use of the word *Catholicos* appeared infrequently in the early church. It referred to the principal bishop of a country who remained under the leadership of his patriarch. It is thought the first use of the term was in the fourth century by the bishop of Armenia within the patriarchate of Antioch. The term became more widely used for the title of leaders or patriarchs of certain autonomous eastern Oriental churches who were no longer in communion with the Catholic Church.

'Ecumenical' comes from the Greek word *oikoumene,* meaning whole world. The Catholic Church has held many Ecumenical Coun-

---

[98] Herbert Thurston, "Catholic," in *The Catholic Encyclopedia*, Robert Appleton Company, 1908. Available at http://www.newadvent.org/cathen/03449a.htm.
[99] Cited in Ibid.

cils constituted by bishops from around the empire under the presidency of the pope or his legates. The Council's decree receives papal confirmation binding all Christians. Up to the fifth century, these Councils included:

- First Ecumenical Council held in Nicaea (325)
- Second Ecumenical Council held in Constantinople (381)
- Third Ecumenical Council held in Ephesus (431)
- Fourth Ecumenical Council held in Chalcedon (451)

'Orthodox', *orthodoxeia* in Greek, signifies right belief or purity of faith. It means the 'right way', correct in opinion or doctrine. The Third and Fourth Ecumenical Councils resulted in the loss from the Catholic Church of a significant number of Christians. Thus, it became necessary to distinguish them: those Christians who upheld the Third and Fourth Ecumenical Councils, rejecting Nestorianism and Monophysitism, were called 'Orthodox Christians'.

Since these two heresies arose in the Eastern part of the Church, and since the Councils that condemned these two teachings were held in that region, the term 'orthodox' was largely used in the East rather than in the West. Still, one could speak of Christians at this time as 'orthodox', whether they resided within the limits of the Byzantine Patriarchate in the East or the Roman Patriarchate in the West.

After 451, it is possible the term 'Melkites' was first used. It was reference to the Christians in the East within the Empire who remained loyal to the Byzantine king and the Catholic faith. These Orthodox Christians became known as Melkites after the word '*melk*', or '*malk*', or '*malkoyo*' for king in Aramaic Syriac. They were royalists or imperialists, loyal to the king, from the 'emperor's party'. By adding the Greek ending *–ites* results in the word *melkites* (malkites) equal to *basilikos* in Greek. The term 'Melkites' became more prominent in use after the arrival of the Arab Muslim conquests in 634-638.

Ethnically, the Byzantine Church comprised not only Greeks but also a mix of cultural backgrounds from Asia Minor and Eastern

Europe. Constantinople as its capital was a large melting pot of ethnicities and cultures. These Greek-Byzantines, when migrating to the Greek-speaking Middle Eastern cities such as Antioch, were sure to have retained their Byzantine church practices.[100]

In Egypt and Africa, the Catholics were led by the Orthodox (Melkite) patriarch of Alexandria. In Egypt, these were generally ethnic Greeks in the city of Alexandria and its immediate surrounds. It may have also been a minor amount of indigenous Copts, but the extent is unknown. In Jerusalem, the Catholics were led by the Orthodox (Melkite) patriarch of Jerusalem. It is not certain what the extent of the ethnic Greek-Byzantine Christian population was in Jerusalem, but likely there was a significant indigenous Aramaic-speaking Christian population.

The Aramaic-speaking world of the patriarchate of Antioch within the empire then constituted the Roman provinces of Syria I and II, Phoenicia I and Phoenicia Lebanon. The Catholics were led by the Orthodox (Melkite) patriarch of Antioch. In the city of Antioch and its immediate surrounds, this included ethnic Greeks-Byzantines and indigenous Syrians. Outside of Antioch, the Catholic population comprised principally the indigenous Aramaic-Syriac speakers. Ethnic Greeks-Byzantines would have been concentrated in the various administrative cities throughout the Middle East to an extent unknown but more likely as minorities alongside the natives.

Up to 1054 AD, the Christians in the Middle East[101] who remained loyal to the Catholic faith have often been identified by Byzantine and Western historians to be 'Byzantines'. However, the overwhelming majority of these Christians were Aramaic-Syriac-speaking. It included the Christians linked to the region of Cyrrhus under Bishop Theodoret and to the region of Apamaea under the monasteries of St Agapetus and St Simon of Cyr, and Beit Maroun after 451. Accordingly, many ancient historical accounts omit any reference to the indigenous Catholic Christians of the Middle East. This has resulted in much con-

---

[100] Chapters 8 and 9 provide more detail.
[101] Defined as excluding North Africa and Asia Minor.

fusion, limited historical accounts, and an unintentional skewing of history from Byzantine and Western-centric historians.

The indigenous tongue of the patriarchate of Antioch was Aramaic-Syriac. So also was its Christian liturgical language. The Syrians, Lebanese, and Palestinians had different cultural, linguistic, and ancestral backgrounds to the Greeks-Byzantines. Their liturgical rites and texts were not the same as the Greek-speaking Byzantines. They saw their Aramaic-Syriac-speaking church as a distinct member of the Byzantine Orthodox communion, but not as a constituent part of the Greek-Byzantine rite and Greek-speaking Church. This is in the same way as Eastern Catholic Churches see themselves today as being in communion with Rome but not as part of the Latin rite and Latin-speaking church.

In terms of population numbers, the Syrian cities of Antioch and Apamaea were at the time of the fifth century likely to be larger than the current Australian capital city populations of Canberra, Hobart, or Darwin. The countryside around these ancient Syrian cities was also densely populated. Bishop Theodoret had hundreds of parishes in the countryside region of Cyrrhus. The East, including Constantinople, was overwhelmingly Christian. There were far fewer Christians in the West at this time. The founder of Western monasticism, the Italian St Benedict, was not born until the year 480.

The use of the term 'Orthodox', following the Great Schism between the Christian churches of Rome and Constantinople in the eleventh century, developed a different context. It labels all Christians in the East who are not Catholic as 'Orthodox'. It perceives them as all practicing in the Byzantine liturgy. It now matters not to mainstream society whether Eastern Christians were previously 'Orthodox' from the Catholic faith or whether they belonged to the non-Chalcedon churches after 451.

Since the Great Schism, this simplistic labelling and perception has unintentionally marginalised the cultural diversity of the ancient Catholic Church. This is particularly so for the various rich traditional Christian denominations of the Middle Eastern Apostolic churches (established by Jesus Christ's apostles) that continue to flourish today. The perception of entire East as 'Orthodox' appears to hold firm in modern times, not only for non-Christians throughout the world, but for western and Byzantine Christians. In order to avoid the confusion in the use of the word 'Orthodox', some today separate the non-Catholic Eastern churches into two main categories, Orthodox (i.e. Byzantine churches), and Oriental Orthodox.

Throughout this book for the period up to the mid seventh century, in order to avoid confusion, terms are used for Catholics such as 'Chalcedonian' and the Monophysites as 'anti-Chalcedonian'. Reference to the term 'Orthodox' is generally limited to the Byzantines after the eleventh century. The term 'Catholic' throughout this study is a reference to the See of Rome led by its patriarch or bishop, the pope, and to any Church in communion with it.

## 5.7 Modern View of Monophysitism

Monophysitism states Jesus Christ had only one nature, divine. Dyophysitism declares Jesus Christ had two natures, physical and divine. The Catholic Church declared monophysitism a heresy in 451. These are very simplified statements. Today, the more commonly held view is that this was a schism (separation) in the Church rather than a heresy, the latter being a corruption in dogma or religious doctrine. It is critical to understand that modern theological views now suggest the 'Monophysites' were not heretics but simply schismatic.[102] That is, this theological divergence created a division or separation in the Church, not a heretical corruption of dogma or religious doctrine.

The Monophysites taught that there is but one Nature of Christ, *mia physis*, because they identify the words *physis* and *hypostasis*. Jesus Christ's Divine and Human nature are united (*mia* – 'one' or 'unity') without separation in a compound nature ('physis'). Hypos-

---

[102] John Chapman, "Monophysites and Monophysitism," *The Catholic Encyclopedia*, Robert Appleton Company, 1911, available at: http://www.newadvent.org/cathen/10489b.htm.

tasis refers to the Incarnation to express that in Christ one person subsists in two natures, the Divine and the human. For this reason, the non-Chalcedonian churches are now more aptly described as Miaphysites believing in the union of two natures rather than Monophysites, the latter rejecting any union, or existence, of two natures.

Similarly, the Nestorian branch that sees Mary not as Mother of God have more recently also been deemed as schismatic rather than heretical. The differences can be best summarised as follows:

**Differing Concepts of Jesus Christ (Christology)**

| Belief System | Personhood | Hypostasis | Nature |
|---|---|---|---|
| Nestorians: | one person | two hypostases | two natures |
| Catholics: | one person | one hypostasis | two natures |
| Monophysites: | one person | one hypostasis | one, divine |

One of the reasons for the dispute was the difference in languages. Translations were problematic. The specialist linguists of today communicate the differences far more adequately. Had the communication barriers been resolved during the fifth century, the history of the Middle East may well have changed course.

In 1984, following a number of meetings since 1971, a common declaration was made between the Catholic Church and the Syrian Orthodox Church. Part of the declaration states:

> Their Holinesses Pope John Paul II and Patriarch Zakka I wish solemnly to widen the horizon of their brotherhood and affirm herewith the terms of the deep spiritual communion which already unites them and the prelates, clergy and faithful of both their Churches, to consolidate these ties of Faith, Hope and Love, and to advance in finding a wholly common ecclesial life.
>
> 3. First of all, Their Holinesses confess the faith of their two Churches, formulated by Nicene Council of 325 A.D. and generally known as 'the Nicene Creeds'. The confusions and schisms that occurred between their Churches in the later

centuries, they realize today, in no way affect or touch the substance of their faith, since these arose only because of differences in terminology and culture and in the various formulae adopted by different theological schools to express the same matter.

Accordingly, we find today no real basis for the sad divisions and schisms that subsequently arose between us concerning the doctrine of Incarnation.

In words and life we confess the true doctrine concerning Christ our Lord, notwithstanding the differences in interpretation of such a doctrine which arose at the time of the Council of Chalcedon.[103]

Accordingly, for the balance of this book, the term Monophysite should be referenced in inverted commas as 'Monophysite', in respect for the oriental churches who appear to have been incorrectly characterized as heretic. However, the inverted commas have been deliberately left out for this book for logistical reasons only.

## 5.8 Beginnings of Rivalry between Rome and Constantinople

At the First Council of Constantinople in 381, a new nominal or titular patriarchate of Constantinople was established. The capital of the Empire was now Constantinople, the 'new' Rome. 'Old' Rome was not represented at the Council and it is understood initially refused to accept the appointment. At Chalcedon in 451, the Council elevated Constantinople to a fully-fledged patriarchate. The patriarch of Constantinople was declared an ecumenical patriarch. The papal legates and later the pope himself once again hesitated to acknowledge the canon of the Council. They saw the see of Constantinople as not Apostolic, unlike Antioch, Alexandria, and Rome. It was uncanonical and secular politics that Rome saw as bringing about its appointment.

---

[103] "Common Declaration of Pope John Paul II and His Holiness Mar Ignatius Zakka I Iwas," 23 June 1984, available at: http://www.vatican.va/roman_curia/pontifical_councils/chrstuni/anc-orient-chdocs/ rc_pc_ christuni_ doc_19840623_jp-ii-zakka-i_en.html.

Constantinople's claim was that it had bishops of the political capital, which justified its advancement: "It was as the emperor's bishops, as functionaries of the imperial Court, that they rose to the second place in Christendom."[104] The power of the See of Constantinople was instantly increased. At the same Council, Jerusalem was given a titular appointment as patriarchate, but only after protest. Constantinople gradually sought to have the other three Eastern patriarchates all unified under its authority to match the one great 'Western unity' under Old Rome.

The emperor was primarily responsible for making the See of Constantinople a centre to rival the capital. As the New Rome, Constantinople saw its patriarch as of equal status to that of the patriarch of Old Rome, and the West saw this as a continual attempt by the emperor's patriarch to become like an Eastern pope and a competing church to match the Western prototype. Old Rome overlooked that the patriarchates in the East were more numerous by virtue of the fact that their Christian populations far outnumbered that under the patriarchate of Rome. The Catholics in Rome may have feared this as the last step before the emperor would transfer all papal rights to the patriarch of the city where he held his court.

Rome, through the pope, tried to hinder Constantinople's new attempts at influence. The Byzantine bishops believed Rome's persistent opposition was unjustified. The emperor backed his bishops in Constantinople. The other Eastern patriarchs were weakened by the continual Monophysite disputes, with Alexandria and Antioch losing many of their flock. The Catholic bishops of Alexandria, Jerusalem, and Antioch could not prevent the growth of Constantinople and began to side with it. Hence, Rome became suspicious of the Middle Eastern Catholics.[105]

This brought about a new conflict for the Catholic Church during this early period of its history, not often reported or emphasised by

---

[104] Adrian Fortescue, "The Eastern Schism," in *The Catholic Encyclopedia*, Robert Appleton Company, 1912, available at: http://www.newadvent.org/cathen/13535a.htm.
[105] Ibid.

historians. The pope in Rome on the one side, and the Byzantine patriarch and emperor in Constantinople on the other, inevitably became opposed. Adrian Fortescue, writing in 1912 for *The Catholic Encyclopaedia*, declared this struggle and animosity would fester for the next six hundred years and become one of the fundamental causes for the great Christian schism between the East and West.[106]

## 5.9  Identity Conflict for Aramaic-Speaking Catholics

Following 451, the Catholic Aramaic-speaking Christians in the East were left in the lurch between two different rivalries. The first was the international religious conflict between the churches in Rome and Constantinople. The Aramaic-speaking Catholics were required to balance their loyalty between the two. The second rivalry related to a local and regional religious conflict between the recently formed independent Syriac Monophysite church and its counterpart in Egypt on the one hand, and the emperor and Catholic Church on the other. The Aramaic-speaking Catholics were required to establish protocols for coexistence with their fellow indigenous Monophysites. Simultaneously, Rome and Constantinople would have pressed upon them as Catholic indigenous to report breaches of the new Catholic doctrine.

The Monophysite church in Egypt was comprised of indigenous Coptics who mobilised as a nationalist church. The Christian minority in Egypt were the ethnic Greeks, principally located in Alexandria, and who dominated the official government positions. They shared the capital with the locals and, to a lesser extent, with other ethnicities and religions.

Some indigenous Egyptians might have remained Catholic, but it would not have been many. There were now two patriarchs of Alexandria. One was the Orthodox (Catholic, Melkite) patriarch who was of Greek-Byzantine ethnic ancestry. The other was the Coptic patriarch of indigenous Egyptian ancestry. As with Egypt, historians have generally painted a picture of the Middle East of the Syrian Orient as

---

[106] Ibid.

forming a nationalistic Monophysite church with a minority of Catholics, namely ethnic Greeks-Byzantines living in the city of Antioch (and scattered around other administrative cities), and a minority of Aramaic-Syriac speakers. This is a great misnomer as will be demonstrated in the following chapters of this book.

After the Council of Chalcedon in 451, a large Aramaic-speaking population of Syria, Phoenicia, Lebanon, and Palestine remained Catholic. They shared the same liturgy, culture, language, and land as the Syriac Monophysites. There was now one perceived theological difference that caused separation between them: whether Christ had one nature or two. The land of the patriarchate of Antioch became completely divided into two main religious Christian sects.

The Syriac Monophysites eventually established their own Syriac patriarch of Antioch shortly after 518. The Catholics remained under the leadership of the Catholic Orthodox (Melkite) patriarch of Antioch. The largest Christian minority in the Roman provinces – Syria I and II, Phoenicia I and II and Palestine I, II and III – were the ethnic Greeks-Byzantines principally in Antioch city and to a lesser extent in other administrative cities. They more than likely shared urban life in Antioch and other administrative cities with the native Aramaic-speakers who were both Catholic and Monophysite and the majority Christian population, and a minor amount of other ethnicities and religions.

Like Alexandria, the Greeks-Byzantines in Antioch city dominated the official government positions. The Catholic (pro-Chalcedon) patriarch of Alexandria led the ethnic Greek-Byzantines as its principal population. Unlike Alexandria, the Catholic (pro-Chalcedon) patriarch of Antioch led the indigenous Catholics as the majority and the ethnic Greek-Byzantine Catholics as the minority. Surely there would have been disagreements over the appointment of the patriarch of Antioch. The indigenous would have liked to see one of their own instated as patriarch. The emperor and patriarch of Constantinople would prefer an ethnic Greek or Byzantine.[107] The Monophysites likely dominated

---

[107] Further research would be useful to document the background of these appointments in the following two centuries.

Eastern Syria, including Mesopotamia and the Euphrates. It is suggested the Catholics formed a smaller part of this population.

Correspondence in the sixth century (dealt with in a later chapter) suggests the western regions of the Roman provinces of Syria, Phoenicia, and Palestine (closer to the Mediterranean coastline and its nearby mountain ranges), comprised significant Catholic populations. The western regions of these seven Roman provinces were roughly along the lines of the ancient Phoenician coast and mountains. The region ran from northern Syria through Lebanon to northern Palestine.

There is a general void in historical reference for this period regarding the Christians in the western regions between northern Syria and Egypt. There is virtually no mention or properly recorded history of the Christians of Lebanon, Phoenicia, and Palestine. Historians have conveniently categorised them as 'Syrian', as part of the previous three Roman ancient provinces of Syria that embodied the whole region. The capital of the patriarchate was Antioch and this was seen as the capital of ancient Syria. After the division of these three provinces into seven in the late fourth century, the practical reference continued that the whole region remained 'Syrian'.

Accordingly, ancient and modern historical accounts give little regard to the terms Phoenicia, Lebanon, and Palestine. In the context of the adherents to the Council of Chalcedon of 451, these historical accounts blend the Lebanese, Phoenicians, and Palestinians as Syrians and therefore Monophysite.[108] This book will support the proposition in the reverse, that is, these Christians in fact remained substantially Catholic and not Monophysite.

The Aramaic-speaking Catholics of the western regions of northern Palestine, Phoenicia and Lebanon were aligned with the Catholics of the western region of northern Syria. They all fell under the leadership of the Catholic pro-Chalcedon patriarch of Antioch. It is not clear after 451 how much influence Constantinople had over the Catholic

---

[108] Even as late as the 1800s, due to Ottoman rule, identification documents for migrants travelling from Lebanon and Palestine to the West reveals they were referred to as 'Syrians'.

patriarch of Jerusalem, as it appears initially the position was titular or nominal. Nonetheless, it would not have changed the view of Palestinian Catholic Christians who were previously led by the patriarch of Antioch until 451. It appears the newly formed patriarchate of Jerusalem, perhaps initially 'nominal', did not extend to the northern half of the western region of Palestine closer to the Lebanon mountain range. It seems this region remained under the patriarchate of Antioch.

The indigenous Aramaic-speaking Catholics were required to delicately balance their religious and day-to-day life around local, regional, and international conflicts. As previously mentioned they were required to establish a balance of loyalty between Rome and Constantinople. Additionally, they were obliged to readjust their life on their own soil in order to seek some form of harmonious co-existence with Christians who were deemed to be 'heretics', but who were their indigenous brothers and sisters.

The Aramaic Catholics could not have been nationalistic but rather needed to be universal in their Christian thinking. Their rationale was not limited to the Middle East, with Antioch as its capital. It extended further to the west in Constantinople with the emperor, and also further to the west again with Rome and the pope. Rome and Constantinople were sure to have been watching the Aramaic-speaking Catholics to confirm they upheld, and often perhaps, enforced the Empire's official Catholic teaching, not only amongst themselves but amongst the 'heretics'. It was inevitable the pope of Rome, the emperor and the patriarch of Constantinople would intervene in local affairs.

The balancing acts required of the Aramaic-speaking Catholics were fraught with danger. The risks could prove unsustainable if Rome, Constantinople, or the Syriac Monophysites became dissatisfied with their performance and relationships. Regardless, the Aramaic-speaking Catholics were left with no choice: they had to learn quickly how to best attempt to manage the fine balance. This may have given them a unique diplomatic skill in the East.

# CHAPTER 6

# THE FOUNDING OF ST MAROUN'S MONASTERY

## 6.1 The Geo-Political Context

St Maroun is currently the earliest recorded 'hypethrite' or ascetic living in the open air. It is not certain exactly where in the region of Cyrrhus, in northern Syria, St Maroun lived as a hermit. Nor is it certain which village settled with the body of St Maroun after his death and for which there was 'a great shrine' and regular 'public festival'. Both Butros Dau[109] and Abou Zayd[110] believe it was the neighbouring village of Brad or Barad in the surroundings of Kfar-Nabo, but there can be no certainty about this.

Christianity was well established in Cyrrhus (or Cyr), the capital of the large district of Cyrrhestica, by the time of the Council of Nicea in 325. The bishop of Cyrrhus claimed Christianity in this region had its beginnings with Simon the Zealot in the first century and housed a magnificent basilica holding the relics of saints Cosmos and Damien who died in 287.[111] By the early fifth century, Theodoret, as the newly elected bishop, inherited hundreds of churches as part of his bishopric in a small but seemingly densely populated diocese. There was not a single trace of heresy in any parish.

The region contained numerous monasteries and anchorites. Many of the anchorites in the region were hypethrites. Cyrrhus was a Roman

---

[109] Butros Dau, *History of the Maronites*, B. Dau, 1984.

[110] Shafiq AbouZayd, *Ihidayutha: A Study of the Life of Singleness in the Syrian Orient: From Ignatius of Antioch to Chalcedon 451 A.D.*, Aram Society for Syro-Mesopotamia Studies, p. 363.

[111] Naaman, *The Maronites*, p. 30.

administrative, military, and commercial centre on the trade route between Antioch and the Euphrates River crossing at Zeugma, leading to Edessa. In later times, it later lacked water, was overburdened with taxes and eventually its resources began to dry up and the population declined.[112]

Apamaea, further south in Syria, was on the Orontes River and adjacent to an immense lake with marshes. During the days of the Greek Empire, it was expanded to be the Seleucid military and revenue centre, and also fortified. The Seleucids had a stud farm there with 30,000 mares (female horses), 300 stallions (male horses) and 500 elephants. Later (after 395 AD) it was the capital of both the Syrian region of Apamaea and the Roman/Byzantine province of Syria Secunda.

Apamaea, about 88 kilometres north-west from Emesa (now Homs), was a metropolis on the intersection of many communication routes. The city may have reached a population of 500,000 at one point. It later became a centre for 'Chalcedonian' opposition to Monophysites in the sixth century, and to Severus of Antioch in particular.[113] Emesa was the metropolis of the Roman province of Lebanese Phoenicia. It lies about 85 kilometres north-east of Tripoli, Lebanon. It also is situated about 25 kilometres from the closest border to modern day Lebanon.

There were many other renowned religious devotees by the name of Maroun or Maron, including a superior of a monastery and a hermit. Naaman cites six others (including those mentioned in 1963 by Syrian Orthodox Patriarch Ignatius Jacob III) but confirms that none of these fit the dates of the St Maroun referred to by Theodoret.[114] Moosa further clouds the waters in his attempts to disconnect Theodoret's Maroun from any link to the Maronite Church.[115] His views will be dealt with in Chapter 7 of this book.

---

[112] Ibid., p. 29.

[113] See next Chapter of this book. Also confirmed by Naaman, *The Maronites*, p. 34.

[114] Naaman, *The Maronites*, pp. 20-21.

[115] Moosa, *The Maronites in History*.

## 6.2 The Monasteries of Marcian, Agapetus, and Simon, 350-400

Theodoret's third chapter of *Religious History* is devoted to Marcian or Marcianius (d. 380s) who was born into a rich and noble family in Cyrrhus around the first quarter of the fourth century. Marcian migrated south to Chalcis, about 86 kilometres north of Apamaea. Theodoret wrote that Marcian's disciples, Agapetus and Simon, later joined him to live in a community of many under his leadership in the "desert" of Chalcis. Theodoret tells us that the desert of Chalcis was a great centre of monastic life under the reign of Constans (337-50). Many ruins of monasteries are still found there today.[116]

By permission of Marcian, Eusebius became their superior. They lived in very small independent cells or huts, barely as large as the body, and surrounded by a fence. The cell was meant to cause continuous torment and Marcian said it was better to eat once per day in the evening for survival only, "for true fasting means continuous hunger."

Agapetus and Simon, as disciples of Marcian, later founded two monasteries in their names at Nikertai,[117] near Apamaea. One of the monasteries consisted of four hundred monks. They put into rules the practices of Marcian. Thereafter, so many hermitages aligned to the monasteries were established, says Theodoret, they were too numerous to count.

Theodoret writes in a chronological and regional order. Accordingly, it appears the two monasteries may have been either the first, or one of the earliest, cenobitic monasteries in the region of Apamaea. Accordingly, it is most likely they were the most distinguished amongst all monasteries in Syria Secunda until the founding of the monastery of Maroun in 452 by the emperor Marcian, as the following chapter of this book will demonstrate.[118]

In parts of Theodoret's passages about Marcian, we are given an

---

[116] Naaman, *The Maronites*, p. 39.

[117] Also known as Nicerte or Nicertae.

[118] See Chapter 7 for further detail. Naaman agrees, *The Maronites*, pp. 41-42.

insight into how the anchorites (hermits) formed into communities
of monks (cenobitic monasteries), which then provided a regulated
form of asceticism that continued to flourish, as the following extracts
show:

> This man had as his fatherland formerly Cyrrhus, which I
> mentioned above, and thereafter the desert; and leaving both
> the one and the other he now has heaven ...
>
> After some time past, he admitted two to live with him:
> Eusebius, who became the inheritor of this sacred cell; and
> Agapetus, who transplanted this angelic rule to the region of
> Apamaea. There is a large and populous village whose name
> is Nicerte. In it Agapetus founded two retreats of philosophy,
> one called after his own name and the other after that of the
> wondrous Symeon, who was conspicuous in this philosophy
> for a total of fifty years. In them there are living even today
> more than four hundred men, athletes of virtue and lovers of
> piety, purchasing heaven with their labours; the legislators of
> this way of life were Agapetus and Symeon, who received
> their laws from the great Marcianus. From these were planted
> innumerable other ascetic dwellings regulated by these laws,
> which is not easy to count; but the planter of them all was
> this inspired man, for he who provided the finest seed would
> fairly be called the cause of the good plants.
>
> At first, as I said, he lived in this voluntary prison on his
> own. Then when he admitted these two, he did not have them
> live with him; for the hut was not adequate for himself alone,
> been extremely small and causing him, whether sitting or re-
> clining, much discomfort: when standing he was unable to
> hold himself erect, since the roof made him bend his head and
> neck; nor when lying down could he stretch out his feet, since
> the cell did not have a length equal to his body. So he told
> them to build another one and bade them live there, singing
> hymns, praying, and reading the divine oracles on their own.
> When more people needed to share in this benefit, he ordered
> another dwelling to be built at a distance and bade those who
> wished to live there. Their teacher was Eusebius, who trans-

mitted the teaching of the great Marcianus. The great Agapetus, when he received the necessary training and exercise and
learned well this athletic skill, departed, as I said, and sowed
the seeds he had received from that godly soul. He became so
notable and celebrated he was counted worthy of an episcopal see, appointed to the charge of a flock and entrusted with
tending his own fatherland ... There came to him from his
fatherland his sister with her son, now a man and a leading
citizen of Cyrrhus ... His philosophy also profited the wonderful Basil who a long time later built his monastic dwelling
near Seleucobelus – it is a city of Syria (near Apamaea) ...

At this season, of course, all were eager to see him. On one
occasion the leading bishops assembled and came to him –
the great Flavian, entrusted with shepherding Antioch, the divine Acacius whom I mentioned above, Eusebius of Chalcis,
and Isidore, then entrusted with governing Cyrrhus – one of
them pre-eminent in virtue. And with them was Theodotus
who held the reins of Hieropolis, glorious for asceticism and
gentleness; present too were some councillors and officials
possessing the spark of the faith ...

Many everywhere built him burial shrines – in Cyrrhus his
nephew Alypius, in Chalcis a certain Zenobiana ... and not
a few others did the same thing, in competition to carry off
this victorious athlete ... (At his request, his body was hidden for fifty years until) each of the shrines mentioned above
had received remains, one of the Apostles (of Marcian) and
the other of martyrs, the heirs of his earthly tent and teaching
were now reassured.[119]

In the above passage, we see a monastic movement and development of rules entirely independent of the movement of the monks
from St Anthony the Great's Egypt. We also know that the monasteries in the Aramaic-speaking world were active and contemplative, in
contrast to the monasteries of St Anthony's Egypt, which appeared
primarily contemplative. We also know that Maroun, the first in his

---

[119] Theodoret, *A History of the Monks*, pp. 37-48.

region and perhaps globally to practise the Christian contemplative life in the open air, established a monastic practice not found in Egypt.

We are informed three monasteries were established from Marcian's inspiration. Two were established by Agapetus in Nikertai in the region of Apamaea, and another by Basil in the city of Seleucobelus near Apamaea. As we will detail in Chapter 7, we find correspondence in the years 517 and 518 referring to the monastery of the Blessed Agapetus, the monastery of the Blessed Basil, and a monastery in Nikertai. The letters clearly indicate these monasteries were later part of a network of monasteries led by the monastery of St Maroun, which was also in the Apamaea region. There can be little doubt, therefore, the monasteries of Agapetus and Basil referred to in this sixth century correspondence are the same monasteries referred to by Theodoret in this passage on Marcian.

The above passage provides direct evidence of monks becoming bishops, and likely patriarchs.[120] We know Theodoret himself was a monk at one of the Agapetus monasteries and later became a bishop. We are informed that Agapetus became a bishop (c. 388) and we know this was of the city of Apamaea.[121] Other monks Theodoret wrote about who came from this anchorite movement also became bishops – one example is Abraham (d. 420s), who preached in Lebanon, and was sent as bishop to the city of Carrhae in Mesopotamia to convert pagans.[122]

We have evidence of a delegation of bishops visiting the hermit Marcian. This included Flavian, bishop from Antioch and almost certainly the patriarch of Antioch. Other bishops came from across Syria including Cyrrhus. Throughout his writings on the thirty monks, Theodoret refers to fifteen different occasions of bishops visiting the hermit monks. It demonstrates not only the importance and influence,

---

[120] For example, see commentary in Chapter 7 on late sixth century Patriarch Flavian II (491-512), not to be confused with Bishop Flavian of Antioch (381-404) referred to by Theodoret.

[121] Theodoret, *A History of the Monks*, p. 47.

[122] Ibid., p. 122 and Price's footnote 1, p. 125.

but the interconnection of the anchorites and monastic movement to the most senior clergy of the Church. It is clear that these hermits remained faithful to the Church. The information also exhibits an organised, close network between senior clergy and monasteries throughout Syria, and likely the patriarchate.

When Theodoret wrote about the monks, it was not just those in his bishopric or see. Of the thirty monks, eight were still alive when he penned his works. Out of these eight monks,[123] it appears he personally visited all but one of them. Four were in Cyrrhus including Maroun's female disciple Domnina, two were in the region of Antioch including Simon Stylite, one in Gabala, and one in Beroea (Aleppo). Once again, this evidences the close relationship between bishops, as Theodoret had crossed over into other bishops' jurisdictions. Indeed, out of the thirty monks reported by Theodoret, only ten were in his jurisdiction of Cyrrhus.

The great importance and influence of the monks and monasteries did not lie only with senior clergy. We have evidence from the above passages of dignitaries and senior officials visiting these anchorite monks. It notes the significant value the senior civic members and officials of the Roman provinces in Syria placed upon the monks. This extended right through to the community as a whole as is noted by the passage relating to Marcian's relics.

Marcian insisted that his companions tell no one where they would bury him when he died. He did not want to be relocated to a prestigious shrine. We know St Anthony the Great in Egypt made the same request. The above extracts provide clear evidence of the popular culture that sought, and housed in shrines, the relics of the saintly anchorite monks. It is clear from Theodoret that shrines of one anchorite were not confined to one village or town; they were spread out in the region. Theodoret notes that even after fifty years from the passing of Marcian, communities were still seeking Marcian's relics.

These passages relating to Marcian provide us with a parallel in-

---

[123] Including Simon the Stylite and Domnina.

sight into what likely took place when Maroun passed away, a short number of decades after Marcian. This evidence presents the certainty of ecclesiastical and religious interconnection between the two Roman provinces of Syria I and II. This relationship was likely also maintained with the immediately adjoining provinces of First Phoenicia (Phoenicia I/Prima) and Phoenicia-Lebanon (Phoenicia II). The chapter on Marcian is but one example of the connection on the one hand in Syria I (in particular the regions of Antioch, Cyrrhus and Chalcis), and on the other in Syria II, in particular the region of Apamaea. Given the populations in this region were overwhelmingly Christian by this time, the religious connection extended to senior ranking civic offices as well as the lay faithful.

Marcian and his followers lived in individual and completely enclosed small cells. Maroun (d. 410-422) was a contemporary of Marcian. He took Marcian's anchorite living to an unprecedented level: it was the open air for Maroun, and no cell. A great 'garden' of anchorites followed Maroun. This included the most famous of them all, St Simon Stylite.

When reporting on Simon Stylite, Theodoret informs us that Simon Stylite entered the monastery of Eusebonas and Abibion (at Teleda) who were disciples of Eusebius, the latter very likely the disciple of Marcian. Simon spent ten years in this monastery. Theodoret reports that of the many monks from this monastery (who were not the active missionary type), Simon had "eighty fellow contestants and out shot all of them."[124] This contest may have applied not just to this one monastery but to dozens, even hundreds.

## 6.3   Female Anchorites, Convents, and Converts

For the first time, likely anywhere in the world, as we will discuss below, we see evidence of not only female hermits, but their existence living in the open air in conformity with Maroun's way of life and philosophy. Theodoret mentions many convents established as a

---

[124] Theodoret, *A History of the Monks*, Chapter 26.

result, each housing hundreds of nuns. As Theodoret instructs us, the open air living for monks and nuns was a heroic contest on a large scale. The history of Simon Stylite, and others Theodoret writes about, implies this practice was widespread amongst many monasteries and convents.

It was not just male monks and monasteries that dominated the landscape. On a number of occasions, Theodoret refers to convents housing nuns, including hermitages governed by the convent. He refers to them in the chapter on Maroun's disciple Domnina. It is clear that following Maroun's leadership, not only did Domnina receive a great many visitors, she set an example for the women who followed her. It seems she may have also founded one or more convents.

In the chapter on Domnina, the concluding chapter for Theodoret's thirty monks, the author praises her and her influence:

> Emulating the life of the inspired Maroun, whom we recalled above, the wonderful Domnina set up a small hut in the garden of her mother's house ...

> But how long can I expatiate in my eagerness to recall all her virtue, when I ought to bring into the open the life of the other women who have imitated both her and those we recalled above? For there are many others, of whom some have embraced the solitary life and others have preferred life with many companions – in such a way that communities of two hundred and fifty, or more, or less, share the same life, putting up with the same food, choosing to sleep on rushmats alone, assigning their hands to card wool, and consecrating their tongues with hymns.

In his concluding comments for that chapter, he gives us an insight into the monastic movement of men and women in the broader East:

> Myriad and defeating enumeration are the philosophical retreats of this kind not only in our region but throughout the East; full of them are Palestine, Egypt, Asia, Pontus, and all Europe. From the time when Christ the Master honoured virginity by being born of a virgin, nature has sprouted meadows

of virginity and offered these fragrant and unfading flowers to the Creator, not separating virtue into male and female nor dividing philosophy into two categories ...

As I have said, numerous are the pious wrestling schools of men and women not only amongst us but also in all Syria, Palestine, Cilicia, and Mesopotamia. In Egypt, it is said, some retreats have 5000 men each.[125]

It is in these comments we can conclude that all the East had flourishing monastic movements. As we have explained previously, ancient references prior to 395 that refer to 'Syria' meant the three ancient Roman Syrian Provinces I, II and III which included Palestine, Phoenicia, and First Syria (the latter housing Antioch city, the capital of the entire patriarchate). Theodoret refers to philosophical retreats of this kind not only in our region but *throughout* the East. If the recently formed provinces of First Phoenicia and Phoenicia Lebanon were to be excluded, he would have said so. It is suggested his reference to Palestine, and not Phoenicia and Lebanon, is of no consequence and merely an unintentional omission.

Theodoret tells us that Domnina had matched the heroic athleticism of others he reported on.[126] On another occasion, in the chapter on the monk Peter the Galatian, Theodoret informs us the athleticism of the male monks was equalled by the female nuns:

There was a certain debauchee, formerly a general. An unmarried girl of marriageable age, who had him as master, left behind her mother and family and fled to a convent that contained a company of athletes – for there are women who compete like men and enter the race course of virtue.[127]

In the chapter on Marana and Cyra, Theodoret once again gives us an insight into the female commitment to monastic life. He informs us these two women founded a small convent on the outskirts of Beroea

---

[125] Theodoret, *A History of the Monks*, p. 187.
[126] Ibid.
[127] Ibid., p. 86.

(Aleppo) and directed it from outside the convent whilst they continued to live in the open air.[128]

It is evident from Theodoret's description of these two female anchorite companions that they were not only from well-to-do families but independent and strong-minded women. It perhaps gives us an example of the free spirit of the women of this era. Theodoret begins his chapter on Marana and Cyra:

> After recording the way of life of the heroic men, I think it is useful to treat also of women who have contended no less if not more; for they are worthy of still greater praise, when, despite having a weak nature, they display the same zeal as the men and free their sex from its ancestral disgrace.
>
> At this point I shall retreat of Marana and Cyra, who have defeated all the others in the contests of endurance.[129]

We are told that these anchorites were from Beroea (Aleppo), they acquired a small place in front of the town after leaving their wealthy families. Their maidservants "were eager to share this life with them, they built a small dwelling outside this enclosure, and in this told them to live." Theodoret believed that the heroics of women anchorites not only matched that of males, but exceeded it.

## 6.4 Catholic Ecclesiastical and Monastic Links in the Patriarchate of Antioch

Given the background set out above coupled with the fact that "Maroun's fame circulated everywhere, attracted everyone from every side," demonstrated by the battle between three towns over his shrine, it is difficult to imagine how a great many of the monks and nuns of the region would not have spoken about Maroun. This equally applies to the senior religious and civic leaders, including Theodoret, as well as the lay population generally. Maroun was a pioneer who set the path for so many including the greatest athletic hero of them all, St Simon

---

[128] Ibid., p. 185.
[129] Ibid., p. 183.

Stylite. He also set the path, through his disciple Domnina, for a great many female anchorites living in the open air in what appears to be a movement that eventually established itself into the regulated living of hundreds of nuns in convents.

In the same way, it is also difficult to understand how St Simon Stylite would not have referred to St Maroun. St Simon belittled himself: to him, he was not worthy and would not have taken any credit for fame. In any event, he was not the pioneer monk of the open air. It is more likely than not that he would have mentioned the foundational practice master, Maroun. Theodoret wrote about Maroun as the first of his type, and Theodoret met with St Simon. Considering this milieu, it is almost unimaginable that St Simon and Theodoret would not have discussed Maroun.

Having personally witnessed many of Simon's miracles, Theodoret became familiar with the area in the vicinity of Simon's pillar. This was Telanissus (now Deir Seman or Qalat Seman not far from Aleppo). From his records we gain an insight into another form of religious organisation. In the chapter on Simon Stylite, Theodoret mentions Bassus as supervisor of well over two hundred disciples who were village priests. Bassus would attend on all of them in their parishes. He ordered them not to have any possessions or purchase any items or accept offerings of money, "but to live indoors and receive the food sent by divine grace."

Price refers to Bassus as having originated from Edessa and states that he was clearly a 'periodeutes', a priest or vicar with no fixed address who acted on behalf of the bishop to supervise rural clergy and their parishes.[130] It is not clear to what extent monasteries played a role in this administration or in servicing these village parishes. However, it is clear that the monasteries played a critical role in the ecclesiastical and religious practice of the Church. After both his parents passed away, Theodoret chose to live and study as a monk in one of the two monasteries founded by Agapetus at Nikertai in the Apamaea region. This was before he was, almost against his will, called away to be-

---

[130] Ibid., p. 174.

come bishop of Cyrrhus in 423. Agapetus himself became bishop of Apamaea in 388.

Naaman believes these foundations likely represent the start of the cenobitic movement in Syria Secunda following the moderate monastic rule of Marcian. The ascetic movement, he says, continued to flourish separately in the region of Cyrrhus with the inspiration of Maroun. Syria was not a single united territory. Aramaic-Syriac monasticism was not monolithic and unlike Greek monasticism did not have one single founder. Syria Secunda represented overtime a religious confederation of monasteries. Theodoret when referring to the number of hermitages or monasteries used the expression "almost beyond counting."

Although not applicable to the wider Aramaic-Syriac world, Naaman was of the view there was at least a confederation of monasteries between Syria Secunda/Apamaea area and the region of Cyrrhus as "it would otherwise be a remarkable coincidence that Theodoret was the only historian of these two monastic movements from northern Syria."[131] Theodoret was not only the historian of both monastic regions, he also personally visited the hermits or their shrines, and visited monasteries of both. He spent time at the celebrated monastery of Teleda, to the east of Antioch. He made repeated visits to a second monastery in Teleda where Simon just left before becoming the famous stylite. He lived and studied at the monastery in Nikertai near Apamaea. Naaman mentions other reasons for the confederation of monasteries including that Agapetus and Simon were both from Cyrrhus and that Cyrrhus – Chalcis – Apamaea went north to south on the same limestone massif as an archaeological unity. It should also be reiterated, the monk Marcian who settled in Apamaea was originally from Cyrrhus as well.

Theodoret chose Apamaea to study. Perhaps it offered a better chance of orthodoxy than the other centres of northern Syria. It was also the Aramaic-Syriac language capital of northern Syria. The intellectual life was possible living in the monastery under Marcian.[132]

---

[131] Naaman, *The Maronites*, p. 64.
[132] Ibid., p. 72.

Theodoret studied at the monastery of Agapetus less than fifty years after its foundation. It became a centre of learning. This fact alone validates the rapid progress and influence of monasticism at the time.

Theodoret informs us Simon, whilst in his monastery at Nikertai near Apamaea, had a combined delegation of leading bishops visit him. They were bishops from Antioch, Cyrrhus, Hierapolis, Cae-sarea (in Palestine), and Chalcis. They attended with councillors and political officials. This provides weight to the importance the Church placed on establishing and maintaining a confederation of monaster-ies and religious in the Syrian region. It also allows us to suggest this monastery in Apamaea may have been a leader in the Syrian network at least fifty years before the founding of Beit (House of) Maroun. It can be no accident, therefore, that Theodoret chose to spend time in the region of Apamaea because of its leadership. Decades later, he must have influenced his fellow religious and bishops for as it is pro-posed by Naaman, it was he who was to influence the Emperor Mar-cian in founding Beit Maroun in Apamaea, and for it to become the lead monastery.

Price refers to Simon (Symeon) from the monastery at Apamaea as presumably the "priest and monk of the territory of Apamea" who was an ally of John Chrysostom and from whom Simon received an extant letter (Ep. 55) around 405. As Chrysostom was particularly interested in Phoenicia, this further supports the proposition in previous chap-ters that Phoenicia, Lebanon (and Palestine) was an important part of the Church's interlink with Syria including Antioch, Cyrrhus, and Apamaea. It also provides support for the proposition that St John Chrysostom wrote to Theodoret's Maroun.

Theodoret was not bishop of Apamaea, though formerly lived in a monastery of the region and also met and wrote about its anchorites and monasteries. It does not follow anchorites and monasteries were not in existence in Phoenicia, Lebanon, and Palestine – as noted above, Theodoret's comments clearly suggest otherwise – it is only that, as discussed in Chapter 5, we do not have a 'Theodoret of Lebanon' (and for that matter a 'Theodoret of Palestine'). Northern Syria was the centre and focus of the anchorite and cenobitic monastic movement by the Church. It was closer to Antioch, the patriarchate's capital.

Perhaps the Aramaic-speaking anchorites and monasteries in other areas may have been less in number. However, this cannot be certain because of historical silence compounded by our inability to locate relevant ancient sources. Perhaps Theodoret left any recordings of anchorites in the region of Phoenicia, Lebanon, and Palestine to some other historian or member of the Church. These regions were a far distance from him, and maybe it was only that the great athletic heroes of the monks of Cyrrhus and Apamaea who set the scene for the fame of the open-air living that drew the special attention. But perhaps it was the centre where the Syrian style of cenobitic monastic living was established.

Naaman's conclusion relating to the confederation of monasteries and monks between Cyrrhus and Apamaea must be correct. However, although it was not relevant to Naaman's study at the time, it will be suggested in the following chapter the region of confederation is likely to have eventually extended to include other areas of the western regions of the provinces of Phoenicia, Phoenicia Lebanon, and Palestine.

Importantly, Theodoret documents Syrian anchorites principally in the regions of Cyrrhus, Apamaea, and Antioch. These included six monasteries in Antioch (founded c. 330-400), two in Cyrrhus (founded 365-390), one in Chalcis, three in Apamaea, and a convent in Aleppo (founded 360-420). However, he also mentions cenobitic monasteries in Osrhoene, Mesopotania (founded c. 320), at Zeugma in the Euphrates (founded c. 350),[133] and as we have seen above, one in Egypt that housed five thousand monks. Although Price states Theodoret was not comprehensive in his list of monks and monasteries, Naaman concludes this was no accident for the region of Cyrrhus and Apamaea as the hermits Theordoret wrote about followed the Antiochian plan and principles relating to the dual physical nature of Christ and "it was this

---

[133] Price, "Introduction," *A History of the Monks.*

same region which was later to become the first cradle of those who were to be called 'Maronites'."[134]

As mentioned previously, Aramaic-Syriac monasticism was a different type of cenobitic monasticism than the Greek and Egyptian practice that followed St Anthony. The Aramaic version would likely have been one in which a monk's life was not only contemplative and inward, away from the world, but missionary and outward, in full communion with the community around it or the community that would establish itself around it. The Aramaic hermits received not only visitors but great crowds, and not at their invitation or pleasure.

By the fourth century at the latest, we begin to see evidence of Aramaic anchorites attached to a monastery. This practice seems to have been first founded by Agapetus and Simon in memory of Marcian. One of their two monasteries at Nikertai near Apamaea was likely to become the leading monasteries in a network of monasteries in Syria.

## 6.5   The Monastery of St Maroun

### 6.5.1   Primary Sources for the Beit Maroun Monastery

Maronite tradition holds that a monastery known as Beit Maroun was built in memory of St Maroun near to Apamaea, in 452, not long after his death in 410-423 AD. Dib, Maronite Bishop of Cairo from 1946, writing in his *History of the Maronite Church* believed the disciples who united around Maroun founded the monastery of St Maroun near to the church (shrine) built in honour of the Saint. He assumes the monastery (and by implication the church housing the shrine) was situated near Apamaea:

> the monastery was situated near the church built in honour of the Saint. Otherwise, it would be difficult to explain why nothing is said sooner about the church which, according to Theodoret, had become a place of pilgrimage. If, on the contrary, we consider the church as a joined to the monastery, the

---

[134] Naaman, *The Maronites*, p. 64.

documents speaking about the latter would have no need to make special mention of the church.[135]

Theodoret completed his writing around 445. He made no mention of where St Maroun's 'shrine' was located. It is more likely it was in Cyrrhus rather than Apamaea as the three disciples of Maroun quoted by Theodoret (James, Limnaeus, and Domnina) were all from Cyrrhus and Maroun "planted for God the garden that now flourishes in the region of Cyrrhus." Dib also informs us that the Arab historian Abu l-Fida (d. 1331) stated the Emperor Marcian expanded the monastery in the second year of his reign, that is, in 452.[136] Dib does not appear to cite the original manuscript of Abu l-Fida, relying on a citation by another author. However, the details of the founding remain uncertain.

Maronite scholar, Abbott Paul Naaman, whose works were translated into English in 2009, believed the foundation date of St Maroun's monastery to be 452. He does not refer to Dib, and offers a differing construction date. Rather than an 'expansion' of the monastery in 452, Naaman believes Abu l-Fida wrote 452 as its foundation date. Vööbus, writing in the 1960s, a leading authority on monasticism in the Syrian orient during this period, interprets the text in the same way as Naaman. As Naaman appears to have cited a copy of the original Arabic manuscript – his translation is adopted for this study.[137] Brock confirms that it is generally accepted the Maronite Church gained its name from the monastery of Mar Maroun founded in 452 by the Emperor Marcian and that thereafter they "were strong defenders of the Chalcedonian doctrinal position against the attacks of the Monophysite opponents of the Council."[138]

---

[135] Dib, *History of the Maronite Church*, p. 4.

[136] Ibid., p. 6.

[137] Translation in Naaman, *The Maronites*, p. 1.

[138] Brock, *Syriac Perspectives on Late Antiquity*, Variorum, 1984, p. 69. In the same citation, Brock states "the theory that the Maronites derive from converts from Monophysitism made by Heraclius in the early 630s rests on a misunderstanding of a passage in Michael the Syrian." See also Brock, *An Introduction to Syriac Studies*, Gorgias Press, 2006, p. 70 and Brock et al., *Gorgias Encyclopaedia Dictionary of the Syriac Heritage*, Gorgias, 2011, under "Maronite."

In 451, the Council of Chalcedon legislated in the Church for the first time rules concerning the founding and establishment of monasteries:

> We have given orders that no one should build a monastery without the approval of the bishop of the region and the owner of the land. We once again remind the monks of the cities and those of the countryside that they should submit to their bishop and that their life is above all a life of peace, fasting and prayer, having nothing to do with the affairs of the State and of the Church.

This rule of the Church was also meant to maintain order, peace and orthodoxy. It notes and confirms all monasteries in the Catholic Church in ancient Christian times from this period were not independent of, but were subject to, the authority of the bishops.

On 28 July 452, the Emperor Marcian issued a strong decree against the monks and followers of Eutychius (directed at the Greek-speaking Monophysite monks) banning them from holding any meeting, building any monastery or living together in monasteries. It was also directed against the Aramaic-Syriac-speaking monks, including those led by Barsauma, Bishop of Nisibis in the eastern Syrian Orient.

The only document that mentions a specific date for the founding of Beit Maroun monastery in the fifth century is from the Arab historian Abu l-Fida (1273-1331) who states in his *Universal History* that during "the second year of his reign, the emperor Marcian (451-57) built the monastery of Maroun in Homs."[139] Abu l-Fida was governor of Hama district during the early fourteenth century. This encompassed an extensive area of northern Syria including Apamaea in the region of which the monastery once stood. Abu l-Fida is the only ancient Arab historian to attribute the origin of St Maroun's monastery to the fifth century.

---

[139] Naaman, *The Maronites*, pp. 1-2 citing the original manuscript in the Royal Library of Paris acknowledging the work of the German scholar Henry Fleischer who translated the work into Latin.

Naaman appears to be the first scholar in Maronite history to fully analyse this citation from l-Fida and dedicates the first chapter of his work to verifying its authority. Naaman provides a thorough scholarly analysis to demonstrate the error of all other historians who date the foundation of Beit Maroun monastery to the reign of the Emperor Maurice (582-602). The leading sources for this error are the Arab historians Ibn al-Atir (839-923) and al-Masudi (d. 956). Al-Masudi (who may have relied on Ibn al-Atir) wrote:

> The twentieth was Maurice, who reigned twenty years and four months. Under his rule there appeared a man of the town of Hamat, in the province of Emesa, called Maroun, to whom the Maronite Christians at our time of writing trace their origin. This sect is famous in Syria and elsewhere. Most of its members live in Mount Lebanon and Mount Sanir at Emesa and in the districts depending on them, like those of Hamat, of Chaizar, of Maarat-al-Noman.
>
> Maroun had a great monastery, which bears his name, to the east of Hamat and of Chaizar, composed of an immense building, surrounded by three hundred cells where the monks lodged. This monastery possessed in the form of gold, of silver and of jewels considerable wealth. It was devastated together with all the cells that surrounded it following the repeated incursions of the Bedouins and the violent actions of the Sultan. It rose near the river Orontes, river of Emessa and Antioch.[140]

Abu l-Fida significantly relies on these two historians in his works. However, when he wrote about the Emperor Maurice, he ignored them. Instead, he agreed with other numerous ancient and authentic documents he had before him that spoke of the monastery as having been founded long before the reign of Maurice. Naaman concludes by doing so, Abu l-Fida accepts Maronite tradition identifying Theodoret's Maroun as the patron of the monastery of Beit Maroun which was later to become the cradle of the Maronite Antiochian Church.[141]

---

[140] Quoted in Naaman, *The Maronites*, p. 173.
[141] Ibid., p. 8.

Naaman indicates that Abu l-Fida was quite precise when determining dates of events related to his region as governor. Accordingly as Dib details, the reliance on Ibn al-Atir (839-923) and al-Masudi (d. 956) by many authors since is an error recognised by historians who cannot be sympathetic to the Maronite cause.[142] It follows then that Maronite tradition should hold firm.

Naaman does not refer to *The Annals of Melkite Patriarch Eutychius* written c. 933-940. Nonetheless, it appears reliance was either on Ibn al-Atir who preceded him or some other source that both Eutychius and Ibn al-Atir had cited. The relevant passage of Eutychius states:

> At the time of Maurice, Emperor of the Romans (582-602), there was a monk named Maron, who affirmed in our Lord Christ two natures but one will, one operation, and one person, and who corrupted the faith of men. Many of those who partook of this doctrine and declared themselves as his disciples were from the town of Hama, of Qennesrin, and of Al-'Awasim ... The followers of his doctrine were called Maronites, from the name Maron. At the death of Maron, the inhabitants of Hama built a monastery at Hama, called it Dair Maron and professed the faith of Maron.[143]

Eutychius makes three fundamental errors. First, as will be demonstrated in Chapter 7 of this book, correspondence in 592 AD confirms Beit Maroun had been in existence for some time prior to the reign of Maurice and in fact more than one hundred years before his reign. Second, as will be demonstrated in Chapter 9, the doctrine of two natures and one will (Monothelitism) was not introduced until 638 AD, well after the end of the reign of Maurice. Third, there is no evidence of a Maroun in this period for which a monastery was built after him.[144]

Perhaps there was confusion between the names Marcian and Mau-

---

[142] Dib, *History of the Maronites.*

[143] Eutychius, *Eutychii Annales*, trans. by Aubrey Stewart, Palestine Pilgrims Text Society, 1895, pp. 57-59.

[144] Dib also discusses Eutychius' passage, see *History of the Maronites*, pp. 31-33.

rice, so that when one historian copied from the next the incorrect attribution of the period to the later emperor continued. Another explanation for the inaccuracy of these quotations may relate to the period of the reign of Maurice. Perhaps there was some event during his reign when the term Maronite was first mentioned. If so, one historian writing centuries later sought to give some explanation and the other historians repeated this assertion. We cannot be sure, but will now turn to the period under Maurice (578-602) for investigation.

Correspondence between Maronites and Jacobites in 592 (set out in Chapter 7) is the earliest available source for the use of the word 'Maronite'. The date clearly fits within the period of the reign of Maurice. It might be that the historian looked for some explanation for the term Maronite around this time but was completely mistaken not only as to the timing of the construction of the monastery, which was at least a century earlier, but also the Monothelite controversy which was half a century later. This is another plausible explanation, but once again is not certain.

Seeking other explanations, perhaps there was some event during the period of Maurice that can assist. John IV was the first Patriarch of Constantinople (582-595) to officially call himself the 'ecumenical patriarch' in documents.[145] This title refers to a universal patriarch and seeks to elevate the bishop of Constantinople to at least equal, or superior, to the bishop of Rome. Any reference to the title for Constantinople had been officially refused by Rome. It had been drafted as the third canon of the Second Ecumenical Council (First Council of Constantinople) in 381 and the twenty-eighth canon of the Fourth Ecumenical Council at Chalcedon in 451.

Pope Pelagius II (579-590) protested and forbade his legate at Constantinople to communicate with John.[146] Pope Gregory (590-604) protested vehemently against the use of the title in long

---

[145] Adrian Fortescue, "John the Faster, and Maurice," in *The Catholic Encyclopedia*, Robert Appleton Company, 1910, available at: http://www.newadvent.org/cathen/08493a.htm.

[146] Ibid.

correspondence addressed first to John, then to the Emperor Maurice, the Empress Constantina, and others. There was also another dispute between John and Gregory. It related to the relics of the head of St Paul. The Court of Constantinople requested it from the pope. Gregory refused and eventually sent part of St Paul's chains.[147] Given the allegiance of the Beit Maroun network to Rome over Constantinople during the Acacian Schism of 471-518, perhaps this was another period of expression of allegiance.

The most remarkable of these available documentary events during the reign of Maurice was therefore the correspondence between the Maronites and Jacobites in 592. There is also a profound contradiction that Eutychius failed to mention: Pope Honorius and the Byzantine emperor decreed the doctrine of Monothelitism; Constantinopolitans and many emperors, as well Eutychius' own predecessor patriarchs of Alexandria, were Monothelite from 638 until 750 and well after the condemnation of it by the Sixth Council in 680-81.[148]

### 6.5.2  The Name 'St Maroun' and the Location of the Monastery

As mentioned earlier, the fame of Abraham of Cyrrhus led Emperor Theodosius (408-450) to summon him. When Abraham arrived, the Emperor found him honourable in his humility, and the empresses made supplications to him, even though he did not speak Greek. In addition to Theodoret's account about Abraham's visit to the emperor, it is reasonable to suggest Abraham possibly mentioned to the emperor, and his sister Pulcheria (the future wife of Emperor Marcian), the memory of St Maroun and others that continued in Cyrrhus, Apamaea, and Lebanon. If so, it is possible Pulcheria's husband Marcian, who succeeded her brother as Emperor, was influenced by the news.

But why would Marcian have built a monastery to St Maroun? As Naaman opines, Marcian was conscious of his dignity as Orthodox Emperor and responsibility for success of the Council of Chalcedon.[149]

---

[147] Ibid.
[148] See Chapter 9 of this book for details.
[149] Naaman, *The Maronites*, p. 13.

Sozomenes, a Greek Christian historian of the time, said Marcian's wife Pulcheria helped build so many churches and monasteries it would take "too long" to document, noting this "pious princess" left rents and revenues for the monks as well.[150] The Council of Chalcedon declared the emperor Marcian the new Constantine and Pulcheria the new Helena and called them "the torch bearers of the orthodox faith."

But as Naaman states, Theodoret himself played the pivotal role in the founding of the monastery of Maroun: he was a former monk at Nikertai (in Apamaea region) both as a young student and later in exile; he was the chief of the 'Eastern party' (Orthodox); the champion of Antioch; the author of *Religious History;* the great victor at Chalcedon in 451; and the friend of the Emperor Marcian and Bishop Domnus of Apamaea. As the Bishop of Cyrrhus, he was in regular contact with the disciples of Maroun in Cyrrhus and the monks from the region of Apamaea. He spent twenty-six months in exile with the monks of Nikertai (about five kilometres to the south of Apamaea). This background allowed him to plan with the monks this new construction.[151]

Theodoret had written to John, Bishop of Germanica, in early 451 that "once the lies have been refuted and truth has triumphed, we propose to flee the worries of affairs *running the bishoporic* and return quickly to the quiet life that is so dear to us." Convincing Emperor Marcian to build such a significant monastery may have meant an intention for Theodoret to retire there. Naaman states that we do not know where Theodoret ended his life having died between 458 and 466, but most think it would have been in one of the monasteries of Apamaea. Given no documents mention the monks of Cyrrhus after Chalcedon or Theodoret's return to Cyrrhus (including no mention by any of his biographers) this may also imply the monks of Cyrrhus moved to Apamaea with Theodoret.[152]

The consensus amongst scholars is that Maroun was the founder

---

[150] Quoted in Ibid., p. 11.
[151] Ibid., pp. 67, 113.
[152] Ibid., pp. 114-115, 129.

of anchorite life in the open air. Even St Simon the Stylite imitated St Maroun's way of life. The movement following Maroun of Cyrrhus flourished everywhere, as Theodoret mentioned, and it must have been significant enough in Cyrrhus to warrant a shrine and church in the region and later a monastery, Beit Maroun, in Apamaea. Apamaea was the town particularly distinguished by its purity of patriotism to the Church. It was a diverse multicultural society, the capital of Syria Secunda. Unlike Antioch, Aramaic culture in Apamaea prevailed over Hellenic culture. It was also a link between the Aramaic-speaking natives of Cyrrhus, Antioch, and Apamaea to form the seat of a solidly united group. Naaman concludes regarding Beit Maroun that its objective,

> was the defence of the Chalcedonian doctrine elaborated by the work of the Antiochians, especially that of Theodoret himself ... The bishops of Apamaea practised the same well-defined religious policy as approved and defended by Theodoret. Among these bishops, special mention should be made of Polychronius, brother of the founder of the School of Antioch, Theodore of Mopseustia. Shortly after its founding, the new monastery flourished to such an extent that all the other monasteries of Chalcedonian Syria admitted its supremacy. It was as Arthur Vööbus, historian of Eastern monasticism, wrote, a solid and impregnable citadel of the Catholic doctrine as defined by the Council of Chalcedon ...

> The monastery of Beit Maroun was founded near Nikertai, in the middle of a religious confederation dear to Theodoret, in a region which offered him, more than any other centre of northern Syria, opportunities for orthodoxy.[153]

As we will examine in the next chapter, an exchange of letters in 517 involving the monks of St Maroun's monastery provide us with more important conclusions. Naaman is succinct in his summary:

> In 517, only 65 years after its foundation, the monastery of St Maroun was already a hive of activity with daughter houses. Thirty monasteries owed to it their origin, setting up

---

[153] Ibid., pp. 126-129.

and organising into a beautifully structured religious order. It is worth noting that all these monasteries were to be found in Syria Secunda, and none were far from Apamaea. All of them acknowledge the leadership of the monastery of St Maroun and conform to its directives. In spite of being more ancient than the monastery of St Maroun, the two monasteries founded respectively by Simon and Agapetus, disciples of the hermit Marcian, who was a contemporary of St Maroun, align themselves with it.[154]

It would be no coincidence then that this monastery "had a well-organised and well-managed library, with two monks in charge of its organization."[155] The relics of St Maroun, or some of his relics, would likely have been transferred about 150 kilometres south to the monastery of Beit Maroun from the church in Cyrrhus region where the body was originally housed.

Regarding the location, Abu l-Fida referred to Homs and not Apamaea. However, Naaman explains that under Islamic rule, Homs was the district for all of northern Syria including the cities of Apamaea, Epiphania (Hama) and Schaizar as far as Chalcis (Qinnisrin). A reference to 'Homs' meant in the region of Homs. This is the same as a reference in ancient documents to 'Apamaea' meaning not just its city but its broader region, or Antioch, often referring to the patriarchate rather than the city. In addition, Naaman also states that of all the surviving ancient documents that mention the monastery of St Maroun, none refer to a monastery in Homs and all agree on locating it in the region of Apamaea and therefore in Syria Secunda, not Syria Prima.[156] The exchange of correspondence in the next chapter deals with many of those documents.

In terms of the geographical context of the monastery today Naaman suggests that it could be places "between Khan Seikhun and Ma'rrat en No'man [where] the ancient site of 'Hirbet Mairun', now

---

[154] Ibid., p. 131.

[155] Ibid., citing the British Museum manuscript add.17.169.

[156] Ibid., pp. 15, 16.

abandoned, is to be found," asking: "Is it possible these ruins are those of the great monastery of Maron described by al-Masudi?"[157] Naaman states the monastery could be somewhere between Apamaea city and Homs city (about 88 kilometres apart) and could have been affiliated to either city but not dependent on any city or village.[158] At the time of the Arab historians' writings many centuries later, the monastery was in ruins and they could speak of it as near either city.

Naaman concludes that although the following hypothesis has a considerable degree of probability, the present means do not allow its verification: "We know that the collection of ruins of an ancient monastery, thought to have been the monastery of Saint Maron, lies near an ancient village called Kaphra Toba. Do we have the grounds for identifying Kaphra Rehima with Kaphra Toba?"[159] There have been many theories from varying authors, Maronite and non-Maronite, about the location of the ancient monastery of Beit Maroun, but its location is still yet to be determined.

---

[157] Ibid., pp. 35-36.
[158] Ibid., p. 18.
[159] Ibid., p. 133.

# CHAPTER 7

# BEIT MAROUN LEADERSHIP IN THE SIXTH CENTURY

## Timeline of Key Dates

| | |
|---|---|
| 440-461 | Reign of Pope Leo I whose theology led to the issuing of the document the 'Tome of Leo', the major foundation for the decree of the Ecumenical Council of Chalcedon in 451 relating to the two natures of Christ. |
| 461-523 | All popes are pro-Chalcedon. |
| 470-488 | Patriarch of Antioch, Peter 'the Fuller', a Monophysite. |
| 471-518 | Acacian Schism between Rome (pro-Chalcedon) and Constantinople (anti-Chalcedon). |
| 474-491 | Emperor Zeno the Isaurian, a Monophysite and the first eastern Roman emperor. |
| 482 | Acacius, Patriarch of Constantinople and Byzantine emperor, Zeno, release the Henotikon, an instrument of union to win back the Monophysites. |
| 491-512 | Patriarch of Antioch, Flavian, thought to be Monophysite but was deposed for failing to condemn Chalcedon. |
| 491-518 | Eastern Roman Emperor Anastasius I, a Monophysite. |
| 511-512 | Fighting raged between Chalcedonian and Monophysite monks in Constantinople and Antioch. |
| 512-518 | 512-518 Patriarch of Antioch, Severus, a Monophysite, likely appointed with support of Emperor Anastasius I. |
| 517 | Massacre of 350 monks from Beit Maroun. |
| 517-518 | Petitions to Pope Hormisdas from monks of Beit Maroun and Syria Secunda. |
| 518 | Syria Secunda Bishops Synod. |
| 518-527 | Eastern Roman Emperor Justin I, pro-Chalcedon. |
| 536 | Council of Constantinople, Beit Maroun monks in attendance. |
| 591 | Conference in Antioch with Beit Maroun monks and Jacobites in attendance. |
| 592 | Correspondence between Beit Maroun monks and Jacobites, first use of the term 'Maronite'. |

## 7.1 Geography and Ecclesiastics of the Patriarchate of Antioch

The patriarchate of Antioch embraced the entire East including parts of Asia. However, the Roman Byzantine Empire ruled only part of the patriarchate to its west. The Persian Empire and others ruled the remainder. The patriarchate territory of Antioch to its west included the following Roman Byzantine Empire provinces and their capitals (before the establishment of the patriarchate of Jerusalem in 451):

- in modern day southern Turkey: Isauria (capital Seleucea, now Silifke); Cilicia I (capital Tarsus, remains Tarsus); Cilicia II (capital Anazarbus, now Cukurova); Euphratensis (capital Heirapolis, now Pamukkale); Osrhoene (capital Edessa, now Sanliurfa); Mesopotamia (capital Amida, now Diyarbakir);

- principally in modern day Syria: Syria I or Prima (capital Antiochia, now Antakya in Turkey bordering Syria); Syria II or Secunda (capital Apamea, about 55 kilometres from Hama); Phoenice II or Phoenice Libanensis (capital Emesa, now Homs);

- Principally in modern day Lebanon but including part of northern Israel and northern Syria: Phoenicia I or Prima;

- in modern day Jordan, Syria, Israel and the Palestinian territories: Palestina I (capital Caesarea, remains Caesarea in northern Israel); Palestina II (capital Bostra, now Bosra in Syria);

- in modern day Jordan and Egypt: Palestina III (capital Petra, remains Petra in Jordan);

- the island of Cyprus, with its capital Constantia (now Salamis in modern day Cyprus).

(Note, refer to Map 2 in Chapter 1). There are many ancient episcopal sees (jurisdiction of bishops) that are no longer in operation but remain titular sees. The *Annuario Pontificio* lists them, and some of those for the patriarchate of Antioch are now listed below. They do not include episcopal sees that still exist such as Beirut and Damascus. The list is not extensive as other episcopal sees are found in ancient chronicles such as Paltas in First Syria whose bishop was present at the Synod of Sidon in First Phoenicia in 512 and was sent into exile with Flavian, Patriarch of Antioch. This information and the lists below provide useful background information to the struggles between the bishops and Patriarch Severus between 512-518.

Ancient episcopal sees of the late Roman province of Syria Prima (I) listed in the *Annuario Pontificio* as titular sees (i.e. no longer operating as a diocese under a bishop) are ten in total:

- Anasartha (Khanasir);
- Bascusus (Baquza);
- Beroea (Aleppo);
- Chalcis in Syria (Qinnasrin);
- Gabala (Jableh);
- Gabula (at the marsh of Al-Jabbul);
- Gindarus (Jandairis);
- Laodicea in Syria (Latakia);
- Salamias (Salamiyah);
- Seleucia Pieria.

Ancient episcopal sees of the late Roman province of Syria Secunda (II) listed in the *Annuario Pontificio* as titular sees (no longer) are eight in total:

- Apamea in Syria, Metropolitan Archdiocese;
- Arethusa (Al-Rastan);
- Balanea (Baniyas);
- Epiphania in Syria (Hama);
- Larissa in Syria (Shaizar);
- Mariamma (Krak des Chevaliers);
- Raphanea;
- Seleucobelus (Seleucopolis).

Ancient episcopal sees of Phoenica Prima (I), as they are listed in the *Annuario Pontificio* as titular sees (no longer) are fourteen in total:

- Antarados;
- Aradus;
- Arca in Phoenicia;
- Botrys;
- Byblus;
- Caesarea Philippi;
- Orthosias in Phoenicia;
- Porphyreon;
- Ptolemais in Phoenicia;
- Rachlea;
- Sarepta;
- Sidon;
- Tyre, Metropolitan Archbishopric;
- Tripolis in Phoenicia.

Beirut was likely a metropolitan archdiocese as well.

Ancient Episcopal sees of Phoenica Secunda/Lebanon (II), as they are listed in the *Annuario Pontificio* as titular sees (no longer are) eleven in total:

- Abila Lysaniae;
- Chonochora (Qara);
- Corada;
- Danaba;
- Euroea in Phoenicia;
- Heliopolis in Phoenicia (Baalbek);
- Emesa (Homs), Metropolitan Archbishopric;
- Iabruda (Yabrud);
- Laodicea ad Libanum;
- Palmyra;
- Damascus, Metropolitan Archdiocese.

For the two Syrian and two Phoenician provinces, there are approximately forty-four ancient sees now titular. There are an additional number that have carried through to the present including Damascus, Beirut and perhaps others. Before 451, there were three Palestinian provinces under the patriarchate of Antioch as listed above. It is estimated there would be approximately thirty ancient episcopal sees for the Palestinian provinces. The present book has not allowed the time to ascertain clearly if all or some of the dioceses under Antioch were transferred to the patriarchate of Jerusalem and the exact nature of jurisdictional borders.

First Phoenicia was known as 'Phoenice I' or 'Phoenicia Prima'. It included the territory from the coast to the peaks of Mount Lebanon on its coastal side. Its capital and metropolis was Tyre. It included most of ancient Phoenicia. To the north it ran to Gabala (modern day Jableh in Syria) on the coast, about in line with Apamaea city inland. To the south it ran to Dora, just north of coastal Caesarea city (modern day Israel).

Second Phoenicia was known as Phoenicia Lebanon ('Phoenice II' or 'Phoenice Libanensis'). Its capital was Emesa on the Orontes River, now Homs in Syria just north of the present Lebanese border. It was about 50 kilometres south of the Syria Secunda city of Epiphania (modern Hama in Syria). Epiphania was also about 50 kilometres south east of Apamaea. Phoenicia Lebanon province embraced the Bekaa Valley, ante-Lebanon mountain, Damascus, Palmyra, and most of southern and central modern day Syria.

Syria Prima province included the cities of Antioch, Beroea (now Aleppo) and Chalcis. Antioch city to its north was the capital of Syria Prima and of the patriarchate and lied on the Orontes River. The patriarch resided in the capital. The province ran coastal south to Gabala (modern day Jableh in Syria). Antioch and Apamaea were about 75 kilometres apart. Apamaea ('Afamiyya' in Aramaic-Syriac and Arabic) was the capital and metropolis of Syria Secunda and had a metropolitan archbishop. It was the largest city of Aramaic speakers in Syria. It also lay on the Orontes River.

The four metropolitan archbishops of the Syrian and Phoenician provinces were those of Apamaea, Tyre, Emesa, and Damascus. The many bishops of each of these cities were under the governance of the metropolitan archbishop. It demonstrates the large populations of these cities at the time. The patriarch of Antioch was likely the metropolitan archbishop of Antioch as well.

## 7.2 The 'Acacian Schism' between Rome and Constantinople

As we have discussed in Chapter 5 of this book, tensions between Rome and Constantinople started to increase after the Council of Chalcedon in 451 with the rise of the influence of the emperor and patriarch of Constantinople. At the same time, the relationship between the Egyptian and Syriac Monophysites on the one hand, and the emperor and Catholic Church on the other, was proving volatile. Between 471 and 518, a schism occurred between the churches of Rome and Constantinople known as the Acacian Schism.

This Schism followed the appointment of Acacius as patriarch of Constantinople in 471. Influenced by the teaching of Timothy, a Monophysite patriarch of Alexandria, Acacius drew up a document as a creed and an instrument of reunion. It was known as the *Henotikon* or 'instrument of union', and was designed to win back the Monophysites. It stated, "Christ is God and man, one, not two. His miracles and Passion are works of one."[160] The *Henotikon* was considered by Rome to be Monophysite and was directed to the Monophysite factions of Egypt and the Middle East as a compromise for reunion with the Catholic Church. Zeno the Isaurian, the first Eastern Roman emperor, enforced it from Constantinople. It coincided with the end of the period of Western Roman emperors.

As we will detail below, from the end of the fifth century to the beginning of the sixth century, the Roman Syrian provinces of Second

---

[160] Quoted in Adrian Fortescue, "Henoticon," in *The Catholic Encyclopedia*, Robert Appleton Company, 1910, available at http://www.newadvent.org/cathen/07218b.htm.

Syria and First Phoenicia appeared as centres of Chalcedonian opposition to Monophysitism and the *Henotikon*. The Roman province of Syria I, or Syria Prima had its capital or metropolis as Antioch in far northern Syria. Some of its episcopal sees (pertaining to the jurisdiction of bishops), included Beroea (Aleppo), Chalcis (Qinnasrin), Gabala (Jableh), and Laodicea (Latakia). Syria II, or Syria Secunda, had as its capital Apamaea (Aramaic/Arabic: *Afamiyya*) in the southern part of northern Syria. It is an area of modern-day Syria closer to the border of Lebanon. Some of its episcopal sees included Epiphania (Hama), Larissa (Shaizar), and Mariamma (Krak des Chevaliers).

It is probable that only a minority of the population in these western areas of the patriarchate adhered to Monophysitism. If Monophysites were present in these areas they may have been persecuted, particularly in Syria Secunda.[161] This persecution would have reversed dramatically under Severus, Patriarch of Antioch from 512-518. Severus was of Greek-Byzantine origin and a known Monophysite. He was installed as Catholic patriarch of Antioch, likely in 512, by Monophysite Emperor Anastasius (491-518). This was after Flavian, the previous patriarch of Antioch, refused to denounce Chalcedon. Immediately upon Severus' appointment he anathematised the Council of Chalcedon.

Emperor Anastasius was succeeded in 518 by Emperor Justin I, who followed the doctrine of Chalcedon. Justin I immediately deposed Severus from his position. Thereafter, pro-Chalcedon patriarchs of Constantinople and Antioch were elected. In the period from about 511 to 518, it appears fighting and occasionally armed battles raged between pro and anti-Chalcedon monks and populations both in Constantinople and Antioch regions. As we will discover, this led to many unfortunate deaths. Under the Emperor Justin I and Pope Hormisdas, both pro-Chalcedon, the schism between Rome and Constantinople ended in 518.

---

[161] Ernest Honigmann, *Eveque et évêques monophysites d'Asie Anterieure Au Vie Siecle*, Peeters Publishers, 1951, pp. 38, 45, 55, 65.

## 7.3  Anti-Monophysitism in Syria, Lebanon, and Palestine

An important primary source for the period of the Acacian Schism is the six-volume work *Ecclesiastical History* completed by Evagrius around 593.[162] Evagrius was born around 535 in the Syria II (Syria Secunda) city of Epiphania on the Orontes River, present-day Hama, not far from Apamaea. As a young boy, Evagrius accompanied his parents to the nearby city of Apamaea, about fifty kilometres to the north, to "adore and kiss" the wood of the Holy Cross.[163] After pursuing his legal career in Antioch, it is suggested he was a legal advisor to Gregory, patriarch of Antioch (570-592) and appeared to have good relations with the emperor's family.[164] *Ecclesiastical History* related to the period from the First Council of Ephesus (431) to a period during Maurice's reign in 593.[165] It is generally accepted that Evagrius was pro-Chalcedon.

Moosa informs us that the Monophysite population in Syria were dominant over the Chalcedonians during the Acacian Schism. This contrasts with Whitby's introduction to the translation of Evagrius' works, which summarises the Monophysite position as follows:

> The strength of the Monophysite cause may be overestimated. In the fifth century the Antiochene diocese had been the bastian of opposition to Cyril of Alexandria ... Monophysite bishops only gained control under Anastasius, and that towards the end of his reign and after a protracted struggle, which showed the limitations of their support; at Sidon in 511 Philoxenus of Mabbug was outvoted by the defenders of Chalcedon. The appointment of Severus as patriarch of Antioch was a Monophysite triumph, but it required consid-

---

[162] Evagrius, *The Ecclesiastical History of Evagrius Scholarasticus,* translated with an introduction by Michael Whitby, Liverpool University Press, 2000.

[163] Evagrius, *The Ecclesiastical History*, p. 224.

[164] Michael Whitby, "Introduction," *The Ecclesiastical History of Evagrius Scholarasticus,* Liverpool University Press, 2000, pp. xiii-xv.

[165] Evagrius noted the devastation and decline of Apamaea province after the invasion of the Persians in 540. He also noted the earthquake in Antioch in 588 and the rebuilding process.

erable energy from him to dominate his see, as his correspondence reveals, and even he could not pressure all his suffragan bishops into conformity.

When Justin I succeeded Anastasius in 518, the situation was bound to change; imperial and ecclesiastical patronage was controlled by Chalcedonians, and first was used against the obstinate ... The construction of a separate Monophysite hierarchy, towards the end of Justinian's reign, stabilised their influence in certain areas, but their bishops, numbering no more than three dozen or so, did not reside in, or control, the cities; some indeed, like John of Ephesus, may rarely have gone anywhere near their titular see. In the Antiochian patriarchate, Monophysite influence was strongest in the eastern parts, and especially in monasteries, sufficiently remote from the metropolitan gaze to be ignored, but these communities were also extremely fragmented; their self-destructive strife was a major concern for John of Ephesus.[166]

In addition, Whitby states the majority of the population in the patriarchate of Antioch adhered to the Chalcedonian doctrine. This is certainly a different picture to that painted by Moosa when he refers to Evagrius.

The eastern parts of the Antiochian patriarchate included the provinces of Mesopotamia, Euphrates, and Osrohoene, the latter with its capital Edessa. From what is known generally in history, it is suggested this would be the area of the patriarchate where the Monophysites may have been in the majority. The Chalcedonians dominated the western part, closer to the Mediterranean Sea and its nearby mountain ranges, as the present discussion will now demonstrate. Brock confirms even after Arab rule in the seventh century, there were sizeable populations of Aramaic Catholics in Syria.[167] The 1932 Lebanese Census may provide further insight. The present day descendants of the Chalcedonians are the Maronites, Melkite Catholics, and Antiochian Orthodox. They totalled 96.7% of Christians resident in Lebanon in

---

[166] Whitby, "Introduction," *The Ecclesiastical History*, pp. xli-xlii.
[167] Brock, *From Ephrem to Romanus*, pp. 157-158.

1924. Syriac Catholic, Syriac Orthodox, Chaldean Catholic and Chaldean Orthodox accounted for 1.6%.[168]

Evagrius informs us that Flavian, archbishop of the city of Antioch and patriarch of Antioch (491-512), had previously practised the monastic life in the countryside of Syria Secunda in a monastery called Tilmognon. When Philoxenus, bishop of Hierapolis (today, Pammaluke in Anatolia, Turkey) attempted, with what sounded like a large group of monks who showed "vehemence," to force Flavian to anathematise the Synod at Chalcedon and the Tome of Leo, the population of Antioch rose up against the monks and slaughtered "a countless number" of them. In a separate incident, the monks of Syria Secunda, who were sympathetic to Flavian because he had practised as a monk with them, came to the city of Antioch to defend Flavian. Evagrius recounts:

> and there also came about another incident not inferior to this (the massacre of the Monophysite monks in Antioch by the city folk)…and so then too events of no small significance took place. And so, either as a result of the former, or of the latter, or indeed of both, Flavian was expelled (by the Monophysite emperor) and condemned to live in Petra, which lies on the borders of Palestine.[169]

It is important to pause here and reflect on the significance to our study of Flavian as a former monk from Syria Secunda under the leadership of Beit Maroun network. It is noteworthy that he went on to be elected patriarch of Antioch in the period of the Acacian Schism. It demonstrates the importance and leadership of training through the Beit Maroun network as the beacon of Catholic orthodoxy for the indigenous in the patriarchate of Antioch.

It also suggests that a significant population of Antioch was anti-Monophysite and anti-Constantinople at the time. Perhaps this was represented by a large number of Aramaic Catholics living in the city

---

[168] Rania Maktabi, "The Lebanese Census of 1932 Revisited. Who are the Lebanese?," *British Journal of Middle Eastern Studies* 26(2), (1999): pp. 219-241.

[169] Evagrius, *The Ecclesiastical History*, pp. 174-175.

of Antioch alongside ethnic Greeks-Byzantines. It may require a re-calibration of conventional thinking that ethnic 'Greeks' dominated the city's population during this period. The events also supports the proposition of a Catholic block in the two provinces of Syria (and broader region including Lebanon, Phoenicia and northern Palestine) that were adherent and loyal to Roman doctrine and the pope rather than Constantinople and the emperor.

The same as for the period of one hundred years earlier during Theodoret's historical accounts, we have once again direct evidence of monks in the region of Northern Syria becoming bishops. How-ever, on this occasion we have proof for one of those monks becom-ing a patriarch. We see Patriarch Flavian having the support of the monks from Syria Secunda and the population at large in Antioch, both of whom came to his immediate support in defending attacks from the Monophysites. We later see Flavian's brother Epiphanius as Archbishop of Tyre become the leading bishop in the patriarchate of Antioch opposed to Severus. The monks of Syria Secunda, led by the Beit Maroun network, were the fiercest opponents to Severus.

Here we have another extraordinary set of correlating events, rep-resenting a continuing pattern that emerges throughout the book. This time we see clear interconnections between the Second Syria monks of Beit Maroun, the pro-Chalcedon patriarch of Antioch (Flavian who was a former monk of the Beit Maroun network), and Flavian's brother Ephipanius as Archbishop of Tyre. This evidences an interconnection between the most strident orthodoxy of the indigenous Catholic popu-lations in the broader area of the western region of the patriarchate of Antioch. Beit Maroun was at its helm. Beit Maroun was also likely to have been closely affiliated with the Greek-Byzantine Catholics in the patriarchate.

Shortly before a 'supposed' Synod in Antioch in 508 or 509, appar-ently Flavian, Archbishop and patriarch of Antioch, at the command of Emperor Anastasius signed the *Henotikon* (decreed by the former Emperor Zeno). Emperor Anastasius then assembled the bishops of Antioch for a synod shortly after. The synod did not specifically anathematise the Council of Chalcedon but put forward four chapters in opposition to it.[170]

In 511, Macedonius was deposed as patriarch of Constantinople partly for refusing to condemn the Council of Chalcedon.[171] In the same year, a Synod of Sidon was attended by all of the bishops of Antioch. Philoxenus, bishop of Hieropolis attempted to have Flavian condemned. Only a minority of nine bishops expressed support for deposing Flavian.[172] Philoxenus travelled to Constantinople to seek emperor Anastasius' support to have Flavian removed.[173]

Count Marcellinus (d. 534) was a well-known Latin chronicler living in Constantinople and a contemporary of the period. The Count records that Emperor Anastasius commanded an assembly of eighty 'unorthodox' (Monophysite) bishops at Sidon in 512, which brought about a rejection of the Council of Chalcedon. Flavian and John (bishop of Paltus in Syria) were exiled into the Fort of Petra where Flavian died a confessor.[174] Based on this information, it is likely in the one-year after 511 Chalcedonian bishops throughout the patriarchate were expelled and replaced by Monophysite bishops in order to achieve the outcome of the vote in 512.

Immediately after the Synod of Sidon, the leaders of the monks of Palestine met in a type of synod to defend Chalcedon. Emperor Anastasius expelled the Chalcedonian patriarch of Jerusalem.[175] Philoxenus and also Soterichus, the archbishop of Caesarea in Cappadocia, were the heads of the Synod at Sidon in 512, which rejected the Council of Chalcedon. Not long after, the Monophysites throughout the patriarchate of Antioch met at another synod under the presidency of Philox-

[170] C.J. Hefele, *A History of the Councils of the Church (From the Original Documents)*, Vol IV, T&T Clark, 1895, p. 87 who cites Theophanes as translated by Mansi. The word in inverted commas 'supposed' was indicated that way by Hefele.
[171] Whitby, *The Ecclesiastical History*, footnote 123, p. 176. Whitby also informs us Macedonius' successor Timothy (511-518) held similar views as Flavian.
[172] Ibid., footnote 106, pp. 170-171.
[173] Ibid., footnote 118, p. 175.
[174] Hefele, *A History of the Councils of the Church*, Vol IV, p. 93.
[175] Ibid., p. 93.

enus. It was at that time Severus was chosen as the new patriarch of Antioch.[176]

Born in a Greek province, Severus was from a well-to-do family. He studied law at a renowned law school in Beirut. After completing his training, he was baptised in a coastal Phoenician city at the sanctuary of the martyr Leonius. He transferred to the monastic life near the city of Gaza. After being driven out of this monastery due to his Monophysite opinions, he migrated to Constantinople and became an acquaintance of the emperor. When writing his synodical decrees, Severus expressly anathematised the findings of Chalcedon.[177]

It should be highlighted that following the Council of Chalcedon in 451, the Monophysites of Syria had not appointed their own patriarch of Antioch. They had not yet formed their own Syriac Monophysite church. Accordingly, they immediately became aligned with Severus. Relying on Evagrius, Moosa informs us only some bishops and priests under his jurisdiction separated themselves from Severus. Moosa states:

> Daww's assertion that the monastery of Marun had actual and judicial authority over all the monasteries in Syria Secunda is without historical foundation; it runs contrary to Evagrius' account that only a few bishops in all of Syria, including Syria Secunda, were opposed to the authority of Severus of Antioch. This indicates that the majority of the bishops in Syria were with their patriarch Severus. After all, despite some opposition, Severus was elected a patriarch of Antioch by a council of bishops held in Sidon in 512. The majority of bishops in Phoenicia, Lebania, Arabia Euphratesia, Mesopotamia, and Syria stood solidly behind him and his doctrine.[178]

However, as stated above, when examining Evagrius closely we see a very different picture to that portrayed by Moosa.

---

[176] Ibid..

[177] Evagrius, *The Ecclesiastical History*, pp. 175-176.

[178] Moosa, *The Maronites in History*, p. 78.

Evagrius goes on to comment that the anti-Monophysite monks from Palestine who wrote their letter to the bishop of Nicopolis (in modern Greece) also reported "that the priests under Apamea distanced themselves from Severus." Whitby explains, after citing *Letters of Severus*:

> although Second Syria was resolutely anti-Monophysite, the metropolitan see of Apamea was currently occupied by Peter, who shared Severus' views. He had probably been chosen in the election referred to by Severus, where the candidates must be orthodox, i.e. hold firmly to communion with Severus himself.

It is likely Severus went about ensuring candidates for bishops were only those who adhered to his views.

This provides a plausible explanation for Moosa's comments that Severus enjoyed support of many bishops as letters of Severus would naturally detail. The view opposed to Moosa is supported by the comments of historian Count Marcellinus and of the historian of the Councils, Hefele. Accordingly, it is highly questionable Moosa is correct in stipulating Severus was 'elected' as patriarch in 512. Contrastingly to the Synod at Sidon in 511, those bishops that had not been replaced by Severus faced expulsion and exile by the emperor at the 512 Synod.

The period in the patriarchate of Antioch from 512-518 under patriarch Severus was unprecedented in its turmoil between a patriarch and his bishops. The bishops, clergy, and monks were subject to expulsion, exile, force, compulsion, and schism. It was the reverse of the period immediately after 451 when the Chalcedonian bishops enjoyed the support of the Emperor. However, the period under Severus was far more hostile. Assuming the provinces of Euphrates, Osrhoene, and Mesopotamia were dominated by Monophysite populations since Chalcedon in 451, and despite the probability of candidates for bishops after 512 being Severus' adherents, we will now attempt to examine the level of support for Severus in Lebanon, Phoenicia, Palestine, and western Syria.

Patriarch Elias[179] of Palestine resisted the Monophysites and Severus with the strong support of local monks.[180] Evagrius sets out a letter from the monks of Palestine to the bishop of Nicopolis. It informs us that in Palestine the people and the monks rose up, and the depositions of Flavian and Macedonius were not accepted nor were the synodicals (synod decrees) of Severus. The letter continues to say some bishops such as Marinus, the bishop of Beirut, had been "brought under control" by Severus:

> others (bishops) consented under force and compulsion to the synodicals of Severus ... others (bishops), after consenting under compulsion, repented and retracted, among whom are those dependent on Apamea; others completely refused to consent, among whom are Julian of Bostra and Epiphanius of Tyre, and some of the bishops, it is said ... Others, however, of the bishops and clergy under Severus have left their churches and fled; among these both Julian of Bostra and Peter of Damascus are living here, as to is Mamas, one of the two who appeared to be leaders of the Dioscorions, by whom indeed Severus was restored; he has condemned their arrogance.[181]

The bishops in Damascus, even though in exile, kept the strong support of the local population. In 517, a large group of anti-Severus monks gathered at the monastery of Maro (Maroun), south of Damascus, and appealed to Pope Hormisdas against their patriarch.[182] Da-

---

[179] A Semitic name, and so likely the patriarch was indigenous and not ethnic.

[180] Whitby, *The Ecclesiastical History*, footnote 123, p. 176.

[181] Evagrius, *The Ecclesiastical History*, pp. 176-177.

[182] Whitby, *The Ecclesiastical History*, footnote 127, p. 177. It is certain this monastery is a different monastery to the monastery of Maroun in Syria Secunda. Moosa, *The Maronites in History*, p. 79 cites Michael the Syrian and Hefele confirming a Monastery of Maroun was also in the district of Sokas in Constantinople. Moosa, *The Maronites in History*, p. 74 cites Doueihi to confirm another Monastery of Maroun was in Batroun in Lebanon – it is proposed by this book it is likely the monastery that housed the skull of St Maroun, also according to Doueihi, brought to it by St John Maroun in the late seventh early eighth century, and from which we now know the Crusaders were given the relic to take back to Italy as discussed in a later chapter.

mascus, as a metropolitan archdiocese, comprised many bishops of the city under an archbishop. By the late sixth century, the city had become the leading centre of learning.[183]

The patriarch of Jerusalem and the Palestinians were opposed to Severus, as we have commented. Outside of Palestine, we have evidence from Evagrius of at least three of the four major cities of the patriarchate outside of Antioch city being opposed to Severus. These were the metropolitan archdioceses of Tyre in First Phoenicia, Damascus in Phoenicia-Lebanon, and Apamaea in Second Syria. It is likely the only other metropolitan archdiocese, Emesa also in Phoenicia-Lebanon, right at the border of Second Syria was likely also to be anti-Severus (as we have evidence stated below its second city Epiphania was resolutely anti Severus). Each of these metropolitan archdioceses had many bishops. The archdioceses in these major cities, most likely housing the most significant populations outside of Antioch city, were therefore the ones opposed to Severus.

In the metropolitan archdiocese of Tyre, the bishops remained very hostile to Severus. Whitby citing from Severus' letters informs us:

> Severus attempted to rally support for his strict doctrinal stands in a series of councils, of which the most important was held at Tyre in 514, where affirmations of loyalty could be obtained; the patriarch of Antioch also had considerable powers of patronage, and could manipulate his financial power and disciplinary authority to obtain agreement. Some areas, such as Second Syria, the province dependent on Apamaea, and individuals such as Epiphanius of Tyre, the brother of the deposed Flavian, remained adamantly hostile ... [see Severus' letters] for disagreements and tension in Second Syria and on the impossibility of receiving Epiphanius back into communion, even if he were to repent.[184]

---

[183] Andrew J. Ekonomou, *Byzantine Rome and the Greek Popes, Eastern Influences on Rome and the Papacy from Gregory the Great to Zacharias, A.D. 590-752*, Lexington Books, 2007, p. 120.

[184] Whitby, *The Ecclesiastical History*, footnote 127, p. 177.

Syria Secunda (Second Syria) province, centred on the Orontes Valley to the south of Antioch, comprised the fiercest opposition to Severus. Years earlier to Severus' installation, as recounted above, we see a rebellion of monks travelling to Antioch to defend Patriarch Flavian. A few decades earlier, the bishop of Apamaea had appealed to Pope Felix about Zeno's *Henotikon*.[185]

Whitby states that Second Syria, was resolutely anti-Monophysite.[186] Evagrius informs us "the priests under Apamaea distanced themselves from Severus," but he doesn't say 'some' as recounted by Moosa. The ancient historian then shares a story about his birthplace:

> Cosmas, Bishop of my own Epiphania (Hama), which has Orontes as its companion, and Severianus, Bishop of nearby Arethusa [on the Orontes River, modern day Ar-Rastan between Homs and Hama], were distressed at the synodical letters of Severus, severed themselves from communion with him, and sent a document of deposition to him while he was still bishop of the city of Antiochus. They entrusted the document to Aurelian, first deacon of Epiphania.[187]

The bishops of Syria Secunda took the matter further than any one else. They officially demanded Severus step down. Upon learning that Cosmas and Severian had written letters of deposition to Patriarch Severus, the Emperor Anastasius instructed his commander, Asiaticus in 'Phoenicia Libanensis', to expel the two bishops from their sees. Evagrius informs us "after Asiaticus reached the eastern regions and found that many adhered to the doctrines of Cosmos and Severianus, and that their cities upheld them most resolutely, he reported to Anastasius that he could not banish these men from their sees without bloodshed."[188] Epiphania (Hama) and Arethusa (Al-Rastan) were both not too distant from Apamaea, and both in Syria Secunda province.

---

[185] Ibid., footnote 117, p. 174.
[186] Ibid., footnote 129, p. 178.
[187] Evagrius, *The Ecclesiastical History*, p. 178.
[188] Ibid.

They were also very close, only kilometres, to the border of Phoenicia Lebanon and its capital Emesa (Homs).

The history recorded by Evagrius, as well as the emperor's commander Asiaticus' refusal to follow the orders of his king, lead us to suggest some important propositions, yet to be considered, it seems, by any other author of Maronite history. The reference to Asiaticus' refusal suggests the threat of bloodshed not only from the many Catholic supporters in Syria Secunda but also in Phoenicia. The commander's refusal to his emperor's orders is significant. His own population may have been anti-Severus.

It is worth questioning why the emperor did not instruct the commander of Syria Secunda or of First Phoenicia, but rather the commander of Phoenicia Lebanon. One plausible explanation relates to geography and the risk of rebellion. A large part of the area of Phoenicia Lebanon extended to the easternmost districts of the Byzantine Empire's border to Persian ruled land. These areas were not part of the previous ancient Phoenicia. Perhaps the populations were less likely Chalcedonian and less likely to rebel against the commander. Nothing is certain.

Immediately after the story relating to Asiaticus, Evagrius recounts an insurrection against the (Monophysite) Emperor Anastasius in 492, the second year of his reign. We are told that Bishop Conon of Apamaea, who was originally an Isaurian, abandoned his episcopacy and joined a campaign with the Isaurians to defeat the emperor's forces. The insurrection was comprehensively destroyed, and nothing is mentioned of the fate of the bishop.[189]

## 7.4 The Massacre of 517

Peter 'the Fuller' was Patriarch of Antioch in 471, 475-477, 485-488. He died in 488. He was a Monophysite and was succeeded by Flavian, who, when refusing to denounce the Council of Chalcedon, was replaced by Severus in 512. From his installation in 512 as patriarch

---

[189] Evagrius, *The Ecclesiastical History*, p. 180.

of Antioch, Severus went about ensuring the appointment of Mono-physite bishops throughout the patriarchate. Syria Secunda proved the strongest opposition to Severus. The monks of the Beit Maroun network, as pro-Chalcedon, led the opposition to Severus.

In 517, the monks of Beit Maroun agreed to attend a meeting with Severus' representative, Bishop Peter of Apamaea. The meeting was arranged to be near the monastery of St Simon the Stylite in Syria Prima. The agreement confirmed that the meeting would take place outside of Peter's territorial jurisdiction, perhaps as a security measure for the Beit Maroun monks.

On their way to St Simon Stylite region, documents record an ambush resulting in the massacre of three hundred and fifty monks from Beit Maroun near St Simon's monastery. Many other monks were wounded. The documentation states some Beit Maroun monasteries were set on fire, others damaged and looted. The massacre led to three sets of correspondence: the monks' petition to Pope Hormisdas in 517; the monk's petition to their bishops in 518; and the Pope's response in 518. These primary source letters are set out further below at the end of this chapter.

### 7.4.1   Correspondence and Petitions

The earliest of the correspondence was the petition to Pope Hormisdas in about 517 (see section 7.7.1 of this chapter). The letter indicates at the time that Emperor Anastasius and patriarch Severus of Antioch, both Monophysite in belief, remained as respective leaders. The letter is signed by a total of 209 archimandrites, priests, and deacons from Beit Maroun monasteries in the province of Syria Secunda. A total of twenty-six names of archimandrites, or superiors of monasteries, are listed. The first archimandrite is listed as Alexander of St Maroun. The other archimandrite names are listed followed by the words 'as above'. This implies their monastery was under the head monastery of St Maroun.

The letter/petition makes it clear the monks were Catholic orthodox and followers of Chalcedon doctrine. They refer to "our most holy and blessed father Leo" and their opposition to those who attack and ridicule "the holy Synod at Chalcedon." The monks of the monasteries led by St Maroun informed the Pope in the petition that they had sent a delegation to Constantinople seeking the support of the emperor. He (king) expelled the delegation "with great mistreatment and he violently threatened those, who would present these (things)."

It appears the Monophysites may have enjoyed the support of Emperor Anastasius and the petition recalls it was someone senior from Constantinople, perhaps the emperor or patriarch, who motivated the attacks stating: "all the depravity and recklessness of such evil people, which is committed against the churches, is arranged through his incitation." It was for this reason the monks then sent their petition to the Pope seeking support and also anathematisation of those who were opposed to the Council of Chalcedon and committed the crimes.

Many Beit Maroun monks were repeatedly forced by their bishops to renounce Chalcedon. The letter to the Pope states:

> The grace of Christ, the Redeemer of us all, has instigated us to take refuge to your blessedness ... you have certainly heard: That Severus and Peter, who have never been counted among the number of Christians, who on each single day have attacked and publicly anathematized the holy synod at Chalcedon and our most holy and blessed father Leo, who think nothing of God's judgment and trample under foot the venerable canons of the holy Fathers, bringing it about that bishops, indeed, are shown as holding the prime authority and forcing us to ridicule the aforementioned holy synod and humiliating us by worthless public prayers.

> Therefore also certain ones of those, who in no way endure the blows brought upon them have gone over because of this and our not so small number of people has in fact almost completely vanished.

Pope Hormisdas responded to the priests, deacons, and archimandrites of Syria Secunda on 10 February 518 (see section 7.7.2 of this Chapter). It appears that at one stage during this period of the Roman-

Greek schism, there may have been confusion, shortly before the massacre, as to whether Beit Maroun monasteries or their monks were briefly aligned with the thinking of the Monophysites. The Pope comments:

> Late, indeed, that you enter on the way of truth, but blessed be God, who does not forget even toward the end, who seizes and heals and does not suffer that the sheep of his flock are continuously torn apart by the rapacity of the wolves which lie in wait ... Therefore, now, at least pursue closely with firm steps the way of the Fathers, to which you are returning.

It may be that the Romans incorrectly believed that the Beit Maroun monks became Monophysite during this period. Rome might have overlooked that the Beit Maroun monks mentioned the Monophysites were "forcing us to ridicule the aforementioned holy synod (Chalcedon) and humiliating us by worthless public prayers." The petition to the Pope informs us that it was the "bishops, indeed, are shown as holding the prime authority" who forced them into these worthless public prayers. The Catholic bishops of Syria were pushed out of office and into silence. The bishops referred to in the petition were no doubt Monophysite. As will be seen later, Severus went about ensuring Monophysite bishops replaced Chalcedonian bishops. The monks of Beit Maroun were humiliated and forced into a public act of obedience to Severus. The news of the public prayers would certainly have travelled to Rome.

The Pope referred to the "confusion" and "mud" of the era. In its violence and turmoil, it is extraordinary that the Beit Maroun monks would have felt so much humiliation that they now decided to publicly oppose their Monophysite bishops. Perhaps this was after delegations to or from Rome to ascertain the varying opinions and for a decision to be made. Certainly, they made a commitment to oppose the bishop of Apamaea, the emperor, the patriarch of Constantinople, the patriarch of Antioch, and perhaps a sizeable population of Monophysites, both Aramaic-speaking indigenous and ethnic Greeks in the imperial administration roles.

For the monks of St Maroun, the truth of their faith was paramount. They knew the dire consequences of aligning their faith with Chalcedon and were in communion with the primary patriarch of the Catholic Church, the bishop of Rome, the Pope. The result was one of virtual isolation from both government and ecclesiastical leaders in their native land who were placed in power as Monophysite partners. Even after the unexpected aggression, the Beit Maroun mission remained peaceful, and publically but not violently defended their theological position.

Despite their isolation, the monks of St Maroun looked to the spiritual refuge of the Pope, thousands of kilometres away, knowing well that Rome was unable to assist physically. The first schism in the Church between Rome and Constantinople followed as a first test of loyalty. The construction of Beit Maroun in the fifth century, and the events during the Acacian Schism, may have shaped the future identity and tradition of these Aramaic-speaking Catholics. Time would tell if the communion with the Church of Rome was unshakable and the traditional Catholic motto 'all roads led to Rome' (in terms of supreme leadership of the Church) was to hold firm.

The third text is the petition from the Beit Maroun confederation to the bishops of Syria Secunda in 518 (see section 7.7.3 of this Chapter). The petition was for the bishops to consider at their synod in the same year. By this time the schism between Rome and Constantinople had ended. Emperor Justin I now ruled and was pro-Chalcedon. The patriarchs of Constantinople and Antioch were restored as pro-Chalcedon. Beit Maroun had renewed their optimism but with moderation. They wrote:

> But as God has now granted a just liberty and graciously allows some much desired hope for our affairs, and has caused a Christian orthodox emperor to rise up for the churches and the whole world, those were oppressed and voiceless must now make themselves heard ... He (God) has restored peace to the world with a good emperor taking care of government; those who endeavoured to loot the straight path of the or-

thodox faith being now set aside, it remains for us to speak, though with moderated voice, of the lamentable conduct of the heretic Severus, as also of the shameful and abominable manner of acting of Peter.

Recounting the journey to meet the Monophysites, they inform us that their mission was "with only peace, union and love, and a just vow in our thoughts, manifesting a purely monastic attitude and intention." They refer to Bishop Peter rising up against the city of Apamaea. Attacks on several monasteries are mentioned including at the locations of Matrona, Oraga, Dorothaea, and Nicerta (the later destroying parts of monastery walls). Combat with arrows is referred to during the battle at the monastery located in Larissa.

Catholic orthodoxy is evident throughout the letter with statements such as "venerable priests here present, the deacons, sub deacons and clergy of the Catholic Church of Apamaea" and seeking the just expulsion of the heretics Severus and Peter. They end the letter asking for the unity in the Catholic Church so that "there may be only one flock and one shepherd, Christ our God." The Beit Maroun monks were in continuous and controversial struggles with the Aramaic-Syriac Monophysites, later known as Jacobites. During the period of the schism between 471-518, the Beit Maroun monks appeared to be the only Aramaic-Syriac Christian monasteries in Syria Secunda who were Dyophysite and Catholic.

A total of eighteen monasteries with the names of their superiors are listed as having executed the petition to the bishops of Syria Secunda. The first signatory is "Alexander, priest and archimandrite of the monastery of the Blessed Maroun," followed by Simon, "priest and archimandrite of the monastery of the Blessed Agapetus." A further sixteen signatures of named archimandrites appear with the names of their monasteries. The monastery of St. Maroun is clearly first ranked amongst all monasteries. A long list of the names and signatures of priests and deacons are included.

Not all monasteries signed both petitions perhaps for the convenience of logistical distances. A total of fourteen names of superiors/

archimandrites that are mentioned in the petition to the bishops, are not mentioned in the petition to Pope Hormisdas. There are only four names of superiors common between the two petitions. Accordingly, it can be deduced there are a total of at least forty monasteries in Syria Secunda under the leadership of Beit Maroun that are mentioned in the two petitions. The texts evidence the pre-eminence of the monastery of Beit Maroun over other monasteries in Syria Secunda (Second Syria).

The monastery of Blessed Agapetus is referred to in the signature clause at the end of the petition to the bishops. It appears immediately after the monastery of Blessed Maroun, in other words second ranked to Maroun but in a confederation. The signatures commence "Alexander, priest and Archimandrite of the Monastery of the Blessed Maron, have made public this letter above ... Simon, by the mercy of God priest and Archimandrite of the monastery of the Blessed Agapetus." The monks of Beit Maroun were fluent in both Greek and Syriac as the letters were signed in Greek.

The beginning of the petition to the bishops also confirms the second ranking of the monastery of Blessed Agapetus even though it notes the name 'John' as second ranked. John is almost certainly the deacon and treasurer of St Maroun's monastery (as seen in the signatures to the petition to the Pope): "To the most reverend Bishops our Lords, to all the Most Reverend Holy Fathers the Bishops of Syria Secunda, from Alexander, John, Simon, Palladius, Procopius, Eugenius Stephanus, and other archimandrites and monks of the region of Apamaea."

In the petition to the Pope, perhaps one year earlier than the petition to the bishops, no monasteries are referred to, only the names of archimandrites. The superior of the monastery of Agapetus, archimandrite Simon, second ranked in the signatures to the petition to the bishops, also appears as Simon ('Symeon') second ranked in the signatures of the petition to the Pope as it opens with: "Alexander, through the mercy of God priest and archimandrite of St Maroun, have prayed. Symeon, through the mercy of God priest and archimandrite, as above. John, through the mercy of God deacon and treasurer, as above..."

As the second ranked monastery, it is safe to conclude Agapetus is the same monastery established in Nikertai by Theodoret's Agapetus, a disciple of Marcian (d. 380). As discussed in Chapter 6 of this book, Agapetus' monastery was reported by Theodoret to be established during the lifetime of Marcian. This was around the same time as the life of St Maroun (d. 410-423). It must follow that the monastery of St Maroun was founded *after* and *not before* the death of St Maroun around 410-423.

This proposition provides a date range of 410-517 (the latter the date of the first petition) for the founding of Beit Maroun monastery. Given its first ranking in the petitions, it must also follow Beit Maroun existed well before 517, even some decades prior. The "fame everywhere and on all sides" of Theodoret's Maroun around the first half of the fifth century coupled with the numerous historical links between Cyrrhus and Apamaea in this period that are set out in this book, clearly supports the evidence discussed in Chapter 6 that the date of the founding of Beit Maroun monastery was 452 as recorded by Abu l-Fida.

With the Monophysite conflict the foremost issue for Christians of the period after 451, it is no coincidence that a little more than sixty years after the Council of Chalcedon, there were at least forty monasteries in Syria Secunda under the leadership of Beit Maroun who were pro-Chalcedon. We recall from the previous chapters, Marcian was originally from Cyrrhus (the region of Maroun's hermitage) before migrating to live as an anchorite in Apamaea region. Marcian's disciple Agapetus, established two monasteries in Apamaea region. The reference in the petitions of 517/518 to the second ranked monastery of Agapetus after Beit Maroun, supports the importance of St Maroun in northern Syria linking two distinct regions from Apamaea to Cyrrhus, the latter where his hermitage was located.

The evidence from Theodoret suggests the monastery of Agapetus may at one time have been a leader and first ranked, but lost this ranking upon the construction of the monastery of Maroun. Given the evidence, once again it leaves little doubt the now first ranked patron of the monasteries of Second Syria, "Blessed Maroun," was the hermit

Theodoret wrote about. Theodoret chose to live and study in one of the monasteries founded by Agapetus.[190] For this reason, and others previously explained, we find a link not only between Apamaea and Cyrrhus, but between Agapetus, Maroun, and Theodoret. There are also links between Theodoret and Emperor Marcian pre- and post-Chalcedon including the founding of Beit Maroun.

As previously reported, we also have seen links between the hermit Maroun and on the one hand the monks and region of Cyrrhus and Antioch, and on the other the monks and region of Phoenicia and Mount Lebanon. These links were established by St Abraham, who was from the 'garden' of Cyrrhus planted by Maroun and nurtured by St Simon the Stylite. There is thus a link between Theodret, Abraham, and Emperor Marcian for the founding of Beit Maroun.

There are many geopolitical links in this period between the area of northern Syria and the western areas of Phoenicia, Lebanon, and northern Palestine. The common bonds were ancient Phoenicia, the geography of the mountain ranges, the Aramaic language and its local dialect, the Aramaic-speaking culture, Christianity, the Aramaic-Syriac liturgy of Antioch, and (as will be demonstrated) the Council of Chalcedon doctrine. For many Phoenicians and Lebanese the nearest metropolis was to the immediate north, Apamaea, the capital of Second Syria.

By 517, only sixty-five years after its founding, the monastery of Beit Maroun was already flourishing. As Naaman states:

> Thirty [this book calculates at least forty] monasteries owed to it their origin, setting up and organising into a beautifully structured religious order. It is worth noting that all these monasteries were to be found in Syria Secunda, and none were far from Apamaea. All of them acknowledged the leadership of the monastery of Saint Maron.[191]

---

[190] As previous chapters have detailed, it was one of two monasteries nearby to each other, both founded by Agapetus, named Simon and Agapetus. It is likely, given the monastery of Agapetus is ranked second after Beit Maroun in the petitions, that the monastery was Agapetus.

[191] Naaman, *The Maronites*, p. 131.

The influence of Beit Maroun monasteries in the region must have been seen such a threat to the Monophysites so as to warrant the atrocities and devastation. The texts establish the orthodoxy of the monks of Beit Maroun. The monks were the leaders of the Orthodox party (that is, partisans of the Council of Chalcedon and of Pope Leo) in Syria Secunda, as recognised at the Council of Constantinople in 536. Beit Maroun was referred to at the Council as 'exarch' or leader of the monasteries in Syria Secunda.[192] Nau informs us:

> The monks of St Maroun spoke Greek and Syriac, for their representatives signed in Greek, the works of St John Maroun, as we have said when publishing them, show a deep knowledge of Greek, and in any case the monastery library, as we shall see later, certainly contained Syriac manuscripts; these monks therefore were entirely suited by their situation, their number, their regularity, and their orthodoxy to enjoy a certain pre-eminence over the other monasteries, both Greek and Syriac.[193]

The earliest reference to these monks and the populus surrounding them being called 'Maronites' was possibly at the Council of Constantinople in 536. The monastery of Saint Maroun, represented by the monk Paul, was referred to as "primate of the Holy Monasteries of Syria Secunda." Paul's signature appeared as: "Paul ... apocrisary of the monastery of the Blessed Maroun, the monastery which governs the holy monasteries of Syria II."[194]

After the Acacian Schism ended in 517, it is of significance that from 529 to 545 the Monophysites considered the monks from Beit Maroun as theological advisors to Ephraim of Amid, the patriarch of Antioch (529-545). It shows their leadership at the time in the patriarchate. The monks promoted the neo-Chalcedonian theology originally documented by Theodoret in the lead up to the Council of

---

[192] Dib, *History of the Maronite Church*, p. 10. Also, Nau in Naaman, *The Maronites*, p. 153.

[193] Nau in Naaman, *The Maronites*, footnote 2, p. 152. It is unfortunate that St John Maroun's works that were published by Nau are yet to be published in English.

[194] Dib cites Mansi, Consil., t. VIII, col. 881, 911, 912, 929, 940, 953, 995, 1022, in *History of the Maronite Church*, p. 78.

Chalcedon. In the eighth century, a Maronite Chronicle invoked the authority of Theodoret in exegesis.[195]

It is often said that the Syriac Monophysites (later known as the Jacobites and today as the Syrian Orthodox Church) were responsible for the massacres of the monks of St Maroun (see for example comments of Nau below). The Byzantine historian, Procupius of Caesarea, tells us Emperor Justinian the Great (reign 527-565) restored the walls of Beit Maroun, which Dib says were torn down by the Monophysites.[196] However, it must be stressed that the extant correspondence makes no direct reference to them.

The Beit Maroun petitions refer to the attackers being "a multitude of unsettled people and contractors," "Isaurians," and "Jews or at least lay persons and even monks." The petitions do not seek the anathematisation of any particular Aramaic-Syriac Monophysite clergy. Other than the name "Faustus" and reference to "even monks," both of whose background we are not entirely sure about, it cannot be settled from the documents whether the Aramaic-Syriac Monophysites themselves were directly involved. Nonetheless, Patriarch Severus is a man of immaculate and saintly character to the Syrian Orthodox Church,[197] and it cannot be suggested a man of such stature and faith would have promoted or participated in such an atrocity.[198]

It is likely that a substantial number of important manuscripts were destroyed during these events. The Beit Maroun monasteries were reportedly attacked, looted, burnt, damaged, destroyed, and three hundred and fifty monks were murdered inside holy buildings. Amongst a plethora of other events over the next centuries, it is the earliest occasion that can suggest the possibility of the destruction of evidence for the hermit St Maroun and also for the founding of Beit Maroun (in the probable event that it had been documented).

---

[195] Naaman, *The Maronites*, p. 130.

[196] Dib, *History of the Maronite Church*, p. 6 quoting De aedific, 1. V, c. IX.

[197] Moosa, *The Maronites in History*, p. 56.

[198] With due respect to the Syriac Orthodox Church, the references in ancient texts to the criminal accusations against Severus have been omitted from this book.

The petitions only refer to the monks in the region of Syria Secunda. As this is where the atrocities took place, perhaps it was not
necessary to mention other monasteries outside the region. On this
basis, it cannot be ruled out that indigenous pro-Chalcedon monasteries outside of Syria Secunda at the time of the petitions may also have
been under the leadership of Beit Maroun. This may have included in
the Roman provinces of First Syria, Lebanon, Phoenicia, and Palestine. However, this is only conjecture until evidence is found. More
possibly there may at least have been a network or close working relationship between them, as will be demonstrated.

The bishop of Tyre's jurisdiction included Lebanon (and modern
northern Israel). Tyre was the capital of the Roman province of Phoenicia Prima (First Phoenicia). It seems during the Acacian Schism, the
archbishop of Tyre became the first in rank of bishops in the See of
Antioch who were opposed to the Patriarch Severus. The archbishop
of Tyre led a bishops' schism in the patriachate from Severus. It is understood all the metropolitan bishops of Tyre, under their archbishop,
were also opposed to Severus. The Christians of possibly half of First
Phoenicia in its southern branch and much of northern Palestine were
likely to have substantially maintained the theology of Rome during
the period of the Acacian Schism. A link developed between Tyre and
Beit Maroun over their rejection of Severus.

During the period of the Schism, it seems the number of monks at
the St Maroun head monastery was significantly reduced. The petition to the Pope informs us: "therefore also certain ones of those, who
in no way endure the blows brought upon them have gone over because of this and our not so small number of people has in fact almost
completely vanished." Not only were the monks massacred but in the
petition to the bishops a significant number were taken prisoner as it
states: "for some they put to death, others they led away into captivity;
some were stripped of their garments and others were taken in triumph
clad in torn rags, as if according to the idea they led a degrading life."

Many monks who were Acacian 'Monophysite' but then joined
Beit Maroun were also taken captive and the monastery of Oraga

where they resided was completely destroyed. The petition to the bishops informs us:

> But if once again we were to recall the deeds formally perpetrated at the monastery of ORAGA, what letter could suffice to enumerate so many wrongs? They did not hesitate at all to knock down the monastery as if they were besieging it and to lead away like prisoners of war the monks who were chanting there because, after having fallen into error, they had finally loved the word of truth and had entered into total communion with us.

The year 2017 marks the completion of this book after twenty years when it first began, and falls on the 1,500th anniversary of the martyrdom of the monks, remembered by the Maronite Church on the 31st of July each year.

### 7.4.2  Aramaic Christian Identity Post-Massacre

After the Acacian Schism and the rule of Severus ended in 518, the certainty of a constant memorial of the massacre of the three hundred and fifty monks would have made the Beit Maroun monks determined to stamp out Monophysitism. Little doubt the emperor, Rome, Constantinople and Antioch would have acknowledged Beit Maroun as the fiercest Aramaic-speaking indigenous opponents to the Monophysites. They would have supported them fully.

It is here we can now speak of the first patriarch of the Syriac Monophysite church. In 518, on the death of Anastasius, Justin I 'took on the purple clothing' as the new emperor. Severus was deposed by Justin I and replaced by the Chalcedonian Paul the Jew in 519.[199] Severus and the Aramaic Monophysites in the patriarchate of Antioch did not recognize the deposition. This formed the basis of two different sequences of patriarchs of Antioch: Chalcedonian as the Catholic patriarch, and non-Chalcedonian as the Aramaic Monophysite patriarch. It was the beginnings of a formal Syriac Monophysite Church. Severus is honoured in the Syriac Orthodox Church as St. Severus the Great

---

[199] Evagrius, *The Ecclesiastical History*, pp. 200-203.

of Antioch. The general perception in history has been that the Syriac Monophysites established their own patriarch of Antioch immediately after 451. This is obviously not the case, as it did not occur until 518.

Persecution of the Monophysites continued for some decades after 518. It seems the fiercest persecution in the empire was in the patriarchate of Antioch by Patriarch Ephraim (d. 545), originally from Amida (now Diyarbakır in Turkey), and was supported by Chalcedonian bishop Abraham bar Khaili, bishop of Amida: "there were arrests, exiles, imprisonments, and some Monophysites were even burnt to death for their faith."[200] At some stage, this persecution must have softened. Evagrius tells us of mixed church congregations of Chalcedonians and Monophysites in front of bishop Abraham bar Khaili, even though the Monophysites did not receive communion.

The Emperor Justinian (d. 564) is reported to have pursued religious unification with the Monophysites in the last years of his reign.[201] Between 561-564, Evagrius notes the emperor "responded to a question from the monastic community of First and Second Syria" relating to a dispute between the emperor and Anastasius, the patriarch of Antioch.[202] This suggests a confederation of pro-Chalcedon monks between the two provinces. Emperor Justinian II continued with attempts at reconciliation with the Monophysites around 568 in the Euphrates and continuing in Constantinople. Theological discussions were ongoing between the emperor and the Monophysite Greek bishops of Constantinople. It appeared Anastasius, the patriarch of Antioch, mediated between the Monophysites and Chalcedonians.[203]

Decades later after the Acacian Schism, the late sixth century saw a preference for coexistence amongst the Eastern Christian populations. Whitby informs us: "Individual Christians were more prepared to live quietly alongside those of a different doctrinal persuasion then the rhetorical of professional argument might suggest." Some monaster-

---

[200] Whitby, *The Ecclesiastical History*, footnote 31, p. 211.
[201] Ibid., footnote 138, p. 250, citing Michael the Syrian.
[202] Evagrius, *The Ecclesiastical History*, p. 252.
[203] Whitby, *The Ecclesiastical History*, pp. 257, 262.

ies in Constantinople began to house both Chalcedonians and Monophysites. Various shared practices became a concern to the Monophysites for fear of losing their faithful to the Chalcedonians. Whitby also
states that group loyalty determined allegiances, but individuals could
be much more flexible. Evagrius observed that Monophysites were located in the Empire's desert frontier regions.[204]

## 7.5 First Available Documentary Reference
## to 'The Maronites'

Jacob Baradaeus (El-Baradei) was the Syriac Monophysite Bishop of
Edessa from 543-578. He was a defender of the Miaphysite movement
that had been established by the patriarch of Constantinople, Acacius,
in 471. He is known for reinvigorating his church such that it became
known after him as 'Jacobite'. We do not have to assume that, at this
time, the Maronites were an independent church by virtue of having
inherited their name (at the latest by the year 592) from their monastic
base of St Maroun. In Semitic terms, it merely would have been for
ease of identification similar to a male referenced by his father's name
– for example, Peter son (Ibn) of Karam. They were a monastic union
with congregations around them, not a church independent of the
Catholic Church. They were certainly leaders of the pro-Chalcedonian
orthodox party. In a sense, the term 'Maronite' was for ease of identification. It may eventually have become a label for those connected to
the pro-Chalcedonian Catholic party.

In 591 a conference was held between the Maronites and Jacobites
in Antioch with representatives of Peter of Callinice, Jacobite patriarch 578-591.[205] The conference followed a conversion of Jacobites to
Maronites to become Catholic. Jacobite Patriarch Denis or Dionysius
of Tell Mahre (d. 845) informs us that two learned and eloquent men,
Probus and John Barbur, accepted the Council of Chalcedon. They

---

[204] Ibid., pp. xli-xlv.

[205] Nau copied the letters from the eighth century manuscript preserved in the British
Museum in London, Add. 12155, fol. 163. Nau's introduction to the exchange of correspondence is provided in Naaman, *The Maronites*, pp. 152-157.

ceased supporting the Jacobite Patriarch Peter of Callinice (d. 591) and provoked numerous defections amongst the Jacobites in the region of Antioch. Probus and John asked the Catholic patriarch of Antioch, Anastasius (559-599), to call for a conference of all the monks of Antioch to show that the doctrine of Peter was in error. It is not coincidental that there is no mention of any other Aramaic Catholic denomination for the new converts other than the Maronites.

Once again, we have evidence of a significant number of Aramaic Monophysites, and likely their monasteries, being absorbed into the Beit Maroun confederation. Most probably after the end of the Acacian Schism in 518, the emperor with the churches of Rome and Constantinople would have ensured a firm consolidation of Catholic orthodox doctrine in the western region of the patriarchate. Beit Maroun would have led the Aramaic-Syriac speaking Catholics with the full support of Rome and Constantinople. By the time of the conference in Antioch seventy years later, Beit Maroun confederation seemed to have completely dominated in the regions of Antioch and Apamaea and perhaps the wider western regions of the patriarchate of Antioch. Syriac scholars such as Brock and Vööbus have confirmed this dominance was also spread across Lebanon (including Phoenicia) and northern Palestine.[206]

It was from the conference in 591 that letters between the Maronites and Jacobites were generated (see below).[207] The letter from the Beit Maroun monks and the reply from the Jacobites provide certainty that by the year 592 the term 'Maronite' was used to refer to the Aramaic Catholics who were under the leadership of the Beit Maroun network of monasteries or who followed their orthodoxy. The letter from the Maronites to the Jacobites when referring to the insults lobbed against

---

[206] This will be discussed in Chapter 9 on Monothelitism.

[207] Nau cites Assemani for his quote of Tell Mahre in *Bibl. Orientalis*, II, 72 in Naaman, *The Maronites*, pp. 154-155. Nau states the manuscript Add. 17169 was written by a certain Sergius in 592 and was brought by the monks of the monastery of St Maroun and placed in their library in the year 745. After the destruction of the monastery a Jacobite monastery held it until 1835 when a Greek named Pacho sold it to the British Museum in London where Nau accessed it.

them states: "It is rich above all insults against the Maronites" and "all these insults now turn to the glory of the Maronites." The Jacobites reply: "you who call him [Christ] double because he has taken on flesh and become man, and he proclaims to you Maronites partisans of the two natures and to all the Council of Chalcedon."

The monks are referred to as "the offspring of the root of Leo," the "plant of the Chalcedon vine," and "the acid germ produced by the vine of Theodoret." The Maronites address themselves as "from the orthodox monks of Beth Maroun, sons of the Catholic Holy Church." These phrases demonstrate the perpetual Catholic orthodoxy of the Aramaic-speaking Maronite monks from the Council of Chalcedon in 451 to the time of the exchange of correspondence in 592 (see sections 7.7.4 and 7.7.5 of this Chapter). It is also notable that there is a reference to Beit Maroun being from "the vine of Theodoret." It provides further support for the many links and interconnections we have spoken about including between Theodoret, Theodoret's Maroun, Cyrrhus, Apamaea, Emperor Marcian, the Council of Chalcedon, and the monasteries of Agapetus and Beit Maroun.

The Jacobites begin their letter of 592 by addressing it to "the five questions sent from the village of Armaz (or Armanez) by the monks of Beth Maron, after their leaving Antioch, to the orthodox monks in the holy monasteries of Mesopotamia." It appears the principal delegates at the conference in Antioch, and principal authors of the letter on behalf of the Maronites, were the monks Philip and Thomas from the village of Armaz in the territory of Apamaea. The Jacobites refer to "Philip and to Thomas, those of Beth Maron" and their response concludes: "End of the solution to the senseless questions of the monks of Beth Maron who are in the territory of Apamaea."

The reference to the territory of Apamaea is likely a reference to Syria Secunda, emphasising the pre-eminence enjoyed by the monasteries over other monasteries in Syria Secunda. In addition, one may also infer the letters provide evidence that the Beit Maroun monastic confederation was over a much broader area than Syria Secunda. Though the Jacobites talk of the monks Philip and Thomas from the territory of Apamaea, this does not mean this was the only territory housing Beit Maroun monks. This proposition is supported by the opening paragraph of the Jacobite response and supported by a report of numerous defections from the Jacobites to the Maronites in the region of Antioch that instigated the conference in Antioch itself.

The authors of the Jacobite response commence their letter by referring to themselves as "the orthodox monks in the holy monasteries of Mesopotamia." This suggests the monastic heartland of the Aramaic-Syriac Monophysites at that time was in Mesopotamia, not in western Syria towards Antioch where the conference was held. This coincides with the influence of Jacob as Bishop of Edessa around the same period.

Nau states the role the Maronites played in this debate, and the tone they adopted in their letters towards the Jacobites, leaves no doubt the Maronites, through the monks of St Maroun, were the leaders of all Catholic orthodox in Syria.[208] The Maronites refer to themselves as "the orthodox monks of Beth Maroun, sons of the Catholic Holy Church." They no longer refer to themselves as first ranked monastery in Syria Secunda. The reference by Nau to all of 'Syria' is likely to have meant ancient Syria, which included Phoenicia, Lebanon, and Palestine.

Nau notes that any reader that feels unsympathetic towards the inquisitions by the Maronites in 592, should be reminded of the harsh acts undertaken a few decades earlier with the massacre of over three hundred Maronite monks. At that earlier time the Monophysites enjoyed the support of Emperor Anastasius, the patriarchs of Constantinople and Antioch, and the bishop of Apamaea. However, as mentioned there is no clear evidence that the Syriac Monophysites committed the atrocities. This is supported by the fact that Maronite reprisals against the Jacobites some decades later were theological rather than physical in nature. In any case, the correspondence of 592 is evidence of Maronite and Jacobite relations without any violence. There are other examples as Nau concludes:

---

[208] Nau copied in Naaman, *The Maronites*, p. 153. He is supported by authors such as Brock as will be seen in the later chapters of this book.

Elsewhere they behave perfectly towards each other as a story shows that we have already published: a periodeute said to a former ascetic unhappily fallen into sin: "I advise you to go down to this monastery of Mar Maron the Blessed, to remain there and to weep there for your sins. For there one finds a monastery life that will do complete penance for the sins committed; in a word, one finds an excellent practice of perfection."[209]

## 7.6 Matti Moosa's Attempts to Undermine Maronite History

Matti Moosa has written extensively on the events dealt with in this book, however, as this Chapter demonstrates, there are multifarious examples in his scholarship that belie bias, selective reading, and the erasure of significant factors in Maronite history. Moosa's personal faith position has directly influenced his reading of history. Moosa, who died in 2014, was not a Maronite, but a proud and faithful member of the Syrian Orthodox Jacobite Church.[210] His agenda is clearly set out on page one of his book in his introduction: "By faith, liturgy, rite, religious books, and heritage, the Maronites were of Syrian Orthodox (Jacobite) origin until the very end of the sixteenth century when they became ultramontane [advocates of the Pope's supreme authority] followers of the Catholic Church."

It may appear as though Moosa has extensively researched Maronite history but, using the same documentation he relies on, one can easily offer an entirely differing deduction. Regrettably, his conclusions run one way almost throughout his entire works. His views reveal an agenda at almost each turn, and the following analysis concludes that his entire works cannot be considered tenable enough to warrant a full formal reply to every one of his hundreds of conclusions, or be accepted as an accurate account of Maronite history.

---

[209] Nau, copied in Naaman, *The Maronites*, p. 157.

[210] See the obituary of Matti Moosa at *Legacy.com*, http://www.legacy.com/obituaries/erietimesnews/ obituary.aspx?pid=173806964.

## 7.6.1 The Massacre and the Primary Sources

On such area of controversy is Moosa's claim that the two petitions of 517 and 518 are inauthentic and the massacre of the three hundred and fifty monks did not take place. In this claim, amongst many others, he is in opposition to many scholars. The following critique outlines a number of the issues with his book. Moosa contradicts himself on numerous occasions. For example, at one stage in his book he refers to the petition to the Pope as admitted to the Council of 536[211] then in another part he denies it. He does however admit the petition to the bishops was known not only to the Council of 536 but to the Syria Secunda Bishops' Synod of 518.

Moosa's principal reason for dismissing the massacre is based on what he sees as an apparent silence in *discussion* on the subject at the Council of Constantinople in 536. Although accepting that the petition to the bishops was admitted to the Council, he states that given the seriousness of the heinous crimes involved it was surprising that it was never discussed. Extraordinarily, after citing an apparent seventeenth century Jesuit writer Labbe, Moosa concludes not only that the petition was invalid but all of the texts of the acts of the Council were defective, incoherent or erroneous.[212]

Moosa admits the records of the Council are incomplete. By his very own admission, there is no proof the Council did *not* discuss the petition to the Pope. The minutes of any Council do not record all of the discussions, particularly in ancient times. The fact that the petition to the bishops and the response from the Pope was part of the documentation of the Council gives credence to the likelihood that they were discussed.

The Council had the particulars of the atrocities. They were referred to in the petition to the bishops. The Council also had the Pope's reply, which by Moosa's own admission was read at its fifth session on 4 June at the request of the Italian bishops and Roman

---

[211] Moosa, *The Maronites in History*, p. 55.
[212] Moosa, *The Maronites in History*, pp. 48, 54.

deacons.[213] The importance of this request cannot be dismissed. The following extracts from the Pope's letter in reply to the monks uses very strong language, clearly showing their awareness of the mayhem [emphases mine]:

> *insanity* of the enemies of God has been laid open and the *obstinate fury* of the unbelievers, who with revived spirit hate the Lord and thereby *wickedly* persecute his members, has *painfully been exposed* ...
>
> the *rapacity of the wolves* which lie in wait ...
>
> the shrewd, *bloodthirsty* and rapacious one ...
>
> These, who abandon his protection, expose themselves to the dangers, by which *they are torn to pieces* ...
>
> Dioscorus and Timothy, the parricide, Peter of Alexandria, Acacius of Constantinople with his followers, also Peter of Antioch, like to the one mentioned beforehand as much in error as in name, but also Severus just the same of the same place and poison, Axenaias of Hierapolis, Cyrus of Edessa, and Peter of Apamea; *they are no longer to be condemned only for their own but also for the destruction of others.*

Comparing the monks' petition to the bishops with the one to the Pope, the petition to the bishops leaves out the actual number of monks massacred but otherwise is detailed in the description of the atrocities. Remarkably, Moosa sees the failure to quote the number of monks killed as justification for alleging both petitions were fraudulent.

As Joseph Azize summarises:

> The records of what happened at the Council of Constantinople in 536, other than the decisions recorded in its canons, are known to be incomplete (even Moosa notes this, which raises the question of how he can rely upon an argument from silence). But, even more directly, the evidence is that either that letter was read and accepted, or one quite similar was. What is certain is that there was read a complaint by monks

---

[213] Moosa, *The Maronites in History*, p. 56.

that Severus and Peter 'had maltreated and even killed many of them' ... So, either the letter of 517 was read, or one the same effect was.[214]

Moosa states the petition to the Pope of 517 was not read or admitted at the Council, only the petition to the bishops' synod of 518, the latter clearly after the end of the Acacian Schism. It is unusual that the petition to the Pope appears directly before the Pope's reply in the collection of papal documents at Rome, but it is not found in the Council documents. The fact that it may have been part of the Council's deliberation is supported by the widely accepted view that the recordings of the Council's meetings were incomplete. However, we cannot forget at least one of the petitions was read.

Had the events related by the monks been untrue and considered so by the Council of 536, its significance should have led the Council to declare the petition to the bishops and the Pope's reply as void. Had there been the slightest suggestion the Beit Maroun monks were fraudsters or had remained Monophysite, the Syria Secunda Bishops Synod of 518 would have stated so and this would have been documented at the Council. Further, an investigation would have been conducted and a condemnation made at the Council.

The petition to Pope Hormisdas and the Pope's letter in reply are preserved in *Collectio Avellana,* amongst the largest collection of Pope Hormisdas' correspondence. *Collectio Avellana* also preserves papal correspondence between the years 367 and 553 AD and is one of the main sources for studying the history of the papacy of Rome in the sixth century.[215] It is therefore untenable to suggest a fraudulent letter to the Pope, and the papal response, would thereafter appear in succession in a collection of papal writings for the period. Ultimately,

[214] Father Yuhanna [Joseph] Azize, "The 350 Martyrs (Part 2): Have We Been Misled," *Under the Sun,* 17 April 2017, http://www.josephazize.com/2017/04/03/the-350-martyrs-part-two-have-we-been-misled/.
[215] Cornelia B. Horn, "The Correspondence Between the Monks of Syria Secunda and Pope Hormisdas in 517/518 AD," *The Journal of Maronite Studies* 1 (4), (1997), http://maronite-institute.org/MARI/JMS/ october97/The_Correspondence_Between. htm.

Moosa's claims seek to undermine the credibility of the churches of Rome and Constantinople at the time.

Considering the turmoil of the era, Moosa's idea that the papal response to the monks' petition was provided without Rome's full investigation or knowledge is implausible. The implication takes aim at the diligence of the papal office, but the acceptance by the Council of the petition to the bishops with the serious tone of the Pope's reply confirms the events in Church history. The Pope's reply read by the Council also confirms the Catholic orthodoxy of the monks of Beit Maroun. The reply demonstrates Rome was tracking the orthodoxy of the Beit Maroun confederation, beyond the information mentioned in their petitions.

In addition, the Pope's written confirmation in 518 of Beit Maroun's orthodoxy contradicts Moosa's suggestion that the Maronites were Monophysite. This is particularly relevant for the period during the Acacian Schism and the eighteen years that followed up to the Council of 536, when the issue of orthodoxy was the most significant in Rome, Constantinople, Antioch, and Alexandria. This book concurs with Azize's assessment of Moosa's arguments:

> Given that Moosa cites the evidence that the Maronites were Catholic at the time of the Crusaders and even attended the Lateran Council of 1215 (see pp. 220-221), his book that no change came before the end of the sixteenth century cannot be maintained.
>
> Further, Moosa's argument turns on the idea that the Maronite practices and teachings which Rome corrected at the time of the Crusades were 'identical to those of the Syrian Orthodox Church ...' (p. 224). However, the doctrines and practices he refers to (e.g. the right of priests to administer chrismation, and the contents of the chrism) were all the common heritage of Christians at the time of Chalcedon. Moosa has succeeded only in showing that the Maronites were an authentically Syriac and Antiochene Church – which we have always claimed ...

To prove that the Maronites had been Orthodox until either the thirteenth or sixteenth century, he would need to show that the Maronites had an Orthodox element in their Church which could not be explained as being from before the Council. He cannot do that, so he asserts it.

He fails to point to one single specifically Monophysite element in Maronite doctrine. Since Monophysitism showed itself precisely in doctrine, to prove a Monophysite origin, he would need to find a distinctively Monophysite element in our doctrine. He fails.

Along the way, he disputes that authenticity of the slaying of the 350 Martyrs, and therefore of the letters by which we know of this tragedy. Moosa needs to do this, because if the monks were slain at the urging of the Monophysite hierarchy, for doctrinal reasons, his argument that the Maronites were Monophysite is even more patently untenable than it already is …

Moosa's book has been considered, and dismissed, by one of the leading scholars of the area. Harald Suermann concluded that the documents were authentic. In *Histoire des origins de l'Église Maronite*, he notes, first, that Moosa is trying to establish that the monastery of Maroun was known before the later Monothelite controversy, and then goes on to lay out all of Moosa's arguments (pp. 102-103) …

Little wonder that Suermann concludes at p. 104: 'Les lettres sont sans doute authentiques' (the letters are without doubt authentic). [216]

Moosa believes that the letter to the Pope and the letter to the bishops relate to two different events, at two different locations and therefore cannot be reliable accounts of the massacre. He states one petition refers to the number of monks massacred and the other doesn't and so they are inconsistent. He believes the massacre did not take place. He also claims there is no evidence the Pope's response is related to the petition from the monks.[217]

---

[216] Azize, "The 350 Martyrs (Part 2)".
[217] Moosa, *The Maronites in History*, pp. 42-43.

These propositions of Moosa must be dismissed. The petition to the Pope refers to one specific event in detail: "when we were going to the pen of the Lord Simeon for the cause of the Church ... they killed three hundred and fifty men from among us." The petition to the bishops details many events at various monasteries, not just the massacre. The petition to the bishops states: "when in truth we were proceeding towards the locality of Kaprokerameh, not far from the venerable temple of the blessed confessor Simon ... For some they put to death ... As for Severus ... he never had enough of the stain of murder." Both the petition to the Pope and the petition to the bishops refer to deaths when the monks were travelling to the area related to St Simon the Stylite. These are not two different places or events as alleged by Moosa.

The petition to the bishops continues:

> Thus [at the monastery of Nikertai], having got into the habit of massacring monks, considering what is abominable in the eyes of men as advantageous profit, he [Severus] got his henchmen, whom he led on the war path in a way not at all religious, to slit the throats of the venerable orthodox monks who had gathered there for a solemn ceremony; then he presented himself at the altar with his hands all bloodied from this deed.

In relation to Moosa's claim that the Pope's reply was not related to the petition, the author Horn makes it clear that the Latin and Greek texts of this correspondence are preserved in succession in the *Collectio Avellana* as letter number 139 for the petition (dated towards end of 517) and number 140 (dated 10 February 518) for the Pope's reply.[218] The letters are only a few months apart. There are no other letters between the monks and the Pope that are preserved. However, the Pope's response indicates a possibility of more than one letter received from the monks. It states at the start, "I have read your highly esteemed letters." However, it is understood the plural 'letters' in an ancient context could be meant as one letter but many words.

---

[218] Horn, "The Correspondence Between the Monks of Syria Secunda and Pope Hormisdas."

Repeatedly, when convenient, Moosa relies on the idea of silence as proof. If a source from history does not mention an event or fact, Moosa often concludes it must not have taken place. Even if the event is mentioned in a text of a Synod or Council, if it is not mentioned by a *historian* Moosa also often concludes it must not have happened. He frequently sets out the facts according to his own interpretation of principal sources, rather than setting out the relevant extracts of the ancient source. His interpretation of sources repeatedly supports his bias.

According to Moosa, if Evagrius did not mention the massacre of the three hundred and fifty monks, so significant an occurrence, it could not have happened. Evagrius was writing more than seventy years after the event. He, like other historians, could not have possibly recorded all events, even in his own time. By Moosa's own admission, the acts of the Council of Constantinople in 536 had written evidence of the massacre through the petition to the bishops, but not the number of monks killed. Whilst six volumes of *Ecclesiastical History* may sound extensive, Evagrius' works are quite brief. They only total approximately three-hundred pages in Whitby's translated edition. We must also remember Evagrius' history covers over two centuries. Though he does not go into detail, after giving us the information about a massacre of monks in Antioch, Evagrius recounts "and there also came about another incident not inferior to this ... and so then too events of no small significance took place."

Further, Whitby informs us in his introduction to Evagrius' works:

> Evagrius reports the violent ecclesiastical disputes of Egypt in the fifth century via his sources, primarily the Zachariah of Mitylene: Egypt is a place of Monophysite discord and disruption, where a patriarch might even be murdered in church and his corpse subject to public humiliation, whereas comparable problems at Antioch are not highlighted.[219]

Whitby adds that all major cities including Antioch had a reputa-

---

[219] Whitby, *The Ecclesiastical History*, p. xix.

tion for violence. Whitby recounts some incidents not mentioned by Evagrius but by another author Malalas: "in 507 victory celebrations of the Green faction had included the destruction of a synagogue, and resulted in the disembowelling of the *praefectus vigilum* (a prefect or governor) ... during Zeno's reign a local monk had incited the mob to attack the Jews and dig up their bones."[220]

The accounts of Evagrius support the petitions from the monks in 517 and 518, and the Pope's response. Both Evagrius and the petitions speak of force and compulsion imposed by Severus. Evagrius' history discusses the recall of the bishops of Apamaea of their support of Severus' anti-Chalcedonian doctrine. The Pope in his response to the monks intimates this exact point. The monks discuss the forced public humiliation. It is plausible the Pope was referring to the bishops, or the monks following obedience to the bishops, when he spoke of them being "late, indeed, that you enter on the way of truth."

Whilst examining Moosa's works, an unscholarly pattern appears. Moosa concludes the recorded acts of the Council, the two petitions of the monks and the Pope's response – as all illegitimate and he dismisses every other author that might be opposed to his view. However, in doing so, he often refers to the works of his own church historians, from the Syrian Orthodox (Jacobite) Church, and describes these authors as "learned." For the sixth century alone, Moosa repudiates the authenticity of ancient manuscripts catalogued by: Guenther's *Collectio Avellana* (preserving papal correspondence from 367-553) held in Rome; Wright's *Catalogue of Syriac Manuscripts in the British Museum;* the recordings of the Councils in *Sacrosancta Concilia*; Schwartz's catalogue *ACO Coll. Sabbaitica*; Hardouin's catalogue; and Mansi's thirty one volumes, *Sacrorum Coniliorum,* held in Italy.

Moosa also dismisses the views of a great many writers, non-Maronite and Maronite, from Doueihi of the eighteenth century to the present scholarship on the topic.[221] On virtually every subject exam-

---

[220] Ibid., footnote 116, p. 174.

[221] Throughout his many chapters related to this topic, he specifically disregards the views of every contemporary non-Maronite writer including Honigmann, Lammens,

ined by Moosa throughout his book the work and conclusions of a multitude of scholars[222] are either directly opposed by Moosa or are completely inconsistent with his findings either on the subject of the massacre, and/or his claim that the Maronites were of Syrian Orthodox (Jacobite) origin until the end of the sixteenth century. In response, scholars Azize, Suermann, and Horn have all addressed and rejected Moosa's claims on these texts of the sixth century, and this book concurs that Moosa's suppositions are imaginary and flawed.

Moosa notes that the Roman Catholic Church each year commemorates the massacre of the martyred three hundred and fifty monks, in addition to the Maronite Church's commemoration.[223] Severus was a patriarch of Antioch and the petition states "As for Severus ... he never had enough of the stain of murder." Despite this, in Moosa's analysis, the massacre could not have taken place. Even though the Aramaic Monophysites are not directly accused in the petitions, Moosa must have believed he still needed to defend them from the crime. The only way he could do this is by dismissing any evidence or commentary that could insinuate their involvement.

Moosa's defence of the Aramaic Monophysites includes a dismissal of any author, ancient manuscript, and the acts of Councils, which make the allegation. This also results in Moosa implying that the many monks from around the Middle East who attended the Council of 536 were frauds. He implicates in this attack, not only the delegate from the confederation of Beit Maroun who signed petitions of anathematization against Severus at the Council in 536, but other monk delegates and co-signatories of the petitions with Paul representing monasteries from Jerusalem, Palestine, Sinai, and Arabia. Moosa once again dis-

---

Frend, Crawford, Dvornik, Gibbon, Downey, Prentice, Vailhe, Cheikho, Torrey, Lent, Bedjan and others. The last three authors relate to Moosa's discussion as to whether St Simon the Stylite was pro or anti-Chalcedonian. See Moosa, *The Maronites in History*, pp. 62-65, 82.

[222] We can add to the above list Vööbus, Brock, Suerman, Noldeke, Festugiere, Price, Tillemont, Horn, Mansi, Wright, Hefele, Atiya, Assemani, Nairon, Hitti, Naaman, Dib, Azize, and Nau.

[223] Moosa, *The Maronites in History*, p. 43-44.

misses their authenticity and relevance to the correspondence between the Maronites and Jacobites in 592 AD: he says if such correspondence ever took place, it could only be attributed to two centuries later.[224]

### 7.6.2 St Simon the Stylite

The two petitions of 517 and 518 from the monks of Second Syria suggest that at the time of the massacre in 517 the monastery and church of St Simon the Stylite the Great or Elder remained in Chalcedonian hands. They mention "for when we were going to the pen of the Lord Simeon for the cause of the Church" and "not far from the venerable temple of the blessed confessor Simon." It would be unusual to venerate Simon and the church and monastery in this way if they were Monophysites. Also, the petition to the Pope contains twenty-six signatures with the name Simon, possibly but not certainly after St Simon the Stylite.

However, Evagrius writing his *Ecclesiastical History* around 593, sets out an extract of a letter decades earlier from St Simon Stylite to Basil, bishop (patriarch) of the city of Antioch. It is clear in the letter that St Simon supported the doctrine from the Council of Chalcedon as he stated:

> Wherefore I too, wretched and worthless, the abortion of the monks, made known to his Majesty my attitude concerning the faith of the 630 Holy fathers who were gathered at Chalcedon, standing by it and being fortified by what was made manifest by the Holy Spirit.[225]

Evagrius confirmed that he also cited a letter from St Simon Stylite to the Emperor Leo, but he did not include it in his work as he said the letter to Basil was more succinct.[226]

The proposition that St Simon was adherent to Chalcedon is contested by Moosa.[227] Nonetheless, it is more likely than not that the

---

[224] Ibid., pp. 84-86. He states the dates should be around the year 727 rather than 592.
[225] Evagrius, *The Ecclesiastical History*, p. 92.
[226] Ibid.
[227] Moosa, *The Maronites in History*, pp. 64-68.

monastery of Qalat Seman and the nearby grand church of St Simon the Stylite built on the site of Simon's pillar, was under the leadership of Chalcedon monks after the death of St Simon in 459. This would have arisen from the emperor's enforcement of Chalcedonian doctrine after 451 and the construction of what some regard as the largest church in the world of its time.

Perhaps during the time of the Acacian Schism, and more particularly at some time during the period of Severus as patriarch of Antioch (512-518), the St Simon Stylite church and monastery may have reverted to the control of the Monophysites. Whitby, who edited and translated Evagrius' works in a publication released in 2000, comments that the monastery of Qalat Seman was probably still in Chalcedonian hands in 517 when Severus' opponents (the monks of Beit Maroun) assembled there. He says "granted that Severus fled from Antioch in 518, there was little time for him to use his power as patriarch to effect a change of allegiance."[228] In contrast, Moosa, whose work was released in 1986, cites a letter from Severus to St Simon monks confirming the monastery was under the jurisdiction of the Monophysite monks who shared the same faith as St Simon Stylite.[229]

Whitby comments that Simon was still regarded as a Chalcedonian, since Severus was required to defend his association with the saint in a speech.[230] Whitby concludes:

> When the monastery came under secure Monophysite control is unknown: assumptions that this occurred during the sixth century are unsafe, and it is quite possible that Chalcedonians were in charge when Evagrius visited the shrine in the late sixth century; the monastery is not among those named in the context of Monophysite discussions in 567/8. The definitive change may have occurred during the Arab invasions, when the monastery was raided in the aftermath of the battle

---

[228] Whitby, "Introduction," *The Ecclesiastical History*, p. xlii.
[229] Moosa, *The Maronites in History*, p. 67 quoting from *The Sixth Book of Select Letters of Severus Patriarch of Antioch*, Part 1, 134-37, and Part 11, 120-23.
[230] Whitby, "Introduction," *The Ecclesiastical History*, p. xlii.

of Yarmuk (636) on the day of the saint's feast; the Mono-physite Michael the Syrian commented that this was a just punishment for the orgies and drunkenness which accompanied these festivals, an indication that he did not approve of the way the shrine was being run at the time. The affiliation of the monks at Qalat Seman cannot be used to support the theory that Chalcedonian patriarchs at Antioch had become detached from their rural hinterland.[231]

Further, Price, in his work on Theodoret, clearly opposes the view St Simon Stylite was a Monophysite. Theodoret had visited Simon Stylite and Price states:

> On several occasions the imperial court requested Symeon's intervention in the great doctrinal disputes of the time. In 432 Theodosius II got Symeon to press John of Antioch to be reconciled to Cyril of Alexandria; in 434 Titus, 'comes domesti-corum', got Symeon to press Theodoret himself on the same issue. Theodoret yielded, though he was deeply distressed by the pressure brought to bear on him. Again after the Council of Chalcedon (451) he advised the dowager empress Eudocia at Jerusalem in favour of Chalcedon and reconciliation with bishop Juvenal of Jerusalem; and in 457 he responded to the emperor Leo's circular letter, again in favour of Chalcedon. Monophysite sources tell of Theodoret personally visiting Symeon after the Council of Chalcedon to press for his support of its Definition.[232]

In his chapter on St Maroun, Moosa mentions an ancient manuscript that refers to the conversion of many pagans from Mount Lebanon through the preaching of St Simon the Stylite. Like other ancient manuscripts, he dismisses this story as apocryphal or fictitious, even though it was recounted by Cosmos, a disciple of St Simon.[233] Avoiding yet another ancient manuscript then allows Moosa to opportunely dismiss any connection between the Maronites of Lebanon and the

---

[231] Whitby, "Introduction," *The Ecclesiastical History*, pp. xlii-xliii.
[232] Price, *A History of the Monks of Syria*, footnote 35, p. 174.
[233] Moosa, *The Maronites in History*, p. 21.

conversion of Lebanese through St Simon the Stylite. He states, "Theodore Noldeke's statement that, 'it is probable the Maronites are the descendants of the converts who accepted baptism after Simon's intercession, as they believed, had freed them from the ravages of wild beasts', is speculation and lacks historical evidence."[234]

Moosa's approach to this story about St Simon the Stylite is far from satisfactory. He also conveniently omits any reference to Abraham (the anchorite from Cyrrhus, from the 'garden' planted by Maroun) who, as recounted by Theodoret, travelled to Mount Lebanon and established what is likely to be a monastic community.

### 7.6.3  St Maroun

Regarding St Maroun, Moosa accepts Theodoret as a reliable historian. However, Moosa states: "The biography of Maroun is very brief and, when compared with his biographies of St Simon the Stylite or even Jacob, a follower of Maroun, it is rather insignificant." He affords Maroun no special place or excellence in the austere life practised by thousands of monks and holy men from the western Egyptian desert to Mesopotamia. Moosa then speaks of St Barsauma as the chief of all anchorites.[235]

Moosa's comments are strikingly inconsistent with what was written about Maroun. Moosa declines to set out any of Theodoret's text on Maroun. The reader must accept Moosa's words of Maroun's insignificance. As Moosa would well have known at the time of writing, his comments are particularly confronting for those who venerate St Maroun.

Many of the previous chapters of this book demonstrate St Maroun's significance, contrary to Moosa's views. Theodoret himself paints the opposite picture to that set out by Moosa. He mentions Maroun's "fame circulated everywhere, attracted everyone from every side." Theodoret goes on to say it was Maroun "who planted for God the garden that now

---

[234] Ibid.
[235] Ibid., p. 18.

flourishes in the region of Cyrrhus." Theodoret makes it clear Maroun was no insignificant figure in Syria.

We find a record of a number of monasteries named after Maroun. In 517, there is a record of anti-Severus monks gathered at the monastery of Maro (Maroun), south of Damascus, and appealing to Pope Hormisdas against their patriarch.[236] There is also a record of a Monastery of Maroun in the district of Sokas in Constantinople and in Batroun, Lebanon.[237]

Moosa relies on Theodoret's brief account of Maroun to propose triviality, but as has been stated elsewhere in this book, one can suggest the reverse, that is, because of his fame at the time it was not necessary to elaborate. It is possible others wrote about Maroun, but their manuscripts have not been located. Further, Theodoret never met Maroun (who died before Theodoret became bishop), but met many of the other anchorites he wrote about in far greater detail.

The author Price, who translated and arranged Theodoret's *Religious History* in English, states in his footnotes at the end of Theodoret's chapter on Maroun:

> Maron ... emerges from the *Religious History* ... as the first influential hermit of the region of Cyrrhus. His pattern of life in the open air, exposed to the extremes of the climate, was imitated by many – James (Chapter 21), Limnaeus (Chapter 22), and others (Chapter 23) – and gave the asceticism of Cyrrhestica a distinctive character, for elsewhere hermits normally lived in cells or caves ... It is it surprising, in view of Maron's importance that this chapter is so brief and sketchy.

Price's comments are contradictory to those of Moosa, and, as he

---

[236] Whitby, *The Ecclesiastical History*, footnote 127, p. 177.

[237] Moosa *The Maronites in History*, p. 79 citing Michael the Syrian and Hefele for the monastery in Constantinople. Moosa at p. 74 cites Doueihi to confirm the monastery in Batroun. It is possible this is the monastery that housed the skull of St Maroun, according to Doueihi, brought to it by St John Maroun in the late seventh early eighth century, from which we know the Crusaders were given the relic to take back to Italy as discussed in a later chapter.

does not cite Moosa in his chapter on 'Identity of the Ascetic Marun', we can easily infer that he does not consider him an expert in this area.

The reference by Moosa to St Barsauma as the chief of all anchorites has no historical basis. Barsauma passed away around 458, after the Council of Chalcedonian in 451 and several decades after St Maroun. He may have been a church father (chief) anchorite for non-Chalcedonian Aramaic monks and also for many monks generally prior to the Council in 451. However, he could not have been a church father anchorite for the Chalcedonian Aramaic monks.

### 7.6.4 Beit Maroun Monastery

In relation to St Maroun's monastery, Moosa errs when stating, "there is nothing to indicate that this Marun (referred to by Theodoret) ever founded a religious community or inspired the name Maronite."[238] Theodoret makes it clear that Maroun had disciples, or followers, as many imitated his lifestyle. The name Maroun inspired the name Maronite, certainly not in Maroun's time, but later through historical circumstances that have been set out in previous chapters and evidenced by the correspondence in 592. St Maroun never established a church, nor did he intend to. It can never be suggested he was the founder of the Maronite Church.

Moosa is incorrect when he comments, "there is no evidence that he (Maroun) or his followers ever built a monastery in his name."[239] There is no suggestion Maroun built a monastery, nor his immediate disciples. However, there is certainly a strong date link between Theodoret's Maroun (d. 410-423), the founding of Beit Maroun in 452 (according to Abdul l-Fida), and the reference to the monastery of Maroun in the correspondence of 517 and 518. There is no other Maroun in this period as significant as Theodoret's. There had to be followers who were inspired by Maroun to arrange the construction of a monastery in his name. Naaman's conclusion is that the principal activists were Theodoret and the Emperor Marcian. There is no other

---

[238] Moosa, *The Maronites in History*, p. 31.
[239] Ibid.

plausible evidence available to counter these claims. Moosa does not offer an explanation as to what other Maroun provided the impetus for the naming of this important Catholic beacon of monasteries in the Syrian orient. He does not because there is no answer.

Moosa is also wrong to conclude there was no Monastery of Maroun in the fifth century in Syria Secunda whose monks were Chalcedonians.[240] The petitions of 517 and 518 completely contradict him, as does the Pope's response. The texts not only confirm a Beit Maroun monastery and extensive network, they also make clear the Catholic orthodoxy of the monks. The Syria Secunda bishops' synod of 518 and the Council of Constantinople in 536 had the monks' petition of 518 before them. The Council would have been very swift in condemning Beit Maroun monks as heretics had they not been Catholic Orthodox. The Pope would have done the same.

By Moosa's own admission, another letter signed by the monks of Beit Maroun was presented to the Council of 536 against Severus of Antioch and Peter of Apamaea by four delegates of monastic communities: two delegates representing the monasteries of Jerusalem and Palestine; one delegate representing the monasteries of Sinai and Arabia; and one delegate, a deacon, representing the monastery of Maroun and all of the monasteries of Syria Secunda.[241] At the end of the petition it is signed:

> Paul by the grace of God, deacon and delegate of the monastery of the blessed Maroun, chief (exarchos) of all the monasteries of Syria Secunda sent by all the abbots and monks of said districts to your piety carrying their petition against the aforementioned heretical acephali and acting on behalf of all the said abbots and monks, I have signed.[242]

One claim emphasised by Moosa to dismiss the validity of the document is that it was not a 'church' custom for deacons to represent

---

[240] Ibid.

[241] Ibid., p. 77.

[242] Ibid., referring to Dau, *History of the Maronites*.

all monasteries. He refers to deacons as the lowest rank of all clerical officers in the church.[243] At the outset, and most strikingly, by using this as grounds to dismiss the document, he implies that the other three delegates representing the monasteries of Jerusalem, Palestine, Sinai, and Arabia were also frauds. This argument cannot be sustained.

Nonetheless, this argument by Moosa contradicts the two petitions by the monks to the Pope and to the bishops that we have discussed in this chapter. First, the petition to the Pope refers to "John ... deacon and treasurer," as second-ranked to the archimandrite of Beit Maroun, not only in that monastery but ahead of all other archimandrites other than for the monastery of Agapetus. Further, in the petition to the Pope, nine archimandrites are referred to as deacons:

> Azizos, the deacon and archimandrite, as above; Antoninus, the deacon and archimandrite; Stephen, the deacon and archimandrite, as above; Julian, the deacon and archimandrite, as above; Nonnus, the deacon and archimandrite, as above; John, the deacon and archimandrite, as above; Macedonius, [the deacon] and archimandrite, as above; Symeonius, [the deacon] and archimandrite, as above; Menas, the deacon and archimandrite as above ...

Additionally, soon after Severus was installed as patriarch, Evagrius informs us "Aurelian, the first deacon of Epiphania" delivered the letter of deposition from two bishops to the patriarch. This is a reference to the deacon being a representative of the exarch (head) monastery of all the monasteries of the city.

At the Council of Constantinople in 536, a deacon administered the proceedings and the minute taking.[244] At the Lateran Council in 679, deacons were in attendance.[245] At the Sixth Ecumenical Council in 680-81 held at Constantinople, we are informed the thirteen legates from Rome included "the deacon John and the subdeacon

---

[243] Ibid.
[244] Hefele, *A History of the Councils of the Church*, Vol IV, pp. 194-195.
[245] Ekonomou, *Byzantine Rome and the Greek Popes*, footnote 125, p. 235.

Constantine."[246] Here we see even a subdeacon representing not just a federation of monasteries, but the Pope. Indeed, the deacon John was later to become a Pope. At the Roman Synod in 721, the 'Oriental' representatives included Archdeacon Petros, and deacons Moschos and Gregorius. At the Roman Synod of 731, there were five deacons present, all of whom were either Syrian or Greek and one of which, Zacharias, was to become a future Pope.[247]

Moosa cannot dismiss the validity of the documents on the grounds that it was not 'church' custom for deacons to represent monasteries. There is more than sufficient evidence of church custom in this ancient period delegating authority to 'deacons' (and subdeacons), even as representatives of the Pope. These persons likely had particular expertise and knowledge of church matters either equal or superior to senior clergy. Thus we can see that Moosa has made a very clear and authoritative statement on church custom, which ultimately has no credibility.

We then find Moosa referring to another letter signed by the monks of Syria Secunda to Pope Agepetus at the Council in 536 that details other complaints against Severus. This had many signatures from different monasteries. One of the signatures was again from Paul as a monk and representative of the monastery of Blessed Maroun. It is not stated whether he is a deacon. Moosa dismisses the validity of the person signing.[248]

Moosa then recounts a memorial document signed by the monks of Constantinople, Jerusalem, Syria, and Palestine submitted to the Patriarch Menace at the end of the fifth session of the Council on 15 May 536. As Moosa notes, the memorial is also signed by the monk Paul representing the Monastery of the blessed Maroun, "the leading monastery in Syria Secunda." The memorial refers to complaints against Severus and Peter. Moosa dismisses the authenticity of the document. He implies all of the monks are frauds.

[246] Hefele, *A History of the Councils of the Church*, Vol V, p. 150; Ekonomou, *Byzantine Rome and the Greek Popes*, p. 203.
[247] Ekonomou, *Byzantine Rome and the Greek Popes*, footnotes 14 and 15, p. 273.
[248] Moosa, *The Maronites in History*, p. 79.

Moosa conveniently excludes any reference to other documents that were read into the Council of 536. After Severus was expelled as patriarch of Antioch, a synod was held at Tyre in 518. Archbishop Epiphanius gave a long description of the complaints against Severus and his Tyrian cleric John Mandrites. Another synod was held by the bishops of Syria Secunda in the same year. The president of the Synod was Cyrus, Bishop of Mariamna (today Krak des Chevaliers). A synodal letter was issued to the 'ecumenical patriarch', John of Constantinople against Bishop Peter of Apamaea and seeking the emperor's sentence of Severus and Peter. Both synodal letters from Tyre and Syria Secunda are found in the acts of the Council of Constantinople in 536.[249]

At the Council at Constantinople (of bishops) in 536, more than eighty abbots and monks from Constantinople, Antioch, and Palestine requested permission to appear before the Council. The Deacon and over notary read out to the Council the written request:

> The priest Marinianus (Marianus), president of the Dalmatius monastery, also exarch of all the monasteries of Constantinople, and the monks from Antioch and Jerusalem, who are here present at the residence, have presented a petition to the emperor, and he has, in accordance with the wish of the petitioners, commanded the reading of the petition in the present assembly, so that they may decide what is in accordance with the laws of the Church. The monks in question and the Referendar Theodore assigned to them by the Emperor now request permission to appear before the Council.[250]

Patriarch Mennas of Constantinople granted the request and the Patriarch had the petition read by a deacon. This petition confirms the reasoning behind the presence of the monks at the ecumenical council

---

[249] Hefele, *A History of the Councils of the Church*, Vol IV, p. 119.

[250] Ibid., p. 194-95. Hefele on p. 203 informs us that after two months following the Council of 536, the bishops of Palestine having returned home, held a synod where forty bishops were present. Hefele's reference to 'Syria' may again suggest Beit Maroun's influence over a wider region.

of bishops and the petitions by the monks and monasteries that were signed for the Council. It also confirms the ancient practice of having one monastery as exarch of all monasteries in a province or even the whole patriarchate. The many petitions during this period, from the monks of Syria Secunda, clearly refer to Beit Maroun as the exarch of all monasteries in Syria Secunda. What is significant again, is a reference in the quote immediately above of "the monks from Antioch." It perhaps suggests Beit Maroun's influence as leading monastery was throughout the patriarchate of Antioch.

C.J. Hefele informs us that the acts of the fifth session of the Council are very voluminous due to the numerous documents read.[251] When examining the references to documentation read at the Council, it appears there are a possible nine documents admitted at the fourth and fifth sessions that related to incidents against the monks and monasteries of Syria Secunda by Severus of Antioch and Peter of Apamaea, nearly all of which refer to Beit Maroun monastery as an exarch of monasteries in Syria Secunda. These are as follows:

- The petition of 518 to the Syria Secunda bishops from Alexander, Archimandrite, monastery of the Blessed Maroun, John, and archimandrites and monks of Apamaea.
- The Pope's reply in 518 to the priests, deacons, and archimandrites of Syria.
- Letter to Pope Agepetus, signed by the monks of Syria Secunda and Paul representing the Monastery of the blessed Maroun, the leading monastery in Syria Secunda.
- A memorial signed by the monks of Constantinople, Jerusalem, Syria, and Palestine submitted to the Patriarch Menace, which confirms Severus and Peter "had persecuted the orthodox [Chalcedonians] ... and had, in an unlawful manner, got possession of the sees of Antioch and Apamaea," likely signed by Paul representing the Monastery of the blessed Maroun, the leading monastery in Syria Secunda.
- A memorial addressed to the Emperor by Paul of Apamaea

---

[251] Ibid., pp. 200-203.

and the other bishops of Syria II (as is normal practice this indicates representation at the Council from Syria Secunda bishops with special permission given to the monks to address the Council).

- A petition addressed to the emperor from the monks of Constantinople, Jerusalem, Syria, and Palestine, likely signed by Paul of the Monastery of the blessed Maroun.

- With other monks from various countries, a petition addressed to the Council of 536 seeking to be heard (as per the quotations set out above).

- The synodal letter of 518 from the bishops of Syria Secunda to John, patriarch of Constantinople.

- The synodal letter of 518 from the bishops of Tyre to John, patriarch of Constantinople.

Extraordinarily, after all of this evidence Moosa still rejects the validity of the four out of nine documents he disclosed, even though the four he disclosed were read at the Council. He informs us: "it is very difficult to accept the historical validity of these charges against Severus" and his followers, it cannot be sure that the same Paul signed all the petitions, Paul was likely a 'lowly' deacon, and "we cannot be sure what monastery of Marun this monk represented."[252]

Moosa admits another letter; one accepted by the Fifth Ecumenical Council of Constantinople in the year 553.[253] He cites Assemani for his reference to confirm two representatives of the Monastery of Maroun attended the Fifth Council convened by Emperor Justinian I. The letter was addressed to the emperor and to Menas, patriarch of Constantinople. Moosa confirms the two delegates presented themselves as representatives of the monastery of St Maroun, "chief amongst the

---

[252] Moosa, *The Maronites in History*, p. 79.

[253] It appears the Council of 536, although an ecumenical Council by virtue that it was represented from across all regions of the Church, has not been listed in church documents as an official Ecumenical Council. Perhaps as this Council was focused on condemning Severus and his followers, it was not a true ecumenical Council. However, there can be no doubt this Council took place.

monasteries of Syria Secunda."[254] Moosa dismisses the authenticity of the document.

The documents read into the Council of 536 are in addition to the following ancient sources for the sixth century referring to the leadership and/or existence of Beit Maroun in Syria Secunda (and/or the massacre):

- The petition to the Pope in 517 from the archimandrites and of other monks of Syria Secunda, and signed first by Alexander, priest and archimandrite of St Maron.
- The letter addressed to the emperor and to Menas, patriarch of Constantinople signed by two delegates of the monastery of St Maroun, and read at the Fifth Ecumenical Council of Constantinople in 553.
- The letter from Beit Maroun monks to the Jacobites in 592.
- The letter from the Jacobites to Beit Maroun monks in 592.

Seven of all thirteen documents were drawn to Moosa's attention by authors such as Butros Dau. Moosa admits citing many of the documents in: *Sacrosancta Concilia*; Mansi, *Sacrorum Coniliorum* and Hefele, *History of the Councils.*[255] However, he dismisses the validity of all these ancient documents as well as the events attributed to Severus of Antioch and Peter of Apamaea. This is despite a total of ten different sets of ancient documents referring to Severus and Peter and signed by representatives from St Maroun on behalf of all of the monasteries of Syria Secunda.

Seven of those documents are also signed by persons other than the monks of Beit Maroun. The other signatories include bishops, the Pope, and monks from Jerusalem, Palestine, Sinai, Arabia, Constantinople and Syria. Moosa implies all the bishops, the Pope and the monks from other countries must be frauds, as well as the monks of Beit Maroun.

---

[254] Moosa, *The Maronites in History*, p. 26, relying on Assemani, *Bibliotheca Orientalis*.
[255] Ibid., pp. 74-80.

The following fifteen events in the sixth century, which are documented in ancient primary sources, are all dismissed by Moosa:

- The massacre of 517.
- Damage to the monasteries in 517.
- Synod of Tyre in 518.
- Synod of Syria Secunda in 518.
- Attendance of Beit Maroun monks to the Council of 536.
- Attendance of Beit Maroun monks to the Council of 553.
- Attendance of Beit Maroun monks and Jacobites at the conference in Antioch in 591.
- Signatures of Beit Maroun representatives that appear eight times.

This makes a total of twenty-eight texts and events in the sixth century judged by Moosa to be implausible. Usually scholars would have only a few ancient texts or events whose interpretation can be debated, but here we have twenty-eight. Nothing further needs to be said about the support of the documentation and events that provide for Beit Maroun and its link, at the latest by 592, to the name Maronites.

However, Moosa then dismisses the connection between Theodoret's Maroun and the monastery of St Maroun. His reasoning is based on Theodoret's Maroun being from Cyrrhus further north in Syria. He provides no explanation as to the identity of the Maroun after which the monastery in Syria Secunda was built. Elsewhere in his works, Moosa allows himself to conclude that St Barsauma was chief of all anchorites, presumably throughout the entire Middle East and for all Chalcedonians and non-Chalcedonians. Yet, he would not grant Theodoret's Maroun, whose "fame circulated everywhere," the small privilege of being recognised within two hundred kilometres from his hermitage. Moosa's logic is incongruous.

This book has provided ample links and interconnections between Theodoret's Maroun and the monastery of St Maroun. It is more than remarkable that these twenty-eight texts and events appear in a short space of time after the death of Theodoret's Maroun and after Emperor Marcian's construction of the monastery of Beit Maroun in 452 (the latter according to Abdul l-Fida). It is also remarkable that no other Maroun of any significance appears in any history other than that of Theodoret. In addition to all of those links, the correspondence of 592, discussed here, puts to bed any doubt.

Moosa accepts the evidence of Dionysius of Tell Mahre (d. 845)[256] about an incident in 629 to conclude that it was the first time any historian had mentioned the monastery of Maroun.[257] This is hugely misleading as has been demonstrated. There are eleven texts from early to late sixth century set out in this chapter of this book[258] that provide evidence of the monastery and its leadership. In addition, one Synod in 518 and two Councils in 536 and 553 accepted not only correspondence but also delegates from the Monastery of St Maroun. This makes a total of sixteen texts and events in the sixth century that referred to the Monastery of St Maroun, its primacy amongst all monasteries of Syria Secunda and its Catholic orthodoxy. Having referred to many of these sixteen texts and Councils, Moosa decides to dismiss their importance or validity because he says (erroneously) no historian had mentioned the monastery of St Maroun before an event in 629 recorded by Tell Mahre.

Regarding the correspondence of the sixth century between the Jacobites and the Maronite monks, the former ask the latter to call on the "whole assembly of Beth Maroun." The Jacobites note they have "shown to our holy fathers" the correspondence for advice. The conference at Antioch in 591, the exchange of letters in 592, and the influence of Beit Maroun were therefore significant to the Jacobites. Still, Moosa does not take this seriously.

Eutychius (d. 941) and al-Masudi (d. 956) claim the monastery of Maroun was founded during the reign of Emperor Maurice (582-602)

---

[256] The abbreviated name 'Tell Mahre' will be adopted in this work.
[257] Ibid., p. 33. See Chapter 9 of this book for detailed discussion.
[258] Including the letter to the Fifth Ecumenical Council of Constantinople in 553 referred to by Moosa.

because of Monothelitism. Moosa knew of the profound inaccuracy of this evidence. Emperor Maurice predated the official introduction of Monothelitism by four decades. Nonetheless, Moosa interprets their evidence to conclude they must have meant a reference not to a Maroun but to a John Maroun in 707, more than one hundred years later. Conveniently, he then dismisses the evidence of Abdul l-Fida who stated Emperor Marcian built the monastery of St Maroun in 452, despite the accurate matching of the emperor's name and the date of his reign.[259]

Moosa contradicts himself by confirming two different dates for the founding of the monastery of Maroun. The first date is 629 relying on an incident in 629 recorded by Tell Mahre. The second date is 707 relying on Eutychius (d. 941) and al-Masudi (d. 956) who recorded the dates as during the reign of emperor Maurice (582- 602) but were mistaken.[260] Again, Moosa cannot be considered a trusted source on this aspect of Maronite history, due to the multiple errors in his scholarship and mistreatment of the evidence.

### 7.6.5 Correspondence between the Jacobites and Maronites

As stated previously, it is no surprise that Moosa dismisses the authenticity and relevance of the correspondence between the Jacobites and the monks of Beit Maroun in 592. The exchange between the Beit Maroun monks and the Syriac Jacobites (by now known in history as the Syriac Orthodox Jacobite Church) in 592 is especially important for a history of the Maronites because it includes the first reference to the word 'Maronite' in any available ancient source. The first chapter of Moosa's book is entitled 'Origin of the term Maronite' and is a calculated rebuke of Maronite identity. He attempts in his opening paragraph and throughout the chapter to make a mockery of Maronite Church historians (the focus of his book from the outset). In Chapter 12, Moosa incorrectly claims there were no 'Maronites' or 'Maronite Church' until the year 727.[261]

---

[259] Moosa, *The Maronites in History*, pp. 32-35.
[260] Ibid., pp. 33, 35.
[261] Ibid., p. 100.

So it follows that in Moosa's account of the 592 correspondence he completely ignores the references to the word 'Maronite'. The word is used twice in the letter from the Beit Maroun monks and once in the letter from the Jacobites. This cannot be other than a deliberate omission by Moosa. It almost certainly cannot be a different interpretation of a word during the translation process. The British Museum manuscript in Syriac, catalogued by Wright, which Moosa refers to, is identical to the manuscript referred to by Nau. Nau translated the text from Syriac into French. The English version of Nau's translation of the 592 letters into French is contained in Naaman's book and is set out below. Moosa does not set out any part of the texts. When reading the texts, it is inconceivable that there could be another translation for the word 'Maronite'.

Moosa says if such correspondence ever took place, it could only be attributed to two centuries later.[262] Once again we see Moosa contradict himself. He acknowledges the evidence proves a conference was held in Antioch in 591 between the Syriac Jacobites monks and former Syriac Jacobite monks that had converted to be Maronite monks – that is now belonging to the Chalcedonian party led by Beit Maroun monastery. Moosa acknowledges that the reference to Peter in the correspondence is a reference to Peter of Callinice, Monophysite patriarch of Antioch who died in 591. By acknowledging these facts, he confirms not only the validity of the date of the correspondence to be 592, but the factual circumstances surrounding the correspondence to be accurate.

Moosa then proceeds in complete contradiction, commenting that "it is incredible no church historian, Syrian or otherwise, has ever mentioned this particular correspondence." Again, Moosa implies the evidence used by many other scholars and attested to throughout this chapter to be fraudulent. To him, if an historian does not mention an ancient manuscript it cannot be accepted as a source. Moosa's irresponsible view, demonstrated earlier, is that even if a document is read into a synod or Council, he does not accept it unless an historian refers to it.

---

[262] Ibid., 84-86.

Moosa opines that if the correspondence of 592 ever took place, it could only be attributed to two centuries later in 727. He confesses the principal reason for the later date is because of his own logic that denies Maronite Church history written by others. He believed the correspondence could only have taken place in the mid-eighth century when the Maronites, (as alleged by Moosa) were defending themselves as Monothelites in a heated dispute with the Melkites. Moosa finds an obscure reference to a Maronite priest Bernard al-Ghaziri who Moosa says correctly dates the correspondence to the eighth century. Moosa does not provide an extract from al-Ghaziri or this source's reasoning.

Moosa remarkably connects the 592 correspondence to a heated Monothelite debate in 727 relating to whether Christ had one divine will or both a human and divine will.[263] It is here we can conclude Moosa once again cannot be trusted on Maronite history. The correspondence in question between the Jacobites and the Maronites makes no mention at all of Christ's will. There is no reference in the correspondence to the word 'will'. It only speaks of Christ's nature. The debate between the Maronites and the Jacobites relates only to their differences over the Council of Chalcedon. As the quote immediately below will reveal, Moosa appeared to have an understanding of the theology of the Monothelite controversy related to Christ's will. It is likely he never properly read the correspondence of 592 and merely copied from the views of others such as al-Ghaziri, not knowing their mistake. Moosa informs us:

> If such correspondence ever took place, it should logically have done so in the eighth century when, as Monothelites, the monks of the Monastery of Marun entered into heated theological argument with other religious groups in Syria (for example the Chalcedonian Melkites) to defend their belief in one will of Christ (Monothelitism). They entered into the same argument with the Syrian Orthodox (Monophysites) to defend their adherence to the faith of Chalcedon as the correspondence shows.[264]

---

[263] This is discussed more fully in Chapter 9.
[264] Moosa, *The Maronites in History*, p. 86.

Yet, he does not supply any part of the correspondence and there is absolutely no reference to the word 'will' or reference to Christ's will in this text.

Moosa's misstatement is extremely disappointing for a supposedly scholarly work that appears to have sought to become a leading authority on the entire Maronite history. A repeated problem throughout his book is that Moosa does not cite original sources (although he makes out he has) but relies on other authors for their interpretations. Most of his work provides no quotations of the ancient sources that contradict his propositions. In any event, on this issue of the correspondence in 592, Moosa's views must be completely set aside.

No doubt the correspondence exchange between the Maronites and the Jacobites must be dated prior to the commencement of the Monothelite controversy. The theology relating to Christ's will was not introduced to the Syriac Jacobites until at least the year 629 according to Moosa.[265] Its formal introduction via the *Ecthesis*, the letter of the emperor Heraclius declaring monotheletism as the official form of Christianity, was not until 639. The correct date of the exchange of correspondence must be around 592 as suggested by Nau and others.

### 7.6.6 The Maronites as 'Monophysite Monothelites'

As detailed above, all twenty-eight texts and events in the sixth century repeatedly validate the Catholic orthodoxy of Beit Maroun monasteries and their adherence to the Council of Chalcedon. They were not Monophysite. According to Moosa's primary reason for stating the texts of 592 must be attributed to some one hundred and fifty years later, he confesses, is because he denies the Maronite Church history written by others. In his view this allows him to maintain that the Maronites were Monophysite and anti-Chalcedon until the sixteenth century. However, in his analysis of the seventh century, he contradicts his own agenda on several occasions.

After dismissing all of the texts and events of the sixth century before him, Moosa informs us in his Chapter 11 that the monks of Beit

---

[265] Ibid., p. 33.

Maroun did not adhere to the doctrine of Chalcedon until the year 629 when they became Monothelite.[266] In complete contradiction to the alleged conversion of 629, he then informs us that the Beit Maroun monks did not adhere to the doctrine of Chalcedon until 745 when a contingent of soldiers persecuted them and forced their conversion.[267] He also tells us that the numerous letters presented to the Councils in 536 and 553 are dubious.

He states that there is no evidence of the monks having defended the doctrine of Chalcedon at the Council of 536 despite admitting a delegate was present and presented petitions against Severus. His arguments of non-Catholic orthodoxy have been dealt with above. Nonetheless, Moosa's comments at this juncture are completely convoluted and contradictory. Further, Moosa has no basis for rejecting, one after the other, a total of twenty-eight texts and events in the sixth century.[268] Once again, silence in documents is no justification for claiming an event did not occur, yet this is the inherently flawed logic employed conveniently by Moosa.

Moosa states repeatedly that the Maronites were Monothelite and must have been Monophysites, (non-Chalcedon adherents) in the first place.[269] He informs us the Maronites became Monothelite but remained Monophysite, that is, the Maronites were 'Monophysite Monothelites', a claim not previously proposed by other authors.[270] His theory is convoluted: theologically, one cannot be both Monothelite and Monophysite. To be Monothelite, one must accept the doctrine of Chalcedon of two natures in Christ. Monothelite is a reference to the one will of Christ accepting His two natures. Also, Moosa's proposition that you can only become Monothelite after being a Monophy-

---

[266] For this he relies on a quote from Tell Mahre.

[267] Moosa, *The Maronites in History*, p. 89.

[268] Moosa's reference to a quote from St Germanos that the Maronites rejected the Fourth, Fifth and Sixth Councils is dealt with in the chapter of this book on Monothelitism.

[269] For example, see Moosa, *The Maronites in History*, pp. 101, 103.

[270] Ibid., p. 159.

site is flawed. On the contrary, one can become a Monothelite believer from being a Chalcedon or non-Chalcedon adherent.

Notably, Moosa states in his Chapter 12 that from 629 until 727 the Chalcedonian Maronites and the Chalcedonian Melkites were both Monothelite but differed in the faith regarding Chalcedon, that is, over whether Christ had two natures or one. This confirms his theory that the Maronites were both Monophysite and Monothelite. However, he appears confused. The difference between the Maronites and Melkites, according to the ancient source Tell Mahre who Moosa relies on, should be over the *two wills* of Christ, not the *two natures* (the latter a reference to the faith position promoted at Chalcedon). Moosa then adds another twist, claiming that after 630 the Beit Maroun monks continued to profess the faith of Chalcedon, but in a Monothelite connotation.[271] He adds his own misunderstanding to an already theologically confusing debate that has never been settled to this day, even amongst the most esteemed theologians.

What is striking in his analysis is the clear reference to Beit Maroun monks being Chalcedonian by the year 629, and not the sixteenth century as stated in his agenda on the opening page of his book.[272] This statement is repeated elsewhere in other chapters. For example, in Chapter 14 he states: "from the above account of Tal Mahri [Tell Mahre] we learn that the Malkites [Melkites] and the Maronites, although Chalcedonians, were separate groups."[273]

The multiple contradictions in Moosa's works around the topic Monothelitism are here summarised. First, he states the Maronites were Chalcedonian but were Monophysite. He misses the point that you cannot be both. Second, he states on page 1 the Maronites were not Chalcedonian until the sixteenth century when, in his many chapters on Monothelitism, he informs us otherwise. Third, he tells us they were Monophysite before 629 dismissing every ancient source that confirms otherwise. Fourth, from the 'apparent' 629 conversion from

---

[271] Ibid., p. 103.

[272] Ibid.

[273] Ibid., p. 115.

being Monophysite to becoming Monothelite, he informs us the Maronites did not have their own patriarch until around 745. He leads us to believe that the Maronites, as Monophysite and Monothelite and distinct from the Melkites, were therefore somehow out in the wilderness, not part of any church, Catholic or Monophysite from 629 to 745.

Contradictions abound in Moosa's work. His theory of Maronite Monothelitism is telling for yet another reason. He clearly refers to the formation of a Maronite identity, "the Chalcedonian Maronites" from 629.[274] This is despite the twenty-eight ancient texts and events of the sixth century referring to the Monastery of Maroun. It is also in complete contradiction to his chapter on Monthelitism. He describes Tell Mahre's account of the Byzantine prisoners introducing the doctrine of two wills in 727, and surmises: "The point is that at this time there were only two major denominations in Syria – the Chalcedonian Malkites [Melkites] and the anti-Chalcedonian Monophysites or 'Jacobites': there were no Maronites." To add to the contradictions, in Chapter 14, entitled 'Establishment of the Maronites as a Separate Church', he concludes "the establishment of a Maronite identity (was) in 745" and also informs us "we may state with certainty that only in the eighth century did ancient writers refer to the Maronites as a distinct Christian sect."[275] Both these statements oppose his earlier statement of the formation of the Chalcedonian Maronites in 629.

Moosa also tells us "the name of the Marun [Maroun] monastery first appears in the time of Heraclius in the first half of the seventh century and in a very particular context – Monothelitism."[276] He states that it was because of Heraclius' persecution of the monastery of Maroun that Beit Maroun became Chalcedonian and their monks then seized the churches and monasteries of the anti-Chalcedonians.[277] Moosa's translation says:

[274] Ibid.
[275] Ibid., pp. 116-117.
[276] Ibid., p. 33.
[277] Ibid., pp. 99-100.

As a result of the persecution of the Orthodox (those who believed in One Incarnate Nature of the Divine Logos and rejected the Council of Chalcedon) many monks accepted the Council of Chalcedon including the monks of Beth Marun (the monastery of Marun) together with the inhabitants of Mabug and Hims.[278]

Moosa's translation related to Heraclius conflicts with the accounts of other sources. Authors such as Gibbon and Migne go as far as suggesting that Heraclius was a Maronite himself having lived in the monastery of Maroun. Further, the opposite translation of Moosa's text is contained in Nau, Naaman, and Dib. Barhebreus (d. 1286), chief bishop of Persia, whilst informing us about the orders from the Emperor for the anti-Chalcedonians to accept the doctrine of Chalcedon, states:

> Since they would not consent, Heraclius was irritated and sent out a decree to the whole Empire: "anyone who will not adhere (to the Council), will have his nose and is cut off and his house pillaged." And so, many converted. The monks of Beth Maroun, of Mabboug and of Emese, showed their wickedness and pillaged a number of churches and monasteries. Our people complained to Heraclius, who did not answer them. This is why the God of vengeance has delivered us through the Arabs from the hands of the Romans. Our churches, it is true, were not restored to us, the conquering Arabs allowed to each sect what they found in its possession. But it is not just a slight advantage for us to be freed from the wickedness of the Romans and the cruel hate towards us.[279]

What is clear from this translation is that many Jacobite monks converted to become Chalcedonian. It is not a direct reference to the

---

[278] Ibid., p. 91.

[279] Dib, *History of the Maronite Church*, p. 11, citing *Chronicon ecclesiasticum*, t. I, ed. Abbelos-Lamy, Louvain, 1872, col. 269-274. Barhebreus (d. 1286) relied extensively on the eighth century *Annals* of Dennis of Tell Mahre, Patriarch of the Syrian Jacobites (818-45). The *Annals* are lost today, but are substantially preserved in the chronicles of Michael the Syrian or the Great, Patriarch of the Syrian Jacobites (1166-1199). Naaman *The Maronites*, p. 155 cites the same passage in Nau's book *Opuscules Maronites* and states that Nau estimates the event to be around 630.

monks of Beit Maroun converting. Certainly these monks, and of Mabboug and Emesa, then took over some Jacobite monasteries. We do not know if the Beit Maroun confederation extended to Mabboug and Emesa before this time. Perhaps it did in the context of what we know, but it is not certain from the quote. What is also clear is that the texts provide no indication of an order from the Emperor Heraclius to observe the Monothelite doctrine, only an order to adhere to the Council of Chalcedon. The edict relating to Monothelitism was not issued until 639. Moosa's conclusion, and Tell Mahre's if Moosa quotes him correctly, ascribing to the date of this incident in 629 as the time of the Beit Maroun conversion to Monothelitism, is untenable.

What is absolutely certain, from both Moosa and the opposing translations, is that there was already a Beit Maroun monastery in existence in 629. This is contrary to Moosa's repeated implication that this monastery *first* appeared at that date. He provides no explanation as to how and when this monastery previously came into existence. For Beit Maroun to be referred to by Syriac Monophysite patriarch Tell Mahre it must have meant the monastery came with significance in the period prior to 629. It must have been established well before this date. Moosa's rebuttal of all of the ancient texts and events of the sixth century proves futile. In addition, Moosa speaks of Tell Mahre's eloquent history for the Syriac Monophysite Church. However, given the significance of Beit Maroun and Moosa's alleged schism from the Jacobite Church during these events, there is no Jacobite account of the existence of the monastery of Beit Maroun within its church before this date. This is an extraordinary contradiction.

In complete reversal, Moosa informs us in Chapter 12, that because no historian wrote about the Maronites until a brief account about them from Tell Mahre in the ninth century, the historian must become the authority, thus we are asked by Moosa to put aside any ancient correspondence and any Council attendance. Further, Dionysius of Tell Mahre happens to be a patriarch from Moosa's own Syriac Jacobite Church. Moosa believes his own patriarch, although writing centuries later, to be completely correct and impartial. However, it is suggested it would be extremely difficult for Tell Mahre to be totally accurate, writing more than two centuries later, and impartial in a historical account of another opposing church, especially considering the bitter conflicts of those centuries.

Moosa attributes the founding of the Maronites to John Maroun (d. 707) who Moosa is adamant was a Monothelite. He misleadingly states and emphasises that the historical sources al-Masudi and Eutychius[280] were 'explicit' that the Maronites were named after him because he was a Monothelite.[281] He says the authors' reference was to his surname only but it is extraordinary for the times to refer to someone by a surname and not their first name.

Moosa informs us that Eutychius and al-Masudi refer to John Maroun as an abbot of a monastery in or near Hama and Shayzar and it was a different monastery to that of the fifth century monastery of Maroun. However, these authors referred to a Maroun in the years of Emperor Maurice's reign (593-602) predating by decades the introduction of Monothelitism and John Maroun. As we have also noted in previous chapters, in the time these historians wrote, Hama was a governing district of the Arab Muslims, which included Apamaea the region of the fifth century Beit Maroun monastery. Moosa conveniently transfers the date quoted by these historians to more than one-hundred years later to slot into his theory.

More problematically, earlier in his book Moosa informs us that the monastery of John Maroun gained notoriety in the early seventh century (626) when its monks adopted Monothelitism. At this time, John Maroun was likely not born and this pre-dates the official introduction of the doctrine by thirteen years. Furthermore, Moosa's claim that the monks of Beit Maroun were Monophysite and later became Monothelite contradicts the Syriac scholars Brock and Vööbus. They accept the monks of Beit Maroun were never Monophysite and were always strong defenders of the Chalcedonian doctrinal position against the attacks of the Monophysite opponents of the Council.

---

[280] Dealt with in Chapter 6.

[281] Moosa, *The Maronites in History*, p. 119.

As stated previously, Brock's considered opinion is that the theory that the Maronites derived from converts from Monophysitism proffered by Heraclius in the early 630s rests on a misunderstanding of a passage in Michael the Syrian.[282] There is also a profound contradiction that Eutychius failed to mention: Pope Honorius and the Byzantine emperor decreed the doctrine of Monothelitism; Constantinopolitans and many emperors, as well Eutychius' own predecessor patriarchs of Alexandria, were Monothelite from 638 until 750 and well after the condemnation of it by the Sixth Council in 680-81.[283]

### 7.6.7 Summary: Moosa's Work Null and Void

This chapter has extensively dealt with Moosa's work, particularly for the formation period of Maronite history. It is acknowledged that Moosa is sometimes correct in demonstrating some inconsistencies between a small number of Maronite historians on certain topics. The historians are mostly non-contemporary. Moosa extensively refers to Maronite authors such as Dau to elaborate on their errors. However, he does not suggest which Maronite history authors are regarded by contemporary Maronite scholars as reliable. Dau is well-known for his extensive research but sometimes unreliable conclusions. Current scholars of Maronite history have sufficiently dealt with previous inconsistencies as Syriac studies have rapidly progressed since Moosa's works.

The agenda and conclusions set out in Moosa's opening chapters, which form the basis for his entire works, are repeatedly proven in this book to be without merit, in contradistinction to the historical evidence. It is no longer of any worth to continue rebutting Moosa, who repeatedly contradicts his own theories. Most notably, for his attempted holistic account of Maronite history, this book argues all of

---

[282] Brock, *Syriac Perspectives on Late Antiquity*, p. 69. See also "Extracts from the Syriac Melkite Chronicle," and "Maronite Chronicle," in *The Seventh Century in the West Syrian Chronicles*, ed. by A. Palmer, S. Brock, and R. Hoyland, Liverpool University Press, 1993 and the *The Hidden Pearl*, 3 Vols. See also Vööbus, *A History of Asceticism in the Syrian Orient*, p. 251.

[283] See Chapter 9 of this book for details.

Moosa's conclusions and his entire work should be regarded as null and void, and dismissed.

## 7.7 Key Primary Sources

### 7.7.1 Petition of the Monks of Syria Secunda to Pope Hormisdas (517)

The following is from the first translation of the text into English, and first modern language translation, published in 1997 by Cornelia Horn in "The Correspondence Between the Monks of Syria Secunda and Pope Hormisdas in 517/518 AD," citing the Latin text CSEL 35 from 1895.[284]

> To Hormisdas, the most holy and blessed patriarch of the whole world, the holder of the See of Peter, the leader of the apostles, the earnest petition and humble prayer of the least (important) archimandrites and of other monks of your province Syria Secunda:

> The grace of Christ, the Redeemer of us all, has instigated us to take refuge to your blessedness ... you have certainly heard: That Severus and Peter, who have never been counted among the number of Christians, who on each single day have attacked and publicly anathematized the holy synod at Chalcedon and our most holy and blessed father Leo, who think nothing of God's judgment and trample under foot the venerable canons of the holy Fathers, bringing it about that bishops, indeed, are shown as holding the prime authority and forcing us to ridicule the aforementioned holy synod and humiliating us by worthless public prayers.

> Therefore also certain ones of those, who in no way endure the blows brought upon them have gone over because of this and our not so small number of people has in fact almost completely vanished. For when we were going to the pen of the Lord Simeon for the cause of the Church, they were

---

[284] For a slightly different translation into English see Naaman, *The Maronites*, pp. 135-137.

lying in wait for us on the way as it had been announced, defiling us, and when they came upon us by surprise, they killed three hundred and fifty men from among us, certain ones they wounded; but others, who could take refuge to the venerable altars, they slayed there and set the monasteries on fire, inciting throughout the night a multitude of unsettled people and contractors and they were wasting all the poverty of the Church through destructive trouble makers of this kind. About the details, however, the writings may instruct your blessedness, which were brought over by the venerable brothers, John and Sergius, whom we had sent to Constantinople, because we believed that revenge might take place for those things which had been committed. Yet he did not think them worth a word, but rather he expelled them with great mistreatment and he violently threatened those, who would present these (things). Therefore it is from here that we, perhaps (too) late, know that all the depravity and recklessness of such evil people, which is committed against the churches, is arranged through his incitation.

We pray, therefore, most blessed one, we go on our knees and ask, that you stand up with fervor and zeal and rightly have pity for the body that is torn to pieces (for you are the head of all) and that you avenge the faith that has been despised, the canons that have been trodden under foot, the fathers who have been blasphemed and such a great synod that has been attacked with anathema.

To you God has given the power and authority to bind and to loosen [Matt 16:19]. Not the healthy ones have need of the physician but the sick [Matt 9:12]. Arise, holy Fathers, come to save us! Be imitators of the Lord Christ, who has come down from the heavens onto the earth to seek the sheep that is going astray, Peter, that leader of the apostles, whose seat you adorn, and Paul, who is the vessel of election, the ones who are going around and have illuminated the world. Great wounds, namely, are in need of greater remedies. For the hired shepherds, when they see the wolves come against the sheep, abandon them so that they are scattered by them [cf. John 10:12], but to you, the true shepherds and teachers, to whom the care for the well-being of the sheep has been committed, the flock come who know their shepherd when they have been freed from the pitiless wild animals and they are following the voice of the shepherd, as the Lord says: 'My sheep hear my voice and I know them and they follow me'. [John 10:3] Therefore, do not despise us, most holy one, since daily we are being wounded by wild beasts.

But so that your holy angel may have complete knowledge, we courageously anathematize with our very petition both all the ones who have been put forth in the libellus and the ones who have been excommunicated by your Apostolic See: We speak, however, of Nestorius, who was bishop of Constantinople, Eutychius, Dioscorus, and Peter of Alexandria, who also has the name Balbus, and Peter, who was named 'the Fuller', of Antioch, and last not least Acacius, who was bishop of Constantinople, the one in communion with them and all, who defend any one of those heretics.

The signatures (note that in the translation cited there is a separate line for each name):

Alexander, through the mercy of God priest and archimandrite of St. Maron, have prayed. Symeon, through the mercy of God priest and archimandrite, as above. John, through the mercy of God deacon and treasurer, as above. Procopius, through the mercy of God priest and archimandrite, as above. Peter, through the mercy of God priest, as above ... Carufas, the deacon, as above.

These signatories include a total of two hundred and nine archimandrites, priests, and some deacons. In addition to the three archimandrites above a further twenty-three archimandrites appear making a total of twenty-six archimandrites. The majority of the archimandrites' names appear towards the end including the very last signature. All of the archimandrites were randomly listed in no particular order and are now listed as follows:

Saulinus, the archimandrite, as above; Flavian, the archimandrite, as above; Daniel, the archimandrite, as above; Symeon, the archimandrite, as above; Isidor, the archimandrite, as above; Eusebius, the archimandrite; Eustasius, the priest, as above; Azizos, the deacon and archimandrite, as above; Antoninus, the deacon and archimandrite; Stephen, the deacon and archimandrite, as above; Julian, the deacon and archimandrite, as above; Nonnus, the deacon and archimandrite, as above; John, the deacon and archimandrite, as above; Macedonius, [the deacon] and archimandrite, as above; Domnus, the archimandrite, as above; John, the archimandrite, as above; Symeonius, [the deacon] and archimandrite, as above; Menas, the deacon and archimandrite as above; Theodorus, the archimandrite, as above; Benjamin, the archimandrite, as above; Daniel, the priest and archimandrite, as above; Abraam, the archimandrite, as above; Symeonius, the archimandrite, as above

Symeonius, the archimandrite was the very last signature. The most common names in the list were Symeon/Symeonius, listed twenty-six times, followed by Sergius, listed thirteen times.

## 7.7.2 Reply of Pope Hormisdas to the Representatives of Syria Secunda (518)

The following text is abstracted from Hormisdas' response to the priests, deacons, and archimandrites of Syria Secunda.[285]

> Hormisdas, to the priests, deacons, and archimandrites of Syria Secunda.

> I have read your highly esteemed letters, by which the insanity of the enemies of God has been laid open and the obstinate fury of the unbelievers, who with revived spirit hate the Lord and thereby wickedly persecute his members, has painfully been exposed: To the extent that it pertains to the recognition

---

[285] For full extract of the text, see Horn, "The Correspondence Between the Monks of Syria Secunda and Pope Hormisdas" and Naaman, *The Maronites*, pp. 138-142.

of your perseverance, I praise God that he preserves the faith of his soldiers in the midst of adversities ...

For we hold as a guaranty the firmness of your faith in its profession up to the individual letters, by which you hurry back from the separative infection through contact with the transgressors to the teachings and instructions of the Apostolic See: Late, indeed, that you enter on the way of truth, but blessed be God, who does not forget even toward the end, who seizes and heals and does not suffer that the sheep of his flock are continuously torn apart by the rapacity of the wolves which lie in wait; he, who through moderation in punishment neither neglects the right to punish his own nor their well-being. But is it a surprise if, after that one and true shepherd has been left behind, the shrewd, bloodthirsty and rapacious one throws the sheep that have been scattered about into confusion with his traps? These, who abandon his protection, expose themselves to the dangers, by which they are torn to pieces. Therefore, now, at least pursue closely with firm steps the way of the Fathers, to which you are returning. The compassion of God will be powerful, also the correction of others for your reward, if they, guided by you toward what is right, enroll. But in all pull yourselves away from the mud, where the heretics are held immersed, and shaking off the impurity of the dust that sticks to all in general who deviate from the apostolic teachings, speak out a condemnation by a pious curse ...

the synod of Chalcedon which has the respect of all; but also is it fitting that we both know and defend the advancements of the venerable Leo which have been set up from the hearts of the apostles themselves. In these the banner of faith, in these the ramparts of truth, in these Christ is recognized, in these the hope and cause of our redemption is preserved ...

Through these councils the poisons of Eutychius and Nestorius have been destroyed, who while they strive against the salvific mystery of the dispensation of the Lord in a conflicting dispute among themselves, agree with a certain sacrilegious smoothness, even though they are different in their statements and of one mind regarding their impiety: one of them does not want the virgin Mary to be the mother of God and therefore he divides in our Lord, what has been united; the other one, while he mingles together what is proper and certain of the appropriate natures, annuls the mystery of our redemption …

Dioscorus and Timothy, the parricide, Peter of Alexandria, Acacius of Constantinople with his followers, also Peter of Antioch, like to the one mentioned beforehand as much in error as in name, but also Severus just the same of the same place and poison, Axenaias of Hierapolis, Cyrus of Edessa, and Peter of Apamea; they are no longer to be condemned only for their own but also for the destruction of others, these who, while they get continuously all wrapped up in the filth of their own opinions, also have defiled others by teaching things which it is evil to pursue.

### 7.7.3 Petition from Beit Maroun Monastic Network to their Bishops (518)

The following is the full text of the petition:[286]

To the most reverend Bishops our Lords, to all the Most Reverend Holy Fathers the Bishops of Syria Secunda, from Alexander, John, Simon, Palladius, Procopius, Eugenius Stephanus and other archimandrites and monks of the region of Apamaea.

The divine Scriptures teach us how the very necessity of things often "serves the moment" [Eccl 3:1]. Therefore during the previous periods we have been silent, forced to be so by the power of those who were in government and by the fury of the heretics. But as God has now granted a just liberty and graciously allows some much desired hope for our affairs, and has caused a Christian orthodox emperor to rise up

---

[286] Naaman, *The Maronites*, pp. 143-148.

for the churches and the whole world, those were oppressed and voiceless must now make themselves heard.

You know in effect to what degree violence follows situations that are impossible or even inexorable. Since God has shown his clemency (he who in his great goodness never leaves his faithful and those who hope in him without counsel, but gives them consolation), He has restored peace to the world with a good emperor taking care of government; those who endeavoured to loot the straight path of the orthodox faith being now set aside, it remains for us to speak, though with moderated voice, of the lamentable conduct of the heretic Severus, as also of the shameful and abominable manner of acting of Peter.

When in truth we were proceeding towards the locality of Kaprokerameh, not far from the venerable temple of the blessed confessor Simon, with only peace, union and love, and a just vow in our thoughts, manifesting a purely monastic attitude and intention, we did not know that we had an enemy in the impious Severus, whom Christianity ignored and never welcomed, and who in no manner or time whatsoever ever took part in the communion of truth, so much was he in the power of the enemy of the truth; most certainly we would have perished when the Jews or at least lay persons and even monks hurled themselves upon us, coming down from the folds of the steep heights... For some they put to death, others they led away into captivity; some were stripped of their garments and others were taken in triumph clad in torn rags, as if according to the idea they led a degrading life. For we ourselves, in truth, we found honour in these events, supporting the trials and holy wounds with firm hope for Christ our God.

But judging such great injustices as only benign, they sent on (to Nikertai) an army of peasants greater in number than the first, making a second assault on the above-mentioned monastery. They destroyed a part of the wall and filtered in taking advantage of the night; they cut the throats of some and rained blows on the greater number, stealing the modest provisions of the monastery in such a way as to put up trophies in the sight of the pious, in answer, they said, to the vehement complaints. And these after their many acts of violence were driven away with great difficulty.

As for Severus, who was the enemy of the whole world and to be more precise of those who contemplate heavenly realities, he never had enough of the stain of murder.

Severus, therefore, not being enough it seems to disfigure the beauty of the world, Peter in his turn rose up against the city of Apamaea and took charge of it, he said, he who should rather have been taught the alphabet and syllables and not dreamt of oracles and sacred rights.

This is why on several occasions he brought the unreasoning petulance of youth into the venerable monastery of Dorothaea, publicly pulling in a crowd of women inclined to enjoying themselves with no holding back. For they were women leading bad lives and not respectable people. Raining blows on the monks of this place, he led them into the town and put them on several occasions in prison.

Who could count the evils already recounted and the harm inflicted on the monastery of Matrona? Even today the features of the Isaurians who followed him and formed his escort are recollected, features which proclaim allowed the enormity of the drama that was enacted that day. And those who pass cannot hold back the tears on seeing the broken doors of the monastery.

And if we dare speak of acts of homicide, for which more than once he misused his own hands and, although seeing the blood staining the altars, dared make offering (the Eucharist), something about which the orthodox will not hesitate to speak-but who on the other hand would not be happy to pass all that over in silence?

But if once again we were to recall the deeds formally perpetrated at the monastery of Oraga, what letter could suffice to enumerate so many wrongs? They did not hesitate at all to knock down the monastery as if they were besieging it and to lead away like prisoners of war the monks who were chanting there because, after having fallen into error, they had finally loved the word of truth and had entered into total communion with us.

The combat of Larissa is known from reliable sources, and the abominable frenzy of Faustus, and the number of those he struck down with impious arrows; likewise, inhabitants of this region know what happened during the attack of Nicerta. What nature endowed with reason could without shedding tears relate how many things were perpetrated in the venerable dwelling of the victorious martyr Antoninus and in how many different ways? Thus, having got into the habit of massacring monks, considering what is abominable in the eyes of men as advantageous profit, he got his henchmen, whom he led on the war path in a way not at all religious, to slit the throats of the venerable orthodox monks who had gathered there for a solemn ceremony; then he presented himself at the altar with his hands all bloodied from this deed.

You have heard in the presence of the most honourable governor of this province the most illustrious Amelius, of the most honourable Narses and several others, what was told by the venerable priests here present, the deacons, sub deacons and clergy of the Catholic church of Apamaea; how he lived in the company of prostitutes and immoral women, what insulting words he pronounced against God, blaspheming in his drunkenness Christ crucified and leading to the sacred pool (font) of Christians women judged still unworthy to receive holy baptism. Further, if we wanted to give details of everything, the present occasion would not be enough and we would need another. Also, leaving aside the many faults of Peter and of Severus, from the tips of our fingers we now expose with timid hesitation the true accusations against them. But it would not be right to pass in silence over the reason for the sorrow of the venerable Julian. In point of fact, as certain stories had been spread around in the sanctuary of St Stephen, when the feast was being celebrated the affirmation venerable man replied that our most pious emperor had a right and holy faith. Peter, enemy of the truth, as if overwhelmed and pierced to the depths of his soul by this word so rightly placed, accused and condemned the emperor, so they say; never did he say a good word, but, impetuous in everything, only opposed here also the Christian and orthodox sentiment of he who after God is the master of the whole universe.

Indeed, how well this is all confirmed; many members of the clergy of Apamaea have affirmed it in the presence of the most honourable governor of the province and of certain illustrious nobles of the metropolis. They also add what tender affection he had for Stephana, the former actress, whom he persuaded by his flattery to throw herself into a convent. At all times he remained continually by her side, finding himself again and indecent place of repose and a dishonest opportunity, that he himself called "teaching and exhortation", thinking to deceive all the superiors and hide the truth; there lies the wrong in which he engaged in this liaison, to speak only discreetly about such a subject.

So we beg and demand Your Beatitude to consider the word of truth that you honour and that at all times you serve with piety and the orthodox purpose worthy of praise of our pious emperor and of our highest magistrates; imitate and follow the holy footsteps of the blessed patriarch of the imperial city and of the holy synod assembled at his sides. Approve the just expulsion of the arch heretic Severus; depose also Peter, whose name we blush to pronounce but which we say driven by necessity. We implore you to depose him and to set him apart from the sacred choir and from the priesthood to which he has been so far completely foreign; for he took on nothing but the external appearance of the priesthood, in illicit fashion.

This being admitted, God will accept your righteous will which is agreeable to him and the great emperor will praise the rectitude of your justice and efface for you the diseases which torment the members of the church.

May you (and to the pleasure of heaven it has already been thus in the past) by procuring for the churches the remedy and apostolate treatment bring the immaculate (faith) of Christians back into order and to its integrity, in order to render glory to God, Lord of the universe, and may hymns and chance unceasing be offered him by the celestial powers as by mankind.

Maybe the just in this way be reunited in the unity of the Church Catholic according to the divine word, that there may be only one flock and one shepherd, Christ our God.

Of the following signatories only the eighteen archimandrites, which appear in random order, are included:

Alexander, priest and Archimandrite of the Monastery of the Blessed Maron, have made public this letter above, signing it with my own hand ...

Simon, by the mercy of God priest and Archmandrite of the monastery of the Blessed Agapetus ...

Procopius of Monastery of the Blessed Theodosius ...

Eugenius of Monastery of the Blessed Heschii ...

Palladius of Monastery of the Blessed Valentinus in Capriole ...

Stephanus of Monastery of the Blessed Theodorus in Vasala ...

Joannes of Monastery of the Blessed Belius ... Maras of Monastery of the Blessed Basilius ... Musilus of Monastery of the Blessed Barsaba ... Sergius of Monastery of the Blessed Tahalasius, Timotheus of Monastery of the Blessed Gaianus ... Simon of Monastery of the Blessed Eugraphius ... Julianus of Monastery of the Blessed Papulis ... Dorotheus of Monastery of the Blessed Cyrillus ... Romulus of Monastery of the Blessed Jacobus (Joannis) ...

Thomas of Monastery of the Blessed Joannis ... Caiumas of Monastery of the Blessed Paullus, Samuelis of Monastery of the Blessed Isaacius ...

Sunt autem et in lingua Syrorum multae et infinitae monarchorum subscriptions.[287]

---

[287] Translated from Latin this reads: "There are an infinite number of signatures from monks with names from the Syriac language."

## 7.7.4 Letter from the Maronites to the Jacobites (592)

The following are extracts from the letter from the monks of Beit Maroun and their questions for the Jacobites:[288]

> Indeed, for five days we have been waiting for you to give us an answer to the five questions concerning which your faith leaves something to be desired, and you have not been able to ... This witness, for which we asked you at Antioch[289] if you are able, and if you have a just and appropriate answer to these five questions that we have raised against you, with the whole town and with the outsiders to be found there as witnesses between ourselves and you, answer us in all piety, according to the chosen doctors and saints, concerning whom there is no division between us and you or any Christian, namely:
>
> First, that the Messiah is not said to be twofold; second, that the Messiah has a composite nature; third, that the nature, the person and the hypostatis are all the same thing in the Messiah; fourth, that Dioscoros, your master, has anathematised Eutychius after having received him in your communion; fifth, show also that you submit to the anathema whoever confesses two natures in the Messiah before the union (of the natures), or in the union, or after the union. That is all ...
>
> Now we have to make known the answer of the Jacobites. It is rich above all insults against the Maronites, but it is nonetheless important, for as we have already said, all these insults now turn to the glory of the Maronites, since their bitter enemies reproach them only with professing the faith of Saint Leo and of the Council of Chalcedon and accuse them of no other error than that of not professing the same faith.

[288] Translated by Nau and cited in Naaman, *The Maronites*, pp. 157-159.

[289] Nau, copied in Naaman, *The Maronites*, p. 158, states in a footnote this is the Greek name for Antioch translated into Syriac. He believes it was probable the letter was written in Greek and we only have a Syriac translation.

### 7.7.5 Response from the Jacobites to the Maronites (592)

This letter of response from the Jacobites to the Maronites is from Nau's translation, quoted in Naaman.[290]

> Response and summary solution to the five questions sent from the village of Armaz [Armenaz] by the monks of Beth Maron, after their leaving Antioch, to the orthodox monks in the holy monasteries of Mesopotamia.

> To the plant of the Chalcedon vine, to the offspring of the root of Leo, to the acid germ produced by the vine of Theodoret and, to say it in a few words, to the sons of the great and principal schism to have taken place in the church, which scatters the members of the Messiah and divides his body into many parts, to Philip and to Thomas, those of Beth Maron ...[291]

> I am astonished by your ignorance, and how can you, you who are the doctors of Ephrem,[292] can you fail to know that (that the Messiah is not said to be twofold) ... If however you wish for a demonstration of these things that are so well-known and evident, address yourselves to St Cyril, about whom alone between us there is no controversy, he been received with complete persuasion of the spirit and recognised as the ax which cuts the artisans of heresies and his teachings believed by us to be Gospel.

> In the great and illustrious letter that he wrote to Nestorius, enemy of God, he seems to say in his definition that the Messiah should not be twofold: "We do not separate the words of the Gospel consecrated to our Saviour in two persons nor in two hypostases, for this one and only Messiah is not double even though he is recognised as from two

---

[290] The letter of response from the Jacobites to the Maronites from Nau's translation is a total of thirteen pages in Ibid., pp. 159-172.

[291] It is suggested by Nau that these names were some of the two principal authors of the letter from the Maronites. Cited in Ibid., p. 159.

[292] Nau in a footnote (cited in Ibid., p. 161) suggests the Maronites might have been advisers of Ephrem, patriarch of Antioch from 529 to 545, who was amongst the harshest persecutors of the Monophysites. If so, Nau suggests, the passage is of great importance.

things which were united in one indivisible unity, just as a man is formed of soul and body but is not therefore double, but one, formed from two. In confirmation of this, we shall call to witness in their time the words of our Saviour which run: Let he who has ears to hear listen, and: That which I say to you I say to all." So in this passage he decides that the Messiah is not twofold and that man cannot be said to be twofold, one from two. ...

you who call him [Christ] double because he has taken on flesh and become man, and he proclaims to you Maronites partisans of the two natures and to all the Council of Chalcedon: "It is not because the Son the Word, in taking on flesh from God [that he was], became man that he should be called double" ...

In fact you say: "show us that the Messiah has one composed nature." You resembled those who remember having dreamt something and then ask somebody to bring what they have dreamt about. When you hear "one incarnate nature," unless because of your ignorance you do not try to understand the word "incarnate" – applied to him who is formed of both, in the simple meaning ...

As you have adjured us to place under the eyes of our fathers your ignominy, that is to say your little letter or your imperfect conceptions that you have sent us from Armaz by Isaac and Simon after burying yourselves secretly in the face of the reprimand (given you) at Antioch, we have done (as you asked) for your salvation and on account of your adjurations. We have shown to the holy fathers who were here that your factum was not worthy of their powerful words like unto the iron which cut stone, as it is written, but they have asked of me and of my young brother Theodore of the monastery of Beth Mar Abaz, to give you the appropriate solution, something that I have done according to my feeble forces- I adjure you also by the holy and consubstantial Trinity which is divided while remaining one and which is one while being divided, to read what we have written, containing the solution of your reproaches before the whole assembly of Beth Maroun ...

End of the solution to the senseless questions of the monks of Beth Maron who are in the territory of Apamaea.[293]

---

[293] In the second last paragraph quoted above, Nau inserts a footnote: The Maronites interpreted 'one nature incarnate' in the sense of 'two natures' for by incarnate (the holy Fathers) announce and recognise a (second) nature.

# CHAPTER 8

# THE SEVENTH CENTURY AND
# THE ARRIVAL OF ISLAM

## 8.1  Introduction to the Period

For Maronite history, the period from the seventh century to the arrival of the Crusades is the most controversial. There are virtually no primary sources available. In the absence of documentary reference to Aramaic Catholics and Maronites, we are left with a limited number of secondary sources, often written by third parties who were commenting on a period of history well before their time. The dearth of detail and the lack of contemporaneity must be given its due weight for the version of events put forward by these ancient writers and thereafter relied upon by later historical and modern historians. Before delving into the discussion, some reflection is provided to situate the reader in the religious, historical, political, and geographical context.

The power struggle between the Monophysites and the Chalcedonians continued in this period. Anastasius succeeded Zeno as Byzantine Emperor from 491 to 518. He was a professed non-Chalcedonian. Severus was appointed by the Emperor as the last of the non-Chalcedonian Patriarchs of Antioch from 512 to 518. He is known as one of the fathers of the Syriac Orthodox Church. From 527 to 545, Emperor Justinian's wife Theodora (apparently a daughter of a Syrian priest) supported the Monophysites. In 533, the Monophysites convinced Justinian to hold a Council and excommunicate the deceased fathers of the dualistic Antiochian doctrine. The anathametisation was also against Theodoret, more than seventy years after his death. However, the Council did not criticise the Chalcedonian doctrine so as to keep the Pope appeased. Many of Theodoret's books were burnt.

241

Ephraim of Amid was Patriarch of Antioch from 529 to 545. The monks of Maroun were his close aids and teachers as evidenced in a letter written by the Monophysites held in the British Museum.[294] By 536, the Chalcedonians had regained their prestige and the delegated monk of Beit Maroun monastery, as the paramount monastery of Syria Secunda, was in attendance at the Second Council of Constantinople in 536. The Monophysites then gradually declined in their importance in the Antiochian region.

Jacob Baradaeus, a Monophysite, was appointed Bishop of Edessa from 543 to 578. One of the fathers and most important figures in the history of the Syriac Orthodox Church, he moved all around the Middle East, Egypt, Persia, and Mesopotamia establishing and strengthening a network of Monophysite ties and ordaining bishops wherever he went. The Syriac Monophysite churches were often called 'Jacobites' by the Chalcedonians because of his influence (incorrectly according to the Syriac Orthodox Church as he was not the founder but a church 'father').

The Christian and Byzantine world redefined the Roman world. Baths and theatre-centred life declined and public worship was promoted above public entertainment. Churches and monasteries, particularly in the East, filled the land. The production of secular literature was on the decline and almost ceased. The separation of church and state reversed and religion and politics became thoroughly embroiled.

During the seventh century, the frontier between East and West ran from the upper Tigris to the middle Euphrates. Rome and Byzantine's enemies had no access to what the Romans called their See. In the previous decades in Europe the Byzantines had struggled to keep back the Slavs, Avars, and Lombards. Constantinople did not protect Italy. The French took over Italy, which would eventually host a rival Western emperor to the Byzantine emperor.

The year 608-609 AD saw the Jews in Antioch rebel against the Christians and kill Anastasios, the patriarch, and many landowners.

---

[294] Naaman, *The Maronites*, p. 131.

The Jews formed a militia and the Byzantine army could not quell them.[295] However, Persia was the empire's greatest enemy. The Persian Empire incorporated Arabia. It conquered Syria (Apamaea, Edessa, and Antioch) in 610-11 from Byzantine Emperor Heraclius. Several years later Palestine and Egypt also fell into Persian hands. Jerusalem would fall to the Persians in 614-15.[296]

The extent of the Persian atrocities in the Middle East before the arrival of the Arabs cannot be underestimated. Theophanes (d. 818) records the Persians killed 90,000 Christians with the assistance of Jews, and then the Jews had bought Christians as slaves and killed them.[297] In the five-week period of the siege of Jerusalem in 614 by the Persians, it is reported there were 66,509 dead with bodies collected from monasteries and churches. The Persians had enslaved or massacred most of the populations of the places they invaded and those who remained were, according to Theophanes, subject to their "yoke ... of bloodthirstiness and taxation."

Clergy and monks were the ones who mostly wrote about the atrocities. The Persians particularly targeted them; even those who posed no threat were killed. Monasteries were plundered and left in ruins. In Nikiu, Egypt, seven hundred monks were massacred. Also in Egypt, one thousand nuns were taken captive and patriarch John of Alexandria had to pay a ransom to have them released. A great number of refugees from the Syrian Orient fled to Alexandria in Egypt where the Catholic Patriarch John became known as the 'Almsgiver'.

To the extent of any tolerance shown, it seemed that the Persians supported the Monophysites over the Chalcedonians. It is possible that, after fierce persecutions, Monophysites saw the Persians as lib-

---

[295] Theophanes, *The Chronicle of Theophanes: Anni mundi 6095-6305 (A.D. 602-813), (Chronographia)* trans. by H. Turtledove, University of Pennsylvania Press, 1982, p. 7.

[296] Ibid., p. 11.

[297] Ibid. Michael the Syrian reports the same number 90,000 perhaps relying on Theophanes, and also states the Christians were bought at a low price by the Jews as slaves, and the Persian king exterminated the Jews in Jerusalem and sent captives to Persia. Michael the Syrian, *Chronicle of Michael the Great, Patrirach of the Syrians*, trans. by Robert Bedrosian, Sources of the Armenian Tradition, 1871, paragraph 121.

erators from Byzantine rule. On the other side, the Persians saw the Chalcedonians as collaborators with Constantinople.[298]

Beginning around 610, the Persians expelled all the Chalcedonian bishops from Mesopotamia and Syria and their churches and monasteries were handed to the Monophysites. Soon after, the Persian king decreed the Chalcedonians should be expelled from the East and permitted the Monophysite bishops to take over their sees. Michael the Syrian, Jacobite patriarch historian, recorded:

> The Episcopal sees everywhere were taken over by our (Monophysite) bishops and the memory of the Chalcedonians disappeared from the Euphrates to the East. The Lord made their inequity fall upon their head: that which they had achieved through the intervention of the Roman Emperor was repaid to them through the intervention of the Persians, kings of Assyria.[299]

It is here we have evidence of a possible mass migration of Catholics from the far Middle East including from the Euphrates region. They are likely to have migrated to the western parts of the patriarchate. It can be assumed that from this point there were very few, if any, Catholics left in the far Middle East and Euphrates area leaving virtually only Monophysite Christians in the region.

After the Persians claimed Antioch in 611, Athanasios, the Syriac Monophysite patriarch of Antioch, wrote a synodical letter to his fellow Monophysite patriarch Anastasius of Alexandria stating: "the world today rejoices in peace and love because the Chalcedonian darkness has passed away."[300] The Monophysite bishops of Syria, who had taken refuge in Egypt because of Chalcedonian persecution, returned to their churches. In reverse, many Chalcedonians fled to Alexandria to leave by ship as refugees principally to Rome.

Scores of monks and nuns, who had seen the worst atrocities within their own monasteries and convents, had gone ahead of the lay refu-

---

[298] Ekonomou, *Byzantine Rome and the Greek Popes*, pp. 55-56.

[299] Ibid., p. 57.

[300] Ibid., p. 58.

gees to Rome before what was perceived soon to be a major Persian onslaught. Constantinople did not appear to be a travel option given the eastern Roman Empire seemed under serious threat. The city of Alexandria remained Byzantine until 619. Outside of Alexandria, the population was Monophysite.[301]

## 8.2 Arrival of Islam in Jerusalem and Antioch 634-638

In 626, Constantinople was besieged by the Persians and Avars. Between 627 and 629, Heraclius had regained from the Persians most of the empire's lost territory. The twenty-six year long war between the Byzantines and Persians was costly to both empires. As a result, both of their resources were severely depleted. During this period, the Arabs began their infrequent incursions into Syria and Palestine.

An unexpected new threat emerged. The birth and rapid rise of Islam and its armies from Arabia. Arriving in southern Syria in 634, the Arabs inflicted heavy losses on Heraclius' troops in battles across the province. In the same year, after a siege that lasted many months, the Arab Muslim conquerors finally took over the great city of Damascus. In 638, the patriarchal capitals of Jerusalem and Antioch fell to the Arabs. The course of history changed.

For centuries the Christians of the Middle East lived in prosperous times. The Aramaic-Syriac-speaking Christians of Roman Middle East (particularly the Catholics after 451) including Palestine, Phoenicia, and Mount Lebanon, had no army and no fighting skill. They were preoccupied with their faith and would have thought the Roman Byzantine Empire was too mighty to ever leave them unprotected. They were unprepared for conquest, let alone one from a new religion. The Persian conquests in Syria and Palestine in the first decades of the seventh century may have sounded the alarm bells, but perhaps not sufficiently enough. The memory of previous Arab incursions around 498 into the Roman provinces of First Syria, First Phoenicia, Phoenicia Lebanon, Third Palestine, and Euphrates must have vanished.[302]

---

[301] Ibid.

[302] Evagrius, *The Ecclesiastical History*, p. 181. Whitby's footnote 138 refers to the

With the Arab Muslim successes, the Middle East Christians now had reason to despair. Their protector, the powerful Byzantine Empire, had perhaps become complacent. A period was to follow of empires at war, famines, earthquakes and plagues, Persian and Arab invasions, and Arab civil wars. Lammens estimates the population of the empire's Middle East at the time of the arrival of the Arab Muslims in the seventh century was approximately one million living in cities and the balance in the countryside. The cities comprised approximately 300,000 persons in Antioch, 117,000 in Apamaea, 50,000 in Beirut, 50,000 in Damascus, and 40,000 in Sidon. The secondary cities of Lattaquieh, Tartus, Byblos, Tripoli, Batrun, Gibla, Tyre, Aleppo, Homs, Hama and Membej totalled approximately 500,000 persons.[303] We cannot estimate what proportion of these populations was Catholic and non-Catholic at the time, nonetheless, the Christian population in the Middle East declined dramatically over the next century from mass emigration to Sicily and Rome, as we shall discuss later.

It is thought that in 610, pro-Chalcedon Emperor Heraclius (610-641) visited Syria and went first to St Maroun's monastery. He gave orders for many Monophysite monasteries to be added to the property of Beit Maroun. This explains the rumours that Heraclius was thought to be Maronite.[304] It is known Heraclius attempted to reunite the Aramaic Monophysites, Copts, Ethiopians, and Armenians with the Byzantines but, according to the Syriac Orthodox Church, with ruthless oppression and the making of many martyrs. With the rapid rise of Islam in the Middle East, the treatment Christians was dependent on factors such as the personality of the rulers and local governors, tolerance levels between faiths, varying degrees of individual and communal Christian resistance, and the varying waves of Islamic fanaticism whether localized or generalized. At certain stages, additional matters influenced Muslim discrimination against the Melkites (Maronites and Byzantines) more than for other Christian denominations.

---

invasions citing Shahid, *Fifth Century*, pp. 121-31.

[303] Dau, *History of the Maronites*, pp. 199-200.

[304] Naaman, *The Maronites*, p. 132, quoting Migne.

## 8.3   The Rapid Rise of Islam

How did the Arabs become dominant so quickly on the Mediterranean side of the Middle East, which was overwhelmingly Christian and under the grand and powerful Byzantine Empire? There are a host of reasons and varying accounts from Arab Muslim, Eastern Christian, and Western historians. A brief outline of some of the many observations from descriptions of battles, seizures, and the conquest is provided here.

The Islamic Prophet Mohammed (570-632 AD) and his lineal ancestors were from a prominent family of the Arabian city of Mecca. They were from the tribe of Quraysh. Many tribes in the region, including the Quraysh, had their own Arabic dialects. This included the Bedouins in the desert. The dialect of Mecca was looked upon as the purest.

Islam gives an account of the prophet Mohammed, at the age of forty around the year 610 AD, retreating to a mountain cave named Hira for several nights of prayer. It was there that he was visited by the Archangel Gabriel and had his first revelation from God. After several years, Prophet Mohammed began preaching these revelations as the messenger of God. Originally he was met with hostility from some tribes of Mecca. He and his followers migrated to Medina (Yathrib) in 622 AD[305] and united the tribes there. Eventually, with a large army of Muslim converts, he conquered Mecca. Two years later he fell ill and died. Before his death, most of Arabia had converted to Islam, and the pagans, Christians, and Jews were forced to either emigrate or convert.

The Muslim Caliphs that followed Mohammed as leaders sent their Arabian tribes to conquer new lands in the name of Islam. The records of battles refer to thousands of foreign slaves, who had converted to Islam as part of the fighting forces. Michael the Syrian records around the year 668, after 80,000 Africans were taken slaves by the Arabs, the Arab forces went to Lebanon and were defeated by the Byzantines where the Arabs lost 30,000 troops in their first defeat.[306] During one

---

[305] This event is known as the Hijra and marks the beginning of the Islamic calendar.
[306] Michael the Syrian, *Chronicle of Michael the Great*, paragraph 133.

of the battles between 692-694, large payments by the Arabs won over 20,000 Slavs who deserted the Byzantines.[307]

The invaders seemingly spared the populations of many of the major cities from massacre. After winning fierce battles in their approach towards the cities, the Muslim armies would surround the city for a lengthy period of time. The siege would continue for months until the city was ready to surrender. Negotiations opened through interpreters. The local population were given several choices. They could depart in safety with as many belongings as they could take, convert to Islam, or remain and pay the Islamic tax known as the *jizya*. Those that refused all of the choices would face death by the sword.

These cities fell to Muslim rule generally via a treaty, most often written and negotiated by the bishop of the city. So long as the *jizya* was paid, the *dhimmis*, or 'peoples of the book' or Abrahamic faith such as Christians and Jews, were allowed to practise their religion in return for protection and as a mark of their submission to Islam. In battles, Muslims were instructed to spare women and children wherever possible. If the soldiers had no family in Arabia, they could marry the locals in the land of conquest. They were also entitled to purchase as many female slaves as they desired.

Abd al-Malik built the Islamic Dome of the Rock on the Jewish Temple Mount in Jerusalem. He minted coins bearing profession of the Muslim faith and sought to institute Arabic as the official language of the new empire. Often, dependent on the local Muslim governor, the increasingly heavy burden of the *jizya* placed unreasonable means on economic existence.

## 8.4   Christians Under Arab Islamic Rule

What is not well known is that the Aramaic-Syriac-speaking Christians and their liturgy constituted the overwhelming majority of the

---

[307] Theophanes, *The Chronicle of Theophanes*, p. 64. Note, in 664-665 Theophanes also records 5,000 Slavs deserted the Byzantines and aligned with the Arabs and settled near Apamaea and the year after the bishop of nearby Emesa was burned alive (p. 48).

population directly affected by the Arab conquest in Syria, Lebanon, Phoenicia, Palestine, Mesopotamia, and Arabia. Scant historical attention has been drawn to the dominance of the Christian population throughout these regions at the time. There is limited to no detail as to their life following the Arab conquest. The Christian populations principally included Catholics, Monophysites, and Nestorians.

The Arab expeditions kept the capture of Constantinople as their goal for almost the next hundred years after initial conquest. They would have sought to restrict or sever communication between Christians of the Middle East and the Byzantine world. In Asia Minor, shifts in population saw the rise of a more rural society, comprised of villages and small market towns protected by castles. This shift to more remote rural lands appeared as a trend for many other Christians throughout the Middle East under Islamic rule.

Public spaces disappeared and buildings as well as peoples huddled together for protection. Dissenters were less and less tolerated. Many became Arab prisoners. Local women became slaves and captives. The Muslim rulers were not sure of their survival in these new Christian lands surrounded as they were by a hostile Christian majority. Arab distrust of the Christian population was ingrained but coexistence had to be the new order of the day. It was from this we see the beginnings of Muslim-Christian relations develop over the following centuries. For example, dependent on the ruler or governor, many of positions of power under Islamic rule began to be held by Christians.

The Arabs did not accept responsibility for internal affairs of the non-Muslim communities under their rule. The churches under Islamic rule therefore tended towards pragmatism. Strong faith competed with behaviour under the rulers. The legal status of the churches became paramount to keep the social solidarity and self-esteem of their Christian communities. The financial basis of the Christian religious institution became important. The church was now more than ever critical in protecting its congregation from the government. This shaped the future identity of the Middle Eastern churches, particularly the Aramaic-speaking Catholics from Palestine, Phoenicia-Lebanon, and the two Syrian provinces. This formation had already taken place amongst the Monophysites due to their hardship under Byzantine rule. In either case, the Christianity of the entire Middle East was one where the lay faithful gathered closely around their monasteries, churches, and clergy. This unique Middle Eastern Christian identity has been retained through the ages and carries on today.

## 8.4.1 The Maronite-Melkites

Orthodox is a Greek word meaning 'the right way' or sound or correct in opinion or doctrine. Those who rejected Nestorianism and Mono-physitism were known as Orthodox, moreso by the Byzantines than by the West. After 451 and the Catholic Church's heresy declarations against Nestorianism and Monophysitism, the only Christians in the East within the Empire outside of Asia Minor who remained loyal to the Byzantine king were the Greek-speaking and Aramaic-Syriac-speaking Christians. After the arrival of the Arabs in 634-638, these Catholic (Orthodox) Christians also became known as the Melkites.[308] As royalists and Catholic-Orthodox they were also referred to in Arabic as 'Rum' or 'Roum' meaning followers of Rome (Rouma), that is Constantinople, the 'New Rome'.

The Maronites were the leading party of Melkite Aramaic-Syriac-speakers in the Middle East. Their liturgical language was not Greek and customs of their church were not Byzantine. The liturgical texts saw their church as a distinct member of the Byzantine orthodox communion but not as a constituent part of the Greek-Byzantine religious customs. This is in the same way the Eastern Catholic churches see themselves today as being in communion with Rome, but not as part of the Latin customs or rites and Latin-speaking church. Accordingly, the Maronites were Melkites or 'Roum' at this time alongside the non-indigenous Greek-Byzantines living in the Middle East.

On the arrival of the Muslim conquerors in the western region of the Middle East, these Catholics were the leading advocates of Chal-

---

[308] For the alternate view that the word 'Melkite' was first used in the fifth century, see Chapter 5.

cedon. As royalists, they were also firmly established as the region's beacon of Christian orthodoxy for the Byzantine Emperor and for the Catholic Church, including the pope in Rome and the patriarch of Constantinople. Beit Maroun monks and their network were perceived as the greatest local and regional Christian threat to the Muslim rulers and governors in the Middle East. Numerous suspicions would have followed as a result of the Maronites' close links to the West, particularly the Vatican, Italy, and France who then led the Catholic world. The Maronites, fully conversant with the price they would have to pay for their faith, would suffer the heaviest form of Islamic persecution.

The Maronite-Melkite isolation as the Catholic beacons of orthodoxy drew attention not just from Muslims, but from the other Christian denominations of the Middle East. In 659, one incident detailed by Bar Hebraeus evidences the difficulties in relations at the time between the Syriac Jacobites and the Maronites. In front of the Islamic Caliph Moawiah in Damascus, discussions had taken place between the Maronites and the patriarch and bishops of the Jacobites. The Maronites had the upper hand and the Jacobite patriarch paid 20,000 dinars in return for protection against "the sons of the Church."[309]

Over the centuries that followed, the Maronites endured martyrdom, the destruction of monasteries, convents, and churches, and numerous relocations of the Maronite patriarchate. Valuable historical records and literature were regularly destroyed, misplaced, lost or left behind in the melee and, of course, survival would have taken priority over the creation of records. The persecution of the Maronites had not only physical consequences but historical. It has resulted in a string of tainted recordings about Maronites throughout the ages, from both Muslim and Christian historians, with a dearth of material from the Maronites themselves.

---

[309] Nau's *Opuscules Maronites* 1899 edition has now recently been published in French by Gorgias Press.

## 8.4.2 The Syriac Jacobite Christians

Christianity spread to Arabia in the first century. Christians suffered persecution within the lands of the Persian Empire. They were suspected at various times as being allied with their Christian brethren just to the west. Nonetheless, the Aramaic-Syriac language and its Christian culture was the clear influence on the Arab Christians, as was its monastic life. The Aramaic-Syriac-speaking monks were known to have established missions in Arabia.

It is said the Christians of the Arabian Peninsula were likely in the great majority Nestorian and Arian. As previously discussed, the Nestorians believed that Mary was the mother of Jesus and not the mother of God, and were declared heretics at the Council of Chalcedon in 451. The Arians, followers of Arius from Alexandria, were declared heretics by the Catholic Church in 381 for their doctrine that Jesus was created later by God than the time of creation and hence is distinct from God the Father.[310] This opposes the Christian doctrine of the Holy Trinity and was said to be closer to the Muslim belief that Jesus is a prophet, but not divine.

The Ghassanid Arabs and their emirs (or princes), the Gafnans, were Monophysite Christians and were commissioned by the Byzantine emperor to secure the border of the Byzantine empire against the attacks of the Arab tribes and their allied Persians. With the arrival of Arab Muslim rule, the Syriac Jacobite Christians had different expectations of Islamic rule to other Christians. They saw the Arabs as saviours from centuries of oppression under the Byzantine and Persian empires.

The Islamic Prophet Mohammed was from the Quraysh tribe from the city of Mecca. Prior to the birth of Islam, it is thought the population of Mecca were split in faith between Christianity and paganism. However, it is likely Christianity would not have flourished to the extent in the Byzantine world being under the rule of the Persian

---

[310] This is based on the Gospel passage from John 14:28 "You heard me say, 'I am going away and I am coming back to you.' If you loved me, you would be glad that I am going to the Father, for the Father is greater than I."

Empire. According to the Syriac Orthodox Church the Christians of Mecca were mostly members of their church. They state the bishop of Mecca was Waraqa Ibn Naufal Ibn Assad (d. 611), the cousin of Khadidga who was the daughter of Khuailid and the wife of Mohammed, Prophet of Islam.

The views of the Syriac Jacobites can perhaps be ascertained through Gregory Bar Hebraeus, bishop of their Church in the thirteenth century. Nau, in his book *Opuscules Maronites*, cites from a Syriac text written by Bar Hebraeus a reference around 630 AD, prior to the arrival of Islamic conquests in Syria, to poor relations between the monks of Maroun and the Jacobites. It was alleged by Bar Hebraeus the Maronite monks had taken possession of some Jacobite churches and monasteries. When the Jacobites complained to the Emperor Heraclius he did nothing about it. Nau quotes Bar Hebraeus as stating: "So the Lord of Vengeance then sent the Arabs to deliver us from the Romans. Our churches were not returned, for each kept what he owned, but at least we were saved from the cruelty of the Greeks and their hatred towards us."[311]

A similar sentiment is shared by the Syrian Orthodox Church (Eastern USA dioceses) which simultaneously also incorrectly asserts all Syrians as Monophysites thus carrying on the repeated void in history that marginalises Aramaic Catholics/Maronites:

> Only through the campaigns of Islam in the first half of the 7th century was it possible to free the East from the Byzantines and the Persians. This happened with the help of the members of the Syrian Church; the original inhabitants of Syria of whom one part was of Aramaic origin who inhabited these areas for generations and another part was of Arabic origin. When the Arab Muslims marched into Syria they were welcomed by the Syrians who saw the new rulers as saviors who freed them from the yoke of the Byzantines because the Byzantines tried by force to assimilate them into the Byzantine Church. This was the church of the empire and membership in it would have meant compulsorily acceptance of

---

[311] Naaman, *The Maronites*, p. 155.

253

the resolutions of Chalcedon: that Christ had two natures, the human eating, drinking and feeling pain and the divine making miracles. This would have been a denial of the dogma of their church fathers. The Syrians were also able through the cooperation with the Arab Muslims to retain their ecclesiastical dogma, the Antiochian See, their churches, monasteries, ecclesiastical inheritance and their liturgy …

The Persian powers in their empire oppressed both West and East Syrians in general to force them under tyrannical policies and Zoroastrian beliefs. Therefore the Syrians under the Byzantine and Persian powers saw the Islamic conquerors as liberators and not as occupiers. The Syrians put great hope in them, not only because the Muslims liberated them from their religious trouble but also because they relieved the Syrians of the burdensome taxes that were placed on their backs. They said, "Praise be to God, who delivered us from the unjust Byzantines and who put us under the rule of the just Muslim Arabs."[312]

The many Arab tribes in Iraq and Syria who were members of the Syriac Orthodox faith "felt obliged to support the Arab Muslims despite the difference of their faith for they were related by blood, language, and culture." Accordingly, they assisted the Muslims against the Byzantines. Initially, the Muslims granted safety and protection to these Monophysite Christians, their churches, and monasteries. As it was under Persian rule, the protection under the Muslims was on the proviso they paid the governor the *jizya* tax in return.

The Syriac Orthodox expectations of Muslim protection in those times (and continuing today) are held in an agreement or covenant between them from the seventh century. It is still retained by the Syriac Orthodox Church and is set out as follows:

He [Muhammad] said: "In the name of Allah, the compassionate, the merciful! This is a writing written by Muhammad Ibn Abdallah to all people as messenger, preacher, admonisher,

---

[312] H.H.I. Zakka I, "A Short Overview of the Common History," *Patriarchal Journal* 33 (146), (1995) pp. 322-344, available at http://syrianorthodoxchurch.org/2010/03/a-short-overview-of-the-common-history/.

and the one responsible so that nothing is kept from the messengers of God. God is powerful and wise. He writes it for the Christians all over the earth who live here or abroad, who speak Arabic or other languages, known and unknown. He gives them a covenant. He who annuls it, who practises the opposite, who oversteps the commandments, annuls the testament of God, denies its agreement, laughs about his religion, and earns a curse whoever he is, a ruler or another Muslim.

When a monk or someone passes through seeking refuge on a mountain, in a valley, in a cave, in a house, on flat land, on sand or in a church, then I with my helpers, relatives, my tribe and my followers will do what they can for him with enthusiasm because he is a member of the community and stands under my protection and I keep all harm from him. The persons affected shall only be taxed with so much tax as they are freely willing to pay without force or pressure; no bishop shall be moved from his bishopric, no monk from his monastery, no hermit from his cell to another city; no one passing through shall be hindered in his traveling. No house, no church building shall be torn down. None of the riches of their churches shall be used either for the building of a mosque or a house for Muslims. Whoever does anything like this violates the testament of God and his messengers. The bishops and God's workers shall be burdened with neither taxes nor fines. I protect them wherever they may be – be they on land or on sea, in the east or in the west, in the north or in the south. They are under my protection and safe from any need ...

Whoever prays to God as a hermit in the mountains or in a blessed place does not have to pay for the sowing, nor the taxes, nor the tithing; one is not allowed to take a part because they only earn their own living and nobody helps them with their harvest. They are also not required to go to sea. The land and estate owners shall not pay more than twelve dirhams per year; none of them shall be burdened with excesses and one shall not debate with them but rather do better than them as a good example, showing mercy and keeping them from tragedies.

When Christianity has come under the rule of Islam then the Muslims shall be satisfied to let them pray in their churches and no obstacle shall stand between them and their inclination to religion. Whoever violates God's testament, who does the opposite, is disobedient before God and his messenger. The Muslims shall be helpful to them, the Christians, with the restoration of their churches and houses. None of them is obliged to carry weapons because the Muslims protect them. Nobody shall offend against this testament until the day of the last judgment and until the end of the world."[313]

### 8.4.3 Aramaic Catholic Migration to Sicily and Rome

As noted previously, the Aramaic-speaking Catholics have been generally left in a void of history since the Council of Chalcedon in 451. The Aramaic-Syriac Monophysites, have sought through their history to wrongly regard themselves as comprising the entire, or almost entire, Aramaic-Syriac native population. From Western and Byzantine spectacles, historians have generally perceived these indigenous peoples to be Monophysite. As demonstrated earlier in this book, it is more than likely the Catholics dominated the population of the patriarchate of Antioch in its western regions.

Following the Persian conquests of the early seventh century, and shortly after the arrival of the Arab Muslims, many Catholic Christians including Maronites remained in colonies in the cities and surrounding countryside of Syria, Phoenicia, Phoenicia, Lebanon, and northern Palestine. Others chose to reduce their family or community's exposure to initially Persian rule, and not long after Islamic rule, and migrated to the West. It is highly unlikely migrants leaving for the West were Monophysite Christians given the West was pro-Chalcedon. Accordingly, migrants leaving the Middle East for the Byzantine

---

[313] Ibid.

world of Europe would almost certainly have been dominated by, if not almost entirely, Catholics.

During the time of the Persian and Arab conquests in the early to mid-seventh century, there was a mass migration to Rome and Sicily of Maronite Melkites (i.e. ethnic Aramaic Catholics) and Byzantine Melkites (ethnic Greek-Byzantine Catholics) from the western regions of the patriarchate of Antioch. This proposition is supported by a progressive analysis during the seventh century of clergy names, funerary inscriptions and public elections in Rome of ethnic eastern popes.

By the beginning of the seventh century there were only a few priests at synods in Rome who had names of an Eastern origin. By 649 at the Lateran Council, nearly one quarter of the names of bishops attending reflected an Eastern origin or ancestry. Thirty years later in 679, over half of the fifteen bishops who attended a synod convened in Rome by the Greco-Sicilian Pope Agatho were Easterners, the same for two thirds of the priests in attendance. At a synod of the Roman Church held on 12 April 732, there were thirty-one clergy present. In addition to the ethnic Syrian Pope, all but one of the seven bishops were of Eastern origin. Eighteen of the nineteen priests had names reflecting an oriental provenance. All five deacons, including the future Pope Zacharias, were unquestionably ethnic 'Syrians' or Greeks. Thus more than ninety percent of the clerics were ethnic Easterners.

Between 701-750, ethnic Greeks in the ranks of the Roman clergy outnumbered Latins by nearly three and a half to one. Excepting one pope, there was an uninterrupted succession of Eastern pontiffs starting from Pope Agatho in 678 and ending with Pope Zacharias in 752. This was a succession of ethnic Greco-Sicilian, Syrian-Sicilian, Syrian, and Greek pontiffs.[314] How did this come about?

Before answering one matter needs explaining. As detailed previously, a reference to Syrian meant the ancient Syrian Orient, which included the western regions of the patriarchate of Antioch. This embodied the seven Roman provinces of Syria, Phoenicia, and Palestine.

---

[314] Ekonomou, *Byzantine Rome and the Greek Popes*, pp. 20, 212, 131, 166, 245-246, 247.

Authors have referred to the emigration from these provinces to be from ethnic 'Syrians' both for clergy and lay. However, the correct reference to them should be 'Aramaic' as a broader more inclusive ethnic and linguistic term. This also included Lebanese.

The Persian and Arab invasions during the first half of the seventh century brought oriental populations to Sicily as refugees. It also became a stepping-stone for migration to the European continent. By the first half of the seventh century, there was a substantial population of Aramaic monks and leadership of the majority of the monasteries in Sicily had passed from Latin to Greek. The Aramaic Theophanes was abbot of the monastery of St Peter *ad Baias* in Sicily. He was one of Greek-Sicilian Pope Agatho's (a former monk himself) delegates to the Sixth Ecumenical Council in 680-681. Theophanes became patriarch of Antioch after Makarios was deposed at the Council, which was attended by 165 bishops and episcopal representatives. By the end of the seventh century, there were four Sicilian popes who were either Greek or Aramaic ethnicity.[315]

Shortly after the Middle Eastern Catholic refugee crisis, Sicily also became a Byzantine Empire military base from 663. It was seen as a strategic position in the centre of the Mediterranean to launch offensives and establishing primary zones of defence. It was considered private imperial property independent of the exarchate of Italy. An imperial court and residence was set up there. It was Italy's richest province, unaffected by wars, and enjoyed considerable economic prosperity throughout the seventh century. It had provided Rome and Italy since ancient times with their principal source of grain. Sicily had been heavily Hellenised since the days of the ancient Greek empire. In the fourth and fifth centuries, the eastern part of Sicily around Messina, Catania, and Syracuse had ethnic Greek majorities. With oriental populations already there, the succession of Justinian emperors' reconquest in the mid-sixth century brought fresh populations of Syrians, Armenians, and Greeks.[316]

---

[315] Ibid., pp. 177-179, 199.
[316] Ibid., pp. 177-179.

There is evidence that after the arrival of the Arabs, the seventh century did not experience a cessation of commerce between East and West, although the volume of trade was reduced. Ancient trade routes, which also carried passengers, remained between Alexandria and Rome. This route made intermediate stops in Sicily, Sardinia, and Naples. Eastern liturgical customs and practices began to influence the Roman liturgy by the late sixth century reflecting a thriving oriental population in Rome and the founding of many Greek and Aramaic monasteries.[317] There is evidence from funerary inscriptions of the Easterners who had immigrated to Rome in the second half of the seventh century occupying important positions within Roman civil and military administrations. So it was not just monks but also the lay from the East who made a profound influence on the Church of Rome and Roman society in this period.

## 8.5  The Maronites in the East and the West

### 8.5.1 Maronite-Melkite Popes

Emperor Constantine IV was aware of the change in Rome's ethnic composition, both in the clergy, monasteries, and lay populations. During the pontificate of Benedict II (684-685), the emperor removed the requirement of imperial approval as a precondition to the consecration of a pope. This meant a return to the ancient practice of the lay population electing the pope. The emperor knew the numbers were in place to assure that Easterners would dominate the papacy. Otherwise he would not have allowed a return to the ancient law.

Benedict II's successor, the Aramaic Pope John V, was the first to be elected by the general population. The succession of ten popes of Eastern descent followed the death of the Greco-Sicilian Pope Agatho in 681. It was testament to Rome's new ethnic composition of Catholic voters. There were five popes of Syrian ethnicity during this period, the rest were either principally Greek or Sicilian.[318] As Andrew Eko-

[317] Ibid., pp. 18, 44-45, 66 (footnote 34), 208.
[318] Ibid., p. 216.

nomou puts it, the Roman liturgy experienced a remarkable adoption of oriental liturgical practices that "was also an unmistakable barometer of the broader cultural influences and changes that Rome and the papacy were about to experience ... ideas whose effect would be to unite East and West rather than to separate them."[319]

Aramaic liturgical culture was a key part of this transformation alongside the Greek-Byzantine. The Aramaic Catholic identity that was shaped in the Middle East of the earlier centuries, namely loyalty to Rome over the emperor in Constantinople, was to hold firm with the decisions of the Aramaic popes. Given their Syrian Orient[320] origin and Aramaic names, it is most likely these popes during the late seventh up to the mid-eighth century were of Maronite (Melkite) ancestry whilst the Greek named popes must have been either Greco-Sicilian or Greek-Byzantine (Melkite) ancestry from the patriarchates of Antioch, Alexandria and Jerusalem rather than Constantinople.

The following discussion references popes who were more likely of Aramaic Catholic indigenous ancestry, that is, originally of Maronite (Melkite) descent.[321] As Ekonomou states, the Eastern popes were notably dedicated to the Church: "Where East and West diverged on religious issues, Constantinople quickly learned that the oriental popes were irritatingly intractable. For whether ethnically Sicilian, Syrian, or Greek, on matters of religion, the Eastern pontiffs never faltered from allegiance to the practices and doctrines of the church of Rome."[322]

Pope John V (685-686) was the first pope of the Byzantine papacy elected by the people. His papacy was marked by (some) reconciliation between the city of Rome and the Empire. John was Aramaic, born in the Syrian Orient in 635 from the patriarchate of Antioch. As a

---

[319] Ibid., p. 166.

[320] This includes Phoenicia, Lebanon, and northern Palestine.

[321] Archbishop Joseph Tawil, *The Patriarchate of Antioch throughout History: An Introduction,* (2001), Sophia Press, pp. 137-147, refers to the line of Aramaic popes as 'Melkite' but makes no reference to them as 'Maronite'. Tawil also lists and sets out details of the Greek Melkite popes.

[322] Ekonomou, *Byzantine Rome and the Greek Popes*, p. 219.

deacon he represented Rome at the Sixth Ecumenical Council of 680-81,[323] and as a Pope had the records of the event thoroughly checked.[324]

During his pontificate, "the Emperor abolished a substantial portion of the taxes due from the papal patrimony in Sicily and Calabria, in addition to eliminating various other imposts, including a surtax on the sale of grain, which the Roman Church was having difficulty paying each year."[325] His tomb praises his efforts against Monothelitism at the Sixth Ecumenical Council: "with the titles of the faith, keeping such vigilance, united the minds so that the inimical wolf mixing in might not seize the sheep, or the more powerful crush those below."[326]

The Eastern popes were popular amongst the Romans as they stood up to the emperor. The Aramaic Pope Sergius (Sarkis) I (687-701) appeared the first to oppose the emperor. Pope Sergius I was a Syrian Oriental from a family in the patriarchate of Antioch who settled in Palermo Sicily.[327] His papacy was dominated by his refusal to accept the Quinisext or Trullan Council of 692. This Council was convened in Trullo in Italy, and attended only by Greek Byzantine bishops and Roman legates, but no Roman bishops. The canons from the Trullan Council varied from Roman customs and were traditions based on the Church of Constantinople. The Romans celebrated Sergius for asserting he would sooner die than agree to anti-Roman customs.

Out of the eighty-five Apostolatic canons, the Roman delegates recognised only the first fifty. Emperor Justinian II sought Pope Sergius' assent to the canons. Unexpectedly the Pope, who was a parish priest only for seven years when elected as Pontiff, refused on the grounds that they were "outside of ecclesiastical usage," "invalid," and that he preferred "to die rather than consent to erroneous novelties." It was clear that even though the Roman pontiff would always

---

[323] H.K. Mann, *The Lives of the Popes in the Early Middle Ages*, Vol. I, Part 2, Kegan Paul, Trench, Truber & Co Ltd, 1925, p. 64 and Mann, *The Lives of the Popes*, Vol II, pp. 657-795.

[324] Ekonomou, *Byzantine Rome and the Greek Popes*, p. 219.

[325] Ibid., p. 217.

[326] Ibid., footnote 233 citing De Rossi, p. 243.

[327] Mann, *The Lives of the Popes*, Vol I, part 2, p. 80.

be a loyal subject of the emperor, he would not be captive in matters of religion.[328]

There is evidence in 691 and 692 of Episcopal representatives of dioceses from the patriarchates of Constantinople, Alexandria, Antioch, and Jerusalem attending the Quinisext Council in Trullo. Pope Sergius was not present at the Council.[329] Emperor Justinian dispatched an imperial order to arrest the Pope. The emperor's notoriously ferocious chief of the Imperial guard, Zacharias, was confronted at the Vatican by military opposition of troops from Ravenna and Pentapolis. Zacharias ordered the city gates to be shut and held the Pope prisoner in the Lateran episcopium. Zacharias took refuge and hid under the Pontiff's bed when the Italian troops entered via St Peters Gate approaching the papal residence. The Pope diffused the crisis with soothing words delivered from a seat just below the portraits of Saints Peter and Paul in the nearby basilica named for Pope Theodore. The pontiff took a gentle approach to the populations outrage and managed to have Zacharias depart with his dignity considerably diminished but his life intact.[330]

During the first three centuries after Christ, ethnic Easterners, particularly Greeks, dominated the papal appointments. It was only between 360 and 382, that Latin replaced Greek as the official liturgical language of the Roman Church. The period from 678 to 752 saw Greek return with increasing frequency in the Roman liturgy. Ekonomou informs us this is no surprise given that it coincided with a period of four Greco-Sicilians in close succession occupying the papacy. Sicily, at the crossroads of the Mediterranean basin, was also a crossroads between Greek and Latin practices and traditions. During this period there is evidence of bilingual chanting and recitation, with the Greek language consistently taking precedence.

There is evidence of both Greek and Aramaic-Syriac liturgical influences. Elaborate papal processions taking place on great feast days

---

[328] Ekonomou, *Byzantine Rome and the Greek Popes*, p. 223.
[329] Ibid., p. 220.
[330] Ibid., pp. 223-224.

were introduced, similar to the Eastern ceremonies. The feast of the Exaltation of the Cross, which was first prominent in Egypt and the Middle East, became an important observance in the Roman Church. It is believed Pope Sergius introduced the feast day and directed a procession in Rome on the day of the celebration of the Virgin Mary's nativity, from the Church of St Adrian to the Church of St Mary Major.

He also decreed on the feast day of St Simon the same procession, and it appears he composed special antiphons to be sung during the litany. They were to be chanted in both Greek and Latin and were of the 'Byzantine' musical style. Pope Sergius also placed great importance on the feast of the Annunciation, also prescribing a procession accompanied by chants and hymns that were unmistakably of Eastern influence.[331] No doubt these were all influenced by the Aramaic Catholic liturgies and religious practices.

We have evidence that Sergius substantially restored and embellished the church of martyred Aramaic Saints Cosmos and Damien (martyred at Cyrrhus around c. 287), originally built in the early sixth century along the Via Sacra by Pope Felix IV. Sergius also restored many other churches throughout the capital. Around this time we have evidence of the church of Roman Christian soldiers, Aramaic Saints Sergius (Sarkis) and Bacchus, martyred during the reign of emperor Maximian (286-305).[332] It is important to reflect on one potential link here: There was a great church in Cyrrhus dedicated to the saints Cosmos and Damien, the region of Theodoret's Maroun. Here we have reference to an ethnic Aramaic pope and a church in Rome in the name of the saints. Once again, there appears a pattern of significant interconnections for this book.

Pope Sisinnius (Sisinn) (708) was born in the Syrian Orient in 650. He was pope for only twenty days before passing away.[333] Also born in the Syrian Orient, Pope Constantine (708-715) was one of the two ethnic Aramaic papal legates sent by Rome (with the Aramaic John

---

[331] Ibid., pp. 261-63
[332] Ibid., p. 210.
[333] Mann, *The Lives of the Popes*, Vol I, part 2, p. 124.

who was later also to become Pope) to the Sixth Ecumenical Council in 680-81.[334] The assembly of Rome united behind the Aramaic Pope Constantine I in 713 who rejected emperor Philippikos' decree reinstating Monothelitism. The pope rejected the imperial portrait, gold coins with his image imprinted, and his commemoration in the mass.

Later, Pope Constantine travelled to Constantinople (Nicodemia) and Philippikos' successor, Emperor Justinian, dropped the demands for the Pope's acceptance of the Trullan canons. After the negotiations, the pontiff celebrated mass on Sunday and Justinian received communion from his hands. It appeared as though it was a reaffirmation of Rome's primacy in the Church. This became known as the so-called Compromise of Nicodemia.[335] It is believed that either of the Aramaic popes Constantine or Gregory III introduced special prayers and hymns on the feast day of the exaltation of the holy cross (of Aramaic influence).[336]

Pope Gregory III (731-741) was born in the Syrian Orient,[337] the fifth Aramaic pope in this period and the second last pope born outside of Europe until Pope Francis in 2013, some 1,272 years later. The last was Gregory's successor, an ethnic Greek pope, Zacharias. Gregory III rebuked the emperors in Constantinople and directed them to abandon iconoclasm and return to the ancient customs of the Church.[338]

The most important contribution made by the East to the liturgy and religious devotion in the Roman Church during this period, according to Ekonomou, is the increasing significance of devotion to Mary. This followed the proclamation by the Council of Ephesus in 431 of 'the Holy Virgin is the Mother of God'. Beginning from the early 560s, the emperors began to invoke the devotion and intercession to the Virgin Mary as the special protector and guardian of the empire and of the city of Constantinople in particular. Greek practice

---

[334] Ibid., p. 127.

[335] Ekonomou, *Byzantine Rome and the Greek Popes*, p. 272.

[336] Ibid., footnote 116, p. 283.

[337] Mann, *The Lives of the Popes*, Vol I, part 2, p. 205.

[338] Ekonomou, *Byzantine Rome and the Greek Popes*, p. 299.

was surely influenced by the devotion to Mary in the Middle East noting the Syriac poems to the Virgin Mary written by St Ephrem (d. 373) and the Aramaic-Syriac poet Jacob of Serugh's (d. 521)[339] *Ode on the Blessed Virgin Mary.*

One of the most famous melodists as part of the many Eastern influences of chant and hymns on the Roman Church was the sixth century Romanus the Melodist. Amongst his many compositions was the *Kontakian*: "today the Virgin gives birth to him who is above all being."[340] He was born in Emesa, Syria, served as a deacon in the Church of the Resurrection in Beirut, and came to Constantinople during the reign of emperor Anastasius. There, he was attached to the church of the Virgin Mary in the Hexi Marmara suburb of the capital.[341] It can be suggested, therefore, that the processions venerating the Virgin Mary throughout Sicily and Italy have their roots from Aramaic-speaking Catholics.

### 8.5.2 Diaconies

Late seventh century Rome saw the birth of charitable institutions known as 'monasteria diaconia', or monastic diaconies. They had their origins from the East and soon they were to serve the poor, the aged, and the ill of Rome.[342] This developed the already established charitable institutions of hospitals and travellers' hostels that existed in Rome prior to the seventh century. The diaconies were prompted by the failure of the civil administration to provide bread for the city's poor. The diaconies, like those established in the East (Constantinople, Syria, Phoenicia, Palestine and Egypt) were located predominantly in the centre of the city and were heavily dependent on the patronage of wealthy people. Nearly all of the Roman diaconies that came into existence from the late seventh century were located at or near churches whose patron saints or congregations were Eastern in faith.[343]

---

[339] Ekonomou records his death date as 523.
[340] A hymn or homily consisting of between 18 to 24 metrically identical stanzas, chanted by the priest from the pulpit with either the choir or congregation joining in the response. See Ekonomou, footnote 140, p. 285.
[341] Ekonomou, *Byzantine Rome and the Greek Popes*, pp. 250-259, 278 (footnote 71).
[342] Ibid., p. 207.
[343] Ibid., pp. 209-210.

Aramaic Pope Sergius I (687-701) founded a diaconie at the church of Saint Maria at the foot of the Capitaline Hill. So too did Aramaic Pope John V gifting a large sum of money to the clergy and monastic diaconies. Pontifical formulas for these charitable works were established in the late seventh century.[344] Pope Gregory III expanded the diaconie charitable institutions for the poor in honour of the Aramaic Saints Sergius and Bacchus and ensured it had sufficient assets to permanently serve the city's poor.[345]

## 8.6   John (Yuhanna) Maroun, First Maronite Patriarch (686-87)

For thirty years from 609, after the Patriarch Anastasius of Antioch was killed by the Persians, the Antioch See (Patriarchate) remained vacant under Persian rule. From about 640 AD the whole of the Middle East, including Syria, Phoenicia, Phoenicia-Lebanon, and Palestine, fell into the hands of the Arabs. Byzantine rule was lost and the masters of the Middle East were no longer Christian.

After the fall of Antioch in 638, the main frontline between the Byzantine and Arab empires was slightly north-west of Antioch city. It is suggested Antioch became the Arab city base of administration for affairs at the frontline. As the prominent leader of the Catholic orthodox in the Middle East, Beit Maroun headquarters and its network was sure to have been under the watchful eye of the Arabs. Perhaps the account of Heraclius' affiliation with the Maronites, including the story of his son Constantine in the mountains of Lebanon, may have added to Arab attention on the Maronites.[346]

---

[344] Ibid., pp. 210 -211.

[345] Ibid., p. 299.

[346] In 634 there was a minor battle in the mountains of Lebanon when the Arab Muslims had attempted to attack Heraclius' eldest son Constantine. Gibbon records the Muslims with "three hundred Arabs and one thousand black slaves" (Edward Gibbon, *The Decline and Fall of the Roman Empire*, Vol. 6, Folio Society, 1985, p. 318. Gibbon relies on historical accounts of various Eastern sources such as the *Annals* of Patriarch Michael the Syrian and Arab historian Abel l-Fida).

Strategically, it is of little doubt the Muslim caliph was required to ensure the Maronite power base was confined, and its large network of monasteries and faithful disengaged from Antioch and the Byzantine frontline. Beit Maroun was in the region of Apamaea, near to the capital and centre of the Roman province, Syria Secunda. In terms of population size, the Melkite (Maronite as opposed to Greek-Byzantine) population would have been far greater in the region of Apamaea than that of Antioch.

While some have suggested communication between the Middle East and the West was completely severed by the Arabs shortly after the time of their arrival in Antioch in 638, and for this reason the appointed patriarch of Antioch resided in Constantinople, not Antioch, it appears there must have been other political reasons for the nominal appointment. There is evidence to suggest communication was not cut, for example Hefele notes the Sixth Ecumenical Council of 680-81 had "bishops from Antioch" present.[347] In 691-692, episcopal representatives of dioceses from the patriarchates of Constantinople, Alexandria, Antioch, and Jerusalem attended the Quinisext Council in Trullo Italy.[348] Further, as noted from the discussion above relating to the Aramaic popes, there is repeated evidence of migration from the Middle East to Sicily and Rome by certain distinguished men, and their families, who were later to become popes.

There are no primary source references to John Maroun. The only history available for him is principally by the seventeenth century Maronite patriarch and historian Estephen (Stephen) Il Boutros El Doueihi (1670-1704)[349] in his book *T'arikh al-Azmina*. Joseph Simon Assemani accumulated further information in the eighteenth century in his *Bibliotheca Orientalis*. Assemani was in charge of the Vatican library. After extensive visits to the Middle East, he assembled more than two thousand ancient works.

Both Doueihi and Assemani were graduates from the Maronite

---

[347] Hefele, *A History of the Councils*, pp. 150-151.

[348] For the events of 680-81, see Chapter 9. For 692, see Ekonomou, *Byzantine Rome and the Greek Popes*, p. 220.

[349] Spelled in various forms including 'Douahi' and 'Doueihy'.

College of Rome. They had an abundance of manuscripts to rely on, both in the College and at the Vatican. Their works are extensive but transcriptions of their work do not indicate the ancient sources on which it was clear they relied upon. The works of Doueihi have been published in various Arabic versions, but it appears there may be differences in translations from the original manuscripts and they may not be entirely accurate transcriptions.

The information relating to John Maroun from Doueihi and Assemani, in general, is consistently recounted in more contemporary Maronite works in English upon which reliance for the work in this book is now placed.[350] Maronite and non-Maronite authors such as Harb and Moosa respectively, have relied on Doueihi's works in Arabic entitled *Tareekh al-Taefat al-Marouniat* published by Rashid al-Shartouni Press, Beirut, in 1890. However, a modern translation of the original manuscripts would allow more accurate references and continuation of further research into Maronite history.

As it stands, it is acknowledged that there may be some inconsistencies or defects in the present versions of Doueihi and Assemani. Accordingly, this study cannot provide with precision an account on the matter and history. However, the salient and consistently matched points of the historical accounts have been selected from the works available in English. In doing so, once again the recurring pattern of Maronite history becomes visible.

The accounts state that John Maroun was born in the village of Sarum (or Sarmaniah) between Antioch and Apamaea.[351] He received the name John 'Maroun' after studying at St Maroun's monastery. Doueihi reports that in 676 AD, John Maroun became bishop of Batroun in north Lebanon residing in the monastery of Kfarhai in its mountain district.

The jurisdiction of Batroun likely included the coastal city of Ba-

---

[350] For example the accounts of Moosa, Dau, and Harb who have cited the published Arabic works of Doueihi, are generally matching.

[351] According to Dau, *History of the Maronites*, p. 207, he had French ancestry who had settled in Antioch several decades prior at the time of the Byzantine battles against the Arab Muslim conquerors.

troun, between Tripoli and Byblos, and its surrounds. It also included a large mountain region above. Doueihi recounts that in 676 when the priest John Maroun was to be consecrated as bishop of Batroun in Lebanon:

> The Pope's delegate came to Antioch to preach the dogma of the two natures and two wills in Jesus Christ. In that time Macarius, the Antiochian patriarch living in Constantinople, professed the official dogma of the Byzantine Empire, that is to say the one will in Jesus Christ. John Maroun attracted by his deeds and faith the attention of the French prince Eugene who presented him to the Pope's delegate. The cardinal consecrated John Maroun Bishop of Batroun and Mount Lebanon with the mission of preserving the Roman Catholic faith in Lebanon …
>
> He [John Maroun] joined his flock in Lebanon, working with the zeal of Apostles for the conversion of non-Catholics. Under the guidance of St Maroun, the Maronite community increased greatly in number, and took possession of Mount Lebanon and the mountain range from Cilicia and Armenia to Jerusalem.[352]

In 685, during a widespread plague in the Middle East, John Maroun visited many cities and villages comforting the afflicted with his prayers. He wrote a special mass celebrated by priests in times of plague.

Since the Lateran Council of 649, when Monothelitism was condemned and the pope Martin I was tortured and exiled (he died a martyr in 655), relations between Rome and Constantinople were at an all-time low. There was a schism in the Church from 649-681, which then extended to 713. As it had from the time of Emperor Heraclius' *Ecthesis* in 638, Constantinople continued to profess the theology of one nature in Christ. The theology of Rome adhered to the dogma of two natures in Jesus Christ.[353]

Syrian-born Theophanes, patriarch of Antioch, died in 686 or

---

[352] Doueihi cited in Antoine Khoury Harb, *The Maronites: History and Constants*, The Maronite Heritage Publications, 2001, p. 74.

[353] The next Chapter deals with this matter in detail.

687.[354] Without consultation, Pope Conon (686-687) installed in his place Constantine, a deacon from the church of Syracuse in Sicily.[355] He abused his position and the Pope sent orders for the emperor's agents in Antioch to arrest Constantine. The Pope wrote to the clergy of Antioch to elect a new patriarch. The bishops met and appointed John Maroun to succeed Theophanes.

The ethnic Aramaic Sergius was elected pope of Rome in 687. Patriarch John Maroun met Sergius' legate in Tripoli, Lebanon. They travelled together to Rome. Pope Sergius confirmed John Maroun as patriarch of Antioch. The residence of Patriarch John Maroun was in Antioch city at the church of St Babilas the Martyr.

When the news of John Maroun's preaching of the 'true faith' (the doctrine of two wills in Christ) reached Constantinople, the Monothelite bishops called on Emperor Justinian II to force Pope Sergius and John Maroun to accept the doctrine of Monothelitism (one will in Christ). Sergius and Maroun refused. The Emperor sent his army commanders, Zachariah and Leo, to arrest the Pope in Rome and John Maroun in Antioch and bring them back in chains. The troops sent to Rome were opposed and defeated by Roman troops.

John Maroun having heard the news of the attack on Pope Sergius, left Antioch for the monastery of St Maroun near Ma'arret en Naaman, on the Orontes River near Apamaea. At this time, John Maroun wrote his treatise on the faith, *Explanation of the Faith*, and sent it to the people of Lebanon. His works were translated from Syriac to Arabic by Maronite Bishop Thomas (d. 1100) of Kfar Thab (a region of Aleppo).[356]

---

[354] The Aramaic Theophanes was abbot of the monastery of St Peter *ad Baias* in Sicily. He was one of Greek-Sicilian Pope Agatho's (a former monk himself) delegates to the Sixth Ecumenical Council in 680-681. Theophanes became patriarch of Antioch after Macarius was deposed at the Council, which was attended by 165 bishops and episcopal representatives.

[355] From 640 to 702 the patriarch of Constantinople, under the influence of the emperor, may have elected the patriarch of Antioch.

[356] Of the two manuscripts of these works written in 1392 (held at Vatican) and 1470 (held at Paris), the latter was translated into French by Nau in his *Opuscules Maronites* in 1899. See Dau, *History of the Maronites*, pp. 330-331.

John Maroun fled to Lebanon and the commander Leo with his forces followed him there. Leo hesitated to arrest John Maroun explaining to the emperor that John Maroun was held in high esteem by the Lebanese and that they would not allow him to be taken. The Emperor imprisoned Leo and sent two more commanders, Marcian and Maurice. John Maroun's nephew, Ibrahim gathered 12,000 armed men and John Maroun left Antioch for Samar Jbail, Lebanon.

In the summer of 694, Marcian and Maurice's forces attacked the monastery of Maroun in Apamaea, killed 500 monks and destroyed its building. They also committed other atrocities and trailed a path of destruction throughout the towns that followed the patriarch. They proceeded to Lebanon. In the meantime, Leo had escaped from prison, arrested Justinian, and took over the reign as Emperor. He allowed the Lebanese governor Sim'an (Simon) to counter-attack the invading Byzantine army at Amiun in Lebanon. The Lebanese killed Marcian and Maurice, and their troops fled. The battle of Amiun resulted in a final separation of the Melkites into the Maronites and the Melkites. The Melkites remained loyal to the emperor who continued to profess one will in Christ, with the Maronites following the Church of Rome adhering to the doctrine of two wills in Christ.

### 8.6.1 Transportation of St Maroun's Relic

The patriarchal seat was relocated from St Maroun's monastery near Ma'arrat-en-Na'aman in the province of Apamaea, to St Maroun's monastery in Kfarhai, Lebanon. Doueihi informs us that when John Maroun settled in Kfarhai, he brought with him St Maroun's skull:

> When Youhanna (John) Maron settled in Kfarhai, he built an altar and a monastery after Saint Maron's name and put Saint Maron's skull inside the altar to heal the faithful. This is why the Monastery is called 'Rish Mro' Syriac for Maron's head.[357]

According to an Italian primary source, a relic of St Maroun, his skull, was gifted to the Crusaders in Lebanon around 1130 AD from the monastery of St Maroun's 'skull' in Kfarhai Lebanon. This is con-

---

[357] Harb, *The Maronites: History and Constants*, p. 46. Harb cites Douehi.

sistent with Doueihi's version about the relic. When considering the documentary sources together in their geographical and historical context and Maronite traditions, it becomes all the more difficult not to accept Doueihi's version about John Maroun as the first Maronite patriarch. St John Maroun passed away in the year 707 at the monastery. His feast day in the Maronite calendar is the 2nd of March.

## 8.6.2 Links to Pope Sergius and Loyalty to Rome

In 678, Emperor Constantine had entered into a thirty-year peace treaty with the Arabs. The Emperor had given up on any hope of reclaiming Egypt, Syria, Phoenicia, Palestine, and Armenia. This was the opportunity for Pope Leo to convene the Sixth Ecumenical Council as Monothelitism was experiencing a substantial resurgence. The patriarchs of Constantinople (Theodorus) and of Antioch (Makarios) were Monothelites and were condemned at this Council.

Rome and Constantinople had experienced a schism from 649 to 681. During this period, Constantinople was officially adhering to Monothelitism – the doctrine of one will of Christ – and Rome, Dyothelitism – the doctrine of two wills of Christ. Although the Sixth Ecumenical Council of 680-81 declared Monothelitism a heresy, it remained prevalent amongst many in Constantinople and the schism was unofficially extended to 715. Theophanes records the Greeks in Alexandria remained Monothelite until 742-43 when the Melkite patriarch Kosmos and his city became Catholic Orthodox, having adhered to the Monothelite doctrine since the time of Patriarch Cyrus during the reign of Heraclius.[358]

Although there is a silence in official accounts, it seems a significant amount of the population of Constantinople after the Sixth Council of 680-81 remained Monothelite despite the view that it had been stamped out because of the Council decree. By the year 713, the emperor declared a return to Monothelitism. It is likely the ethnic Greeks

---

[358] Theophanes, *The Chronicle of Theophanes*, p. 107. Doueihi's account opposes the commonly held view which places reliance on Tell Mahre, that the separation of Melkites was a result of the Maronites being Monothelite and Maximite Melkites not. This is dealt with in detail in Chapter 9.

(or Greek minded) in Antioch followed their counterparts in Constantinople, which gives more weight to the account given by Doueihi. It is for these reasons it is suggested in this study that an East-West division did not end in 681 but continued in the Church until after 713.

Before becoming Pope of Rome, Aramaic-born John was a deacon who represented Rome at the Sixth Ecumenical Council of 680-81. Four years later, after becoming Pope in 685, suspicions remained high about Constantinople's acceptance of the Council. Pope John V feared that the acts of the Sixth Ecumenical Council had been falsified as they had left the Imperial archive without the Emperor's knowledge. He convened a synod of high-ranking civil and ecclesiastical officials and asked that the text of the Council records be read in their presence for them to confirm it was a true and accurate profession of the faith.[359]

Even though it appeared Rome and Constantinople were again united in 681, tensions remained. Pope John V's fears were validated after he passed away. In 711, Emperor Philippicus Bardanes rejected the Sixth Ecumenical Council's decree. Aramaic born Pope Constantine refused to recognize Bardanes. The Emperor called a synod of Constantinople in 712. The synod re-established the dogma of Monothelistism and condemned the Sixth Ecumenical Council. It demonstrated that a significant part of Constantinople's clergy and population remained Monothelite after the decree of the Council in 681.

On the death of Pope Conon after only eleven months in office (686-687), a dispute arose, sometimes in combat, over the election of his successor. There were two candidates each backed by supporters. Because of the dispute a third candidate, Sergius, was proposed. The majority of the population supported the ethnic Aramaic priest Sergius who was then elected, though not without further conflict, as pope over the candidacy of the archpriest Theodoros. Following the conflict leading to Sergius' consecration, the battles for succession to the papacy ceased for the next half a century as long as 'Byzantine' authority prevailed in Italy.[360]

---

[359] Ekonomou, *Byzantine Rome and the Greek Popes*, p. 219.
[360] Ibid., p. 217.

As noted above in the summary of Pope Sergius (see Section 8.5.1), he rejected the canons decreed at the Council of Trullo in 692. This brought him into dispute with the Emperor who sought his arrest. Doueihi gives an independent account of the dispute with the Emperor's attempted arrest of Sergius and John Maroun. It is very difficult to see how Doueihi, writing almost one thousand years later, would have fabricated such detail especially since he was well regarded in Rome as a Maronite and a scholar. A graduate of the Maronite College, Doueihi would go on to become a Maronite patriarch with close links to the pope: he would not have allowed himself to be discredited.

The common ethnic Aramaic ancestry of Pope John V, Pope Sergius, Patriarch Theophanes,[361] and John Maroun provides support for Doueihi's account. Rome would have been eager to ensure an ethnic Aramaic, John Maroun, would succeed as patriarch his ethnic Aramaic predecessor. It is no coincidence these popes and John Maroun all stood up to Constantinople and the emperor. There was a significant ethnic Aramaic and fervently Catholic population in Rome that began to publicly elect ethnic Aramaic popes. As recounted above, they were part of the Roman population that stood up to the emperor's commander Zachariah.

We know from Count Marcellinus (d. 534) that such ethnic communities were closely networked amongst themselves in any of the cities to which they migrated. Places of worship played an important part in this. As Marcellinus recounts, Constantinople during the sixth century was divided into ethnic conclaves: the Greeks, Latins, Macedonians, Goths, Armenians, Cappadocians, Jews, Alexandrians, Isaurians, Africans, and Amidans. The Latins were further divided into Italians, Africans, and Illyrians of which Marcellinus was from the latter. In 505, the bishop of Amida (modern Diyarbakır in Turkey)

---

[361] The Aramaic Theophanes was abbot of the monastery of St Peter *ad Baias* in Sicily. He was one of Pope Agatho's (Greek-Sicilian and former monk himself) delegates to the Sixth Ecumenical Council in 680-681. Theophanes became patriarch of Antioch after Makarios was deposed at the Council, which was attended by 165 bishops and episcopal representatives.

was elected by citizens of Amida who resided in Constantinople, the Imperial capital.

The precedent over the previous two centuries of Beit Maroun and the Maronites acting as the beacon of Catholic Orthodoxy in the Middle East must be considered in the account of John Maroun. The loyalty to Rome over Constantinople was unshakeable. The pope was, and would always be, their primary patriarch. Given the record of fidelity to Rome over the previous centuries, it is difficult to accept the Maronites would have deviated in the seventh century. Knowing the tradition and history of Beit Maroun's struggles, particularly during the Severus era, it is also difficult to accept that the Maronites would have remained Monothelite after direct communication with Rome.

Naturally, official church documents do not record all events and undercurrents. They are required to remain religiously and politically sensitive. Accordingly, the evidence for John Maroun and Pope Sergius' actions in opposition to Constantinople may be difficult to locate. Yet, it seems likely that Doueihi and Assemani were privy to some seminal information, and Doueihi's account of the events is supported by additional evidence.

As will become clear in the following chapter on the subject of Monothelitism, it seems unlikely that the Syriac Jacobite Patriarch Tell Mahre (d. 845) would have been able to understand the complexity and intricacy of these events if he was living in the time of John Maroun, but even more so hundreds of years later when he actually wrote his account. He was writing from afar in the Syrian Orient. He was not connected to the Church of Rome or Constantinople. His Church was persecuted by the Emperor and often the Chalcedonian party. No Syriac Jacobite hundreds of years before him would have been able to track the movements of synods, armies, and papal legates from hundreds of kilometres away. His accounts about the Maronite Church and Beit Maroun must be therefore assessed with considerable caution.

### 8.6.3 Maronite Patriarchal Succession

The Maronites who remained part of the Beit Maroun confederation headed by the Patriarch John Maroun stayed loyal to Rome. Accordingly, through unintentional circumstances, John Maroun became the first Maronite patriarch. Doueihi records after John Maroun (686/7-707), his nephew Kyrios was appointed Maronite patriarch from 708-715. Following his election, the pallium of patriarchal confirmation was received from Pope Constantine. Patriarch Kyrios was buried at St Maroun's monastery in Kfarhai, in the Batroun district of Lebanon.[362]

From 702 to 742, the Greeks in Constantinople no longer appointed a patriarch of Antioch and the See of Antioch was left vacant. There was no other patriarch of Antioch in this period. Theophanes records this was a result of the Arabs not allowing the appointment.[363] Having many ancient manuscripts before them, one must assume Patriarch Doueihi and Assemani were able to provide a reasonable account about St John Maroun and the succession of Maronite patriarchs thereafter.

Dionysius of Tell Mahre substantiates the election of Maronite patriarchs in this period in his *Annales*, written around 840. He refers to an incident which had taken place in 745-746 AD at the monastery of St Maroun. This is the earliest text in existence in which the phrase 'Maronite Patriarch' appears. Tell Mahre commented: "The Maronites remain as they are; they ordain a patriarch and bishops of their monastery."[364] Dib states the ancient document reverts to a very distant date to the period when the See of Antioch was unoccupied. The word

---

[362] Details of patriarchs taken from Doueihi and Assemani in their series of Maronite patriarchs, cited in Dau, *History of the Maronites*, p. 228.

[363] Theophanes, *The Chronicle of Theophanes*, p. 107.

[364] Dib, *History of the Maronite Church*, p. 43. Moosa's translation 'remain as they are today' allows Moosa to claim that it was only from 745 that the Maronites established as a separate church. However, Moosa implies the Maronites were Syriac Orthodox (Jacobite) until the end of the sixteenth century. Moosa's views cannot be accepted as consistent or reliable as they are incongruous with documentary evidence, Maronite traditions, and as the previous chapter has argued, stem from poor scholarship.

'remain' implies the Maronites were this way previously to 745 AD, governed by a patriarch and bishops.

Not surprisingly, Moosa's convoluted interpretations uses the same passage adding the word 'today' to state that the Maronites did not elect a patriarch before 745.[365] His translation states: "and the Maronites remained as they are *today* consecrating for themselves a patriarch and bishops from their monastery" [emphasis mine].[366] The operative words used by both translations are 'remains' for Dib and 'remained' for Moosa. Accordingly, Moosa's translation brings the same conclusion as Dib's.

Thanks to Tell Mahre's text, says Dib, the Maronite patriarchal succession is incontestable. Dib continues with an important critique on the patriarchal origins:

> Although the origins of the Maronite Patriarchate remain in shadows, the text of Tell Mahre furnished nevertheless a serious support to the tradition that the establishment of the Patriarchate goes back to the latter years of the seventh century. The scholarly patriarch Stephen Douaihi [Doueihi] preserves this tradition. He has listed the Maronite patriarchs from John Maroun, the first of the line (who should not be confused with Saint Maroun, the founder of the Church, up to himself [1670-1704]).

> He tells us that he has taken his information from the following documents: a paper dated in 1313 which was found among the papers of his predecessor, George of Beseb'el (d. 1670); a letter written in 1495 by Gabriel Ibn al-Qela'I; lists given to him by the Bishop of 'Aqoura, George Habqouq; a very ancient diaconcicon, where the deacon at the dyptichs proclaims the names of all the Patriarchs ...

> The circumstances at the time of the birth of the Maronite Patriarchate render its creation as incontestably legitimate. The church of Antioch did not have a ruler; the Maronite monks, leaders in the situation, were able to provide one; they did so,

---

[365] Moosa, *The Maronites in History*, p. 135.
[366] Ibid., p. 114.

and the action cannot be alleged to be against any canonical rule. Furthermore, if there had been any doubt about its legitimacy, the Holy See would not have failed to condemn it as Pope St Martin in 649 condemned Macedonius of Constantinople (titular Patriarch of Antioch at the time) ...

The documents that we have studied lead us to believe that the Maronite patriarchs have always born the title of Antioch ... Far from failing to recognise this right of the Maronite patriarchs, Rome has positively recognised its legitimacy. The Bull of Innocent III Quia Divinae Sapientiae of 1215 furnished the oldest testimony on this subject: "By our apostolate authority, we grant to you and your successes the use of the pallium according to your approved customs, which you and your predecessors in the Antiochene Church have been known to have." The patriarchal jurisdiction recognised by Innocent III had been exercised by Maronites in this see before Jeremias who took possession about 1199.[367]

However, it is important to point out that Dib and other authors cannot be correct when they state St Maroun was the founder of the Maronite Church. As has already been stated, St Maroun had no intention to found a Church. Beit Maroun was a monastery built and founded around 452 AD in his honour, as its patron Saint, and as a church father for the Aramaic-speaking Chalcedonian Christians of Antioch. The followers of this monastery, and the network of monasteries behind it, had come to be known through the ages as Maronites only by circumstance, not intention.

Of all modern historians of the Maronites, Moosa, whose ancestry is Syriac Orthodox, is almost alone when he says, relying on two tenth century historians (Sa'id Ibn Batriq and Arab Abu al-Hasan al-Masudi), the Maronite Church was named after John Maroun and not St Maroun. Moosa also goes to great lengths attempting to demonstrate that John Maroun was not a Patriarch of Antioch. These views are in stark contrast to the conclusions of Professors Brock and Vööbus, regarded as the foremost scholars of Syriac studies. At no time has

---

[367] Dib, *History of the Maronite Church*, pp. 44-45.

the appointment of a patriarch of Antioch from Beit Maroun been disputed in any Church Council or has there been any text found disputing it. There is no evidence from the Holy See in Rome in that period, or since, of any canonical rule or condemnation of the appointment of Maronite patriarchs starting from 686 or 687.

## 8.7 The Aramaic Catholic Military Response to Islam

### 8.7.1 The Mardaites' Army and the Byzantine-Arab Treaties

Little is known about the history of the Mardaites or al-Jarajimah, a Christian group living near the Arab-Byzantine border.[368] It is suggested they were a military movement in the seventh century gaining the most strength in its latter half (650-700). The Jarajimah people were so-called from their chief city al-Jarajimah in the Amanus (al-Lakkam) region of Antioch. The Arab historian Al Baladhuri (d. 892) comments: "All Jarajimah are inhabitants of a city on Al-Lukam Mountain, between Bayas and Boukah, called Jarjimah ... When Abu-'Ubaydah invaded Antioch, he attacked Jarjimah, but a treaty of peace was concluded between its inhabitants and Abu-'Ubaydah."[369] It is most probable they were also known as the Mardaites by the Byzantines.[370] The Greek historian Theophanus (d. 818) said the Mardaites operated from the Amanus mountains of northern Syria through to Jerusalem with Lebanon their focus of attacks on the Arabs. Perhaps this was at the time of internal Arab conflicts between Caliph Mu'awiyah and Imman Ali.

In the context of this discussion, it must be noted that the Byzantines and Arabs continued to have tense relations in this period. Several treaties were negotiated between the two, for example, in 646, the sea battle at Acre (in Phoenicia) resulted in the deaths of 23,000 men from Byzantine forces and a treaty was arranged wherein the emperor

---

[368] It has been suggested Mardaites is synonymous with the word 'Marda', and means 'free heroes of high stature'. See Dau, *History of the Maronites*, pp. 210-211. Moosa refers to the term as 'rebels'.

[369] Dau, *History of the Maronites*, p. 211.

[370] Michael the Syrian, *Chronicle of Michael the Great*, paragraph 132.

paid taxes to the Caliph not to attack Constantinople and the Arabs withdrew from Acre. The taxes were not paid, and the Arabs raided Acre again. The taxes began to be paid and a further treaty was arranged whereby the Arabs withdrew from Syria. A treaty in 658-9, led to Muawiyah (the Umayyad Caliph from 657-680AD) paying "the Romans" 1,000 nomismata, a horse, and a slave per day.[371] Constantinople was frequently besieged by the Arabs during the years 674-78 and 717-18.[372]

In his *Chronographia* the Greek historian Theophanes (d. 818) states in relation to an army division of the Byzantines:

> In this year (677-78), the Mardaites invaded Lebanon and conquered it from Mt Mauros (Black Amanus Mountains between Antioch and Tarsus) to the holy city (Jerusalem) overpowering its most important centres. Many slaves, natives, and prisoners fled to them, so in a little while there were many thousands of them.

> When Muawiyah (the Umayyad Caliph from 657-680AD) and his advisers learned this they were quite discomfited as they reckoned that the Roman Empire was watched over by God. Muawiyah sent ambassadors to the autokrator (emperor) Constantine asking for peace, and even promised to pay the Emperor a yearly tribute.

> When the Emperor had received these envoys and heard their request, he sent the patrician John (surnamed Pitiziguadis) back to Syria with them, as he had spent a long time in government and was highly experienced and prudent. His purpose was to negotiate with the Arabs in a suitable fashion and to agree on peace terms. Muawiyah, who had convened an assembly of his emirs and members of the tribe of Qurash received him with great honour when he arrived in Syria.

> After long peace talks between them, it was agreed by each

---

[371] Theophanes, *The Chronicle of Theophanes*, p. 46.
[372] Turtledove, "Introduction," in *The Chronicle of Theophanes. Anni mundi 6095-6305 (A.D. 602-813), (Chronographia)* trans. by H. Turtledove, University of Pennsylvania Press, 1982.

of the two that there should be a written peace accord with an oath. The terms were for an annual tribute, with the Romans being furnished 3000 nomismata, fifty prisoners and fifty high bred by the Agarenes. These terms agreed upon by both sides created a firm peace between Romans and Arabs for thirty years. After they had made the two general written treaties (and the oaths) and had given copies to each other, this highly acclaimed man (who has been mentioned in many contexts) return to the emperor-with many gifts as well ... There was absolute freedom from care in both East and West ...[373]

In this year [684-85] there was a famine and a great plague in Syria, and Abd al-Malik [the Caliph] conquered its people. While the Mardaites were attacking Lebanon, and the plague was at its height, Abd al-Malik sent envoys to the Emperor asking for the same peace terms which had been requested during the reign of Muawiyah. He agreed to pay the same 365,000 nomismata, the same 365 slaves and likewise the same 365 high bred horses ...[374]

In this year [686-687] Abd al-Malik sent envoys to Justinian to secure peace. It was arranged on these terms: the Emperor would keep the Mardaite troops out of Lebanon and stop their attacks, and Abd al-Malik would give the Romans 1,000 nomismata, a horse and a slave each day. Also, both sides would share equally the tribute from Cyprus, Armenia and Iberia. The Emperor sent the magistrianos (senior civil servant from the imperial court) Paul to Abd al-Malik to secure the arrangement. There were written sureties with witnesses; the magistrianos, who was treated with honour, returned.

The Emperor sent messengers who seized 12,000 Mardaites, mutilating the Roman state. For all the cities in the heights from Mopsuestia to fourth Armenia, which are now inhabited by the Arabs, had grown weak and depopulated from the Mardaites attacks. After they were transplanted, Romania

[373] Theophanes, *The Chronicle of Theophanes*, pp. 53-54.
[374] Ibid., p. 59.

suffered all sorts of evils at the hands of the Arabs up until the present day ...[375]

In this year [687-88)] there was a famine in Syria, and many men entered Romania. The Emperor went to Armenia and there received the Lebanese Mardaites, putting an end to his stout wall.[376]

Although there is no reference in these passages to Maronites, the author Dau suggests a link between the Maronites and the Mardaites. Moosa disagrees.[377] Michael the Syrian records:

In the ninth year of Constantine [677 AD], some villainous troops arose from the Byzantines, went and dwelled at Mount Lebanon, and were declared rebels. The Syrians called them 'chur'chans'. They seized all the territorial from Mount Lebanon to Black Mountain. (Perhaps it is for this reason the Iberians/Georgians are called 'chur'chans' by the Franks, since they had rebelled from service to the Armenians and from religious unity to them). The Arabs arose and wiped out these rebels.

In 685, Caliph Abd al-Malik was troubled by rebels at this time and made a peace treaty with Justinian for ten years promising 1000 dahekans per year, a horse and a servant ... The Armenians helped the Byzantines. For a second time Lebanon became the dwelling place of rebels, this time 12,000 of them, cavalry. The Romans removed them and brought them to Rome.[378]

It is worthy of note that in a Maronite Chronicle of the debate at Damascus in 659 between the Jacobite Patriarch and one of his bishops on one side, and the Maronites on the other, in the presence of the future caliph Muawiyah, there is no mention of the Maronites as

---

[375] Ibid., p. 61.

[376] Ibid., p. 62.

[377] Dau, *History of the Maronites*, pp. 210-214. Moosa, *The Maronites in History*, pp. 174-193.

[378] Michael the Syrian, *Chronicle of Michael the Great*, paragraph 133-34.

Mardaites.[379] It appears almost conclusive from the various ancient sources including Theophanes and Michael the Syrian, and more modern historians such as Bury, that the Maronites were not Mardaites. Rather the Mardaites were foreigners from Asia Minor.

After quoting a manuscript written in 1315 AD, Doueihi informs us:

> Yusif became governor of Byblos and Mount Lebanon. Yusif went to Armenia accompanied by 12,000 horsemen and conquered the Persian army ... Afterwards, Yusif led his army to Al-Beqa [Bekaa valley in Lebanon] and invaded the land of Muawiyah [the Muslim Caliph in Damascus who died in 680 AD].
>
> After Yusif, Yuhanna became king and took possession of the entire Holy Land. He went from Lebanon to Mount Carmel, accompanied by a huge army, seeking the conquest of Jerusalem. Having fought many victorious battles against the Muslims, he returned to Lebanon and lived in Baskinta.[380]

It is not clear if Yusif was Lebanese, but he was a governor of one of its districts. The passage does not state Yusif took 12,000 soldiers *from* Lebanon and in any event refers to the battles against the Persian army not Arabs. It is possible the Emperor required him to leave his position as governor and lead an army division. It is possible he met that army division somewhere along the way to Armenia. If the account in the above passage is correct, Yusif returned to the Bekaa valley of Lebanon with his army division and then on to the Holy Land.

As noted by Theophanes in the aforementioned passage, in 686-687 Abd al-Malik renewed with Byzantine Emperor Justinian II (reign 685-695 and 705-711) the thirty-year peace treaty which had been made with Justinian's father Constantine, but with slightly varied

---

[379] Dib, *History of the Maronite Church*, p. 12, cites the chronicle as found in Nau, *Opuscules Maronites*, pp. 6 and 36 for the first and second part of the Syriac text respectively. See also Brock et al., *The Seventh Century in the West-Syrian Chronicles*, pp. 29-35.

[380] Dau, *History of the Maronites*, p. 213, citing Doueihi.

terms. The Caliph agreed to pay 1000 nomismata and the daily tribute of one horse and one slave. They agreed to divide between them the revenues of Armenia, Iberia, and Cyprus. Bury informs us part of the treaty terms that Justinian agreed to was to remove the Mardaites who were placed in the Lebanon area in 676 (or 677) by the emperor, stating:

> [The Mardaites] were a perpetual thorn in the side of the caliphs from their homes in Lebanon. These mountaineers 'rendered unsafe and uninhabited all the mountain towns of the Saracens from Mopsuestia to the Fourth Armenia'. They were, however, Monothelites, and this fact made the Roman government look on them with disfavour, in spite of the services which they rendered in weakening the common enemy. And so Justinian did not demur to a measure, which really meant, in the chroniclers words, a maiming of the Roman power, by removing 'the brazen wall', that is the Mardaites. We are not informed how the measure was executed; but it must be remembered that these Christian outlaws considered themselves the subjects of the Emperor, and it was perhaps at the instance of Constantine IV that they entered it the high lands of Syria. Certain it is that the Mardaites, to the number of 12,000, were transferred to Romania. Of these some more settled in Thrace, others in Asia Minor, while others were enrolled in the army, and Justinian proceeded in person to the Armenian provinces in order to superintend the disposal of the immigrants …

> Other transplantations and immigrations, as well as those of the Mardaites, took place in the reign of Justinian. A famine in Syria (687) induced a number of the natives to migrate to Romania. I have already mentioned the transportation of the slaves to Asia Minor, and although most of these were formed into a military body, some were doubtless settled as agriculturalists in the north-western provinces on the Propontis. To the same regions the emperor also designed to transplant part of the population of Cyprus. Cyprus, by the new arrangement which had been made with Abd Al-Malik, was

half Roman and half Saracen territory; and Justinian wish to leave the whole island to the rival power without surrendering the Roman tributaries.[381]

This account from Bury confirms perhaps another wave of Aramaic migration to 'Romania'[382] in 687 following a famine. He also refers to the Mardaites as bought "slaves" and "subjects of the emperor" who formed into a military body and who shifted out of Lebanon. During the arrival of the Mardaites into Arab held lands in 677-78, the emperor and patriarch of Constantinople were Monothelite. It would follow that the slaves employed by the emperor as a military wing were of the same religious persuasion, Monothelitism. Their transportation to the Aramaic-speaking Catholic belt in Maronite heartland has caused confusion for historians (aside from Bury) as to whether they were Maronites, and if the Maronites were Monothelite. The immediate removal of the Mardaites from this region to fight elsewhere allows the firm conclusion that as slaves they were under the full control of the emperor and were not Maronite.

Syrian Orthodox Jacobite Patriarch Dionysus of Tell Mahre (d. 845) informs us:

> In the ninth year of Constantine [676 AD] there were invaders, Byzantine Mardaites, that is to say heroes, called by the Syrians Jarajimah. They took possession of the land from the mountains of Galilee to the Black Mountains and all the Lebanese mountains. The Muslims suffered a great deal from them.[383]

Moosa's translation of the same passage states:

> In the ninth year of Constantine (Pogonatus), *rumoye* (soldiers), known as Maridoye (Mardaites or Marada), that is

---

[381] J.B. Bury, *A History of the Later Roman Empire from Arcadius to Irene*, Vol. II, MacMillan & Co., 1889, pp. 320-21. Bury's sources include Theophanes (760-817).
[382] Turtledove, *The Chronicle of Theophanes*, p. 34, in a footnote, refers to 'Romania' as the land of the Roman/Byzantine Empire.
[383] Quoted in Dau, *History of the Maronites*, p. 211.

highway robbers, whom the Syrians called Gargumoye (in Arabic Jarajima) came to Mount Lebanon and occupied the area from the Mount of Galilee to Mount Ukomo (the Syriac word for black, that is, the Black or al-Lukam Mountain). They always came out to plunder and for this purpose they were dispatched by the Romans (Byzantines) against Lebanon. Eventually, the Arabs overcame them, killing some and plucking out the eyes of others.[384]

These are two extraordinarily divergent renderings of the same text. Moosa's account is far more colourful and if Moosa is correct it supports the view that the Patriarch of Tell Mahre was a partisan historian. What is certain is that both Theophanes and the Patriarch Dionysus speak of Mardaites occupying a large area from the holy land to near Antioch and aligned with the Byzantine army. It is significant the passages of Theophanes and Dionysus do not mention the Maronites. Had the Maronites been Mardaites, it is highly likely they would have stated so. This is particularly the case for Dionysus who had referred to the word 'Maronites' in his works. It is therefore reasonable to conclude the Maronites were not Mardaites.

Writing in the late nineteenth century, Bury tells us the Mardaites were Monothelite Christians, but he does not refer to them as Maronites. We understand from Bury that he relied on numerous ancient sources. This provides us with the basis for a further suggestion. The passages from Theophanes and Dionysus make it clear that Mardaites were not natives of Syria, Lebanon, or Palestine, but came from another region. It is plausible they were Monothelite as Bury suggests and over time they have been mistakenly conflated with the Maronites. It must be recalled that a substantial number of Byzantines in Constantinople, and likely their ethnic counterparts in the patriarchate of Antioch, remained Monothelite and the Mardaites appeared to have their origins in nearby Asia Minor.

If Doueihi's version of events is correct, the date of 676 for the pa-

---

[384] Moosa, *The Maronites in History*, p. 190, taken from the same French edition and same page as Dau.

pal legate discussions with John Maroun about the two wills of Christ, and the election of John Maroun as bishop of Batroun at the same time, remarkably coincides with the arrival of the Mardaites a year later. Constantinople had perhaps sought to counter the influence of Rome in the Middle East by sending forth the Mardaites as Mono-thelites. Another remarkable fact is the departure of the Mardaites in 686-87 at the same time as Doueihi's account of the election of John Maroun as patriarch of Antioch. It was from this moment, perhaps in spite of Rome, the emperor appeared to abandon the Middle East (ex-cepting Antioch city) for the payment of tributes by the Arabs. Theo-phanes says that up to this time the Arabs had grown weak and their population had depleted.[385] The Middle East could well have remained in Byzantine hands but for the withdrawal under Emperor Justinian II, who was only seventeen at the time.

During the reign of Justinian II, Byzantine coins began to feature an image of Christ, an image unacceptable to the Arab Muslims. Pre-viously the caliphs had been paying the emperors in Byzantine coins with Roman emperors' heads imprinted. In 691-92, the Caliph Abd Al-Malik had his own coins printed with verses of the Koran. Justin-ian refused to accept payments in Arab coins or in gold and broke the peace treaty, as he was also anxious to re-settle the island of Cyprus and did not understand that the Arabs sought to maintain the treaty to stop Mardaite inroads. For these actions, Theophanes regarded Justin-ian as foolish and lacking in sense.[386]

The battles of 692-94 were a result of deliberate attacks by Em-peror Justinian's forces on the Arabs following what Justinian saw as a breach of the thirty-year peace treaty signed in 678 by his father Constantine. During one of those battles, via large payments the Arabs won over 20,000 Slavs who deserted the Byzantines, who had previ-ously acted as mercenaries fighting for them in Caesarea area.[387] They

[385] Theophanes, *The Chronicle of Theophanes*, p. 61.
[386] Ibid., p. 63; Bury, *A History of the Later Roman Empire*, p. 322.
[387] Theophanes, *The Chronicle of Theophanes*, p. 64. Note, in 664-665 Theophanes also records 5,000 Slavs deserted the Byzantines and aligned with the Arabs and settled

were defeated and the Slavs requested an oath and came under Arab rule. The Arabs settled 7000 of them in Antioch and Cyrrhus, giving them women and goods.[388]

Michael the Syrian says that in 695 the Byzantines came to Antioch to battle the Arabs and were defeated and conquered. Both sides lost many but the Byzantines moreso. The total number slain on both sides was 400,000. In 696/697, the Arabs minted gold coins for the first time without images of their Caliphs.[389] Abd al-Malik appointed two military commanders who were merciless in their rule, stirring up fierce persecution against Christians.[390] It seems that from this time, the Byzantines had abandoned the Arab treaties and the entire Middle East to the Arabs. From then, the Christians of the Middle East began to experience aggressive intolerance from Muslims.

### 8.7.2 The Maronite Indigenous Army Division

Heraclius was Byzantine Emperor from 610 to 641. When visiting Syria early in his reign, documents suggest his first visit was to the monastery of St Maroun, the head of the Chalcedonian party. He declared his pro-Chalcedonian preference and gave orders for many of the Monophysite monasteries to be passed to the control of Beit Maroun. Historians such as Gibbon and Migne propose Heraclius was a Maronite, formerly a monk resident at Beit Maroun.[391] There can be no certainty about this. In fact, it appears the first suggestion about the will of Christ was from the Jacobites who introduced the concept to Heraclius when he visited Hierapolis. The emperor referred the com-

---

near Apamaea and the year after the bishop of nearby Emesa was burned alive (p. 48).

[388] Michael the Syrian, *Chronicle of Michael the Great*, paragraph 134.

[389] Turtledove, *The Chronicle of Theophanes*, footnote 133, p. 63; Michael the Syrian, *Chronicle of Michael the Great*, paragraph 135-36.

[390] Michael the Syrian, *Chronicle of Michael the Great*, paragraph 135-36.

[391] Naaman, *The Maronites*, p. 132, cites P.G. Migne, III, col. 1089. The historian Edward Gibbon was of the view Heraclius was introduced to the concept of Christ's one will when he stayed at the monastery of St Maroun in 'Emesa' (Gibbon, *The History of the Decline and Fall of the Roman Empire*, Vol., 6, p. 73). This subject is dealt with further in the next Chapter.

ments back to Patriarch Sergius of Constantinople who, with Cyrus, Bishop of Phasis, confirmed Christ had one will.[392]

If the visit to Beit Maroun did take place, it may have coincided with the deliberate beginnings of a restructuring of the empire's army divisions in the Middle East with the support of Beit Maroun's confederation of monasteries. If the visit did not take place, it is plausible, with the advent of the Persian and Arab conquests of the early seventh century, that the Byzantine emperor would have supported the Melkite (Maronite) populations in forming an indigenous military wing. The Persians had just taken many parts of Syria and were converging on Antioch (which fell in 611 to the Persians). The Persians had broken through the Syrian border, which was under the protection of the Ghassanids, Arab Monophysite Christian tribes aligned with the Byzantines. Heraclius had to strategically regroup and restructure.

Heraclius' visit to Beit Maroun may have coincided with a declaration of substantial financial support and supplies of arms. Perhaps it was the founding, or reinforcement, of a substantial Maronite military contingent as part of the region's Byzantine army divisions. The Maronites were the leading Catholic confederation in the Middle East. They could supply loyal troops from their faithful to the emperor if necessary and to defend themselves. This likely made them unique and distinct from any Byzantine foreign contingent, for example the Mardaites. Being indigenous to the region, they provided a combined commitment not only to defend their church, but their families and ancestral land.

Shortly after the fall of Damascus in 634 to the Arab Muslims, Heraclius' eldest son Constantine was stationed with forty thousand men at Caesarea, the civil metropolis of the three provinces of Palestine. This was only a short distance to the Phoenician port city of Akko and the mountain ranges above which were linked to Mount Lebanon. Constantine was then recalled to the Byzantine Court in withdrawal. The emperor's son retreated to the mountains of Lebanon. He was

---

[392] Theophanes, *The Chronicle of Theophanes*, p. 31.

289

speedily attacked by "three hundred Arabs and one thousand black slaves."

No doubt Constantine had significant military forces with him that warranted the presence of the initial and then much greater Muslim army divisions. Constantine's forces in the Lebanon mountains may have been a contingent that accompanied him from Caesarea. There could also have been troops already stationed in the mountains of Lebanon who provided aid. It is even possible the Maronites formed a large part of the emperor's forces that were amassed at Caesarea. As the leading indigenous Catholics in the region, they would likely have been engaged to support the local faithful in military wings or to join with divisions of the Byzantine army. The Beit Maroun network of faithful were likely well placed to lead the local forces. Nonetheless, the Arab Muslim squadrons arrived and defeated Constantine.[393]

The Caesarea incident may give weight to Hercalius' family's partiality to the Maronites and close working relationship between them. Constantine would not have entered the Lebanese mountain range unless he knew a great part of the native Christian population was not hostile. They had to be from the Chalcedonian party, predominately led by the Beit Maroun network. The account of Constantine's retreat to the Lebanese mountains also supports the view that the Aramaic-speaking Catholics (Melkites/Maronites) were well entrenched in that area at this time. The relationship between the emperor and the Maronites would likely have soured at some stage after Hercalius' reign, as we shall see through other events that unfolded.

It would be naive to think that the Aramaic Catholic population would not take action to defend their lands from the Persians and Arabs. Joining, or aligning with, the Byzantine army to form a formidable defence was logical. Unfortunately, standard historical accounts, which are typically Byzantine and Arab-centric, do not provide an insight into the detail of what actually took place.

---

[393] Gibbon, *The History of the Decline and Fall of the Roman Empire*, Vol. 6, p. 318. Gibbon relies on historical accounts of various Eastern sources such as the *Annals* of Patriarch Michael the Syrian and Arab historian Abel l-Fida. Gibbon refers to the 'snowy mountains of Lebanon'.

A Maronite Chronicle written around the year 664 provides insight into the influence of the Maronites during the early Arab conquest period as they were not required to pay a tax:

> In the same month [June 659 AD] the bishops of the Jacobites, Theodore and Sabukht came to Damascus and held an enquiry into the faith with the Maronites in the presence of Muawiya. When the Jacobites were defeated, Muawiya ordered them to pay 20,000 denarii and commanded them to be silent. Thus there arose the custom that the Jacobite bishops should pay that sum of gold every year to Muawiya, so that he would not withdraw his protection and let them be persecuted by the members of the [Orthodox] church. The person called 'patriarch' by the Jacobites fixed the financial burden that all the convents of monks and nuns should contribute each year towards the payment in gold and he did the same with all the adherents of his faith.
>
> He bequeathed his estate to Muawiya, so that out of fear of that man all the Jacobites would be obedient to him.
>
> On the ninth of the same month in which the disputation with the Jacobites took place, on a Sunday at the eight hour, there was an earthquake ...
>
> In [661], many Arabs gathered at Jerusalem and made Muawiya king and he went up and sat down on Golgotha; he prayed there, and went to Gethsemane and went down to the tomb of the blessed Mary to pray in it ...
>
> In July of the same year the emirs and many Arabs gathered and proffered their right-hand to Muawiya. Then an order went out that he should be proclaimed king in all the villages and cities of his Dominion and that they should make acclamations and invocations to him. He also minted gold and silver, but it was not accepted, because it had no cross on it. Furthermore, Muawiya did not wear a crown like other kings in the world. He placed his throne in Damascus and refused to go to Mohammed's throne.[394]

---

[394] "The Maronite Chronicle," in Brock et al., *The Seventh Century in the West-Syrian Chronicles*, pp. 29-35.

The debate between the Maronites and Jacobites took place in 659, and this chronicle provides us with some critical information. It occured almost two decades before the arrival of the Mardaites to Syria, Lebanon, and Palestine. It is clear that the Maronites were still Melkite (loyal to the Roman Byzantine emperor) and adherents of the 'Orthodox' Christian faith.[395] It is not clear at this time whether this faith was Monothelite and in line with Constantinople, or Dyothelite and in line with the doctrine of Rome.

It seems from the passage the Maronites were a notably more dominant Christian sect than the Jacobites, perhaps both in terms of numbers and also influence, as the Jacobites required Arab Muslim protection from persecution by the (Orthodox) Catholics. The Maronites were not required to pay a tax which indicates some form of treaty held with the Arabs – perhaps their own or one that was under the Byzantine-Arab treaty of 658-9 recorded by Theophanes where the Arabs agreed to payment of daily tributes.[396] It then becomes plausible that the Maronites had their own regional military wing at the time in alliance with the emperor and prior to the arrival of the Mardaites.

Under the treaty of 646 the Arabs agreed to withdraw from Syria. The treaty could support a proposition arising from the Maronite Chronicle of 664 that implies the majority of the population in the former Byzantine region of the Middle East may have remained Christian at this time. The Maronites were not required to pay the Muslim *jizya* tax.

Doueihi refers to a text from a sixteenth century Maronite historian Ibn al-Qilai who talks about "the Maronites and their prince who lived in Baskinta" and appears *not* to correlate the Mardaites with the Maronites:

> The Maronites lived in Mount Lebanon where they spread their authority on the mountains and neighbouring coasts. They were loyal to the Roman Church and to their Patriarch ...

[395] Ibid., pp. 29, 35.
[396] Theophanes, *The Chronicle of Theophanes*, p. 46.

[c. 690] After Prince Yuhanna was killed in Qab Elias, the Maronite army accompanied by its leaders headed to the mountain where they fought against the Muslim army in Al-Mrouj. The Muqaddam (Prince) Semaan won the battle but the war continued for thirty years. Another battle took place at Nahr-el-kalb. Meanwhile, Muqaddam Semaan was in Bikfaya. When he heard about the battle, he led an army of 1500 soldiers and headed to Nahr-el-kalb where he victoriously fought the enemy …

Prince Semaan of Baskinta visited Prince Yusif of Byblos in the presence of Patriarch Gregorios. The meeting had the solemn form of a general Maronite Council, assembling all forty Maronite bishops, headed by the Maronite patriarch, from the boundaries of Akkar to those of the Shouf. They confirmed Semaan as Prince of Kisrawan and granted him great support in the event of war with Muslims.[397]

Doueihi informs us that Prince Semaan's uncle Kisra succeeded him in many victories over the Muslim armies. He was recognised by the Maronites as a national hero. The Lebanese mountain district of Kisrawan was named after him.[398]

It is possible the Maronites established a separate military wing. Perhaps at one stage this wing may have aligned with the Mardaites who were an occupying foreign force of the Byzantine emperor. However, if Doueihi's account is correct relating to John Maroun, this is less likely, and at present none of these propositions are certain. What is more certain, as will be set out in later chapters, is that there is clear and abundant evidence that allows for the safe conclusion that many Maronites *remained* in Syria, Phoenicia, Phoenicia-Lebanon, and Palestine after the dispersion of the Mardaites. Accordingly, the Maronites were not part of the disbursement.

It is likely, after 687-95, the influence of the Maronites in the former Byzantine Middle East diminished rapidly and persecution against

---

[397] Harb, *The Maronites: History and Constants*, p. 70, citing Doueihi.
[398] Ibid.

them by the Islamic rulers increased. Concurrent with these events are the closing of borders and the restriction of movement for Maronites and Christians generally between northern Syria (from Apamaea region in the north) and Antioch after the Byzantine Empire's devastating loss to the Arabs in Syria around 692-95. One therefore needs to be cautious in reading historical accounts of commonly held views that there was intense persecution commencing immediately after the Arab Muslim conquests of Middle East in 634-638. It is apparent from the evidence that this may not have occurred until after 692-695.

## 8.8  Summary

To recap, the churches of Rome and Constantinople had been bitterly divided for a number of decades over the Christological debate as to whether Jesus Christ had one will, divine (Constantinople's position), or two wills, human and divine (Rome's position). A schism occurred between the churches of Rome and Constantinople from 638 after the release of the emperor's *Ecthesis*, which declared Monothelitism (that Christ has two natures but one will) to be the official doctrine of the empire. In 649, the Lateran Council, which the patriarch and bishops of Constantinople did not attend, declared the one will in Christ dogma a heresy, and Pope Martin I was taken prisoner from Rome, tortured, and was to die a martyr (discussed more fully in the following chapter).[399]

Constantinople directly controlled patriarchal appointments of Antioch, contrary to convention and canon law. The patriarch of Antioch resided in Constantinople and may have not visited Antioch (for example, Macarius who was deposed by the Council in 681 but apparently had never visited Antioch). Pope Martin I's encyclical letter of 649 declared null and void Constantinople's appointments of patriarchs of Antioch and Alexandria.

---

[399] Many historians refer to Pope Martin as being murdered by the emperor. However, Theophanes (*The Chronicle of Theophanes*, p. 46) records Pope Martin died in exile as a confessor.

Despite the Lateran Council decree of 649 emanating from Rome, Constantinople remained, in the main, Monothelite. It was not until 681 that the theology of one will in Jesus Christ was officially declared heretical by the Church. This occurred during the Sixth Ecumenical Council (Third Council of Constantinople). Only a handful of religious representing the Romans were present. It must have taken some time thereafter before the bitter relations between the two churches were restored. We know that many clergy in Constantinople continued to adhere to the one will in Christ doctrine even after the Sixth Ecumenical Council.

In this environment, Rome set out to support the Maronites as Catholic Orthodox. There was a large ethnic Aramaic population in Rome, and ethnic Aramaic popes were being elected. The Aramaic community in Rome would likely have lobbied the Vatican to support the Aramaic-speaking Catholics and Beit Maroun in the Middle East. Together with the Greek clergy, the Aramaic clergy in Rome dominated. Back in the Middle East, tensions had been rising within the Melkites over loyalty to Constantinople or Rome. The faction supporting the leadership of John Maroun looked to Rome. The more Greek-centric faction looked to Constantinople and the emperor. The Maronites could no longer be called 'Melkites' as their loyalty shifted to Rome, in opposition to the emperor.

If Doueihi's account of John Maroun is correct, it must follow that Rome was intent on restoring the convention of the appointment of the patriarch of Antioch. It did so by allowing John Maroun to be elected. John Maroun, in declaring his loyalty to Rome by becoming patriarch of Antioch and then travelling to Rome, became an enemy of Constantinople. In 694, the Byzantine emperor, seeing the election of John Maroun as a violation of his rule, had his army attack St Maroun's monastery in Syria, killing five hundred monks.[400] He sought to

---

[400] Harb, *The Maronites: History and Constants*, p. 76, citing Doueihi, instructs us that the Mardaite Prince Simon of Lebanon joined with the Byzantine army and defeated the Arabs. 'As a token of gratitude, the Byzantine Emperor sent Patriarch John Maroun a royal flower along with a letter thanking his Holiness and his brave followers'. Harb puts the date of this as 669 and relates it to the reign of Emperor Tiberius. This

capture John Maroun who then fled to Lebanon, where the Byzantine army followed. Doueihi reports most of the population of Lebanon rallied around John Maroun.[401]

Naturally, there is likely to be some defects in the historical account of Doueihi. Nonetheless, Arab and Western-centric historians have generally presumed throughout history that the Byzantine forces in the Middle East were completely crushed after the Arab conquests of 634-638. We are also led to understand that the Byzantine and Arab emperors did not communicate, and that Christians virtually went into hiding. It seems possible from the texts drawn on here that this convoluted history tells a different story.

Islamic rule in the seventh century appears not to have been ironclad and as fanatic after their initial conquest. There appears consistent dialogue between the caliph and the emperor. There was a peace treaty between them from 650 to 653. After its expiry, the Arab fleet set sail from Tripoli in Phoenicia in 655 to begin their incursions on Cyprus, Rhodes, Cos, and Crete.[402] There was another peace treaty in 678, discussed above, that required annual payments and accordingly regular contact between the opposing sides. As mentioned in the brief account of the Mardaites, extraordinarily several of the treaties negotiated between the Byzantine emperors and Arab Muslim caliphs allowed the Byzantine army divisions to return well into Arab held territory. Given the tensions between the Caliph (Sunni) and Iman Ali (Shiite) elsewhere in the Middle East at the time, it is feasible borders and roads were open or easily penetrable, and so the Byzantines and Mardaites were able to roam.

Hence, travel between the Middle East and the western Roman Empire was not as restricted as one would have imagined. Notably,

---

cannot be correct. Harb has erred. John Maroun was not elected patriarch until 685 and not elected bishop until 676. Further, the event contradicts Doueihi's recount that the emperor was opposed to John Maroun from his inception as patriarch, which must be preferred. It is more plausible the gift of the royal flower was at a date before 685, that is, before John Maroun was patriarch.

[401] Dau, *History of the Maronites*, p. 223.

[402] Ekonomou, *Byzantine Rome and the Greek Popes*, p. 166.

not long after the commencement of Islamic rule in the Middle East between 634-638, a number of Middle Eastern-born ethnic Aramaic men travelled to Rome and later became Popes. Pope John V was born in 635 within the patriarchate of Antioch. He was the first in all succeeding popes thereafter not to require the emperor's consecration before being installed as the patriarch of Rome. The other Aramaic popes included Pope Sergius I, Pope Sisinnius, Pope Constantine, and Pope Gregory III. With their range of birth years as between 635-669, travelling to the West from the Middle East was clearly open during Islamic rule in this period.

We are also informed by historians that the Christians, and particularly the Maronites, suffered waves of extreme persecution. However, it appears in the early days of Islamic conquest this may not have been the case. Harb states, for example:

> The Maronites' determination to be independent of Byzantine authority led the Umayyads to change their attitude. In his 'History of Damascus', Ibn Acaker mentions that several caliphs lived and died in Maronite monasteries. Abdul Malik bin Maran (685-705) used to spend spring in St Maroun's monastery near Damascus; Omar bin Abdul Aziz (717-720) used to stay in St Simon's monastery near Aleppo and was buried there. In addition the weddings of some Umayad princes were held in St Maroun's monastery.[403]

Bizarre contradictions are in abundance for this period. We cannot be sure exactly what took place. It would be useful for research to be undertaken in Rome to ascertain if there are any records of the journeys, for example, to Antioch and Tripoli, of the papal legates during this time. There may be an obscure reference in the Vatican records to John Maroun's visit to Rome with the papal legate. Perhaps Doueihi and Assemani recorded their sources in their original manuscripts and these have been missed in the transcriptions. There is of course much further research required on these matters and others.

---

[403] Harb, *The Maronites: History and Constants*, p. 76, citing Ibn Acakir, *History of Damascus*.

Nonetheless, it is clear once again the Maronites could not have been Monophysites as suggested by the author Moosa and could not have descended from Arabia as suggested by the author Salibi. If Doueihi's version is preferred, the Maronites formed a stronghold in the mountains of Lebanon under St John Maroun. The Maronites established a military organisation as a separate body to the church. It protected their faithful as the leading Catholics in the region in communion with the Church in Rome and with the Pope as its primary patriarch. Whether or not the Maronites had formed a military alliance with the Mardaites, they must have maintained some form of military resistance in the mountains of Lebanon and north-western Palestine for close to the next four hundred years. It would be otherwise difficult to explain why, on the arrival of the Crusaders in the late eleventh century, the chronicler William of Tyre records more than 40,000 Maronite soldiers (discussed in Chapter 11).

It is not clear what proportion of Maronites remained on the coast and in the mountains after the end of the seventh century. As Lebanon's coastal plains are generally quite narrow, settlements could have been on the fringe of the cities in the lower mountain range leading all the way to the high summits of the mountains. Contrary to conventional thinking, William of Tyre's comments, referring to the cities, may imply that the Maronites continued to populate the coastal cities in the eleventh century. Perhaps the military remained in the mountains with a more significant Maronite population. The Maronite existence in Akko (or Acre, in present Israel) on the arrival of the Crusades in the eleventh century demonstrates that in fact the Maronites were not traditionally confined to Syria and Lebanon. Once again, we see evidence of Maronite links to indigenous ancient Phoenician roots.

On the balance of the present evidence, it would be difficult to reverse the following finding from the texts and commentary before us: the Maronites were still the Catholic beacons of Orthodoxy in the Middle East during the seventh century. The unexpected shock for the seventh century is that the Maronites also became the beacons of Orthodoxy in Rome amongst the popes, monks, clergy, and the lay faithful. There was an even closer bond between Rome and the Maronites. In the following chapter we will further examine the question of whether or not the Maronites were really Monothelites and explore how the relationship between Rome and the Catholics of the Middle East fared under Islamic rule.

# CHAPTER 9

# THE LEGEND OF MARONITE MONOTHELITISM

## 9.1 Christological Debates of the Seventh Century

The seventh century saw for the first time intense ecumenical activity from the Catholic Church in Rome and Constantinople and from the Byzantine emperor. They sought to win back the non-Chalcedonian churches. Language barriers had diminished and there was a better understanding between the 'Monophysites' and the Catholics, but much discussion of 'right' Christological understandings. To reiterate the key positions: Monophysitism states Jesus Christ had only one nature, divine; Dyophysitism declares Jesus Christ had two natures, physical and divine; and Miaphysitism holds that in the one person of Jesus Christ his divinity and humanity are fully united as one nature. Monothelitism (as opposed to Monophysitism) states Jesus Christ had two natures but only one will, divine.

### Diagram: Differing beliefs in nature and will of Christ

| Belief System | Nature of Christ | Will of Christ |
|---|---|---|
| Monophysitism | one nature: divine | |
| Dyophsyitism | two natures, divine and human | |
| Miaphysitism | divine and human natures are united as one | |
| Monothelitism | two natures, divine and human | one will |
| Dyothelitism | two natures, divine and human | two wills, divine and human |
| Miathelitism | two natures, divine and human | divine and human wills are united as one |

Today, many Catholic theologians suggest the 'Monophysitism' of the churches who did not ascribe to the Chalcedon decree (the 'non-Chalcedonian churches') can be more aptly understood as 'Miaphysitism'. Two schools of thought had developed on the two wills of Christ. One was the conventional and more popular thinking of two distinct wills, and the other, the union of two wills, Miathelitism. Both are correct doctrine. The union of two wills was not condemned at the Sixth Council in 680-681 and was clearly accepted as theologically sound.

Those that dismissed both these two will Christologies were Monothelites. Miathelitism, which may have been attributed to the Maronites, has been misunderstood as Monothelite only because it was not the conventional and more popular Christology. Monophysitism was declared a heresy by the Catholic Church in 451 at the Council of Chalcedon (Fourth Ecumenical Council). The introduction of the theology of Monothelitism by Constantinople was thought to be the key in bringing the disparate churches back in communion. However, in 681, at the Third Council of Constantinople or Sixth Ecumenical Council, Monothelitism was rejected as heretical. The accusation of Monothelistism against the Maronites is a legend that has been repeated by historians since ancient times. The principal reasons are discussed here, after setting out the key events and theological debates relevant to this issue.

Politics, war, and historical church divisions played a large part in the complexity and misunderstandings of this period. The patriarchs of Constantinople and Antioch were directly influenced by the Byzantine emperor and the Byzantine Court repeatedly intervened in church affairs. The Byzantine Church attempted to affirm the See of Constantinople as at least equal or first in the Christian Church, in primacy to the Patriarch of Rome.

The tension between the Greeks and Romans was exacerbated by the long vacancy in the See of Antioch. Not long after the murder of Patriarch Anastasius II in 609, the Persians ruled Antioch until 628 and the Arab Muslims from 638. From 609 to 639, the patriarchal see of Antioch remained vacant. This was despite the Byzantine Empire regaining control of Antioch between from 628 until 638. After 639, Constantinople appeared to begin the practice of electing a titular or nominal patriarch that never resided in Antioch. It may be that the vacancy was the result of the Muslim Caliphs not allowing the appointment of the patriarch of Antioch from Constantinople. Or perhaps it gave Constantinople a reason to diminish the role of Antioch thereby increasing Greek-Byzantine influence and better positioning Constantinople in its attempts to have equal or primary standing to the patriarch of Rome (the pope).

### 9.1.1  The Lateran Council of 649 and Surrounding Events

Between 634 and 638, Pope Honorius had been misconstrued with confirming "one will of Christ" in a letter responding to Patriarch Sergius of Constantinople. It is thought the introduction of this theology was ecumenical in its thinking. It was an attempt to reunite the 'Monophysites' with the Catholic Church as it was understood they believed in one nature of Christ, divine. In conformity with the words in Pope Honorius' letter, Sergius composed the *Ecthesis*, or exposition, issued by the Emperor Heraclius from Constantinople in 638. The *Ecthesis* ordered all persons to "confess one will in our Lord," and to avoid the expressions "one operation" and "two operations." This became known as Monothelitism – the belief in two natures in Christ but only one divine will. Pope Honorius and Patriarch Sergius died in 638. In the same year, the patriarchal capitals of Jerusalem and Antioch fell to the Arabs. Emperor Heraclius retreated and his reign ended in 641.

In 648, Byzantine Emperor Constans II decreed the 'Typus', protecting from legal prosecution Monothelites and Dyothelites and forbidding any dispute on the issue. The Typus contained a denial of the doctrine of two wills in Christ. One year later in 649, Pope Martin I convened the Lateran Council, which condemned as heresies the *Ecthesis* of Emperor Heraclius and the Typus of Emperor Constans II. The Lateran Council was a Roman synod, not an ecumenical Council of bishops from around the world. Accordingly, its decrees did not represent the whole of the Church. The Lateran condemnation only emphasised the schism between the churches of Rome and Constantinople. It condemned Constantinople's promotion of the theology of one will and, adding to the confusion within the Roman Church, the infallibility of the Pope was questioned when Pope Honorius was declared a heretic at the Council.

Pope Martin I's encyclical letter in 649 was issued throughout the whole Church. The Pope declared invalid Constantinople's appointment of Macedonius as Patriarch of Antioch (639-654) and Peter as Patriarch of Alexandria (appointed 640). Macarius succeeded Macedonius as patriarch of Antioch from 654-681 and he resided in Constantinople and not Antioch.[404] The Pope also gave orders for the papal vicar in the East to depose heretical bishops in the patriarchates of Antioch and Alexandria and substitute new bishops who were 'Orthodox'.

Emperor Constans II retaliated. The Pope was asked to accept the *Ecthesis*, but he refused, so the emperor had Pope Martin I taken by force from Rome and kept as prisoner in Naxos and then Constantinople. There he was publically ridiculed and was kept prisoner in close and cruel confinement in prison for ninety-three days suffering from hunger, cold, and thirst. Pope Martin was publically stripped of nearly all his clothing, loaded with chains and dragged through the streets of the city of Constantinople. He was sent into exile in 655 to Crimea where he died six months later. Many historians have claimed that the emperor murdered Pope Martin however, Theophanes states Martin died a "confessor" (martyr) whilst exiled by the emperor.[405] He is a saint in the Catholic Church and is honoured by the Byzantines as a successor to St Peter.[406]

Constantine Pogonatus succeeded Constans II as the new emperor. Whilst fully occupied with the empire's wars with the Arabs, he was

---

[404] Brock, *Syriac Perspectives on Late Antiquity*, pp. 322, 323, 343. In the same pages Brock confirms the See of Antioch remained vacant from 609-639.

[405] Theophanes, *The Chronicle of Theophanes*, p. 46, where he also records other proponents of the two will doctrine, including Maximus the Confessor (d. 662) who had his tongue and hand cut off on the emperor's orders, died martyrs to their orthodoxy.

[406] Francis Mershman, "Pope St. Martin I," in *The Catholic Encyclopedia*, Robert Appleton Company, 1910, available at: http://www.newadvent.org/cathen/09723c.htm.

determined to reconcile the Sees of Rome and Constantinople. In 678, he summoned the Sixth Ecumenical Council (the Third Council of Constantinople), which ran from 680-681 and declared Monothelitism a heresy.

Beit Maroun's thinking or stance before 638, is unknown. After 638, there is no evidence the Maronites did not adhere to the official Church teachings as result of Pope Honorius' letter and the *Ecthesis*. The fall of the Middle East to the Arab Muslims in the same year as the *Ecthesis*, and the varying difficulties of war and communication with Rome and Constantinople faced by the Middle Eastern Catholics, complicates what subsequently occurred. Rome's Lateran Council of 649 declaring Monothelitism as a heresy without a full ecumenical council declaration, and Pope Martin's arrest, imprisonment, torture, and exile by the emperor, added to the confusion and chaos. The events that unfolded for the Middle East Catholics relating to the Monothelite controversy are thus relatively obscure, both in the decades leading up to the Council of 680-81 and thereafter. According to Doueihi's version of events, when John Maroun was selected bishop of Batroun in 676, the Maronites were at that time adhering to the doctrine of two wills in Christ.

The condemnation of Pope Honorius as a Monothelite has been questioned by Catholic theologians since the eighteenth century. The issue of the 'personal' infallibility of the Pope has also played its part. Honorius was judged by the Council on the wording in his letter to Sergius. The more widely held view today is that the letter falls under the definition of *ex cathedra* – that is, it refers to infallible teachings of the papacy, but was incorrectly worded. Thus, the thinking of the Pope was actually orthodox in terms of a definition of faith.[407] Until recent times, he was misunderstood to be a Monothelite.

### 9.1.2  The Sixth Ecumenical Council of 680-681 and the Fallout

Between 638 and 681, the Church was in complete chaos. Confusion reigned amongst clergy and the faithful regarding the theology of the

---

[407] John Chapman, "Pope Honorius I," in *The Catholic Encyclopedia*, Robert Appleton Company, 1910, available at: http://www.newadvent.org/cathen/07452b.htm.

will of Christ and loyalty to either Church. The Arabs ruled the Middle East and were threatening to take Constantinople. To whom were the Catholics of the Middle East to express their allegiance – Rome and the Pope, or Constantinople and the Emperor? As they did during the Acacian schism (471-518), the Maronites who were indigenous and Aramaic-speaking opted for Rome and the Pope. Once again, they proved to be the beacon of Catholic orthodoxy in the Middle East.

The Sixth Ecumenical Council at Constantinople in 680-681 was the most important Catholic ecclesiastical event of the seventh century. The Aramaic Theophanes was abbot of the monastery of St Peter *ad Baias* in Sicily. He was one of Greek-Sicilian Pope Agatho's (a former monk himself) delegates to the Sixth Ecumenical Council in 680-681.[408] Under Pope Agatho (678-681), the Emperor Constantine IV may have engineered the Council of 680-81. Initially it was not a council but a conference. The delegation Pope Agatho sent was an impressive one, containing two future Popes (John V and Constantine), and a synodical decree signed by one hundred and fifty bishops condemning Monothelitism. When the Emperor Constantine IV saw this, he then ordered his new Patriarch, George I, to make it a council and invite his bishops and metropolitans.[409] The Council anathematised Pope Honorius I (625-638) and the papal delegates made no objection at the time. However, delicate negotiations had been necessary to secure their acquiescence.

Most authors have maintained not one Catholic bishop from Egypt, Syria, or Palestine was present. Many historians believe this was a result of Arab rule that had severed their communication lines, however, the acts of the Council of 680-81 indicate the patriarch of Alex-

---

[408] Ekonomou, *Byzantine Rome and the Greek Popes*, pp. 177-179, 199. Theophanes became patriarch of Antioch after Macarius was deposed at the Council. It is not clear how the election process occurred and whether bishops from Antioch took part or whether it was an appointment.

[409] J.D.N. Kelly, *Oxford Dictionary of the Popes*, Oxford University Press, 1986, pp. 77-78. If there were no bishops from the patriarchate of Antioch present at the Council of 680-81, assuming Hefele's recording of its minutes are incorrect, perhaps this rapid transformation as a full 'ecumenical council' might be one reason for the lack of bishops present from Antioch.

andria and bishops of Constantinople and Antioch were present.[410] It seems there were no abbots or monks (including Beit Maroun representatives) in attendance at the Council; the delegates were principally bishops. At the Council of 536, special permission was required for abbots or monks of monasteries to attend. In any event, there was no reference to, or declaration against, Beit Maroun or the Maronites at the Sixth Ecumenical Council.

At this council, Pope Honorius, Patriarch Sergius of Constantinople, Melkite Patriarch Cyrus of Alexandria, and Patriarch Macarius of Antioch, amongst others, were deemed heretics for their Monothelitism. Some authors have suggested Bishop Germanus initially voted in support of the dogma of one will of Christ (he must have changed his vote as he was not condemned at the Council). He later became patriarch of Constantinople in 715 and adhered to the dogma of two wills in Christ.

Patriarch Macarius of Antioch, declared a Monothelite heretic at the Council, was also misunderstood to be a Maronite, although he was never appointed by the bishops in the patriarchate of Antioch and had likely never met them. He was appointed by, and resided in, Constantinople. It appears there is no record of him ever visiting Antioch.[411] Accordingly, it has been assumed that the Maronites must have been the only Monothelites after the Council in 681. This ancient legend of Macarius being a Maronite has carried through to modern times. No author or Maronite apologetic has made that clear. As will be seen in Chapter 11 on the Crusades, the Crusader chronicler De Vitry states "The author of this error was a Bishop of Antioch named Macarius."

The most prominent theologian to promote the doctrine of two wills was Maximus the Confessor. In a letter to a priest in Cyprus, Maximus exonerated Pope Honorius. He stated that Honorius believed the human will could not be contrary to the divine will. Explained in

[410] Hefele, *A History of the Councils*, p. 151.
[411] Francis Joseph Bacchus, "Macarius of Antioch," in *The Catholic Encyclopedia,* Robert Appleton Company, 1910, available at: http://www.newadvent.org/cathen/09483b.htm; Brock, *Syriac Perspectives on Late Antiquity*, p. 70.

another sense, Christ's will could not make two decisions, one human decision, and one divine decision. There was only one decision made, divine.

After the Council decree of 681, Rome questioned the minutes of the Council and several years later called another Council to confirm the correct minutes. Theophanes records disputes over the acts (minutes) of the Council for four years.[412] Pope John V of Rome had previously acted as a deacon representing Rome at the Sixth Ecumenical Council. Four years later, after becoming Pope in 685, suspicions remained high about Constantinople's acceptance of the Council. Pope John V feared that the acts of the Council had been falsified as they had left the Imperial archive without the Emperor's knowledge. He convened a synod of high-ranking civil and ecclesiastical officials and asked that the text of the Council records be read in their presence to confirm it was a true and accurate profession of the faith.[413]

It is said that during the reign of Pope Conon (686-87), Emperor Justinian II (685-695 and 705-711) restored the Monothelite Theodore as Patriarch of Constantinople.[414] In 711, Emperor Philippicus Bardanes rejected the Sixth Ecumenical Council's decree. Pope Constantine refused to recognize Bardanes. The Emperor called a synod of Constantinople in 712. The synod re-established the dogma of Monothelistism and condemned the Sixth Ecumenical Council.[415] In 713, Bardanes was dethroned by Anastasius II and the new emperor restored orthodoxy. Constantinople Patriarch John VI wrote the Pope a long letter of apology and confirmed the Pope's primacy over the Catholic Church.

The Greeks in Alexandria remained Monothelite until 742-43 when the (Melkite) patriarch Kosmos and his city became Catholic Orthodox, having adhered to the Monothelite doctrine since the time of Pa-

---

[412] Theophanes, *The Chronicle of Theophanes*, p. 59.
[413] Ekonomou, *Byzantine Rome and the Greek Popes*, p. 219.
[414] Kelly, *Oxford Dictionary of the Popes*, p. 81.
[415] Michael the Syrian, *Chronicle of Michael the Great*, paragraph 136; Ekonomou, *Byzantine Rome and the Greek Popes*, p. 272.

triarch Cyrus during the reign of Heraclius.[416] Not long after another Byzantine Emperor, Constantine (c. 744-750), was reported to be a Monothelite.[417] It is possible that significant amounts of the populations of Constantinople and Alexandria remained Monothelite, despite the view that it had been stamped out because of the Council decree.

Historians have been distracted by Macarius, who was not a Maronite, rather than focusing on the Maronites. Greek historians and rivals of the Maronites around the time of the Council of 680-681 and beyond have managed to divert attention away from Constantinople and referred to the Maronites as a deviation, targeting them as the creators and single heirs of Monothelistism. It may also have been part of an ongoing attempt to drive a wedge between the Maronites and Rome in order to tamper or remove the Aramaic Catholic influence from the Middle East. A re-writing of history on this subject is clearly warranted. Given what seems to be Arab Muslim severity in restricting communication between the Middle East and the West intensifying from around 695, these events seem to have coincided with Rome's loss of communication and eventually any memory of the Maronites until the Crusades more than four hundred years later.

The consolation for the Maronites of having the attention on Macarius is the significance ancient historians placed on the prominence and leadership of the Maronites in the patriarchate of Antioch during this period. The implication is that they were its only indigenous Catholics at the time. Hence, the claim by many historians that the Maronites are not only responsible for the birth of Monothelitism but were the only Monothelites after 681, up until the twelfth century when they were officially confirmed as reunited with the Catholic Church, is striking. On the contrary, the evidence points to the church of Constantinople and the emperor, as Catholics, officially introducing the doctrine throughout the empire in 638 and maintaining it for over four decades until the Sixth Council. Thereafter, evidence discovered during the course of this book clearly supports the first time proposi-

---

[416] Theophanes, *The Chronicle of Theophanes*, p. 107.

[417] Michael the Syrian, *Chronicle of Michael the Great*, paragraph 143.

tion that the Monothelite doctrine remained part of Constantinopolitan and Alexandrian societies for at least one hundred years until 750 AD. This is despite the emperor, patriarch, and bishops of Constantinople agreeing to decree it a heresy at the Council of 680-681.

## 9.2 Alleged Monothelite Connections

From 634 to 713 there was substantial tension and constant struggle between Rome and Constantinople in relation to the Monothelite doctrine. There must have been significant confusion in the Church, not only relating to church teachings but a conflict of loyalty between Rome and the pope on the one hand, and Constantinople and the emperor on the other. The era is one of the most controversial and complex in the ecclesiastical history of the Christian church. For Aramaic Catholic and Maronite history, the question of whether the Maronites were Monothelites from 681 up to the arrival of the Crusades has been contentious. Unfortunately, the little evidence available is itself full of ambiguities and contradictions.

One should understand that from the birth of Christianity to shortly before this period, the overwhelming majority of Christians in the world would have lived in the Middle East, not the West. Prior to the Persian invasions, the Christian populations and theologians of the Middle East were foremost committed to their faith and doctrine rather than defense of their lands. Simultaneously, most were repeatedly dedicated to peaceful resolution of doctrinal disputes and unification of the Church. The passionate commitment of Christians to their faith and intellectual understanding in this period can be demonstrated by a comparison with contemporary Christians. The typical Christian today does not consider whether Jesus Christ had one or two natures and one or two wills: even if these doctrines were put to them, it is doubtful they would appreciate their meaning, relevance, or importance.

The debate over the will of Christ is principally one for highly intellectual theologians. There has been confusion even amongst them. As Catholics, Pope Honorius (misunderstood to be a Monothelite), Patriarch Sergius of Constantinople, Patriarch Cyrus of Alexandria, and Patriarch Macarius of Antioch believed in the one will of Christ. The Byzantine Emperor Heraclius, in his decree known as the *Ecthesis*, officially introduced the Christology of one will, Monothelitism, in 638. It became the official teaching of the empire from 638 until 649 and until 681 the Romans adhered to the doctrine of two wills in Christ, and Constantinople the doctrine of one will. Though it was later to be declared a heresy at the Sixth Ecumenical Council by the Catholic Church in 681, there is evidence to suggest a large part of the population of Constantinople including emperors continued to practise Monothelitism until 750 despite its condemnation.

In the same way as modern theological opinion has suggested the Miaphysitism of the non-Chalcedonian churches is not a heresy, a similar approach must apply regarding Monothelitism. Accordingly, even if the Maronites were Monothelites (and this chapter determines they were not), they could never have been heretics: their Catholic orthodoxy remained intact. Nonetheless, we will examine here the circumstances that have led to the incorrect assumption that the Maronites, by allegedly maintaining Monothelite beliefs, deviated from the teachings of the Catholic Church, including their alleged connections with Heraclius and Macarius and the findings of the Maronite College of the medieval era.

### 9.2.1 Emperor Heraclius and Beit Maroun

Heraclius was Byzantine Emperor from 610 to 641. When visiting the Middle East early in his reign, his first visit was to the monastery of St Maroun, the head of the Chalcedonian party. Naaman, says of the visit, thought to have been in 610:

> On the same occasion, the emperor, who did not hide his pro-Chalcedonian preferences, gave orders to add to the property of the monastery of St Maroun, a great part of the property belonging to the Monophysite monasteries. Such actions explain the rumours according to which Heraclius was thought to be a Maronite.[418]

---

[418] Naaman, *The Maronites*, p. 132, citing P.G. Migne, III, col. 1089.

Gibbon notes that this visit included an "expansion of the monastery" with Heraclius' support. He gives no date but incorrectly states it was the Maronites who introduced the emperor to the theology of one will. Perhaps Heraclius studied at Beit Maroun. He could be unfairly described as a Maronite due to his favouritism towards them as the leaders of Catholic orthodoxy in the Middle East. No explanation is certain. However, Heraclius was of Armenian descent.[419]

The indigenous Melkites (Maronites) were the leading Catholic orthodox party in the Middle East and accordingly the only indigenous Christians who could supply loyalty and if, necessary, troops to the emperor. The emperor may have declared substantial financial support and supplies of arms to the Maronites. Nonetheless, it appears some Monophysite monasteries came into the hands of the Maronites at this time.

Barhebreus tells us the order from the Emperor of the merger came after the victories against the Persians from 622-628. Whilst visiting Edessa and then Mabboug (Hierapolis) in 630-31, the Emperor pressed the Monophysites to accept the Council of Chalcedon and Barhebreus states:

> Since they would not consent, Heraclius was irritated and sent out a decree to the whole Empire: 'anyone who will not adhere (to the Council), will have his nose and ears cut off and his house pillaged'. And so, many converted. The monks of Beth Maroun, of Mabboug and of Emese, showed their wickedness and pillaged a number of churches and monasteries. Our people complained to Heraclius, who did not answer them. This is why the God of vengeance has delivered us through the Arabs from the hands of the Romans. Our churches, it is true, were not restored to us, the conquering Arabs allowed to each sect what they found in its possession. But it is not just a slight advantage for us to be freed from the wickedness of the Romans and the cruel hate towards us.[420]

---

[419] W. Kaegi, *Heraclius Emperor of Byzantium*, Cambridge University Press, 2003, p. 214.

[420] Dib, *History of the Maronite Church*, p. 11, citing *Chronicon ecclesiasticum*, t. I, ed. Abbelos-Lamy, Louvain, 1872, col.269-274. Barhebreus (d. 1286) relied ex-

The date of the visit to Beit Maroun is therefore likely to have been after Heraclius' troops stormed back to Antioch in 628. One or more other visits could have also taken place shortly after the fall of Damascus to the Arab Muslims in 634 and before the fall of Antioch in 638.

The author Moosa provides a completely different translation of the above quote stating:

> As a result of the persecution of the Orthodox (those who believed in One Incarnate Nature of the Divine Logos and rejected the Council of Chalcedonian) many monks accepted the Council of Chalcedon including the monks of Beth Marun (the monastery of Marun) together with the inhabitants of Mabug and Homs.[421]

Moosa informs us that it was at this time the Beit Maroun monks became Chalcedonian. Brock rejects that view and states "the theory that the Maronites derive from converts from Monophysitism made by Heraclius in the early 630s rests on a misunderstanding of a passage in Michael the Syrian."[422] Brock confirms that it is generally accepted the Maronite Church gained its name from the monastery of Mar Maroun founded in 452 by the Emperor Marcian and that thereafter they "were strong defenders of the Chalcedonian doctrinal position against the attacks of the Monophysite opponents of the Council."[423] Nothing is known about the extent or duration of Beit Maroun's expansion, or the force that may have been applied during the process.

Michael the Syrian (and Dionysius of Tell Mahre) record Heraclius first introduced the theology of the will of Christ when he visited the Monophysites in Hierapolis in 630. Remarkably, Theophanes states

tensively on the eighth century *Annals* of Dionysius of Tell Mahre, Patriarch of the Syrian Jacobites (818-45). The *Annals* are lost today, but are substantially preserved in the chronicles of Michael the Syrian or the Great, Patriarch of the Syrian Jacobites (1166-1199). Naaman, *The Maronites*, p. 155 cites the same passage in Nau's book *Opuscules Maronites* and states that Nau estimates the event to be around 630. See also, Kaegi, *Heraclius Emperor of Byzantium*, pp. 213-214.

[421] Moosa, *The Maronites in History*, p. 91.
[422] Brock, *Syriac Perspectives on Late Antiquity*, p. 69.
[423] Ibid. See also Brock, *An Introduction to Syriac Studies*, p. 70.

the reverse: that the first suggestion about the will of Christ was from the Jacobites who introduced the concept to Heraclius in Hierapolis. The emperor referred the comments back to Patriarch Sergius of Constantinople (Syrian born with apparent Jacobite ancestors) who, with Cyrus, Bishop of Phasis, confirmed Christ had one will.[424] Furthermore, rather than a number of churches and monasteries being passed to the Maronites, sources like the thirteenth century chronicle of Michael the Syrian only records the Cathedral of Edessa.[425]

Dib informs us the first seeds of this teaching appeared about 616 in negotiations between Sergius, Patriarch of Constantinople and Theodore, Bishop of Pharan, amongst others.[426] Sergius then wrote his letter to Pope Honorius in 634. The Sixth Ecumenical Council in 681 condemned Sergius as a heretic and confirmed about the letter: "Sergius sometime bishop of this God-preserved royal city who was the first to write on this impious doctrine;"[427] Migne records a visit to Beit Maroun by Hercalius around 610, almost two decades prior to the *Ecthesis*.[428] No other account on the subject of the Monothelites attributes the introduction of the dogma to Beit Maroun. Indeed, one author suggests it developed in Alexandria.[429] Gibbon's tainted comments must be dismissed, as the only real evidence associating Monothelitism with Heraclius is the *Ecthesis* of 638.

Through the theology of one will of Christ, Constantinople began to attempt reunification of the Monophysites with the Catholic Church. The theology of one will gained ground amongst the Coptic Monophysites in Egypt. Any Maronite retention of Monophysite and

---

[424] Theophanes, *The Chronicle of Theophanes*, p. 31.

[425] Michael the Syrian, *Chronicle of Michael the Great*, paragraph 122-23. See also Kaegi, *Heraclius Emperor of Byzantium*, p. 214.

[426] Dib, *History of the Maronite Church*, p. 16, citing *S. Maximi confessoris disputatio cum Pyrrho*, Migne, t. XCI, col. 289,332.

[427] Quoted in *Acts of the Third Council of Constantinople*, in *Nicene and Post-Nicene Fathers*, trans. by Henry Percival, ed. by Philip Schaff and Henry Wace, Second Series, Vol. 14, Christian Literature Publishing Co., 1900, available at: http://www.newadvent.org/fathers/3813.htm.

[428] The year 610 according to Migne, as cited by Naaman, p. 132.

[429] Chapman, "Monothelitism and Monothelites," in *The Catholic Encyclopedia*.

Monothelite manuscripts from this seventh century period may suggest one explanation for the Catholic Church's delay, after arrival of the Crusaders, in accepting back the Maronite Church in communion.

The alleged lack of purity in liturgical texts led to a Jesuit Father Eliano's report to Rome from Lebanon (1578-1582) that certain Maronite liturgical and theological books contained doctrinal errors. We are also aware that in 581, there was a significant conversion of Jacobites to Maronites, which may also have led to retention of Jacobite documents. Following Father Eliano's report, Maronite Patriarch Sarkis requested Pope Clement VIII send a delegation to undertake a new enquiry. The Jesuit delegate, Dandini, was sent to Lebanon in 1596. He found the books claimed by Eliano to contain errors were in fact from the Syrian Jacobites (Monophysites) rather than Maronite books. They were found in some Maronite libraries as resource material. Thus, the accusations of Eliano of doctrinal error amongst the Maronites were proved false.[430]

### 9.2.2   Macarius of Antioch at the Sixth Council

Towards the end of his account on the Maronites, Gibbon mentions patriarch Macarius of Antioch at the Synod of Constantinople as holding firm to the theology of one will in Christ. It is left to the reader to accept the narration as Macarius representing the Maronites at the Sixth Ecumenical Council of Constantinople in 680-681. It appears a widespread view that Macarius, as patriarch of Antioch, had to be a Maronite. The only Catholic patriarchs of Antioch after 451 were from the Chalcedonian party, which, over time, was led by Beit Maroun network. Given that Macarius was deposed and declared a Monothelite heretic by the Council of 681 the assumption follows that the Maronites must have been Monothelite. This legend formed one of the two fundamental bases for all ancient accounts thereafter. It has continued to be repeated throughout the ages and infiltrated modern texts though it is a profoundly flawed opinion.

---

[430] Dau, *History of the Maronites*, p. 439, citing *Girolamo Dandini, Missione apostolica al Patriarca e Maronite del Monte Libanon*, Cesena, 1656.

Gibbon did not, in fact, make this specific statement. His submission was only that, even though he had no basis for assuming so, the Maronites introduced the theology of one will. It is typical of his intentional narration style, but unbeknown to the reader this lures them into accepting his bias as true fact. It seems Gibbon was aware Constantinople was adhering to the dogma of one will in Christ. He states it was "propagated amongst the Greeks and Syrians." He may have been unaware that since the arrival of the Arabs several decades prior to the Council of 680-81, the patriarchs of Antioch were appointed by the patriarch of Constantinople, under the influence of the emperor. Their appointments must have contradicted canon law. As it does today, the election of the patriarch appeared to require a vote of the bishops of the patriarchate. The emperor, however, often intervened.

All of the patriarchs of Antioch in the seventh century after 640, including Macarius, resided in Constantinople.[431] They were not Maronite and were not elected by the bishops of the patriarchate of Antioch. There is no evidence Macarius, patriarch of Antioch from 656 until 681, or any other of these patriarchs visited Antioch.[432] Despite the prominence in the Middle East of the Beit Maroun confederation, there was no reference at the 680-681 Sixth Ecumenical Council to Maronite presence, any decree against the Maronites, or Macarius representing the Maronites. If Macarius represented all the bishops of the patriarchate, it is extraordinary there was no condemnation of any of them.

Macarius, as Antiochian patriarch, had always been under the authority and instructions of Constantinople and most likely he never met with any Maronites. At the Sixth Council Macarius was the lone voice of any senior clergy or bishop opposed to the Dyothelite theology. Priest Constantine of Apamaea made a special request to be heard at the Council, and his submission was examined at length. He was deposed not for promoting Monothelite theology, but for a new mediation doctrine invented himself. The Council called it a "new Man-

---

[431] Bacchus, "Macarius of Antioch," in *The Catholic Encyclopedia*.
[432] Brock, *Syriac Perspectives on Late Antiquity*, p. 70.

ichaean" and "new Apollinarian" principle and he was expelled from the hearings.[433] Constantine did not claim his Monothelitism from the authority of the religious leaders in the region of Apamaea, where Beit Maroun was centred, nor did he mention Beit Maroun. The priest did confirm that he had taken his authority from Macarius.[434] He sought to find ground for conciliation to unite the divided churches.

At the Council, "he admitted freely that before His death Christ had possessed two wills, but he said that He lost on the cross, together with His flesh and blood, His human will. This last point the priest Constantine had learned from Macarius."[435] Macarius' answer to the Council was very different. At the eighth session, the Emperor demanded he accept the teaching of the holy and Ecumenical Synod and profess

> That in our one Lord Jesus Christ, our true God, there are two natures unconfusedly, unchangeably, undividedly, and two natural wills and two natural operations; and all who have taught, and who now say, that there is but one will and one operation in the two natures of our one Lord Jesus Christ our true God, we anathematise.

The answer of Macarius was, "I do not say that there are two wills or two operations in the dispensation of the incarnation of our Lord Jesus Christ, but one will and one theandric operation."[436] Macarius completely denied the union of wills and the two wills, and was deposed.

Importantly, the Council of 680-81 was before John Maroun was elected patriarch of Antioch. The consolation for the Maronites of

[433] Hefele, *A History of the Councils*, Vol. V, pp. 172-173. Those declared Monothelite heretics by the Council were: Theodore of Pharan, Sergius, Cyrus, Honorius, Pyrrhus, Paul, Peter, Macarius, Stephen, Polychronius, Apergius of Perga. Extracts from the *Third Council of Constantinople*.
[434] Dib, *History of the Maronite Church*, p. 17, citing Mansi, t. XI, col. 618-19.
[435] Dib, *History of the Maronite Church*, p. 17. The view of Dib and *The Catholic Encyclopedia* is that the priest Constantine was not deposed for this view. This contrasts with Hefele's view that the same priest was deposed from the Council.
[436] Ibid.

having the attention on Macarius is the significance ancient historians placed on the prominence and leadership of the Maronites in the
patriarchate of Antioch during this period. It implies they must have
been the only indigenous Catholic Melkites in the patriarchate with
the ethnic Greek Catholic Melkites, both led by the Beit Maroun party.

It is here we can further detect the ongoing undertones of conflict between Rome and Constantinople. Immediately after Macarius'
deposition, Rome appeared to have negotiated with and temporarily
silenced Constantinople and the emperor over the Monothelite issue.
It is not certain but they may have temporarily restored the democratic
practice of patriarchs to Antioch being elected by bishops, hence over-
riding Constantinople's former authority and interference over the appointment. This would not have been pleasing to Constantinople and
the displeasure was to come to a head with the emperor's attack on,
and attempted arrest of, Pope Sergius around 692 and the official re-
introduction of Monothelitism in 711.

As part of this review, further research is necessary to carefully
examine the accuracy of many details surrounding the events of this
time. This would include but is not limited to: citation of the full acts
of the Council of 680-681 including the presence of bishops from
Antioch; any information about the appointment and residency of
Macarius, void of Antioch connections; the appointment or election
of Theophanes; events following Theophanes' death; the severing of
what appeared to be communication ties between Antioch on the one
hand and Rome and Constantinople after the heavy Byzantine loss to
the Arabs around Syria in about 692-695;[437] and the vacancy in the
see of Antioch from about 702. On present evidence, Doueihi and Assemani's accounts of the events relating to John Maroun remain the
most plausible.

One legend that may have been the cause of attribution of Monothelitism to the Maronites around the time of Macarius and the Sixth

---

[437] Brock suggests "Syria was effectively cut off in the seventh century from the
Greek-speaking world by the Arab invasions." See Brock, *From Ephrem to Romanus*,
p. 159. As detailed elsewhere this book suggests this was more likely after 692-695.

Council relates to the Mardaites. As discussed in the previous chapter, they were Byzantine bought 'slaves' or mercenaries from Asia Minor around 677-78 who formed into a military body run by the emperor during the last half of the seventh century. The emperor and patriarch of Constantinople were Monothelite, and so their slaves or mercenaries were likely of his same religion. Because the Mardaites were transported into the Aramaic-speaking Catholic region, they have become conflated with the Maronites, who in turn have become conflated with Monothelitism.

## 9.3   The Maronite-Melkite Connection

Prior to the late seventh century or early eighth century, it is reasonable to propose all Melkites in the patriarchate of Antioch were a confederation of Catholics, partisan to the Chalcedonian party. The most prominent leader of this party, particularly for the indigenous Aramaic speakers, was the Beit Maroun monastic network. The term 'Melkite' meant they were royalists, that is, loyal to the king.

The Melkites included both ethnic 'Greek' (Byzantine) and indigenous Aramaic speakers. The ethnic Greeks were primarily in the city of Antioch and scattered in smaller numbers principally in the Byzantine administrative cities of the patriarchate of Antioch. They generally consisted of Greek colonists (and their descendants), mainly foreigners sent out from Constantinople as government officials who spoke Greek and until the Arab conquest had the strong support of the government and the army.[438] Until the mid-eighth century many of their monks came from the major Greek-speaking cultural centres of Byzantium.[439]

The ethnic Greek Melkites were bilingual in Greek and Aramaic-Syriac and up to the fifth century Greek was the dominant liter-

---

[438] Adrian Fortescue, "Melchites" in *The Catholic Encyclopedia*, Robert Appleton Company, 1911, available at: http://www.newadvent.org/cathen/10157b.htm.
[439] Samuel Noble and Alexander Treiger (eds), *The Orthodox Church in the Arab World 700-1700. An Anthology of Sources*, Northern Illinois University Press, 2014, pp. 20-23.

ary language after which Aramaic-Syriac began to appear in texts.[440] Their liturgical language was Greek until the tenth century.[441] There is evidence in cities like Antioch that during mass Greek was instantly translated to Aramaic as part of the service. There is also evidence from the early Arab period of liturgical texts side-by-side in both Greek and Syriac. However, soon Greek appeared in Syriac characters, indicating it had become the secondary language.[442] The liturgy was Antiochian until the tenth or eleventh century, rather than Byzantine (Constantinopolitan).[443] It is likely ethnic Greek Melkites utilised Byzantine church architecture including the iconostasis, as well as some Byzantine customs.

In addition to documentary evidence, there would be a host of sociological reasons to support the proposition ethnic Greeks maintained Greek language in their church services up to the seventh century. Communities were proud of their heritage as they are today. Greek was the language and often the ethnicity of the emperor. Greek became the official language of the empire in the sixth century.[444] Antioch was well known as a Greek-speaking city, the capital of the patriarchate, and the closest city of the patriarchate to the Greek-speaking world. It is unlikely the ethnic Greeks in Antioch would have been willing, in any generation, to give up their heritage. This all tilted the royalist term 'Melkite' in their favour. They eventually took over the exclusive expression and use of the term as loyal to and conforming to the emperor's views.

The indigenous Aramaic-speaking Melkites (known as Maronites sometime during the fifth to sixth century) were located throughout

---

[440] Brock, *From Ephrem to Romanos*, pp. 149-153.
[441] Archbishop Joseph Tawil, *The Patriarchate of Antioch Throughout History: An Introduction*, Sophia Press, 2001, p. 43.
[442] Ibid., pp. 158-59.
[443] Brock et al., *Gorgias Encyclopaedia Dictionary of the Syriac Heritage*, p. 285.
[444] In 425, the university in Constantinople had fifteen professors of Latin and sixteen professors of Greek. In 535 Greek took over from Latin as the official language of the state (Count Marcellinus, *Count Marcellinus and his Chronicle*, trans. by B. Coke, Oxford University Press, 2001, pp. 84-86).

the Byzantine provinces of the patriarchate of Antioch, including the capital Antioch and other cities. In the cities they were bilingual also speaking and writing Greek, particularly the educated who would have held some government posts. The indigenous would have constituted almost all of the population in the towns and countryside. After the construction of Beit Maroun by the Emperor Marcian in 452, it appears as convention that indigenous Aramaic-speaking clergy and monks were educated in Greek as well as Aramaic-Syriac. By the early fifth century at the latest, there is evidence of indigenous Melkites as metropolitan archbishops as well as being electing patriarchs of Antioch.

After the arrival of the Arab Muslims at Antioch in 638, the Melkites (Maronites and Byzantines) may have temporarily had contact with Rome and Constantinople severed. The Arabs would have identified them as loyal to the Byzantine emperor. The Syriac scholar Brock states the reference to the term 'Melkite' during this period appeared to be one and the same as Maronites (i.e. belonging to the party led by Beit Maroun) or Maronite Melkites.[445] Brock suggests that over time subsequent events led to the Melkites (ethnic Greek Byzantines) dominating the cities with the Maronites retreating into Lebanon.[446] However, this view can be contrasted with the evidence demonstrated throughout this book of substantial Maronite colonies remaining in cities outside of Lebanon such as in Aleppo, Damascus, and Akko (Acre).

Up to the seventh century, the Catholics in the patriarchate of Antioch, including to an extent unknown in the island of Cyprus, were principally of two ethnicities, united as one in faith. Initially they may have practised two slightly different liturgies, one Greek Byzantine and the other Aramaic-Syriac, but both as Antiochian rites. The languages and architectural styles and some customs were different. There is evidence some churches and monasteries practised a combined liturgy. Outside of Cyprus and outside of the city of Antioch, the patriarchate of Antioch was almost exclusively of the Syriac rite.

---

[445] Brock, *Syriac Perspectives on Late Antiquity*, p. 69.
[446] Brock, *The Seventh Century in the West-Syrian Chronicles*, pp. 26-27.

The communities in the city of Antioch were multicultural in faith, language, and ethnicity. The Christian denominations coexisted in relative harmony. Ethnicities included Armenian, Jewish, and Arab. They may have included Europeans such as the French. After the arrival of the Arabs, the city would have included Muslims. Through cross-cultural marriage, the ethnic Greek Melkites would likely have had a minority of people with mixed ethnicities including indigenous Aramaic ancestry. This would apply in reverse for the Maronites who would have had a minority of ethnic Greek ancestry. The Maronites adhered to the Catholic Church teachings. They were the prominent leaders of the Chalcedonian party in the patriarchate especially for the indigenous. The ethnic Greeks were also aligned to the party.

Prior to 638, there were discussions amongst theologians about the will of Christ, however, it was not until 638 with the *Ecthesis* of Emperor Heraclius, that official teaching throughout the Empire was that Christ had one will, divine. This decree was in the same year and virtually the same time as the fall of Antioch, the last Syrian frontier of the Byzantine Empire. A 'Maronite Chronicle' from 659 informs us the Maronites remained Melkite at that time, loyal to the emperor, and so were likely still Monothelite.[447]

### 9.3.1. Formation of Melkite/Antiochian Orthodox Church

The process of separation of the ethic Greek-Byzantine Melkites and Maronite Melkites is extremely obscure.[448] According to Doueihi, a division occurred amongst the Melkites after the election of John Maroun as patriarch of Antioch in 686-87. It related to the doctrine of two wills and the election of John Maroun as patriarch of Antioch. Now those supporting Rome and the doctrine of two wills could not be called 'Melkite' – they were Maronites. They were no longer loyal

---

[447] For more on this see Brock, *The Seventh Century West Syrian Chronicles*, pp. 29-35.
[448] Brock agrees in a private email to the author of 3 May 2017. See also Cyril Charon (Korolevsky), *History of the Melkite Patriarchates (Volume I), Pre-Modern Period (869-1833)*, trans. by John Collorafi, ed. by Bishop Nicholas Samra, Eastern Christian Publications, 1998, p. 2, who dates the history of the Melkite Patriarchate of Antioch with Nicholas I from 847 AD.

to the emperor. Those supporting Constantinople and the emperor re-tained the title of Melkite. This coincided with the Byzantine-Arab peace treaty of the same year resulting in the withdrawal of Byzantine troops from the Middle East in exchange for annual payments by the Arabs.

Douehi's account is the opposite to Tell Mahre's version. A de-tailed technical analysis of Douehi and Tell Mahre's written record-ings are set out later in this Chapter. In this context, it is important to keep in mind that a substantial population in Constantinople including the emperor remained Monothelite until at least the early 700s and the Greeks in Alexandria as Melkites remained Monothelite until 742-43.[449]

Tell Mahre's explanations of the division of the Melkites contain several contradictions. Each account describes the Melkites as Mono-thelites and bases their dispute over the introduction of the doctrine of two wills which, he states, resulted in a division into Melkites and Maronites. In one account he states the division in the Melkites was in 727. In another account he states the division was in 745. Tell Mahre's first two accounts can be contrasted with his third. Tell Mahre com-ments that in the mid-eighth century there was a dispute between the Maronites and the Melkites over possession of the great cathedral in Aleppo where fighting took place inside the church building. The Muslim governor of the city ordered a wooden petition to be erected in the middle of the church so each group had its own section. The women joined in the fighting that took place inside the church build-ing. The two groups reconciled and became the followers of Maximus, maintaining the doctrine of two wills in Christ.[450]

Michael the Syrian, writing in the twelfth century about an event in the early eighth century, states that he relies on ninth century Tell

---

[449] See Chapter 8 of this book.

[450] Moosa, *The Maronites in History*, p. 102. Moosa suggests on the same page: "with the exception of the congregation of Aleppo, (the Maronites) remained Monothelites and maintained one will in Christ." Moosa's views are not reliable. The passage from Tell Mahre adds weight that the incident was more likely to be between 638-649 and the allegations of Monothelitism attributed to the Maronites is a legend.

Mahre as a key source. We do not know how much Michael the Syrian embellished Tell Mahre's works. However, we do know the partiality was substantial with phrases directed at the Chalcedonians such as: "wickedness," "filled with demons," "impious," "evil," bishops as "wicked and depraved men," and epidemics killing 36,000 people in Amida because of their adherence to Chalcedon.[451] It is also stated after the Monophysite Patriarch Severus was deposed from Antioch in 518, "fire fell from heaven and burned the royal palace in that city. Nor did the fire cease for six years. Indeed, it burned the entire city, to the point that it seemed that the fire itself was alive."[452] This may sound like strong language today, but it was more typical of the period when writing about rival churches.

As demonstrated previously in this book, the Maronites were a constant rival to the Syriac Jacobites of which both Michael the Syrian and Dionysius of Tell Mahre belonged. The contradictions and confusion of Tell Mahre's accounts and our knowledge of historical circumstances give credence to the likelihood that his references relate to a period before 727. It also gives credence to Doueihi's account as being more reliable. Tell Mahre informs us a bitter dispute also took place at the same time over the Trisagion prayer in the liturgy (explained in more detail below). It then becomes difficult to determine whether the separation occurred because of the dispute over the Trisagion or the will of Christ.[453]

The most plausible set of circumstances from this complex issue and the clash of evidence between Doueihi and Tell Mahre is suggested as follows. After 638 the Melkites/Maronites were adherents of the doctrine of the *Ecthesis* (one will in Christ), the official dogma of the empire and of Pope Honorios. At some stage, between the Lateran Council decree of 649 and the official Ecumenical Council decree of 681, they adopted the doctrine of two wills in Christ, possibly as a result of direct influence from the Church of Rome. This was not pleas-

[451] Michael the Syrian, *Chronicle of Michael the Great*, paragraph 105.
[452] Ibid., paragraph 88.
[453] See discussion in Brock, *The Seventh Century West Syrian Chronicles*, pp. 25-27.

ing to those Melkites, probably ethic Greek Catholics both in Antioch city and in the administrative Byzantine cities throughout the patriarchate, who wished to remain loyal to the emperor. John (Yuhanna) Maroun was elected patriarch of Antioch in 686-7, but the Emperor opposed his appointment. This elevated the differences between the Melkites-Maronites: those who wished to remain loyal to the emperor kept the title Melkites, and the Maronites who wished to remain loyal to the Pope of Rome lost the title Melkites.

Maronite Melkite and Greek Melkite liturgical and canonical texts did contain numerous Monothelite references. This was the official teaching of the Pope and the Empire immediately upon the arrival of the Arab Islam conquest in 638. It is remarkable that by the ninth century these texts are only the minority, both in Maronite and Melkite Churches,[454] despite constant references to the Maronites being Monothelite until the twelfth century. It is extraordinary that Tell Mahre (or Michael the Syrian) refers to the Greek Melkites favouring the two wills of Christ as the reason for separation from the Maronite Melkites in 727 or 745, yet the Greek Melkite texts remained Monothelite two centuries later.

In any event, those who severed ties from Beit Maroun were seen as remaining loyal to the emperor. They kept the title of Melkite. Their population would likely have been substantially the ethnic Greeks centred on the cities of Antioch and Jerusalem and smaller ethnic Greek settlements around the patriarchate. In about the eighth century, when the caliphs regained full control of the Middle East, the Melkite-Maronite communication with Constantinople and Rome would have been crippled or severed. It is from this period they would have begun to experience an increase in persecution by the Muslim rulers. In the *Annals* of Tell Mahre he records the Caliph Marwan II (reign 744-750) in 745 permitting the Melkites to elect a patriarch, Theophilactos ben Qanbarah, but that previous requests were denied.

The Maronites were spread throughout northern Palestine, Leba-

---

[454] Brock, *Syriac Perspectives on Late Antiquity*, p. 345.

non, and northern Syria. Maronite presence and communication with Antioch would have declined, certainly after this incident. From the eighth century, the Maronites and Melkites suffered under Islamic rule in addition to being persecuted as Christians. The Melkites faced hardship for their allegiance to the emperor, remaining principally in the cities. The Maronites suffered for their likely retention of a military organization, eventually based in the Lebanon mountains, and attempting isolation and opposition to Islamic rule. Based on Doueihi, this Maronite military body had also previously provided a formidable opposition to the Muslim armies. Not long after the early eighth century, it appears Rome had lost formal contact with the Middle East.

The Maronites, remaining under the leadership of Beit Maroun confederation of monasteries and their appointed patriarch of Antioch, were no longer referred to as Melkite. Their physical means of affiliation with Antioch was diminished, not just by the Arabs, but by the Byzantine Melkites. With the overwhelming majority of the Maronite population located in northern Palestine, Lebanon, and in lower northern Syria (nearer to the border of Lebanon), another new chapter in the history of the Maronites was established.

From the late eighth century the new Greek genre of liturgical poetry, the canon, began to be translated by the Greek Melkites into Syriac (and eventually reaching the Syrian Orthodox as well). Some Greek texts began to be translated into Arabic in the late eighth century. In the tenth to twelfth centuries, the Constantinople liturgical rite replaced that of the Melkite Antiochene rite, and this involved translations of large numbers of liturgical texts from Greek into Syriac and Arabic.[455] The Greek Melkites were therefore tri-lingual. Syriac remained the liturgical language from the tenth to seventeenth centuries after which it was abandoned for Arabic.[456] It seems that for the Melkites, communication with Constantinople and Rome was fully restored in the middle of the tenth century when the Byzantine Empire regained control of Antioch. For the Maronites, restoration of contact

---

[455] Ibid.
[456] Tawil, *The Patriarchate of Antioch Throughout History*, p. 43.

with the West most likely occurred with the arrival of the Crusades in the late eleventh century.

Amidst the turmoil and chaos of the seventh and eighth centuries, obscuring the details of the separation of the Maronites and Melkites and leaving many contradictions in the limited sources available, both the Melkites and Maronites can legitimately claim Catholic Orthodox succession to the patriarchate of Antioch from this time. Up to around 1054 AD, the Christians in the East of the Empire who remained loyal to the Catholic faith were known to the Byzantines as the 'Orthodox'. They were placed into the category of being in unison with the Church's teaching. However, the Melkite succession was interrupted when they became Byzantine (Greek) Orthodox for many centuries after the Great East-West Schism between Rome and Constantinople in the eleventh century.

Since the great East-West schism, the West's popular use of the term 'Orthodox' took on a different meaning. It became a reference to all non-Catholics of the East, including those churches, such as the Syriac Orthodox Jacobites and the Coptic Orthodox, who were not part of the Catholic Church prior to the eleventh century Byzantine-Roman split in the Catholic Church. In the Middle East, the term 'Roum' remains today generally a reference to the Greek (Antiochian) Orthodox. You occasionally hear Melkite Catholics referred to as *milkiyyu*. The common expression for the Melkites is 'Roum Catholique', literally translated as 'Orthodox Catholics', but meaning Byzantine Catholic. It is a religious rather than ethnic reference.

The Greeks have traditionally dominated the position of patriarch of Antioch for the Byzantine Orthodox Church in the Middle East. Since the formation of the Melkite Catholic Church in 1724, the patriarch of the Antiochian Orthodox Church and its high clergy until 1898 remained ethnic Greek but more recently are entirely native to the Middle East. The patriarch of Jerusalem is still an ethnic Greek up until today.[457]

---

[457] Timothy Ware, The Orthodox Church, Penguin Books, 1997, pp. 134-135.

## 9.4 Assessing the Sources

### 9.4.1 The *Annals* of Dionysius of Tell Mahre (d. 818) cited by Michael the Syrian (d. 1199)

The Chronicle of Michael the Syrian, Syriac Jacobite Patriarch from 1166-1199 set out the *Annals* of Syriac Jacobite Patriarch Dionysius of Tell Mahre. Here it is suggested that around 727 AD Greek prisoners arrived in Syria and instigated a discussion concerning the doctrine of two wills. It proposes the Melkites (Maronites) believed in the doctrine of one will in Christ in accordance with official Church dogma before communication ties were severed by Arab Muslim conquest, not long after 638 when Antioch fell to the Arabs. The relevant passage from Tell Mahre is as follows:

> Although we have already spoken of the heresy of Maximus (Maximus the Confessor) and of the manner in which Constantinus (Constantine Pogonatus) introduced it in the churches of the Romans, after it had been wiped out by his father, Constant, we ought now to take note of the schism which survived among them (the Chalcedonians) in this year 727 regarding this heresy and the expression who has been crucified. In the Roman territory, this opinion continues since the time of Constantinus, **but in the regions of Syria, it was not admitted**. It is being sown now by prisoners and captives that the troops of Taiyaye (Arabs) have led into and placed in Syria. No doubt, because of their esteem of the Empire of the Romans, those who have allowed themselves to be perverted by this opinion (Dyothelitism) and accepted it were especially the bishops and the chiefs.

> One of them was Sergius, son of Mansour, who oppressed many of the faithful who were at Damascus and Emese. Not only did he make them remove the expression 'who was crucified' from the Trisagion, but he drew also many of ours (Syriac Jacobites) into his heresy. This heresy perverted also the Sees of Jerusalem, Antioch, Edessa and other towns, that the Chalcedonians had occupied since the time of Emperor Heraclius...

The monks of Beth Maron (Maronites) and the Bishop of this Monastery, and some others, did not accept this opinion (the two wills), but the majority of the (towns) people and their bishops did. How many anathemas (were delivered), how many fights up to the present cannot be enumerated nor reckoned. In the discussions, the Chalcedonians of the party of Beth Maron insulted the Maximites: 'You are Nestorians, the companions of the pagans and the Jews. You do not say that Christ is God, that He was born of the Virgin, that He suffered and was crucified in the flesh, He is an ordinary man, an individual person, abandoned by God, who feared and dreaded His death and cried: "My Father! If it be possible, would that the chalice pass from Me, nevertheless your will and not mine be done," as if one and another were the wills of the Father and the Son; that is, there would therefore be in Christ two wills separated and opposed, or even enemies, and battle one against the other'.[458]

The most important passage of the text is highlighted in bold font above, and has been subject to multiple translations. The translation of three scholars, Moosa, Brock, and Dib, are as follows:

"it was not at all known in Syria" (translation of Moosa);

"it had not been accepted in Syria" (translation of Brock);

"it was not admitted in Syria" (translation of Dib).

The consequences of these translations will be discussed below.

One should be cautious in relying on the text set out by Tell Mahri for many reasons including:

- The Chronicle of Michael the Syrian is a third party source. It relies on Tell Mahre as a secondary source. It is not known to what extent, if any, Michael the Syrian embellished Tell Mahre's works.

- Tell Mahre was not a witness in the period 727 – he lived

---

[458] Dib, *History of the Maronite Church*, pp. 18-19. Dib cites the chronicle of Michael the Syrian. The word '(towns)' has been inserted from Brock's translation in *Syriac Perspectives on Late Antiquity*, p. 69.

more than one hundred years after. He also lived almost two hundred years after the intensive period of the controversy relating to the will of Christ.

- The Chronicle of Michael the Syrian is written nearly six hundred years after the introduction of the belief of one will in Christ.

- The secondary source relied upon by Michael the Syrian, i.e. the *Annales* of Tell Mahre, have not been located.

- Both Michael the Syrian and Tell Mahre were Syriac Orthodox (Jacobites) and often their church did not look favourably upon the Maronites. Further, they looked at the issue from the eyes of Monophysites.

- The translation of this text relied upon by modern historians is disputed and has three vastly different interpretations.

- At the debate between the Maronites and the Jacobites in 658-59 before the future caliph Mo'awiah, there was no reference to the energies or wills in Christ.[459]

- Tell Mahre makes no mention of the doctrine from the decree of the Third Council of Constantinople in 681. He only refers to the Maximites. This is a reference to the followers of Maximus the Confessor and to a period prior to the Lateran Council decree of 649. After the Council of 681, the talk would not have been about Maximus but about the Council. Prior to 649, there would have been many Byzantine prisoners of the Arabs. It appears more likely that the date of the event Tell Mahre refers to is between the issue of the emperor's *Ecthesis* in 638 and the Lateran Council condemnation in 649 or up to the Council of 680-81. This opinion is supported somewhat by an implication from the scholar Brock. He confirms Maximus hardly rates a mention in the acts of the Council of 680-81.[460]

- We are led to believe by the text that there was no communication between the Middle East on the one hand and

---

[459] Dib, *History of the Maronite Church*, p. 17, citing Tell Mahre in Michael the Syrian and Germain of Constantinople (715-730).

[460] Brock, *Syriac Perspectives on Late Antiquity*, p. 343.

Constantinople in Rome after the emperor's issue of the *Ecthesis* in 638. It appears from texts set out further below in this chapter and from events recorded in the previous chapter, this is clearly not correct. Further, Theopanes records the Byzantine – Arab treaty of 678, three years before the Sixth Council, brought peace and freedom from care in the East and West.[461]

- We know there are practically no contemporary sources that can assist us for the period of the late seventh century and early eighth century.
- Brock cites evidence that the doctrine of two wills controversy had been admitted into Syria (the Middle East) rather earlier than 727.[462]

Moosa interprets the text to read that all of the Christians throughout the Syrian Orient were Monothelites after Emperor Heraclius imposed Monothelitism as a new doctrine in 638. He states any mention of two wills did not occur in the Middle East until 727 when Greek prisoners arrived. Remarkably, Moosa utilises this same text to conclude that the monks of Maroun knew of the Sixth Ecumenical Council (Third Council of Constantinople) prior to 727.[463] Thus, Tell Mahre's text leads us to believe there was no debate in the Middle East at the time Monothelitism was introduced, which is Moosa's argument also. That there was no discussion until 727 must be rejected as inconsistent with Church convention and the typical intellectual debates of the faithful especially as one cannot understand the theology of either one will or two wills without understanding the principles of the other.

Brock translates Tell Mahre's passage with its most important words reading "it had not been accepted in Syria." He states that, contrary to the views of well-meaning apologists for the Maronite Church, the Dyothelite-Monothelite issue was well entrenched throughout Syria-

---

[461] Theophanes, *The Chronicle of Theophanes*, pp. 53-54.

[462] Brock, *Syriac Perspectives on Late Antiquity*, p. 70.

[463] Moosa, *The Maronites in History*, pp. 101-109.

Palestine prior to the arrival of Greek prisoners in 727. The previous chapter of this book confirms communication and travel between the Middle East and the West was open.

Tell Mahre complains there was "no bishop from Egypt, Syria, Palestine or Armenia" present at the Sixth Council. Brock has suggested this implies *all* the Chalcedonians (i.e. the present Maronites and Melkites) in these regions were Monothelite until 727, they were opposed to the Dyothelite theology, and Tell Mahre (via Michael the Syrian) is implying that if these bishops had been present at the Council the declarations would have been different.[464] Every historian appears to have relied on Michael the Syrian's comments and this has multiplied the confusion over the topic. For example, Brock comments, "though he [Macarius] lived far from his flock, thanks to the political situation, was at least representative of their opinions. It is also significant that the only Syrian who was present at the Council and who intervened, was also opposed to Dyothelite theology."[465]

It is noteworthy that there is no mention of Phoenicia or Lebanon. Also, Brock flags a contradiction in Tell Mahre's passage citing a letter in 720/721 of Sophronius, Patriarch of Jerusalem, noting he was one of the main defenders of Dyothelite theology and this was before Tell Mahre's date of 727 as the first acceptance of the Dyothelitism. Other contradictions include, as previously stated, that the Greeks in Alexandria remained Monothelite until 742-43 and a substantial part of the population in Constantinople remained Monothelite until 750 including at least two emperors.

Although utilising a different translation, Dib takes the same view as Moosa that the doctrine of two wills was not known in Syria before 727. Based on Dib and Moosa, the Melkites were asked to accept, as hearsay, the oral account of Byzantine prisoners related to the belief in two wills of Christ. It was passed from the frontline to Antioch and much further to the south of northern Syria. There is no reference to these prisoners being clergy (i.e. priests or monks). The prisoners

[464] Brock, *Syriac Perspectives on Late Antiquity*, p. 70
[465] Ibid.

were likely not to have known the date, the decision or detail of the Council's decree.

Tell Mahre does not mention the 'doctrine' of the Catholic Church, or the Council meeting in Constantinople. The information imparted by the prisoners may have been the belief in two wills after 649, rather than a doctrine of two wills. Tell Mahre does inform us that the introduction of the debate over two wills caused a schism in the Melkite Church in 727. One group preferred the explanation of two wills by Maximus the Confessor; the other group opposed that explanation. The two groups became known on the one hand as Maximites, adhering to the dogma of two wills in Christ, and the other Maronites, adhering to one will in Christ.

Critically, Moosa refers us to a passage from Tell Mahre describing an incident from 745:

> In the year (745) Marwan the King (Caliph) of the Arabs permitted the Chalcedonians (Malkites) to consecrate a patriarch for their denomination who was Theophilact Ibn Qanbara from Harran. Theophilact was Marwan's goldsmith. He obtained from the Caliph an order for troops to persecute the Maronites. When he arrived at the monastery of Marun he harassed its monks to accept the doctrine of Maximus and desist from reciting the Trisagion with the phrase "Thou who wast crucified for us." Agonised by affliction, the monks promised Theophilact that on the next day they would submit to his order ... And the Maronites remained as they are *today* consecrating for themselves a patriarch and bishops from their monasteries. They are distinguished from the followers of Maximus for the belief in one will in Christ ... But they accept the Council of Chalcedon ... Finally, Andrew the Maronite obtained an order from the caliphs and built a church for the Maronites in Manbij. They then became separate from the followers of Maximus. And many disgusting and abominable affairs happen between these two groups.[466]

---

[466] Moosa, *The Maronites in History*, p. 114.

Once again, Tell Mahre's reference to Maximus is most likely to a time earlier than 727. Tell Mahre informs us that before the separation of the Melkites in 745 there was no Chalcedonian patriarch of Antioch. This is implausible. This also contradicts his own passage regarding the incident in 727 which implied the same dispute and that the separation took place in 727 not 745.

As previously noted, Moosa's translation of this text relating to the ordination of a Maronite patriarch varies from that of Dib. Moosa inserts the word 'today' and says there was no Maronite patriarch before 745. However, the interpretation of the text allows a conclusion that the Maronites had their own patriarch prior to this event in 745 and were resisting the appointment of a patriarch by the Maximites. It was the Maximites who sought permission to have a patriarch not the Maronites. Remarkably, Tell Mahre says this patriarch was the Caliph's goldsmith. This cannot be accepted as a reliable account. Furthermore, the Caliph attempted to force the Maronites to recognise the appointment of a Melkite patriarch and to cease to elect their own patriarch, but they refused.[467]

Dib's rendition of events, relying on Tell Mahre's text, is that in the eighth century the Melkite Chalcedonians, that is the Maronites, became spilt into two. The first group were the Maximites, Melkite Chalcedonians who were followers of the Dyothelite doctrine preached by Maximus the Confessor. They separated themselves from Beit Maroun and the traditional Melkite patriarch of Antioch. The second group were the Maronites, the Melkite Chalcedonians who were followers of the Dyothelite doctrine opposing Maximus. They were already known as and remained Maronite, but were misunderstood to be Monothelites.[468]

Dib states that both the Maximite Melkites and the Maronite Melkite were Antiochian and adherents to the doctrine of two natures in Christ decreed in 451. Both agreed Jesus Christ had two wills but differed on its meaning. Had their communication not being cut from

---

[467] Dau, *History of the Maronites*, p. 206, citing Michael the Syrian.
[468] Dib, *History of the Maronite Church*, p. 15.

Constantinople and Rome, the dispute would not have arisen. Likewise, had they been able to attend or read the decree of the Council in 681. In the difficulties of the times, they must be forgiven for the misunderstandings.

Dib argues that even though both groups agreed that Jesus Christ had two wills, their arguing indicates a general lack of understanding. The confusion about the Maronites then spread. The first relevant extant written account in the East we have today is that of Eutychius (Sa'id Ibn Batriq), Melchite (Maximite) Patriarch of Alexandria (933-940). His comments were followed in the West by the Crusader chroniclers. And so, says Dib, the "legend of Maronite Monothelitism was born, developed, and incorporated into history."[469]

Dib provides a useful insight to other factors:

> The introduction of Byzantine usages in the church of Antioch widened the breach which separated into two camps the defenders of the Fourth Ecumenical Council. Known at first by the name of Chalcedonians, they were later called by their adversaries by the name of Melkites (the Emperor's party), because of the bonds which tied them to Constantinople.

> However, this name Melkite, given to Timothy Salofaciol, Bishop of Alexandria, who died in 482, was used in Syria, we believe, only after the arrival of the Arabs. It is encountered, for the first time, in the letters of the Nestorian patriarch, Timothy I (d. 823). It was applied to all the Chalcedonians. A writer of the elevnth century, Habib Abou-Raita, Jacobite Metropolitan of Tagrit, tells us that one distinguished between the Melkite Chalcedonians who are Maximites and the Melkite Chalcedonians who are Maronites. However, the former group was drawn more and more to Constantinople; they abandoned the rite and usages of Antioch and adopted those of Constantinople.

> Also, in the succeeding years the name Melkite was reserved exclusively for them. The Maronites, here after having their

---

[469] Ibid., pp. 20-41.

own patriarch, were faithful to the rite and the discipline of Antioch and became separate from the Byzantinized Melkites.[470]

Brock, after considering a Syriac text on Maximus the Confessor, agrees with the theory that the Maximite Melkites broke off from the Maronites.[471] He suggests that up to the early eighth century all the Chalcedonian communities of Syria-Palestine were Melkites (aligned to the Emperor) and represented by the Maronites.[472] Brock suggests they were Monothelites from the time of Heraclius, conforming to Church teachings. After 727, those believing in two wills broke away from the Maronite Melkites as Maximite Melkites. He states that for this reason Monothelite theology is preserved in much later Melkite liturgical and canonical books.

Brock also comments that Monothelite theology views were only found among a minority of Melkites and Maronites from the ninth century onwards and notes: "Furthermore, when looking at the whole controversy, it should be remembered that almost all our information about it comes from Dyothelete sources, and as seen through Dyothelete spectacles."[473] Brock's analysis fits generally with Dib's explanation. It can be said the Maronites were misunderstood as Monothelites after 727, though, on the whole, they were not.

## 9.4.2 Doueihi (d. 1704) and The Maronite College of Rome

For the present topic it is necessary to quote once more Doueihi on the 676 consecration of the priest John Maroun as bishop of Batroun in Lebanon:

The Pope's delegate came to Antioch to preach the dogma

---

[470] Ibid., pp. 47-48.

[471] Brock, *Syriac Perspectives on Late Antiquity*, p. 345.

[472] Ibid., chapters XII, XIII, p. 343. Brock's reference to Syria-Palestine is assumed to include Phoenicia and Lebanon. It should be noted that after the Maximite Melkites formed their church, it is probable Chalcedonians from northern Palestine, including the areas formerly under the patriarchate of Antioch, remained Maronite and Melkite. The ethnic Greeks centred in Jerusalem were more likely to have constituted Maximite Melkites.

[473] Brock, *Syriac Perspectives on the Late Antiquity*, p. 71.

of the two natures and two wills in Jesus Christ. In that time Macarius, the Antiochian patriarch living in Constantinople, professed the official dogma of the Byzantine Empire, that is to say the one will in Jesus Christ. John Maroun attracted by his deeds and faith the attention of the French prince Eugene who presented him to the Pope's delegate. The cardinal concentrated John Maroun Bishop of Batroun and Mount Lebanon with the mission of preserving the Roman Catholic faith in Lebanon ...

He (John Maroun) joined his flock in Lebanon, working with the zeal of Apostles for the conversion of non-Catholics. Under the guidance of St Maroun, the Maronite community increased greatly in number, and took possession of Mount Lebanon and the mountain range from Cilicia and Armenia to Jerusalem.[474]

If Doueihi is correct that the Pope's delegate visited John Maroun in 676, John Maroun, as a bishop and former monk of Beit Maroun, would have been well aware from at least that time of Rome's adherence to the belief in two wills in Christ.

Further, as stated in the previous chapter, Doueihi refers to Patriarch John Maroun's visit to Rome in 687 as coinciding with the Byzantine-Arab treaty where the emperor's forces withdrew from the Middle East. If John Maroun's visit took place then, the patriarch must have known of Constantinople's decree of the Third Council in 681 declaring Monothelitism a heresy. It is difficult to argue that John Maroun would thereafter not have his Maronite faithful in the patriarchate follow Church doctrine. Though only theories at this stage, the following propositions are now put forward as a plausible explanation for the events that would follow. It is based on the relevant texts we have from Doueihi for the period.

Rome and Constantinople had been bitterly divided on the will of Jesus Christ for many decades. Constantinople directly controlled patriarchal appointments of Antioch, contrary to convention and canon

---

[474] Harb, *The Maronites: History and Constants*, p. 74, citing Doueihi, p. 63.

law. The patriarch of Antioch resided in Constantinople and never visited Antioch. John Maroun, declaring his loyalty to Rome in becoming patriarch of Antioch, and then travelling to Rome, became an enemy to Constantinople.

The Emperor issued a 'death warrant' for John Maroun. Constantinople was determined to terminate John Maroun's life, the same way it did for Pope Martin I who opposed the emperor in 649. John Maroun was hunted down in Syria, Beit Maroun was attacked, and he fled to Lebanon. The emperor's forces followed him and the Maronite military wing stationed in Lebanon defeated the emperor's forces. Based on Doueihi, we must assume the Maronites could no longer be called 'Melkite' or royalists after the appointment of Patriarch John Maroun in 686-687 and the adoption of the doctrine of two wills in 676, as they were no longer loyal to the emperor. It is at this point, around 676 or after 686-687 rather than 727 as alleged by Tell Mahre, that there must have been a division in the Melkites.

The new Maronite theology negotiated and deemed acceptable by Rome was the union of two wills. In the East, the Maronites were misunderstood to be Monothelites. After the appointment of John Maroun in 686-687, the Melkites who wished to remain loyal to the emperor kept the title of Melkite. They would have been substantially the ethnic Greeks centred around the administrative cities including Antioch and Jerusalem. From about the eighth century, when the caliphs gained full control of the Middle East, the Melkite and Maronite communication with Constantinople and Rome respectively would have been crippled or severed. It is from this period they would have begun to experience an increase in persecution by the Muslim rulers. The Maronites who remained part of the Beit Maroun confederation headed by Patriarch John Maroun, were loyal to Rome. They were spread throughout northern Palestine, Lebanon, Phoenicia and northern Syria. Maronite communication with Antioch would have declined.

Unfortunately, examination of the issues in this book does not cite the original of Doueihi's works, and the references to the documents he relied on, as they are not in English. For almost all authors whose works are in English attributing Monothelitism to the Maronites, it appears they have failed to consider Patriarch Doueihi's references to John Maroun noted above. They may have also failed to consider this in the context of the seventeenth and eighteenth century critiques by Nairon and Doueihi, and later Darian and Dib that followed in the twentieth century on the moral sense of Monothelitism. On consideration of all of the information and the various authors' views on the subject set out above, the most plausible account appears to be that of Doueihi's. While Brock, Moosa, and Dib have not questioned the 727 date of Tell Mahre, this book suggests a reconsideration by scholars.

### 9.4.3 Clashes Between the Sources

The Maronite College of Rome was established in 1584. Maronite students and graduates of the College began modern comprehensive analyses of the abundant ancient texts they had at hand. They were trained and fluent in various languages. In the late seventeenth century, two graduates explained that the Monothelitism that has been attributed to the Maronites was a Christology other than that condemned by the Catholic Church.[475] This preceded the beginnings of modern opinion in the west on the orthodox thinking of Pope Honorius.

The Maronite College of Rome graduates, Faustus of Naironus and Estephen (Stephen) Doueihi, undertook their works in Latin.[476] Doueihi was later to become Maronite patriarch, and is a key source for this book. They safeguarded the orthodoxy of the Maronites as Catholics. They confirmed that the Maronites believed in the union of two wills in Christ. This has been more recently examined in the works of Ma-

---

[475] Dib, *History of the Maronite Church*, p. 15 describes this as a 'moral Monothelitism' or a moral union of two wills in Christ.

[476] Ibid., citing Faustus of Naironus, *Dissertatio de origine, nomine, ac religione maronitarum* and Doueihi, *Defense de la nation Maronite*, ms. Vat. Syr. 396, fol. 25-27. According to Dau, *History of the Maronites*, p. 593, Faustus of Naironus is Latin for Murhej Nayrun in Arabic. He was born in Rome. His father was born in Ban or Bain, northern Lebanon.

ronite Archbishop Joseph Darian (d. 1920) and Pierre Dib, Maronite Bishop of Cairo from 1946.[477]

Dib devotes a whole chapter of his book to the Monothelite question. He found that after 727, the Maronite Church accepted the doctrine of two wills but it was not in perfect accord with the final Church Council decree a few decades earlier. He states the Maronites were unable to have access to the eloquence of the conciliar definitions from 680-681, as they were cut off. He affirms it was not until 727 that the Dyothelite controversy was re-admitted in Syria by prisoners of the Arabs. As we have seen, this theory, based on Tell Mahre, cannot be correct.

Dib quotes four texts to support his conclusion the Maronites were not Monothelite after 727. Although the texts suggest a moral sense of belief in one will of Christ, not in perfect accord with the decree of 681, they were different from that which was condemned by the Council. The first is a passage from a Maronite missal used in the eleventh century, and which was held by Doueihi. Part of that passage states:

> (Jesus) has entered the world by miracle and marvelously,
> In the union of two natures truly.
> Having one person, he had one will doubly
> With the properties of two natures indivisibly
> the natures remained in one hypostasis divinely.
> Recognised without separation nor confusion.
> By His Divine nature, He performed wonders divinely.
> By His human nature, He endured suffering humanely.
> Paul has said: he has become like us entirely
> Except sin, in equity, impiety, truly.[478]

Dib explains: "It proclaims the doctrine of two natures in the unity of one person, with each nature acting on its own ... He possesses a

---

[477] Dib, *History of the Maronite Church*, p. 15 cites Darian J., *The Substance of the Proofs Concerning the Situation of the Maronite People, from the Beginning in the Fifth Century to the Thirteenth Century* (in Arabic) from 1912.

[478] Ibid., p. 21, citing Ms. Vat. Syr. 396, fol. 24.

double will, but this will is one in the sense that the human faculty is irreversibly submitted to the divine."[479]

A second text comes from the ancient canonical collection of the Maronites translated from Syriac into Arabic in about 1059 and known by the name *Book of Direction*, or *Book of the Law* or *Book of Perfection*. Dib, citing a 1402 copy of the document from the Vatican, translates the text:

> He (Jesus) resembled us in all things except sin … He has one person and two intellectual natures; He is God and man … We do not believe however that He is two, two Christs, two persons, two wills and two energies. Far from it! … He is perfect God … and perfect man. The Melkites and the Maronites are divided on the question of the will (in Christ), the Melkites profess two wills, the Maronites one; and each party brings forth arguments to support its book … The Maronites say (to the Melkites): these two wills that you profess in Christ ought to be either conformed or opposed to each other. If they are conformed to each other one ends up with one will; but if they are opposed to each other, it follows that the divine nature wills what the human nature does not will, and the human nature wills what the divine nature does not will. If this is so, there would be division and opposition, resulting in two (persons in Christ); and therefore (Hypostatic) union would not exist anymore, the Trinity would become a quaternity and one would find himself reduced to the point of view of Nestorius and his opinions on Christ.[480]

Dib makes it clear that the author of this document did not know the doctrine of the Sixth Ecumenical Council in 680, declaring Monothelitism a heresy. He states the Maronite position in the document was: "the human will in Christ would not be denied, since Christ possessed our whole nature, except sin. What is denied, is the possibility of a conflict in Jesus Christ opposing the human will to the divine will, for if the two wills 'are conformed to each other, one ends up with one

[479] Ibid., p. 21.
[480] Ibid., p. 22, citing Vat. Syr. 133, fol. 21, vol. 31.

will'." In other words, the two wills are so united that one would not notice an exterior distinction between them. In summary, this passage of the *Book of Direction* recalls for us the account of Tell Mahre: the Maronites and the Melkites had been united in the same religious faith; they divided on the question of the two wills, the Maronites having understood the two wills as adverse and opposed to each other.[481]

The third text Dib utilises is a response addressed by the Patriarch of the Nestorians, Timothy I (d. 823), to the monks of St Maroun. It provides evidence that the Maronites understood Monothelitism to be the moral union of two wills, divine and human, in Christ.[482] The fourth text was composed in Arabic in 1089 by Maronite bishop, Thomas of Kaphartab. It is known by the name *Ten Chapters* and was addressed to John IV, Melkite Patriarch of Antioch. Dib notes this text is usually quoted in support of the proposition that the Maronites were Monothelite. However, he states that such conclusion is a superficial reading of the passage. Thomas does not appear to deny or doubt the human will for he declares that Christ has subjected entirely to the Divinity "the weakness of the will of His body" and that Christ has said: "I have not come to do the will of my humanity."[483]

Dib concludes:

> This is the doctrine of the Maronite Church. The physical will of Christ has never been denied. It is the idea of a conflict between the two wills of God man that one does not wish to admit. The expression of this idea is confused, but it is necessary to search for the cause in the ignorance of the conciliar definitions of 680-81. Even in the elevnth century, the Maronites were totally unaware of the Sixth Council. It is Thomas of Kaphartab who tells us: "Never have the Councils spoken of two wills." The Maronites were so convinced of it that they regarded themselves united in faith to the 'Franks', that

---

[481] Ibid., p. 24.

[482] Ibid., citing Cod. Borgiano, Syr. 31 of the Vatican, fol. 306.

[483] Ibid., p. 24, citing preserved copy No 203 in the Syriac collection of the *Bibliotheque Nationale* of Paris written in 1470, fol. 90, 93, 103, 105.

is, to the Latins, and found themselves in perfect accord with orthodoxy. This is why, they welcomed with open arms the first Crusaders who arrived in Lebanon in 1099, and rendered them precious services. Then, having learned of the doctrine of the Sixth Ecumenical Council, they hastened to profess explicitly the dogma of the two wills. As it was explained by the Fathers, this dogma was in close accord with the idea the Maronites had of the Incarnation. This is the so-called conversion of the Maronites, as told by the famous historian of the Crusaders, William of Tyre ...

Taken separately, we recognise voluntarily that certain Maronite texts, liturgical and other, can be cited in favour of Monothelitism. But texts cannot be considered in isolation; it is necessary to make a comparative study before drawing final conclusions. But, if one looks at all of the Maronite texts together, and even if one takes the other documents and puts them in their historical context, one would end up with this conclusion: Monothelitism condemned by the Sixth Council was not that of the Maronites. They had wished to proclaim only the moral union of two wills in Christ. Their inexact expression would not be understood otherwise by anyone who had carefully examined the diverse documents relating to this question ...

Moreover, if one considers the situation of the Maronites, a small group surrounded by heretics and infidels, disrupted by centuries of oppression and terror, one should not be surprised to encounter some surprises and material errors due to ignorance. Circumstances of time and place should not be forgotten when one passes judgment on the Maronite question. There were no schools of theology, nor other centres of culture. Threats and trials of all sorts absorbed their attention. However, in spite of their constant care to be ready to defend themselves against several religious and political enemies, they never lost sight of their duty to be faithful to the Church of Rome. This explains why, in the course of the ages, the Maronite clergy and people received always, with deference, the orders and directives of the Holy See.[484]

One can see the potential conflict between the historical facts presented by Doueihi and the historical facts Dib sets out in the final passage above. Following the passages on John Maroun from Doueihi, the greatest concern is the following reference from the text immediately above: "It is Thomas of Kaphartab who tells us: 'Never have the Councils spoken of two wills'." Once again, we find a bizarre contradiction. There could be many plausible, but complex explanations. One could be that in the turmoil of the seventh century, Thomas was simply unaware of the Council three centuries prior and the other explanation relates to a belief the moral union of two wills was in Thomas' eyes as different to two wills. Regardless, whether or not the Maronites were aware of the Council decree of 681, they maintained a belief in two wills of Christ, and Dib's analysis of Tell Mahre demonstrates that the Maronites were not Monothelite in the terms set out at the Sixth Ecumenical Council decree.

Doueihi refers to John Maroun's seventh century discussions with papal legates relating to Christ's nature of two wills. Tell Mahre's account, found in Moosa and Dib, is that the theology of two wills in Christ was not known in Syria prior to 727. Based on Brock, Tell Mahre's account is that all of the Melkites rejected the Dyothelite theology prior to 727. In either event, the two pieces of evidence between Douihi and Tell Mahre are a complete clash. We do not have any other sources to consider relating to this particular subject. Only Doueihi or Tell Mahre can be correct, not both.

It is proposed in this book, contrary to the conventional thinking on Tell Mahre's quote, the year 727 was not the first time the theology of two wills was accepted by the Melkites. As discussed previously, there is evidence it had been adopted in the patriarchate of Jerusalem by the latest in 720-721. Keeping Doueihi's account aside, one cannot be blind to the intricacies of the debates and decrees raging through-

---

[484] Ibid., pp. 25-27.

out the previous century. To suggest otherwise undermines Church convention and the intellectual capacity of the faithful at the time. A discussion about one will in Jesus Christ cannot be understood without considering whether Jesus Christ had two wills. It is a logical starting point particularly given the schism in the Catholic Church after 451 decreeing one nature in Jesus Christ as a heresy.

Tell Mahre was writing more than one hundred years later than the alleged event in 727. He was also a Monophysite Syriac Jacobite and was likely biased against Beit Maroun after the disputes between the two during the Acacian Schism of 471-518 and during Heraclius' reign from 610-641. He makes no mention of the doctrine from the decree of the Sixth Ecumenical Council in 681, and refers only to the Maximites. It appears Tell Mahre has not accurately recorded dates and historical facts. It is probable that Tell Mahre's reference to prisoners being brought in by the Arabs, and opening the discussion of two wills in Christ, took place at the chaotic, highly complex, and confusing period between 638 and 680. It is much more likely the dispute developed amongst the Melkites about the nature of Christ's will at this time, and that this is the period Tell Mahre was referring to, though he mistakenly reported the date. He, like many other historians of the time, is likely to have been unintentionally negligent in the recording of his dates and the names of emperors attached to the date.

Thus, the accuracy of Tell Mahre's statement about the introduction and or the adoption of the theology of two wills in 727, cannot be accepted. Nor can Tell Mahre's implication that the Maronites remained Monothelite after 727. There are too many evidentiary sources in contradiction. The numerous texts conflict with Tell Mahre's version include Greek, Syriac, and Arab historical accounts, referred to in this Chapter and the previous Chapter. They recall events relating to John Maroun's visit to Rome, the papal legates in Syria and Lebanon with John Maroun, the Byzantine army incursion into Syria against the Mardaites, the treaties between the Muslim caliphs and Byzantine emperors, the silence about Monothelitism in the Maronite and Jacobite debate before the Muslim caliph of 656-8, and knowledge in the West of the Mardaites. It follows then that, until proven otherwise, we must also accept Doueihi's recording of papal legates visiting Antioch in 676 to preach the doctrine of two wills, and John Maroun visiting Rome in 687. Hence, John Maroun and the Maronite Church knew of the decree of the Third Council of Constantinople in 681 and adopted Rome's theology.

Whether one adopts the facts stipulated by Tell Mahre or those by Doueihi, it leads to the same conclusion reached by the Maronite theologians and historians Nairon, Doueihi, Darian, and Dib. The Maronites believed in the moral union of two wills, which was not condemned by the Six Ecumenical Council. Independently and contrary to the conventional assumption, Patriarch of Antioch, Macarius, who was condemned as a Monothelite heretic at the Council, did not represent the Maronite Church. Accordingly, the Maronites have been misrepresented as Monothelites.

In a final consideration of comparable reliability between Tell Mahre and Doueihi, the following factors need to be acknowledged. Michael the Syrian in the twelfth century (stating he relied on Tell Mahre writing in the ninth century) was without the skill of a more modern historian and without a plethora of ancient sources before him. He no doubt had a bias against the emperor, the Chalcedonians, and Beit Maroun in particular, as many of his texts in this book has shown. Michael the Syrian and Tell Mahre were Syriac Orthodox Jacobite patriarchs. Their recording of the history of these events close to two hundred and five hundred years before them and hundreds of kilometres away is without reference to ancient sources.

Steven Doueihi was trained in the late seventeenth century at the Maronite College of Rome. He studied at various Roman universities. At the same time he went about researching every available document relevant to his Maronite people, especially a large number of manuscripts in the library of the Maronite College of Rome. He continued discovering manuscripts when he returned to Lebanon to be ordained as a priest in 1655. As a young priest, Doueihi persisted in his research accumulating manuscripts in Aleppo where he spent one year and in Cyprus where he was to become Bishop of Nicosia in 1668.

Doueihi had the most modern techniques at the time taught to him in recording history impartially and dependent on ancient sources. He had available, both at the College and the Vatican nearby, an abundance of ancient manuscripts that had been pinpointed to Maronite history by previous College graduates as well as himself and fellow graduates at the time. These ancient sources were not only from the East but were from ancient Rome. Patriarchs before him were graduates of the College of Rome and had undertaken much work in preparation for their successors. In 1670, Doueihi was chosen as Maronite Patriarch. As a patriarch with close ties to Rome and under public and professional scrutiny due to his high position, he would not have promoted his works if they included fabricated events.

Not all the sources Doueihi relied upon are clear in the translations of his works made more than a century ago. Perhaps this was an oversight by the translators and editors or perhaps they were not diligent in recording the quotations used. Perhaps he set out the sources as an appendix and this was left out in the transcription edition. It becomes ever more so critical that the Maronite Church returns to his original manuscripts and confirms the accuracy of their translation.

### 9.4.4 The *Annals* of Eutychius (d. 940)

The *Annals* of Eutychius, Melkite Patriarch of Alexandria from 933 to 940, inform us:

> At the time of Maurice, Emperor of the Romans (582-602), there was a monk named Maron, who affirmed in our Lord Christ two natures but one will, one operation, and one person, and who corrupted the faith of men. Many of those who partook of this doctrine and declared themselves as his disciples were from the town of Hama, of Qennesrin, and of Al-'Awasim ... The followers of his doctrine were called Maronites, from the name Maron. At the death of Maron, the

inhabitants of Hama built a monastery at Hama, called it Dair Maron and professed the faith of Maron.[485]

This appears to be the primary reference for most historians asserting the Maronites were Monothelites. Arab Muslim historians, such as Abu al-Hasan al-Masudi in the tenth century, have relied on the passage. So too have the Crusader chroniclers William of Tyre and Jacques de Vitry, and the eighteenth century historian Edward Gibbon. They claim the Maronites were Monothelite until one hundred years after the arrival of the Crusades when they were reunited in communion with the Catholic Church. However, Brock summarises:

> It is well-known that the early history of the Maronite church is shrouded in obscurity thanks to the paucity of sources, but that nevertheless much ink has been spilt on the subject with the aim of proving or disapproving the 'perpetual orthodoxy' of the Maronite Church, in the light of mediaeval accusations that it was of heretical – in other words, monothelete – origin, accusations which are first clearly found in the tenth century writer Eutychius.[486]

The difficulties with any reliance on Eutychius' text are numerous:

- 'Maro', 'Maron', or 'Maroun' was a common name in the Aramaic-Syriac speaking world. It means 'our Lord' or 'small Lord'. Various authors have suggested that the Maro referred to by Eutychius is either the fourth century Maroun or the Maronite John Maroun. Those authors' views are quickly dismissed when one looks at the date St Maroun died in about 410 and John Maroun in 707. Neither could be the Maroun that Eutychius refers to during the period 582-602.

- The Third Council of Constantinople was not convened specifically against the Maronites and there is no record of any condemnation of the Maronites by that Council.

---

[485] Eutychius, *Eutychii Annales*, trans. by Aubrey Stewart, Palestine Pilgrims Text Society, 1895, pp. 57-59.
[486] Brock, *Syriac Perspectives on the Late Antiquity*, p. 68.

- The time of Emperor Maurice predates by decades the introduction of the belief in one will of Christ.
- Eutychius does not quote any source or authority upon which he makes such claim.
- A tenth century Coptic bishop wrote a treatise refuting the writings of Eutychius concerning Christian doctrine.[487]
- The document is not a primary source. Eutychius was writing from Alexandria, a considerable distance from the Maronites. There is no evidence he had any contact with their monasteries or any followers of Beit Maroun.
- Eutychius as a Melkite was a rival of the Maronites. The Melkites had their justification for dismissing the legitimatacy of the Maronite patriarchs.
- John Maroun, whom tradition holds as the first Maronite patriarch in 685 and who died in 707, has been singled out as the Monothelite founder of the Maronite Church. However, the evidence is clearly weighted to suggest otherwise. Having died twenty years before Tell Mahre's account of the arrival of the Byzantine prisoners, John Maroun could not have known that the Catholic belief was now two wills in Christ, if Tell Mahre is correct. Further, John could not have been the Maronite founder as there is documentary reference to 'Maronites' centuries earlier.
- There is also a profound contradiction that Eutychius failed to mention: Pope Honorius and the Byzantine emperor decreed the doctrine of Monothelitism; Constantinopolitans and many emperors, as well Eutychius' own predecessor patriarchs of Alexandria, were Monothelite from 638 until 750 and well after the condemnation of it by the Sixth Council in 680-81 as detailed further above in this Chapter.

Writing about the Monothelite question, the eighteenth century historian Edward Gibbon in a footnote informs us he relies on the account of Euytchius. Gibbon speaks unfavourably about the Maronites when informing us of Heraclius' visit to Beit Maroun:

---

[487] Moosa, *The Maronites in History*, p. 35.

In the style of the Oriental Christians, the Monothelites of every age are described under the appellation of Maronites, a name which has been insensibly transferred from a hermit to a monastery, from a monastery to a nation. Maroun, a saint or savage of the fifth century, displayed his religious madness in Syria; the rival cities of Apamaea and Emesa disputed his relics, a stately church was erected on his tomb, and six hundred of his disciples united their solitary cells on the banks of the Orontes.

In the controversies of the Incarnation they nicely threaded the orthodox line between the sects of Nestorius and Eutychius; but the unfortunate question of one will or operation in the two natures of Christ was generated by their curious leisure. Their proselyte, the emperor Heraclius, was rejected as a Maronite from the walls of Emesa; he found a refuge in the monastery of his brethren; and their theological lessons were repaid with the gift of a spacious and wealthy domain. The name and doctrine of this venerable school were propagated among the Greeks and Syrians, and their zeal is expressed by Macarius, patriarch of Antioch, who declared before the Synod of Constantinople, that, sooner than subscribe the two wills of Christ, he would submit to be hewn piecemeal and cast into the sea.[488]

Gibbon's commentary on the Maronites being Monothelite is fundamentally flawed. He refers to Maroun living in the fifth century and in a footnote he refers to Eutychius for this even though, as demonstrated above, Eutychius states Maroun lived in the late sixth century. Gibbon thereby contradicts himself. He also appears to repeat the dubious idea that Heraclius introduced the one will in Jesus Christ – this has been discussed above and has been shown to be highly unlikely,

---

[488] Gibbon, *The History of the Decline and Fall of the Roman Empire*, Vol. 6, p. 72. In a footnote as part of this passage, Gibbon mentions Euytches' opinion is supported by Jacobites and Latins. Elsewhere in his book, he mentions that the Jacobite sources relied on are Michael the Syrian and Bar Habreus – see further below in this Chapter for the relevant texts. Gibbon also refers to passages found in the methodical table of Pocock. For the Latins, see later Chapter of this book on the Crusades.

with more tenable sources, prior to the *Ecthesis*, being the Jacobites, or even discussions from Alexandira. Gibbon's tainted comments must be dismissed as the association of Monothelitism with Heraclius only becomes clear with the *Ecthesis* in 638. In addition to his reliance on an unreliable source, his throwaway claim "Monothelites of every age are described under the appellation of Maronites" merely compounds the confusion rather than investigating the development of the identifier 'Maronite', discussed in this book.

### 9.4.5 *Kings of Roum* by Abu Al-Hasan Al-Masudi (d. 956)

Al-Masudi wrote in the *Kings of Roum* (c. 590) of the founding of the monastery of Maroun documenting the date to the reign of emperor Maurice (582-602). He wrote:

> [In] the twentieth was Maurice, who reigned twenty years and four months. Under his rule there appeared a man of the town of Hamat, in the province of Emesa, called Maroun, to whom the Maronite Christians at our time of writing trace their origin. This sect is famous in Syria and elsewhere. Most of its members live in Mount Lebanon and Mount Sanir at Emesa and in the districts depending on them, like those of Hamat, of Chaizar, of Maarat-al-Noman.
>
> Maroun had a great monastery, which bears his name, to the east of Hamat and of Chaizar, composed of an immense building, surrounded by three hundred cells where the monks lodged. This monastery possessed in the form of gold, of silver and of jewels considerable wealth. It was devastated together with all the cells that surrounded it following the repeated incursions of the Bedouins and the violent actions of the Sultan. It rose near the river Orontes, river of Emesa and Antioch.
>
> Maroun expressed opinions not in conformity with Christian faith, for example on the subject of the will. He had many adepts. We have already described his belief. Together with Melkites, the Nestorians and the Jacobites, he admitted the Trinity, but he differed from them by counting two natures in

the Messiah, one person and one will, and opinion intermediate between that of the Nestorians and that of the Melkites. This is what we have explained, together with other things, in our book 'Doctrines on the Foundations of the Religions'. One of the secretaries, known by the name of Kais the Maronite, is the author of an excellent book on chronology, the origin of the world, the prophets, books, cities, nations, the kings of Roum and others, and their histories. He ends his work with the caliphate of Mouktafi (901); I do not know of the Maronites composing any other book on these same matters.[489]

The text is flawed for the same reasons stated above in relation to the text of Eutychius. They can be briefly repeated as follows: St Maroun died in about 410 and John Maroun in 707 when compared to the Maroun that al-Masudi refers to during the period 582-602. The time of Emperor Maurice predates by decades the introduction of the belief in one will of Christ. Some scholars attribute St Maroun, the founding of the monastery of Maroun, and the Maronites to the reign of emperor Maurice (582-602). They rely on the Arab historians Ibn al-Atir (839-923) and al-Masudi (d. 956). In his writings, Abu l-Fida (1273-1331) quotes as his sources Ibn al-Atir and al-Masudi, but ignores their history and dates relating to St Maroun. Accordingly as Dib details, this is an error recognised by historians who cannot be sympathetic to the Maronite cause.[490]

### 9.4.6 St Germanus (d. 730) and St John of Damascus (d. 756)

There are two other texts that are, to a lesser extent, relied upon to assert that the Maronites were Monothelites – the first from St Germanus, Patriarch of Constantinople (d. 730) and second from St John of Damascus (d. 756). St Germanus, in his treatise 'De Hæresibus et Synodis' (c. 735), writes:

There are some heretics who, rejecting the Fifth and Sixth-

---

[489] Naaman, *The Maronites*, p. 173.
[490] Dib, *History of the Maronite Church*, pp. 15-41.

351

Councils, nevertheless contend against the Jacobites. The latter treat them as men without sense, because, while accepting
the Fourth Council, they try to reject the next two. Such are
the Maronites, whose monastery is situated in the very mountains of Syria.[491]

Dib records that in complete contradiction in a later passage Germanus goes on to say that the majority of the Maronites not only rejected
the Fifth and Sixth Councils but also the Fourth Council of Chalcedon
in 451. Furthermore, contrary to Germanus the Maronites (of Beit Maroun) accepted the Fifth Council as they were represented there. This
book demonstrates ample evidence of Maronites being not only pro-
Chalcedon but in fact the leaders of that party.

Nonetheless, Germanus' passage above is theologically inconsistent.
His reference to the Maronites' rejection of the Fourth, Fifth and Sixth
Council appears to take the theological line that Chalcedonians (adherent to the Fourth and Fifth Councils) who then rejected the Sixth Council as Monothelite were then theologically retrospectively rejecting the
previous two Councils. He is alone in the attribution of this view, which
can be called 'Monophysite Monothelitism'. The only modern author
that appears to adopt this Christology is Moosa, and his views on this
specific issue have been critiqued in detail earlier of this book.

Some authors have suggested that St Germanus said that the Maronites rejected the Sixth Ecumenical Council doctrine that declared
Monothelitism a heresy.[492] But one can easily conclude differently.
Brock states that this is an ambiguous and muddled passage[493] perhaps
for the contradiction discussed previously. We also know the Council
made no reference to the Maronites and they were not present at the
Council. This evidence also conflicts with the evidence of Tell Mahre,
which implies the Maronites had no knowledge of the Council Decree

---

[491] Quoted in Jérôme Labourt, "Maronites," *The Catholic Encyclopedia*, Robert Appleton Company, 1910, available at: http://www.newadvent.org/cathen/09683c.htm.
The comments of Labourt in general about the Maronites are outdated and should not
be accepted.
[492] Moosa, *The Maronites in History*, p. 208; Labourt, "Maronites."
[493] Brock, *Syriac Perspectives on Late Antiquity*, p. 68.

of 681. Germanus was from a rival church of the Maronites and likely sought to dismiss the legitimacy of the Maronite patriarch.

Again, in relation to St John of Damascus, the very brief reference he makes to the Maronites is used as evidence that they rejected the Sixth Council.[494] For an opposing and detailed opinion, see Dib's explanation where he assessed the related texts.[495] As Brock suggests there is no clear or unambiguous evidence demonstrating that the Maronites openly rejected or found fault with the Sixth Council.[496] Undoubtedly once again the legend of Macarius representing the Maronites forms the basis of Germanus' view or that the Maronites' union of two wills was misunderstood as Monothelitism. There can be no other explanation.

## 9.5  Summary

For the seriousness of the claim that the Maronites were heretics in the context of the understandings of the seventh century, the burden of proof should be of the highest standard. The test of beyond reasonable doubt would apply. Based on the investigation in this and the next chapter, the evidence fails the heresy claim. Adopting the lesser standard of proof, namely the balance of probabilities, the analysis also finds the Maronites were not heretics in this period.

The very little evidence available allows the conclusion to be reached as follows. During the Monothelite controversies of the seventh and early eighth centuries, the Maronites at no time severed their union with the Catholic Church. They upheld the primacy of the patriarch of Rome, the Pope and believed in the moral union of two wills in Jesus Christ: this was not condemned by the Council of 681. From about the late seventh century or early eighth century, communication ties between Rome and the Maronites were severed due to Islamic rule. The ties were restored upon the arrival of the Crusaders at the end of the eleventh century.

---

[494] Moosa, *The Maronites in History*, pp. 208-210; Labourt, "Maronites."
[495] Dib, *History of the Maronite Church*, pp. 27-31. Dib also refers to Assemani's refutation of St John of Damascus' claim.
[496] Brock, *Syriac Perspectives on the Late Antiquity*, p. 68.

Due to Muslim rule and fluctuating levels of persecution, the Christians of the Middle East had been preoccupied with survival rather than documenting their history. For the few historians and individuals that may have compiled histories, their documents have mostly perished, been destroyed because of persecution, or lost. The history of this period is therefore generally obscure. The spotlight of world historians has never been able to properly point to the church history of this region of the Middle East for the period from seventh to eleventh century. This includes for churches other than the Maronite Church. Financial support for comprehensive scholarly studies is required to examine and illuminate the many complexities and fascinations for this period. Until such time, the propositions put forward above, and in other chapters of this work, are an appropriate and plausible historical account. However, given the complexity of this topic and the contradictions in the evidence, there can be no absolute certain conclusions.

# CHAPTER 10
## ARAMAIC CATHOLIC CULTURE
## IN THE MEDIEVAL PERIOD

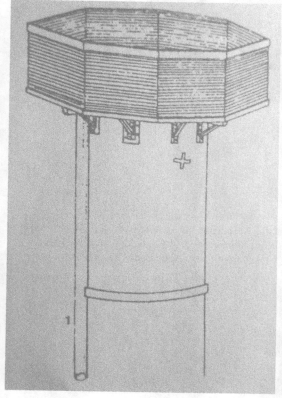

Left: A model of St Simon Stylite's pillar from the mid fifth century mimicked by other Christian Stylites throughout the Middle East and Arabia pre Islam. The diameter of the pillar was just over one metre with timber planks at the top making a square type platform of about two metres by two metres with timber balustrades around it, resembling in a later period the balcony of an Islamic minaret. There was also a ladder for those who wanted to climb to the top.

Right: Typical Islamic minaret likely to have been influenced by the prototypes of the many Stylites' manner of living who imitated St Simon and preached from the towers. The Aramaic church open colonnette timber bell towers also may have been an inspiration for the minaret as was the later enclosed towers of the Stylites.

Aramaic Maronite Madonna – Rabulla Gospel 586AD and Our Lady of Ilige, 10th century – both evidencing the pre Islamic Aramaic style of female dress and likely influenced Islamic dress culture (Image taken from Father Abdo Badwi's works).

Left: Maronite nun (name withheld), Mother Superior of a fully enclosed cloistered convent in Lebanon. The female neck and chest cover was typically Aramaic in style pre dating Islam. Right: Iranian Muslim female tourist visiting Our Lady of Lebanon, Harissa, Lebanon. Note the similarity in head dress with Maronite nun on left. (See women in crucifixion scene further below for more commentary). Photos taken in 2005 by the author.

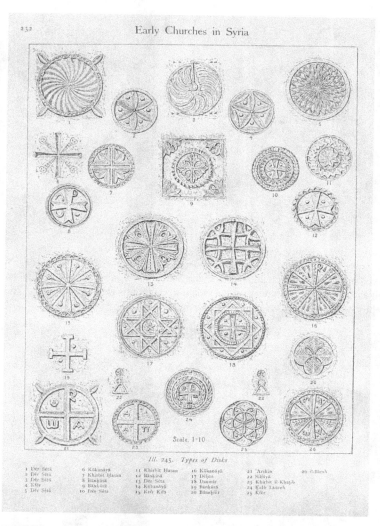

*Ill. 245. Types of Disks*

| | | | |
|---|---|---|---|
| 1 Dêr Sêtâ | 6 Kôkanâyâ | 11 Khirbit Hasan | 16 Kôkanâyâ | 21 'Arshin | 26 il-Bârah |
| 2 Dêr Sêtâ | 7 Khirbit Hasan | 12 Bânkûsâ | 17 Dêhes | 22 Siljâyâ |
| 3 Dêr Sêtâ | 8 Bânkûsâ | 13 Dêr Sêtâ | 18 Dauwâr | 23 Khirbit il-Khatib |
| 4 Kfer | 9 Bânkûsâ | 14 Kôkanâyâ | 19 Bânkûsâ | 24 Kalb Lauzeh |
| 5 Dêr Sêtâ | 10 Dêr Sêtâ | 15 Refe Kfs | 20 Bânakjlûr | 25 Kfer |

Types of Aramaic equal armed crosses and disks from the fourth to early seventh century AD found throughout the ancient Syrian Orient and documented during the American archaeological expeditions to Syria in 1899-1900 (Butler, H.C. *Early Churches in Syria Fourth to Seventh Centuries*, 1921, p. 232). Note, the various types of equal armed crosses including Disks 8 and 12 likely replicated by the Knights of St John Hospitallers (originally established to treat the injured Crusaders). The Knights' emblem became more widely known in the sixteenth century after they settled in Malta and hence the name 'Maltese Cross'.

Maarat Namaan, northern Syria. Typical fourth to early seventh century AD equal arm cross in the UNESCO declared Ancient Villages of Northern Syria. These stone carved motifs adorned churches, the exterior of buildings, front entries of houses as well as stone coffins. They are also evident throughout Lebanon such as in the sixth century churches of St Mamas in Ehden and Deir al-Qal'a in Beit Mery.

The earliest illuminated motif of a Christian cross in existence today – from the Rabbula Gospels, 586AD (original in full colour from negatives of Fr. A. Badwi).

From left: Emblems most likely replicating ancient Aramaic equal armed motifs: Lebanese Maronite Order of monks, Knights of St John (Crusaders) eight pointed 'Maltese Cross', today's St John Ambulance emblem and Australian Red Cross emblem.

Kadisha Valley, North Lebanon. Former Maronite patriarchal residence, Monastery of Qannoubine, can be spotted one third from the bottom towards the left.

Typical flat roofed Maronite village church (Niha, North Lebanon) with introduction of metal bell tower post 11th century Crusades in many instances likely replacing timber bell towers.

359

Typical house, Sejilla, Northern Syria, 4th -5th century AD. Note the lavish stonework of fourth to early seventh century AD house in the UNESCO declared Ancient Villages of Northern Syria. The houses had advanced sanitary plumbing with pipes connected to sewers or reservoirs. The bathrooms had wash hand basins. These buildings were still intact at the time of the photo taken by the author in 2005 in one of the ancient towns, Serjilla.

Fifth century town of Serjilla, Northern Syria. H.C. Butler one hundred years ago commented that the degree of advancement in sanitation and personal cleanliness in the houses of these towns 'is an index of the progress in civilisation of Syria in the fourth and fifth century, considerably in advance of large parts of Europe in the early twentieth century'.

360

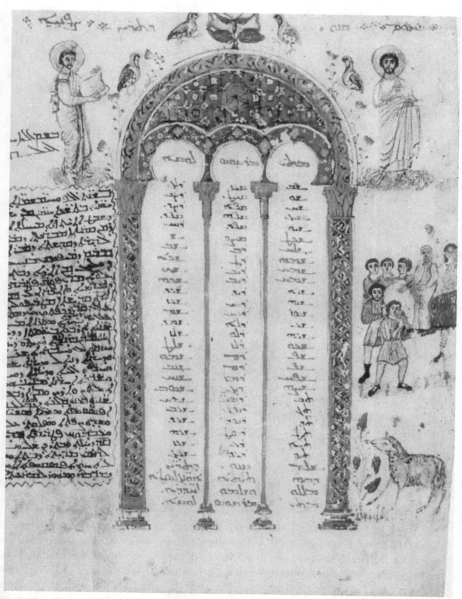

Rabbula Gospel illumination, 586 AD, which evidences inward tapered architectural arches, pre Islamic period. The gospel images are all in colour (from negatives of Fr. A. Badwi).

The scene of the Crucifixion-Resurrection of Jesus Christ from the Rabbula Gospels, 586AD. The large number of full colour illuminations within this manuscript are the world's and Syriac's most ancient illuminations of the Gospels in existence today. They contain the earliest illuminated motif of a Christian cross and scene of the crucifixion of Jesus Christ available from any ancient source. It is possible the many illustrations influenced Byzantine iconography. Note the headdress of the three Aramaic women at the top left, typical of the pre Islamic period and today characteristically worn as traditional clothing for Muslim women. (Images from negatives of Fr A. Badwi).

## 10.1 Aramaic Catholics in Palestine, Lebanon, Phoenicia, and Syria

Foreign rulers and empires have come and gone since ancient times. In various periods the political boundaries of 'Lebanon', the 'Holy Land', 'Palestine', and 'Israel' have changed. For example, ancient upper Galilee extended to the south of Mount Lebanon. Ancient and Roman Phoenicia extended well into what is now modern day northern Israel and much of coastal northern Syria. During the Crusades the kingdom of Jerusalem extended to Beirut. Followers of Christ in his lifetime were present in all these areas.

Leaving political boundaries aside, as has been stated previously, geographically southern Lebanon including Tyre and Sidon is part of the Holy Land. Christ preached and performed miracles at the base of and around Mount Lebanon. Lebanon is therefore part of the Holy Land. It is mentioned approximately seventy times in the Old Testament, was the place of Jesus Christ's first miracle in Cana (two other towns in northern Israel apparently make the same claim), and Jesus preached around the cities of Tyre and Sidon. Tradition holds the Virgin Mary retreated to a hilltop (modern Maghdouche) whilst Jesus Christ preached in Sidon.

Antioch and Jerusalem were inextricably linked for the Jews and so for the first Christians. The Christians of the Roman Byzantine provinces of Palestine, which included Jerusalem, were under the patriarchate of Antioch until the establishment of the patriarchate of Jerusalem in 451. Accordingly, the church liturgy in Jerusalem for the indigenous population became by its nature dominated by Aramaic language and Antiochian influences. The populations in and around Jerusalem and Galilee looked north to Antioch, not only for church leadership in the form of their patriarch, but for liturgical and theological leadership.

In the early to mid-fifth century, between the death of St Maroun (d. 410-423) and before the establishment of Beit Maroun monastery (452), one cannot dismiss the possibility of the existence of, at least, a loose network of Aramaic (Syriac) speaking Christian populations tied to Antioch who were from Jerusalem, Galilee, Lebanon, Phoenicia and Syria. Over time many of these Christians became part of a network of faithful connected by the monks from Cyrrhus, Apamaea and Antioch region in Syria (e.g. St Abraham and later St Simon the Stylite). More remotely, the link may have also been through contemporaries and imitators of St Maroun from northern Syria such as two anchorite women, Marana and Kyra. They travelled to the Holy Land as Theodoret informs us:

> eager one day to contemplate the places hallowed by Christ's salvational sufferings, (they) ran to Æolia (Jerusalem) without having eaten for the whole trip, but once in the Holy City and their devotions made, they had some food then fasted the whole way back, which is no less than twenty days walk.[497]

Historians remain relatively silent about an Aramaic Syriac-speaking population of the Holy Land, Palestine, Lebanon, and Phoenicia in this period and after. As we have seen historians were and still remain generally Hellene, Latin, and Syriac Monophysite focused in their documentation and thinking. The majority of the Aramaic Syriac-speaking Catholic indigenous population from the Holy Land would have followed the Dyophysite doctrine of the Council of Chalcedon. We know further south in Egypt, within the patriarchate of Alexandria outside of the capital city, the Christians in the main were Monophysite.

After 452 the 'Chalcedonian Orthodox' populations around Jerusalem were part of the Chalcedonian party. Following the Acacian Schism in 471-518, between Rome and Constantinople and the Council of Constantinople in 536, it seems a confederation formed in the region which was attached to the network of Beit Maroun monasteries that appeared to lead the Chalcedonian party throughout the patriarchate of Antioch. The Chalcedonian party were known as Melkites, loyal

---

[497] Theodoret, *A History of the Monks*, pp. 193-185.

to the emperor. Over time, Beit Maroun followers were interchangeably known as Melkites and Maronites.

There is a reference to the so-called Omar Decree of 638 that mentions the Maronites in the Holy Land in that year.[498] Further studies would be warranted in this area. However, some weight, albeit light, should be given to the Decree to assist in the present topic. Additional sources, such as the Crusader chronicles, will be dealt with in the next chapter to explore the story of Maronites at this time.

One chronicle tells of Maronite assistance to the Crusaders in their route to the Holy Land. The Chronicles confirm the Maronites were stationed in Akko, presently Acre in northern Israel. Considered in context, it adds weight to the proposition that Maronite colonies were present further south than Mount Lebanon, and throughout the Holy Land. It seems reasonable to suggest that without such colonies the Crusaders' gratitude towards the Maronites for the success of the route to Jerusalem would not have been so highlighted. Further, Seward (citing Fulcher de Chartres) wrote of how only twenty years after the arrival of the Crusaders in Jerusalem in 1099 "there was a large native Christian population, Maronite, Melkite, Syrian and Armenian" and inter-marriage was taking place with the French Crusaders.[499]

The Maronite descendants of Syria are relatively unknown. Through their Maronite parishes and dioceses these offspring are numerous throughout Syria. Their history appears to have been substantially neglected by historians up to now. Sadly, the recent Syrian war has displaced a great many of them. Documentary evidence shows continuation of Maronite colonies in locations such as Aleppo even after the destruction of Beit Maroun (the final destruction at the latest by early tenth century).

We do know that the Maronites were the direct and formidable op-

---

[498] The reliability of this source may be compromised since the text was written in 1625, almost a thousand years after the decree was issued.
[499] Desmond Seward, *The Monks of War – The Military Orders*, The Folio Society, 2000, pp. 9-12.

position to the Syriac Monophysites. The Jacobite references are constant indicating the Maronites were the only Aramaic Catholics. There is no reference to any other Aramaic Catholics. The Maronites are the focus of the events recorded in Syria under Patriarch Severus in 512-518 including the massacre of the three hundred and fifty Beit Maroun monks. The Maronites and Jacobites met at a conference in 591 and exchanged letters after. The Maronites were from the Chalcedon party, the vine of Leo. Many Jacobites converted to Maronites shortly before this conference. The Jacobite Patriarchs, Tell Mahre (d. 845) and Michael the Syrian (d. 1199), refer to the take over in 628-630 of Jacobite monasteries by the Maronites at the order of the emperor Heraclius. We read of a conference at Damascus in 658-659 between the Jacobites and Maronites in the presence of the future Muslim Caliph and the Maronites having the upper hand.

In the ninth century, a Maronite community existed in the region of Aleppo (ancient Beroea), ruled by Bishop Thomas of Kaphartab and in 1140, a Maronite bishop, Simon took the episcopal see of Aintab, which is north of Aleppo.[500] In addition to Aleppo, we know the number of Maronite communities that remained on the plains and shores of the Orontes River slowly reduced over time. This included in areas such as Apamaea (near Hama), Epiphania (Hama), Emesa (Homs), and Antiochia (Antakya, Turkey).

There are many links between Beit Maroun and Lebanon that have been set out in previous chapters. It is timely to set out an additional link. The reference to Maronites in the exchange of correspondence of 592 between the Maronites and the Jacobites as followers of Beit Maroun, and the reference to the Maronite Patriarch in the incident of 745 described in the *Annals* of Dionysius of Tell Mahre, also assists to explain the tradition of a historical link between Beit Maroun and Lebanon. The reference to the followers of Beit Maroun as Maronites was first made explicit by Patriarch Doueihi in the seventeenth century, saying the first Maronite Patriarch, St John Maroun (d. 707), "built

---

[500] Dib, *History of the Maronite Church*, p. 53.

an altar and a monastery after Saint Maroun's name and put Saint Maroun's skull inside the altar to heal the faithful." There is evidence this monastery dates back to that time and was still in existence at the time of the Crusades.

Yet, it would be a surprise to learn St John Maroun was the first to establish a Maronite colony in Lebanon. Documentation of the life of St Abraham and St Simon the Stylite reveals the fifth century Aramaic-Syriac monastic links to Lebanon discussed in this book. This is not to say Maronite colonies became non-existent outside of Lebanon in the period of the late seventh and early eighth century. There is evidence that suggests Beit Maroun in Apamaea region was not finally destroyed until the tenth century, in 935. It may have suffered extensive damage in the seventh century, according to Doueihi, but was perhaps rebuilt.

By the time of the arrival of the Crusades in the eleventh century, the only Christians who had their patriarch residing in Lebanon were the Maronites. Comparatively, there are far fewer towns or villages today in the mountains of Lebanon that are Syriac Orthodox, Melkite Catholic, or Antiochian Orthodox. Today, the genealogical descendants of the Catholic (Chalcedonian 'orthodox') populations of the Middle East after the Council of Chalcedon in 451 can only be the Maronites, Melkite Catholic, and Antiochian Orthodox. As the evidence shows, there may have been some conversions up to the seventh century (and after the Crusades) from Jacobites to Maronites, but it is suggested overall this is likely a minority.

As modern-day Lebanon is the heartland of the Maronites, Maronite history tends to focus on this region. However, a detailed study of Maronite history in other countries such as Syria is warranted. Unfortunately, any attempt at present to undertake this task is made difficult due to the ongoing civil war in Syria. In addition, there surely remains an abundance of Maronite history in Cyprus and the Holy Land to be explored. Much work is ahead, in addition to that still required for Lebanon.

367

## 10.2  Iconography

### 10.2.1  The Rabbula Gospels c. 586

Before printing presses were invented in the seventeenth century, many monks would spend their days and years as missionaries writing copies of the Gospels and the Bible for distribution. The sixth century Rabbula Gospels are in the Syriac Peshitta, or simple vulgate form, that is the day-to-day language of that time. The Gospels are accompanied by colour illustrations to over 292 folios. These are the world's and Syriac's most ancient illuminations of the Gospels in existence today. The manuscripts date to around 586 AD and also contain the earliest illuminated motif of a Christian cross and scene of the crucifixion of Jesus Christ available from any ancient source in existence. It is possible the illustrations influenced Byzantine iconography.

The signature of the monk Rabbula from the monastery of Beit Zaghba appears on the manuscript. It is accepted this monastery was in northern Syria in the neighbourhood between Apamaea and Antioch. From its time in this monastery to the eleventh century, its whereabouts is not known, but later may have come into the possession of Maronite monastics in Lebanon, such as Our Lady of Mayfouq in the Ilige Valley of the Byblos region from the eleventh century until 1497. Thereafter it was held at the seat of Our Lady of Qannubin in the Qadisha Valley until 1652. It moved to Britain, then the National Library of France, then finally in 1747 to the Mediceo-Laurentian Library in Florence where it remains today. For preservation, it is currently in a special air and humidity controlled dark room unable to be accessed to the public: only microfilm versions can be purchased from the library housing it.

The scholars Carlo Cecchelli, Giuseppe Furlani, and Mario Salmi in their 1959 book *The Rabbula Gospels* undertook the first modern detailed analysis of the manuscript. Father Abdo Badwi in his 2013 book *Iconographie Et Peinture Dans L'Eglise Maronite* provides a more recent analysis of the Rabbula Gospels. Father Abdo Badwi, from the Lebanese Maronite Order, is Dean of the Department of Syriac and Antiochian Sciences, Faculty of Religious and Oriental Studies, at the University of the Holy Spirit, Kaslik, Lebanon. He is also a leading scholar in the Syriac art world. Badwi is often called upon by the Syriac Orthodox Church and the Maronite Church for his expertise. He possesses copies of the negatives of photographs of the Rabbula illuminations taken some decades ago by an Italian photographer.

In his book *The Liturgical Year Iconography of the Syro-Maronite Church*, Badwi details his attentive study of the Rabbula ancient illuminations, their liturgical origins, and spiritual inspirations. He does so in the context of Christian art and other available ancient manuscripts of illuminations. Badwi informs us Rabbula's most original art themes are of The Nativity, The Epiphany, The Crucifixion-Resurrection, The Ascension, and The Pentecost. He states:

> It presents us through its marginal and full page miniatures the iconography of the Syro-Occidental liturgical year in its embryonic stage ... It represents the period of transition between Paleo-Christian [early Church] art and Iconographical art and it is a basic element for the Christian Iconography.

> The origin of its roots is in the Syro-Aramean Hellenistic world in Doura-Europos, Palmyra, Edessa and other metropolis of the Arameo-Hellenistic world.[501]

Badwi enlightens us of the many characteristics of the miniatures:

> popularity and simplicity; far from the Byzantine hieratism and the naivity of primitive art; the colours are vivid; the graphic is well studied; the composition is monumental even if the execution is in the miniature; the drawing is executed from right to left like the Syriac script; more than one hand has executed the work.

Badwi states the Rabbula Gospel book remains a large source of

---

[501] Abdo Badwi, *The Liturgical Year Iconography of the Syro-Maronite Church*, University of Saint Esprit, 2006, pp. 25-26.

inspiration for liturgical art in the Syriac world and universal church. Giving priority especially to the Syriac, Maronite, and Antiochian heritage, Badwi uses the Rabbula illuminations and many other ancient illustrations for inspiration to produce his own contemporary sacred artwork of forty modern magnificent icons for the Maronite Church's liturgical year. A radiant, distinctive, and beautiful cross drawn in the Rabbula folios is now often referred to as the 'Rabbula Cross'.

The Maronite author Dau devotes a whole chapter of his book to claims that the Rabbula Gospels are from the Aramaic-Syriac-speaking Chalcedonians, and hence are a Maronite work. He draws on the example of the Rabbula crucifixion scene to attest to the double nature of Christ as human and divine – that is, as proof that the work was by the Maronites and not the Monophysites. Dau states that Christ crucified was not represented on the cross by the Monophysite manuscripts before the thirteenth century as they followed their great Church fathers Philoxenes of Mabbug, Severus of Antioch, and Peter Foulon (Peter of Apamaea) who were adverse to holy images. The cross without a crucified Christ was tolerated, but the alternative was considered to represent the person or human nature of Christ.

However, Dau may go too far when he comments on the picture in Folio 14a:

> The most ancient picture of St Maroun is to be found in the Maronite codex, the Rabbula Gospels returned in the year 586, about 180 years after the death of St Maroun, in the Maronite convent of Mar Youhanon of Beth-Zaghba. St Maroun is the first on the left in this picture, and wears a hood adorned with precious stones, sign of his dignity as founder of a large monastic community. The Syriac word written near him Moran is a variant of his name found in many Maronite and non-Maronite texts and traditions.[502]

Cecchelli, Furlani, and Salmi, referring to Folio 14a, comment on the inscription 'Maron' to the right of Christ having been handwrit-

---

[502] Dau, *History of the Maronites*, p. 166.

ten at a later time: "in the left margin written in black vertically in a writing later than the Gospels. The word means our Lord."[503] They continue:

> It is not easy to identify the figures of this scene, which we called the presentation. Garucci following a conjecture of Assemanus has suggested identifying them as St James the apostle, St Ephraim and two abbotts ... The one in fact definitely looks like a monk (also emphasised by the hood which has a cross on it).[504]

Brock differs in his view of Folio 14a:

> there is an image of Christ enthroned, approached by four men, two of them presenting books with veiled hands. It is very likely that they should be identified as members of the monastery at Beth Zagba offering this very book to Christ, under the protection of two patron saints.[505]

Certainly, the Maronites had an interest in the work. The Maronite Patriarchs commenced documenting the possession of the Rabbula Gospels on the manuscript itself at least since the eleventh century. Having no recording beforehand cannot be taken to mean they did not possess it previously. No other Aramaic-Syriac church can or has laid claim to Rabbula Gospels. On balance of probabilities, the fact of possession alone supports the view Rabbula was a monk in a Beit Maroun networked monastery.

## 10.2.2  Maronite Madonna: Our Lady of Ilige

The painting, known as the Maronite Madonna or Our Lady of Ilige, dates from the tenth century and depicts the Madonna holding the infant Jesus in her arms. It hangs in the Maronite Church of Our Lady at Ilige in Mayfouk, Lebanon and was attached to the monastery and

---

[503] C. Cecchelli, G. Furlani, M. Salmi, *The Rabbula Gospels*, Urs Graf, 1959, p. 15.
[504] Ibid. Footnote 260 states: "Macler suggests the hooded figure as Aaron dressed as high priest and the other figure as Moses. This to us is truly mistaken."
[505] Brock (ed.), *The Hidden Pearl: The Syrian Orthodox Church and its Ancient Aramaic Heritage*, Vol. II, Gorgias Press, 2001, p. 231.

later Maronite Patriarchal seat from the years 1120 to 1440. Badwi, who has been influenced by both this icon and the iconography of the Rabbula to produce his own modern works of art, explains:

> The icon of Mary Mother of God is inspired from the icon-ographical tradition of the Hodiguitria (The Conducting Virgin icon type attributed to St Luke). Mary shows us the way of salvation with her right hand, the Lord seated on her left hand. She blesses us with her right hand together with her Son who is carrying the Bible. The Child resembles his mother and their eyes are open with an eternal gaze. The oval opening of the Virgin's veil and the Ephodita (white bandage that oriental women wear under their veil) in the form of a cross, at the level of her forehead and eyes, are characteristic of Syriac Iconography.[506]

It is said the two small star like holes in the painting (one above the forehead of Our Lady and one on her right shoulder) are actually from bullets fired at it by Ottoman soldiers in later times. The two circles at either end at the uppermost of the painting, with the faces inside, may be inspired by the top of some Rabbula illuminations to represent the sun and moon as symbols of the movement of seasons, months, weeks, and days.

The icon of Our Lady of Ilige is from a period after the Monothelite controversy of the seventh century and prior to the arrival of the Crusades and both Mary and the infant Jesus with two fingers protruding from the rest of the right hand. This symbolises the two natures of Christ – divine and human – and perhaps advocates the theology of two wills. Even though they may have believed in two natures of Christ, if the Maronites were Monothelites it is difficult to accept they would have allowed any reference in their churches to an image or icon that portrayed two fingers to suggest two wills. It may support the theory that the Maronites were not Monothelites. It could also suggest the Maronites were still following the practice of making the sign of the cross the same way the Byzantine Orthodox continue to do to the present time.

---

[506] Badwi, *The Liturgical Year Iconography of the Syro-Maronite Church*, p. 48.

The Byzantine Churches today, whether Orthodox or Catholic, make the sign of the cross with their right hand by forehead to chest, then from right to left (Catholics from left to right), with the thumb, index and middle fingers joined in honour of the Trinity (Catholics with open hand). The other two fingers are pressed to the palm, in honour of Christ's two natures, divine and human, in one Person. Could it be that up to the time of the Crusades, the Maronites did the same? This tenth century painting may indicate this possibility. There is evidence the use of two fingers by the Maronites continued until the fifteenth century.[507]

### 10.2.3 Iconoclasm

Given the Maronites appear to have been cut off from Rome and Constantinople by the eighth century, it seems they were not impacted by the Byzantine Iconoclasm controversies of the eighth and ninth centuries – this may also add another layer of complexity to the Monothelitism debate. The Iconoclasm schism between Rome and Constantinople may have commenced with Justinian's introduction of Christ's image on imperial coins in 695. It was in full swing with Pope Gregory II's rebuttal in 727 of Emperor Leo's order to remove imagery. This is notably the same year as Tell Mahre records a split between the Maronite Melkites and Maximite Melkites. If Doueihi is correct, and if there was any form of contact with Rome (for which there is no evidence), the Maronites would have taken Rome's position, that is, support for the use of images and icons against those opposed to the use of religious images – the 'Iconoclasts' – led by the emperor in Constantinople.

The first Iconoclasm schism lasted until about 787. The Greek Melkites of the Middle East must have supported Constantinople to have retained the label of Melkites. However, the evidence for this period contains contradictions. Theophanes records that in 762-73, Kosmas, bishop of Epiphania (near Apamaea), apostasized from the

---

[507] Mentioned by Gabriel al-Qilai (d. 1516) in Mar Dumit Garshuni manuscript MS 454 (cited in Moosa, *The Maronites in History*, p. 146).

Catholic faith and adhered to the Byzantine emperor Constantine's opposition of holy icons. The patriarchs of Antioch, Alexandria, and Jerusalem anathematised Kosmas.[508] Based on documents from 736 and 836, Ignatius Dick states these three Melkite patriarchs were officially opposed to the emperor and the iconoclasts, and thus aligned themselves with Rome.[509] If so, it follows that they were technically not Melkite during these periods but rather non-indigenous Middle Eastern Greek Catholics.

## 10.3  Aramaic-Syrian Architecture

### 10.3.1  The 'Dead Cities'

Northern Syria is one of the main archaeological regions of Syria. Architecturally, it is an archaeological Christian splendour of the world today. Many of the 'Dead Cities', known as the 'Ancient Villages of Northern Syria', were listed as World Heritage sites by UNESCO only in 2011. It shows how belated is the interest in this history. The more widespread awareness of the sites probably only came to attention following the recent Syrian civil war, commenced in the same year as the listing. The other UNESCO World Heritage sites of Syria include: the Ancient City of Aleppo, the Ancient City of Bosra, the Ancient City of Damascus, the Crusader castle Krak des Chevaliers, Qal'at Salah El-Din and the Site of Palmyra. The Syrian Civil War from 2011 to the present has unfortunately resulted in many of these sites being pillaged and damaged to an extent unknown.[510]

The ancient villages of Northern Syria have been regularly reported by UNESO as in danger of destruction since the Syrian civil war,

---

[508] Theophanes, *The Chronicle of Theophanes*, p. 123.

[509] Dick Ignatius, *Melkites, Greek Orthodox and Greek Catholics of the Patriarchates of Antioch, Alexandria and Jerusalem*, Sophia Press, 2004, p. 21.

[510] Some of the many listed heritage sites are: Jebel Sem'an 1 [Qal'at Sem'an] 3,700 hectares; Jebel Sem'an 2 [KafrNabo], 2760 hectares; Jebel Sem'an 3 [Sinkhar] 380 hectares; Jebel Zawiyé 1 [Ba'uda] 3,200 hectares; Jebel Zawiyé 2 [Rouweiha] 530 hectares; Jebel al-A'la [QalbLozé] 460 hectares; Jebel Barisha [Deirouné] 580 hectares; Jebel Wastani [Kafr Aqareb] 680 hectares.

which is also a regional and international war. In 2013, there were repeated UNESCO emergency press releases sounding warnings to the warring parties and the world about these sites. The sites have been in the midst of the heaviest fighting between regime forces and rebels, many of whom are reported to be Islamic fundamentalists from abroad. The nearby cities of Aleppo and Idlib are centres for many of these sites and so have seen the fiercest fighting of the present war. Almost unknown to all but a few including few Maronites, is that many of these heritage sites owe their origins to the Maronite and perhaps to a lesser extent the Syriac Orthodox churches. We can only pray the war and senseless loss of life will end soon and the damage from the war to these sites will be minimal.

The dead cities in travel guides to Syria, better described as abandoned towns, are labelled by William Dalrymple in *From the Holy Mountain* as 'Byzantine', though they date back close to time of St Maroun and St Simon Stylite.[511] It is believed there are some 750 sites ranging from single monuments to nearly whole villages complete with houses, churches, baths, and even wine presses. Their abandonment around the early seventh century coincides with the onset of the Persian and Arab invasions and conquests. The sites are relatively still largely unexplored and undocumented.

What is certain is that these so-called Byzantine dead cities, which were relatively intact before 2011, are not 'Byzantine' at all. They actually belong to the Antioch Aramaic-Syriac speaking churches. Their only connection with Byzantine is the period of time that they flourished – simultaneous with the glory of the Byzantine empire – and that they were within the land of the empire. Other than that, they are distinctly Aramaic-Syriac in architecture and culture. The groundbreaking American archaeological expeditions to Syria in 1899-1900 resulted in resident scholar Butler stating:

> One might almost say that a renaissance of the art of architecture was brought about by the Syrian architects of the fifth

---

[511] William Dalrymple, *From the Holy Mountain. A Journey in the Shadow of Byzantium*, Flamingo, 1998.

and sixth centuries, showing a remarkable degree of independence of any influence from the capital of the Byzantine empire. This individual and vigorous style grew and progressed
until abruptly cut off in the early years of the seventh century ... The Syrian churches, while they may have boasted
of mosaics and wall paintings, were not dependent, as the
Byzantine churches were, upon these superficial adornments
for beauty of affect and, even in their ruins, present examples
of careful composition and design, both exterior and interior,
adorned with a wealth of purely architectural ornament, all
wrought in a simple, truthful and beautiful use of natural
building materials.[512]

Butler goes on to suggest that these Syrian churches had an important impact on the design of Hellenistic and European churches.

Some of these towns may have a Syriac Orthodox Jacobite heritage but it is quite unlikely. For one thing, the western region of
ancient Syria was probably dominated by Aramaic Catholic Christians who were Chalcedonian adherents. Second, the more amenable
Jacobite relationship with the Persians and Arabs around the time of
the incursions into Syria do not gel with the abandonment of these
towns when the Persian and Arab forces invaded. In addition, we
have evidence for mass Aramaic Catholic migration to Rome and
Sicily around this time. The Ancient Villages of Northern Syria that
were abandoned in the early seventh century are far more likely than
not to be Aramaic Catholic and accordingly substantially Melkite-
Maronite.

Indeed, as Dau has claimed, a great deal of these 'dead cities' and
their churches would have been Maronite.[513] There were many monasteries that fell under the leadership of St Maroun's monastery (though
we do not know its exact location, we know the monastery was in
Syria Secunda). These churches and monasteries were the rallying

---

[512] H.C. Butler, *Early Churches in Syria Fourth to Seventh Centuries*, Leyden, 1921,
pp. 3-4.
[513] Dau, *History of the Maronites*, pp. 253-278.

point in both the political and ecclesiastical spheres. The Antiochian Aramaic-Syriac churches, which included the Maronites as they do today, rally and centre a great deal of their life around their monks, nuns, priests, bishops, and patriarch.

The greatest church built in the fifth century, that of St Simon Stylite (d. 459), provides an example of Maronite-Jacobite ambiguity in this region. This wonder, outside of Aleppo, was still relatively intact before the Syrian War from 2011. Dau has claimed that this is a Maronite Church, pointing to a Syriac inscription at St Simon that recognises St Maroun as their father.[514] In some instances, Dau exaggerates his conclusions although he is diligent in extracting source material. It is for this reason he is often not relied upon, yet on this occasion parts of his conclusions may have merit. To the contrary, the Syriac Orthodox Jacobite Church claim St Simon Stylite as one of theirs, however, it is highly likely St Simon Stylite supported the Council of Chalcedon, as suggested by Beit Maroun correspondence in 517. At some stage after the Acacian Schism it may have passed from the Maronites into the hands of the Syriac Orthodox Jacobite Church.

### 10.3.2 Architectural Styles

The Middle East, the birthplace of Christianity, possibly preserves more ancient Christian buildings than any other part of the world. The evidence lies in the Ancient Villages of Northern Syria. One reason might be the large districts where Christian communities were thriving and were subsequently deserted early in the seventh century and have remained in that condition ever since. Butler implies it is no coincidence that these towns were abandoned with the arrival of Arab Muslim conquest. These districts and their substantial ruins have never been subsequently reoccupied to this day possibly because of the combined effects of their remoteness and decline in fertility of the land.[515]

---

[514] Ibid., p. 277.

[515] See the commentary in Butler, *Early Churches in Syria*, the summary of Butler's expeditions to Syria from 1899-1909.

During the fourth and fifth centuries, while Italy and Greece were being subject to conquest by the Goths and Vandals with little architectural development, the Middle East was enjoying peace and prosperity, producing churches, public buildings, private villas, and tombs of significant dignity and beauty. Now ruins in modern day northern Syria and within the ancient Roman province of Arabia, these remnants tell of a very large and well-to-do middle class. The thousands of residences were well-planned, richly decorated, had two or more storeys, and contained large rooms, balconies, stables, and elaborately ornamented entrance doors and gateways. They are surrounded by public baths, chapels, churches, and monasteries. There is evidence of large numbers of wine and olive presses, industries, and market places and bazaars. The huge number of tombs they erected are likely the most notable group of ancient funeral structures known in history.

The fifth century saw the commencement of a great era of church building and a renaissance in the art of architecture of Syrian architects, independent of any Byzantine influence. Like the Byzantine churches, the Aramaic-Syriac churches boasted mosaics and wall paintings but unlike Byzantine architecture, Aramaic-Syriac churches were not dependent on their styles for beauty of effect. These churches were complete with a wealth of purely architectural ornament both in the interior and exterior using natural building materials combining simplicity, veracity, and beauty. This is what distinguished them from other forms of Christian architecture, such as the Hellenistic form. It should be noted that unlike Hellenistic art's rich and abundant sculptural decoration, Aramaic architecture is almost wholly without any figurative and representational forms and the ruins of the Christian churches disclose no fragments of freestanding sculpture. The roofs were made of timber, arches and apses were employed, and many of these architectural themes continue today in Maronite churches.

One can speculate how this architecture would have developed if it was not later subject to Islamic rule. What is certain is that the Milan edict in 313, declaring religious tolerance, gave the Aramaic-speaking Christians the chance to accentuate their own oriental influences on architecture rather than a purely classical Hellenistic/Roman influence. This coincided with rich Christian symbolism in the elaborate ornamentation. Within almost three hundred years from the Milan edict to the time of Arab Muslim conquest, the Roman Middle East was able to blossom in its full glory. Every one of the smallest communities possessed a house of Christian worship and even small villages could boast three or four churches.

In the minor arts, Butler suggests that the style and iconography of Syriac illuminated manuscripts, such as the Rabbula Gospels, was as a result of the influence of the Hellenistic Christian centres of Antioch and Alexandria and between them the monastic centres of Syria and Upper Egypt. Badwi would disagree with this analysis. However, in relation to architecture, Butler says the situation was reversed. He says that where Alexandria and Egypt had the more authoritative tradition in the minor arts, 'Syria' had the richer and more permanent stone architecture that grew directly out of the indigenous style of the region. He says that the prothesis and the diaconicon passed from Syria into Egypt and in the case of the flanking chambers became a common feature of the early churches of North Africa. Nothing had ever been produced in Christian architecture to match a church equal to that of St Simon Stylite's or other provincial churches in northern Syria at the time.

### 10.3.3  Churches and Monasteries

Prior to the arrival of the Crusaders there are instances where we are informed a monastery was built without reference to the existence of a previous hermitage(s). This implies that the hermitages connected to the cenobite community were built later to service those monks who desired the complete solitary life. The monastery of Qannoubin (Kannoubin) in the Qadisha (Kadisha) valley of Lebanon may be one such example. The word Kannoubin or Koinobion means cenobium or group of monks living together. Patriarch Doueihi tells us Emperor Theodosius built the monastery around 375. Others believe the monastery was built by the monk Theodosius (c. 423-529), one of the founders of monastic life in a community, who also built a monastery in Palestine and was known as a Kannoubian.[516] It is possible there may have been hermitages – already in place prior to its construction and thereafter the monastery was built.

Not far from Qannoubin, also in the Qadisha valley is the Monastery of St Anthony of Qozhaiyya (Kozhaya). The word Kozhaya is of Syriac origin and means 'treasure of life'. The valley of Qadisha was named after the words valley of the 'sainted' or 'sacred' in Syriac. Oral histories passed down by the monks of the monastery from the Lebanese Maronite Order inform us that there were Christian hermits living there around the time of St Anthony the Great (251-356) and that St Anthony himself visited them from Egypt with one of his disciples, Bishoi. The oral history has it that there were one or two years in the life of St Anthony where his whereabouts were not known and during this time he made his visit to the hermits in Qadisha. They believe the abandoned cell of Bishoi still stands in the cliff next to the present monastery as testament to this event.

The Qadisha valley is dotted with both abandoned and currently used hermitages. One hermitage, Our Lady of Hawqa, is presently occupied by the Colombian born priest Father Dario Escobar, mentioned in Chapter 5. The Crusader Brocard in 1183 mentioned the monasteries and numerous churches in the valley.[517] Sader comments that in 1997 there were hundreds of grotto-hermitages in the Qadisha being documented by Lebanese spelaeologists (cave scientists).[518]

Around the twelfth and thirteen centuries, there is documentary evidence from the Crusaders of the principal Maronite monasteries spread over Mt Lebanon. They included: Our Lady of Yanouh (in Batroun region); Our Lady of Abel (Habil), near Gibilet (Jbail); St Elijah and Notre Dame at Lehfed; St Maroun of Kfarhai; St Anthony of Kozhaya; St Sergius of Hardin (destroyed 1440); St Demetrius near Becharre; St Cyprian of Caphiphoun; St George of Kafar; Sts Sergius

---

[516] Harb, *The Maronites: History and Constants*, p. 54.
[517] Youhanna Sader, *Painted Churches and Rock cut Chapels of Lebanon*, Dar Sader, 1997, p. 40.
[518] Ibid.

and Bacchus (Bakhos) near Ehden.[519] There are obvious omissions such as Qannoubine.

The monasteries of northern Syria, particularly the church connected with the great St Simon the Stylite monastery, had profound influence upon ecclesiastical architecture of the sixth century in the Byzantine world. Butler says that more than any other buildings in Christian history between the third and twelfth century, the northern Syrian churches illustrate a conscious effort to produce a beautiful exterior effect with the interiors naturally taking care of themselves. Typical of these churches was the apse in semicircular form covered with a half dome of cut stone rather than timber. Practically all of the churches in the Middle East were orientated with the sanctuary facing east.

Butler also notes that rich hangings played an important part in these Syrian churches. Sockets in walls evidence wooden fixtures for the support of these hangings. The wall hangings distinguish the interior of the Aramaic-speaking churches from the Greek Byzantine form. The Greek Byzantine form contains the iconostasis wall in front of the altar. The Aramaic-Syriac form, without an iconostasis, still provided a richness of colour in the interior taking its own unique style with wall hangings and evidence in some churches of painting over plaster on the roof and mosaic pavements on the floor.

It is no wonder that with the arrival of the Arab Muslims, who were typically aniconic and opposed imagery, most traces from these Syrian ancient sites of any sculpture or imagery were lost. There is some evidence of human and animal depictions in the churches of the Middle East. Butler reports that the earliest example in the world of the Madonna and Child lies on a lintel of a church in Khanasir in an ancient area of north-eastern Syria.

The ornamental architecture of the Middle Eastern churches is nowhere more glorified than in the carving or mouldings on stone of symbolic discs to which hundreds of examples can be found on buildings still standing. These discs are not of Christian origin but can be

---

[519] Ibid.

found previously in pagan buildings. However, Butler confirms that they are distinctively Syrian in style. The Aramaic-speaking populations used them in Antiochian Aramaic-Syriac-speaking churches of the Maronites and the Syriac Orthodox, to infuse Christian symbolism in their ornamentation as well as the distinctive equal-armed cross surrounded by a round laurel. The Lebanese Maronite Order uses these symbols today as do some Syriac Orthodox monasteries.

They are generally circular in nature and the cross, almost equal-armed, in one form or another is the chief motive of each design. It is often converted into monograms of Christ by the addition of a P to the head of the cross. The quadrants between the cross and a circle are filled with various symbols, such as the lily, the rose, the dove, the lamb, and the wafer. The enclosing circle is most often a wreath incised or in relief. They can be found not only in the interior and exterior of churches and monasteries but also on the top of doorways and windows to houses. Often they are found on the keystones above doorways. Not mentioned by Butler or any other scholar, is the possibility of these discs influencing the Crusaders in their art and Christian symbolism thereafter, for example, in the style of the Maltese cross, St John Ambulance cross, pharmacy cross, hospital cross, and the Red Cross (discussed further in section 10.4.1).

It should be noted that Constantinople was the civil, not the ecclesiastical or religious head of the Middle East. It could be said that the architectural aims of Constantinople and the Middle East were opposed. Antioch was proud of the apostolic origin of her patriarchal see and jealous of any interference from the political capital. Her patriarchs were often opposed to the patriarchs of Constantinople. The emperors alone had power to control them and often failed. The architects from Constantinople clearly developed a school of architecture in which the dome was the principal form and brick the main material. The aim of the architects of the Middle East was to perpetuate the stone tradition – the dome and cross vault was rare, the arches were less bulky and the dosseret, so characteristic of Byzantine architecture, was almost non-existent. Although both forms of architecture treated carved ornament with colour, one school believes this originated in the Middle East, thereafter influencing Byzantium.

The architecture of churches and buildings of each region in the Middle East, although possibly having a minor common foreign influence, had little in common with each other. The architecture of the Holy Land was different to that of Arabia, and likewise the Holy Land and Arabia different to the architecture of northern Syria. Some variation in forms probably had to do with the different types of stone available. In northern Syria (including Lebanon) the buildings had intricate patterns carved into limestone, the most ideal stone for this kind of work. It allowed for detail in doorways and door caps, treatments around windows, mouldings, and entablatures with almost every form of richly carved ornament imaginable. In the southern Syrian Orient and Arabia the buildings were almost devoid of carving and intricacy because the basalt used is very hard. Although this did change slightly in the Arabian area with the advent of Christian symbolism in ornamental work, it is possible that stone choice impacted on the less ornamental style of Islamic stonework.

Throughout the Middle East, many Christian inscriptions on churches commemorated a saint. The most favoured saint among the Aramaic Christians was their own Sarkis (in English Sergius), martyred about the beginning of the fourth century. Churches were built in honour of his name as the patron saint including St Bacchus. The second most important or popular Aramaic saint was St George – the Aramaic martyr of the persecutions under Diocletian. St George was put to death in Palestine and is still greatly revered by the Christians. As noted in the part of this book on the Aramaic popes and Aramaic migration to Rome, Sergius, and George became popular names amongst Romans.

Before referring to the saint in the dedication of the inscription, many inscriptions began with the words "there is One God and His Christ and the Holy Spirit," "In the Name of the Father, Son, and Holy Spirit" or "Holy Mary, Mother of God, help ..." (referring to the name of the builder of the church). Numerous inscriptions provided the name of a Jewish prophet such as Moses, the great law-giver of the Jews. Apart from churches being built as memorials, many others were also built in fulfillment of vows made by individuals, groups, or families. Some of these traditions regarding memorials continue today even in the Latin Church.

In northern Syria there are a significant number of ancient churches (forty five out of hundreds), which contain a *bema*. This is a large horseshoe shaped platform in the centre of the nave of the church. It is a particular feature of the architecture of the west Aramaic-Syriac dialects rather than east Aramaic-Syriac dialects. There is some archaeological evidence that its origins are from the synagogue architectural tradition. It has been recently suggested that this altar, being a peripheral altar rather than the main altar, was used as a way to display or use a saint's relic during services and linked to the display or veneration of the relic during the liturgy/mass. This is a distinct feature of Aramaic architecture not found in other Christian architecture.

An aspect of the Syrian churches that is distinct from other Eastern churches is that there is no iconostasis – that is, no wall of icons separating the nave from the sanctuary. Syriac church architecture takes a more simplistic form. Aramaic monasticism also took its own practice with in most cases little influence from its Greek counterpart. The Aramaic-Syriac language, the sacred melodies, and the liturgy of the Syrian-Aramaic Antiochian churches are also distinct from the Byzantine Church. They do not have any Greek origins.

On a passing note, perhaps one of the striking and little known differences between some, and possibly in ancient times, all Aramaic-Syriac churches and Byzantine churches was the kneeling for prayer with prostration, which today is resembled by Muslims praying. Dalrymple tried to popularise this comparison in his book *From the Holy Mountain* when he witnessed in the mid 1980s Syriac Orthodox congregations in Turkey and Syria "praying like Muslims." Syriac and Byzantine church traditions do however share other traits, perhaps mysticism being the most common when compared to the Latin (Roman) Church.

## 10.4 Influence on Western and Christian Aesthetics

At the time when Middle Eastern architecture was at its height, France and Italy housed masses of ethnic Aramaics – mostly merchants and ecclesiastics – who held prominent positions in the economic and religious life of the West. There are ample chronicles and inscriptions from as early as the third century of 'Syrians' in Gaul (a former region including France, northern Italy, Belgium, Germany west of the Rhine, and the southern Netherlands). When the Arab conquest cut Western Christianity off from the Middle East, these Syrian craftsmen, traders, and churchmen could not return to their homeland and therefore would have continued to influence Western-style culture and architecture. Butler suggests that the Romanesque facade with its two flanking towers, which provides us with the modern-day Western style of church, was influenced by the Aramaic towered façade.

### 10.4.1 The Equal-Armed Cross and Modern Emblems

As mentioned in Section 10.3.3 above, one of the most remarkable points of influence of Aramaic culture on Christian aesthetics and modern Western symbolism is the equal-armed cross. The Crusaders would have been familiar on their journey and long occupation of the Middle East seeing many of the seventh century abandoned villages of northern Syria. Within this feast of archaeological remains, still standing today, are hundreds of examples of equal-armed crosses with circular reliefs. Similar and other types of equal-armed crosses are found in abundance in Maronite Churches of Lebanon dating back to the sixth and seventh century.[520] They seem to be typical only to the region of the Middle East including Lebanon. Some scholars have incorrectly referred to these pre-Crusade crosses as 'Maltese crosses', although the Maltese cross is not known to pre-date the Crusade era.

The Order of the Hospital of St John the Baptist, also known as the Knights of St John or the Knights Hospitaller established themselves in Jerusalem during the Crusades. At one stage their nursing work accommodated one thousand pilgrims per year. Their hospitals

---

[520] For example, see Sader, *Crosses and Symbols in ancient Christian art of Lebanon.*

and guesthouses later spread to all over the Crusader kingdoms. They would later form a military organization around 1187.[521] This is only five years after the date William of Tyre attributes to the Maronite union with Rome. It may be of little coincidence the Maronites had a substantial population in Acre prior to the arrival of the Crusades and subsequently the Knights of St John became stationed there in an imposing fortress like monastery and then the Maronites and Hospitallers joined forces. The Hospitallers were part of the occupation of the three locations of the last Christian resistance before the final fall of the Crusades – in Akko, Krak des Chevaliers (near Homs) and Tripoli, all three in the heart of Maronite strongholds. When King Louis landed at Akko in the Holy Land in 1250 he was received by a contingent of twenty five thousand Maronites. On the fall of Akko in 1291, the Maronites followed the Hospitallers to the Greek island of Rhodes and no doubt were part of a large contingent that made up the Hospitallers and influenced the use of the equal-armed cross.

It is thought a variation to the Aramaic and Maronite cross, the Maltese Cross, was first introduced in the mid-sixteenth century when the Knights migrated to Malta after the fall of Rhodes. These crosses are today incorporated in various ambulance logos throughout the West. In Australia for example, that includes St John's ambulance services and the various state government run ambulance services. It may have been an influence for the Red Cross logo. It is not inconceivable to suggest the Middle East crosses, were the inspiration for these western medical service crosses. Similarly one could suggest the Maronites, who joined the Order of St John Hospitallers in tens of thousands, were influential not only for the form of the Christian cross logo, but hospital practice and military organization of the Knights. Perhaps the black robes worn by the Order of St John until 1248 were also influenced by the Maronites. This is when the robe (surcoat) became black with a white cross and then later replaced by a red surcoat with white cross.

---

[521] Seward, *Monks of War*, p. 19.

## 10.5  Influence of Aramaic Christian Culture on Islam

Before the birth of Islam, Aramaic-Syriac monks were responsible for the conversion of many Arabs to Christianity. Vööbus states: "It must be said that one cannot understand the sudden rise of the Islamic culture without the factor of all the accomplishments of the Syrian culture in the formation of which Syrian monasticism played the most important role."[522] In other words, the exposure of Aramaic-Syriac Christianity in Arabia significantly assisted the local population, pagan and otherwise, in their immediate understanding and acceptance of Islam. In the new religion of Islam, Jesus was a prophet-messenger. Without the presence of Aramaic-Syriac Christianity (and Judaism) in Arabia, the rapid rise of the Muslim faith cannot be understood.

### 10.5.1  Islamic Architecture

Certainly the Christian architecture of Syria and Arabia influenced not only the styles of Christian architecture in other countries but also the aesthetics of Islam. It is generally agreed that metal bells, and therefore bell towers, were not introduced into Latin churches before the seventh or eighth century. But the East had its own form of church bell well before. The Eastern church bell was the *nakus* or semantron, an instrument of two suspended logs made to swing toward each other and touch, producing a booming sound. It is thought this was housed in the top of towers to produce the sound necessary to call the worshippers together. Many of the churches in the Middle East, particularly in northern Syria in the ancient villages abandoned around the time of the Islamic conquests, contain remnants of towers that likely would have been used for this purpose. They had large openings separated by colonnettes in the top storey, resembling the top storeys of minarets. Butler states it is probable they were the prototypes from which the Islamic minarets took their form.[523]

Other towers in the Middle East contained watch or signal towers of a military character but these were not connected to the churches.

---

[522] Vööbus, *A History of Ascetism in the Syrian Orient*, Vol. I, p. viii.
[523] Butler, *Early Churches in Syria*, pp. 210-211.

Many other churches in the Middle East, including in Arabia, from the fifth to the seventh century contained towers with a distinct chamber at the top. The chamber comprised small windows, cupboards in the top storey, and overhanging constructions to pull up supplies and for sanitary discharge with clay pipes leading to the ground. Butler, over a hundred years ago, believed that these were the towers of the hermits who imitated St Simon. They did this by separating themselves from the world living shut up in towers instead of being exposed upon pillars. Butler says:

> One of the Arab poets of the sixth century signals the Christian monk in his menerah, whose night lamp shines far out over the desert. The word *menorah*, means, among other things, a lighthouse and a minaret; therefore it is probable that the poet was referring to one of these same towers which was the retreat of some holy man.[524]

One can imagine how these hermits would have preached from these towers to the pilgrims who would have been as fascinated with this person as they were with all the other ascetics. St Simon Stylite's pillar had a diameter of just over a metre and was between sixteen and eighteen metres high. It had timber planks at the top making a square type platform of about two metres by two metres with timber balustrades around it, resembling in a later period the balcony of an Islamic minaret. Typical of many stylite pillars, there was an earthenware pipe leading from the top platform to a pit at the bottom for the lavatory. There was also a ladder for those who wanted to climb to the top. The top levels of these stylite towers resemble the top storeys of Muslim minarets. Butler concludes that these church minarets were the prototype from which the Muslim tower took its form. This is a very plausible explanation. It is extraordinary it has not been researched further by modern day scholars.

The Rabbula illuminations depict a form of oriental arch that may have been used in the Aramaic-Syriac Christian architecture at the time. This arch continues its inner circular form at the bottom of

---

[524] Ibid.

both ends rather than stopping as a perfect semi-circle. Butler points to some evidence this arch was also found in the region prior to the birth of Jesus. It is now more common to Islamic buildings and is sometimes identified, incorrectly, as having its origins from the Islamic arch. However, one can still see today the arch in some Christian churches and buildings in use in the Middle East and Lebanon including in Maronite churches.

## 10.5.2 The Aramaic Language

There has been recent suggestion in the western academic world that Aramaic-Syriac Christianity had an important cultural and linguistic importance for the Koran.[525] They also suggest that Aramiac-Syriac, transmitted through a Christian medium, had a fundamental influence on those who created written Arabic. The legitimacy of these propositions should be examined more carefully from the part of Islamic and Syriac scholars.

One key example of linguistic influence, mentioned in Chapter 2, is the identification of Christian hermits of the Middle East with martial motifs, e.g. as soldiers in a holy war against the devil and whose weapon was prayer. In the modern day clash of fundamentalisms, coupled with, for the first time in history, the rapid increase of Muslim populations in the West, perhaps the context of this warfare terminology in the setting of the Middle East and its period of time around the birth of Islam, can be put into perspective as impacting upon the Islamic idea of *jihad* or 'holy war'. That is, not physical warfare against fellow humans, but rather the individual's own spiritual and personal fight against the enemy, the devil, as a common theme amongst the three monotheistic religions of Judaism, Christianity, and Islam in the context of Middle Eastern culture. This shared vocabulary has the potential to promote an understanding in the West of the Middle East, Islamic ethics, and mutual respect, co-existence, and harmony amongst the Abrahamic faiths.

---

[525] Based on Christoph Luxenberg's book, *The Syro-Aramaic Reading of the Koran: A Contribution to the Decoding of the Language of the Koran*, Hans Shiler, 2007.

### 10.5.3 Religio-Cultural Customs

St John Chrysostom tells us the stylites said their prayers and Bible reading five times a day standing – the chanting of Psalms before the cock crow, prayers at 9am, noon, 3 pm, and sunset. The regularity provides us with a parallel to the basis of Muslim prayer times. Though it is rarely commented upon it is striking how similar the prostrations of Muslims during prayer are to the traditional prostrations of the Aramaic Syriac Christians including the many anchorites of north Syria in the early centuries. These Christian prostrations can be still found today in the Syriac Orthodox Church.

It is likely that the modest dress code of the early seventh century Christians of the Middle East impacted on the development of scarf wearing amongst Muslim women. This is today still a firm part of many Islamic cultures, and can be seen in many variations such as the *hijab*, designed to wrap around the head and neck to cover a woman's hair and chest. The oval opening of the Virgin Mary's veil depicted in the sixth century Rabbula Gospels with its Ephodita (white bandage that oriental women wear under their veil) were characteristic of Syriac iconography at the time.[526] The Aramaic-Syriac tradition of modest dress and veils for women can be seen depicted in the Rabbula Gospel through the icon of Our Lady and the women in the scenes of the Crucifixion and Resurrection. The Rabbula Gospel images pre-date Islam by more than half a century.

Mary (Mariam), the mother of Jesus, holds a special place in Islam. She is the only woman referred to by name in the Koran and is mentioned numerous times. She is referred to as being chosen above all women of creation acknowledging God created Adam without parents and the birth of Jesus (Issa) was from a mother with no father. Mary's son Jesus is mentioned as a 'prophet' and a 'messenger'. In Islam, Mohammed is the final messenger.

In 2007, as the only country in the world to declare a joint Christian-Muslim religious feast, Lebanon declared 25 March as a nation-

---

[526] Badwi, *The Liturgical Year Iconography of the Syro-Maronite Church*, p. 281.

al holiday to be celebrated by Christians and Muslims for the Feast day of the Annunciation, that is, the announcement by the archangel Gabriel to Mary that she would conceive and become the mother of Jesus. Under the patronage of the Maronite Bishop of Australia, His Excellency Bishop Antoine-Charbel Tarabay, Christians and Muslims in Australia descendant from the Middle East, both religious and faithful, are now also celebrating this feast day together.

## 10.6   Christian Culture Under Islamic Rule

### 10.6.1 Overview

With the arrival of the Arab Muslim conquerors towards the middle of the seventh century, it has been estimated that half the world's Christian population became subjected to Muslim rule.[527] For many decades after the initial conquest, the Umayyad Caliphs kept the Byzantine administrative system and also Greek as the official government language. Those Christians with knowledge of Greek in the cities of administration retained a certain social prestige and influence, particularly if they had worked for the previous Byzantine administration.

Coinage with images of Christ, replacing images of the emperors, were in turn replaced with verses of the Koran under Caliph Abd al-Malik (685-705). The emperor Justinian rejected this move and 692 saw a series of battles between his forces and those of the Arabs. The triumphant Arabs settled their Slav mercenaries in the areas of Antioch and Cyrrhus. In battles against the Byzantines in Antioch, casualties were severe. It seems as though from this time, the Byzantines had abandoned the Arab treaties and the entire Middle East to the Arabs. From then, Christians of the Middle East began to undergo fierce persecution. In due course, the (Byzantine) Melkite Christians, aligned to the emperor in Constantinople, were to suffer a great deal for their attachment to the king who led the enemy of the Arabs.

Some authors have reported Abd al-Malik declared Arabic as the

---

[527] Noble and Treiger, *The Orthodox Church in the Arab World*, p. 3.

official language of the administration. Theophanes (d. 818) suggests this decree came in 707-708 when Caliph al-Walid (the son of Abd al-Malik) robbed the Catholic Church in Damascus and stopped the use of Greek in the public record books of the departments ordering they be written in Arabic instead. Theophanes records the public finance minister of Palestine at this time was a Christian.[528] Theophanes also informs us that because of language barriers the scribes remained Christian even up to his time. Caliph al-Walid (705-715) decreed around 711-713 that Christians who did not convert to Islam be taken into churches and killed.[529]

In Jerusalem, Abd al-Malik constructed the Dome of the Rock on the Temple Mount. It was designed to rival the Church of the Resurrection (the Holy Sepulchre) and was decorated with Koranic style verses that opposed the doctrines of the Trinity and the Incarnation. In Damascus, al-Walid demolished the (Byzantine Melkite) Cathedral of St John the Baptist, which previously had defined prayer areas for both Christians and Muslims, and constructed the great Umayyad Mosque. During the construction of the mosque, John the Baptist's relic of his head was apparently found in a crypt and on al-Walid's orders a special column was erected in the mosque in honour of the relic as the Muslims revere John The Baptist as one of the prophets. The shrine remains in place today.[530]

Mosques began to dominate the public space marginalising the previous ubiquity of church buildings. Christians became second-class citizens. Caliph Umar II (717-720) introduced the 'Pact of Umar' under which Christians could maintain their 'protected' status as *dhimmis*. In addition to paying the *jizya* tax, the 'Pact' prohibited Christians from building new churches or repairing old ones. Christians were not allowed to convert Muslims or endeavour to discourage family members, including spouses and next-of-kin, from converting to Islam. They could not teach their children the Koran or imitate Muslim cloth-

---

[528] Theophanes, *The Chronicle of Theophanes*, pp. 64, 73.
[529] Michael the Syrian, *Chronicle of Michael the Great*, paragraph 136.
[530] Noble and Treiger, *The Orthodox Church in the Arab World*, p. 17.

ing, speech, or behaviour. They were forbidden from riding horses or carrying swords and were required to wear distinctive dress, including a special belt called the *zunnar*. Future Muslim rulers, such as Abbasid caliph al-Mutawakkil (847-861) and Fatimid caliph al-Hakim (996-1021), enforced the 'Pact' with great brutality. Even in modern times the 'Pact' has been used as validation for refusing the building and repair of churches including in Egypt.

Restricting the public presence of Christians was taken a step further by Umayyad caliph Yazid II (720-724) who forbade the public display of crosses and icons and called for their destruction.[531] Additional laws related to Christians included: their testimonies should not be admitted; they were forbidden to ride on saddled animals; and should a Muslim kill a Christian he would not die as a result but could pay a blood price of a thousand (or five thousand) drams. He also made a law that all Arabs (including Christians) should not drink wine.[532] As a result of the prohibition to ride on saddled animals, it is from this time we can assume travel for Christians was severely limited. It may also have been directed against the remnants of any Christian militia, potentially those aligned to the Maronite Church.

It is likely a great many Maronites and other Christians at this time retreated to secluded areas such as the mountain region of Lebanon. Persecution intensified under the last Sunni Umayyad caliph, Marwan II (745-750), especially when the Shiite Abbasids under Abul-Abbas seized the Caliphate from Marwan. In 750, "the soldiers of Abdullah bin Ali spread terror by killing many Jews and Christians."[533] The Maronites from the Mount Lebanon district of Jebbet al-Munaytra complained to the Abbasid governor of Baalbek about high taxes and the petitions were dismissed. Led by Bandar, a Maronite militia proceeded towards Baalbek and assaulted some villages in the Bekaa valley. They suffered heavy losses in an ambush and in return the Abbasids seized the fort of al-Munaytra, killing and capturing many inhabit-

---

[531] Noble and Treiger, *The Orthodox Church in the Arab World*, pp. 17-18.
[532] Michael the Syrian, *Chronicle of Michael the Great*, paragraph 139.
[533] Harb, *The Maronites: History and Constants*, p. 78, quoting Arab historian Makki.

ants. The Baalbek legislator, Imam Abdul Rahman al-Ouzai (707-774) wrote a letter to the governor of Baalbek expressing indignation at the killing of innocent villagers. After the al-Munaytra rebellion, the Abbasid Caliph Abu Jaafar al Mansur (754-775) implanted Arab tribes in the Lebanese mountains to restrain Maronite expansion from the north and Byzantine raids from the sea.

Many military confrontations occurred between the Maronites and these tribes, particularly the Tannukhi. The Tannukhis were instructed by the caliph to protect the coastal region and the mountains overlooking Beirut from Maronite invasions. The battle of Nahr-al Mot, near Beirut, resulted in the Maronites withdrawing to the north. It was at this time the first Islamic Arab emirate of Tannukh was established in Lebanon. It lasted for eight centuries until the beginning of the Ottoman rule.[534]

In 756-757, Theodore the Melkite patriarch of Antioch was exiled for being (falsely) accused of revealing Arab affairs in letters to Constantinople. In the same year, Abd Allah decreed for all Arab lands that no new churches were to be built, the cross was not to be displayed and that Christians should not enter into religious discussions with Arabs. In the following year, taxes were increased on the Christians, and "all monks, solitary monks and pillar sitters (who are pleasing to God)" had to pay taxes. He also sealed the churches' treasuries and brought in Hebrews to sell them; they were purchased by freedmen.[535]

In 760-761, a Syrian named Theodore led a rebellion against the Arabs in the villages outside of Heliopolis (Baalbek) in Lebanon. Both sides suffered substantial losses. Eventually, the Lebanese were defeated and all those who were with Theodore were killed, but he fled.[536] In 762 the seat of the caliphate transferred from the Umayyads of Damascus to the Abbasids of Baghdad. Administration and court models shifted from Byzantine to Iranian and in literature from Bedouin Arab to Persian in culture. The Abbasids promoted the con-

---

[534] Ibid., p. 80, quoting Arab historians Ibn Acakir, al-Balaziri and al-Shidyaq.

[535] Theophanes, *The Chronicle of Theophanes*, p. 119.

[536] Ibid., p. 121.

version of non-Arabs to Islam resulting in mass conversions. A west Syriac chronicle (c. 775) from the region of Tur Abdin (present-day south-eastern Turkey), reports entire villages of up to three hundred at a time converting without compulsion.[537] Apostasy from Islam was punishable by death under Islamic law. There are accounts in the eighth and ninth centuries of a number of Byzantine Christians in Syria and Palestine who converted to Islam, then reverted back to Christianity, and were martyred at the hands of Muslim officials, as well as a Muslim who converted to Christianity and was martyred for publicly proclaiming his conversion.[538]

Theophanes records contact between Constantinople and Antioch and Alexandria in 784-785 noting a temporary peace treaty with the Arabs.[539] In 872, Ahmad Ibn Tolon, the Turkish ruler of Egypt, overthrew the Abbasid Empire in Palestine, Syria and Lebanon. In 935, the Akhshidi replaced the Tolonians and in 969 the North African Ismaili branch of the Shiite Fatimid Empire overthrew the Tolonoians. During the reign of Fatimid Caliph Al Hakim bi Amrellah (996-1021), Christians suffered humiliating persecutions and thousands of churches were demolished including the Church of the Holy Sepulchre in Jerusalem. This resulted in most of the Byzantine Melkite Christians emigrating from Alexandria, and a large number of monks from Palestine, to Constantinople. It is said this is one of the events that mobilised Christian Europe to launch the Crusades to liberate the Holy Land.[540]

## 10.6.2   The Destruction of the Beit Maroun Monastery

There is evidence in a Syriac manuscript written in 581, stored in the British Museum, that the Monastery of St Maroun was still in existence around the middle of the eighth century. A note in that year, placed on the Syriac manuscript, read that the manuscript came to the

[537] Noble and Treiger, *The Orthodox Church in the Arab World*, pp. 20-21.
[538] Ibid., pp. 23-24.
[539] Theophanes, *The Chronicle of Theophanes*, p. 145.
[540] Harb, *The Maronites: History and Constants*, p. 80.

library of Beit Maroun in 745.[541] The monastery remained active in 791 as noted in a letter written to the monks by the Nestorian patriarch, Timotheus I.[542]

Jacobite Patriarch of Antioch, Dionysius of Tell Mahre (d. 845) wrote in his *Annales* "They [the Maronites] ordain a patriarch and bishops from their monastery" giving weight that the monastery was still in existence in his lifetime.[543] However, there is evidence suggesting the monastery was destroyed during the reign of the Sultan around the time of the Arab historian al-Masudi (d. 960):

> there was dedicated to him (St Maron) a great convent, located in the east of Hamah and Chizar. It was a splendid building. Around it were three hundred cells, inhabited by monks ... That convent was sacked ... by the many raids of the Arabs and by the cruelty of the Sultan. It is situated on the shore of the Orontes, the river of Emese [Emesa] and Antioch.[544]

Dib states there is no mention of the monastery in any writings after al-Masudi.[545] Dib refers to Patriarch Doueihi's seventeenth century comment that John Maron II definitively transferred the Maronite Patriarchal residence to Lebanon in 939.[546]

---

[541] Dib, *History of the Maronite Church*, p. 6.

[542] Dib refers to the letter as preserved in the Chaldean monastery of St Hormisdas near Algosch in the Doicese of Mosul –a copy can also be found at the Vatican.

[543] Dib, *History of the Maronite Church*, p. 7, cites Michael the Syrian.

[544] Citied in Guita Hourani, "Saint Maron's Relic 'Ornament of the Divine Choir of Saints'," *The Journal of Maronite Studies*, 1997, http://www.maronite-institute.org/ MARI/JMS/january97/Saint_Marons_ Relic.htm. The English translation by Hourani is from the French translation of 1897 by Cara de Vaux. Naaman's version is quoted in full in Chapter 9.

[545] Dib, *History of the Maronite Church*, p. 7.

[546] Ibid., p. 47.

# CHAPTER 11

## THE IMPACT OF THE CRUSADES

### Timeline of Key Events

| | |
|---|---|
| 1054 | Generally accepted date for the Great Schism between Eastern and Western Catholics. Maronites become the only Catholics in the East. |
| 1095 | Council of Clermont launches the crusades to recover the Holy Land and to re-establish safe pilgrimages from the West. |
| 1098 | Passage of the Crusaders (1098) through the coasts of Syria and Lebanon to Jerusalem – the 'Holy Land'. |
| 1099 | Crusaders take over Lebanon and Jerusalem. Maronites assist Crusaders to Jerusalem. |
| 1120 | Maronite Patriarch moves from Yanouh, Lebanon to Our Lady of Ilige in Mayfouk. |
| 1130 | Maronites in Lebanon gift and entrust to an Italian Count on pilgrimage to the Holy Land the skull of St Maroun – the most important and only surviving bodily relic of the Maronites' patron saint. |
| 1182 | Maronites introduce minor Latin influences into liturgy to express loyalty to Rome. Maronites confirmed in communion with Catholic Church in Rome. |
| 1183 | Maronites from Lebanon (including Upper Galilee) expand to Jerusalem. |

## 11.1  Introduction to the Period

Since its early foundation, the Catholic Church was made up of a diversity of traditions and disciplines (rites or churches) not uniform in practice but all united in the one faith. These sets of customs grew up around the five major centres of the early Christian church which were important cities in the Roman Empire: Rome in Italy, Antioch in

397

Syria (now Antakya in Turkey near the border of Syria), Alexandria in Egypt, Byzantium (later Constantinople, now Istanbul in Turkey) in Asia Minor, and Jerusalem in today's Israel. Each of these centres had a patriarch. The Roman patriarch, the pope, as successor to St Peter who died in Rome, is the primary patriarch of the Catholic Church.

For a substantial part of the first one thousand years of Christianity, the Roman or Latin rite was simply one rite of many that was practised in the multicultural Catholic Church. During the first five centuries of Christianity, the Catholic congregation of the Roman liturgy in Western Europe and Britain were far outnumbered by the Catholic congregation of differing liturgical customs in the East. A bishop from the East often occupied the papal seat.

The declarations by the Catholic Church in the fifth to seventh centuries relating to two of the most well-known 'heresies', Nestorianism and Monophysitism, caused the formation of a number of Middle Eastern Christian churches who broke away from the sees of Rome and Constantinople. The population of the Middle East was almost entirely Christian during this time. Debate amongst them was intense and they were passionate about their faith. Rome and Constantinople remained in direct communication with the Christians in the Middle East.

By the year 638 the Arab Muslims had overtaken the Middle East. By the early eighth century, it appears Muslim rule severed communication between Christians of the Middle East and their counterparts in Constantinople and Rome. From 635 to 1918 AD, a period of almost 1300 years, the Maronites and Christians of the Middle East were under the succession of Islamic empires ruled by caliphs or sultans, some of whom were moderate in their tolerance of Christians while others promoted their fierce persecution. The only exception to Islamic rule was the Crusader's period between 1098 and 1289 (apart from the reconquering of Antioch by the Byzantines from 969 to 1085). The land of the Maronites and of Middle Eastern Christians was subject to continual battles between at least seven competing Islamic rulers from different regional areas, ethnic backgrounds and beliefs – both Shiite and Sunni.

The Great Schism between the churches of Rome and Constantinople in 1054 was the culmination of a long estrangement. Timothy Ware records the schism was long developed over two principal theological matters. First, Rome's Papal claims to universal supremacy rather than primacy of honour with Constantinople demanding that final decisions on matters of faith rest with a Council representing all the bishops of the Church. Second, the dispute over the Filioque in the Nicene Creed with the Byzantine Church opposed to the addition of the words "and the Son" after the words "I believe in the Holy Spirit, the Lord, the giver of life, who proceeds from the Father."[547]

After the great schism of 1054 between Western Catholicism and Eastern (in essence Greek Byzantine) Catholicism, the Crusaders were sure that there were no longer any Catholics in the entire East. They believed the Latin Christian customs and traditions emanating from Rome were now the only true rites that existed in the Catholic Church. Since this time Roman Catholics have generally regarded themselves as the only proper Catholics.

In 1095, not long after the great schism, the Council of Clermont launched the first Crusades by 'Western' British and European Latin Catholics known as the Crusaders. They were to recover the Holy Land and to re-establish safe Catholic pilgrimages from the West to the birthplace of Christ without the threat of Muslim persecution. The Crusaders were highly apprehensive of Eastern Christianity. In saving the lands of the Middle East and the Holy Land from Islam, they sometimes turned their minds to saving the souls of the 'heretics' in the East and showing them the 'error' of their ways – but they did this from Euro-centred and Latin-centred minds, maintaining every suspicion about the customs of these Eastern Christians and their allegiances. Their approach was to match Eastern Christian groups to

---

[547] Timothy Ware (Bishop Kallistos of Diokleia), *The Orthodox Church*, Penguin Books, 1997, pp. 44 and 49..

a heresy and, since the Maronties had been separated from Rome for four hundred years, the Crusaders relied upon on other rival Middle Eastern Christian denominations for reports and historical accounts to match them to their alleged deviation.

On their journeys, the Crusaders divided the seized lands and created four kingdoms for European nobles: Jerusalem (extending to Jbail in north Lebanon), Tripoli (from Jbail to Maraclea in northern Syria), Antioch (from Maraclea to Tarsus in modern Turkey), and Edessa (extending beyond the Euphrates). Within these kingdoms Latin bishops were elected, as were Latin patriarchs of Jerusalem and Antioch. Struggles for power ensued between the Crusaders themselves. The Eastern population were caught in the midst.

These Latin-Roman Catholic Crusaders often attempted to impose their religious customs and traditions on the Eastern Christian population. The Maronites, who sought to be loyal to the Catholic Church, but also to maintain their Eastern Aramaic-Syriac Antiochian practice, were probably the most misunderstood by the Crusaders. Immediately upon the Crusaders' arrival to Lebanon, it is reported in the Crusaders' chronicles that the Maronites came down from the mountains, congratulated them, advised them on the safest route to Jerusalem, and fought alongside them. In 1130, a little over thirty years after the Crusaders arrival, the Maronites gifted and entrusted to an Italian Count on pilgrimage to the Holy Land, the skull of St Maroun. Importantly, this was the Maronite's only remaining relic of the patron saint of their Church and so a significant expression of their loyalty to Rome.

Despite these symbolic deeds, the Crusaders likely remained highly suspicious of the Maronites for several reasons: they were slow to distinguish them from the other Syrian Christians; the Maronites were not Latin either in custom or language; and caution and time was required in observing Maronite liturgical customs which likely were differed from the contemporary official Catholic Church principles given the Maronites' long seclusion from the Latin church. During this period of 'observation', the Crusaders believed they found the necessary heresy for the Maronites – Monothelitism. They relied on a historical account of tenth century historian, Melkite Patriarch Eutychius, demonstrated in this book to be heavily flawed. In addition to the impact upon Maronite liturgy, the Crusaders' paper chronicles have also had significant impacts on the history of Maronite Catholicism during the seventh century Monothelite controversy. The more relevant extracts of primary sources are set out below.

It was not until 1182 that the Crusaders' chronicles record an acceptance by the Crusaders and Rome of the communion between the Maronites and the Catholic Church. It was acknowledged that during these times and thereafter the Maronites, in token of their obedience to Rome, commenced following many of the religious and liturgical customs of the Latin Church. For many centuries later, the Vatican actively pursued the further 'Latinisation' of the Maronite liturgy and traditions.

The prominence of the Maronites, as leading Aramaic Catholics who gained increasing momentum during the fifth to seventh centuries, attracted the attention and rivalry of other Christian denominations. The rivalry was reignited after the arrival of the Crusaders in the late eleventh century and for most of the centuries that followed. Maronite loyalty to Rome during all these periods would have exacerbated any animosity from the opposition. Those writing through the lens of an opposing church could not therefore have been impartial in their accounts about the Maronites, and many would have looked to some form of self-justification of their own church positions. In some instances authors would likely seek to undermine the relationship between Rome and the Maronites by an adverse allegation. This must be given its due weight when considering any evidentiary sources.

## 11.2   Key Sources for the Period

### 11.2.1  William Of Tyre

William of Tyre, born probably in Palestine of a French or English family, died in about 1190. He was at one stage Chancellor to the Latin kingdom of Jerusalem and was also Latin Archbishop of Tyre (in Lebanon). In the West, he is one of the most relied upon historians for a general history of the Crusades and the Kingdom of Jerusalem down to 1184 having written twenty three books in Latin, together entitled *A History of Deeds Done Beyond the Sea*. The English translated extracts from his books relating to the Maronites are set out below. It should be noted that William of Tyre was writing almost a century after the first arrival of the Crusaders in Lebanon.

The Maronites assist the Crusaders (c. 1098-1099):

> The governor of Tripoli obtains a treaty from the Christians, at the cost of much money and many gifts. By the advice of the faithful living in those parts, the leaders choose the shore route ... High up on the lofty range of Lebanon, whose towering summits rise far above those cities of the East which I have just mentioned [Akko, Tripoli, and Byblos], lived certain Syrian Christians.

> These people had come down to offer their congratulations to the pilgrims and to pay them their tribute of brotherly affection. Since they were well acquainted with the country or about, the leaders called these people and consulted with them, as experienced men, about the safest and easiest road to Jerusalem. In all good faith the Syrians carefully considered the advantages and the length of the various routes leading thither and finally recommended the shore road as the most direct. By following this, the pilgrims would also be able to have the assistance of the ships, which would follow the army as it in advanced.[548]

The massacre of the Maronites (c. 1137):

> The count of Tripoli is slain at the Mount of the Pilgrims through the treachery of some of his own people. He is suc-

---

[548] *A History of Deeds Beyond the Sea*, Vol. I, completed about 1189AD by William of Tyre, trans. by E. Atwater, E.A. Babcock, and A.C. Krey, Columbia University Press, 1943, pp. 330-331. (Footnote 29 from the translator at this point quotes: "These were Maronite Christians whose later affiliation with the Roman church is told by William. Although William does not refer to a specific date when this event occurred, on reading of the chapter this book suggests it at about 1098-99 AD.")

ceeded by Raymond, his son, who avenges the death of his father.

Not long after this, Baswaj, commander of the army of Damascus, invaded the land of Tripoli. Count Pons marched valiantly forth against him with all his forces. The two armies met near the fortress called Mount of the Pilgrims, and a fierce battle was fought. But the lives of his army were broken and put to fight, and the Count himself was taken prisoner. Through the treachery of the Syrians who lived on the heights of Lebanon, he was betrayed and put to death. He left a son, Raymond, who, as his heir, succeeded him in the care of the county. Gerald, Bishop of Tripoli, was also captured at this time. He remained in captivity for a while without being recognised, but at last a prisoner held by the Christians was given in exchange for him and he was restored to his former liberty. In this battle some of the nobles of Tripoli fell, but the great majority of those slain were from the middle class.

After the death of his father, Raymond collected the remnant of the cavalry and with a strong body of foot soldiers in addition went up to Mt Lebanon with great valor. Then he seized and carried away in chains to Tripoli as many of those men of blood, with their wives and children as he could find. For he considered them guilty of his father's death and responsible for the general massacre of the Christians, since by their persuasive words they had drawn that powerful man into the plain of Tripoli. Accordingly, to avenge the blood of those who had fallen in battle, he visited upon them divers tortures in the presence of the people, and, in just proportion to the enormity of the crime which they had committed, he caused them to suffer death in its most cruel forms.

Such were the first proofs of valor which were given by the young count, whereby he won the affection of all his people and universal approval.[549]

---

[549] William of Tyre, *A History of Deeds Beyond the Sea*, Vol. II, trans. by E. Atwater, E.A. Babcock, and A.C. Krey, Columbia University Press, 1943, p. 82. Although William does not refer to a specific date when this occurred, this book suggests it was about 1137.

William of Tyre refers to a betrayal "through the treachery of some of his own people ... the treachery of the Syrians who lived on the heights of Lebanon," in relation to one battle in about 1137 between the forces of Christian Count Pons of Tripoli and the Army of the Muslim commander of Damascus Baswaj. Count Pons was taken prisoner and put to death. It is likely these Syrians were Muslim under the Count's rule as William states they were responsible for the general massacre of Christians and the murder of Count Pons, the father of Raymond. The Christians massacred by the Syrians were likely Maronites as they were the only Christian denomination supporting the Crusaders in this early period of arrival of the Crusaders. On reading the next chronicle below, we see the Maronites described as being "of great service to the Crusaders in the difficult engagements which they so frequently had with the enemy."

The Maronites and "the heresy of Maro:"

> At this time, while the kingdom was enjoying a temporary state of peace, as has been related, a race of Syrians in the province of Phoenicia, near the Lebanon range, who occupied territory near the city of Jbail, underwent a wonderful change of heart. For almost fifty years [sic: it should be five hundred years][550] these people had followed the heretical doctrines of a certain Maro, from whom they took the name of Maronites. They had separated from the church of the faithful and had adopted a special liturgy of their own. Now, however, by divine leading, they were restored to their right minds and abandoned their heresy. They repaired to Aimery, the patriarch of Antioch, the third of the Latin patriarchs to preside over that church, renounced the error by which they had been so long enslaved, and returned to the unity of the catholic church. They adopted the orthodox faith and pre-

---

[550] This quote is taken from the translation of William of Tyre's Chronicles held at Sydney University Library and is likely to be a typing error. Although the original Latin version has not been cited for this book, most authors quoting this passage from the original Latin version quote the reference to five hundred years. It is a typical example of historians overlooking human error by relying on translations.

pared to embrace and observe with all reverence the traditions of the Roman church.

These people were by no means few in numbers; in fact, they were generally estimated at more than forty thousand.[551] They lived, as has been said, in the bishoporic of Jbail, Botron, and Tripoli, on the slopes of the Lebanon mountains. They were a stalwart race, valiant fighters, and of great service to the Christians in the difficult engagements which they so frequently had with the enemy. Their conversion to the true faith was, therefore, a source of great joy to us.

The heresy of Maro and his followers is and was that in our Lord Jesus Christ there exists, and did exist from the beginning, one will and one energy only, as may be learned from the sixth council, which, as is well-known, was assembled against them and in which they suffered sentence of condemnation. To this article, condemned by the Orthodox church, they added many other pernicious doctrines after they separated from the number of the faithful. Now, however, as has been stated, they repented of all these heresies and returned to the Catholic Church, under the leadership of their patriarch and several of their bishops. These leaders who had hitherto led their people in the waves of iniquity, now displayed equal zeal in piously guiding them as they returned to the truth.[552]

## 11.2.2  Jacques De Vitry

Jacques de Vitry was born in France and died in 1240. He was bishop of Akko and was later appointed patriarch of Jerusalem. He wrote *The History of Jerusalem* extensively giving an account of conditions in the Holy Land during the Crusader period of his time. Below is the English translation of what he wrote in Latin about the Maronites.

---

[551] Generally a reference in those times to number of men or fighting men.

[552] William of Tyre, *A History of Deeds Beyond the Sea*, Vol. II, p. 458. William does not give a specific date but this book suggests it was about 1180-1182 AD. Also, footnote 25 from the translator quotes: "This union of Maronites with Latins has continued down to the present-day."

## Description of the Maronites and the charge of heresy:

There are some people who dwell on the mountains of Lebanon, in the province of Phoenicia, not far from the city of Biblium. They are numerous, use bows and arrows, and are swift and skilful in battle, and are called Maronites, after their teacher, one Maro, a heretic, who taught that Christ had only one will and one energy. The author of this error was a Bishop of Antioch named Macarius, who, together with his followers, was condemned as an arch-heretic, and cast out of the Church of Christ's faithful people bound with the chain of anathema, by the sixth Synod of Constantinople, in which one hundred and fifty fathers of the church assembled ...

Now the aforesaid Maro, who was foolishly blinded by an illusion sent by the devil, had many followers in his error, who are called Maronites, and for five hundred years were cut off from Holy Church and from communion with the faithful, and celebrated their Sacraments by themselves apart: yet afterwards they turned their hearts, and in the presence of the venerable Father Amalric, Patriarch of Antioch, professed the Catholic Faith, abjured the aforesaid error, and followed the customs of the Church of Rome.[553] Hence, whereas all Eastern prelates save only the Latins do not use rings and pontifical mitres, nor carry pastoral staves in their hands, nor use bells, but are wont to call the people to church by beating a wooden board with a staff or hammer, these aforesaid Maronites, in token of their obedience to Rome, follow the customs and rites of the Latins. So their Patriarch was present at the General Council at the Lateran (1216 AD) which was held with much solemnity in the reign of the venerable Pope Innocent III. They use the Chaldaean alphabet and the common Saracen speech.[554]

---

[553] A note from the translator states: "In 1182; the full submission of the Maronites to the church of Rome dates from about 1600." No explanation is given by the editor and his view is inconsistent with the bulls and letters from the Roman Pontiffs discussed here.

[554] Jacques de Vitry, *The History of Jerusalem*, completed around 1240, trans. by Au-

De Vitry states in this passage "the author of this error was a Bishop of Antioch named Macarius." As noted in Chapter 9 of this book, Macarius was not a Maronite. He was appointed as patriarch of Antioch by Constantinople. The allegation repeats one of the many misleading legends about the Maronites.

### 11.2.3  Evidence for the Gifting of the Skull of St Maroun (1130 AD)

According to Ludovico Jacobilli, in 1130 an Italian abbot was on a pilgrimage to the Holy Land. He brought back to Italy the holy skull of St Maroun. The abbot, Michel Degli Atti, a noble and then Count of Opello, gifted the relic to the abbot (or rector) of the Holy Cross Monastery of Sassovivo. Abbot Michel promoted reverence for St Maroun – St Mauro in Italian – and the relic to such an extent that a great devotion to the saint sprang up throughout all of Italy and spread to Eastern Europe. Since this time the holy skull has remained in the region of Foligno in Italy, near the famous town of Assisi. The crypt at Sassovivo is still dedicated to St Maroun and two towns in Umbria, Italy, celebrate his feast day each year.

Evidence of the gifting and its date have been assessed by Guita Hourani as the following:

> Luigi Jacobilli in his book Vite De'Santi e Beati Dell'Umbria (1656)[555] asserts that in the year 1130 AD, Saint Maron's skull was again moved – this time to Foligno, Italy. The Bibliotheca Sanctorum records the following:
>
> In regard to the relics of St Maron, Jacobilli affirms that the Saint's skull is now preserved in Foligno after being transferred three times. The first transfer was in 1130, when Abbot Michel of the Croce di Sassovivo while on a pilgrimage to the Holy land, brought back the skull of the honored Saint from a Maronite monastery in Syria. A short while after, and at the request of the same Abbot, the skull was moved from Sassovivo to a church erected in honor of the

---

brey Stuart, Palestine Pilgrims Text Society, 1896, pp. 79-80.
[555] Hourani, "Saint Maron's Relic," citing Luigi Jacobilli, *Vite de'Santi e Beati dell'Umbria*.

Saint in a nearby town of Volperino. The third transfer was in 1490 when the relic of the Saint was moved from Volperino to the Cathedral of Foligno where it was placed in a silver statue. The authenticity of the first transfer [from Syria to Sassovivo] is recorded in the Chronicon Monasterii S. Crucis Saxivivi, the other two transfers are noted in the archive of the Church in Volperino and the Town Hall of Foligno.[556]

The country of Lebanon was generally known as part of Syria in the ancient historical context. The passing of the relic from what is understood in Maronite tradition to be none other than the monastery of the skull of St Maroun in Kfarhai, Lebanon, happened some thirty years after the arrival of the Crusaders. This sheds new light on the chronicles of the Crusaders relating to the Maronites and their heresy claims.

It would be highly probable, given the close relationship between the Maronites and the Crusaders, that St Maroun's relic was gifted to them rather than being forcibly taken. The passing of the relic is documented at a point in history more than fifty years prior to the communion with Rome (around 1180-1182) noted by William and de Vitry. On the Crusader's part, it would be unlikely they would have accepted the relic of an honoured saint from a Maronite monastery belonging to a heretical church, some fifty years prior to the stated return to communion with Rome documented by William and de Vitry.

From the thirteenth century a new authentication of apostolic papal letters was introduced with a metal seal made originally from lead. It was given the term *bulla* in Latin (bull in English) because of its bubble or boil (raised embossed) appearance. Thereafter the term 'Bull' was also often used for papal letters predating the lead seal.[557] The first reference to the St Mauro (Maroun) Church in Italy was made in the

---

[556] Ibid.
[557] Herbert Thurston, "Bulls and Briefs," in *The Catholic Encyclopedia*, Robert Appleton Company, 1908, available at: http://www.newadvent.org/cathen/03052b.htm.

Bull of Pope Innocent II of 1138.[558] Unfortunately, William of Tyre missed this critical detail half a century before he attributes the Maronite communion with Rome. It may well be that the Roman declaration of the communion was at this time in 1138: further examination of the Bull is required.

It is likely, therefore, that the Maronites expressed their loyalty to Rome and were in communion with the Catholic Church much sooner than documented by William and de Vitry. It is also highly probable that the gift was the only remaining relic the Maronites had of their patron saint. It evidences at least what Maronite tradition holds as their expression of perpetual and unbroken loyalty to Rome after being cut off from the West for four hundred years. This is further supported by the Maronites who, upon the arrival of the Crusaders, immediately provided assistance for the Crusader route to Jerusalem.

## 11.3 The Church of Rome and the Maronites

In 1215, Maronite Patriarch Irmya al-Amshiti participated in the Lateran Council of Rome. Following the Crusades, he was the first Maronite patriarch to visit Rome. It is likely this led to the first available evidence of Rome's formal recognition of the legitimacy of the Maronite patriarchs in the Bull of Pope Innocent III *Quia Divinae Sapientiae* in 1215: "By our apostolate authority, we grant to you and your successors the use of the pallium according to your approved customs, which you and your predecessors in the Antiochene Church have been known to have." However, patriarchal jurisdiction had been exercised by Maronites in this see before 1199.[559]

In 1256, Pope Alexander IV confirmed the Bull of Innocent III. There are many other examples of papal confirmation of Maronite patriarch legitimacy: Pope Innocent IV (1353-1361); Pope Eugene IV (1431-47); Pope Nicholas V (1447-55); Pope Calistus III (1455-58);

---

[558] Maria R.P. Marzetti, "Volperino, Italy, Celebrates Saint Maron's Feast Like a Phoenix Rising from the Ashes," *The Journal of Maronite Studies*, (1998), http://www.maronite-institute.org/MARI/JMS/october98/ Volperino_Italy.htm.

[559] Dib, *History of the Maronite Church*, pp. 44-45.

*Virtutum Deus* letter of Pope Paul II in 1469; Bull of Pope Leo X in 1515; amongst others.[560] It is worth noting that Pope Leo X was not aware in the early sixteenth century of any apostolic letters from previous Roman Pontiffs that confirmed former Maronite patriarchs. It appeared Rome had little interest in the East at that time. Pope Leo X requested evidence from the Maronites of previous papal approvals. The originals were supplied by the Maronites and the many confirmations noted in the previous paragraphs above were referred to in Pope Leo X's Bull to the Maronite patriarch in 1515.[561]

Whilst there may have been claims that the Maronites were Monothelite prior to 1182 (the date William of Tyre attributes to the communion) and prior to the Bull of 1215, the reasons for this claim are evident in William (based on Eutychius) and de Vitry (based on Macarius being declared heretic at the Council in 680-681). The error and legend of these claims has been demonstrated in Chapter 9. If in the twelfth and thirteenth century it was possible for Rome, with impartial interpreters, to properly examine Maronite liturgical texts, it could also have mistaken the theology of the union of two wills as heretical though it would be not be understood today as a challenge to doctrine.

### 11.3.1 Influence of Roman Customs on the Maronites

As confirmed by Jacques de Vitry in the passage above, it is generally accepted that after centuries of distance from the Catholic Church, the arrival of the Crusades re-established contact between Rome and the Maronite Church. This brought with it significant benefits to the Maronites, both immediate and long-term. There were, however, several adverse impacts at the same time, two of the most notable being the pressure the Crusaders and Rome placed on Maronites to Latinise their customs and rites, and the chronicles produced by the Crusaders which include accusations of heresy against the Maronites.

William of Tyre states: "They [the Maronites] adopted the orthodox faith and prepared to embrace and observe with all reverence the

---

[560] Ibid.
[561] Ibid., p. 46.

traditions of the Roman church." Jacques de Vitry thought the same stating they "professed the Catholic Faith, abjured the aforesaid error, and followed the customs of the Church of Rome." As can be seen from these texts, being loyal to Rome in the eyes of the Crusaders meant not only adhering to doctrine but abandoning the Maronite liturgy and customs for those of the Roman rite.

We know that after the arrival of the Crusaders, the Maronites frequented the Latin churches and celebrated on the altars using the articles of the Western clergy.[562] Churches and paintings began to be influenced by Roman style, and formal church bell towers and metal bells began to appear on top of Maronite churches.[563] Following the visit of Cardinal Peter of Amalfi, at the time of the Bull of Pope Innocent III, *Quia Divinae Sapientiae* of 1215, the pope wrote to the Maronites:

> Having seen that you were lacking in certain things, the Cardinal took care to supplement them by the fullness of apostolic authority in ordering you ... to use at baptism the form which consists in triple immersion but one invocation of the Trinity; to have bishops alone administer the sacrament of Confirmation; not to use any substance other than Balsam and oil in the preparation of Chrism ... Being obedient sons you have accepted all these things with humility and submission. Approving these prescriptions and ordering that they be inviolably observed, we take you, brothers and sons ... with the churches constituted in your provinces, under the protection of the Blessed Peter and ourselves ... and we decree that the prelates located in the Maronite territories wear the vestments and the insignia that are proper to them, according to the manner of the Latins, and conforming in all things and with more care to the customs of the Roman church.[564]

---

[562] See letter from Father Gryphon written from Rome to the Maronites in 1469 cited by Henri Lammens, "Frère Gryphon," *Revue de l'Orient chrétien*, IV (1899), pp. 94-95. See also letter of Gabriel Ibn al-Qela'i to Patriarch Simon of Hadeth written in 1494 in Lammens, "Frère Gryphon," pp. 99-100.

[563] See Dib's references, *History of the Maronite Church*, pp. 63-64.

[564] Translation taken from Ibid., pp. 62-63.

Reading the above extracts it may appear that the Maronites at the time of the Crusades abandoned all their traditional Aramaic-Syriac Antiochene Chalcedonian rites and customs for the Latin Roman rite. However, this contrasts with another passage from the same Bull: "By our apostolic authority, we grant to you and your successors the use of the pallium according to your approved customs, which you and your predecessors in the Antiochene Church have been known to have."[565]

There are also texts many centuries outside the Crusades period relevant to this topic. It appears that until 1592 the Latinisation of the Maronite Church was only superficial and touched on external practices such as the use of metal bells rather than timber bells, the wearing of Latin vestments by the clergy, and the wearing of a ring and mitre by bishops. Dib states:

> But that the work of Eliano and Dandini (papal legates from Rome) marked the point of departure of a systematic Latinisation, touching the very substance of cult. What they undertook was continued by the incessant activity of diverse factors, until a solid, definitive change was achieved.
>
> Patriarch Joseph el-Ruzzi, a daring and resourceful man, was himself an inconsiderate Latiniser; he sacrificed a great number of the venerable practices to copy better the usages of Rome. He defied the opposition of a strong part of his subjects by decreeing certain modifications.[566]

There is some suggestion or evidence that the same Father Eliano, a Jesuit priest mentioned in this passage, supervised the burning of the books and manuscripts of the Maronite rite alleging they contained heresies. In 1606, the same Patriarch Joseph el-Ruzzi as above promulgated the Gregorian calendar. Thus the Maronites were the first Eastern Christians to abandon the use of the Julian calendar.

Eventually, it is likely at some point after the fifteenth century the Maronites ceased making the sign of the cross the same way that the Byzantines and the Greeks still do today – that is, as a symbol of the

---

[565] Ibid., translation from p. 45.
[566] Ibid., p. 105.

two natures of Christ from the 451 Council of Chalcedon with the two smallest fingers pressed against the palm to represent the two natures of Christ, and the other two fingers pressed against the thumb to represent the Trinity. According to Moosa, Ibn al-Qilai wrote in the fifteenth century that the Maronites at that time were still making the sign of the cross with the thumb and two fingers (as distinguished from the Monophysites such as the Syrian Orthodox [Jacobites] who still make the sign of the cross with one finger today to indicate the oneness of the natures of Christ contrary to the Christology of Chalcedon).[567] Maronites continue today to make the sign of the Cross in the Roman/ Latin practice – with an open hand.

Following the Council of Florence ending in 1439, the Church of Rome entrusted the Franciscan monks in Syria, Lebanon and Palestine with responsibility in observing and attending to the affairs of the Maronite Church. We know from two of these Franciscans, Fra Gryphon (d. 1475) and Francesco Suriano (d. around 1481), that there were other distinct eastern practices in the Maronite Church that Rome was seriously concerned to stamp out and saw as deviations to the Latin practice. Moosa, from his perspective as a Syriac Orthodox Jacobite, suggests these may have included ancient Syriac practices such as the rights of the priests and are a useful comparison to the following Syriac Orthodox Church practice without Latinisation:

- To anoint the baptised with the holy chrism.
- To administer the Holy Eucharist to infants after their baptism.
- To use reserve Sacraments in Lent.
- To administer both elements, the bread and wine, on ordinary days.[568]

The Lebanese Council for the Maronite Church of 1736, although emphasising the use of the Syriac language first and the Arabic lan-

---

[567] Mentioned by Gabriel al-Qilai (d. 1516), cited in Moosa, *The Maronites in History*.
[568] Cited in Moosa, *The Maronites in History*, p. 236. See next footnote for Moosa's unreliability.

guage second in church services, instituted many Latin practices. Moosa, once again looking through Jacobite spectacles, suggests they were a deviation from ancient Syriac practices such as:

- Baptism should be performed not by immersion according to the custom of the eastern churches, but by only pouring water over the head of the baptised.

- Contrary to the ancient eastern custom, a confined woman who has given birth to a child is allowed to attend church before forty days have lapsed since the date of her delivery.

- Baptism and confirmation should be performed separately and confirmation is the exclusive right of the bishops.

- Unleavened bread should be used in the Eucharistic service, according to the custom of the church of Rome.

- The priest should not cover his head (that is, what was usually worn by the officiating priest according to the custom of eastern churches) while celebrating the mass.[569]

After sustained efforts from Rome since the Lebanese Council of 1736, the Maronite Church prohibited the practice of mixed monasteries from 1818. This was the long-standing ancient practice of the Aramaic-Syriac Antiochian monks and nuns who shared the same monastery land, goods, and authority but lived in separate quarters or buildings.[570]

In the *Maronite Rite: A Catechism* written in 1972, it states: "many factors, such as the Crusaders, the Roman delegates and the Roman Seminary in Rome, contributed to the Latinisation of the Maronite liturgy."[571] Since Vatican Council II (1963-1965), the Maronites have gradually returned to many of their traditional rites and liturgical customs. For example, baptism and confirmation are now once again

---

[569] Ibid., p. 272. It is anticipated Moosa is correct in citation but as demonstrated by this thesis he has proved to be a very unreliable source. His citation has not been checked.
[570] This may have been suggested by Moosa and requires verification.
[571] Monsignor Joseph Abi Nader (ed.), *Maronite Rite: A Catechism*, Maronite Apostolic Exarchate, 1972, p. 15.

performed at the same time. The Latin traditions generally have been removed from the Maronite liturgy. However, many of the Roman rituals and traditions are now so entrenched that it will be very difficult to revert to the ancient Aramaic-Syriac Antiochian Chalcedonian customs in their completeness. For example, Maronite parishioners in the West would *not* so readily agree to:

- Not kneel in the church during the liturgy (mass) and thereby allow the removal of the kneeling rests from the pews (this was attempted in Australia in one parish in the 1990s and completely resisted by the parishioners).

- Making the sign of the cross the same way as the Greeks and Byzantines with index and middle finger pressed against the thumb representing the Trinity and the two other fingers pressed against the palm representing the divine and human nature of Christ in the one person.

- Remove the metal bells from their churches.

- Have the entire mass service in the Aramaic-Syriac language.

It is also unlikely the Maronite bishops would forego the wearing of the Latin mitre on their heads (a tall triangular shaped usually golden coloured liturgical headdress) instead of the traditional Toubia (a much smaller circular black coloured headdress), although the vestments worn during the liturgy are generally Aramaic Syriac in origin.

Interestingly, after Vatican Council II, the Roman/Latin rite was 'modernised' both in its liturgy and language (from Latin to the *lingua franca* of each country). For the liturgy, this has been the opposite for the Maronite Church since that time – that is, it has moved more towards a return to its ancient liturgy. However, Vatican Council II had no real impact on language for the Maronites, the dominant tongue of its homeland now being Arabic, the liturgy in Arabic had already been in place for centuries though it did retain several parts in ancient Syriac.

## 11.4  Claims of Monothelitism Against the Maronites

The main reference for historians for the source of the claim of heresy against the Maronites comes from *The Annals* of Eutychius (also known as Sa'id Ibn Batriq, d. 941), who was a Melkite patriarch of Alexandria. Writing more than three hundred years after his date of reference, this is a secondary source and the relevant extract states:

> At the time of Maurice, Emperor of the Romans (582-602), there was a monk named Maron, who affirmed in our Lord Christ two natures but one will, one operation, and one person, and who corrupted the faith of men. Many of those who partook of this doctrine and declared themselves as his disciples were from the town of Hama, of Qennesrin, and of Al-'Awasim ... The followers of his doctrine were called Maronites, from the name Maron. At the death of Maron, the inhabitants of Hama built a monastery at Hama, called it Dair Maron and professed the faith of Maron.[572]

It is important to note the period of Emperor Maurice preceded the introduction of the Monothelite decree by emperor Heraclius in 638. The issues relating to the unreliability arising from the text are extensively dealt with previously in Chapter 9 and elsewhere.

We can suggest with confidence that William of Tyre utilised this text of Eutychius and accordingly duplicated his errors. William of Tyre, referring to another history in his prologue, writes: "As the principal source for this we have used the work of the venerable patriarch of Alexandria, Seith, son of Patricius."[573] William also mentions the heretic Maro, which is a clear reference to a citation of Eutychius who suggested this Maro lived during the reign of Maurice (594-602). Eutychius' reference does not fit with St Maroun (d. 410-423) or John Maroun (d. 707) or even the Monothelite controversy (declared a heresy in 681). It is generally accepted that Jacques de Vitry relied on William of Tyre for much of his writings, and appears

---

[572] Eutychius, *Eutychii Annales*, pp. 57-59.
[573] William of Tyre, *A History of Deeds Beyond the Sea*, Vol I, p. 56.

to have simply repeated again this faulty heresy charge against the Maronites.

These Crusader authors misunderstood or knew little about the Syrian Christians. There is little reference from both the Crusader chroniclers discussed here about the indigenous population to which it appears they were either indifferent or prejudiced against. It appears they may not have been able to differentiate for some time between the varying denominations of Syrian Christians even one hundred years after the arrival of the Crusaders. For example, William reported massacres of Christians without identifying the group.

Contrary to what William of Tyre implies, the Sixth Council of Constantinople was not convened specifically against the Maronites and there is no record of any condemnation of the Maronites by that Council. De Vitry intimates that the only rightful custom and tradition of the Catholic Church is that of the Latin/Roman rite. His final comment incorrectly states that the Maronites "use the Chaldean alphabet" (a reference perhaps to the eastern version of Syriac, not the western Syriac form used by the Maronite and Syriac churches).

Both texts of William and de Vitry are not primary sources relevant to the period of the Monothelite controversy some five centuries previous and after the Maronites were cut off from Rome. The Monothelite charge and also the Maronite communion with Rome date of 1180-82 are questionable when fifty years earlier in 1130 the Crusaders accepted the gift of St Maroun's skull, which would have meant the acceptance of a relic belonging to a 'heretic' church.

### 11.4.1  The Legacy of Monothelitism Charges

The inaccuracy of William of Tyre's 'heresy' charges against the Maronites, copied from Eutychius, and repeated by Jacques de Vitry, has continued even with current historians. Edward Gibbon, in his well-known *History of the Decline and Fall of the Roman Empire*, writes scathingly of the Maronites in this period:

In the twelfth century the Maronites, abjuring the Monothelite error were reconciled to the Latin churches of Antioch and Rome, and the same alliance has been frequently renewed by the ambition of the popes and the distress of the Syrians. But it may reasonably be questioned whether the union has ever been perfect or sincere; and the learned Maronites of the college of Rome have vainly laboured to absolve their ancestors from the guilt of heresy and schism.[574]

And in the twentieth century, Stephen Runciman, in his three volume work, *A History of the Crusades*, follows William of Tyre in stating that the Maronites were the surviving adherents to the Monothelite doctrine and only agreed to submit to the supremacy of the Roman See in about 1180 (note once again the obvious slurs against the Maronite church):

> In the kingdom itself the heretic sects were of little importance outside of Jerusalem, where almost all of them kept establishments at the holy sepulchre ... The Crown protected their rights ... In the county of Tripoli the chief heretic church was that of the Maronites, the surviving adherents of monothelite doctrine. With them the western Church acted with rare tact and forbearance; and about 1180 they agreed to admit the supremacy of the Roman See, provided that they might keep their Syriac liturgy and customs; nor did they renounce their radical doctrine of Christ's single will. The negotiations, of which too little is known, were ably managed by the Patriarch Aimery of Antioch. The admission of this first Uniate Church showed that the Papacy was ready to permit divergent usages and even doubtful theology, provided that its ultimate authority was recognised.[575]

William Dalrymple in his 1997 bestseller *From the Holy Mountain, a Journey in the Shadow of Byzantium,* clearly relying on William of Tyre, Gibbons, and Runciman, regurgitates the heresy charge against

[574] Gibbon, *The History of the Decline and Fall of the Roman Empire*, Vol VI, pp. 72, 73.
[575] Steven Runciman, *A History of the Crusades*, Vol. 2, Cambridge University Press, 1952, p. 322.

the Maronites.[576] Dalrymple shows no less a lack of understanding concerning other aspects of the Maronite Church. It should be noted his bibliography does not provide as a reference the reading of any author who has supported the 'Maronite' position. And if the legacy of the heresy charges should have stopped there, it hasn't: it has now worked its way into the travel guidebooks on Lebanon and the Middle East.[577]

However, there are assessments of Maronite history and of the period and sources in question that have emphasised the faulty logic of Eutychius and his parrots. Dib, who deals at length with the legend of Maronite Montheletism in his *History of the Maronite Church* summarises:

> This accusation has spread to the East and the West, especially through Eutychius of Alexandria, William of Tyre, and Jacques de Vitry; the first was the source of the second, and the second the source of the third. The letter *Quia Divinae Sapientiae* of Innocent III is misunderstood and consecrates, in the eyes of numerous writers, the heterodox origin of this people. And so, this is how the legend of Maronite Monothelitism was born, developed, and incorporated into history.[578]

In addition, Robert Crawford says:

> It has been shown that, in all probability, William of Tyre's reference, based on the writings of Eutychius, to an heretical Maro was to Maro of Edessa and not to the fourth century St Maro or the John Maro who died about 707 AD. It has also been shown that the Sixth Council of Constantinople was not convened specifically against the Maronites and that there is no record of any condemnation of the Maronites by that Council. Thus, it is not correct to state, in reference to the Maro (or Maros) of the Maronites, that 'The heresy of Maro

---

[576] Dalrymple, *From the Holy Mountain*, p. 197.
[577] For example, see both the Lonely Planet guide to Lebanon for 2001, pp. 13, 15, and the Footprint Handbook, *Syria and Lebanon*, from 2001.
[578] Dib, *History of the Maronite Church*, pp. 15-41.

and his followers is and was that in our Lord Jesus Christ there exists, and did exist from the beginning, one will and one energy only, as may be learned from the Sixth Council, which, as is well-known, was assembled against them and in which they suffered sentence of condemnation'.[579]

Finally, Father Anthony Salim aptly summarises the Maronite position:

In history, some people have claimed, based on some liturgical texts they had seen and misinterpreted, that Maronites at one time believed that there was only one will in Jesus – the divine ... However, these Maronite texts only emphasise this truth: that Jesus was wholly conformed to the Divine Will, which directed and guided perfectly his human will, while leaving it free ...

Jesus' life was lived according to the saving will of God for all human beings ... Jesus accepted this will and plan and lived it out with faith and obedience to the Father.[580]

### 11.4.2   Closing Comments on the Monothelite Legend

From the available evidence we can make the following suggestions, many of which have not been raised by previous authors or historians. It is likely the overwhelming majority of Christians today would not be aware of the Catholic Church's decrees (applicable not only to the Catholic Church but the Greek Orthodox and Byzantine Churches as well) that Christ has two natures and two wills. Those who would become aware, like many in the ancient Christian world, would probably be confused. The debate is a highly complex, sophisticated, and a sensitive theological one even amongst modern clergy.

The confusion of the theological debate is further compounded by the complex web of relations between other eastern Christian denominations and the Maronite Church. Whether clergy, parishioners, or au-

[579] Robert W. Crawford, "William of Tyre and the Maronites," *Speculum* 30(2), (1955: pp. 222-228.
[580] Anthony Salim, *Captivated by Your Teachings: A Resource Book for Adult Maronite Catholics*, E.T. Nedder Publishing, 2002, p. 39.

thors of any text were both Maronite and Monothelite could not and cannot today always be certain. Perhaps some Maronites (as Melkites) would have been, and some Maronites not, Monothelite. Further, the Syriac Jacobites and Tell Mahre's 'Maximite Melkites' either attended Maronite parishes or at least shared the same Church. There would have been much confusion for observers and later historians as a result.

For example, at the request of the Byzantine Emperor Heraclius (610-641) the followers of Beit Maroun, as they were called at that time Maronite, took over some Syriac Jacobite churches. As a result many parishioners attending Maronite churches may well have being perceived to be Syriac Jacobites or vice versa. It would have also meant that some parishes of the Maronites retained Syriac Jacobite literature and some Jacobites became Maronites.

Moosa cites evidence from 1242 AD for about forty Syriac Jacobite monks living in the heartland of the Maronites in the Qadisha Valley and the Faradis monastery near the village of Ban.[581] According to Moosa, the Maronite priest al-Qilai in his Zajaliyya of the fifteenth century refers to many incidences concerning the Syriac Jacobites: al-Qilai cites the Jacobites still in the Lebanon mountains, disputes between Maronites and Jacobites, a rare incident of a Maronite becoming Jacobite including the Muqaddam Abd al-Mun'im of Bsharri.[582] Moosa also states that after the death of Muqaddam Abd al-Mun'im of Bsharri in 1495, the Syriac Jacobites of the Lebanon mountains gradually became Maronites. Moosa cites a number of Syrian Orthodox Jacobites living in Hardin in the Batrun district until the eighteenth century. It is the oral histories of the clergy today that remind us the Maronites and Jacobites shared the same churches in Hardin.

Even the Greek Byzantine Melkites (Maximite Melkites according to Tell Mahre), who later supposedly followed the Sixth Ecumenical Council doctrine of two wills, had Monothelites amongst them opposed to the Sixth Council. In the eighth century, the Maximite

---

[581] Moosa, *The Maronites in History*, p. 227.
[582] Ibid., pp. 236-239.

Melkites shared the main cathedral of Aleppo with the Maronites. Rajji states that Monothelite views were found among only a minority of Melkites and Maronites in the seventh and early eighth centuries. Brock in disagreement with Rajji, does state that Monothelite theology views were definitely only found among a minority of Melkites and Maronites from the ninth century onwards.

Even in the modern period debate has raged over the technical theological details of the arguments of key figures involved in the Monothelite controversy. For example, Pope Honorius was condemned by the Sixth Ecumenical Council of 680-681 for being a Monothelite. At the time of Vatican Council I (1869-1870) Honorius figured in every pamphlet and every speech on ecclesiastical subjects. Many argued at the Vatican Council I that the Pope Honorius' belief was *not* Monothelite. Alternatively, a great debate also raged as to whether the previously declared heresy of Monotheletism (over a thousand years before the meeting of Vatican Council I) should be overturned because of papal infallibility. Eventually, the Council held that the Pope's letter to Sergius, the Patriarch of Constantinople at the time was not *ex cathedra*.

Pope Honorius is possibly the only Pope in history that has been condemned for his doctrinal belief. However, *The Catholic Encyclopaedia* (2006) states in their entry on Pope Honorius that even then, in the nineteenth century, the Church's position on this matter was subject to change:

> Bishop Hefele before 1870 took the view that Honorius' letter was not strictly heretical but was gravely incorrect, and that its condemnation by an ecumenical council was a serious difficulty against the 'personal' infallibility of the popes. After his hesitating acceptance of the Vatican [Vatican Council I] decrees he modified his view; he now taught that Honorius' letter was a definition ex cathedra, that it was incorrectly worded, but that the thought of the writer was orthodox ... These views of Hefele's, which he put forth with edifying modesty and submission as the best explanation he could give of what had previously seemed to him a formidable difficulty, have

had a surprisingly wide influence, and have been adopted by many Catholic writers.[583]

Nonetheless, in closing this argument we must be mindful of the proofs that have been offered throughout this book to show that affiliations between Monothelitism and the Maronites have almost always been faulty and flawed. The historical details of the relevant eras are, at many turns, complicated and unclear, but in addition, as Brock reminds us, "when looking at the whole controversy, it should be remembered that almost all our information about it comes from Dyothelete sources, and as seen through Dyothelete spectacles."[584]

In addition to the exploration of this issue in this book it should be noted that the Vatican has never decreed that the Maronite Church was Monothelite. Applying standards of proof, this book demonstrates that there is not sufficient evidence to conclude that the Maronite Church was Monothelite. It is therefore fair to say that the Maronite Church is the only Eastern Church that can claim a perpetual communion with the See of Rome and the Catholic Church. Historical texts cannot clearly, unambiguously, and satisfactorily prove otherwise. After the arrival of the Crusaders in the eleventh century, the Maronites were certainly the only eastern Christians in perpetual communion with the See of Rome until 1724 when the first of many other eastern Christian Churches began their perpetual communion with Rome.

## 11.5 Patriarchates and Churches of the East Before and After the Crusades

The period of the Crusades and the great schism of the eleventh century between East and West saw numerous changes in the various churches of the patriarchate of Antioch and elsewhere in the East. The following breakdown notes some of the impact of the events of this tumultuous time on the Patriarchs and churches of this region, and gives some indication of their development into the modern period.[585]

---

[583] Chapman, "Pope Honorius I," in *The Catholic Encyclopedia.*
[584] Ibid.
[585] This information relating to Eastern Catholic Churches is based on CNEWA web-

## Maronite Patriarch of Antioch

*Before the Crusades:* Chalcedonian, Catholic Orthodox until the great schism and in communion with the universal Catholic Church. Communication with the Catholic Church cut off due to Arab Islamic rule in the late seventh or early eighth century. Its liturgy is Antiochian in the western form of Syriac.

*After the Crusades:* Catholic and in communion with Rome. The church is the only Eastern church that can claim an unbroken union with the Catholic Church. The Maronite Church is the only Eastern Catholic church today not to have an Orthodox counterpart. It is the only Eastern Catholic Church that can claim to have always recognised the patriarch of Rome as the primary patriarch and Pope. It is the only Eastern Catholic Church that can claim an unbroken succession of Eastern Catholic patriarchs to the Christian world's first patriarchate, the See of Antioch, established by St Peter.

## Melkite and Antiochian Orthodox Patriarch of Antioch

*Before the Crusades:* Chalcedonian, Catholic Orthodox – in communion with the universal Catholic Church. Patriarch resided in Constantinople or Antioch after the Arab Muslim conquests of the seventh century. The church was known as Melkite by the end of the seventh or early eighth century after a division from the Melkites-Maronites. The Byzantine Empire reconquered Antioch from about 960 to 1085. It was at this time the Melkites were likely to have commenced a transformation of their liturgy to Byzantine. Following the Schism of 1054, the Melkites were no longer in perpetual communion with the universal Catholic Church. By the end of the thirteenth century their liturgy was completely Byzantine.

*After the Crusades:* Since about the time of the great East-West schism in the eleventh century, it was known as the Antiochian Orthodox Church and was no longer in communion with the Catholic Church. The liturgy (customs as opposed to language) of the Antiochian Orthodox Church may have been originally Antiochian in the western form of Syriac, but since about the thirteenth century the liturgy has been Byzantine. In 1724, part of the congregation established the Melkite Catholic Church as an Eastern Catholic Church recognising the patriarch of Rome as the primary patriarch and Pope. The Melkites have had an unbroken succession of Eastern Catholic patriarchs since that time.

### Syriac Patriarch of Antioch

*Before the Crusades:* Non-Chalcedonian, 'Monophysite', and not Catholic – that is, in terms of not being in communion with the universal Catholic Church since 451. Its liturgy is Antiochian in the western form of Syriac.

*After the Crusades:* In 1782, part of the congregation separated to form the Syriac Catholic Church as an Eastern Catholic Church recognising the patriarch of Rome as the primary patriarch and Pope. The Syriac Catholic Church has had an unbroken succession of its Eastern Catholic patriarchs since that time. The non Catholic church is known today as the Syriac Orthodox Church.

The Malankara Jacobite Syriac Orthodox Church of India is headed by the Syriac Orthodox Patriarch of Antioch. Its jurisdiction included the Indian sub-continent such as modern day Pakistan and Afghanistan, established by Thomas the Apostle in the first century. The Syriac church of Edessa was from where Christianity spread to the Far East. In 1912, part of the congregation separated to form the Indian Orthodox Church. The Malankara Orthodox Syriac Church of India has its roots from the Syriac Orthodox Church.

The Syro Malankara Catholic Church was established in 1930 as an Eastern Catholic Church recognising the patriarch of Rome as the primary patriarch and Pope. This church has an unbroken succession of its Eastern Catholic patriarchs since that time. All these Churches had the ecclesial traditions of the Aramaic-Syriac-Antiochian language and liturgy.

One also needs to consider the Catholicos (heads) of other church-es established in the controversial political and religious times of the early centuries after Christ not linked to the traditional patriarchates. Their communities broke ties with the Catholic Church and include:

### Armenian Apostolic Church

Non-Chalcedonian. Communion with Catholic Church was broken in 451. The Armenian Apostolic Church considers Monophysitism a heresy but disagrees with the formula de-fined by the Council of Chalcedon. In 1742, part of the con-gregation separated to form the Armenian Catholic Church in full communion with Rome as an Eastern Catholic Church recognising the patriarch of Rome as the primary patriarch and Pope. This Catholic church has an unbroken succession of its Eastern Catholic patriarchs since that time.

### Assyrian Church of the East

Officially the Holy Apostolic Catholic Assyrian Church of the East. Non-Chalcedonian, but claims by others to be Nesto-rian are contentious. Union with Catholic Church was broken either in 431 or 451. Its liturgy is Antiochian in the eastern form of Syriac. The Ancient Church of the East was estab-lished as a separate church in 1964 as a result of a schism in the Assyrian Church of the East.

### Chaldean Catholic Church

Today a Uniate church in union with the universal Catholic Church. The congregation was formally part of the Assyr-ian Church of the East. The thirteenth century witnessed Do-minican and Franciscan Catholic missionaries amongst the faithful of the Assyrian Church of the East. This resulted in a series of individual conversions of bishops and brief unions with the Church in Rome including in 1553. In 1830, Pope Pius VIII confirmed Metropolitan John Hormizdas as head of all Chaldean Catholics, with the title of Patriarch of Babylon of the Chaldeans, with his see in Mosul in modern day Iraq. It is in full communion with Rome as an Eastern Catholic Church recognising the patriarch of Rome as the primary patriarch and Pope. This church has an unbroken succession of its Eastern Catholic patriarchs since that time.

## Syro-Malabar Church

From the Indian coast of Malabar; was in full communion with the Assyrian Church. Malabar became a Portuguese colony in 1498. Since that time, the church was in regular dialogue with Rome. In 1923, the Syro-Malabar Catholic Church was established in full union with Rome as an Eastern Catholic Church recognising the patriarch of Rome as the primary patriarch and Pope. This church has an unbroken succession of its Eastern Catholic patriarchs since that time.

Before the arrival of the Crusades and the schism of the eleventh century, the various churches of the patriarchates of Alexandria (and all of Africa) were:

## Greek Patriarch of Alexandria

Chalcedonian, Orthodox, and in communion with the Catholic Church until the eleventh century schism. The Church was Byzantine.

## Coptic Patriarch of Alexandria

Non-Chalcedonian, Monophysite, and not in communion with the Catholic Church after 451. Known today by two churches – the Coptic Orthodox Church and the Coptic Catholic Church. Their liturgy is Coptic with some Byzantine influence.

Before the arrival of the Crusades (and before the great schism of the eleventh century between East and West), the various churches of the patriarchates of Jerusalem were:

## Greek Patriarch of Jerusalem

Chalcedonian, Orthodox - in communion with the Catholic Church.

## Armenian Patriarch of Jerusalem

Non-Chalcedonian, not Orthodox – that is, in terms of not in communion with the Catholic Church. This position came after 638 apparently when Constantinople failed to appoint a patriarch upon the conquest by Arab Muslims.

Not in order of ranking, the following mentioned patriarchate and relevant to the period immediately prior to the arrival of the Crusades is:

**Patriarch of Constantinople**

Greek, Chalcedonian, Orthodox, and in communion with the Catholic Church.

**Patriarchate of Rome**

The primary patriarchate of all five patriarchates and the residence of the primary Patriarch, the Pope. Latin, Chalcedonian, Orthodox, and in union with the Catholic Church.

After the schism of 1054 the term Orthodox took on a new meaning. The ethnic Latins and their churches in Constantinople were sacked. The Greeks continued to call themselves the Greek Orthodox Church. They became known as Orthodox. Since then the term Orthodox has taken on a further meaning to include all the Eastern churches that are not in communion with Rome, whether they are schismatic or heretical. It often refers to all of the Eastern churches whether or not they were the followers of the Catholic Church doctrine up to the great East-West schism of the eleventh century.

The Coptic Orthodox Church, the Syriac Orthodox Church, and the Armenian Orthodox Church are examples that are not Catholic or Byzantine but see themselves as Orthodox. Doctrinally, even today, the Byzantine churches have no major theological differences with the Catholic Church. For example, both remain Dyophysite and Dyothelite. Accordingly, for those churches that are not Eastern Catholic, often the general expressions used are 'Orthodox' for the Byzantine churches and 'Oriental Orthodox' for the other Eastern churches.

## 11.6 Summary

The Crusades brought about a renaissance of the Maronite Church including in religious art and architecture. Many churches and paintings still exist today as a testament to the period. However, the Maronite union and loyalty to Rome, and the Latinisation of some (or much) of their liturgy and rituals was not without burden. The other Eastern Christian denominations, for example the 'Greek' Antiochian Orthodox, ridiculed the Maronites and set the Turkish rulers out to persecute them. Father Jean Boucher visiting Qannoubin in 1612 said 'the Greeks had skinned them... the Turks ... nibbled at their bones'[586]. This was but one documented case of the difficulties faced by the Maronites (in this instance as late as the seventeenth century) for their Latinisation and communion with Rome. One could only imagine the derision not only from the other Eastern Christians, but also the Muslims, four hundred years earlier by the Maronites aligning themselves to the Crusaders on their arrival and simultaneously as the only Eastern Christians expressing their loyalty to Rome.

The approach amongst the Catholic Church at the time of the Crusades, that Western Roman Catholicism was the only correct Catholicism, unfortunately has reverberated amongst a great many Roman Catholic parishioners today who form the overwhelming majority of Catholics in the world. This perception persists even in the secular media of the West. For example in Australia, when the late Pope John Paul II was critically ill shortly before his death in 2005, the headline captions on ABC (Australian Broadcasting Company) news were "Roman Catholics around the world pray for their Pope," explicitly excluding other Catholics from the anxious faithful. But this is not just a Western notion. A Palestinian Christian, who was a former primary and high school student with the Franciscans in the West Bank, a Latin Catholic from the Holy Land and tour guide in 2005 in Jerusalem for Catholic tourists, firmly believed the Maronites could not possibly be *really* Catholic because they were not 'Latin' practising Catholics like him.[587]

This attitude or belief remains so even though from Vatican Council II (1963-1965), the Catholic Church finally decreed, eight hundred years after the arrival of the Crusades, that the Eastern Catholic

---

[586] Cited in Dib, *History of the Maronite Church*, p. 106.
[587] Tour guide for the author in 2005. Most indigenous Latin Catholics in the Holy Land establish their succession of Latin rite Christianity back to the period of the Crusades.

Churches, whilst still remaining in communion with Rome, as much as those of the West, are rightfully and duty-bound to rule themselves in accordance with their own established disciplines. This was a clear acknowledgement by the Vatican that Eastern Catholic rites and their churches have existed from the very birth of the Christian church and their rites have never been inferior to the Roman rite. It is the confirmation of the communion of all Christian customs in the one Catholic Church. It acknowledges the Church, as a universal church, was multicultural from its inception.

# CHAPTER 12

# THE MARONITES UNDER MAMLOUK AND OTTOMAN RULE

## 12.1 The End of the Crusades

After the Crusaders lost Jerusalem in 1244, King Louis IX of France launched the Seventh Crusade to Egypt. On his way, he landed in Cyprus welcomed by thousands of Maronites, five thousand of which accompanied him to Egypt.[588] In 1250 King Louis landed at Akko (Acre) in the Holy Land and was received by a contingent of "twenty five thousand Maronites" as well as "beautiful horses."[589] The King wrote to the Maronite Prince stating: "We, and those who follow us on the throne of France, promised to give you and your nation protection equal to that given to the French, always doing whatever is necessary for your happiness."[590]

The Franks had already been grouped in Lebanon, driven back by the enemies as they slowly lost their control over other areas. The Maronites showed their hospitality and the French used Lebanon as a centre of their defence to try and hold on to the Latin Kingdom. King Louis IX returned to France in 1254 after his mother died. His time in Syria and Lebanon is fondly remembered by the Maronites.

Upper Lebanon fell in 1267 and the Arab historian Makrizi (1364-1442) reported: "The troops stormed many caves and presented the prisoners and booty to the Sultan (of Egypt). He commanded that the captives be decapitated, the trees cut, and the churches destroyed."[591]

---

[588] Harb, *The Maronites: History and Constants*, p. 86.
[589] Harb sets out a copy of the letter in French, Ibid., p. 86.
[590] Ibid.
[591] Dib, *History of the Maronite Church*, p. 64.

The Maronites grouped around their Patriarch at Hadeth, but the Patriarch was captured. The French castles and areas began to fall rapidly, one after the other. Tripoli was still held in 1277 and Acre fell in 1291, just after the fall of Beirut. The French knight Guy de Lusignan acquired the island of Cyprus in 1192 for the French to find refuge and many Maronites from the Holy Land and Syrian Orient followed. The Maronites also followed the Catholic military order the Hospitallers to the Greek island of Rhodes.[592]

When the Hospitallers, who occupied Rhodes (including Bodrum on the famous tourist coast of modern day Turkey) and the Greek island of Kastelorizon, lost their 'new Jerusalem' (Rhodes) and the archipelago to the Turkish Sultan Suleiman in 1522, they moved to Crete taking with them their two precious relics (the icon of Our Lady of Philermo and the hand of St John the Baptist), their archives, and the key to the city of Rhodes.[593] The Sultan agreed to supply ships for all who wanted to leave Rhodes. For those staying he assured them no churches would be turned to mosques and Rhodians would have freedom to worship and be free from taxes for five years. The Sultan asked the grand master Hospitaller Philippe to enter Turkish service and he replied: "a great prince would be dishonoured by employing such a renegrade." The Sultan later said how sorry he was to make "that fine old man" leave his home.[594]

## 12.2 The Mamlouk Muslim Period (1291-1516)

In 1268 the Mamlouks (the Muslim Turks) conquered Antioch. Patriarch Doueihi informs us that in 1283 "an army of the Mamlouk Sultan Qalaoun penetrated into the remotest strongholds of the Maronites, Ehden, Besharri, Hadath el-Jibbet. They besieged Ehden, which fell after forty days."[595] They captured the Maronite Patriarch Daniel el-

---

[592] Ibid., p. 65.

[593] Seward, *The Monks of War*, p. 200.

[594] Ibid.

[595] Harb, *The Maronites: History and Constants*, p. 88.

Hadshiti who was martyred and they demolished the fort at the top of Ehden Mountain.

The Maronites were subject to Mamlouk persecution moreso than their Christian counterparts. This was due to their allegiance to the Mamlouk enemy, the Crusaders. Most Maronites would have fled the coast to their traditional lands and strongholds in the Lebanon mountains and amongst the cedar forests. This left the abandoned churches and monasteries nearer to the coast, including in the Koura and Tripoli, to the Orthodox Christians, who were less of a Christian population than the Maronites and less of a threat to the new rulers.[596]

Sader mentions that Peter Embriaco, the Lord of the Gibelets (Crusaders from Genoa in Italy who had been handed the kingdom of Gebail'or Gebelet – that is, Jbail/Byblos), signed a treaty with the Mamlouk Sultan of Egypt, entitled the *seigneury* of Gibelet. This provided provisional protection for the Maronites.[597] The Crusader's last post of the Latin kingdom of Levant was Akko. After its fall in 1291, French ships would sail up and down the eastern Mediterranean coast threatening attack. The new rulers, the Mamlouk Sultans, made sure the Christians and especially their closest allies, the Maronites, were once again cut off from the West. Documentation provides evidence that no relations were permitted between foreigners and the local Christian populations. Accordingly, there were no letters between Rome and the Maronite Patriarch for a considerable period of time.

Tripoli was one of six Syrian kingdoms (or *mamlakat*) of the Mamlouks headed by a *naib*. The Maronites having grouped themselves in northern Lebanon under the direction of their patriarch, divided into autonomous districts headed by chiefs called *mouqaddamin*. They answered to the naib of Tripoli. The office of mouqaddamin became hereditary and were mostly ordained as subdeacons to have priority over

---

[596] Sader, *Painted Churches and Rock cut Chapels of Lebanon*, p. 40, suggests that, in turn, the Orthodox Christians abandoned their monasteries and rock cut chapels of the Holy Valley of Kadisha to join their brothers on the coast.
[597] Ibid., p. 40.

the laity of the Church.[598] The other six Syrian mamlakats (or niabats) were Damascus, Aleppo, Hama, Safad, Karak (Transjordan). This is a return again to the term 'Syria' that generalises the populations of this Middle Eastern region.

The Maronite Ibn al-Qilai provides a description of battles taking place between the Mamlouks and the people of the Lebanese mountain during the early period of the Sultanate. The Druze, other Levantine monotheists, joined forces with the Maronites against the Mamlouks.[599] Shiites were also involved in the battles as allies to their Lebanese brothers. Eventually the Mamlouks succeeded. They demolished many villages and towns as well as Maronite churches and monasteries.[600]

The Crusaders continued their attacks on the Lebanese and Egyptian coasts. In 1365, following a crusader attack on Alexandria in Egypt, the Mamlouks captured Maronite Patriarch Gibrail of Hajula in the Lebanon mountains and burned him alive near the mosque of Tilan in Tripoli. However, Doueihi, in referring to the Mamlouk period overall, states: "reports of this age point out that the just rule of the mouqaddamin lived to prosperity and to the building of numerous churches and schools."[601]

Originally the Maronite mouqaddamin resided in the district of Batrun-Byblos. After the complete submission of the Maronites following a long period of contention, in 1388 the residence was moved to the district of Besharre. Immediately, and for the first time, the Sultan appointed a non-Maronite mouqaddamin, Deacon Yaacoub. Prevailing facts and circumstances might suggest he was a Jacobite. It is a possible prelude to an expansion of Jacobites into the region after this time.

The Christian, Muslim (Shiite), and Druze allegiance during the early Mamlouk Sultanate period can be attributed as the first formal multi-faith military and nationalistic movement in world history. It

---

[598] Dib, *History of the Maronite Church*, p. 68.
[599] Harb, *The Maronites: History and Constants*, p. 90.
[600] Ibid., p. 92.
[601] Ibid., p. 94.

evidences social cohesion and a functioning multi-cultural society, which would form the basis of Lebanese independence six hundred years later.

### 12.2.1 Arrival Of The Franciscans

In the fifteenth century, Rome began to focus its mind back to the East but this time in the form of apostolic rather than military conquest. The brothers from the Order of St Francis, the Franciscans, were entrusted with the principal missionary role and commenced their residency in the Middle East including in Lebanon. They also began returning to Rome from Lebanon with their reports.

In 1439, the superior of the Franciscans of Beirut, Brother John, returned to Tripoli from Rome. News of the Council of Florence of 1439, and the prospects of reunification between the Greeks and Rome, spread to the Sultans who thought that the West were planning to reconquer the Holy Land. They prohibited Brother John from meeting the Maronite patriarch. However, he did and the Sultan's soldiers went on a burning and pillaging rampage against the Maronites in retaliation. They especially targeted and destroyed the monastery of Mayfouq in 1440, the seat of the Patriarch.

The Patriarch decided to move the patriarchal seat to the monastery of Qannoubin. It was close to Besharre, the base of the Maronite mouqaddamin, and offered improved protection from the tyranny of the Mamlouk governor of Tripoli. To capture an image of the new patriarchal seat, even over a century later, the voyager M. e la Roque (writing in 1689) wrote of Qannoubin: "It is a large building, very irregular, hewn into rock: the church is dedicated to the Blessed Virgin ... the rest of the building consists of the patriarchal apartment which is undistinguished, with many rooms for the religious ... all is very poor."[602]

Just prior to the destruction of Mayfouk, Pope Eugenius IV sent the papal pallium of confirmation, a miter, and a chasuble to the Maronite Patriarch Yuhanna al-Jaji in 1440 whilst he was in Mayfouq. Although we know that the use of the papal pallium (official vestment)

---

[602] Dib, *History of the Maronite Church*, p. 73.

of confirmation to the Maronite patriarch commenced formally in the year 1215, Harb states that from 1440 this papal confirmation became traditional and, not long after, Rome began using the term 'Patriarcha Antiochienis' instead of 'Patriarcha Maronitarum'. Harb mentions that Patriarch Butros al-Hadathi (1468-1492) was the first to benefit from this new title in 1469.[603] Assuming Harb is correct, and there is no reason to believe otherwise, this was a clear acknowledgement from Rome that the Maronite church was the only church in the East perpetually loyal to Rome after the 1054 schism. Hence, the ancient title of 'Patriarch of Antioch and all the East' was resurrected.

By 1444, the Franciscans were accompanied to Rome by not only Maronite delegates but those of the Druze religion. In this year, Rome appointed permanent apostolic commissioners for the Maronites, Druze, and some Melkite/Antiochian Orthodox who had been in negotiations with Rome to re-establish their communion as Catholics. Brother Peter of Ferrara from the Maronite Monastery of the Holy Saviour in Beirut was made the first commissioner and Andrew, Maronite Archbishop of Nicosia (Cyprus), was made commissioner there.

The Franciscan Brother Gryphon, who studied Arabic and Syriac at the monastery of Mount Sion in Jerusalem, was appointed in 1450 to the mission of Mount Lebanon accompanied by Brother Francis of Barcelona. Although helping to build new churches for the Maronites, at the same time Gryphon is well-known for 'reforming' what he saw were the 'errors' of the liturgical ways of the Maronite Church as not being in conformity with Western practice. The legacy of the Monothelite charges in the chronicles of William of Tyre and Jacques de Vitry must have lingered in his mind as it also may have amongst the Latin Catholics of Europe. The author Father Lammens believes that Gryphon must have seen some Jacobite errors as they were the neighbours of the Maronites, sharing the same language, a common liturgy and perhaps as history has shown in many instances, sharing their churches.[604]

---

[603] Harb, *The Maronites: History and Constants*, p. 94.
[604] Dib, *History of the Maronite Church*, p. 70.

Gryphon returned to Rome twice to report about the Maronites. On one occasion whilst in Rome, he wrote back to the Maronites on behalf of the Pope:

[T]here are throughout the world many unbelieving Christian sects. The Maronites, we know, have no accord neither with the unbelievers, nor the Nestorians, nor the Jacobites, nor the Greeks, but they consider all these sects as heterodox. From time immemorial the Maronites have solemnly mentioned the Roman Pontiff and have not included the personages of any other confessions. Your ancestors have established this custom, because they were in accord with the Pope of Rome and united in the same belief. That in the territories of the Franks – Rhodes, Cyprus, Tripoli, Beyrouth, Jerusalem – the Maronites from antiquity have frequented the churches of the Franks; they consecrate and make the sign of the cross as the Franks do; they confess and receive communion at the churches of the Franks and received presents from them such as miters, etc. ... Furthermore, more than 250 years ago, Patriarch Jeremias, his priest and people joined themselves to the faith of the Franks.[605]

Gryphon returned to Lebanon and eventually became the representative of the Holy See to the Maronites.

## 12.2.2 The Late Fifteenth Century

Dib cites Doueihi to inform us that during the second half of the fifteenth century the Maronite territories enjoyed intermittent peace thanks to the work and intelligence of the mouqadammin. The Maronites were in large numbers. The village of Hadchit had twenty priests. The town of Besharre had as many churches as days in the year. Schools flourished and there were more than one hundred and ten Maronite copyists.[606]

Yet, the relative peace was often broken. Franciscan Brother Alex-

[605] Ibid., p. 71.
[606] Ibid., p. 74.

ander, the pope's legate to the Maronites, wrote from Qannoubin to the pope in 1475 about the cruelty inflicted upon them:

> In the midst of this nation (Maronite) live the Saracens ... Their tyranny knows no rest; also, in all the parts of Lebanon, there is only desolation, provoking tears. Under the pretext of raising a certain tribute that they call gelia, they (the agents of the authority) despoil the poor mountain people of all that they have; afterwards, they beat them with rods, inflicting all sorts of torments to extort from them what they do not have. Against these vexations, there is only one recourse possible, apostasy. Many might have fallen if it had not being for the pious charity of their Patriarch (Peter Ibn Hassan) who came to their aid. Dismayed at the peril to the souls of his sheep, he gave over all the revenues of his churches to satisfy the greed of the tyrants. The door of the (Patriarchal) monastery was walled up; sometimes he was obliged to hide, as Popes Urban and Sylvester, in the caves hollowed out of the earth.[607]

This was also likely to be a period of Jacobite expansion in the Jibbett area of North Lebanon. It was probably brought about by the Sultan's earlier appointments of a non-Maronite (Jacobite perhaps) as mouqaddamin. It may also be attributed to the natural protection Lebanon and its rugged mountain provided to so many religious and ethnic groups.

In the late fifteenth century the Maronite mouqaddamin of Besharre, Abd al-Mon'en Ayoub II (1472-1495) declared his favouritism towards the Jacobites and built them a church near his home. The Maronite Patriarch Peter, called Ibn Hassan, was opposed to him and in 1488 "the inhabitants of Ehden, known for their bravery, resorted to force, following a battle provoked by Abd al-Mon'en Ayoub himself, routed his followers and cleared the area of his agitators."[608] Harb reports that this was a battle between the Maronites and the Jacobites. Seven years later in 1495, Abd al-Mon'en Ayoub died and was suc-

---

[607] Ibid., p. 75.
[608] Ibid., p. 74.

ceeded by his son who remained faithful to his Maronite ancestors. The Monophysite Jacobites were forced to flee from the Jibbett area in the north of Lebanon.[609]

The Maronite, Gabriel Ibn al-Qelai, was born in 1450 in the village of Lehfed in the Jbail (Byblos) district. Brother Gryphon chose him and two other Maronites to become Franciscans in Jerusalem. Thereafter, as the first Maronites sent to the West to study, they studied in Venice and Rome. Brother Gabriel returned to Lebanon serving and instructing the Maronites. Within three years he wrote 456 letters setting out the errors of the Monophysites. He also accused Besharre mouqadammin, Abd al-Mon'en Ayoub, of betraying the religion of his ancestors in person. He composed *zajaliat* (popular sung poetry) and composed and translated into Arabic many works of theology, history, and pontifical letters addressed to the Maronites, and canon law. It appears as though his zajaliat were particularly directed at keeping the faithful's minds loyal to the Roman church and thereby resistance against any Jacobite infiltration. He was consecrated as the Maronite Bishop of Nicosia in 1507, remaining in his bishopric until his death in 1516.[610]

Of al-Qelai, Dib writes:

> Ibn al Qelai was the first Maronite to read the Latin works on the religious origins of his nation. He defended with vigour the perpetual orthodoxy of the Maronites and his example was followed by later writers. He exercised a profound influence on the life of the Maronite Church. He is considered among the principal precursors of the effective Latinisation of the liturgy and discipline.[611]

It is ironic that whilst defending the perpetual orthodoxy of the Maronites on one hand, on the other Ibn al-Qelai ushered in the most significant period of Latinisation of the Maronite liturgy. Embracing Maronite faithfulness to the Catholic Church since the arrival of the

---

[609] Harb, *The Maronites: History and Constants*, p. 94.
[610] Dib, *History of the Maronite Church*, pp. 75-76.
[611] Ibid., p. 76.

Crusades was often at the expense of their own rich indigenous liturgy, perhaps unintentionally promoting the concept of superiority of the Latin liturgy. It would take almost a thousand years in the form of the Second Vatican Council of the 1960s to officially commence the reversal of that direction.

## 12.3  Lebanon in the Ottoman Muslim Period (1516-1918)

The Ottoman Muslim Turks took Constantinople from the Byzantines in 1453. Under Selim I they took Syria in 1516 from the Mamlouks. The Ottomans were named after Osman, a tribal leader, and had formed as a contester for the Middle East in the thirteenth century in Anatolia, modern-day Turkey. Their Islamic empire extended from the thirteenth century into Europe and reached the height of its power in the sixteenth and seventeenth centuries, only collapsing in the twentieth century.

The civil administration of niabat under the Mamlouks became known as the *pachaliks* governed by the *pasha*. Syria was divided between Damascus, Aleppo and Tripoli. The Damascus government (*wilayat*) included the districts (*sanjaks*) of Sidon and Beirut as well as other districts of Palestine. The sanjak of Tripoli included North Lebanon, and in Syria, Homs, and Hama. A delegation of Lebanese princes went to Damascus swearing obedience to the Sultan who confirmed them in their fiefdoms. They included Fakhr-al-Din I Ma'an from the Chouf, Assaf al-Turkmani of Kisrawan, and Jbeil Harfush of the Bekkaa, and the Chihabs of Wadi Taym.[612] There was no military service required to the Sultan.

Two years before the Ottoman conquest of Lebanon, the Maronite Patriarch wrote to Pope Leo X: "We are located among infidels and heretics, we suffer persecution; our goods are despoiled and we often fall under the whip."[613] In 1514, Pope Leo sent the first of three missions to the Maronites in Lebanon. After receiving reports back, he called them "roses amongst the thorns."

---

[612] Harb, *The Maronites: History and Constants*, p. 96.
[613] Dib, *History of the Maronite Church*, p. 178.

For a long period of time, the Mediterranean coastal cities lost their importance as trade ports under Turkish rule. Coupled with the refuge of the Lebanese mountains from the brutality of the Turkish governors, this meant a significant development of the mountain areas in terms of population, economy, culture, and politics. The Maronites continued to be governed by their mouqaddamin from the Besharre region. He answered to the wilayat of Tripoli. He was responsible for collecting the tax for the Ottomans and obviously wielded power and diplomatic advantage with the rulers.

In 1527, Patriarch Moussa al-Akkori (1524-1567) sent a delegation to the French Emperor Charles V seeking for Lebanon to be freed from the Ottomans. The letter from the Patriarch read: "For four years we have been imploring your Majesty to help us acquire our independence, as we have fifty thousand well-trained archers perfectly ready to serve you in this war for independence."[614] The Emperor was unable to assist. Consequently, the Maronite Patriarch successfully petitioned Sultan Suleiman the Magnificent (1520-1566) for special autonomy for the Maronites. One should read this in the context of a treaty signed a few decades prior (in 1536) between King François (Francis) I of France and Sultan Suleiman. The 1536 treaty gave protection to 'Western' Latin Catholics in the Ottoman Empire. Though the patronage of France was originally established during the Crusades, this laid the basis for the economic, political, and religious protection of the Maronites, the only non Latin Catholics in the East.

The Ottoman Turks found on arrival in Lebanon a ruling feudal system of individual emirs or dynasties from various ethnicities and religions. They allowed the status quo to remain. The special autonomy offered to the Maronites allowed them to continue to be governed directly by their mouqaddamin, principally from Becharre. These freedoms likely attracted many immigrants to Lebanon from other regions under Turkish occupation.

The events and sources for the period represent the third time in history that the Maronites were the only Christian denomination in

---

[614] Harb, *The Maronites: History and Constants*, p. 98.

the Middle East to have what appeared to be a regular independent military wing that resisted Islamic conquest or rule. The first of the two earlier occasions was upon the arrival of the Arab Muslim conquests in the seventh century, and the second was upon the arrival of the Crusaders in the late tenth century. The events that took place in the Mamlouk period of rule also provide weight for the beginnings of a Maronite tradition of promoting Lebanese of all faiths to co-exist harmoniously as one nation, seeking foreign assistance wherever necessary but never accepting foreign rule.

### 12.3.1  Ma'an Dynasty and Prince Fakhr-al-Din (1516-1697)

The Druze emir Fakhr-al-Din II (1598-1635) was from the Ma'an family of the Chouf mountain area of Lebanon. He was hidden by his mother from Ottoman troops in the Christian district of Kesrawan, and was raised under the care of the Maronite family of Khazen. He rose to power to monopolise Lebanon for the profit of his dynasty. Fakhr-al-Din sealed a union between the Maronites and the Druze, bringing prosperity and peace and allowing arts and literature to thrive. He strove for an independent Lebanon. He was known as the Prince (or Emir) of Saida (Sidon). His principal adviser was a Maronite, Abou Nader el Khazen.

Because he was seen as a threat to the empire, Fakhr-al-Din was exiled to Italy in 1613. There he met with Maronite scholars, one of whom acted as his intermediary in the Medici Court. The Maronite Patriarch Yuhanna Makhlouf had appointed Bishop George as the emir's representative to the Papal See. During this time, Fakhr-al-Din signed a secret treaty with the Duke of Tuscany, Ferdinand I de Medici to wage a military campaign to free the Holy Land from Turkey. The treaty required that Ferdinand obtain from the Pope a bull commanding Maronites to be on the side of Fakhr-al-Din in future wars. Fakhr-al-Din returned from Italy in 1618.

Maritime activity began to flourish between the Orient and Europe via the ports of Beirut and Sidon. Fakhr-al-Din helped the silk industry by encouraging the Maronites from North Lebanon to the Chouf and

Kisrawan regions. He promoted production and protection of the trade managing to modernise Lebanon following European progress. The economy of the country was flourishing and the Emir favoured Christians. Doueihi comments that the Maronites enjoyed freedom during this period: "They held their heads high, built churches, rode saddled horses and wore white headdresses. Moreover, missionaries came from Europe and resided in Mount Lebanon. Most of the army of the Prince, his ministers and his collaborators were also Maronites."[615]

The Capucin, Father Eugene Roger, reported on the Maronites and their relationship with Prince Fakhr-al-Din, who was a close friend to Roger:

> The Prince, who had a great esteem for the Maronites and the Maronite church, did not want to rule on the Maronite cases. He left to their Patriarch the task of making them respect the laws, and settling their conflicts ... (the Patriarch) used to bring the contentious parties to stand before him, and settle their conflicts. They used to accept his judgment as God's words. Thus, the Turks were unable to interfere in the conflicts arising among the Maronites.[616]

The Maronites even joined the military for Fakhr-al-Din as the Italian voyager Dominco Magri wrote in 1624: "the permanent army of Fakhr-al-Din was composed of 20,000 Maronites and 12,000 Druze."[617] The Chief of the army was the Maronite Abu Nader el Khazen. The Ottomans may have become suspicious of Fakhr-al-Din's close allegiance to the Maronites and Christians and his independence tendencies again. In 1633, they ordered the Ottoman pashas to attack the Lebanese prince. He was captured and taken to Istanbul where he was executed in 1635.

In addition, Maronite loyalty to Rome would have been of continual concern to the Ottomans. In 1643, Father Thomas Vitali visited Lebanon and reported: "They are Catholics most loyal to the Apostol-

---

[615] Ibid., p. 108.
[616] Ibid., p. 112.
[617] Ibid., p. 109.

ic See, and they are the only community in the East to maintain their faith, and preserve the virtues that characterised their ancestors."[618] This special relationship jeopardised the Maronite relationship with the Ottomans. The Maronites were known as 'Franjs' or French, meaning the pope's followers and were considered spies of Rome. Even the papal envoy Dandini in 1596 had to change his name and conceal his identity.

The Ottomans targeted the Maronites via the hereditary nature of the office of mouqaddamin. They made it competitive and in 1655 conferred it on the Shiite (or Metoulite) family of Hamada who had risen to power in the area. The Pasha of Tripoli supported the Hamada successors of the Shiites in attacking Christian areas of North Lebanon, causing more migration of Maronites to Druze areas of the Chouf and even Shiite areas of the South whose sheiks were more favourable than their Shiite brothers in the North. A major proportion of Maronites fled at this time to take refuge south in the district of Kesrawan, past the river Nahr Ibrahim and down to the villages of the coast.[619]

In 1660, the pashalik of Saida (Sidon) was created to watch over the south of Mount Lebanon with pashalik of Tripoli remaining to watch over the north of Lebanon. King Louis XIV sent a letter to his ambassador in Istanbul in 1670, confirming French protection of the Maronites and seeking for the Sultan intervene to stop the oppression of the Maronites by local Turkish governors.[620] In 1675, Patriarch Doueihi moved his seat from our Lady of Qannoubin to the monastery of Mejdel-Meoush in the Chouf because of attacks from the Hamadi Shiites. He remained there under protection of the Ma'an prince for three years.

The Ma'an dynasty of the Chouf kept their autonomy as the Turks and their Sultan became preoccupied with threats of attack from Europe. The Maronite's loyalty remained to the Ma'an as successors of Fakhr-al-Din. These princes also had an alliance with the Chihab emirs of Waddi Tayham, a neighbouring district.

---

[618] Ibid., p. 114.

[619] Dib, *History of the Maronite Church*, pp. 84-85.

[620] Harb sets out the letter in French, *The Maronites: History and Constants*, p. 99.

## 12.3.2 Chihab Dynasty (1697-1842)

The emir Ahmad from the Ma'an family died in 1697 leaving no adult male offspring. The Ma'ans were Druze of faith. A new emir from another dynasty had to be elected. Accordingly, the lords of Lebanon met at Somqannya (between Deir al-Qamar and Moktara) to elect a successor to govern Lebanon. They elected Emir Bashir I from the Chihab family. The Chihabs were Sunni Muslims descendant from the Arab tribe of Qoraish who came to Lebanon in the thirteenth century to fight against the Crusaders. They settled in Hasbaya. During the late seventeenth and early eighteenth century political blocks or parties had been established. The Chihabs belonged to the Qaysi party.

The Chihab emirs renewed good relations with the pashas of Tripoli and Saida, who were also Sunni Muslim. The emirs increased their popularity in Lebanon by appointing other emirs and sheiks. In 1711, the new governor of Lebanon, Haidar Chihab, brought a new feudal system to the mountains of Lebanon, dividing up new areas under his control. This included the Maronite emirs from the families of the Khazen, Hobaich, Dahdah, Khoury, Bitar, and others. Maronite confidence grew and they sought to take back North Lebanon from the rule of the Shiites. By 1777, this was accomplished and the Maronite sheiks of the region from the families of Karam, Aouad, Daher, and others took control.[621]

Haidar Chihab moved the seat of the emirate from Hasbaya to Deir al-Qamar. The Ottoman *wali* of Sidon deposed him and elected Prince Yussef Alam-Eddin from the opposition Yamani political party. Haidar fled to be with his Qaysi party allies in Ghazir, namely the Khazen and Hobaish families in the region of Kesrawan. The new Prince Yusuf followed Haidar to Ghazir, conquered the town and setting it aflame. Haidar fled to Hermel but his sons remained in hiding under the protection of the Khazen family.

In 1729 Haidar's son Melhem became the Prince and added Beirut as the second capital of the emirate after Deir al-Qamar. During his reign, a conflict arose between two Druze dynasties – the Jumb-

---

[621] Dib, *History of the Maronite Church*, p. 88.

lats and the Yazbekis. The Khazen Maronites supported the Jumblats. The Hobaish and Dahdah Maronite dynasties supported the Yazbekis. Prince Melhem abdicated to his brothers Ahmad and Mansour. After this time Melhem's sons, Yousef and Qassem, converted to become Maronites and so too followed many of the Chihab family dynasty. This opened the doors for other Muslim dynasties to convert such as the Bellama family who were head of the region of Matn. Emir Bashir II (1789-1840) was the first Prince of Lebanon (1831-1840) to declare his Christian faith publicly. This contributed significantly to the prospering of the Maronite church.

In addition to maintaining the power over Lebanon, the Maronites bettered their political and economic fortunes. The status of the Druze was in dispute. Rome and European Catholic missions supported the Maronites, the latter maintaining good relations with Europe. The Maronites also multiplied their crops of mulberry trees producing more silk for export. At the same time, the Maronite emirs began making substantial donations to the church and establishing religious causes. The Chihab emirs, as governors of Lebanon, kept their good relations with the Ottoman authorities. Mount Lebanon, compared to other parts of Syria, became a land of refuge though subject to the mercy of the pashas.[622]

### 12.3.3 The Massacres of Maronites and Christians in 1840-1860

The author Colonel Charles Churchill, British Consul to Ottoman Syria (including Lebanon) in the 1840s, believed that since Turkish rule from 1521 the mountains of Lebanon exercised a virtual independence and that up to 1840 the Druze and the Maronites lived together "in the most perfect harmony and goodwill."[623] However, from 1840, a series of events led to these relations promptly deteriorating.

Leading up to 1840, Lebanese autonomy once again threatened the rule of the Sultan and his Pashas. Emir Bashir Chihab II was exiled to

---

[622] Ibid.
[623] Charles Churchill, *The Druzes and the Maronites under the Turkish Rule From 1840 to 1860*, Bernard Quartich, 1862, pp. 24-25.

Egypt. Later the Egyptians conquered Lebanon from the Ottomans for two years. The Maronites regarded their Egyptian ruler Mohammed Ali as a liberator who removed the traditional restrictions imposed on Christians and Jews and put them on equal footing with the Muslims. The Druze were opposed to rule from Egypt. This followed a turbulent period of power struggle between the Druze and the Maronites over the appointment of the Lebanese emir.

When the Egyptian ruler declared compulsory conscription in his army, the Maronite Patriarch Hobaish (1823-1845) opposed the decree. The Maronites and the Druze aligned once again. They assembled with the Muslims at Antelias in 1840 to discuss their grievances and swore an oath at the Maronite Church altar of St Elias to stay united and fight for their independence or die. They elected the Maronite sheik Francis Khazen as their rebel leader and defeated the Egyptian occupiers in a brutal war in 1840.

We now see the beginnings of significant and numerous competing foreign influences over the factions in Lebanon, which has continued into modern times. The Russians were supporting the Greek Orthodox in the Levant, the Austrians were supporting the Greek Catholics (Melkites), the French were supporting the Maronites, and the British were supporting the Druze. Tensions were mounting over the Lebanese Emirate between the Maronites and the Druze. In 1841, clashes took place. The Shiites sided with the Maronites. The Greek Orthodox backed the Druze. Bashir III (1840-1842) from the Chihab dynasty was the Lebanese Emir at the time. The Ottomans and the British became increasingly concerned about French influence over the Maronites and Lebanon generally. The Ottomans intervened and exiled Bashir III bringing an end to the Christian Chihab dynasty of Lebanon after almost one hundred and fifty years.

The Maronite patriarch then disputed the feudal domination of the Druze lords over the Maronite population in majority Druze areas. In 1841 armed battles arose between the Druze and Maronites with both sides suffering heavy casualties. A massacre of Maronites took place in Deir El Kamar and the burning of surrounding Maronite villages, monasteries and convents. The Greek Orthodox generally aligned themselves with the Druze to attack the Maronites. Churchill cites letters confirming that the Turkish conspired with the Druze to allow the massacres and plundering of villages and violation of women. The Druze received military supplies from the Turks and with five hundred Turkish soldiers and thousands of Druze militia set out against all Christians in the town of Zahle and surrounding villages burning buildings and massacring hundreds of people. This encouraged a general Muslim uprising and fanaticism against Christians all over Ottoman Syria with extensive burning of villages around Damascus.[624]

The Turks appointed their own Omar Pasha as governor of Lebanon who was aligned with the Austro-Hungarians. Omar Pasha's reign was brutal and caused deep divisions between Christians and the Druze. Both the Druze and Maronites were opposed to the appointment and formed an alliance for an insurrection and rebellion against the Turkish government. The Turks attacked the Druze and Maronites. Accordingly, with the support of the British and the Sultan, the Austrians proposed that Lebanon be divided into two governments: Maronite to the north and Druze to the south. This was aimed at destroying the Lebanese Emirate. The proposal of a divided Lebanon succeeded in 1843 when the Turks agreed to allow the appointment of both a Druze and Christian governor (kaimmakan) of Lebanon at the start of 1843.[625]

Whilst the Maronites formed the large majority in the north of Lebanon, they were also in considerable numbers in the south and there were many mixed villages of both Maronites and Druze. Anarchy ensued and the Maronites in the south were subject to significant persecution. The Greek Orthodox Christians refused to be governed by the Maronite governor preferring governance under the Druze. The Druze insisted the Maronites in their region be governed by the Druze governor. The Maronites resisted. Assassination and reprisals continued. France and Austria sent relief funds to the Maronite patriarch as result of the severe impact of the Civil War.

---

[624] Ibid., pp. 50, 55-57, 60.
[625] Ibid., p. 79.

The French and British empires were competing against each other for favour with the Lebanese people. The British were unable to form an alliance with the Maronites because the latter maintained their traditional ties to the French. The British turned towards the Druze to counter the French influence. The French supported the demand by the Maronites for an undivided and autonomous Lebanon to be returned to the Chihab dynasty. In 1845 another civil war broke out between the Maronites and the Druze. The Maronites set out and burned fourteen Druze villages. Turkish authorities came to the aid of the Druze and another massacre of Maronites and Christians ensued with the burning of Maronite villages. For the next fifteen years the Druze oppressed the Christians.[626]

The Turks organized a *madjlis* or council in 1845 represented by one judge and one counsellor from each sect in the region: the Muslims (Sunni), Druze, Maronite, 'Greek' (Orthodox), 'Greek Catholic' (Melkite), and only a counsellor from the Metoualis (Shiite) as "they have a judge in common with the Muslims."[627] This appeared to be a liberal measure for the relevant groups to preside over judicial, financial, and administrative affairs. But the feudal organization under the Chihabs was no longer in practice and the Turks achieved the breakdown of Lebanese sovereignty, bringing Lebanon back under the direct rule of the Pasha.

In 1856 the Sultan Abdel Majid declared the abolition of the feudal system throughout the Ottoman Empire and sought to establish equality amongst all communities. The Maronites in Kisrawan, supported by their Patriarch Boulos Massaad and the clergy under him, revolted against their feudal lords. They declared a rebellion in 1858. This was the first social movement in the Levant. The Druze continued to have their sights set on ruling Lebanon.

This was the background and lead up to a very tragic sectarian civil war for three weeks between late May and June 1860 where the Christians, especially the Maronites constituting the overwhelming

[626] Ibid., pp. 91-94, 135.
[627] Dib, *History of the Maronite Church*, p. 91.

majority in Lebanon, came under physical attack. Churchill states that the Druze had been secretly conspiring with local Turkish authorities for a number of weeks prior, arranging Ottoman Government support for the commencement of a massacre of Christians and the burning of their villages in the Druze districts of Mount Lebanon. He also records evidence through a confidential agent of the British Consul of a plan declared in 1840 by the Turkish pasha in Damascus to exterminate Christians of Ottoman Syria by using the local Muslim and Druze populations as mercanaries in order to maintain supremacy. It was stated in the documentation that by having the locals do the deed the Turks could maintain their innocence amongst Europeans. Churchill believes the British government was also implicit in this plan.[628]

The 1860 civil war was sparked by a village dispute that arose between Druze and Maronite neighbours in the town of Beit Meri and which led to deaths on both sides. The Druze escalated the matter and began to burn Christian villages. This time the Greek Orthodox Christians aligned with the Maronites. Maronite delegations to Druze leaders requested avoidance of another civil war but the requests were dismissed. From late May 1860, the Druze, in full agreement and with the physical support of Turkish troops, began a furious onslaught burning Christian villages and massacring Christians including women and children.[629] The Turks would signal comfort to the Christians that the Turkish authorities would protect them from the Druze and Turkish soldiers would lure the Christians from surrounding villages that were being burnt into major town squares. They would ensure no place to escape and then let the Druze loose to undertake the massacres. Kurds and Muslims joined in the atrocities and the Druze were congratulated by them for leading the slaying.

As it did in 1840, the Druze massacre of Christians incited Muslims to now rise up against the Christians in their quarter of Damascus. This took place over three days and once again the Turkish Pasha falsely promised protection to the Christians luring them into the city

---

[628] Churchill, *The Druzes and the Maronites*, pp. 137, 140-141, 223.
[629] Ibid., p. 146.

square allowing massacres and crimes to be committed by the Arabs, Kurds and Druze. The Pasha himself supervised the massacres and the burning of villages. However, it should be noted there are records of some Druze sheiks and the Prince of Damascus offering refuge to Christians at the time. The Muslim uprisings against Christians then spread throughout Syria and Palestine including Aleppo as well as all of Lebanon. Consul generals stationed in Ottoman Syria from the imperial powers of England, Austria, France, Prussia and Russia intervened. Around late June 1860 each day would witness thousands of Christians board European boats for Alexandria, Scyra and Athens.[630]

The British objected to the arrival of French troops on 16 August 1860 who landed in Lebanon shortly after the massacres. The British requested the pacification of the country be left to the Turkish authorities. Churchill states this showed Britain's implicitness in the massacres quoting British correspondence declaring that so long as the Druze and Christians existed as two races no permanent security could be obtained. He also states Britain was complicit in throwing Lebanon into confusion and disorder to give the Ottoman Empire strength and independence.[631]

Churchill records the Maronite districts of Lebanon at the time contained about 1000 villages and a population of about 500,000. During the three weeks of pillage, he documented Mount Lebanon had 5000 Christians massacred and 200 villages burnt. He also records within Ottoman Syria generally, including Lebanon, the sum total of "all these accumulated horrors induced by the Turks" were:

- 11,000 Christians massacred;
- 100,000 sufferers by civil war;
- 20,000 desolate widows and orphans;
- 3000 Christian habitations burnt to the ground;
- 2 million pounds sterling worth of property destroyed.[632]

---

[630] Ibid., pp. 199, 200, 214.
[631] Ibid., pp. 251, 257.
[632] Ibid., pp 199, 219.

Dib cites one eyewitness account:

> in sum, 7771 persons of every age and sex were killed in the space of 22 days! Three hundred and sixty villages were destroyed, 560 churches torn down, 42 monasteries burned, 23 schools that would usually handle 1830 students were destroyed.[633]

The Sultan sent his Foreign Minister Fouad Pasha to settle affairs, distribute relief to the homeless Christians and to conduct trials to execute the guilty participants of the massacres. Nonetheless, Churchill informs us those responsible for the crimes were in the main absolved, even after investigation forced upon the local Turkish authorities by the Europeans, with not one person punished for the crime.[634] This period marked the beginning of the first mass migration of Maronites since the Crusades. It was this time to the 'new West' namely, the Americas (North, Central, and South America), the Caribbean, and, to a lesser extent, Australia.

The three Massabki brothers – Francis, Abdul-Moti and Raphael –were martyred on 10 July 1860 in Damascus for refusing to denounce their Christian faith whilst seeking refuge in a Franciscan monastery. These Maronite lay persons one of whom was married, were beatified by Pope Pius XI in 1926 and with other Maronite saints are dealt with in more detail by Azize in his book.[635] The Maronite saints, St Na'amtallah Al Hardini (1810-1858), St Charbel (1828-98) and St Rafqa (1832 - 1914) all lived through these massacres and hardships.

### 12.3.4  Mutasarrifat Period (1861-1914)

Father John Hadj, a Maronite member of the *madjlis*, drafted a report of the massacre and distributed it throughout Europe and especially France. Christian Europe convened a conference at Paris resolving to send six thousand French soldiers to protect the Christians and Ma-

---

[633] Dib, *History of the Maronite Church*, p. 92.
[634] Churchill, *The Druzes and the Maronites*, p. 243.
[635] Azize, An Introduction to the Maronite Faith, pp. 377-412

ronites and to provide relief work. The French proposed the Organic Laws of 1861 to re-establish the ancient Lebanese organisation under a native authority. An international commission representing Britain, France, Russia, Austria and Prussia convened in Beirut to discuss and settle the proposal. The Ottomans and the British watered down these laws. Two autonomous regions of Mount Lebanon were established known as *moutasarrifat*. They were to report directly to the Sultan without the intermediary of the pashas.

At the head of the two moutasarrifat was a governor nominated by the Sultan and approved by Britain and Europe. An administrative Council elected by the Lebanese communities assisted the Governor. A Lebanese gendarmerie was formed to maintain public order with French instruction. The High Commissioner of Turkey, Fouad Pacha, appointed the famous Maronite Joseph Karam from Ehden as the chief of the sub-prefecture (known as the *qaimaqamat*) for the Christians. However, the Commander in Chief of the foreign expedition, General de Beaufort d'Hautpoul, intervened requesting that the High Commissioner choose Emir Madjid from the Chihab family, the son of Bashir. Instead a Turk, Daoud Pacha, was appointed as Lebanese governor.

Believing the interests of his country were at stake, Joseph Karam declined offers in the new government. He was subsequently imprisoned and exiled to Syria. When the appointment of governor was to be renewed three years later in 1864, Karam returned to seek appointment and led a resistance group. They were outnumbered and Karam left Lebanon in 1867 under French protection. He became a local hero, and his body remains revered in the main church of Ehden.

In the same year, Patriarch Mas'ad made the second *ad limina* visit to Rome of a Maronite patriarch. The first was by Jeremias al-Amchiti (d. 1230). From Rome the Patriarch went to Paris where Napoleon III welcomed him. The Patriarch then travelled to Istanbul and the Sultan Abdul-Aziz "offered him hospitality in a palace where care had been taken to install a chapel."[636] From that time until 1914, the diverse religious groups of Lebanon lived in relative harmony.

---

[636] Dib, *History of the Maronite Church*, p. 167.

In 1890, John Hadj, the former judge for the Christians of Lebanon on the *majdlis*, was elected Maronite patriarch. One of his first actions was to transform the modesty of the patriarch's fortress type residence in the ancient monastery at Bkerke to a palace type building which contained "a new residence, a church, a library, special salons, and rooms serviced by large corridors ... conceived in a sober but elegant style of striking beauty." Hadj also built a new summer residence at Diman. This elevated the status of the patriarch and as Dib puts it:

> To these residences, during the reign of John Hadj, came religious and civil authorities of the East; prelates of all rites, consuls, pashas, governors, emirs, sheiks, and notables of all races and nationalities. The president of the French Republic decorated him with the Legion of Honour and the Sultan of Turkey with the Mejidie of the first-class and the Grand Osmanie cordon – something no other patriarch had obtained.[637]

The external aspect of office was of secondary importance to Patriarch Hadj. His principal goal was spiritual order. He tried to promote the progress of the Maronite people in all spheres: religious, social, and intellectual. He vigorously pushed for the establishment of schools, discipline of the clergy, and diverse works which would raise the standards of living for his flock. His pastoral letters witnessed this solicitude. It was at this time, if not before, that the Maronite clergy founded schools next to each monastery and, where there was no monastery, beside the village Church in the shadow of an oak tree.

To supplement the existing four national Maronite seminaries in Lebanon, Patriarch Hadj established, for the first time, a seminary that belonged solely to patriarchal authority. The formation of the clergy was one of his greatest priorities even outside Lebanon. Accordingly, he re-established the Maronite College of Rome in 1891 after

---

[637] Ibid., p. 170.

a long non-operational period and subsequent dilapidation. Monsignor Hoyek was appointed by Patriarch Hadj for the foreign mission. Hoyek appealed to the French for funding and visited the Sultan in Istanbul obtaining from him 500 Turkish pounds in gold. The Pope donated 150,000 francs to the cause.[638]

At the same time, Hoyek had successfully lobbied the French authorities for a Maronite college in France. The French government opened the Chapel of Marie de Medici at Petit Luxembourg in Paris for the Maronites. The Patriarch named a procurator and eight scholarships were awarded to students. Elias Hoyek, as Archbishop of Acre in Palestine, was also successful in the Holy Land when the Patriarch established a church and house in Jerusalem in 1895.

After the death of Patriarch Hadj in 1898, Hoyek was appointed Patriarch. He was a former student of the Oriental seminary of Ghazir founded by the Jesuits. He was also a former student of the College of the Propaganda in Rome where he received a doctorate in theology. One of his first acts was to build a grander style summer palace at Diman, the same way his predecessor built a grand winter palace at Bkerke. The summer palace was to overlook the holy Valley of Qadisha including the former patriarchal residence and monastery at Qannoubin.

### 12.3.5 First World War (1914-1918)

As soon as the First World War commenced, the foreign consuls present in the Ottoman Empire were sacked. The moutasarrifat two state system in Lebanon, which was under the guidance of the combined European powers, ended. Ottoman troops entered Lebanon and converted the monasteries of Mar Chaya in Brumana and St John al Qalaa into military forts because of their strategic locations. Aley, as a strategic mountain position, became the Ottoman Army headquarters for Beirut and Mount Lebanon. In 1915, Jamal Pasha abolished the administrative Council of Mount Lebanon and formed a military court at Aley. This court exiled leading Lebanese figures including religious

---

[638] Ibid., p. 172.

such as the Archbishop of Beirut Boutros Chabli and the Antiochian Orthodox Bishop of Beirut, Germanios Msarrah.

Documents found by the Turks in the sacked French consulate of Beirut showed that prominent Lebanese were plotting with the help of France to liberate Lebanon. Consequently, the Turks arrested, exiled, imprisoned, and executed many of them without distinction between Christians and Muslims. The first martyr was killed in 1915 and was the Maronite parish priest Yousef al Hayek from Sin el-Fil. In 1916, twenty-five leaders were publicly hanged in Beirut in the square that until now is known as Martyr's Square in the centre of Beirut.

During the war thousands of people in Lebanon died of famine and disease. The Turks had oppressed the Lebanese by confiscating their crops and cattle and prohibiting the import of grain. They also blocked land and sea routes from foreign aid thereby preventing the receipt of assistance from families who had emigrated. Inflation was rampant and a locust plague destroyed the agricultural crops.

Maronite Archbishop Boulos Akl (General Vicar of the Maronite Patriarchate) had secretly raised money from the French Governor of the Arwad Island (off Syria), from Lebanese emigrants in Egypt and from around the world. Eventually, the Turks found out and sentenced him to death *in absentia*. In this desperate time, Abbott Ignace Dagher of the Lebanese Maronite Order negotiated to raise money for assistance. With the approval of the Patriarchate, the Order mortgaged all its properties to the French government for one million gold francs. The money was sent in instalments from France via special routes and distributed to the poor. Jamal Pacha attempted to arrest the Maronite Patriarch Hoyek. The Patriarch sought the support of Pope Benedictus XV who subsequently arranged for the intervention of the Austrian Emperor who was allied to the Ottoman Sultan.

The War ended in 1918. One third of the Lebanese population had died. Competing political movements had been fermenting in Lebanon for decades prior. The first was for Lebanese nationalism and independence with the return of important traditional parts of the country's land: this was supported by the great majority of Christians. The second was Arab nationalism shared with other countries based on language and cultural heritage. This was supported by many Muslims, moreso the Sunnis who sought a Muslim Arab state. The Christians who supported this concept wanted it to be a secular state in nature. The third movement was for Syrian-Arab nationalism stretching over Syria, Lebanon, Palestine, and Iraq, to form 'Greater Syria'. This concept was designed to be inclusive of Muslims and Christians. All three movements shared the common goals of opposing Turkish rule and gaining freedom.

### 12.3.6 Lebanese Independence

The administrative Council of Lebanon was reconstituted in December 1918. It brought back all of the Lebanese sects under the former moutasarrifat system. They sent a delegation of seven members to the Peace Conference in Paris in February 1919, but the delegation returned to Lebanon without a resolution. Another Lebanese Administrative Council was held in Baabda. It issued a unanimous proclamation affirming: "the political and administrative independence of Lebanon in its historical and geographical boundaries including the parts previously usurped."[639] They instructed the Maronite Patriarch Hoyek to head the second Lebanese delegation to the Peace Conference, scheduled later in the year. The memorandum to this Conference included a request "for a French mandate in Lebanon granting the inalienable rights of the Lebanese to ultimate sovereignty."[640] The French Prime Minister Clemeceau wrote to Hoyek confirming France's approval and the Patriarch was given a hero's welcome upon his return to Lebanon.

Patriarch Hoyek is also well-known for providing mentoring and practical counsel in conformity with divine teaching. He insisted on devotion to the Sacred Heart and to Mary the Mother of God. He arranged for the construction of Our Lady of Lebanon in Harissa in 1921

---

[639] Harb, *The Maronites: History and Constants*, p. 150.
[640] Ibid.

and the expansion of the cult of Mary via this new centre of pilgrimage. This remains a hub for both Christian and Muslim Lebanese pilgrims today and tourists from the Middle East and around the world. The Patriarch also established in 1895 the first congregation of teaching women, The Maronite Sisters of the Holy Family, who today have a significant presence in Sydney, Australia through their schools and nursing homes.

Muslim Lebanese figures who wanted a broad Arab state refused the independent Lebanese entity under French control, given it was separated from Syrian nationalism. The Arabic author al-Jisr states that Muslims who were accustomed to being part of an Islamic state were now to become a minority governed by Christians and foreigners, and saw Greater Lebanon as the defeat of the Arab movement by Christian Europe.[641] Around this time, the French waived the return of the loan from the Lebanese Maronite Order since, as Prime Minister Clemenceau declared, "the French Government did not want to be less generous than a community of 600 monks."[642]

On 1 September 1920, the independent 'State of Greater Lebanon' was declared by the French and established under their mandate. This was ratified by the League of Nations in 1922 and the boundaries of Lebanon as they are presently were defined in its Constitution in 1926. In his conclusion to his book, Harb comments on this moment:

> What had been achieved on September 1st was not only a physical entity but also a cultural and spiritual one nourished by the Lebanese soil and values. The Maronite Nation's existential commitment to the land has rendered it a Geographical Nation coincident with the Lebanese Nation as a whole.

> The Maronite Patriarchate, confirming its intimate relationship between the Maronites and the Lebanese land, adopted the motto: 'The Glory of Lebanon is given unto him'. This motto, which adorns the entrance of the Patriarchate, is the

---

[641] Ibid., p. 152.
[642] Ibid., p. 146.

testimony of faith in Lebanon as a whole, for Lebanon cannot be but a unified and unifying whole. Moreover, the motto is a firm testimony of an everlasting Maronite faith in Lebanon, a land of liberty and values, the Land of Man.

## 12.4   Religious History in Ottoman Times: Assistance, Influence, Latinisation, and Persecution

Although the Ottomans had conquered the Middle East in 1516, it was not until 1570-1571 that they conquered the island of Cyprus and took it from under the Venetians. Maronites were massacred and many of the living fled to Lebanon. Others followed the Venetians to Malta.[643] The Maronites who remained in Cyprus had to answer to the Sultan's governor and, as Ristelhueber writes, also to the Greeks who were no less difficult. The troubles from the Greeks would likely have been because the Maronites were the only Catholics left on the Island.

Around 1580, Jesuit priests Fathers Dandini and Eliano visited the Maronites in Cyprus and noted they were reduced to a population of about 1,500 and nineteen villages. France intervened to lighten their suffering, but by 1686 there were no more than one hundred and fifty people amongst eight villages.[644] The Jesuits who visited the Maronites in Cyprus were part of two pontifical delegations Rome had sent to Lebanon between 1578 and 1582. This was the first official contact between the Jesuit Order and the Maronites. The goal was also to attempt to bring other Christians back in communion with Rome.

The leading Jesuit delegate at the time, Father Eliano, had caused the Vatican to believe that he led the Maronites to communion with Rome. This is the justification for a very limited number of scholars who claim, incorrectly, that the Maronites were still Monothelites until this time. Dib deals with the Monothelitism claims of Eliano extensively in his book. Eliano demanded the burning of books and

---

[643] This was potentially the second wave of migration of the Lebanese to Malta, the first being when it was colonised by the Phoenicians around the seventh century BC.
[644] Dib, *History of the Maronite Church*, pp. 176-178.

manuscripts of the Maronite liturgy contending that they contained errors in the Catholic faith. It was later found that many of the Maronite books were part of a library of Jacobite books and did not belong to the Maronite Church liturgy. One can only imagine how much of the heritage of the Maronite church was lost at that time.

Pope Clement VIII arranged a new mission to Lebanon to clarify the issue, led by Father Girolamo Dandini. On his arrival to Qannoubin, Patriarch Sergius el-Ruzzi (the brother of his predecessor) was vehement in his defence of the accusations made against the Maronites. The Latinisation of the Maronite Church became priority. There were Maronites who were reluctant, some even to the point of refusal, to accept the transformation. On occasion, this included the patriarch. Eventually, Dandini brought two hundred copies of the Romanised Maronite missal to the Maronite Synod at Qannoubin in 1596, marking a significant move in the Latinisation of the Maronite Church. This was less than a century since the last major program of Latinisation led by Maronite Ibn al-Qelai (d. 1521).

In 1614, King Louis XIII of France founded an Arabic and Syriac choir at the College of France. The Maronite, Gabreil Sionita, professor at the College of Sapienza and a former student of the Maronite College of Rome, was appointed as its first head. Other Maronites were to succeed him including Abraham of Ekel or Al-Haqiliani and then Faustas Nairon from Ban in Lebanon. Al-Haqiliani and Faustas' brother Nairon are attributed to the first catalogue of oriental manuscripts held at the Vatican.

In 1635, George Amira was elected Maronite Patriarch, and was the first patriarch to have been a student of the Maronite College in Rome, where he was a schoolmate of the later elected Pope Urban VIII. Pope Urban had called Amira "the light of the Eastern church."[645] Patriarch Amira continued the process of Latinisation of the liturgy. He also worked for Latin Catholic missions in the East and offered the monastery of Saint Eliseus in the region of the Cedars to establish

[645] Ibid., p. 108.

the Carmelites in 1643. Under his reign the St Ephraim Maronite College was also founded at Ravenna in Italy. It appeared that Patriarch Amira aroused discontent amongst the conservative Maronites for his Latinisation tendencies.[646]

The traditional ties between the Maronites and the French established during the Crusades had returned in this period. It can be summarised by reference to a passage from the writings of French scholar Ristelhueber from 1925:

At the beginning of the seventeenth century, the French influence was solidly established in Lebanon on a double basis, religious and commercial. In the religious sphere, the development of our (French) commercial relations with the Levant, and the traffic in silk from Lebanon in particular were the origin of our frequent relations with this region, and then the cause of the rapid expansion of our influence. To the consuls and the missionaries fell the task of collaborating in the work that Louis XIV had fixed as the goal of his oriental policy; to develop French commerce and to protect the Catholic religion. Nowhere better than in Lebanon is it possible to follow this double activity. Reports of consuls, relations of missionaries, reports of merchants and voyagers, the works of savants contributed to making the Maronites known in France. We (the French) became interested in this little people who, in its misfortune, placed its hope in us. Such misfortune and confidence touch the heart of the French. The court was moved by the distress of the Lebanese at the same time that it witnessed their attachment to France. The desire to better the lot of the Catholics of the East by intervening in their favour was always a tradition of our kings. To speak the truth, nothing in the capitulations (with the Ottomans in 1535) conferred on them such a right. According to France, they concerned the protection of the Holy Places and religious strangers. But, for a long time, by an extension of the right of protectorate, they were equally exercised for the benefit of the indigenous Catholics themselves. Without ever recognising it formally, the sultan had admitted it in fact. It was for our representatives in the Levant a question of tact, moderation, and circumstance. On condition that it not be invoked abusively, the patronage of France over the Oriental Catholics little by little past into custom. The Maronites had particular need of this assistance to which they have made appeal.[647]

This passage may imply there were other Eastern Catholics in the Middle East. However, it is worth interjecting at this point to again emphasize the fact that the Maronites were the only perpetual indigenous Catholics in the East at the time of the seventeenth century.

Despite the strong ties, the French were unable to protect the Maronites from extreme and repeated religious persecution. Examples are provided in various texts, only two of which are now selected. The first is an account by Father Jean Boucher who visited Qannoubin in 1612. It also gives an insight into the intermittent struggles with other Christian groups:

> The Greeks molest them (the Maronites) all the time. The Patriarch told me at Qannoubin when I was there, that the Greeks by three years of lies had cost them more than 10,000 sekins they were condemned to pay the Sultan to make satisfaction for the disobedience of which they had been falsely accused by the Greeks. Then, when the Greeks had 'skinned' them, the Turks who remained at Tripoli 'nibbled at their bones'.[648]

Another account of the voyage of the Chevalier of Arvieux to Qannoubin to visit Patriarch George Besebel in 1660 sheds light on the customs and hospitality of the Maronites. At the same time it details the direct persecution of the Patriarch:

> Qannoubin, or cenobium in Latin, and monastery in French, is the patriarchal monastery where the patriarch of the Maronites resides ... We were received by the bishops and religious ... Other brothers went to announce our arrival to the

---

[647] English translation, ibid., pp. 176-177.
[648] Ibid., p. 106.

patriarch. He was hidden in a grotto far away, very secret, of difficult access and well covered, where he does not go out during the day but only at night. This is because the inhabitants of these mountains were at war with the Pasha of Tripoli, who had asked for a large sum of money which they had judged was not proper to give him. The Pasha would often send the Turks to take the patriarch and lead him to him, not doubting that when he would have him in his hands, all the Maronites would sell everything to ransom him from prison ... their life was ordinarily extremely frugal ... they fast often and very austerely; they work very hard and rise at night to chant the Office, with excellent melodies and perfect harmony ...

Afterwards, we were taken each to his proper cave, where we had found the mats and covers we had brought with us ... This prelate ... was modestly dressed in a robe of cheap cloth, and wore a large turban of blue cotton. Formerly he had worn white, but he was obliged to take blue after the Turks became masters of the country and appropriated to themselves the sole right of wearing a white turban ... all the Maronite prelates lead a very regular and austere life; they live poorly and take only what the earth gives them by the work of their hands. They do not put on the display of the prelates of Europe. They are ornated with virtue and not with rich clothes, embroidery, gold, or silver. They have only crosses of wood, but they are bishops of gold. All the Christians have an infinite respect for them, and a blind obedience to all the commands. They kiss the hands of archbishops, bishops, and priests, and the feet of the patriarch ...

The church is beautiful and large, cut in the rock. In the sacristy there is a large tableau of King Louis XIV. At supper, the patriarch had spoken to us of him and assured us that they regarded the King as their most powerful and zealous protector, and that they offer special prayers to him every day at Mass and in the Office... We went to the bottom of the Valley of the Saints, where we saw an infinite number of caves, which are the residences of the holy anchorites whose lives would be a source of admiration for all generations to come ... The bishops and the religious continued their good care and politeness towards us with so much profusion.[649]

In 1659, texts provide an account of the goods of the Maronites being despoiled and their infants taken away and sold as slaves. The Patriarch attempted to buy them back but was obliged himself to flee to escape death by sword from the assassins.[650]

In 1670, Steven Doueihi was chosen as Patriarch. He was born in 1630 in Ehden, in the mountains of North Lebanon. Doueihi was sent to the Maronite College of Rome by Patriarch Amira. He studied at various Roman universities and went about researching every available document relevant to his Maronite people, especially the large number of manuscripts in the library of the Maronite College. He continued discovering manuscripts when he returned to Lebanon to be ordained as a priest in 1655. As a young priest, Doueihi persisted in his research accumulating manuscripts in Aleppo where he spent one year and in Cyprus where he was to become Bishop of Nicosia in 1668. Doueihi is the first Maronite historian whose full works have been preserved. He was required to flee as Patriarch because of the many struggles including persecution from, not just the Turks, but the Metoualis (Shiites) who controlled parts of North Lebanon and at various times had no respect for the office of Maronite Patriarch.

Other Christian sects also showed hatred to the Maronites in his period. Doueihi wrote to Pope Innocent XI: "We are hated even more because of you."[651] Dib informs us around this period of history there is evidence that Muslims had made couplets so that their children take evil pleasure in singing whenever they encountered Christians.[652] Doueihi turned to France and Louis XIV to renew "his orders to his ambassador at Constantinople, the marquis de Ferriol, to obtain from

---

[649] Ibid., p. 106.

[650] Ibid., p. 179.

[651] Ibid., p. 119.

[652] Ibid., p. 123.

the Sultan what would be more advantageous to religion in the territory of the Maronites, and to show his protection to its inhabitants."[653]

Doueihi had several disagreements with the Franciscan missionaries' interference in Maronite affairs, and Rome agreed with him. He did not stop to work for the cause of other Christian sects to be in communion with Rome. The scholar and leader, Dib reports on Doueihi:

> He was not content with multiplying centres of religious life. Up to then, the monasteries had lived under an exclusively autonomous regime. He wished to introduce the plan of the modern Western orders with centralised authority, and on June 18, 1700 he was happy to approve the first constitutions of reform communities.[654]

He died at the monastery of Qannoubin in 1704 aged seventy-four.

In the late seventeenth century, we have yet another account of the ongoing persecutions by the pashas of Tripoli. It speaks of tortures inflicted on Sheik Younes, the head of the Maronite family of Rezq, who died a martyr for his religion:

> It was unfortunately not an isolated fact. All of Lebanon groaned under the exactions of the Turks. Their violence knew no limits. They destroyed villages, dispersed the inhabitants, hurled fathers of families into prison, hung women to trees. Without respect for the sacerdotal dignity, the patriarch and bishops were also insulted. In order to escape new affronts, they 'dressed in secular clothes' and had to flee to the rocks in the high mountains.[655]

Patriarch Joseph el-Khazen convened a Maronite Synod at the monastery of Loaisah in Kesrawan Mount Lebanon in 1736. This established the constitutional law for the Maronite church. The Maronites wrote to Rome and asked that Father Joseph Assemani be appointed as the pontifical legate to the synod. Rome was particularly

---

[653] Ibid., p. 119.
[654] Ibid., p. 120.
[655] Ibid., p. 179.

interested in reforming the mixed monasteries of monks and nuns (an ancient Christian monastic custom in the East where they would live on the same land but cloistered apart simply, usually in individual buildings), the establishment of eparchies (dioceses), the rights exercised on distribution of the holy oils, and the giving of Orders. Prelates of other Eastern Christian churches were in attendance at the Synod as were the Jesuits, Franciscans and two consuls of France.

The issue of the separation of mixed monasteries was the most heated and was drawn out for several years thereafter. It involved opposing delegations to Rome promoting their differing views and questioning whether or not Rome should confirm the Synod. Rome ultimately approved the legitimacy of the Synod. The Synod gave the Maronite Church a complete and definitive law: any new monasteries were exclusively male or female. However, many existing monasteries remained as they were until after another Synod in 1818. As Dib puts it:

> Above all, the practice of mixed monasteries did not imply any greater danger for virtue than the presence of sisters in the Episcopal residences and seminaries of the West did to the observance of vows or the obligations of the clerical state. The local authorities did not see the urgency of reform. Obstacles in the material order also hindered realization. In addition, in imitation of the second Council of Nicaea, the Synod of Mount Lebanon tolerated the monasteries already existing, but on condition that the monks and nuns lived in two sets of buildings, entirely separate.[656]

The issue of the patriarchate being divided into dioceses or eparchies, each with a resident bishop, was also controversial. Before the Synod of 1736, the bishops generally lived near to the patriarch as his vicars or lived in a monastery or hermitage. This fresh appointment required bishops to find a new residence, which was a political and economic obstacle. After 1835, the residence within the eparchy became strictly observed.

---

[656] Ibid., p. 162.

# CHAPTER 13
# MODERN MARONITE IDENTITY

## 13.1 Lebanon in the Interwar Period

Since the mass emigration of Maronites to Sicily and Rome in the seventh century and their exodus with the Crusaders in the thirteenth century, the next major wave of emigration of Maronites from Lebanon and Syria to the West was after the massacre by the Druze in the 1860s. The next wave of mass emigration was immediately after the First World War (1914-1918). Many Armenians migrated to Lebanon at this time to escape the atrocities being committed under the Ottoman regime. The administrative Council of Lebanon of 1919 sent delegations to the Peace Conferences in Paris in 1919. They requested "a French mandate in Lebanon granting the inalienable rights of the Lebanese to ultimate sovereignty." The French Prime Minister Clemenceau wrote to the Maronite Patriarch confirming France's approval. On 1 September 1920, the independent 'State of Greater Lebanon' was declared by the French and under their mandate. This was ratified by the League of Nations in 1922 and the present boundaries of Lebanon were defined in its Constitution in 1926.

Because of religious sensitivity, the last census taken in Lebanon was in 1932. At this time, Christians constituted 59% of the population including emigrants abroad and 50% of the population excluding emigrants. Maronites made up almost two thirds of the Christian population. In the overall number of citizens of just over one million in Lebanon and abroad, Maronites were the largest religious group at 34%. Thereafter the other main confessional groups were: Sunni 19%; Shiite 16%; Greek Orthodox 13%; Greek Catholic 7%; Druze 6%; and Armenians 3% (all numbers from the census have been rounded off).

Citizens abroad constituted close to one quarter of the total cen-

467

sus population with Christians at 85%. Of those abroad, Maronites made up 50% of the emigrants.[657] The total percentages for all Christians resident in Lebanon in 1932 comprised the following: Maronites 57.3%; Greek Orthodox 19.5%; Greek Catholic 11.8%; Armenian Orthodox 6.6%; Protestant 1.73%; Armenian Catholic 1.5%; Syriac Catholic 0.7%; Syriac Orthodox 0.68%; Chaldean Catholic 0.14%; and Chaldean Orthodox 0.05%. Jews constituted 0.5% of the total resident population of Lebanon at this time.[658]

Lebanon obtained independence in 1943. A National Pact of the same year required Parliamentary representation to be: a president who was a Maronite Christian, prime minister as Sunni Muslim, speaker as Shiite Muslim, and Deputy Speaker and Deputy Prime Minister as 'Greek' (Antiochian) Orthodox. British and allied troops occupied Lebanon until the end of World War II in 1945. The last French troops withdrew in 1946. This saw another wave of Maronite emigration from Lebanon to the West. The last mass emigration of Maronites from Lebanon was during the Lebanese Civil War between 1975-1990.

### 13.1.1  Arab League and President of Lebanon

The League of Arab States, more commonly known as the Arab League, was formed in Cairo on 22 March 1945 with six members: Egypt, Iraq, Transjordan (renamed Jordan in 1949), Lebanon, Saudi Arabia, and Syria. In the same year, Yemen joined as a member. Currently, the League has twenty-two members. As well as countries from the Middle East and North Africa, the African countries of Sudan, Somalia, Mauritania, Comoros, and Djibouti are member states of the Arab League of Nations. The League has become a modern political and regional identity embodying those persons living in its member countries whose national language is Arabic. Although Christians in Lebanon are now estimated to be less than 50% of the population, the

---

[657] Rania Maktabi, "The Lebanese Census of 1932 Revisited. Who are the Lebanese?," *British Journal of Middle Eastern Studies* 26 (2), (1999): pp, 219-241.

[658] Ibid.

legacy of the Lebanese 1932 census lives on. It is for that reason we see the President of Lebanon remaining a Christian and a Maronite Catholic. He is also the only Christian head of state in the Middle East with a seat on the Arab League of Nations.

## 13.2 Maronites in The Middle East: History and Today

### 13.2.1 Lebanon

Lebanon is full of hundreds if not thousands of Maronite churches, monasteries, convents, hermitages, villages, towns, traditional city suburbs, and shrines. It has also a sizable Maronite population the exact quantity of which is unknown but present estimates are about a quarter of the Lebanese population. Estimates are that the Lebanese population today would be approximately 5.5 million, with a further 2 million Syrian refugees and 0.5 million Palestinian refugees. It is estimated that Christians account for about 40% of the current population with about 55% Muslim and the balance mainly Druze.

### 13.2.2 Syria

After the death of the hermit Maroun (d. 410-423) in the region of Cyrrhus in northern Syria, Theodoret informs us "a bitter war" broke out over his body and it was finally laid to rest in a "great shrine" at a nearby village "that was well populated." Beit Maroun monastery in the region of Apamaea was built under the instructions of the Byzantine Emperor Marcian in 452. It became the leading monastery of the Chalcedonian party (Catholic adherents to the Council of Chalcedonian 451) in a network of monasteries in the region of northern Syria. Over the next two centuries, this leadership expanded to the western regions of Syria, Phoenicia, Phoenicia, Lebanon, and northern Palestine. It was the members of that party who became known as Maronites, the first documentary evidence referring to them by that name dates to the sixth century.

There is evidence of a Maronite community in the region of Aleppo in the ninth century and in another region north of Aleppo in the middle of the twelfth century. Al-Masudi, the Muslim Arab historian, refers to Maronites in the Orontes valley in the tenth century.[659] The Maronite communities in Syria remain until this day with their fate unknown since the commencement of the Syrian War in 2011. As of 2011, twenty-four Maronite parishes exist in Syria. Little of the history of these Syrian parishes is known in the broader Maronite community. After the Arab Muslim conquests of the seventh century there appears to be no available information on the Maronite Church in Syria, at least in English. Further studies are warranted.

### 13.2.3 Cyprus

As part of the patriarchate of Antioch, it is possible Maronites began migrating to Cyprus during the Arab Muslim conquests of the seventh century. However, no documentary evidence can be found to support this proposition. There is evidence of a Maronite monastery in Cyprus in the ninth century that was still functioning in the first half of the twelfth century. Documentary records dating from 1121, 1141, and 1154 are the basis for these findings. They provide evidence of a Maronite monastery by the name of St John of Kouzbande that was already established on the island.[660] Dib also informs us that the first documentary reference to Maronite groups in Cyprus were from the ninth century.[661]

After the Crusaders lost Jerusalem in 1244, King Louis IX of France launched the Seventh Crusade to Egypt. On his way, he landed in Cyprus and was welcomed by thousands of Maronites, five thousand of who accompanied him to Egypt.[662] Guy de Lusignan, who was King of Jerusalem from 1186 for a short period, until it fell to Saladin in 1188, acquired the island of Cyprus in 1192 from the Order of the Knights Templars. The French found refuge there after the fall of the Crusades and many Maronites and Christians from the Syrian orient followed.

A further Maronite migration to Cyprus occurred at the end of the

---

[659] Dib, *History of the Maronite Church*, p. 53.
[660] Ibid., pp. 52-53.
[661] Ibid., pp. 72-73.
[662] Harb, *The Maronites: History and Constants*, p. 86.

thirteenth century with the defeat of the Crusaders in Tripoli and the Holy Land.[663] A great number of Maronites came to Cyprus after the Crusades. According to Stephen of Lusignan around 1192 they were the largest community after the Greeks and had a bishop and counted up to seventy-two villages.[664] According to Patriarch Doueihi, the Maronite patriarch would consecrate the bishop of Cyprus, send him the holy chrism and send a legate every ten years to receive the tithes.[665] A Maronite population of 80,000 in Cyprus in the year 1340 has been cited in documents.[666] The French Fra Gryphon in 1469 wrote "(we know that) in the territories of France, Rhodes, and Cyprus ... the Maronites, from ancient times, frequent the churches of the Franks and celebrate on their altars with the same articles."[667]

In 1570-1571 the Ottomans took over the island of Cyprus, which was at that time under the rule of the Venetians. Maronites were killed and survivors either fled to Lebanon, followed the Venetians to Malta, or stayed in Cyprus under the command of the Sultan's governor and neighbouring Greeks. By 1580, their populations were reduced to less than two thousand, and little more than a century later, less than two hundred. There was another mass migration of Maronites to Cyprus during the period of the Lebanese civil War between 1975-1990. Most have now returned to Lebanon. Today there are ten Maronite parishes in Cyprus including in all its main cities. The Maronites hold a permanent seat in the House of Representatives of the Parliament of Cyprus.

### 13.2.4  Israel, Palestine, and the Holy Land

The so-called Omar Decree of 638 refers to the Maronites in the Holy Land in that year.[668] This has been discussed in more detail in previ-

---

[663] Dib, *History of the Maronite Church*, pp. 65, 77.
[664] Ibid., p. 77.
[665] Ibid., p. 79.
[666] Harb, *The Maronites: History and Constants*, p. 92.
[667] Dib, *History of the Maronite Church*, p. 79.
[668] Louis Wehbe, "The Maronites of the Holy Land: A Historical Overview," *The Journal of Maronite Studies* 5 (2), (2001), available at: www.maronite-institute.org/MARI/JMS/january01/docs/MaronitesEnglish.doc.

ous chapters as well as Maronite colonies present in the Holy Land, in the north, at the arrival of the Crusaders. What is more certain and documented is that many Maronite colonies were either expanded or founded in the Holy Land following the Crusades.

Commenting on Latin Syria after the arrival of the Crusades, Seward mentions some fascinating cultural insights into the population at the time:

> The Crusaders stormed Jerusalem in July 1099.
>
> Those who stayed in Palestine were mainly French, and the state they created reflected the feudalism of their own land. It came to include four great baronies: the principality of Galilee, the county of Jaffa and Ascalon, the lordship of Kerak and Montréal, and the lordship of Sidon, together with twelve smaller fiefs. There were also three lesser states: the principality of Antioch and the counties of Tripoli and Edessa ...
>
> There was a chronic shortage of manpower, while the desert frontier was far from impenetrable, holding water and fodder. The 'Franks' placed their trust in sea power and fortresses. Genoese, Pisan and Venetian fleets soon controlled the sea ... their owners often settling in the coastal towns.
>
> There was a large native Christian population, Maronite, Melkite, Syrian, and Armenian. In about the year 1120, Fulcher de Chartres wrote of how "Some of us have married Syrians, Armenians or even baptised Saracens ..." and how his people were no longer Frenchman, but Palestinians who were accepted by the natives as fellow countrymen. Morfia, the Queen of Baldwin II himself, was the daughter of an Armenian prince. Many officials and merchants were Christianised Arabs, while great barons employed Moslem secretaries. But if European visitors talked of poulains, Syrian born Franks, it is too much to say that a new Franco Syrian race had been born. The local Christian churches were treated with contemptuous tolerance, patriarchs of the Latin rite being installed at Jerusalem and Antioch. French was the

language of administration, and the ruling classes remained French. This was Europe's first colony.

Nevertheless, to the Franks Jerusalem was home. The king dressed in a golden burnous and keffiyah, and gave audiences sitting, cross-legged, on a carpet. Nobles wore turbans and shoes with upturned points, and the silk, damasks, muslin, and cotton that was so different from the wool and furs of France. In the towns they lived in villas with courtyards, fountains and mosaic floors, reclining on divans, listening to Arab lutes and watching dancing girls. They ate sugar, rice, lemons, and melons, washed with soap in tubs or sunken baths, while their women used cosmetics and glass mirrors unknown in Europe. Merchants, grown accustomed to bazaars, veiled their wives, and professional wailers were seen at Christian funerals. Coins bore Arabic inscriptions.[669]

From a Maronite perspective the author Wehbe provides us with much insight into the Maronite history of the Holy Land since the Crusades:

When King Godefrey had sent the news of Jerusalem's fall, Maronites representing Patriarch Joseph el-Gergessi joined the king's ambassadors (Arce 1973: 261).

Thousands of Maronites joined the Order of the Knights of Saint John in Jerusalem, Acre, and Cyprus. In the hierarchy that the Frankish authorities established in the Holy Land, 'Maronites came immediately after the Franks and before the Jacobites, Armenians, Greeks, Nestorians and Abyssinians. Moreover, they were admitted into the Frankish middle class and shared the civil and juridical privileges offered to the Latin middle class' (Ristelhueber 1925: 58).

In 1179, after the end of the schism caused by the double papal election of Alexander III and Victor IV, the Latin Patriarch of Antioch, Amaury of Limoges, received the obedience of the Oriental Franks toward Alexander. The Maronites of Jerusalem took the same oath of allegiance ...

[669] Seward, *The Monks of War*, pp. 9-12.

> In 1310, when the Knights of Saint John conquered Rhodes, an armed force of Maronites accompanied them from Jerusalem …
>
> Towards 1320, Armenian historian Aitoun noted that, in Jerusalem, Maronites formed one of the most important Christian colonies.[670]

Maronite relations with the Franciscans in the Holy Land were intimate. Ludolf De Sudheim, a pilgrim from 1336 until 1341, notes having assisted in many consecrations of Maronite bishops performed by Latin archbishops. Maronites celebrated in the churches of the Franks, on their altars, and with their vestments.

It is likely the Maronites possessed a place in the Church of the Holy Sepulchre (built over the location where Christ is thought to have been buried). In his book on his voyage to the Holy Land in 1621, Deshaye, ambassador of Louis XIII, "counts the Maronite Nation among the communities that had oratories in the Saint sepulchre." In the same century, Patriarch Doueihi celebrated two ordinations in the Grotto of the Cross.

It seems many Maronites in the Holy Land may have become Latin Catholics from the time of the Crusades. In the seventeenth century the Franciscans prohibited the Maronites from practising their own ecclesiastical customs (for example, the use of incense and abstaining from eating meat on Wednesdays) and arranged an order from the Cadi of Jerusalem authorising Christians of any rite to change their profession to the Latin Catholic rite, promising lucrative employment in return. Doueihi, recognising that the number of Maronites were diminishing in the Holy Land because of conversions to the Latin rite, entered into an agreement that the Maronites were entitled to practise their own rites in freedom. He also arranged for the construction of a Church in Nazareth.

The Maronites could also be found in Jaffa (now Tel Aviv) in 1099, accompanying the arrival of the Crusaders from Lebanon. From

---

[670] Wehbe, "The Maronites of the Holy Land."

around 1559, they came in organized numbers during the late eighteenth century from Lebanese towns such as Bkassine, Sidon, Jbail, and Bekfaya. However, Latin priests met their religious needs until 1855 when two monks from the Lebanese Maronite Order arrived and founded a monastery and church in the old town of Jaffa near the harbour. The Order built fifty apartments in the city in 1982 for families. In 1982, the Lebanese Maronite Order also bought property in Bethlehem, one hundred and seventy metres from the Church of the Nativity. They transformed it into a pilgrim's inn, sewing room, and chapel.

In Nazareth, the Maronites seem to have come and gone since the Arab Muslim conquests of the seventh century. The earliest documentary evidence points to their presence during the Crusades. There is evidence they were required to evacuate the town at the end of the thirteenth century when it became exclusively inhabited by Muslims. Documents confirm they returned to the town in the seventeenth century with other Christian denominations when it was under the Lebanese government of Fakhr-al-Din I Ma'an. Haifa, towards northern Israel, has the largest Maronite parish in the Holy Land. The city has remarkable similarities in geography and mountain range to the Lebanese coastal city of Jounieh, a traditional Maronite region.

Prior to 1996, the Maronites of the Holy Land were under the diocese of the Maronite Archbishop of Tyre. Because of the closing of the Israel-Lebanon border in 1967, following the Arab Israeli six-day war, visits by the Archbishop of Tyre to the Holy Land became infrequent. Since 1996, a new episcopate was established for Haifa and the Holy Land. Wehbe reports this has brought much energy to the Maronite Church in the Holy Land with the parish of Haifa as its most active. The ancient Phoenician port city of Akko, known as Ptolemaïs in the third century BC and later known as the Crusader stronghold of Acre, is also in northern Israel. This is one of the closest coastal Israeli cities to Galilee. The Knights of St John were stationed there in an imposing fortress like monastery. The Maronites were in Akko prior to the arrival of the Crusades, as documented by William of Tyre.[671]

---

[671] See Chapter 11 of this book. Wehbe overlooks this historical representation when

475

The Maronite village of Kfar Bar'am (or Birim or Ber'em) is situated three kilometers from the inland Israeli-Lebanese border. It had 1,050 inhabitants according to the census in November 1948. Two weeks later the Israeli army entered the village and ordered the population to leave, promising to let them in again within two weeks when their military exercises were over. They were unable to return. In 1953, the village was dynamited and destroyed. The refugees scattered to the nearby towns of Jish, Haifa, and Akko.[672] The same fate struck the Maronite village of Mansoura in northern Israel, whose descendants are currently scattered in Fassouta, Eilaboun, and other villages and practise the Melkite rite.[673]

The Maronite Sisters of Saint Theresa of the Christ Child (Sainte Thérèse de l'Enfant Jésus), established in the Holy Land in 1981 including at Jerusalem and in particular the parish of Jish where many refugees are living. Today, fourteen Maronite parishes exist in Israel and Palestinian Territories.

### 13.2.5 Egypt

Egypt currently has four Maronite parishes. According to the *L'Osservatore Romano*, the newspaper of the Holy See, there are around 20,000 faithful in Egypt today, and the Maronites have a considerable history in this region:

> The documented presence of Maronites in Egypt dates back to 1639. In the 18th century the Holy See appointed two Maronite priests to serve as advisers to the Franciscans who came from the custody of the Holy Land to evangelize Egypt because 'no one knows the land and mentality of the Copts like the Maronites.[674]

---

he states in his article that the Maronites came from Lebanon and settled in this city towards the end of the seventeenth century. Patriarch Michael Fadel from 1741 until 1753 was a former Maronite serving priest in the city.

[672] Wehbe, "The Maronites of the Holy Land."

[673] Ibid.

[674] *L'Osservatore Romano*, Weekly Edition in English, 1 March 2000, pp. 6-7, available at: http://www.ewtn.com/ library/CHISTORY/EGPTCATH.HTM.

## 13.2.6 Jordan

In Jordan there is one parish Church, St Charbel, built recently in the capital Amman.

## 13.2.7 Kuwait

Religious freedom is enshrined in the constitution of Kuwait. However, it is an offence to proselytize to Muslims. There are reportedly 140,000 Catholics in Kuwait, nearly 70,000 Orthodox, and 50,000 Protestants. Maronites, who are mainly from Lebanon, attend the Catholic Cathedral in Kuwait City. There is a Maronite Order or Congregation of nuns serving the community.

## 13.2.8 Dubai

In Dubai there is one Maronite parish Church of St Mary, built recently, apparently with the generous financial assistance of the (Muslim) Emir of Dubai.

## 13.2.9 The Khazens and Feudal Lords

Numerous books have been written about the Maronite feudal lords from the Keserwan district of Lebanon, the el Khazen or the Khazen family. Around 1590, the Druze Prince Fakhr-al-Din al-Ma'ani II, succeeded his father Korkomaz to the Chouf Emirate. This Prince spent most of his youth among the Maronite Khazen family of Keserwan.[675]

In 1858, a Firman or royal decree was issued announcing equality among all citizens and annulling the privileges of the feudal lords. As a result of this Firman, Maronites in Kesrouan revolted against their Khazen lords and demanded social equality. Then leader Tanios Chahine was the first to issue proclamations on behalf of the 'Lebanese Republic'. The Maronite clergy, themselves poor, enlightened the peasants and crystallised their popular movement. The patriarch and the European Consuls intervened to restore order and to return the Lords to their homes after having lost their feudal privileges. The Turks and foreign powers conspired to rekindle the strife.

[675] Harb, *The Maronites: History and Constants*, p. 98.

## 13.3 The Communion Of Churches: Maronites Leading From The East

Since the Council of Florence in 1444, which saw much dialogue and decrees between Rome and the non-Catholic Eastern churches, the Vatican has mostly been active in devoting resources to the communion of churches. Maronites, as the only Eastern Catholics who have had perpetual communion with Rome since the period of the great schism in the eleventh century, played an important part in seeking communion of other Eastern churches with Rome. Throughout history, the Maronites have especially opened their arms to the Syriac Antiochian churches that share a common liturgy. In particular, even though there have been many struggles with the Syriac Orthodox Church (Jacobites) since the fifth century, Maronite churches and villages have been shared with them.

At the initiation of the Maronites, the Vatican sponsored the establishment of the Maronite College of Rome in 1584. Shortly after, Rome (with the Maronites playing an integral role) began plans to formalise the establishment of a missionary movement in the East for churches to return to Catholicism. Following his voyage to Lebanon in 1596, Jesuit Father Dandini reported to Pope Clement VIII that the Maronite people were the vanguard of the Catholic missions in the East.[676] The Pope wrote to the Maronite Patriarch and to the Archbishop of Ehden thanking them for the services of two Maronite students from the Maronite College in Rome for assisting the Chaldean Patriarch in sending a legate to the Pope.[677]

In 1622 the 'Congregation de Propaganda Fide' was formed to coordinate Rome's missionary activity with the churches of the Middle East. The promotion of Catholicism in the Ottoman Empire became a foreign policy priority of the French and the Vatican. Aleppo and the Lebanese port cities of Tyre and Sidon became the chief centres of Roman Catholic activity in the Levant. In the seventeenth century, the Maronites welcomed the Jacobite Andre Akidjan as a priest, sent him

---

[676] Dib, *History of the Maronite Church*, p. 190.
[677] Ibid., p. 187.

to the Maronite College of Rome, appointed him Bishop of Aleppo and eventually he became the first Patriarch of the Syriac Catholic Church in 1662.[678] However, because of the Ottoman support for the Syriac Orthodox, the Syriac Catholics were forced underground and the communion with Rome was broken until 1782.

In 1724, there was a dispute amongst the Antiochian Orthodox (Melkites) over the entitlement of their seat to the patriarchate of Antioch. The Melkites who became in communion with Rome suffered persecution especially in Aleppo. Many of them took refuge in Lebanon and were assisted by the Maronite Patriarch. They were welcomed at the Maronite monastery of St Anthony Qazsaya in the Qadisha valley. Maronite Patriarch James Aouad at the time had to take refuge at St Anthony as the Antiochian Orthodox of Koura in North Lebanon and their Patriarch denounced the Maronite Patriarch for his support of the Melkite Catholics informing the Pasha of Tripoli that Aouad and these Catholics were traitors to the Ottoman Empire and should be tried for treason. The Pasha's troops pillaged the monastery of Qannoubin and imprisoned its monks and the Patriarch's brother.[679] Rome recognized the election of the Melkite Greek Catholic Patriarch of Antioch in 1729.[680]

Shortly after this assistance, the Melkites began to challenge the Maronites over the next hundred years for honouring both St Maroun (d. 410-423) and John Maroun (d. 707) as saints, and took their complaints to Rome. This resulted in disagreements between the Maronites and Melkites. The Melkite complaints led to investigations by Rome, which confirmed Maroun's sainthood and gave indulgences for the sainthood of John Maroun (the Melkites had accused him of being Monothelite).[681] The events provide testament to the ongoing challenges the Maronites faced, even from their new fellow Easten Catho-

---

[678] Ibid., p. 188.
[679] Ibid., pp. 188-189.
[680] CNEWA, *The Melkite Catholic Church*, www.cnewa.org.
[681] Moosa, *The Maronites in History*, pp. 167-169. Given the modern view that Monothelitism could not be a heresy, even if John Maroun was a Monothelite, he should be accorded full status as a saint.

479

lics. These difficulties appeared from as early as the fifth and sixth centuries, likely due to the Maronite prominence through the ages as a sizeable and influential Christian denomination in the region from northern Palestine through Lebanon to northern Syria. Notwithstanding, since the eighteenth century there has been a close relationship between the Maronites and Melkites, even more so today.

Later in the early eighteenth century the Maronite Patriarch was again involved in assisting the Patriarch of the Nestorians to profess the teaching of the Catholic Church in 1735. There was an intermittent period of Chaldean communion with Rome from 1551 to 1830 for Nestorians who became Catholic. However the union has remained unbroken from 1830. The same dedication of Maronites to communion of churches was equally applied to the Armenians when 'the Maronites opened their arms'. The Armenians' communion with Rome has remained unbroken since 1749. The famous Maronite from the College of Rome, Joseph Simon Assemani, and his nephew Stephen Awad worked for the communion of the churches in Egypt and elsewhere in the early 1770s as recounted by Assemani himself.[682]

Dib's conclusion for this period is fitting:

> These indications suffice to show the activity of the Maronites in promoting communion. An assembly held at Aleppo in the eighteenth century which brought together the heads of different Christian confessions of this city: Maronites, Melkites, Syrians, Armenians and the superiors of the Latin religious communities, declared that the Maronite church was the refuge of all the Oriental peoples. One should add: and the worker for reproachment with the non-Catholics.[683]

The Maronites, who have traditionally been dominant in terms of the numbers of Christian religious population in Lebanon, have continued to promote the communion of the churches. Lebanon is seen as an inspiration of hope for Christians in the Middle East and for co-existence with all faiths. Through Maronite encouragement, Lebanon

---

[682] Dib, *History of the Maronite Church*, p. 189.
[683] Dib, pp. 189-190.

has hosted, welcomed, embraced, and nurtured with open arms the richness of the Oriental church and their congregations. It is Maronite influence that has helped in so many instances bring communion. Opus Libani, established by Pope John Paul as a synod of Catholic churches in the Middle East gives testament to the communion as does the number of Eastern Catholic Patriarchs residing in Lebanon.

The various members of Opus Libani are:

- The Maronite Church under the Patriarch of Antioch and all of the East. The Patriarch's residence is in Bkerke, Lebanon.

- The Melkite Greek Catholic Church under the Patriarch of Antioch and all the East, of Alexandria and of Jerusalem. The Patriarch's residence is in Raboueh, Lebanon.

- The Armenian Catholic Church under Patriarch of the Catholic Armenians. The Patriarch's residence is in Bzoummar, Lebanon.

- The Coptic Catholic Church under the Catholic Coptic Patriarch of Alexandria. The Patriarch's residence is in Egypt.

- The Catholic Chaldean Church under the Patriarch of Babylon for the Catholic Chaldean. The main seat of the Patriarchate is in Baghdad (Iraq) but the Patriarch has a residence in Beit – Mery, Lebanon.

- The Latin Catholic Church under the Latin Patriarch of Jerusalem. The Patriarch resides in Jerusalem.

- The Syriac Catholic Church under the Patriarch of Antioch and all the East of the Syrians. The Patriarch's residence is in Beirut, Lebanon.

The current Maronite Patriarch Rai, and as Cardinal of Rome, has headed the Vatican's ecumenical movement and rapprochement with Eastern Churches as a member of the Pontifical Congregation for Eastern Churches. As of February 2013, in a very short space of time since installation as Patriarch, he had conducted pastoral visits to Cyprus, Antioch (Turkey), Iraq, Egypt, Jordan, Romania, India, Damascus in Syria and Russia. There is a strong and close working ecumenical movement today between all Christian churches from the Middle East – Catholic, Orthodox, and Oriental Orthodox.

### 13.3.1 Maronite Religious Institutes

Before 1695 all Maronite monasteries and convents were autonomous. Many were also double monasteries housing monks and nuns. A list of the modern Maronite orders and congregations are:

- The Lebanese Maronite Order (LMO) or Baladites. Founded in 1695. St Charbel and St Nimtallah El Hardini belonged to the order.
- Lebanese Maronite Nuns. Affiliated with the Lebanese Maronite order. St Rafka belonged to the order.
- Order of Antonines. Also known as the Order of St Isaiah. Founded 1700.
- Order of Aleppine. Originally part of the Lebanese Maronite Order. Formally approved 1770.
- The Congregation of Lebanese Missionary Fathers or the Lebanese Missionaries (Kreimists) founded 1865
- Antonine Maronite Sisters.
- The Congregation of the Maronite Sisters of the Holy Family. Founded 1895.
- Congregation of the Maronite Sisters of St Therese of the Child Jesus (St Therese de Lisieux).
- Religious Missionaries of the Blessed Sacraments.
- Various Maronite congregations of Latin rites and orders including the Capuchins, and Jesuits. Also the Maronite Poor Clares of Yarze following St Francis and St Clare of Assisi.
- Four convents *sui juris* (independent with full legal rights) –
  - Our Lady of Hakle founded in 1572,
  - St John the Baptist Hrash founded 1716.
  - The Maronites of the Visitation following the rules of St Francis de Sales. They have two convents, one in

Aintura (established 1747) and one in Zouk Mikayel known as 'The Annunciation' (established 1836). Both convents were founded by the el Khazen family and are two of the three remaining Maronite enclosed cloistered convents in Lebanon. The other cloistered convent is our Lady of the Fields at Dlpeta. They are under the Patriarch's authority. They are strictly enclosed and each convent is autonomous.

### 13.3.2 Aramaic-Syriac Churches and Other Churches of the East

Today, there are five Churches in the Middle East representing the Syriac language and liturgy: the Maronite Church; the two Syriac branches of Syriac Orthodox Church and Syriac Catholic Church; the two branches of the Church of the East, the Chaldaean Catholic Church and the Assyrian Church. The last two have their roots from Christians of Mesopotamia who were within the territory of the Persian Empire rather than the Roman Byzantine Empire.

Although the Maronite and Syriac liturgies have certain distinct traits, Chahwan informs us:

As far as concerns the anaphoras in particular, the Maronite Church and the Syrian Church (in both of its branches) have always used the same anaphoras, having in common the same Syro-Occidental tradition. This tradition had already been formed in essence before the schism between the Christians of the Patriarchate of Antioch following the Council of Chalcedon (451). After this, there co-existed, within the one Patriarchate, a Chalcedonian community, from which the Maronites come, and a non-Chalcedonian community which is the origin of the Syrian Church.

Even after the schism, the two communities continued to share the same language and culture, and were thus able to exchange liturgical manuscripts which could be utilised by one another, and so continued to reciprocally influence one another.[684]

---

[684] Fr. Najem Chahwan in his article *The Mass in the East and the Theology of the Anaphoras*, Kaslik, Lebanon, 2010-11.

In 1990, the Catholic Church promulgated the Code of Canon Law of the Oriental Churches for the twenty-one Catholic Oriental Churches. This new code of 1,546 Canons (rules or ecclesiastical laws) is the first for all of the Oriental Churches. Despite their different rites, it is common to all of them. The Catholic Churches with oriental rites are the following:

- Alexandria
  - Coptic (from 1741).
  - Ethiopian (from 1930).
- Antiochian
  - Malankarese (1930).
  - Maronite (the only Eastern Church that can claim unbroken union).
  - Syriac (from 1782, intermittent communion from 1662).
- Byzantine
  - Albanian
  - Bulgarian
  - Georgian
  - Greek
  - Hungarian
  - Italian-Albanian
  - Melkite (1724) (Orthodox branch is known as the Antiochian Orthodox under the Orthodox Patriarchate of Antioch and All the East).
  - Romanian
  - Russian
  - Ruthenian
  - Slovakian
  - Ukrainian
  - White Russian
  - Yugoslavian

- Chaldaean
    - Chaldaean (from 1830, intermittent union from 1551).
    - Malabarese
- Armenian (from 1749, intermittent union from 1444).

From the great schism of the eleventh century and certainly from 1182 to 1724, the Maronite Patriarch was the only perpetual Eastern Catholic Church patriarch. The office of the Latin patriarch of Antioch, established in 1098 at the arrival of the Crusades, was abolished by the Vatican in 1964. However, the office of the Latin Patriarch of Jerusalem, also established after the arrival of the Crusades, remains.

In terms of the Syriac Antiochian Churches there are only a relatively minor number of divisions. In terms of the Eastern Churches overall the divisions are far less than the divisions of the Western Christian churches since the Protestant reformation of the early sixteenth century. In comparison, Protestantism has hundreds of individualistic churches around the world whilst the Eastern Christians have maintained their traditional and broader communal and hierarchical approach. The Maronites have no Orthodox counterpart. Despite the more recent communions with Rome, the Eastern Catholic churches are generally less in number than the orthodox branch from which they were established. In the context of Christians living in countries that are part of the Arab League, the Coptic Orthodox of Egypt would be the largest Church.

## 13.4  Maronite History in Italy

Maronite migration to Britain and Europe has been in small numbers since the mid to late 1800s and while London and Paris have the main parishes, Italy, and of course Rome, has long been important to the Maronites. There are multiple links the Maronites have to Italy, historically and today. After many centuries of separation, the Crusades opened the road to Rome for the Maronites once again.

485

In 1199, Jeremias al Amchiti was appointed Maronite Patriarch and became the first Patriarch to visit Rome in 1213 assisting at the Fourth Council of the Lateran. A painting in his honour performing a miracle was kept at St Peters in Rome, was restored in 1655, and was visited by Patriarch Douaihi when he was in Rome.[685] In a letter written by Maronite Gabriel Ibn al Qelai to the Patriarch Simon of Hadeth in 1494 he informs us: "When King Godfrey had taken Jerusalem (several centuries earlier), he sent this news to Rome. His ambassadors were joined by envoys of the Patriarch Joseph Al Gargasi, and they brought back a cross and miter."[686] He also confirms the Maronite tradition of the Patriarch requesting pontifical confirmation of his election. He indicated there were fifteen letters sent by the Holy See. Today, there are only eight or nine that remain in existence.[687]

Since the twelfth century, the towns of Sassovivo, Volperino, and Foligno in Italy have housed relics of St Maroun, and the first two towns celebrate him today in festivals. The Rabbula Gospels, which were in the possession of the Maronite patriarchs, were deposited in the Mediceo-Laurentian Library in Florence in 1747, where they remain today.[688] Rome was the site of the Maronite College that produced several key Maronite figures, patriarchs, and scholars.

Today, the Vatican houses numerous Maronite manuscripts and St Peter's Basilica has a statue of St Maroun, and Rome attracts Maronite pilgrims every year. Tour groups have converged on Rome from Maronite parishes all over the world over the last few decades for the canonisation of the Maronite saints from Lebanon, the monk Charbel, nun Rafqa, and monk Nemetallah. Catholics of the Maronite Church may be comforted to discover that Italy helps conserve their own rich Eastern past and simultaneously cements the communion between the Holy See of Peter in Rome and the See of Antioch which was also

---

[685] Dib, *History of the Maronite Church*, p. 61.
[686] Ibid., p. 59. Ibn al Qelai states his sources as the archives of the Maronite Patriarchate and those of St Peter in Rome.
[687] Ibid., p. 62.
[688] See 10.2.1 for a discussion of the Rabbula Gospels.

founded by St Peter before he went to Rome and for which the Maronite patriarch claims succession.

## 13.4.1 Relics of St Maroun

St Maroun, the patron saint for the Maronites, died around 410-423 AD and his relics, especially the skull, were carried by his followers to the Beit Maroun monastery, built in 452 AD in northern Syria. Tradition has it that the first Maronite patriarch of Antioch, Patriarch John Maroun, settled in Kfarhay in the Batroun region of Lebanon at the beginning of the eighth century and placed St Maroun's skull inside the altar of the monastery there to heal the faithful.

According to Ludovico Jacobilli, in 1130 an Italian abbot, on a pilgrimage to the Holy Land, brought back to Italy the holy skull of St Maroun.[689] The abbot, Michel Degli Atti, a noble and then Count of Opello, gifted the relic to the abbot (or rector) of the Holy Cross Monastery of Sassovivo in Umbria. Abbot Michel promoted reverence for St Maroun – St Mauro in Italian – and the relic to such an extent that a great devotion to the saint sprang up throughout all of Italy and spread to Eastern Europe. Since this time the holy skull has remained in the region of Foligno (in Italy) near the famous town of Assisi. A crypt at Sassovivo is still dedicated to St Maroun and also in the town of Volperino in Umbria, both celebrating his yearly feast day.[690]

A church was built on land that the monastery owned at Volperino, east of Sassovivo, around 1135 and became the centre of religious devotion to St Maroun. It was dedicated to St Maroun and adorned with several frescoes depicting him. It probably housed the relic from 1138, the same year the first reference to St Mauro (Maroun) Church in Italy was made in the Bull of Pope Innocent II.[691] The relic was transferred to the Duomo (Cathedral) of Foligno in 1490. It was subsequently

---

[689] Hourani, "Saint Maron's Relic," translates *Bibliotheca Sanctorum, Instituto Giovanni XXXIII Della Pontificia Universita Lateranense*, 1967, columns 1195 and 1196.

[690] "St Maron," *Key to Umbria: Foligno*, http://www.keytoumbria.com/Foligno/St_Maron.html.

[691] Marzetti, "Volperino, Italy, Celebrates Saint Maron's Feast."

encased in a silver reliquary (in 1499) that represents the tonsured and wounded head of a young deacon. This reliquary was transferred back to Sassovivo in 2000, when the crypt at St Maroun's was re-opened after the damage from the earthquake of 1997. It was stolen in 2005 but recovered and brought back to the Cathedral of Foligno where it remains in the crypt and can be viewed by request.[692] On August 17 and 18 of every year for the feast of St Maroun the reliquary is transported from the Cathedral of Foligno to the village of Volperino, during which a large crowd follows the relic in a procession through the town.

In 1887, Bishop Youssef El-Debs reports in his book that during his stay in Italy the Bishop of Foligno gave him some relics of St Maroun's skull. A small relic was also gifted again in 2000 when Maronite Patriarch Sfeir was in Italy. The relic was placed in a replica statue (to that in Foligno) at St Maroun's monastery at Kfarhay in 2000. This is the monastery tradition holds was established by St John Maroun in the late seventh or early eighth century and where he originally placed the skull of St Maroun. A new marble statue is being prepared for housing St Maroun's relic at Kfarhay in a miniature of the St Maroun statue in front of St Peter's Basilica. Temporarily, the relic has been placed in a carved wood image of the head of Jesus Christ at the front of the monastery Church at Kfarhay.

### 13.4.2 Maronite College of Rome

In 1584, a significant event in Maronite relations with Rome occurred when Pope Gregory XIII founded the Maronite Seminary of Rome. At the inauguration Pope Gregory XIII said: "We open this college-seminary for the Maronites of Mount Lebanon, who are holding fast to the Catholic faith and to unity with the Roman Church, unlike the other Orientals, who are not united with her." Maronite clergy attended various universities in Rome to further their ecclesiastical education and the College was used as a community residence. This opened a new era of cultural, scientific, and religious co-operation and under-

---

[692] "St Maron," *Key to Umbria: Foligno.*

standing between East and West. Several graduates from the seminary went on to hold important posts throughout Europe including teaching posts in Eastern languages in universities, translators, and custodians of libraries. Moreover some forty bishops were among the graduates, twelve of whom became patriachs. Patriarch Douehi (1630-1704), a graduate from the school, is the first Maronite historian to whom full records are in existence, and whose works have been discussed throughout this book.

In 1610, a graduate of the college introduced the Syriac typeset to the Kozhaya Monastery in the Qadisha Valley of Lebanon. In 1624, Patriarch Youhanna Makhlouf, another graduate, founded the first two schools of higher education in Lebanon in Haouqa and Bkarkasha. The establishment of the seminary and natural flow-on of regular direct contact in Rome between Maronite eastern Catholic and western Roman Catholic clergy may well have led Western missionaries to Lebanon such as the Capuchins in 1626, the Carmelites in 1635, and Jesuits in 1656.

In 1635, George Amira was elected Maronite Patriarch. He was the first patriarch who was a former student of the Maronite College of Rome. He had been a schoolmate at Rome of the later elected Pope Urban VIII. Under his reign a Maronite College was also founded at Ravenna in Italy under the name of St Ephraim.[693]

Pope Clement XI founded in Rome in 1707 the monastery of St Peter and Marcellus, which served as a College for the Maronite monks from the monastery of St Anthony (of Qazahya) in the Qadisha Valley of Mount Lebanon. It was also to serve as a hospice for Maronite pilgrims. In 1753, the house was transferred to near St Peter in Chains and was named after St Anthony the Great. Dib records it as still in existence in 1962.

The Maronite clergy graduating from the Maronite College of Rome paved the way for an intellectual renaissance in the Near East and by the nineteenth century Lebanon was reportedly the most advanced region in the whole Ottoman Empire in the field of learning.

---

[693] Dib, *History of the Maronite Church*, p. 110.

It is not clear why the college closed in 1799. Dau submits that Napoleon destroyed the college but this has been dismissed as an unreliable version. It appears the college in that location came into the hands of the Italian government and was then privately owned. The college from 1584-1799 was located between Vicola dei Maroniti and Via dei Maroniti, or the Street of Maronites. It is an honour for all Maronites that Rome has named two streets after them. The church of the old college is now a restaurant on this street.

Approximately a hundred years later the closure of the college, Archbishop Elias Hoyek (later Patriach 1899-1931) relentlessly worked for three years travelling to Rome, France, and other countries to lobby and raise funds to re-establish a new Maronite college. He succeeded on 1 January 1894 when the building at 18, Via Porta Pinciana in Rome was purchased and the first twelve students came from all over the Lebanon, Syria, and Cyprus. After another short closure, this Maronite College of Rome re-opened again in October 2001. The College is currently owned by the Maronite Church.

It is likely the College in Rome was an inspiration in the late nineteenth century for the then Bishop Hoyek to successfully lobby the French authorities for a Maronite college in France. The French government opened the Chapel of Marie De Medicis at Petit Luxembourg in Paris for the Maronites. The Patriarch named a pro curator and eight scholarships were awarded to students.

### 13.4.3 The *Bibliotheca Orientalis* at the Vatican

Youssef Assemaani was from Hasroun, North Lebanon, and is one of the most distinguished products of the Maronite College of Rome. He promoted the richness of the Oriental churches opening the eyes of the scholars of the West to the cultural and Christian wealth of the East. In 1715 Pope Clement XI sent Assemaani to the East to collect manuscripts. On his way back to Rome in 1717 a ship bearing some of the Oriental treasures was sunk in a storm and it is possible a large amount of Maronite manuscripts were lost. However he assembled in the Vatican library one of the finest and greatest Oriental collections in the world and it is still used today as a major source of information on the churches and nations of the East. The collection called the *Bibliotheca Orientalis* at the Vatican library includes manuscripts in Syriac, Arabic, Hebrew, Persian, Turkish, Greek, Coptic, and Ethiopic.

In 1736 Assemaani was appointed as Pope's Legate to the Maronite Synod in Lebanon. Assemaani became director and custodian of the Vatican library in 1737 and held that office for thirty-one years until his death at the age of eighty-one in 1768. In the same year, a fire destroyed most of his works, which he spent a lifetime writing on the manuscripts. He is responsible for numerous books, collections, catalogues, reports, and calendars, all of which are too great to list here. He was fittingly consecrated Archbishop of Tyre Lebanon two years before his death in 1766.

His nephew Joseph Simon Assemaani (d. 1768) also gathered a large amount of manuscripts for the Vatican. So too did his nephew Stephen, Archbishop of Apamaea Syria and prefect of the Vatican library (d. 1782), his nephew Joseph Aloysius, and his grand-nephew Simon. The Vatican library owes a great volume of its collection of manuscripts from the East to the Maronites because of the Assemaanis, Al- Haqiliani, Fautsas Nairon, Andrew Scandar, and Gabriel Hawa.[694]

## 13.4.4  Patriarchs and Orders in Rome

Italy has nine orders and congregations of monks, priests, and nuns who originate from Lebanon and Syria and who adhere to the Maronite liturgy. Most of these orders have missions around the world. A great many also have permanent representations in Rome, as does the Patriarch. The Patriarch's representative resides in the building of the current Maronite College. Some of the other representations are as follows:

- The Lebanese Maronite Order
- The Mariamite Order
- The Antonians
- The Lebanese Maronite Missionaries or Kreimistes

---

[694] Dib, *History of the Maronite Church*, pp. 183, 188.

### 13.4.5 Sculpture of St Maroun at St Peter's Basilica

On 24 February 2011, Pope Benedict XVI blessed a new sculpture of marble, located outside St Peter's Basilica dedicated to St Maroun. In his left hand he holds a small Maronite style church and at his feet is an inscription in Syriac of a psalm. The sculpture is over fifteen feet high and weighs 55,000 pounds. Its presence in the Vatican is highly symbolic. Cardinal Angelo Comastri said at the unveiling ceremony that it is a gesture of affection and gratitude towards the Maronite Church "that has suffered so much over the centuries." Father Abdo Badwi can be attributed to the design of the statue.[695]

## 13.5 Maronites Outside the Patriachate of Antioch and All of the East

It has been almost one thousand years since the arrival of the Crusades in the Middle East, and the establishment for the first time of the Latin Church in the jurisdiction of the East. It has also been more than 1300 years since the Aramaic speaking Catholics from the Middle East, along with the Greeks from Byzantine lands, dominated the Catholic population of Rome, its clergy, monasteries, and papacy. These Easterners substantially influenced the liturgical and religious practices of the Latin Church in the late seventh and early eighth century.

Today, we are now witnessing the establishment of the Eastern churches in the West. Although there are many jurisdictional challenges resulting from the Eastern Catholic churches sharing in the jurisdiction of the Roman Catholic churches, the new migration has brought a renewed vigour for the Catholic Church and for the diversity of Christianity in Western nations. Many of the issues for Maronites in the West similarly apply for other Eastern Catholic Churches on Western shores.

The Maronites have been an important part of this Eastern Chris-

---

[695] Dean of Sacred Art and Head of the Department of Syriac and Antiochian Sciences, Faculty of Religious and Oriental Studies, at the (Pontifical) University of the Holy Spirit, Kaslik, Lebanon.

tian migration to the West. Indeed, it comes as a great surprise as the ink was being penned to this paragraph to think those who have their ancestry from Maronites are the largest number of Eastern Catholics in the West and conversely, the Maronites are the largest number of any Eastern Catholic church living in the Middle East. They have migrated all over the Western world. The overwhelming majority of Maronite ancestry populations in the West, starting from the 1800s, are baptised Roman Catholics and not practising Maronites. Due to historical circumstances,[696] it has only been more lately the Maronite Church has been able to begin in earnest to send missionaries from the Middle East to serve the faithful in the West.

With a long history of partnership between the Middle Eastern Maronites and Rome (as well as France), the greater number of Maronite missionaries in the West today allows us to witness many first-time events for the Maronite and Roman churches on Western shores. Particularly in the English-speaking world there are official collaborations between schools, seminaries, parishes and social services. The Maronite bishops, as for other Eastern Catholic bishops, belong to the Catholic Conference of Bishops in Western countries that have substantial active Maronite populations. Both Maronite and Roman Catholic clergy co-celebrate at the altar for many cross-cultural weddings. In Sydney more recently, Maronite clergy have been engaged to serve mass in the Roman rite for a local Roman Catholic parish. With a rapid expanding population of non-Middle Eastern/non- Maronite ancestry this time exposed to the Maronite rite, the Maronite Church in the West is better placed to facilitate and serve the growing numbers.

### 13.5.1 African Maronites

There are Maronite colonies throughout Africa, the most substantial being in South Africa with a Lebanese Maronite Order mission and school.

---

[696] For example, the cessation of centuries old Islamic rule in Lebanon at the end of the WWI, thereafter WWII and the Lebanese Civil War from 1975-1990.

## 13.5.2 North and South America

Mass migration to North, South and Central America, Canada, and the Caribbean commenced after the 1860s. As at 2011, there were seventy-four Maronite parishes in the USA and Canada including thirty-two priests and religious not of Lebanese or Middle Eastern ancestry. The USA is now up to its 57th annual Maronite convention.

There are many Maronite parishes and colonies throughout Central and South America. It is often said there are more people of Lebanese (majority Maronite) descent in South and Central America than Lebanon. Some reliable estimates put the population of Lebanese ancestry in the West at more than eight million. However, with the majority of them of Maronite ancestry only approximately 15% would attend Maronite Catholic church with the remaining part of the Roman Catholic Church.

Maronites (and other Eastern Catholics such as the Melkites) fuse quickly into the Roman Catholic Churches. This is particularly so in Central and South America for several reasons including:

- Latin Catholics have traditionally constituted up to 95-100% of the population.
- Maronites have no issue attending Latin Catholic mass and canon law allows attendance at any Catholic Church.
- Maronite missions have been lacking particularly in the early days of mass migration of Maronites from the mid to late 1800s.
- A general perception from Western Catholics that Roman Catholicism is the only Catholicism.

Accordingly, most Maronite descendants living in Central and South America are Latin Catholics. Brazil, with the largest number of descendants from Maronites and Lebanese outside Lebanon (in the several million perhaps) has very few practising Maronites.

The estimates at the end of 2012 for practising Maronites (as opposed to a much large number of ancestral Maronites) were as follows.[697] The USA had two dioceses with a total of sixty parishes and

---

[697] CNEWA, *The Maronite Catholic Church*, www.cnewa.org.

ninety-nine priests serving about 75,000 Maronite faithful. Canada had fourteen parishes for about 80,000 faithful. Buenos Aires in Argentina had three Maronite dioceses with an estimated 700,000 faithful. Sao Paolo in Brazil had 468,000 members and Mexico City about 150,000 faithful. For these estimated 1,318,000 Maronites in the Americas, there were only seventeen parishes served by forty-eight priests. Colombia, Venezuela, and the Caribbean are known to have large populations of Maronite ancestry but no Maronite churches.

### 13.5.3  St Maroun in Russia

In 2013, a relic of St Maroun was gifted to Moscow's Annunciation Cathedral in the presence of Maronite Patriarch Cardinal Rai and the Orthodox Patriarch of Moscow and All the Russias Patriarch Kirill I during the fourth century saint's feast day according to the Orthodox calendar. A gift from the Holy See, the relic was given to Patriarch Rai by the Apostolic Nuncio to Moscow on his arrival in the Russian capital. The relic is a bone fragment from the skull of the saint preserved in the Foligno Duomo, Italy. For the Vatican, this ecumenism of holiness is part of the process of rapprochement with Eastern Churches of which Patriarch Rai is currently responsible as a member of the Congregation for Eastern Churches.[698]

### 13.5.4  Australian Maronites

Migration to Australia commenced in the mid 1800s after the 1860 massacre by the Druze in Lebanon. This was at a period when the modern state of Lebanon did not exist. Travel documentation confirms that most of the migrants originated from the Ottoman district of Mount Lebanon in Syria and they were called Syrians or Ottomans.

The Maronite Heritage Centre in Sydney reports:

> In 1889 the number of Maronite Catholics in Australia had reached a critical mass to justify the establishment of a Ma-

---

[698] Fady Noun, "A Relic of St Maron Given to Moscow's Annunciation Cathedral," *AsiaNews.it*, 28 February 2013, http://www.asianews.it/news-en/A-relic-of-St-Maron-given-to-Moscow's-Annunciation-Cathedral-27263.html.

ronite mission with two priests, Father (later Monsignor) Joseph Dahdah and Father Abdullah Yazbeck were sent. When they arrived Cardinal Moran attached them to the Latin rite churches of St. Vincent de Paul in Redfern and Our Lady of Mount Carmel in Waterloo from where they attended to the spiritual requirements of the Maronites. It was reported in 1897 that: A move for [sic] their own church began early in 1894 when a chapel was set up in a private house in Raglan Street Waterloo and was blessed by Bishop Higgins. Although inadequate this chapel served the community with the Latin Rite until the completion of the first Maronite Catholic Church in Elizabeth Street Redfern in January 1897.

A newspaper article appeared in Sydney reporting on the official opening of the first Maronite Catholic Church in 1897:

> In relation to Cardinal Archbishop (Moran) blessed and opened the pretty little church in Elizabeth street Redfern, which had been erected with the sanction of his Eminence to meet the spiritual wants of the Maronite residents in the city and suburbs ... everything possible had been done to give the church a picturesque appearance ... Arch of foliage and flowers ... displayed draperies with welcome greetings painted thereon ... rich carpets and rugs all the way from the Holy Land, were spread within the sanctuary enclosure.[699]

As for the Americas, a further mass wave of migration occurred to Australia post-World War I, post-World War II and then during the Lebanese Civil War 1975-1990. Currently nineteen parishes and mass centres are found in Australia. Some of the mass centres are found in Latin Catholic churches by special arrangement with the Latin Church.

For many of the early centuries after Christ, the Middle East region comprised an overwhelming majority of Christians through-

---

[699] Quoted by S. Thompson, "1880-1930 Redfern Maronite Heritage Centre Collection," *Migration Heritage Centre*, 2007. http://www.migrationheritage.nsw.gov.au/exhibition/objectsthroughtime/maronites/index.html.

out the world. Descendant from the birthplace of Christianity, most Australian Christians with ancestral links to the Middle East are either: Maronites (Catholics of the Aramaic liturgy closest to that practised by Jesus Christ); those affiliated with the Byzantine liturgy being Melkites (Catholic) and Antiochian Orthodox; and Coptic Orthodox.

The Maronites and Melkites established their missions and first churches in the inner city of Sydney between 1888 and 1897,[700] the Antiochian Orthodox between 1911-1913,[701] and the Coptic Orthodox in 1969.[702] The Maronites, Melkites and the Antiochian Orthodox have historical and liturgical links to the ancient city of Antioch (now Antakya in modern day Turkey) where Saint Peter established the first Patriarchate before establishing the office of the Roman Patriarch (the later to become the primary patriarch governing as Pope from Rome). Antioch is also the location where the disciples of Jesus Christ were first called Christians (Acts 11:23-26).

For 1954, Price estimated the religious composition of the Lebanese community in Australia to be: 88.5% Christian including 70% Catholic (Maronite and Melkite) and 18.5% Orthodox; 4% Muslim; and 3% Druze.[703] The first substantial wave of Lebanese immigrants was between the 1880s and 1930s and the second wave from the late 1940s to the early 1970s. The third substantial wave came after the start of the Lebanese civil war in 1975 and, coinciding with the official end to the White Australia policy, saw an increase in migration of Muslims from around the world including Lebanon and the Middle

---

[700] Rev. G. Abdullah, *The Maronite Church in Australia: A Study of a Local Church and its Place in the Communion of Local Churches*, Masters Thesis, Catholic Institute of Sydney, 2005; Melkite Catholic Eparchy of Australia and New Zealand, *History of the Eparchy*, 2009, http://www.melkite.org.au/history.aspx.

[701] Nicholas Shehadie, *A Life Worth Living*, Simon & Schuster, 2003; Antiochian Orthodox Archdiocese of Australia, New Zealand and the Philippines, *History of Antiochian Orthodoxy in Australasia*, 2007, http://www.antiochianarch.org.au/HistoryofAntiochianOrthodoxyinAustralasia.aspx.

[702] Matthew Attia, *Coptic Orthodox Church of Australia 1969-1994*, Copt, 1995.

[703] C.A. Price, *Lebanese in Australia: Demographic Aspects*, Australian National University, 1983.

East. Although they are not nationalistic churches, in Australia most Maronites, Melkites and Antiochian Orthodox have ancestral links to Lebanon but many also have ethnic backgrounds from The Holy Land (modern-day Israel and the occupied Palestinian Territories), Syria and to a lesser extent Jordan, Egypt, Cyprus and Turkey. Descendants from Lebanon form the majority of Australian Christians with ancestry from the Middle East.[704]

The overwhelmingly number of Maronites in Australia (as for other Catholics descendant from the Middle East) attend Roman Catholic schools and parish churches and a great many are baptised Roman Catholic.[705] For many throughout the year, attendance at mass rotates between the nearest ancestral church parish and the local Roman Catholic parish. There are a number of Roman Catholic nuns, priests, monsignors and bishops in Australia who are of Middle Eastern ancestry. For all Catholics descendant from the Middle East, any or all of the combination of these phenomena has taken place in many Western countries since substantial migrations commenced in the mid to late 1800s. This traditional fusion and communion in the relationship between Eastern and Western Catholics explains why census statistics for those responding 'Maronite' are completely unreliable and would only represent a fraction of the true numbers. As most answer 'Catholic', they are counted that way in the Census figures. It is estimated there are 150,000 practising Maronites in Australia.[706]

For the first time in the history of the Catholic Church, the relics of three Eastern Catholic saints (Maronite) arrived on Australian shores in October and November of 2005 with an entourage of religious. There was scant mention of the event as a news item despite significant numbers of press releases by the Maronite Church of Australia.

---

[704] Australian Bureau of Statistics, *Ancestry by Religion for 'Australia' 2001 Census*, 2006, report especially commissioned by the author.

[705] These paragraphs can be found in an earlier work. See: Peter El Khouri, *Keeping up 'Appearances'. Australia 2013: Ancestry and Ethnic Descriptors – After the Cronulla Riots*, Palmer Higgs, 2012.

[706] Census estimate undertaken by Maronite Eparchy of Australia, 2012. See also CNEWA, *The Maronite Catholic Church*.

The Maronites represent the largest Christian denomination in Australia from Lebanon and the Middle East and form a significant part of the Christian majority (when compared to Muslims) of Lebanese ancestry in Australia.

Indeed, this was the first time the relics of any Eastern saint had come to Australia – Catholic, Orthodox or Oriental Orthodox – and the first time the relics of these saints left Lebanon. Wide press coverage may have helped the great bulk of Australians better understand the 'Lebanese' community, its diversity and its contribution to Australia and possibly assisted in averting the Cronulla Riots that were to follow shortly after. Nonetheless, through Maronite parishes, word of mouth and media coverage in Catholic press, tens of thousands of Catholics and Christians, from Eastern and Western customs had the privilege to witness the blessings.

It has become well-known that two of the largest Catholic parishes in the world are in Sydney. Both of them are Maronite. They are St Charbel's parish at Punchbowl and Our Lady of Lebanon at Harris Park/Parramatta. It is estimated each parish services about 20,000 practising Maronites. On Good Friday, the congregations for each of these parishes swell to between 5,000 and 10,000 parishioners for one mass attendance. There are several Maronite orders and congregations of monks, religious and nuns undertaking missionary work in Australia. They operate a number of primary and high schools, and nursing homes. The current Maronite Bishop of Australia is His Excellency Bishop Antoine-Charbel Tarabay. Previous Maronite bishops of Australia were the late Archbishop Abdu Khalife, Bishop Joseph Hitti, and Bishop Ad Abi Karam.

## 13.6   Ethnicities and Future Ancestry

### 13.6.1   Arab 'Ethnicity'?

Arabs are, for the most part, not descendants of the Bedouins, the nomadic peoples of the desert regions of North Africa and the Levant.

The historical enculturation of the term 'Arab' used throughout the ages has resulted in an ambiguous term. This is perhaps an effect of Western and Byzantine historical writings. The Arab Muslim invasions of the seventh century were not principally constituted by Bedouins, but more likely came from the men from the cities and the sedentary settlements of the surrounding countryside. The environment of the desert could not sustain the great army needed to take on the might of both the Persian and Byzantine empires. The Muslim prophet, Mohammed, was born in the city of Mecca and later lived in the city of Yathrib, which he renamed Medina. The Prophet Mohammed himself was therefore never a nomad or Bedouin.

Apart from a small proportion, almost all of those who are now called 'Arab' peoples commonly descend from the populations of permanent cities, towns, and villages in the Middle East rather than the more confined desert area of Arabia. The term 'Arab', since the birth of Islam in the seventh century, has usually meant a person from the Arabic-speaking world. In contemporary society, its linguistic context has spread to include a modern political and regional identity embodying those persons living in the member countries of the Arab League whose national language is Arabic. Very recently, some scholars of ancient Middle Eastern Christian history have declared Christians of the Middle East to be 'Arab Christians' suggesting: "to the degree that they underwent Arabization but not Islamization, Middle Eastern Christians are Arab Christians."[707] In other words, by the simple fact they adopted Arabic as their spoken language a thousand years ago, these Christians are classified as Arabs.

However, most of the Arab Muslim conquered region of the seventh century did not speak Arabic. The language of the Islamic Koran, Arabic, became the official language of the caliphate and its civil administration in the eighth century. This explains why many in the Arab world reject the notion of 'Arab ethnic' ancestry. Also, embracing the geopolitical and linguistic notion, close to the entirety of an estimated three hundred million people living in the 'Arab' region today could

---

[707] Noble and Treiger, *The Orthodox Church in the Arab World*, p. 3.

not claim nomadic ancestry or true ethnic Arabian ancestry. The percentage of Arabic-speaking persons having nomadic ancestry is likely to be far less than the percentage of Australians who can claim convict ancestry, perhaps a very nominal percentage.

Within the member nations of the Arab League, there are many ethnic communities who do not affiliate with the ethnic term 'Arab', even though Arabic may be their official language and first tongue. The largest Christian denominations descendant from the Middle East today, the Maronites and Copts, generally do not aspire to be of Arab 'ethnic' ancestry. However, those Christians living in the Middle East within countries today who are Arab League members are referred to as Arab Christians. This is a reference to the geopolitical block of Arabic speaking countries. Nonetheless, it should only be used in those regional terms rather than the nomadic and ethnic context that all too often is insinuated. For those Christian descendants from the Middle East now living in the West (a significant number and for several generations), the Western media has often spoken of them as 'Arab Christians': this is clearly inappropriate for Christians living outside the geopolitical Arab world.

It cannot be denied some Maronites, but only a very fractional minority, may have Arabian ethnicity. Many scenarios can be espoused but only a few will now be mentioned. 'Arabia' in the pre-Muslim seventh century had two meanings. One Arabia was under Byzantine rule and the other under Persian rule. Byzantine 'Arabia' was closer towards the Mediterranean, no further east than modern Syria and Jordan. In fact, the Roman Byzantine province of Arabia was far from the Arabian peninsula. The peninsula is defined today as containing the countries of Kuwait, Bahrain, Qatar, the United Arab Emirates (UAE), Oman, Yemen, and Saudi Arabia at its centre. These areas were under Persian rule.

It is generally accepted that Arab Christian tribes from the Arabian peninsula were almost entirely Monophysite. There may have been very few Christians, if any, who were adherent to the doctrines of

Chalcedon, and had migrated from Persian ruled Arabia to Byzantine land before the birth of Islam, as they would have been persecuted. After the Arab Muslim conquests of the Middle East in the seventh century, some of the Arab Christian tribes may have migrated as far as the western regions of the Middle East closer to the Mediterranean coast of Syria, Lebanon and Palestine. If they did, perhaps over the ages some of them may have joined the Maronite Church.

Later, some may have been Muslims of ethnic Arab ancestry who converted. For example, the great Chihab dynasty of Lebanon (1697-1842) was originally Sunni Muslim, descendant from the Arab tribe of Qoraish who came to Lebanon in the thirteenth century to fight against the Crusaders. There is evidence some of them converted to become Maronites in the eighteenth century. Accordingly, there are many contradictions with use of the term 'Arab'. It is regarded as synonymous and one and the same as Arabic speaking people, nomads and Bedouins, Muslims, ethnic descendants of Arabia, ethnic descendants of the desert, Middle East and more recently terrorists. The concept of 'Arab Christian' adds to the contradictions and confusion.

### 13.6.2   Lebanese Ethnicity and Maronite Ancestry

Lebanon, like many countries in the Middle East, is an ancient land and one of the first melting pots in history for mixed ancestry. For over 1200 years up to around 300 BC, the Phoenicians' maritime trading empire had their principal port cities in what is now modern day Lebanon. They traded all over the Mediterranean and had many colonies including Malta, Sardinia (Italy), Carthage (in modern day Tunisia), and Cadiz on the Atlantic tip of south-western Spain. Recent historical investigations point to the Phoenicians crossing the Atlantic thousands of years ago and influencing culture in Central and South America, and no doubt intermingling with the population.

Within the Middle Eastern region, ancient Biblical accounts tell of hundreds of thousands of foreign workers involved in construction, stone quarrying, and cedar and cypress trade around Phoenicia. The cedar provided the Phoenicians with the finest timber for constructing their seafaring ships. With a large labour intensive economy powered by cedar logging and its trade, many from afar would have migrated to Phoenician land, as they did for the construction of Solomon's temple. Once settled, its attractive geography, climate, beauty, abundant snow fed water reservoirs and springs, fertile land, papyrus trade and a long-standing history of a vibrant, easily adaptable and cosmopolitan population would have inspired them to remain. This was the beginning of a wider cross-cultural mix of Phoenician population. The same can be said of a broad area of ancient Syria that was fertile and a strategic location for trade routes.

Lebanon throughout history has been the subject of numerous lengthy foreign occupations and conquests – ancient Greeks, ancient Romans, ancient Persians, Arab Muslims, Egyptian Muslims, European and British Crusaders, Turkish Muslims and Ottomans, the French in post-World War I, Western allied forces including Australian soldiers in World War I and II, and many United Nations mandates including the more recent mandate of 15,000 soldiers from 2006. During all these occupations, inter-marriage would have and has taken place. There was a mass migration of Maronites to Sicily and Rome in the seventh century fleeing Persian and Arab Muslim conquest of the Middle East. For two hundred years between approximately 1100–1300 AD, the Crusaders mixed with the local Christian and Catholic (Maronite) population sharing the use of old and newly built churches and no doubt celebrating on the altar many mixed ancestral marriages. At the end of the Crusades, thousands of Maronites accompanied the Crusaders' withdrawal to Cyprus, Rhodes, Crete, and Malta. In modern times, we know of offspring living in both Lebanon and Australia from mixed marriages between Lebanese women and Western allied soldiers resident in Lebanon during World War II.

The Maronite Church is an Eastern, Aramaic-Syriac, Antiochian, non-nationalistic universal church. It has been well placed throughout history, as part of the Aramaic-speaking Catholic church in the patriarchate of Antioch and the East, for its faithful to naturally develop a true ethnic mix. It is accepted that Lebanon has been the cradle of the

Maronite Church for much of its history and has provided protection for its patriarch. The same analogy applies for Catholics (including Maronites) who see Italy, the Vatican and the pope as the cradle for leadership and inspiration of the universal Catholic Church. However, the Maronite Church is not a 'Lebanese church' or a nationalistic church like many Orthodox churches such as the Greek, Macedonian, or Russian.

Maronite expansion to the West has witnessed a rapid change outside of the traditional jurisdiction of the Maronite patriarchate in its ethnic mix, more than any other time in history. As a general phenomenon for all ethnicities, the inter-ethnic marriage and inter-religious marriage is and has been taking place in most Western nations. This is a dynamic time for the Maronites to hold on and expand the rich and beautiful Aramaic Catholic liturgy in the West.

Simultaneously, the rapid change requires a rapid response and there lies one of the most challenging issues for the dynamic of the Maronite Church in the West. The Maronite Patriarchal Synod held in Lebanon from 2003 to 2006 was particularly mindful of the Church in its global expansion. One of its multitudes of recommendations concerning the expansion was to foster communion and solidarity between the cradle of the Church, the Maronites of Lebanon, and the Maronites in the expansion based on the principle of unity in diversity.[708] Likewise, the first international Maronite youth convention was held in Sydney in 2008 to coincide with World Youth Day Sydney 2008. There were over three hundred delegates from all over the world.

Australia is one of the most multicultural nations in the globe. The Maronite Church in Australia, as for the Americas, is witnessing many parishioners who are not of Middle Eastern or Maronite ancestry. In many of its parishes, a significant number of marriages are a cross-culture of ethnicities and Christian denominations. It raises a new identity issue for future generations. It is hoped this book will assist the future generations of Maronite ancestors in answering many of their queries.

---

[708] Maronite Patriarchate, *Maronite Patriarchal Synod. Texts and Recommendations*, Maronite Patriarchate, 2008, p. 143.

The Maronite Church must learn from the many millions in Central and South America who are unaware of their Maronite ancestry as the Church was not equipped in the 1800s and early 1900s to deal with the expansion. However, it can deal with the expansion today. The rich heritage of the indigenous Aramaic Catholic liturgy that has been retained by the Maronites should be able to flourish in the Catholic and Christian communities across the globe for all people to be enriched.

# CONCLUSIONS

This book has aimed to fill a series of voids in the history of Christianity in the Middle East, in particular, that of the Syriac-Aramaic Catholics of the Levant and the growth, development, and impact of the Maronite Church. Historical studies of this period, religion, and area have typically focused on aspects such as the Greek-speaking populations, the ascetics of Egypt, and the formation of the Roman Catholic and Eastern Orthodox Churches. Instead, this book turns the focus to the Aramaic and Syriac-speaking peoples, the existence of the first open-air hermits in the Syrian Orient, and the Eastern Catholicism and Aramaic-Syriac traditions of Antioch that formed the Church of the Maronites. It has also sought to correct the numerous misconceptions that pervade common understandings of the Christianity of the past and today, such as the idea that all Catholics are Roman Catholics, Eastern Christians are all Byzantine Orthodox, and that the Middle East and Arab World is inherently Muslim.

Furthermore, the work of historian Matti Moosa has been taken to task for obscuring and misrepresenting the details of the history of the Maronite Church: yet another obstacle for acknowledging the role of this Church in the region. This book has intended, therefore, to present an alternative history to that promoted by Moosa and various misunderstandings, one that draws on ancient evidence and modern scholarship to uncover the roots of the Maronites. In doing so, it focuses on the long-running relationship this Church has had with the Holy See of Rome, and additionally shed new light on the ways in which Aramaic Catholics have impacted upon not only Christian culture, but the culture of the Middle East more broadly.

Chapters 1 and 2 of this book have provided an overview of the geographical, cultural, religious, and political context of the early centuries of Christianity in its birthplace of the Middle East. Jesus Christ's native tongue, Aramaic, and melodies chanted by the early Christians

506

indigenous to the Middle East have been preserved in the liturgy of the Maronite Church, the largest Christian denomination in the world to retain this connection. Chapters 3 and 4 provided detailed overviews of key figures and primary sources of the period and areas of Syria, Phoenicia, Lebanon, and Palestine, highlighting the developments in asceticism and monasticism. St Maroun, for whom the Maronites are named, was the earliest recorded 'hypethrite' or ascetic living in the open air and inspired many with his pious lifestyle.

Chapters 5 and 6 place the emergence of the Beit Maroun monastery in a time of great turmoil for the Church. Beit Maroun was established in Apamaea in 452 (but was first recorded in the early sixth century as an institution for followers of St Maroun and the Catholic Church). Amidst schisms, factions, imputations of heresy, and rising tensions between patriarchs, popes, and emperors of the East and West, Beit Maroun soon became a leading light in a confederation of monasteries for Catholic Orthodoxy and the Aramaic-speaking Christians of the Syrian Orient. Its monks would be subject to persecution and violence over the years. Chapter 7 explores the leadership role the monastery took in the sixth century and the strong Orthodox Catholic position its monks took against rival groups. When Rome and Constantinople were divided from 471-518 and again from 639-713, Beit Maroun loyalty reverted to Rome. Both primary and secondary sources are analysed here with particular attention paid to refuting the claims made by Moosa, based on his biased reading of the evidence.

Chapter 8 investigates the relationship between the Maronites, other Middle Eastern Christians, and the new influx of Muslims and subsequent Islamic leaders of the Middle East in the seventh century. In this period the first Maronite Patriarch, John Maroun, was installed as were a series of Maronite-Melkite popes and patriarchs following this. Such Eastern clergy were markedly dedicated to Rome and the maintenance of their Chalcedonian Christology. However, under the control of the Islamic caliphs, Christians were variously persecuted, and communication with Rome broke down.

In the seventh Christian century, tensions between Rome and Constantinople and private treaties between Byzantine emperors and the newly emerged Arab Muslim caliphs suggest how the Middle East's religious make-up, as the world's heartland of Christianity, was to be considerably altered into the future.

In Chapter 9 we delve into the accusation that the Maronites were Monothelites after this was deemed unorthodox at the Council of 680-681, and even well into the medieval period. Causes for this misconception are manifold, including misleading affiliations with figures who were allegedly proponents of Monothelitism, confusion with groups they shared heritage with such as the Melkites, and a generally clouded understanding of the theological topic at hand. Here again the sources for this controversy are assessed for their strengths and weaknesses. Ultimately, it is shown, the Maronites did not profess a heretical or Monothelite theology.

The culture of Aramaic Catholics in the medieval period is discussed in Chapter 10 and its influence on the architecture, language, and customs of Western Christian and Islamic society is highlighted. Examples are provided such as the succession of Maronite popes in Rome, Western hospital emblems, the Muslim hijab and the minaret tower of mosques. During this time Christian culture was, in turn, impacted upon by Islamic culture, not the least the Arabic language and otherwise various customs, the subject of which would require a separate thesis. After the destruction of Beit Maroun in the tenth century, the Maronite patriarchal seat became entrenched in the Lebanon mountains.

In Chapter 11, the impact of the Crusades on the Maronites in particular and their relationship with Rome is analysed. This study indicates that the Maronites continued to be accused of holding heretical beliefs for centuries. Again it is argued that, when the evidence is considered, the legend of Monothelitism amongst the Maronites has been skewed and is rendered null.

Chapter 12 follows the Maronites under the rule of the Turkish dynasties of the Ottoman and Mamlouk and, with a focus on Lebanon, traces this up to Lebanese Independence in the twentieth century.

Chapter 13 then broadens the focus to look at the Maronite Church on a global scale: in the Middle East, in Italy, Australia, and beyond. To round off this study, this Chapter closes with some comments on the connections between ethnicity, culture, and faith. This book's exploration of the history and identity of the Maronite Church intends to form a nexus of these elements to allow modern Maronites (and anyone else interested in this subject) a window into their heritage.

The book also tracks the modern day religious descendants of the first Christian converts –Jews, indigenous Aramaic and Coptic speaking gentiles, and even the Greek (Antiochian/Melkite) colonists living in the Middle East. Maronites are Catholics from the first patriarchate established by St Peter in Antioch – the city where Christ's followers were first called Christians – on his journey to Rome, and they are heir to the Aramaic-speaking Jews who were the first converts to Christianity. The Maronite Church emerged inadvertently as a church in the late seventh century and survived tumultuous periods in Christian heritage, persecution under Islamic control, and centuries of separation from their papal home to become today the largest religious denomination in Lebanon and the only Eastern Christians and Aramaic-speaking Church that can claim perpetual communion with the Pontifical See of Rome and the Catholic Church.

Prior to the Crusades, the Maronites can claim their loyalty to Rome was constant despite their communication broken by Islamic rule. Following the re-establishment of contact with the West through the Crusades and the formalisation of ties once again, it became tradition that the first act of every new Maronite patriarch appointed would be (and is to) profess fidelity to the see of Rome and to seek pontifical confirmation of the appointment. In return, Rome would send a legate providing a letter of confirmation of the election to the see of Antioch and also the pallium. Although a controversial proposition for some, the Maronites are the only Eastern Church and Aramaic-speaking Christians that can claim the inheritance from the first century of a perpetual link of loyalty between the patriarchate of Antioch and Rome. Since the Crusades until the eighteenth century (when some other Eastern churches returned in communion with Rome), the Maronite Church is the only Eastern Catholic Church whose patriarch can claim the perpetual ancient title of patriarch of Antioch and all of the East.

As for heads of other Christian communities, the Maronite patriarch was given temporal (historical) rights by the successive conquerors – the Arabs, Crusaders, Mamlouks, and Ottoman Turks. This gave rise to a type of judicial administration only found in the East known as the *Nomocanons*, a mix of canon law and civil law. It gave the patriarch some autonomy, and the opportunity to reinforce the spirit of his church and its place in the nation, a patriotism that would go on to shape the modern state of Lebanon.

Dib says this mix of canon and civil jurisdiction gave the patriarch and bishops an independence and freedom that none of the heads of other Christian communities in the East had. The clergy and the faithful recognised no other authority as ruling their affairs. It was either the patriarch or his bishop that would decide or arbitrate on a matter. Therefore, as Dib states, the religious life of the Maronites,

> is intimately tied to their civil and national life. It is mixed with it. There is hardly a matter of importance where the patriarch does not appear ... Absorbed in the trials, they (the patriarchs) scarcely had the opportunity to keep the records of the church. Also some of their writings did not survive.[709]

For almost 1,400 years Maronites have lived amongst people of many faiths. These include: Muslims be it Sunni, Shiite, or Alawite; Druze; Jews; and Christians – be it Syriac, Armenian, Chaldean, Greek Orthodox, Greek Catholic, Assyrian, or Latin. The deep interconnection between Maronite Catholics with the Melkite, Antiochian Orthodox, and the Syriac churches becomes transparent. From the initiation of Islamic conquests in the seventh century up to the arrival of the Crusades, it appears the Maronites were the only Christian denomination in the Middle East to have what appeared to be a regular independent military wing that sought to resist Islamic conquest and rule.

---

[709] Dib, *History of the Maronite Church*, pp. 49-50.

In the fourteenth century during Mamluk Muslim rule, Maronites began a Middle East tradition promoting harmonious co-existence amongst faiths as one nation and equals, seeking foreign assistance wherever necessary but not foreign rule. The Christian, Muslim (Shiite) and Druze allegiance in this period can be attributed as the first formal multi-faith military and nationalistic movement in world history. It evidences social cohesion and a functioning multi-cultural society, which formed the basis of Lebanese independence six hundred years later.

Given the ever-changing foreign rulers of the Levant, the Maronites have learnt over time sound diplomatic skills. The ability to manage this interaction has been led by the patriarch, bishops, and leaders of the laity. This long history has been passed down to each generation making the Maronites well placed to continue the diplomacy for peace and coexistence and be at the forefront of multicultural and inter-faith affairs in the new global environment of the third millennium. In the words of Pope John Paul II during his visit to Lebanon in 1997: "Lebanon is more than a country, it is a message."

# SELECT BIBLIOGRAPHY

## Historical Sources

**Al-Masudi (d. 956).** "Book of the Warning and of the Revision." In Paul Naaman, *The Maronites. The Origins of an Antiochene Church. A Historical and Geographical Study of the Fifth to Seventh Centuries.* Minnesota: Cistercian Press, 2009.

**Aphrahat.** *The Demonstrations of Aphrahat, the Persian Sage.* Translated by Adam Lehto. Piscataway: Gorgias Press, 2010.

**Athanasius.** *Life of St. Anthony of Egypt.* Translated by David Brakke. New York: Garland, 2000.

**H.C Butler (d. 1922).** *Early Churches in Syria, Fourth to Seventh Centuries.* Edited by E.B. Smith. Michigan: Adolf M. Hakkert 1929.

**Church Councils (451-787).** *A History of the Councils 451-787 AD of the Church (from the original documents).* Vols IV and V. Translated by C.J. Hefele and edited by W. Clark. Edinburgh: T & T Clark, 1895.

**Church Council (680-681).** "Acts of the Third Council of Constantinople." In *Nicene and Post-Nicene Fathers*, Vol. 14, trans. by Henry Percival, ed. by Philip Schaff and Henry Wace, Second Series. Christian Literature Publishing Co., 1900. Available at: http://www.newadvent.org/fathers/3813.htm.

**Charles Churchill (d. 1877).** *Mount Lebanon, A Ten Years' Residence from 1842 to 1852.* London: Saunders and Otley, 1853.

*The Druzes and the Maronites under the Turkish Rule From 1840 to 1860.* London: Bernard Quartich, 1862.

**John Chrysostom (d. 407).** "36th Epistle." In Shafiq AbouZayd, *Ihidayutha: A Study of the Life of Singleness in the Syrian Orient: From Ignatius of Antioch to Chalcedon 451 A.D.* Oxford: Aram Society for Syro-Mesopotamia Studies, 1993.

**Jacques de Vitry (d. 1240).** *The History of Jerusalem.* Translated by A. Stuart. London: Palestine Pilgrims Text Society, 1896.

**Dionysius of Tell Mahre (d. 845).** See citation for Michael the Syrian.

512

**Eusebius (d. 339).** *The Ecclesiastical History of Eusebius Pamphilus, Bishop of Cesarea, in Palestine.* Translated by Christian Frederick Cruse. New York: Thomas N. Stamford, 1856.

**Eutychius (d. 940).** *Eutychii Annales.* Translated by Aubrey Stewart. London: Palestine Pilgrims Text Society, 1895.

**Evagrius (d. 594).** *Ecclesiastical History of Evagrius Scholarasticus.* Translated by Michael Whitby. Liverpool: Liverpool University Press, 2000.

**Count Marcellinus (d. 534).** *Count Marcellinus and his Chronicle.* Translated by B. Coke. Oxford: Oxford University Press, 2001.

**Abu l-Fida (d. 1331).** "Universal History." In Paul Naaman, *The Maronites. The Origins of an Antiochene Church. A Historical and Geographical Study of the Fifth to Seventh Centuries.* Minnesota: Cistercian Press, 2009.

**Maronite Chronicle (c. 664).** In S. Brock, S. Palmer, A. Hoyland (eds), *The Seventh Century in the West-Syrian Chronicles.* Liverpool: Liverpool University Press, 1993.

**Michael the Syrian (d. 1199).** *Chronicle of Michael the Great, Patrirach of the Syrians.* Translated by Robert Bedrosian. New Jersey: Sources of the Armenian Tradition, 1871.

**Petition of the monks of Syria II (518).** In Paul Namaan, *The Maronites. The Origins of an Antiochene Church. A Historical and Geographical Study of the Fifth to Seventh Centuries.* Minnesota: Cistercian Press, 2009.

**Pope Hormisdas (d. 523).** In Cornelia B. Horn, "The Correspondence Between the Monks of Syria Secunda and Pope Hormisdas in 517/518 AD." *The Journal of Maronite Studies* 1 (4), (1997), http://maronite-institute.org/ MARI/JMS/october97/ The_Correspondence_Between.htm.

**Rabbula (c. 586).** *The Rabbula Gospels.* Translated and edited by C. Cecchelli, G. Furlani, and M. Salmi. Olten and Lausanne: Urs Graf, 1959.

**Sozomen (d. 450).** *A History of the Church in Nine Books, from A.D.324 to A.D.440.* Translated by E. Walford. London: S. Bagster, 1846.

**Syriac Manuscript, MS160 (c. 473).** In Robert Doran (trans.), *The Lives of Simeon Stylites.* Minnesota: Cistercian Press, 1992.

**Syriac Manuscript Add. 12155, fol.163 (c. 592).** In Paul Naaman, *The Maronites. The Origins of an Antiochene Church. A Historical and Geographical Study of the Fifth to Seventh Centuries.* Minnesota: Cistercian Press, 2009.

Theodoret (d. 457). *A History of the Monks of Cyrrhus of Syria by Theodoret of Cyrrhus*. Translated by R.M. Price. Kalamazoo: Cistercian Press, 1987.
Theophanes (d. 818). *The Chronicle of Theophanes*. Translated by H. Turtledove. Philadelphia: University of Pennsylvania Press, 1982.
William of Tyre (d. 1186). *A History of Deeds Done Beyond the Sea*. Translated by E. Atwater, E.A. Babcock, and A.C. Krey. New York: Columbia University Press, 1943.

## General Christian History

AbouZayd, S. *Ihidayutha: A Study of the Life of Singleness in the Syrian Orient: From Ignatius of Antioch to Chalcedon 451 A.D*. Oxford: Aram Society for Syro-Mesopotamia Studies, 1993.
Antiochian Orthodox Archdiocese of Australia, New Zealand, and the Philippines. *History of Antiochian Orthodoxy in Australasia*, 2007, http://www.antiochianarch.org.au/ HistoryofAntiochianOrthodoxyinAustralasia.aspx.
Atiya, A.S. *A History of Eastern Christianity*. London: Methuen, 1968.
Attia, M. *Coptic Orthodox Church of Australia 1969-1994*. Sydney: Coptic Orthodox Publications, 1995.
Bacchus, F.J. "Macarius of Antioch." In *The Catholic Encyclopedia*. New York: Robert Appleton Company, 1910. Available at: http://www.newadvent.org/ cathen/09483b.htm.
Barret, D. *World Christian Encyclopaedia*. New York: Oxford University Press, 1982.
Brock, S.P. *Syriac Perspectives on Late Antiquity*. London: Variorum Reprints, 1984.
*From Emphrem to Romanus. Interactions Between Syriac and Greek in Late Antiquity*. Oxford: Routledge, 1999.
*An Introduction to Syriac Studies*. Piscataway: Gorgias Press, 2006.
Brock, S.P. (trans.). *The Syriac Fathers on Prayer and Spiritual Life*. Kalamazoo: Cistercian Press, 1987.
Brock, S.P. (ed.). *The Hidden Pearl: The Syrian Orthodox Church and its Ancient Aramaic Heritage*. 3 Volumes. Piscataway: Gorgias Press, 2001.
Brock, S.P. et al. *Gorgias Encyclopaedia Dictionary of the Syriac Heritage*. Piscataway: Gorgias Press, 2011.
Brock, S.P. et al. *The Seventh Century in the West-Syrian Chronicles*. Liverpool: Liverpool University Press, 1993.

**Bury, J.B.** *A History of the Later Roman Empire from Arcadius to Irene*, Vol. II. MacMillan & Co., 1889.

**Charon (Korolevsky), C.** *History of the Melkite Patriarchates (Volume I), Pre-Modern Period (869-1833)*, translated by John Collorafi, edited by Bishop Nicholas Samra. Fairfax, Virginia: Eastern Christian Publications, 1998.

**Chapman, J.** "Pope Honorius I." In *The Catholic Encyclopedia*. New York: Robert Appleton Company, 1910. Available at: http://www.newadvent. org/ cathen/07452b.htm.

"Monophysites and Monophysitism." *The Catholic Encyclopedia*. New York: Robert Appleton Company, 1911. Available at: http://www. newadvent.org/ cathen/10489b.htm.

**Pope John Paul II and His Holiness Mar Ignatius Zakka I Iwas.** "Common Declaration of Pope John Paul II and His Holiness Mar Ignatius Zakka I Iwas," 23 June 1984. Available at: http://www.vatican. va/roman_curia/pontifical_councils/chrstuni/anc-orient-ch-docs/rc_pc_ christuni_doc_19840623_jp-ii-zakka-i_en.html.

**Dalrymple, W.** *From the Holy Mountain. A Journey in the Shadow of Byzantium*. London: Flamingo, 1998.

**Dawood, N.J.** (trans.). *The Koran*. London: Penguin, 1993.

**Dick, I.** *Melkites, Greek Orthodox and Greek Catholics of the Patriarchates of Antioch, Alexandria and Jerusalem*. Roslindale, Massachusetts: Sophia Press, 2004.

**Ekonomou, A.J.** *Byzantine Rome and the Greek Popes, Eastern Influences on Rome and the Papacy from Gregory the Great to Zacharias, A.D. 590-752*. Lanham, Maryland: Lexington Books, 2007.

**Fortescue, A.** "Henoticon," in *The Catholic Encyclopedia*, Robert Appleton Company, 1910, available at http://www.newadvent.org/cathen/07218b. htm.

"John the Faster, and Maurice," in *The Catholic Encyclopedia*, Robert Appleton Company, 1910, available at: http://www.newadvent.org/ cathen/08493a.htm.

"Melchites." In *The Catholic Encyclopedia*, New York: Robert Appleton Company, 1911. Available at: http://www.newadvent.org/cathen/ 10157b. htm.

"The Eastern Schism." In The Catholic Encyclopedia. New York: Robert Appleton Company, 1912. Available at: http://www.newadvent.org/ cathen/13535a.htm.

**Gibbon, E.** *The Decline and Fall of the Roman Empire.* Vols 1-8. London: The Folio Society, 1985.

**Harvey, Susan A.** "Revisiting the Daughters of the Covenant: Women's Choirs and Sacred Song in Ancient Syriac Christianity." *Hugoye: Journal of Syriac Studies* 8, pp. 125-149.

**Kaegi, W.** *Heraclius Emperor of Byzantium.* Cambridge: Cambridge University Press, 2003.

**Kelly, J.D.N.** *Oxford Dictionary of the Popes.* Oxford: Oxford University Press, 1986.

**Lammens, H.** "Frère Gryphon." *Revue de l'Orient chrétien* IV (1899): pp. 68-104.

**Maalouf, A.** *The Crusades Through Arab Eyes.* London: Saqi, 1984.

**Mango, C.** *Byzantium, The Empire of the New Rome.* London, Weidenfeld & Nicolson, 1980.

*The Art of the Byzantine Empire.* Toronto, Toronto University Press, 1986.

**Mann, H.K.** *The Lives of the Popes in the Early Middle Ages.* Vol. II. London: Kegan Paul, Trench, Truber & Co Ltd, 1925.

**Melkite Catholic Eparchy of Australia** and New Zealand *History of the Eparchy,* 2009. http://www.melkite.org.au/history.aspx.

**Mershman, F.** "Pope St. Martin I." In *The Catholic Encyclopedia.* New York: Robert Appleton Company, 1910. Available at: http://www.newadvent. org/ cathen/09723c.htm.

**Noble, S., & A. Treiger** (eds) *The Orthodox Church in the Arab World 700-1700. An Anthology of Sources.* Illinois: Northern Illinois University Press, 2014.

**Runciman, S.** *Byzantine Civilisation.* Vols 1-3. London, Edward Arnold, 1933. *A History of the Crusades.* Vols I-III. London, Cambridge University Press, 1954.

**Russell, N.** (trans.). *The Lives of the Desert Fathers, The Historia Monarchorum in Aegypto.* Kalamazoo: Cistercian Press, 1981.

**Seward, D.** *The Monks of War – The Military Orders.* London: The Folio Society, 2000.

**Shehadie, N.** *A Life Worth Living.* Roseville, NSW: Simon & Schuster, 2003.

**Tawil, J.** *The Patriarchate of Antioch throughout History: An Introduction.* Boston, Massachusetts: Sophia Press, 2001.

**Thurston, H.** "Bulls and Briefs." In *The Catholic Encyclopedia.* New York: Robert Appleton Company, 1908. Available at: http://www.newadvent. org/ cathen/03052b.htm.

**Trimingham, J.S.** *Christianity Among the Arabs in Pre-Islamic Times.* Beirut, Librarie de Liban, 1979.

**Waddell, H.** *The Desert Fathers.* London: Constable, 1936.

**Ware, T.** *The Orthodox Church,* London, Penguin Books, 1997.

**Zakka I, H.H.I.** "A Short Overview of the Common History." *Patriarchal Journal* 33 (146), (1995): pp. 322-344. Available at: http://syrianortho-doxchurch.org/ 2010/03/a-short-overview-of-the-common-history/.

## Maronite Related

**Abdullah, G.** *The Maronite Church in Australia: A Study of a Local Church and its Place in the Communion of Local Churches.* Masters Thesis, Catholic Institute of Sydney, 2005.

**Amash, P.J.** (trans.). *The Church of St Simeon the Stylite and Other Archaelogical Sites of Simeon and Halaqa.* Damsacus: Sidawi Printing House, 1990.

**Awit, M.** *The Maronites, Conscience of the Church.* New York: M. Awit, 1980. *The Maronite Patriarchate History and Mission.* Lebanon: Arab Printing Press, 1996.

**Azize, J.** *An Introduction to the Maronite Faith.* Redland Bay, Queensland: Connor Court Publishing, 2017.

**Badwi, A.** *The Liturgical Year Iconography of the Syro-Maronite Church.* Kaslik, Lebanon: University of Saint Esprit, 2006. *Iconographie Et Peinture Dans L'Eglise Maronite.* Kaslik, Lebanon: University of Saint Esprit, 2013.

**Beggiani, S.** *Introduction to Eastern Christian Spirituality – The Syriac Tradition.* Scranton, Pennsylvania: University of Scranton, 1991. *The Divine Liturgy of the Maronite Church. History and commentary.* Glen Allen, Virginia: Saint Maron Publications, 2002. *Aspects of Maronite History.* Glen Allen, Virginia: Saint Maron Publications, 2003.

**Cragg, K.** *The Arab Christian. A History in the Middle East.* London: Mowbray, 1992.

**Crawford, R.W.** "William of Tyre and the Maronites." *Speculum* 30 (2), (1955): pp. 222-228.

**Dau, B.** *History of the Maronites.* Lebanon: B. Dau, 1984.

**Dib, P.** *History of the Maronite Church.* Detroit: Maronite Exarchate, 1962.

**Doran, R.** (trans.). *The Lives of Simeon Stylites.* Kalamazoo: Cistercian Press, 1992.

**Eparchy of St Maron.** *The Maronite Catholic Church.* Glen Allen, Virginia: Saint Maron Publications, 2002.

**Finn, E.** *These are My Rites, A Brief History of the Eastern Rites of Christianity.* Collegeville, Minnesotta: Liturgical Press, 1980.

**Harb, A.K.** *The Maronites. History and Constants.* Lebanon: The Maronite Heritage Publications, 2001.

**Hourani, G.** "Saint Maron's Relic 'Ornament of the Divine Choir of Saints'," *The Journal of Maronite Studies*, 1997, http://www.maronite-institute.org/ MARI/JMS/ january97/Saint_Marons_Relic.htm.

**Lebanese Maronite Order of Monks.** *The Blessed Nimitallah Kassab Al-Hardini.* Lebanon: Five Star Photography, 1998.

**Leroy, J.** *Monks and Monasteries of the Middle East.* London: Harrap, 1963.

**Mahfouz, J.** *Short History of the Maronite Church.* Translated by S. Foukx. Lebanon: J. Mahfouz, 1987.

**Maronite Archbishopric of Cyprus.** *The Maronite Icons. Modern Sacred Art.* Beirut: Dar Sader Publishers, 1999.

**Maronite Patriarchate.** *Maronite Patriarchal Synod. Texts and Recommendations.* Bkerke, Lebanon: Maronite Patriarchate, 2008.

**Marzetti, M.R.P.** "Volperino, Italy, Celebrates Saint Maron's Feast Like a Phoenix Rising from the Ashes." *The Journal of Maronite Studies*, (1998), http://www.maronite-institute.org/MARI/JMS/october98/Volperino_ Italy.htm.

**Moosa, M.** *The Maronites in History.* New York: Syracuse University Press, 1986.

**Naaman, P.** *The Maronites. The Origins of an Antiochene Church – A Historical and Geographical Study of the Fifth to Seventh Centuries.* Piscataway: Cistercian Publications, 2009.

**Price, R.M.** (trans.) *A History of the Monks of Syria, by Theodoret of Cyrrhus.* Kalamazoo: Cistercian Press, 1987.

**Sader, Y.** *Painted Churches and Rock cut Chapels of Lebanon.* Beirut: Dar Sader, 1997.

*Crosses and Symbols in Ancient Christian Art of Lebanon.* Beirut: Dar Sader, 2006.

**Saad, A.** *The Seventy Sixth. Mar Nasrallah Boutros Cardinal Sfeir Vol I (1986-1992).* Translated by N. Nasr. Lebanon: Entire East Publications, 2005.

**Salibi, K.** *Maronite Historians of Medieval Lebanon.* Beirut: Nawfal, 1959.

**Salim, A.** *Captivated by Your Teachings. A Resource Book for Adult Maronite Catholics.* Arizona: E.T. Nedder Publishing, 2002.

**Sfeir, P.** *Blessed Nimattullah Kassab Al – Hardini. His life, Words and Spiritualities.* Tranlsated by K. Akiki. Lebanon: Lebanese Maronite Order, 2000.

**Tarabay, A.C.** et al. *The Maronite Church Roots and Mission.* Lebanon: Kreim Printing Press, 2014.

**Tayah, W.P.** *The Maronites.* Miami: Bet Moroon Publishers, 1987.

**Thompson, S.** "1880 – 1930 Redfern Maronite Heritage Centre Collection." *Migration Heritage Centre,* 2007. http://www.migrationheritage.nsw.gov.au/exhibition/objectsthroughtime/ maronites/index.html.

**Vööbus, A.** *A History of Ascetism in the Syrian Orient.* Vols I-III. Louvain: Secretariat Du Corpusco, 1960.

"The Contribution of Ancient Syrian Christianity to West European Culture." *Journal of the Syrian Academic Studies* 2 (1988): pp. 8-14.

**Wehbe, L.** "The Maronites of the Holy Land: A Historical Overview," *The Journal of Maronite Studies* 5 (2), (2001). Available at: www.maronite-institute.org/ MARI/JMS/january01/docs/MaronitesEnglish.doc.

**Zayek, F.M.** *Rafka. The Blind Mystic of Lebanon.* Massachusetts: St Bede's Publications, 1980.

## History of Lebanon and Syria

**Azize, J.** *The Phoenician Solar Theology.* Piscataway: Gorgias Press, 2005.

**Ball, W.** *Syria – A Historical and Architectural Guide.* New York: Intelink Books, 1998.

**Butler, H.C.** *Publications of American Archaeological Expeditions to Syria.* New York: Architecture, 1903.

*Publications of the Princeton University Archaeological Expeditions to Syria.* New York: Leyden, 1920.

**Burns, R.** *Monuments of Syria: A Historical Guide.* London: I.B. Tauris, 1992.

**Cobban, H.** *The Making of Modern Lebanon.* London: Hutchison, 1985.

**El Khouri, P.** *Keeping Up 'Appearances'. Australia 2013: Ancestry and Ethnic Descriptors – After the Cronulla Riots.* Victoria: Palmer Higgs, 2012.

**Fisk, R.** *Pity the Nation: Lebanon at War.* Oxford: Oxford University Press, 1992.

**Harb, A.K.** *Lebanon. A Name Through 4000 Years. Entity and Identity.* Lebanon: Lebanese Heritage Foundation, 2003.

**Hitti, P.K.** *Lebanon in History.* London: Macmillan & Co, 1957.

*History of Syria, Lebanon and Palestine.* London: Macmillan & Co. 1957

*A Short History of the Near East.* Princeton: D. Van Nostrand Company, 1966.

*The Near East in History: A 5000 Year Story.* Princeton: D. Van Nostrand Company, 1966.

**Hourani, A.** *A History of the Arab Peoples.* London: Faber & Faber, 1991.

**Kennedy, H.** "Antioch and the Villages of Northern Syria." *Nottingham Medieval Studies* 32 (1988): pp. 65-90.

**Littmann, E.** *Publications of the Princeton University Archaeological Expeditions to Syria.* New York: Leyden, 1934.

**Luxenberg, C.** *The Syro-Aramaic Reading of the Koran: A Contribution to the Decoding of the Language of the Koran.* Berlin: Hans Shiler, 2007.

**Maktabi, R.** "The Lebanese Census of 1932 Revisited. Who are the Lebanese?." *British Journal of Middle Eastern Studies* 26 (2), (1999): pp. 219-241.

**Mansfield, P.** *A History of the Middle East.* London: Viking, 1991.

**Price, C.A.** *Lebanese in Australia: Demographic Aspects.* Australian National University, Canberra, 1983.

**Salibi, K.** *A House of Many Mansions: the History of Lebanon Reconsidered.* London: IB Tauris, 1988.

## Travel Guides

**Footprint Syria and Lebanon.** Bath: Footprint Handbooks, 2001.

**Lonely Planet Middle East.** Melbourne: Lonely Planet Publications, 2003.

**Lonely Planet Syria.** Melbourne: Lonely Planet Publications, 1999.

**Lonely Planet Lebanon.** Melbourne: Lonely Planet Publications, 2001.

**Skeels, F. and L.** Highways and Byways of Lebanon. Reading and Beirut: Garnet and Geo Projects, 2000.